D1072405

Biodata Handbook

Biodata Handbook

Theory, Research, and Use
of Biographical Information
in Selection and Performance Prediction

EDITED BY
Garnett S. Stokes,
Michael D. Mumford,
and William A. Owens

Foreword by Marvin D. Dunnette

CPP BOOKS
Palo Alto, California
A Division of Consulting Psychologists Press, Inc.

Library of Congress Cataloging-in-Publication Data

Biodata handbook : theory, research, and use of biographical information in
    selection and performance prediction / edited by Garnett S. Stokes,
    Michael D. Mumford, and William A. Owens.
        p.   cm.
    Includes bibliographical references and index.
    ISBN 0-89106-063-4 :
    1. Employee selection--Biographical methods. 2. Prediction of occupational
    success--Biographical methods. 3. Scale analysis (Psychology) I. Stokes,
    Garnett S. II. Mumford, Michael D. III. Owens, William A.
    HF5549.5.S38B56   1994
    658.3'14--dc20   93-38878
                                                                              CIP

Printed in the United States of America
First edition
    First printing, 1994

98 97 96 95 94   10 9 8 7 6 5 4 3 2 1

*This book is dedicated to the memory of Edwin R. Henry,
who was a staunch and visionary champion of biodata.*

Contents

Foreword

Publication of this *Biodata Handbook* constitutes a landmark in defining fully the underlying theory, practical usefulness, and scientific basis of biographical information. Although the idea of using background data for predicting occupational success extends back nearly a century (Ferguson, 1961), it was not until the mid-1960s that William A. Owens, Jr., stepped forward to the challenge of championing not only the practical usefulness of biographical information but also its important role as the basis for a scientific discipline of human behavior (see, in particular, Owens, 1968, 1971).

By that time, Owens had already joined forces with a passionate spokesman for the use of biodata, Ed Henry, to whom this volume is dedicated. Together, they staged a groundbreaking conference that brought together most of the top applied researchers of the time (Henry, 1966). Proceedings of the conference were published in a widely circulated and influential report (Owens & Henry, 1966).

From those beginnings, over the last quarter century, Owens and his students have defined and extended the domain of biodata and its uses for both applied prediction and scientific understanding (see, in particular, Owens, 1976; Owens & Schoenfeldt, 1979; Mumford & Owens, 1987; Mumford, Stokes, & Owens, 1990; and Mumford & Stokes, 1992).

Publication of this *Biodata Handbook* marks a juncture, serving not only to outline current knowledge of the practical and scientific bases of biographical information but also to provide a framework for extending our knowledge substantially in the years ahead. The editors and authors of the chapters of this *Handbook* have succeeded admirably in fulfilling these dual purposes.

—Marvin D. Dunnette

REFERENCES

Ferguson, L. W. (1961). The development of industrial psychology. In B. H. Gilmer (Ed.), *Industrial psychology* (pp. 18–37). New York: McGraw-Hill.

Henry, E. R. (1966). *Research conference on the use of autobiographical data as psychological predictors.* Greensboro, NC: The Richardson Foundation.

Mumford, M. D., & Owens, W. A. (1987). Methodology review: Principles, procedures, and findings in the application of background data measures. *Applied Psychological Measurement, 11,* 1–31.

Mumford, M. D., & Stokes, G. S. (1992). Developmental determinants of indvidual action: Theory and practice in application of background data measures. In M. D. Dunnette & L. M. Hough (Eds.), *Handbook of industrial and organizational psychology* (2d ed., vol. 3, pp. 61–138). Palo Alto, CA: Consulting Psychologists Press.

Mumford, M. D., Stokes, G. S., & Owens, W. A. (1990). *Patterns of life history: The ecology of human individuality.* Hillsdale, NJ: Erlbaum.

Owens, W. A. (1968). Toward one discipline of scientific psychology. *American Psychologist, 23,* 782–785.

Owens, W. A. (1971). A quasi-actuarial basis for individual assessment. *American Psychologist, 26,* 992–999.

Owens, W. A. (1976). Background data. In M. D. Dunnette (Ed.), *Handbook of industrial and organizational psychology.* Chicago: Rand McNally.

Owens, W. A., & Henry, E. R. (1966). *Biographical data in industrial psychology: A review and evaluation.* Greensboro, NC: The Richardson Foundation.

Owens, W. A., & Schoenfeldt, L. F. (1979). Toward a classification of persons. *Journal of Applied Psychology, 64,* 569–607.

Preface

FIVE YEARS AGO Robert Most at Consulting Psychologists Press (CPP) contacted Bill Owens (Doc), Mike Mumford, and me about writing a book on biodata to follow up on our chapter in the second edition of the *Handbook of Industrial and Organizational Psychology*. The three of us met in Doc's office at the Institute for Behavioral Research, University of Georgia, and we hammered out a list of potential topics for such a book. We then brainstormed regarding potential authors, consulting with other colleagues for recommendations. In some cases, multiple authors had contributed a great deal to a topic area, making the choice of a single individual to author the chapter on that topic unclear. In other cases, very little research existed so there were no obvious "experts" on the topic. Consequently, we needed to identify authors who wanted to branch out and pursue biodata in a new arena or from a new perspective. After much thought, we developed our list and presented our ideas to Bob Most, who enthusiastically supported the direction of our book. We three editors divided up the work, with each of us contacting potential authors for specific chapters.

As a first time editor of a book and as a researcher fascinated by individual differences, I was intrigued, amused, and sometimes horrified at the differences among authors in responding to deadlines. Some chapters arrived early; some arrived very late. One important chapter in the book was extremely late, but when it arrived, it clearly was an excellent addition to the book. As a result of my experience as an editor, I've learned quite a bit about responding to such deadlines when they are imposed on me!

As a strategy for dividing up the work, Mike, Doc, and I reviewed each chapter that arrived and provided the author with feedback for revisions. I then edited each revised manuscript. Authors made a number of revisions prior to going to press, including updating citations until the very last moment. The result is a comprehensive and informative group of chapters on the use of background data in organizations. The authors have done an outstanding job both in clarifying the work of the past and in suggesting avenues for future consideration. The authors' contributions to the field of psychology and to background data will be recognized for many years to come.

A book is not edited without a great deal of support. Along the way, I was pleased to have the help of those at CPP. Bob Most, Lee Langhammer Law, and Kathy Hummel were my primary contacts at CPP. I greatly appreciated their enthusiasm, assistance, and patience.

My coeditors have been wonderful as well. Mike Mumford, my friend from graduate school and continuing research colleague, provided excellent suggestions for authors in reviewing each of the chapters. Both Mike and I greatly valued the input of Doc, our mentor and friend. Mike and I were Doc's last two Ph.D. students before he retired at the University of Georgia. We feel very fortunate that we have been able to maintain such close ties with him since his retirement and our forays into the academic world. Doc's wisdom and guidance are evident throughout this book, and his influence on our lives as applied psychologists is pervasive. One could not ask for a kinder, more helpful and supportive mentor.

There are others who certainly deserve mention. Thanks to my graduate students, who listened to me as I discovered the intricacies involved in obtaining the required permissions for chapters and all the other things that come up when one is responsible for a book. Thanks to the UGA psychology department secretaries, who copied and typed and took myriad phone messages from authors. And finally, thanks to Marv Dunnette for his support and reviews of chapters for this project. His support of the *Biodata Handbook*, along with that of Bill Owens, is warmly appreciated.

—Garnett S. Stokes

Introduction and History

Garnett S. Stokes
University of Georgia

In 1988 ED FLEISHMAN referred to background data (biodata) as a new frontier in the area of performance prediction. Although biodata have been used as a selection tool for most of the 20th century, exciting new research and developments in the legal arena over the last few years have led to a resurgence of interest in the use of background data as an alternative to cognitive ability tests and as a powerful selection tool in its own right. This book represents the most recent research on background data, and it provides both the researcher and the user with vital information for understanding and using background data in a number of domains, such as selection in the public and private sectors, vocational counseling, career development, and job classification.

The background data form of today may bear only slight resemblance to the job application blank from which it originated. Apparently, the first known mention of using a standardized method of assessing life history came in a 1894 meeting of the Chicago Underwriters. Colonel Thomas L. Peters of the Washington Life Insurance Company of Atlanta proposed that one way to improve the selection of life insurance agents would be to ask applicants a series of standard questions regarding their life experiences, such as where they lived, how many places they had lived in during the last ten years, what their marital status was, how many dependents they supported, their previous experiences selling life insurance, and so on (Ferguson, 1961, cited in Owens, 1976). This form is regarded as the "granddaddy" of biodata questionnaires.

Not long afterwards, procedures for the quantification of responses to life experience questions were published. Woods began in 1915 with an empirical analysis of the responses of both good and poor salespersons to an application blank, and Scott in 1917 included a personal history record in his *Aids in the Selection of Salesmen* (cited in Mumford & Owens, 1987). An explicit description of analysis and weighting procedures for biodata items appeared in Goldsmith's (1922) article on the use of life history data for identifying successful salespersons. Over the next few years, a number of articles appeared advancing the empirical methods used for biodata item analysis and weighting procedures (Kenagy & Yoakum, 1925; Manson, 1925) as well as expanding the use of biodata to jobs other than sales (Anonymous, 1925; Viteles, 1932; see also Owens, 1976).

The present day multiple choice format emerged around the time of World War II, and the military enjoyed considerable success with their use of background data to predict success in military training (Guilford & Lacey, 1947). Findings from studies conducted in the military attested to the successful use of biodata (Levine & Zachert, 1951; Parish & Drucker, 1957; Roy, Brueckel, & Drucker, 1954). The weighted application blank also became increasingly popular in the civilian sector (England, 1961, 1971).

In spite of the large number of positive findings on the use of background data for selection, most of the work that had been done into the 1960s and 1970s focused on maximizing prediction, with little regard for the use of biodata in gaining an understanding of the antecedents of success and failure in various occupations. The crossroads may have come at a conference chaired by Henry (1966), one of the early champions of the biodata approach, entitled "Research Conference on the Use of Autobiographical Data as Psychological Predictors." At this conference, it was concluded that increased prediction using biodata might only be achieved by learning more about the causal relationships underlying items that are predictive.

Although there had been some work in this area that preceded the 1966 conference reported by Henry in 1966 (Berkeley, 1953; DuBois, Loevinger, & Gleser, 1952; Siegel, 1956a, 1956b), since that conference, a number of researchers have tackled the issue of developing a conceptual understanding of biographical information. Increasingly, researchers have conducted factor analyses of their biodata items or developed other methods for developing homogeneous clusters of items to attempt a greater understanding of their meaning (e.g., Baehr & Williams, 1968; Eberhardt & Muchinsky, 1982; Klimoski, 1973; Matteson & Osburn, 1970; Morrison, 1977; Morrison & Sebald, 1974; Russell & Domm, 1990).

Probably the most comprehensive and influential investigations of life history information and its meaning were conducted by William A.

Owens. His developmental-integrative model served as a framework for investigating subgroups of individuals with similar life experiences identified through their responses to an extensive biodata form given to them as college freshmen. His pool of biodata items and the subsequent factors derived from them using principal components analysis were criterion-free, and they provided a structure of biodata constructs unmatched until this day. The factors have been found to be predictive of a large number of criteria of interest in organizations, including job satisfaction, career choice, and career success. The factors were scored and used in a Ward and Hook (1963) hierarchical clustering program to identify subgroups and assign membership. The subgroups have been found to capture unique variance beyond that obtained from factor scores alone. Some of these are further described in a chapter by Hein and Wesley in the present volume. Further information about the details of this study may be obtained from Owens and Schoenfeldt (1979) and from Mumford, Stokes, and Owens (1990).

Thus, the charge of "dustbowl empiricism" has frequently been made against users and researchers of biodata, but such charges are not likely to be true of most biodata proponents today, nor were they necessarily true of many of the biodata researchers of the past. Increasingly, biodata researchers are developing more rational methods for biodata item development and scoring. Attention is being focused on accuracy and fakability, and measurement issues are receiving renewed attention. The importance of theory as a basis for biodata investigations is increasingly recognized. This book provides a look at the state of the art in each of these important areas.

The chapters in the book provide an overview of both the present and the future of biodata. The book has been divided into five sections. Practical advice for item development, use of job analysis, and the definition of biodata are provided in the first section of the book. Then, in the second section, practical issues of scoring are addressed, and the reader is provided with extensive descriptions and comparisons of empirical, rational, and factorial methods for scoring biodata inventories. The subgrouping method and its utility for selection and classification is also described. In the third section, issues in the validation and application of biodata inventories are discussed. Methods of validation are discussed and issues of generalizability are described. Also, several chapters are devoted to the use of biodata in different arenas, including its use in blue collar selection and in the federal government. Other general selection issues are addressed, and there is an update on legal issues of importance to users of biodata forms. Finally, faking is addressed, and ways of reducing its impact are noted. The fourth section contains chapters that cover general applications of biodata to organizations, including the use of biodata in a career development system, and ways of dealing with utility are addressed. Finally, in the last section, theoretical issues in the measurement area, in vocational interest, in personality, and in developmental psychology are reviewed. The chapters in this book offer the researcher and the user a comprehensive assessment of the state of the art, providing a substantial amount of information to guide research and application. It is clear from these chapters that the future of biodata research seems to be very bright indeed.

REFERENCES

Anonymous. (1925). A method of rating the history and achievements of applicants for positions. *Public Personnel Studies, 3,* 202–209. (Methods and data credited to Gertrude V. Cope.)

Baehr, M. E., & Williams, G. B. (1968). Predictors of sale success from factorially determined dimensions of personal background data. *Journal of Applied Psychology, 52*(2), 98-103.

Berkeley, M. H. (1953). A comparison between the empirical and rational approaches for keying a heterogeneous test. *USAF Human Resources Research Center Bulletin,* 53–54.

DuBois, P. H., Loevinger, J., & Gleser. G. C. (1952). The construction of homogeneous keys for a biographical inventory. *USAF Human Resources Research Bulletin,* 52–58.

Eberhardt, B. J., & Muchinsky, P. M. (1982). Biodata determinants of vocational typology: An integration of two paradigms. *Journal of Applied Psychology, 67*(6), 714–727.

England, G. W. (1961). *Development and use of weighted application blanks.* Dubuque, IA: William C. Brown.

England, G. W. (1971). Development and use of weighted application blanks (Bulletin No. 55). Minneapolis: University of Minnesota, Industrial Relations Center.

Fleishman, E. A. (1988). Some new frontiers in personnel selection research. *Personnel Psychology, 41,* 679–701.

Goldsmith, D. B. (1922). The use of the personal history blank as a salesmanship test. *Journal of Applied Psychology, 6,* 149–155.

Guilford, J. P., & Lacey, J. I. (1947). Printed classification tests. *AAF Aviation Psychology Research Program Reports* (No. 5). Washington, DC: Government Printing Office.

Henry, E. R. (1966). *Research conference on the use of autobiographical data as psychological predictors.* Greensboro, NC: The Creativity Research Institute, The Richardson Foundation.

Kenagy, H. G., & Yoakum, C. S. (1925). *The selection and training of salesmen.* New York: McGraw-Hill.

Klimoski, R. J. (1973). A biographical data analysis of career patterns in engineering. *Journal of Vocational Behavior, 3,* 103–113.

Levine, A. S., & Zachert, V. (1951). Use of a biographical inventory in the air force classification program. *Journal of Applied Psychology, 35,* 241–244.

Manson, G. E. (1925). What can the application blank tell? *Journal of Personnel Research, 4,* 73–99.

Matteson, M. T., & Osburn, H. G. (1970). A Fortran program series for generating relatively independent and homogeneous keys for scoring biographical inventories. *Educational and Psychological Measurement, 30,* 664–671.

Morrison, R. F. (1977). A multivariate model for the occupational placement decision. *Journal of Applied Psychology, 62*(3), 271–277.

Morrison, R. F., & Sebald, M. L. (1974). Personal characteristics differentiating female executive from female nonexecutive personnel. *Journal of Applied Psychology, 59,* 656–659.

Mumford, M. D., & Owens, W. A. (1987). Methodology review: Principles, procedures, and findings in the application of background data measures. *Applied Psychological Measurement, 11*(1), 1–31.

Mumford, M. D., Stokes, G. S., & Owens, W. A. (1990). *Patterns of life history: The ecology of human individuality.* Hillsdale, NJ: Erlbaum.

Owens, W. A. (1976). Background data. In M. D. Dunnette (Ed.), *Handbook of industrial and organizational psychology.* Chicago: Rand McNally.

Owens, W. A., & Schoenfeldt, L. F. (1979). Toward a classification of persons [Monograph]. *Journal of Applied Psychology, 63,* 569–607.

Parish, J. A., & Drucker, A. J. (1957). *Personnel research for Officer Candidate School* (USA TAGO Personnel Research Branch Tech. Rep. No. 117, 1–22).

Roy, H., Brueckel, J., & Drucker, A. J. (1954). Selection of army and air force reserve training corp students. *USA Personnel Research Branch Notes, 28,* 1–9.

Russell, C. J., & Domm, D. R. (1990, April). *On the construct validity of biographical information: Evaluation of a theory-based method of item generation.* Paper presented at the annual meeting of the Society of Industrial and Organizational Psychology, Miami.

Siegel, L. (1956a). A biographical inventory for students: I. Construction and standardization of the instrument. *Journal of Applied Psychology, 40,* 5–10.

Siegel, L. (1956b). A biographical inventory for students: II. Validation of the instrument. *Journal of Applied Psychology, 40,* 122–126.

Viteles, M. (1932). *Industrial psychology.* New York: Norton.

Ward, J. H., & Hook, M. E. (1963). Application of a hierarchical clustering procedure to a problem of grouping profiles. *Educational and Psychological Measurement, 23,* 69–81.

BIODATA
ITEM
DEVELOPMENT

Owens (1976) noted that "biodata items are much more likely to validate if they are knowledgeably beamed at a specific target" (p. 614). However, few guidelines exist in the literature on how to generate items for a biodata inventory. The chapters in this section provide useful information for defining the nature of biodata items and sources for their development. Nickels addresses the issue of defining biodata items, noting that the single characteristic that sets biodata apart is the use of retrospective self-report to develop a general description of a person's life history. He reviews a taxonomy of items recently proposed by Mael (1991) and suggests that biodata items should be constructed using a well-defined framework of antecedent behaviors and experiences. He reviews several recent attempts to develop biodata inventories using such a framework, and suggests that our current lack of understanding concerning the predictive power of biodata items stems from the absence of an empirically tested nomological network to support the development and applications of biodata measures. Item development, he argues, needs to be focused on well-defined performance dimensions.

Whereas Nickels develops an argument that biodata items should have construct, content, and criterion-related validity, Russell attempts to provide ways to develop such items. Russell reviews six possible sources for biodata item development derived from Mumford and Owens (1987), and he argues that three of these provide a plethora of information for biodata item development. These are the human development literature, life history interviews with incumbents, and typical factor loadings of biodata items. He then reviews theories in three general areas: personality, vocational interest and job choice, and leadership and human development theory. In each area, he discusses specific techniques for deriving items based on the theory, providing specific examples of items. Finally, Russell discusses item characteristics that may influence both reliability and validity, noting the necessity for examining both item characteristics, such as heterogeneity and response formats, and theoretical rationale in order to understand the best techniques for adequately capturing relevant individual difference constructs.

Finally, Fine and Cronshaw focus specifically on the role of job analysis in establishing the validity of biodata and in providing a source of information for item development. They make a strong case for the use of job analysis in terms of both legal and validity issues. Although they discuss the utility of other job analysis procedures for biodata inventory development, they focus on functional job analysis (FJA) as a tool for developing biodata items, and they provide specific examples of how biodata items could be written from the information obtained from FJA.

REFERENCES

Mael, F. A. (1991). A conceptual rationale for the domain and attributes of biodata items. *Personnel Psychology, 44,* 763–792.

Owens, W. A. (1976). Background data. In M. D. Dunnette (Ed.), *Handbook of industrial and organizational psychology.* Chicago: Rand McNally.

The Nature of Biodata

Bernard J. Nickels

University Research Corporation

Because the situations to which individuals are exposed change over their life span, it cannot always be assumed that people will behave in the future as they have in the past (Lerner & Tubman, 1989). Most psychologists, however, would grant that prior behavior and experiences act to condition, or shape, future behavior and experiences (Owens & Schoenfeldt, 1979). As a result, applied psychologists have displayed an abiding interest in the potential applications of life history information (Dailey, 1960; Galton, 1902).

Biodata items, in which individuals are asked to recall and report their typical behaviors or experiences in a referent situation likely to have occurred earlier in their lives (Mumford & Owens, 1987), represent a standardized paper-and-pencil technique for collecting life history information. Few applied psychologists question the predictive efficiency of biodata scales. Reviews by Asher (1972), Ghiselli (1973), Hunter and Hunter (1984), Mumford and Owens (1987), Owens (1976), and Reilly and Chao (1982) indicate that biodata will predict a wide range of criteria, from leadership performance to employee theft, that typically yields cross-validities between .30 and .40.

Biodata measures represent excellent measurement tools producing respectable validities in the prediction of performance in industrial and educational settings (Ghiselli, 1973; Reilly & Chao, 1982). Reilly and Chao (1982), for example, reviewed a number of studies involving a variety of occupations, including clerical, management, scientific, and military personnel. The job-performance factors investigated in these studies included tenure, training, productivity, and performance ratings. The reported cross-validities ranged from .25 to .50. Additionally, Barge (1987) has identified several other recent reviews that have provided evidence in support of the predictive effectiveness of biodata measures.

Unfortunately, we currently have a limited understanding of the processes through which biodata measures obtain their predictive power, despite their reported validity (Barge, 1987; Mumford & Owens, 1987). To date, there exist very few generally accepted constructs that define and perhaps organize the content domain being measured. Furthermore, the characteristics presumed to be responsible for the predictive power of these instruments have not been explicitly stated and tested. The theories that do exist concerning the specific domain being addressed by biodata measures have tended to be rather informally stated, and subsequently, empirical testing of these theories has traditionally been absent.

It should be no surprise, then, that a limited understanding prevails with respect to exactly what biodata items measure. Mumford and Owens (1987) have suggested that this lack of understanding may be due, at least in part, to the fact that "in their satisfaction with the resulting validity coefficients, investigators have often lost sight of the psychological principles underlying the development and application of biodata measures" (p. 2).

BIODATA'S DEFINING CHARACTERISTICS

The use of biodata is a measurement strategy that is deeply rooted in the past behaviors and experiences of the individual. More specifically, biodata items require people to describe behaviors and events occurring earlier in their lives. Biodata, like other life history measures, are used based on the assumption that a person's past behaviors and experiences are a potential predictor of his or her future behaviors and experiences. This does not suggest that *all* future behavior can be predicted by past experience, but rather that knowledge of previous experiences will allow some prediction of future behavior, given that the individual's prior learning history will make the occurrence of some forms of behavior more probable than others (Mumford & Owens, 1987). More directly stated, biodata measures may predict performance across so many aspects of behavior as well as they do because responses to biodata items may serve to capture previous manifestations of the constructs and mechanisms that ultimately determine predictive relationships with criteria.

But what exactly constitutes a biodata item? Unfortunately, there is insufficient agreement among practitioners to provide a single and precise definition. Therefore, I will offer a brief summary of some previous taxonomies of variables on which biodata items tend to differ from study to study. The most recent of these taxonomies was presented by Mael (1991). Mael points out that many previous efforts to identify what is (and is not) included under the biodata rubric have been unsystematic. He further suggests that while some researchers have attempted to address these issues (Asher, 1972; Mumford & Owens, 1987; Mumford & Stokes, 1992), much of this research is ignored or challenged by others.

The primary purpose of Mael's article, however, is to integrate current perspectives on biodata in an attempt to clarify the domain of biodata items. To this end, Mael identified ten attributes of biodata that could be used to classify items. These dimensions are history, externality, objectivity, firsthandedness, discreteness, verifiability, controllability, equal accessibility, job relevance, and invasiveness.

According to Mael, these ten dimensions represent three general categories of biodata attributes. The first category includes the *history* dimension. This category, which will be discussed later, really defines the domain of biodata. Additionally, this historical perspective is one of the primary distinctions between biodata and temperament or personality items. As previously stated, biodata is a measurement strategy that is deeply rooted in the *past* behaviors and experiences of the individual. Thus, biodata items should refer to events that have already occurred or continue to occur (e.g., historical). They should not include broad statements about a person's overall disposition or about hypothetical behaviors or situations.

The second category of item attributes proposed by Mael (1991) included what can generally be thought of as *methodological variables* used to ensure the accuracy of the information being obtained. These item attributes include externality, objectivity, firsthandedness, discreteness, and verifiability. *Externality* refers to the extent to which the item addresses observable events (e.g., behaviors that can be witnessed by an outsider) rather than internal events (e.g., behaviors that are not readily witnessed such as attitudes or value judgments). Similarly, the *objectivity* of the item refers to the extent to which the item focuses on recalling and reporting fact-based information rather than on reporting the more subjective interpretation of the event. For example, a highly objective item might inquire about the number of times a student was called to the principal's office, while a more subjective item would inquire about how he or she felt during those visits.

The third attribute in this category is *firsthandedness*. This attribute refers to the extent to which the item seeks information that is directly and personally available to the respondent rather than an evaluation of the respondent's behavior by others. The fourth attribute in the category is *discreteness*. This refers to the extent to which the item seeks information about a single event or a simple count of the number of times something occurred (e.g., number of times elected) rather than a summary response (e.g., average time spent in office). The final attribute in the category is *verifiability*. This refers to the extent to which the accuracy of responses to the item can be verified. This particular attribute is discussed in detail by Lautenschlager in a later chapter of this book.

Mael's (1991) third and final category of item attributes includes attributes pertaining to *legal and moral issues* surrounding the content of biodata items. These attributes are controllability, equal accessibility, job relevance, and invasiveness. In this context, *controllability* refers to the extent to which the item addresses events that were under the direct control of the respondent (e.g., prior behaviors), as opposed to events over which the respondent had little or no control (e.g., demographics, parental behavior). The second attribute in this category is *equal accessibility*. This refers to the extent to which the events or experiences addressed in the item are equally accessible to all potential respondents. Prior microcomputer usage, for example, is potentially less accessible for the socioeconomically disadvantaged.

Job relevance covers the extent to which the items solicit information that is clearly related to the job. Although Mael's discussion focuses on the use of biodata as a selection instrument, I think this attribute could be expanded to include more global situations (and relabeled *situational relevance*). In any case, this attribute focuses on the manifest similarity between the content of the item and the criterion of interest (e.g., face validity). The final item attribute in Mael's (1991) taxonomy is *invasiveness*. This attribute refers to the extent to which the item content is sensitive to the respondent's right to privacy. In other words, invasiveness addresses whether the respondent will consider the item content to be an invasion of his or her privacy. Items inquiring about religious affiliations, marital status, or dating habits are examples of items that are potentially invasive.

The preceding summary is intended to give the reader a sense of the multifaceted and complex response that must be given to the seemingly simple question, What exactly is biodata? The short answer is that it is many different things to many different people. The long answer is the reason for this book. Unfortunately, with the exception of the historical perspective required in biodata items, there is no clear-cut, indisputable evidence to support a definitive position on any of the attributes identified in Mael's (1991) taxonomy. Previous attempts (Asher, 1972; Barge, 1987; Cascio, 1982) to clarify some of the ambiguity surrounding biodata by developing similar descriptive taxonomies of item attributes have proven unsuccessful. Despite the efforts of these authors, biodata items still differ greatly from application to application. I believe this is due, in part, to the unresolved controversy surrounding the definition of precisely what constitutes a biodata item—a controversy I'm sure will continue for some time.

A FEW COMMENTS ON SCALING STRATEGIES

If there is a single characteristic of biodata measures that sets them apart from other life history measures, it is the use of a retrospective self-report (Mikesell & Tesser, 1971) to formulate a general description of a person's life history. This description is derived from an individual's responses to questions about behavior and experiences in a number of discrete situations likely to have occurred earlier in his or her life. In response to these questions, individuals are asked to recall their behavior and experiences in the referent situation and then select the response option that provides the best available description of their typical behavior and experiences. These observations led Mumford and Owens (1987) to conclude that "whenever a biodata item predicts performance, it must also represent a developmental antecedent or a sign for later performance" (p. 3). This suggests that biodata items capable of capturing significant past behaviors and experiences are a minimal requirement if a biodata measure is to display adequate predictive power (Mumford & Owens, 1987). Because multiple prior behaviors and experiences are typically required to maximize predictive power, however, it is often necessary to find some technique for combining these items into a meaningful pattern (Mumford & Owens, 1987).

A number of such techniques have proven useful when scaling biodata items for use in performance prediction, including rational scaling, factorial scaling, subgrouping, and empirical keying (Mumford & Owens, 1987; Owens, 1976). Although each of these techniques has its own unique merits (Mitchell & Klimoski, 1982; Schoenfeldt, 1989; Schrader, 1975), traditionally the most common method of defining these patterns has been through the empirical keying approach, where items or response options are weighted on the basis of their ability to predict differential performance (England, 1971; Lecznar & Dailey, 1950).

Generally speaking, *empirical keying* is a scaling procedure used to select and weight biodata items on the basis of the item's ability to differentiate individuals or discriminate the members of a criterion group from members of a reference group. In so doing, empirical keying defines general patterns of differential behavior or experience related to the specific criterion under consideration. Item selection is typically completed through a correlational or nonparametric analysis to identify item scores or response patterns that predict group membership. Items are then assigned differential weights based on the direction and magnitude of the observed relationship. These weights are used to form a composite response score, which can then be correlated with criterion performance to determine overall predictive power. Finally, the observed correlations are cross-validated on an independent sample to control for sample-specific results (Mumford & Owens, 1987; Wesley, Mumford, & McLoughlin, 1987).

Although the criterion-related validity of empirical keys is well documented (Asher, 1972; Ghiselli, 1973; Mitchell & Klimoski, 1982; Mumford & Owens, 1987; Owens, 1976), the use of such keys is not entirely free from difficulties. For example, empirical keying provides a description of a general pattern of development in reference to a specific criterion, which implies that the generality of any empirical key is limited by the generality of the criterion measure. This limitation includes external validity for groups not explicitly measured. Additionally, the predictive power of an empirical key will be limited by the nature of the criterion used to define it (Mumford & Owens, 1987; Thayer, 1977).

It has also been suggested that the predictive power of measures formulated on purely empirical grounds may be unduly sensitive to transient applicant pool characteristics (Dunnette, Kirchner, Erickson, & Banas, 1960; Schwab & Oliver, 1974; Wernimont, 1962). Along somewhat different lines, Mumford and Owens (1987), O'Leary (1973), and Pace and Schoenfeldt (1977) have argued that empirical keying may lead to inappropriate inferences concerning the performance of certain individuals if nonconstant or noncommon life history influences are operating in certain subgroups.

Consideration of these facts led Owens (1976) to argue that a broader and more general descriptive system could be formulated through the identification of modal patterns of individual development without reference to a specific criterion. This process would not only alleviate the aforementioned difficulties, it would also minimize the necessity of developing new keys for each criterion of interest.

The scaling technique Owens developed, known as *subgrouping,* is more general than empirical keying, thus making it particularly useful in situations where prediction of several criteria is necessary. Generally speaking, subgrouping is a statistically based classification procedure in which groups of individuals displaying similar characteristics are identified. When this approach is used in the context of biodata, individuals displaying similar patterns of past behaviors and experiences are grouped together. Differences in the characteristic patterns of behavior and experiences across subgroups can then be established and used to predict differences in performance.

Like empirical keying, subgrouping begins with a comprehensive set of biodata items capable of capturing significant behaviors and experiences.

These items are administered to a large sample of individuals, and responses are summarized through principal components analyses, resulting in a profile of scores on each of the relevant components for every individual. The similarity between an individual's profile and the profiles of all other gender group members is then assessed to identify subgroups of individuals (Feild & Schoenfeldt, 1975). The ability of subgroup membership to predict performance in a variety of domains is then examined. Data from a variety of field studies (Owens & Schoenfeldt, 1979) have demonstrated that these general developmental patterns are strongly related to performance on criteria across a wide range of traditional domains, including perception, cognition, attitudes, values and motives, social pressures, and learning and memory.

The important similarity between empirical keying and subgrouping is that both use biodata items to capture differential patterns of past behaviors and experiences that are highly predictive of future differences in criterion performance (Owens, 1976, 1978; Owens & Schoenfeldt, 1979). The important distinction between these two is that the end result of empirical keying is the inclusion of a set of biodata items that define specific differential patterns of behavior and experiences linked to a specific criterion, whereas the end result of subgrouping is the inclusion of a set of biodata items that identify more general patterns without reference to a specific criterion. Both, however, rely on the ability of a set of biodata items to successfully capture differential patterns of past behavior and experience, which may then serve to discriminate differential criterion performance.

THE IMPORTANCE OF THEORY

Regardless of the scoring method, biodata measures typically use patterns of item responses as predictors of later external performance. It has been repeatedly demonstrated (Kavanagh & York, 1972; Mumford & Owens, 1987; Quaintance, 1981; Williams, 1961) that biodata items developed on the basis of specific hypotheses about the dimensions underlying performance are much more likely to produce significant relationships with external criterion performance measures than items for which such hypotheses were lacking. Additionally, Mumford and Owens (1987) have identified several item-pool characteristics that are likely to result in poor prediction or misleading inferences. One such concern is that item pools that fail to capture significant antecedents will subsequently fail to predict future performance due to deficiency in the predictor space. A second concern is that inclusion of prior behaviors and experiences that are irrelevant to criterion performance will unnecessarily contaminate the predictor space. A third concern is that a failure to capture relevant shifts in experiential patterns across gender, race, or age groups will result in a biased set of predictors.

These concerns suggest that biodata items should be constructed using a well-defined framework of antecedent behaviors and experiences. Such a framework will serve to assist the practitioner in (a) widening the domain of what is thought to be a significant antecedent, (b) assessing the relevance of the included antecedents with respect to the criterion measures, and (c) accommodating known differences among groups. Clearly, this suggests that well-constructed biodata measures should start with an adequate definition of the domain of relevant antecedent behaviors and experiences. This domain definition will then provide a solid foundation for item development (Mumford & Owens, 1987).

In the past, the domain to be assessed by biodata measures has generally been established primarily through criterion-related validation strategies. This was due largely to the prevalent reliance on empirical keying (Pace & Schoenfeldt, 1977). Strictly speaking, no a priori, substantive justification was necessary for including biodata items in an empirical key. Instead, item retention was justified by demonstrating a significant relationship with criterion performance. Unfortunately, when coupled with the tendency of some investigators to select items on the basis of convenience, this empirical bent has become a source of some consternation (Korman, 1968). In fact, Dunnette (1962), Henry (1966), and Owens (1976) have argued that this unadulterated empiricism may have actually stymied theory development and the subsequent generation of general laws relating life events to work performance.

As yet, there has been very little research effort aimed at establishing methods to ensure the systematic identification of the content domain. The empirical keying approach, by virtue of its focus on a particular kind of criterion performance, may have contributed to this failure to establish a general theoretical framework required for routine application to biodata item development strategies (Mumford & Owens, 1987; Schoenfeldt, 1989).

PREVIOUS THEORY-BASED STUDIES

When one considers the fundamental nature of such a defining framework, it is surprising that only a few notable efforts have served to demonstrate how one might go about establishing the content of biodata measures. In a relatively early effort, Himmelstein and Blaskovics (1960) provided a sound prototype for the systematic identification of the content of biodata measures. In their study, which involved the prediction of combat effectiveness, the nature of job performance was assessed, and hypotheses were formulated about the kind of life history constructs conditioning future performance. Biodata items were then developed to provide an adequate sample of behavior and experiences in situations that would either (a) call for the prior expression of an attribute or (b) contribute to its development. For example, the authors hypothesized that risk taking was an important construct and subsequently developed an item that asked about willingness to play poker. Finally, these items were scaled, criterion measures reflecting hypothesized behavioral relationships were specified, and the measure's relationship to these substantively relevant forms of behavior was assessed.

A few more recent efforts have provided some important extensions of this general approach. Russell, Mattson, Devlin, and Atwater (1988) identified several dimensions thought to underlie performance of naval officers. Naval academy students were then asked to write narrative essays that described past performance on these dimensions. A content analysis of the events the students identified was conducted and used as the basis for the generation of biodata items. Using a somewhat different approach to identify the dimensions underlying performance, Schoenfeldt and Mendoza (1988) administered a biodata instrument intended to evaluate several hypothesized dimensions of managerial performance. A subsequent LISREL analysis supported the existence of most of their dimensions. Although their methods differed, both Russell et al. and Schoenfeldt and Mendoza used well-formulated hypotheses about the attributes (dimensions) underlying performance as a basis for their item development efforts.

Others have suggested that stronger inferences concerning the meaningfulness of biodata items might be generated by showing that the scale yields an interpretable pattern of relationships with other substantively relevant measures (Hough, 1984; Owens, 1976), or by demonstrating that items measure behaviors and experiences that are performance-relevant (Mitchell, 1986; Mumford & Owens, 1987; Pannone, 1984; Russell et al., 1988). Pannone (1984), for example, used a sample of electricial technicians to evaluate the utility of using job-analysis task statements as biodata items. In this study, the applicants were asked to rate their previous work experience on each task. Pannone's results confirmed the utility of this approach in the identification of performance-relevant dimensions to include in biodata instruments.

The preceding studies suggest that careful consideration of the dimensions thought to underlie performance will assist the item writer in the systematic development of biodata items in relation to these dimensions. This, in turn, will enhance the meaningfulness and substantive interpretability of those items. Thus, developing biodata items intended to tap prior behavior and experiences in relation to a systematic underlying dimensional framework should not only provide a necessary interpretative framework, it should also provide the structural guidelines needed for systematic sampling (vis-à-vis items) of relevant prior behavior and experiences. One implication of this notion is that it should be possible to formulate stronger or more meaningful item pools by orienting item development around performance-relevant life history constructs.

Nonetheless, direct attempts to identify and define the psychological constructs (dimensions) underlying the predictive power of biodata measures have been notably absent in the biodata literature. As noted by Mumford and Owens (1987), biodata measures may be said to display validity to the extent that the items in the measure successfully capture a representative sample of the prior behaviors and experiences that contribute to the development of differential levels of criterion performance. The development of criterion performance, however, is typically a complex and multifaceted phenomenon that is subject to variation across developmental phases and subpopulations (Lerner & Busch-Rossnagel, 1981). The content of the biodata measure, therefore, should not be derived solely from observable similarity between the item content and the criterion in question (Mumford & Owens, 1987).[*]

EXPANDING THE THEORETICAL DOMAIN TO FURTHER OUR UNDERSTANDING

Biodata items capture differential patterns of antecedent behaviors and experiences that can be used to make targeted predictions about criterion performance. Thus, an adequate representation of relevant antecedent behaviors and experiences must exist in the content of these items. This is true regardless of whether any particular set of antecedents may look as though it should be a good predictor of criterion performance. It is inappropriately restrictive to exclude from measurement a given antecedent behavior because it may not appear to be job related. To do this would be to maintain that predictors that lack face validity must also lack predictive power.

Traditional biodata research has, for one reason or another, failed to address potentially relevant dimensions of past behavior and experiences,

---

[*]As Owens, 1976, has noted, having $100,000 of insurance at age 25 does not have the same implications as having $100,000 of insurance at age 50.

while attempting to explain the predictive power of biodata items. This observation holds true despite consistent evidence to show that biodata items formulated on the basis of specific hypotheses concerning antecedent behaviors yield better relationships with external criteria than do items that are developed in the absence of such hypotheses (Kavanagh & York, 1972; Quaintance, 1981; Williams, 1961). Perhaps the consistency in these findings stems from the fact that hypothesis-based items are more likely to capture differences in the relevant patterns of antecedent events responsible for the predictive power of the item.

Although biodata scales have consistently proven effective in performance prediction, a recurring criticism of this technique has centered around a lack of understanding with respect to the exact nature of what is being measured by biodata scales. In this chapter, I have proposed that the current lack of understanding concerning the predictive power of biodata items stems from the absence of an empirically tested nomological network to support the development and application of biodata measures.

Broadly speaking, this chapter argues that by systematically identifying performance relevant attributes (and developing biodata items in relation to these attributes), we will do much to enhance the interpretability of biodata measures. Biodata measures that are developed based on a systematic underlying set of hypotheses need not rely solely on predictive evidence to establish their meaningfulness or their usefulness.

I have also suggested that the traditional pattern of limiting biodata items to those displaying a high similarity to the criterion of interest is overly restrictive. Perhaps our previous inability to create an adequate nomological network is due, in part, to the fact that the constructs underlying successful prediction have not been fully represented. In this chapter, I suggest that it is absolutely imperative that a wider range of past behaviors and experiences be represented in the content of biodata items because biodata items derive much of their predictive power from individual differences in these behaviors and experiences. Expansion of the nomological network surrounding biodata to include a broader range of relevant antecedent behavioral and experiential dimensions will not only improve the predictive power of biodata measures but will also improve the current understanding of the success of biodata as a predictive device.

For one reason or another, however, the application of such basic construct validation principles has proven difficult in the construction and evaluation of biodata measures, except in the limited sense that any criterion-related validation study represents a form of construct validation. As noted earlier, this state of affairs might be attributed to our lack of understanding of what exactly is being measured by biodata scales (Mumford & Owens, 1987). The ability to present a theoretical framework to account for the predictive power of biodata items against both general developmental patterns and discrete criteria might prove useful in resolving this issue. Multiple models might be formulated capable of serving this purpose. The important factor is that the use of a well-formulated model, in conjunction with established job analysis techniques, such as *Functional Job Analysis* (Fine, 1988), occupational reinforcers (Borgen, 1988; Dawis & Lofquist, 1984), or Fleishman's ability requirement scales (Fleishman & Mumford, 1988), might further define the domain of constructs thought to condition differential performance.

Additionally, such a framework can be used to minimize deficiency, contamination, and bias by targeting item development on those constructs (dimensions) most relevant to the performance variables of interest (Mumford & Owens, 1987), while simultaneously producing guidelines for the application of systematic item development techniques (Russell, Mattson, Devlin, & Atwater, 1988). Finally, to the extent that relevant constructs are appropriately specified, and items reflecting or contributing to the development of these attributes are obtained, one would expect that inferences drawn from use of the resulting instrument would manifest stronger construct, content, and criterion-related validity.

This points to the possibility of employing systematic theoretical frameworks to generate biodata items capable of capturing situation-relevant prior behaviors. This will, of course, provide an additional basis for drawing inferences concerning the likely meaningfulness of the performance inferences derived from biodata measures.

CONCLUSION

In summary, this chapter suggests that biodata items should be developed based upon a well-formulated specification of the domain of behaviors of interest. Such a theory-based approach will serve to provide a stronger basis for drawing inferences concerning the meaningfulness of these items. It should be recognized, however, that the principles of item development outlined herein can also be used to address a number of other criticisms traditionally leveled against biodata measures. First, by focusing item development on performance-relevant dimensions, transient applicant-pool characteristics are unlikely to exert any great influence on the validity of empirical keys. This will greatly enhance the confidence with which use of these keys can be extended beyond the development sample to the larger population of interest.

Second, use of the procedures suggested herein alleviates the need for evidence of a scale's meaningfulness based solely on its observed relationship to the criterion in use. By focusing item development on performance-relevant dimensions, evidence of the scale's meaningfulness can be extracted from other studies, as well as from existing knowledge about known relationships between the dimensions being evaluated and other constructs and/or measures.

Third, some degree of criterion-related validity is likely to be insured by the use of content and construct valid items. Traditionally, biodata measures have focused item development on those aspects of behavior demonstrating a manifest similarity to the criterion at hand. The expansion of this fairly constrained set of items to include items intended to measure those behavioral or experiential antecedents thought to underlie observed differences in manifest performance will allow an opportunity to capture content and construct areas previously left unmeasured. This will thereby alleviate, or at least minimize, the potential for content deficiency or underrepresentation of key variables. Similarly, an expressed focus during item development on those dimensions thought to underlie differential performance almost certainly will improve the criterion-related validity of these measures.

Not only will these procedures do much to eliminate some of the more common criticisms leveled against biodata scales, they will also serve to enhance the substantive value of biodata measures. By targeting item development on well-specified dimensions, for example, validity generalization efforts become more plausible. A logical extension of validity generalization efforts would be the subsequent availability of general item pools for use in multiple studies. This would do much to alleviate the traditionally significant costs to the practitioner associated with developing a unique item pool for every application.

Additionally, if biodata items capture antecedents of performance, then careful examination of the results obtained in a number of different studies might prove extremely useful in attaining at least a preliminary understanding of the developmental events conditioning differential criterion performance. Information of this sort might in turn prove to be highly useful in both theory development and the specification of optimal developmental interventions. In fact, in a much broader sense, this same information might even prove useful in future attempts to identify the development of various differential characteristics.

Taken as a whole, these observations indicate that the use of substantive constructs in the development of biodata items may do much to enhance the validity and utility of the resulting measures. Given this conclusion and its grounding in standard psychometric theory (Messick, 1989), one must ask why this strategy is not a routine application. As I pointed out earlier, however, the application of substantive constructs in measurement is contingent upon the availability of a theory specifying the kind of attributes that contribute to observed differences. Until recently, our limited understanding of the forces shaping differential life histories has made it difficult, if not impossible, to specify the kind of constructs that should be employed in developing biodata measures.

Because biodata measures seek to define quantitative developmental patterns (Mumford & Owens, 1987), it is necessary to attain an understanding of the kind of constructs contributing to the predictive power of biodata measures. I hope that this chapter has provided an initial illustration of how a theoretical understanding of differential developmental patterns might contribute to the emergence of more sophisticated techniques for the construction of biodata items and validation of biodata measures. It is only through the progressive refinement of systematic theoretical models that biodata will be able to live up to its promise as one of applied psychology's best tools for the description and prediction of individual performance.

REFERENCES

Asher, E. J. (1972). The biographical item: Can it be improved? *Personnel Psychology*, *25*, 251–269.

Barge, B. N. (1987, August). Characteristics of biodata items and their relationship to validity. In *Biodata in the 80s and beyond*. Symposium conducted at the 95th annual meeting of the American Psychological Association, New York.

Borgen, F. H. (1988). Occupational reinforcer patterns. In S. Gael (Ed.), *The job analysis handbook for business, industry, and government* (pp. 902–916). New York: Wiley.

Cascio, W. F. (1982). *Applied psychology in personnel management* (2d ed.). Reston, VA: Reston.

Dailey, J. T. (1960). Life history as a criterion of assessment. *Journal of Counseling Psychology*, *7*, 20–23.

Dawis, R. V., & Lofquist, L. H. (1984). *A psychological theory of work adjustment: An individual-differences model and its applications*. Minneapolis: University of Minnesota Press.

Dunnette, M. D. (1962). Personnel management. *Annual Review of Psychology*, *13*, 285–314.

Dunnette, M. D., Kirchner, W. K., Erickson, J., & Banas, P. (1960). Predicting turnover among female office workers. *Personnel Administration*, *23*, 45–50.

England, G. W. (1971). *Development and use of weighted application blanks* (Bulletin No. 55). Minneapolis: University of Minnesota, Industrial Relations Center.

Feild, H. S., & Schoenfeldt, L. F. (1975). Development and application of a measure of students' college experiences. *Journal of Applied Psychology*, *60*, 491–497.

Fine, S. A. (1988). Functional job analysis. In S. Gael (Ed.), *The job analysis handbook for business, industry, and government* (pp. 1010–1035). New York: Wiley.

Fleishman, E. A., & Mumford, M. D. (1988). The ability requirements scales. In S. Gael (Ed.), *The job analysis handbook for business, industry, and government* (pp. 917–935). New York: Wiley.

Galton, F. (1902). *Life history album* (2d ed.). New York: Macmillan.

Ghiselli, E. E. (1973). The validity of aptitude tests in personnel selection. *Personnel Psychology, 26,* 461–477.

Henry, E. R. (1966). *Research conference on the use of autobiographical data as psychological predictors.* Greensboro, NC: The Creativity Research Institute, The Richardson Foundation.

Himmelstein, D., & Blaskovicks, T. L. (1960). Prediction of an intermediate criterion of combat effectiveness with a biographical inventory. *Journal of Applied Psychology, 44,* 166–168.

Hough, L. M. (1984). Development and evaluation of the "accomplishment record" method of selecting and promoting professionals. *Journal of Applied Psychology, 69,* 135–146.

Hunter, J. E., & Hunter, R. F. (1984). Validity and utility of alternative predictors of job performance. *Psychological Bulletin, 96,* 72–98.

Kavanagh, M. J., & York, D. R. (1972). Biographical correlates of middle managers' performance. *Personnel Psychology, 25,* 319–332.

Korman, A. K. (1968). The prediction of managerial performance: A review. *Personnel Psychology, 21,* 295–322.

Lecznar, W. B., & Dailey, J. T. (1950). Keying biographical inventories in classification test batteries. *American Psychologist, 5,* 279.

Lerner, R. M., & Busch-Rossnagel, N. A. (1981). Individuals as producers of their own development. In R. M. Lerner & N. A. Busch-Rossnagel (Eds.), *Individuals as producers of their own development: A life span perspective* (pp. 1–36). New York: Academic Press.

Lerner, R. M., & Tubman, J. G. (1989). Conceptual issues in studying continuity and discontinuity in persons across life. *Journal of Personality, 57,* 343–373.

Mael, F. A. (1991). A conceptual rationale for the domain and attributes of biodata items. *Personnel Psychology, 44,* 763–792.

Mikesell, R. H., & Tesser, A. (1971). Life history antecedents of authoritarianism: A quasi-longitudinal approach. *Proceedings of the 74th Annual Convention of the American Psychological Association, 6,* 136–137.

Messick, S. (1989). Validity. In R. L. Linn (Ed.), *Educational measurement* (pp. 13–104). New York: Macmillan.

Mitchell, T. W. (1986, April). *Specialized job analysis for developing rationally-oriented biodata prediction systems.* Paper presented at the annual meeting of the Society for Industrial and Organizational Psychology, Chicago.

Mitchell, T. W., & Klimoski, R. J. (1982). Is it rational to be empirical? A test of methods for scoring biographical data. *Journal of Applied Psychology, 67,* 411–418.

Mumford, M. D., & Owens, W. A. (1987). Methodology review: Principles, procedures, and findings in the application of background data measures. *Applied Psychological Measurement, 11,* 1–31.

Mumford, M. D., & Stokes, G. S. (1992). Developmental determinants of individual action: Theory and practice in applying background measures. In M. D.

Dunnette & L. M. Hough (Eds.), *Handbook of industrial and organizational psychology* (2d ed., vol. 3, pp. 61–138). Palo Alto, CA: Consulting Psychologists Press.

O'Leary, L. R. (1973). Fair employment, sound psychometric practice, and reality. *American Psychologist, 23,* 147–150.

Owens, W. A. (1976). Background data. In M. D. Dunnette (Ed.), *Handbook of industrial and organizational psychology* (1st ed., pp. 609–644). Chicago: Rand McNally.

Owens, W. A. (1978). Moderators and subgroups. *Personnel Psychology, 31,* 243–247.

Owens, W. A., & Schoenfeldt, L. F. (1979). Toward a classification of persons. *Journal of Applied Psychology, 64,* 569–607.

Pace, L. A., & Schoenfeldt, L. F. (1977). Legal concerns in the use of weighted application blanks. *Personnel Psychology, 30,* 159–166.

Pannone, R. D. (1984). Predicting test performance: A content valid approach to screening applicants. *Personnel Psychology, 37,* 507–514.

Quaintance, M. K. (1981). *Development of a weighted application blank to predict managerial assessment center performance.* Unpublished doctoral dissertation, George Washington University, Washington, DC.

Reilly, R. R., & Chao, G. T. (1982). Validity and fairness of some alternative employee selection procedures. *Personnel Psychology, 35,* 1–62.

Russell, C. J., Mattson, J., Devlin, S. E., & Atwater, D. (1988, April). *Predictive validity of biodata items generated from retrospective life experience essays.* Paper presented at the annual meeting of the Society for Industrial and Organizational Psychology, Dallas.

Schoenfeldt, L. F. (1989). *Biographical data as the new frontier in employee selection research.* Paper presented at the annual meeting of the American Psychological Association, New Orleans.

Schoenfeldt, L. F., & Mendoza, J. L. (1988, August). *The content and construct validation of a biographical questionnaire.* Paper presented at the annual meeting of the American Psychological Association, Atlanta.

Schrader, A. D. (1975). *A comparison of the relative utility of several rational and empirical strategies for forming biodata measures.* Unpublished doctoral dissertation, University of Houston.

Schwab, D. P., & Oliver, R. L. (1974). Predicting tenure with biographical data: Exhuming buried evidence. *Personnel Psychology, 27,* 125–128.

Thayer, P. W. (1977). Somethings old, somethings new. *Personnel Psychology, 30,* 513–524.

Wernimont, P. F. (1962). Reevaluation of a weighted application blank for office personnel. *Journal of Applied Psychology, 46,* 417–419.

Wesley S. S., Mumford, M. D., & McLoughlin, L. M. (1987). *On the robustness of background data keys.* Unpublished manuscript.

Williams, W. E. (1961, April). *Life history antecedents of volunteers versus non-volunteers for an AFROTC program.* Paper presented at the meeting of the Midwestern Psychological Association, Chicago.

2

Generation Procedures for Biodata Items
A Point of Departure

Craig J. Russell
Louisana State University

The purpose of this chapter is to help future investigators generate biodata items that demonstrate both construct- and criterion-related validity. It is my belief that such efforts will ultimately lead to the development and evaluation of theories of performance prediction (see Campbell, 1990). The first part of this chapter is devoted to convincing the reader of the merits of such an effort. Theories of life history events, such as they are, are described in light of the absence of any operational guidelines for biodata item generation. I argue that the gap between theories of life history and operationalizations (i.e., biodata item content) presents a major opportunity for scholarly contribution to a theory of performance prediction, or, as borrowed from Fleishman's (1988) discussion of similar issues, a "new frontier."

The second part of this chapter provides explicit examples of two item generation procedures applied to three theories of individual differences (personality, vocational interest, and leadership). This section portrays a number of item generation efforts I have been involved in over the past decade. On my first involvement with biodata, I found the absence of published instruments and keys to be a major barrier to entry. I hope this section will give the novice biodata researcher a number of alternate points of departure.

The third section describes how item content might affect other aspects of biodata items. These include item reliability, heterogeneity, behavioral discreteness, and behavioral consistency.

IMPORTANCE OF BIODATA ITEM CONTENT

Recent research efforts involving biographical information typically start with a brief overview of meta-analytic results supporting biodata criterion-related validity (e.g., Hunter & Hunter, 1984; Reilly & Chao, 1982; Schmitt, Gooding, Noe, & Kirsch, 1984). Biodata research conducted prior to the introduction of meta-analytic techniques usually referenced Ghiselli's (1966) survey of test validities. Each biodata study would then describe the particular aspect or issue to be examined. Recently, these have included examinations of alternate scoring procedures (Mitchell, 1992; Mitchell & Klimoski, 1982), the susceptibility of biodata items to faking in applicant versus incumbent samples (Hogan & Stokes, 1989; Kluger, Reilly, & Russell, 1991), the effect on criterion-related validity of biodata response distortions (Trent, 1987), the generalizability of item validities across jobs (Rothstein, Schmidt, Erwin, Owens, & Sparks, 1990), and the consistency of biodata factor structures over time (Neiner & Owens, 1982).

However, until Mumford and Owens (1987) published their review of methods in biodata technology, guidelines on how to generate items were not available in the literature. Few investigators provided any direction on how to construct an item that could be expected to demonstrate criterion-related validity. Almost no investigators have described explicitly how to develop items that could subsequently be used to test theory-based hypotheses (for an exception, see Kuhnert & Russell's [1990] description of how Kegan's [1982] constructive/developmental theory of adult development might be used to generate biodata items).

That is not to suggest that efforts at developing models or theories of *constructs* underlying biodata items have not taken place. Owens' (1968, 1971) developmental-integrative model suggests that prior life events are sources of individual development and integration (i.e., the meaning a person derives from an event) that influence future knowledge, skills, abilities, and motivation. Mumford and Stokes (1991) have extended this approach to an ecology model describing a longitudinal sequence of interactions between the environment, a person's *resources* (human capital, skills, abilities), and a person's *affordances* (needs, desires, choices). Stokes, Mumford, and Owens (1989) demonstrated that "prototypes" of individuals could be empirically identified that "create their own organized subenvironments consisting of various activities and experiences with which a self-propagating developmental trajectory...crystallizes, or becomes predictable" (p. 512). Mael (1991) elaborated the ecology model, using social identity theory to explain how biodata items tap situations in which "a person associates with a...psychological group," taking on "(to varying degrees) the syndrome of aspirations, preferences, values, and self-perceptions that are endemic to group members" (p. 768).

These models are valuable conceptualizations of the construct domain underlying life history items. However, they fail to provide strong guidance for operationalization—that is, explicit direction in how to design paper-and-pencil life history inventories to predict specific criteria. Consequently, characterizations of biodata research as atheoretical empiricism will remain until the loop is closed—that is, until support is found for specific linkages between theory, item content, and criterion performance measures (see Dunnette, 1962; Guilford, 1959; Henry, 1966).[1]

At first glance, rational keying procedures for biodata instruments might provide such a linkage (see Hough & Paullin's chapter in this volume). These procedures involve generation of specific a priori hypotheses about how item responses should be related to a criterion based on subject matter experts or investigators' subjective judgments (see Mitchell & Klimoski, 1982). Unfortunately, none of the applications of rational scoring techniques were derived from nomological networks of hypothesized relationships among constructs (two of which include biographical information and job performance). In other words, rational scoring techniques are not excessively burdened with elaborate theory. This criticism should not be considered too harsh, as the field is generally plagued with a lack of accepted theories that explicitly link the content domains of job and person (Bobko & Russell, 1991; Burke & Pearlman, 1988; Dunnette, 1966).

Yet somehow investigators have been able to generate instruments that consistently yield criterion-related validities among the highest reported in the literature (Reilly & Warech, 1990). Further, Owens and his colleagues have demonstrated that subjects' biodata item responses exhibit coherent factor structures and relationships over time (Mumford & Owens, 1982, 1984; Mumford, Wesley, & Shaffer, 1987; Neiner & Owens, 1982; Owens & Schoenfeldt, 1979; Shaffer, Saunders, & Owens, 1986; Stokes, Mumford, & Owens, 1989). These results suggest that systematically scored biodata items capture consistent aspects of antecedent developmental processes that causally influence subsequent job performance. Simultaneous exploration of construct domains underlying criteria and biodata items may provide the answer to Campbell's (1990) call for a theory of "experience."

This growing body of biodata research caused Fleishman (1988) to recently label biographical information as one of the new frontiers in personnel selection. Numerous authors over the years have called for more theory-based investigations of biodata measurement technologies (Bass, 1990; Dunnette, 1966; Henry, 1966; Owens, 1976; Reilly & Chao, 1982; Toops, 1948, 1959). Meta-analytic results suggest that limited resources can be directed away from efforts to establish criterion-related validity at every job site. Now more than ever, these research resources can be refocused toward more theory-based efforts that *simultaneously* target prediction and explanation. One of the most promising points of departure into this "new frontier" is at the level of biodata item development.

APPROACHES TO DEVELOPING
BIODATA ITEM CONTENT

In this section, specific item generation procedures are described in the context of three theories of individual differences. Item generation procedures outlined by Mumford and Owens (1987) are reviewed, and then two specific techniques are applied to theories of personality, vocational choice, and leadership.

PROCEDURE BEHIND ITEM GENERATION

Mumford and Owens (1987) described six methods or sources of biodata item development: (a) the human development literature, (b) life history interviews with incumbents, (c) typical factor loadings of biodata items, (d) known life history correlates of various job specifications, (e) biodata items with known predictive validities, and (f) items generated from the investigators' general psychological knowledge. The latter three sources of biodata items are derived from existing item pools and/or rely solely on investigators' imagination and subjective judgments. Though useful for developing criterion-valid selection instruments, tapping existing biodata item pools without some theoretical rationale does not enhance our understanding of why observed criterion-related validities exist.[2] Though these three procedures will undoubtedly be used in the iterative nature of theory testing, item development, and theory development, it is unlikely that they will provide useful *initial* points of departure for theory development and criterion prediction.

In contrast, the first three sources provide rich sources of information for biodata development. The first three sources reflect two thrusts: theory (the human development literature) and procedure (interviews and factor interpretations).[3] This section attempts to link existing *theories* of individual differences with *procedures* for biodata item development. No attempt was made at being comprehensive or even representative in choosing theories related to job performance. Consequently, I sampled from literatures in personality theory, vocational interests and job choice, and human development/leadership. Theories of personality and vocational interest were chosen as two points of departure because they are convenient: They both are noncognitive with histories of scale development similar to those of biodata (Barge, 1988). The leadership literature (and the emerging human development literature focusing on leader development) was chosen because theoretical approaches to leadership are arguably as close to a theory integrating construct domains found in the job and individual as we have in the field of industrial and organizational psychology. Further, recent work by Kuhnert (Kuhnert & Lewis, 1987; Kuhnert & Russell, 1990; Russell & Kuhnert, 1992) provided a model of how leaders develop *and* guidelines on how to develop biodata items that reflect critical stages of that development.

Following discussion of each theory or construct domain, specific *procedural* suggestions and examples of how to generate biodata items are provided. Procedures including post hoc interpretation of item factor structures and life history interviews/essays are described as alternate techniques for actual item generation.

Alternatively, equally viable points of departure (theory-based and nontheory-based) could have been chosen from many other arenas. For example, the job constructs of involvement with data, people, or things could be used as a basis for item development procedures. One could also target specific knowledge, skills, and abilities (KSAs) required of a job, working backward to identify the prior life events that influence their acquisition in much the same way that the typical structured interview is conducted (see Russell, Mattson, Devlin, & Atwater, 1990). However, the sheer volume of approaches to jobs and people precludes an exhaustive survey of alternate theories or models that could serve as points of departure for biodata item generation. The topic areas chosen serve as good examples for outlining item generation procedures.

THEORY-BASED METHODS FOR DEVELOPING ITEM CONTENT

Personality Theory

Most investigators in personnel selection abandoned personality tests long ago, based on conclusions drawn by Guion and Gottier (1965) and the discouraging results of Ghiselli's (1966, 1973) surveys of criterion-related validity. Only recently has interest been revived among applied investigators. For example, efforts by Pulakos, Borman, and Hough (1988) indicate that personality scales chosen on the basis of careful job analysis procedures can yield meaningful incremental criterion-related validities.

Briefly by way of review, Allport (1937) and Murray (1938) conceived of personality in terms of traits manifesting themselves as consistencies in behaviors across a variety of situations. Without reviewing the trials and tribulations that have characterized personality theory over the last 50 years, five personality characteristics that consistently emerge across studies are now viewed as capturing most of the variance in existing measurement instruments.[4] These Big Five characteristics include Extroversion/ Surgency, Agreeableness, Conscientiousness, Emotional Stability, and Culture (see Digman, 1990; Digman & Inouye, 1986). A recent meta-analysis of 49 criterion-related validity studies using the Big Five personality character- istics resulted in average validities ranging from .22 for Conscientiousness to .08 for Agreeableness and Emotional Stability, again indicating that it may be premature to abandon these measures (Barrick & Mount, 1991).

Regardless of their criterion-related validity in selection contexts, the Big Five have substantial evidence of construct validity (Digman & Inouye, 1986). This evidence takes the form of interpretable factor structures, consistency in factor structures over time, and convergent and discriminant validity (see Digman, 1990; Digman & Inouye, 1986). Given that these Big Five behavioral consistencies exist and are related to job performance, how can we generate examples of antecedent life events that (a) are related to differential rates of developing Big Five personality characteristics (e.g., demonstrate convergent and discriminant validity among the Big Five) and (b) demonstrate criterion-related validity?

As noted earlier, the techniques described here will involve factor interpretation and life history interviews/essays. Mumford and Owens described factor interpretation in terms of biodata item factor structures. However, in this application we are faced with factors of personality scale items. It should be feasible to use the Big Five factors (or, for that matter, any other post hoc interpretations of empirically derived factors) to develop biodata items. For example, at least two of the Big Five seem to be capturing some notion of affect (e.g., Agreeableness and Emotional Stability). Using simple notions of frequency of exposure to an experience as well as inputs, process, and outcomes of that experience, it is not difficult for an investigator to generate examples of past situations that might influence these two factors.

Specifically, consider the following items derived for purposes of selecting a retail store manager:

- How often have you been very unhappy with some product or service you purchased for your home? (exposure)

- How often has a clerk or salesperson said something that really irritated you? (input)

- How often have you been very nervous or tense in helping a customer who had a complaint? (process)

- How often have you resolved to try to remain calm after getting upset about something a co-worker did? (outcome)

The position of retail store manager was chosen just to provide a point of reference for the applicant pool (e.g., those out of school who have had some meaningful work/life experiences prior to being considered for the position). Exposure, inputs, process, and outcomes were chosen as an initial taxonomy of ways people might differ in their prior experiences that can be expanded or contracted as item generation proceeds. The taxonomy is taken, with minor changes, from Campbell, Dunnette, Lawler, and Weick's (1970) person-process-product model of managerial performance (see Russell & Domm, 1990, for an initial use of this taxonomy to generate biodata items). Regardless, each item has a specific hypothesized construct that it should be related to (i.e., the notions of happiness, irritation, and resolution to remain calm found in these items would be expected to capture aspects of Agreeableness and/or Emotional Stability). Further, each item has constructs that it should not be related to (the other three members of the Big Five) *and* a content domain (customers and co-workers) that should overlap with aspects of the criterion job performance domain (working with others in a retail sales work environment).

This kind of investigator-dependent item generation can be engaging to the investigators (try thinking of some items related to personal integrity or any deeply held value about "right" and "wrong"—we will come back to this in the section on leadership). However, there is always the risk of contamination or deficiency due to limits of the investigators' imaginations. An alternate procedure that I prefer involves the use of life history interviews or essays with incumbents, hence, shifting the role of subject matter expert (SME) to individuals who are closer to having actually experienced any biodata constructs of interest.[5] Russell, Mattson, Devlin, and Atwater (1990), Russell and Domm (1990), and Siegel (1956) demonstrated that criterion-valid items can be generated from essays written by incumbents about prior life experiences. Russell (1990) demonstrated how criterion-valid life history information can be systematically obtained through tape-recorded life history interviews. Essay and interview questions can be structured to target facets of life episodes that incumbents feel influenced their capacity to perform their jobs. These questions would address environmental circumstances (e.g., task requirements, availability of resources, presence of obstacles, assistance received from others), cognitions (perceptual processes, information gathered, ways information was combined), affect (attitudes, beliefs, values, valences present when the episode started and/or after the episode was complete), behaviors engaged in, task outcomes, and what was learned from the life episode (cognition, affect, and behavior change). Russell et al. (1990) described specific follow-up questions focusing on aspects of the target job of U.S. naval officer, whereas Russell (1990) used 42 pages of structured life history interview questions targeting job choice, job environment, major accomplishments, major disappointments, obstacles encountered/ overcome, specific behaviors engaged in, what was learned from each job tour, and any affect associated with job experiences.

In the case of the Big Five Extroversion/Surgency scale, we could ask incumbent retail store managers who had been recently hired (i.e., those most similar to the applicant pool) to describe prior life experiences (work-related or nonwork-related) in which they had been required to be particularly vocal, secretive, cautious, adventurous, or sociable (aspects of the Extroversion/Surgency dimension). Again, each essay or interview could be structured to prompt respondents for descriptions of the circumstances in which they found themselves, what they thought and felt at the time, what they did, what outcome occurred, and what they feel they learned from the situation. Thus, a pool of life experiences can be generated that *are not* dependent on the imaginations of the investigators.

Regardless of the technique used, it would appear that the Big Five personality variables are capturing behavioral consistencies that demonstrate criterion-related validity *and* construct validity (Barrick & Mount, 1991; Digman, 1990). The techniques just described provide a means of developing biodata items that might be expected to augment both construct- and criterion-related validities. I would not be surprised if future investigators find that a subset of past behavioral consistencies common to work-related roles (as well as their antecedents and consequences) exhibits much higher criterion-related validity than that reported by Barrick and Mount (1991), yet is readily interpretable in terms of the Big Five constructs.

Vocational Interest and Job Choice

Holland's (1973) model of vocational choice is a direct application of personality theory. Briefly, Holland believed that an individual's similarity to six personality types—Realistic, Investigative, Artistic, Social, Enterprising, and Conventional—could be used to place the individual into vocational groups. Similar to Mumford and Stokes' (1991) ecology model, Holland's (1973) view is that individuals' choices of a vocational type is a function of their environments, personal abilities, and desires.

Osipow (1973) criticized Holland's theory for not indicating how these personality types developed, though some research has addressed this issue. A large number of studies in the early 1960s examined how biodata items were related to the career paths of engineers, lawyers, physicians, and other professionals (see Albright & Glennon, 1961; Chaney & Owens, 1964; Kuhlberg & Owens, 1960). Not surprisingly, engineers and lawyers tended to have different histories of interpersonal success and differential performance in quantitative versus language courses (see Kuhlberg & Owens, 1960).

More recently, Eberhardt and Muchinsky (1982, 1984), in a large-scale survey, found that prior life experiences captured through a biodata instrument can accurately predict vocational type. Holland's use of personality characteristics to identify vocational types lends itself to the biodata item generation procedures described in the previous section. Given meta-analytic results suggesting that biodata instruments are among the most accurate predictors of voluntary turnover, it would appear that life history items are *also* stable predictors of the motivational states reflected in vocational and job choices.

Placing the motivational process of vocational and job choice into an expectancy theory framework provides a different point of departure for the identification of life history events. Items might be developed that reflect events influencing individuals' expectancies, instrumentalities, and valences in some prior work or goal-oriented activity. Although Kuhlberg and Owens (1960) report differences in prior life experiences between engineers and lawyers, it would be of theoretical and practical interest to identify which facets of prior developmental processes are actually related to the way people choose jobs or career paths.

For example, it would be interesting to know which situations—home, school, part-time job—have the greatest impact on work-related expectancies, instrumentalities, and valences (EIV) in high school and college students. What kind of role models at home, school, or part-time employment have the greatest impact on EIV? Is it the mere presence of these role models, or is some opportunity for a particular *type* of role model interaction necessary? Again, life history essays targeting role models and role model interaction could be used to obtain an initial set of biodata items. Relationships between items reflecting specific role model characteristics and environmental circumstances with work-related EIV would be of great value for theory development, vocational guidance, and personnel selection.

Equally interesting to applied researchers *and* employers is the exact nature of early developmental experiences that contribute to later career performance. For example, companies like General Electric and Westinghouse would be interested in knowing which approach to performance management influences EIV that cause engineers to continue as practicing engineers rather than opting for career tracks in technical sales or management.

In the context of vocational decisions to leave a job or career path, Russell and Van Sell (1986) demonstrated that within-subjects policy-capturing research designs are much more likely to accurately forecast voluntary turnover decisions than the currently popular between-subjects longitudinal panel surveys (e.g., Williams & Hazer, 1986). Russell and Van Sell developed regression models of how each employee weighs and combines various facets of his or her job in arriving at a decision to quit. Further, using a cluster analysis technique, they were able to identify groups of incumbents who were similar in the relative weights they assigned to different aspects of the job. For purposes of selection/classification (requiring prediction) and career guidance (requiring explanation), it would be of interest to identify different biographical experiences that influence these weights.

For example, the following items might be expected to be related to how individuals weigh scheduling flexibility and pay fairness in their decisions to quit a job:

- How often did you miss your parents when you were growing up because they were away at work? (H_0: affects valence of flexible work schedules.)

- How often while you were in school did you work part-time jobs but still didn't have as much money as you needed? (H_0: affects development of a "need" norm and may affect the valence perceptions of subsequent pay levels.)

- How often have you continued to work at something even though you weren't getting the reward you originally thought you were going to get out of it? (H_0: affects development of capacity to identify other valent outcomes in a work situation.)

Again, my preference would be to use a combination of life history essays and interviews targeted at prior life events that affect motivation to pursue a particular line of work or to continue on a job even after conditions of work have changed. The following essay questions, given to first-year college students, might yield responses that can be used to develop items demonstrating construct- and criterion-related validity with subsequent measures of career choice/job choice/turnover:

- Please describe some job or task you have worked on (related to work, school, or any other situation you may have encountered) in which the situation changed yet you continued to participate. Please be sure to describe what things changed, how you *initially* felt about the changes, how you *ended up* feeling about the changes, why you thought you could deal with the changes, and how the changes influenced what you were getting out of the situation.

- Please describe some situation in which you had to decide between different types of projects or activities in which to take part. Examples would include choosing among elective courses in school, choosing among different summer jobs, or choosing among different colleges to attend. These choices can be very difficult for some people. How did you make yours? How did you know what you wanted? How did you know you could do it? How did you know what to expect from each alternative? What did you learn that will prompt you to do things differently the next time you have to make a choice like this?

By decomposing the events into sequences of exposures to different environments and responses to the environment (e.g., cognitive, affective, and behavioral components of attitudinal response as described by Kiesler, Collins, & Miller, 1969, and Kretch & Crutchfield, 1948), we should be able to generate biodata items that are accompanied by specific hypothesized relationships with subsequent levels of motivation that are directly reflected in career and job choices.

Leadership and Human Development Theory
Kuhnert and his colleagues recently used a theory of adult development to describe how individuals acquire skills as transactional and transformation leaders (Kuhnert & Lewis, 1987; Kuhnert & Russell, 1990; Russell & Kuhnert, 1992). Using Kegan's (1982) model of adult development, Kuhnert and Lewis (1987) distinguished between the concepts of *object* and *subject* at different stages of development. The process or structure through which an individual makes sense of his or her experiences in the world is called the *subject* . The metaphor most commonly used in referring to the subject is that of a lens. In contrast, the content of the experiences (what is being viewed through the lens) is called the *object*. Kegan (1982) hypothesized that as humans mature, the way in which they make sense of things (subject) and the things they pay attention to (object) change. The six stages of development described by Kegan are characterized by the subject of earlier stages becoming the object of later stages.

For instance, at Stage 3, Kegan describes the subject in terms of interpersonal mutuality—the rules of interaction or exchange (e.g., equity, equality) that individuals use to view the world. The object is the individuals' knowledge of their own and others' needs, wishes, and interests. Hence, Kuhnert and Lewis (1987) argued that the Stage 3 adult has the foundation needed to be a transactional leader—one who influences followers by managing contingencies.

At Stage 4, Kegan (1982) described individuals who have developed to the point where they can stand back and view the rules of the exchange— what was subject in Stage 3 becomes object in Stage 4. The new subject consists of deep-seated values or ideology held by individuals through which they view the exchange. Hence, whereas in Stage 3 the content of the exchange was viewed through a lens consisting of the rules of exchange, in Stage 4 deep-seated values make up the lens used to view the rules of exchange. A Stage 3 individual would have difficulty violating a rule of exchange in some interaction with a subordinate, whereas a Stage 4 individual would be able to violate the rule of exchange *if that violation was congruent with some deep-seated value.* For example, Stage 4 leaders would routinely violate some trust with a subordinate or take action that was detrimental to their own good because of some overarching, higher-level value (e.g., doing what is "right" versus doing what is in the leader's or others' best interests).

Kuhnert and Lewis (1987) used these stages of development as a framework to describe how people acquire transactional and transformational leadership skills. Transformational leaders influence others by inducing a relatively permanent shift in their values, beliefs, and goals— that is, their beliefs about what is right (Stage 4). The transactional leader influences others through the careful management of inducements and contributions to meet both the organization's and employees' needs (Stage 3).

Kuhnert and Russell (1990) argued that how people make sense out of their past life experiences should reflect their stage of development. A logical means of operationalizing what is subject and what is object—a person's stage of development—is to use items that capture aspects of that person's life history. They use an existing criterion-valid biodata item taken from Russell et al. (1990) as an example:

> On a group project, many times a person is not pulling his or her own weight. Sometimes you have to discuss this with the person. How often did these discussions "work out" and resolve the problem?

Kuhnert and Russell (1990) argued that different ways of viewing and responding to this situation should discriminate between Stage 3 and 4 leaders. Two subsequent items provided by Kuhnert and Russell that describe the same situation but in which the item ends with either "I pointed out it wasn't fair to the other individuals in the group" or "I explained how the individual was letting him or herself down" should yield different response patterns from Stage 3 and 4 leaders. Stage 3 leaders should indicate they often engage in the former action and seldom in the latter action. Stage 4 leaders should indicate they engage in each action with about equal, and high, frequency.

These constitute examples of biodata items accompanied by explicit hypotheses derived from established psychological theories of adult development and leadership. Again, post hoc interpretation of factor structures, as well as life history essays, could be used to ensure a rich pool of items reflecting critical developmental episodes that might signal points of change from one stage to the next. For example, Russell et al. (1990) and Russell and Domm (1990) interpreted the dominant biodata factor in their item generation efforts as capturing life problems or negative life experiences. Interestingly, recent ethnographic work on key events in executives' lives by Bobko, McCoy, and McCauley (1988) and Lindsey, Holmes, and McCall (1987) indicates that having worked under a very stressful, obnoxious boss (an unpleasant life experience) is commonly cited as a key developmental period by many upper-level managers. Future item development efforts might ask incumbents for life history essays about aspects of negative life events.

ITEM CHARACTERISTICS

In this final section I shall discuss issues related to item characteristics that are independent of item content. Item characteristics are interpreted broadly to include, for example, characteristics of the accompanying instructions, choice of response formats, and item tone (negative versus positive; see Asher, 1972, for an overview of different item characteristics). I shall discuss the relationship of these features to random and systematic response error and item validity, though few definitive studies have addressed these issues.

IMPACT ON RELIABILITY

Numerous reasons for the presence of error in biodata item responses have been suggested. Van Rijn (1980) listed faking, errors in memory, carelessness, and response bias as potential sources. Response biases might include selective memory of certain types of life experiences and maturation effects that cause changes in how prior perceptions, cognitions, attitudes, values, or beliefs are recalled at a later point in time. However, as we shall see, many of these biases may indeed represent error variance resulting from meaningful life experiences that occur at a later date, as revealed in Kuhnert and Lewis' (1987) discussion of changes in subject and object during leader development.

The heterogeneity of biodata items usually dictates that split-half reliabilities and other estimates of internal consistency reliability generally will be low (see Owens, 1976; Siegel, 1956). Additionally, if England's (1961) vertical percent difference method of item scoring is employed (which, as Devlin, Abrahams, & Edwards, 1992, demonstrated, yields the highest cross-validities compared to five competing methods), high test–retest correlations could conceal a shift in mean response. Such a shift would have a drastic effect on resultant biodata scores obtained using England's procedure.

Owens, Glennon, and Albright (1962) avoided these concerns by examining 43 subjects' response consistency to 200 items. An interval of approximately two months lapsed between administrations. Owens et al. developed four rules or principles to describe why some items received consistent (or inconsistent) responses. These rules referred to item brevity, graduated or continuous response scales, presence of an "escape" response, and the use of neutral or pleasant undertone to the item stem. To my knowledge, none of these post hoc interpretations of why some items yielded consistent responses has been evaluated for its relationship to item reliability or validity.

Shaffer, Saunders, and Owens (1986) replicated and extended this effort in a test–retest design over a five-year period combined with an independent measure of life experiences. They examined both test–retest reliabilities and t tests of differences in mean value for factor scores and item responses. Shaffer et al. (1986) reported consistent evidence of high test–retest reliability for both factors and items. However, approximately one-third of the factors demonstrated significant shifts in mean response. Slightly over 30 percent of the items demonstrated a significant shift in mean response over the five-year period, while over 26 percent of the items were significantly different from an independent assessment of the same life history experiences. Shaffer et al. also presented evidence suggesting that objective to moderately subjective items (as opposed to highly subjective items) are not likely to demonstrate mean shifts.

Unfortunately, in designs of this nature, it is very difficult to separate random error (e.g., careless responding, failure of memory, etc.) from Campbell and Stanley's (1963) description of history and maturation effects. That is, lack of test–retest reliability and/or shifts in mean response for biodata items or factors may result from specific events that occur between administrations or from changes in the respondent. History and maturation effects are exactly what is hypothesized by Mumford and Stokes' (1991) ecology model as the causal process underlying the predictive power of biodata items.

Hence, it may be that items exhibiting the most change in how prior life experiences are recalled over time are those with the highest criterion-related validity, simply because these items are more reflective of critical developmental episodes. It is not surprising that studies of accuracy in biodata item responses using test–retest procedures and/or independent verification yield mixed results (Mumford & Owens, 1987). Simple shrinkage in criterion-related validity upon cross-validation should measure the amount of random error in biodata item responses. I am unaware of any studies examining the effect of manipulating item characteristics on shrinkage in cross-validities. Items influenced by history and maturation effects that truly contribute to validity but detract from traditional measures of reliability (e.g., Shaffer et al.'s test–retest reliabilities and *t* tests) should survive cross-validation.

Finally, a discussion of the impact of item characteristics on reliability would not be complete without noting widespread concerns about one source of nonrandom error, that is, faking (see Fleishman, 1988). Numerous authors have reported evidence of faking (Cascio, 1975; Colquitt & Becker, 1989; Keating, Paterson, & Stone, 1950; Mosel & Cozan, 1952), while others have failed to find evidence (Goldstein, 1971; Hogan & Stokes, 1989; Trent, Atwater, & Abrahams, 1986; Weiss & Dawis, 1960). Indeed, Trent (1987) found that the ability of respondents to detect and respond to the keyed option contributed to criterion-related validity regardless of what their true response might have been. Apparently, in some applicant pools the cognitive capacity to detect and fake the desired response correctly forecasts performance.

In the face of these mixed results, some authors have suggested that the only way to eliminate faking is to rely on verifiable biodata items. However, Mumford and Owens (1987) speculated that choice of keying procedure (item keying versus option keying) may be causing the mixed results. A recent lab study by Kluger et al. (1991) tested this speculation, finding that option keying caused biodata scores not to be inflated due to bias caused by knowledge of the target position and general social desirability, though such biases did contribute to random error variation. Item keying, however, did result in inflated biodata scores. Kluger et al. (1991) suggested that to reduce inflation of random error, future researchers should examine the effect on response bias of instruction sets explicitly warning respondents that attempts to fake will not be fruitful.

IMPACT ON VALIDITY

Few investigators have evaluated how item characteristics affect criterion-related validity. Recently, Barge (1987, 1988) reported the results of a study examining how three biodata item characteristics are related to item validity independent of item content. Barge found that heterogeneity, behavioral discreteness, and behavioral consistency of biodata items could be reliably rated and, using job performance and training criteria, found that these properties were related to criterion-related validity.

Item heterogeneity refers to the distinction between items that capture multiple characteristics or environmental events (e.g., school performance) versus items that narrowly reflect a single characteristic. *Behavioral discreteness* refers to the distinction between items that address "a single, perhaps verifiable, behavior rather than a more abstract or summary characteristic" (Barge, 1987, pp. 3–4). Finally, *behavioral consistency* refers to the degree of congruency between the content domain of the biodata item and the content domain of the target job—that is, the degree to which the item is a *sample* as opposed to a *sign* (Wernimont & Campbell, 1968).

While Barge (1987, 1988) found real differences in the criterion-related validity of items varying on these dimensions, it remains to be seen whether these differences are replicated with different sets of items. Specifically, Barge used 103 items out of the 118 items in the short form of Owens' *Biographical Questionnaire* (BQ; Owens & Schoenfeldt, 1979). This instrument was derived from an initial set of 2,000 items generated to reflect 52 pages of item categories (e.g., dependency, aggression) that the team of investigators viewed as capturing a broad array of inputs and behaviors. Do item heterogeneity, behavioral discreteness, and behavioral consistency influence construct- and criterion-related validity for items reflecting life history construct domains other than those found in the Owens' *Biographical Questionnaire* (e.g., those relevant for the selection of middle managers)? Future research will need to examine simultaneously both differences in theoretical rationale for item content and variability in item characteristics. It may be that a number of items with characteristics exactly opposite from those reported by Barge (e.g., homogeneous, nondiscrete sign items) are needed to accurately measure certain critical constructs or life events that are not reflected in the short form of the BQ.

CONCLUSION

The focus of this chapter has been on the generation of biodata items with content that can be traced to some theory or model. The goal of such efforts is to close the gap between theory, item content, and criterion performance measures. Theories focusing on person characteristics (personality theory), motivation (vocational choice), and the development of individuals into leaders were discussed. Any one of a number of alternative approaches could have been chosen, and the reader should consider it a challenge to identify causal, developmental life experiences that will confirm (or fail to confirm) his or her favorite theory or model.

Life history essays/interviews and post hoc factor interpretations have been featured as means of item development—obviously, many others are possible. I have been fascinated by autobiographies that describe major life-influencing events. For example, Armand Hammer (1987) attributed many of his early career decisions to the circumstances surrounding his father's illness. Dr. An Wang (1986) paused to reflect on basic values of right and wrong while negotiating with IBM on the sale of rights to his memory cores in the early 1950s.

Owens (1976) commented on the possibility of abstracting items from biographies, but expressed concern that it would not be an efficient method of item generation. Fortunately, microcomputer-based text search software has been developed that, like data base searches in library archives, could be used to target passages of text dealing with specific themes and issues (see Gephardt & Wolfe, 1989). Imagine the biodata sampling possibilities such a tool would provide when combined with the computerized biography section of the Library of Congress!

Research indicates that personality, vocational choice, and leadership models, among others, provide fairly accurate representations of nonrandom individual differences. Unfortunately, many empirical examinations of these theories and others conclude with a statement that "the results are consistent with the theory," even though no criterion of organizational interest was predicted. In contrast, biodata inventories consistently demonstrate criterion-related validities as high as any competing predictor. We need to close the gap between what has been characterized as an atheoretical measurement technology and the many substantive theories of industrial and organizational psychology. Toward this end, methods of theory-based biodata item generation comprise a major research opportunity.

A portion of this chapter was written while I held a visiting appointment at the Krannert Graduate School of Management, Purdue University. I would like to thank Philip Bobko and Marvin Dunnette for their valuable comments and suggestions.

NOTES

1. This criticism is common to many "noncognitive" domains and is not unique to biodata research. For example, Eberhardt and Muchinsky (1982) made a similar observation regarding Holland's (1973) use of personality types to explain underlying vocational interest—that is, that viewing personality at any point in time as a function of genetic and current/past environmental factors is too general to be of much use.

2. Nickels and Mumford (1989) recently completed a study examining the construct- and criterion-related validity obtained in using a priori theory-based guidelines to select biodata items from an existing pool. While this is a perfectly viable approach, the focus of this chapter is on biodata item development, not biodata item selection.

3. Though I would argue that the sixth source of items, investigators' general psychological knowledge, permeates the other five sources, especially in the interpretation of factor loadings.

4. See the chapter by Mary Tenopyr in this volume for a more extensive treatment of the roots of the Big Five.

5. I faced this problem when trying to decide how to develop items capturing biographical information for purposes of selecting midshipmen for the U.S. Naval Academy (Russell, 1986). As a member of the thirty-something generation, I was *very* uncomfortable with the idea of trying to generate item content reflective of life history events for teenagers today.

REFERENCES

Albright, L. E., & Glennon, J. R. (1961). Personal history correlated of physical scientists' career aspirations. *Journal of Applied Psychology, 45,* 281–284.

Allport, G. W. (1937). *Personality: A psychological interpretation.* New York: Holt, Rinehart and Winston.

Asher, E. J. (1972). The biographical item: Can it be improved? *Personnel Psychology, 25,* 251–269.

Bass, B. M. (1990). *Bass and Stodgill handbook of leadership* (3d ed.). New York: Free Press.

Barge, B. N. (1987, August). *Characteristics of biodata items and their relationships to validity.* Paper presented at the annual meeting of the American Psychological Association, New York.

Barge, B. N. (1988). *Characteristics of biodata items and their relationship to validity.* Unpublished doctoral dissertation, University of Minnesota, Minneapolis.

Barrick, M. R., & Mount, M. K. (1991). The Big 5 personality dimensions and job performance: A meta-analysis. *Personnel Psychology, 44,* 1–26.

Bobko, P., McCoy, C., & McCauley, C. (1988). Towards a taxonomy of executive lessons: A similarity analysis of executives' self-reports. *International Journal of Management, 5,* 375–384.

Bobko, P., & Russell, C. J. (1991). A review of the role of taxonomies in human resource management. *Human Resource Management Review, 1,* 293–316.

Burke, M. J., & Pearlman, K. (1988). Recruiting, selecting, and matching people with jobs. In J. P. Campbell & R. J. Campbell (Eds.), *Productivity in organizations* (pp. 97–142). San Francisco: Jossey-Bass.

Campbell, D. T., & Stanley, J. C. (1963). *Experimental and quasi-experimental designs.* Chicago: Rand McNally.

Campbell, J. L. (1990). Modeling the performance prediction problem in industrial and organizational psychology. In M. D. Dunnette & L. M. Hough (Eds.), *Handbook of industrial and organizational psychology* (2d ed., vol. 1, pp. 687–732). Palo Alto, CA: Consulting Psychologists Press.

Campbell, J., Dunnette, M. D., Lawler, E. E., & Weick, K. (1970). *Managerial behavior and performance effectiveness.* New York: McGraw-Hill.

Cascio, W. F. (1975). Accuracy of verifiable biographical information blank responses. *Journal of Applied Psychology, 60,* 576–580.

Chaney, F. B., & Owens, W. C. (1964). Life history antecedents of sales, research, and general engineering interests. *Journal of Applied Psychology, 48,* 101–105.

Colquitt, A. L., & Becker, T. E. (1989, April). *Faking of a biodata form in use: A field study.* Paper presented at the meeting of the Society of Industrial and Organizational Psychology, Boston.

Devlin, S. E., Abrahams, N. M., & Edwards, J. E. (1992). Empirical keying of biographical data: Cross-validity as a function of scaling procedure and sample size. *Military Psychology, 4,* 119–136.

Digman, J. M. (1990). Personality structure: Emergence of the five-factor model. *Annual Review of Psychology, 41,* 417–440.

Digman, J. M., & Inouye, J. (1986). Further specification of the five robust factors of personality. *Journal of Personality and Social Psychology, 50,* 116–123.

Dunnette, M. D. (1962). Personnel management. *Annual Review of Psychology, 13,* 285–314.

Dunnette, M. D. (1966). *Personnel selection and placement.* Belmont, CA: Wadsworth.

Eberhardt, B. J., & Muchinsky, P. M. (1982). Biodata determinants of vocational typology: An integration of two paradigms. *Journal of Applied Psychology, 67,* 714–727.

Eberhardt, B. J., & Muchinsky, P. M. (1984). Structural validation of Holland's hexagonal model: Vocational classification through the use of biodata. *Journal of Applied Psychology, 69,* 174–181.

England, G. W. (1961). *Development and use of weighted application blanks.* Dubuque, IA: Brown.

Fleishman, E. A. (1988). Some new frontiers in personnel selection research. *Personnel Psychology, 41,* 679–701.

Gephardt, R.P., & Wolfe, R.A. (1989, August). Qualitative data analysis: Three microcomputer-supported approaches. In *Academy of Management Best Papers Proceedings 1989.* Washington, DC: Academy of Management.

Ghiselli, E. E. (1966). *The validity of occupational aptitude tests.* New York: Wiley.

Ghiselli, E. E. (1973). The validity of aptitude tests in personnel selection. *Personnel Psychology, 26,* 461–477.

Goldstein, I. L. (1971). The application blank: How honest are the responses? *Journal of Applied Psychology, 55,* 491–492.

Guilford, J. P. (1959). *Personality.* New York: McGraw-Hill.

Guion, R. M., & Gottier, R. F. (1965). Validity of personality measures in personnel selection. *Personnel Psychology, 18,* 135–164.

Hammer, A. (1987). *Hammer.* New York: Putnam.

Henry, E. (1966). Conference on the use of biographical data in psychology. *American Psychologist, 21,* 247–249.

Holland, J. L. (1973). *Making vocational choices: A theory of careers.* Englewood Cliffs, NJ: Prentice-Hall.

Hogan, J. B., & Stokes, G. S. (1989, April). *The influence of socially desirable responding on biographical data of applicant versus incumbent samples: Implications for predictive and concurrent research designs.* Paper presented at the annual meeting of the Society for Industrial and Organizational Psychology, Boston.

Hunter, J. E., & Hunter, R. F. (1984). Validity and utility of alternative predictors of job performance. *Psychological Bulletin, 96,* 72–98.

Keating, E., Paterson, D. G., & Stone, C. H. (1950). Validity of work histories obtained by interview. *Journal of Applied Psychology, 34,* 1–5.

Kegan, R. (1982). *The evolving self: Problem and process in human development.* Cambridge, MA: Harvard University Press.

Kiesler, C. A., Collins, B. E., & Miller, N. (1969). *Attitudinal change: A critical analysis of theoretical approaches.* New York: Wiley.

Kluger, A. N., Reilly, R. R., & Russell, C. J. (1991). Faking biodata tests: Are option-keyed instruments more resistant? *Journal of Applied Psychology, 76,* 889–896.

Kretch, D., & Crutchfield, R. S. (1948). *Theory and problems in social psychology.* New York: McGraw-Hill.

Kuhlberg, G. E., & Owens, W. C. (1960). Some life history antecedents of engineering interests. *Journal of Educational Psychology, 51,* 26–31.

Kuhnert, K. W., & Lewis, P. (1987). Transactional and transformational leadership: A constructive/developmental analysis. *Academy of Management Review, 12,* 648–657.

Kuhnert, K. W., & Russell, C. J. (1990). Using constructive developmental theory and biodata to bridge the gap between personnel selection and leadership. *Journal of Management, 16,* 1–13.

Lindsey, E., Holmes, Z., & McCall, M. (1987). *Key events in executive lives.* Greensboro, NC: Center for Creative Leadership.

Mael, F. A. (1991). A conceptual rationale for the domain and attributes of biodata items. *Personnel Psychology, 44,* 763–792.

Mitchell, T. W. (1992, April). *A priori biodata to predict teamwork, learning rate, and retention.* Paper presented at the annual meeting of the Society of Industrial and Organizational Psychology, Montreal.

Mitchell, T. W., & Klimoski, R. J. (1982). Is it rational to be empirical?: A test of methods for scoring biographical data. *Journal of Applied Psychology, 67,* 411–418.

Mosel, J. L., & Cozan, L. W. (1952). The accuracy of application blank work histories. *Journal of Applied Psychology, 36,* 365–369.

Mumford, M. D., & Owens, W. A. (1982). Life history and vocational interests. *Journal of Vocational Behavior, 21,* 330–348.

Mumford, M. D., & Owens, W. A. (1984). Individuality in a developmental context: Some empirical and theoretical considerations. *Human Development, 27,* 84–108.

Mumford, M. D., & Owens, W. A. (1987). Methodology review: Principles, procedures, and findings in the application of background data measures. *Applied Psychological Measurement, 11,* 1–31.

Mumford, M. D., & Stokes, G. S. (1991). Developmental determinants of individual action: Theory and practice in the application of background data. In M. D. Dunnette & L. M. Hough (Eds.), *Handbook of industrial and organizational psychology* (2d ed., vol. 3, pp. 1–78). Palo Alto, CA: Consulting Psychologists Press.

Mumford, M. D., Wesley, S. S., & Shaffer, G. S. (1987). Individuality in a developmental context II: The crystallization of developmental trajectories. *Human Development, 30,* 291–321.

Murray, H. A. (1938). *Explorations in personality.* New York: Oxford University Press.

Neiner, A. G., & Owens, W. A. (1982). Relationships between two sets of biodata with 7 years separation. *Journal of Applied Psychology, 67,* 146–150.

Nickels, B. J., & Mumford, M. D. (1989). *Exploring the structure of background data measures: Implications for item development and scale validation.* Unpublished manuscript.

Osipow, S. H. (1973). *Theories of career development* (2d ed.). Englewood Cliffs, NJ: Prentice-Hall.

Owens, W. A. (1968). Toward one discipline of scientific psychology. *American Psychologist, 23,* 782–785.

Owens, W. A. (1971). A quasi-actuarial prospect for individual assessment. *American Psychologist, 26,* 992–999.

Owens, W. A. (1976). Background data. In M. D. Dunette (Ed.), *Handbook of industrial and organizational psychology* (1st ed., pp. 609–644). Chicago: Rand McNally.

Owens, W. A., Glennon, J. R., & Albright, L. E. (1962). Retest consistency and the writing of life history items: A first step. *Journal of Applied Psychology, 46,* 329–331.

Owens, W. A., & Schoenfeldt, L. F. (1979). Toward a classification of persons. *Journal of Applied Psychology, 64,* 569–607.

Pulakos, E. D., Borman, W. C., & Hough, L. M. (1988). Test validation for scientific understanding: Two demonstrations of an approach to studying prediction–criterion linkages. *Personnel Psychology, 41,* 703–716.

Reilly, R. R., & Chao, G. T. (1982). Validity and fairness of some alternative employee selection procedures. *Personnel Psychology, 35,* 1–62.

Reilly, R. R., & Warech, M. W. (1990). *The validity and fairness of alternatives to cognitive tests.* Berkeley, CA: Commission on Testing and Public Policy.

Rothstein, H. R., Schmidt, F. L., Erwin, F. W., Owens, W. A., & Sparks, C. P. (1990). Biographical data in employment selection: Can validities be made generalizable? *Journal of Applied Psychology, 75,* 175–184.

Russell, C. J. (1986). *Review of the literature and development of a biodata instrument for prediction of naval officer performance at the U.S. Naval Academy* (Contract No. DAAG29-81-D-0100). San Diego: Navy Personnel Research and Development Center.

Russell, C. J. (1990). Selection of top corporate leaders: An example of biographical information. *Journal of Management, 16,* 71–84.

Russell, C. J., & Domm, D. R. (1990, April). *On the construct validity of biographical information: Evaluation of a theory-based method of item generation.* Paper presented at the annual meeting of the Society for Industrial and Organizational Psychology, Miami.

Russell, C. J., & Kuhnert, K. W. (1992). Integrating skill acquisition and perspective taking capacity in the development of leaders. *Leadership Quarterly, 3,* 109–135.

Russell, C. J., Mattson, J., Devlin, S. E., & Atwater, D. (1990). Predictive validity of biodata items generated from retrospective life experience essays. *Journal of Applied Psychology, 75,* 511–523.

Russell, C. J., & Van Sell, M. (1986, August). *An examination of the processes underlying models of job choice and turnover* (winner of the Ghiselli Award for Research Design). Paper presented at the annual meeting of the American Psychological Association, Washington, DC.

Schmitt, N., Gooding, R. Z., Noe, R. A., & Kirsch, M. (1984). Meta-analysis of validity studies published between 1964 and 1982 and the investigation of study characteristics. *Personnel Psychology, 37,* 407–422.

Shaffer, G. S., Saunders, V., & Owens, W. A. (1986). Additional evidence for the accuracy of biographical information: Long-term retest and observer ratings. *Personnel Psychology, 39,* 791–809.

Siegel, L. A. (1956). A biographical inventory for students: Vol. I. Construction and standardization of the instrument. *Journal of Applied Psychology, 40,* 5–10.

Stokes, G. S., Mumford, M. D., & Owens, W. A. (1989). Life history prototypes in the study of human individuality. *Journal of Personality, 57,* 509–545.

Toops, H. A. (1948). The use of addends in experimental control, social census, and managerial research. *Psychological Bulletin, 45,* 41–74.

Toops, H. A. (1959). A research utopia in industrial psychology. *Personnel Psychology, 12,* 189–225.

Trent, T. (1987, August). *Armed forces adaptability screening: The problem of item response distortion.* Paper presented at the annual meeting of the American Psychological Association, New York.

Trent, T. T., Atwater, D. C., & Abrahams, N. M. (1986). *Biographical screening of military applicants: Experimental assessment of item response distortion.* Paper presented to the Tenth Psychology in the DOD Symposium, Denver.

van Rijn, P. (1980). *Biographical information and scored application blanks in personnel selection.* Washington, DC: U.S. Office of Personnel Management, Personnel Research and Development Center, Alternatives Task Force.

Wang, A. (1986). *Lessons: An autobiography.* Reading, MA: Addison-Wesley.

Weiss, D. J., & Dawis, R. V. (1960). An objective validation of factual interview data. *Journal of Applied Psychology, 44,* 381–385.

Wernimont, P. F., & Campbell, J. P. (1968). Signs, samples, and criteria. *Journal of Applied Psychology, 52,* 372–376.

Williams, L. J., & Hazer, J. T. (1986). Antecedents and consequences of satisfaction and commitment in turnover models: A reanalysis using latent variable structural equation methods. *Journal of Applied Psychology, 71,* 219–231.

3

The Role of Job Analysis in Establishing the Validity of Biodata

Sidney A. Fine
Sidney A. Fine Associates

Steven Cronshaw
University of Guelph, Ontario, Canada

INTRODUCTION

This chapter describes the role of job analysis in establishing the validity of biodata. It is divided into three sections. In the first section, traditional approaches to biodata development are described, with particular attention given to how these approaches conform to the professional standards and principles on which industrial psychologists rely. In the second section, one approach to biodata development and validation is presented that fully meets professional standards and principles. This approach is based on functional job analysis (FJA).[1] Several other job analysis methods are briefly reviewed with respect to their suitability for biodata development as well. In the third section, implications of the FJA approach for biodata research and practice are discussed.

TRADITIONAL APPROACHES
TO AND USE OF JOB ANALYSIS

Job analysis has a critical role to play in the validation of biodata (biographical information blanks, or BIBs). However, in elucidating that role, it is first necessary to describe the traditional methods used to validate BIB predictors. First, we will review some key concepts from validation theory. Then we will describe two approaches used by industrial psychologists to validate BIB predictors: (a) the criterion-related/construct-oriented validation approach and (b) the content-oriented validation approach. Finally, some recommendations for the use of job analysis will be presented.

BASIC VALIDATION CONCEPTS

As stated in the *Standards for Educational and Psychological Testing* (AERA, APA, & NCME, 1985), validity refers to "the appropriateness, meaningfulness, and usefulness of the specific inferences made from test scores" (p. 9). Industrial psychologists have adopted this definition in the *Principles for the Validation and Use of Personnel Selection Procedures* (Society for Industrial and Organizational Psychology [SIOP], 1987), extending it to a wide range of predictors that include biographical data forms and scored application blanks. Although validity is presented as a unitary concept, evidence for BIBs or any other predictor can be accumulated in a number of ways. More specifically, three validation strategies are proposed in the *Standards* and the *Principles* for the purposes of accumulating evidence to support inferences concerning the validity of selection predictors. These three validation strategies will now be briefly discussed.

The first strategy is commonly referred to as the *criterion-related strategy of predictor validation*. Criterion-related evidence usually consists of an empirical demonstration of a relationship between a selection predictor (e.g., a score on a BIB) and one or more measures of job performance behavior, referred to as criteria. The second strategy, *construct-oriented strategy of predictor validation,* requires the industrial psychologist to provide a logical argument, along with supporting empirical research, to support the contention that a given selection predictor assesses a construct or set of constructs. These constructs are defined in the *Principles* as "theoretical constructions about the nature of human behavior" (p. 25) and can be construed to include such psychological characteristics as sociability or introversion. The third strategy, *content-oriented strategy of predictor validation,* involves the psychologist in the specification of a content domain, followed by careful construction of a measurement instrument to assess that content domain. Job analysis is a prerequisite to all three strategies, although the type of information collected in the job analysis may differ between the strategies, depending on objectives of the validity study.

CRITERION-RELATED/CONSTRUCT-ORIENTED VALIDATION

Biographical information blanks have a long history as a selection method, including the identification of military officers during World War II (Owens, 1976). Much of the work done on biodata in recent years was performed by William Owens and his colleagues at the University of Georgia. The rationale behind the development of biodata measures is quite simple: Life history information is a good predictor of the future job behavior of individuals or, more precisely, of the job behavior of groups of individuals sharing the same life background and experiences. The biodata methodology is, however, somewhat more complex than this simple rationale would suggest. Therefore, some explanation of this methodology is needed if the role of job analysis in BIB construction and validation is to be satisfactorily explained.

Schoenfeldt (1974) describes the typical approach taken to develop and validate biodata measures. His assessment-classification model of manpower utilization is summarized in Figure 1. As the figure shows, this model has three components: (a) the assessment of individuals, (b) the measurement of jobs, and (c) the matching of individuals to jobs through statistical procedures. The assessment of *individuals* is accomplished through the use of a specially designed biodata form. The measurement of *jobs* is accomplished through a job analysis. The validity of the biodata predictor is established, according to Brush and Owens (1979), by examining the relationship of life history subgroups (S_1, ...,S_L) as assessed by the biodata instrument, to a criterion. One key criterion against which life history data has been validated is success or satisfaction within job family, where job families are represented as F_1, ...,F_M in Figure 1.

The above description of the validation process undertaken in the development and implementation of biodata instruments is clearly criterion-related in nature. However, the development of biodata instruments also involves, implicitly, elements of construct-oriented validation as well. That is, biodata developers seek to classify individuals into the life history subgroups in Figure 1 through the profiling of life history dimensions assessed by the biodata instrument. These life history dimensions, each consisting of several biodata questionnaire items and empirically derived through the use of factor analysis, represent constructs as described in the

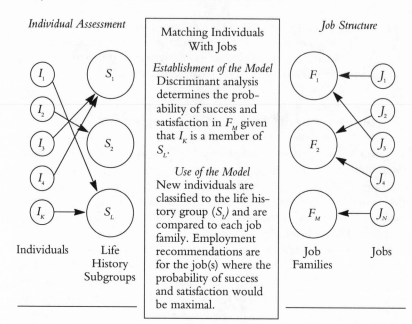

Individual Assessment

FIGURE 1   Schoenfeldt's (1974) Assessment-Classification Model of Manpower
Utilization

From "Utilization of Manpower: Development and Evaluation of an Assessment-Classification Model for Matching Individuals With Jobs" by L. F. Schoenfeldt, 1974, *Journal of Applied Psychology, 59*, pp. 583–595. Copyright 1974 by *Journal of Applied Psychology*. Reprinted by permission.

Principles. These life history constructs are variously described in terms such as "warmth of parental relationship," "academic achievement," or "social introversion" (e.g., Schoenfeldt, 1974). The labeling of the contructs is heavily influenced by the researchers' interpretation of the conceptual communality among the several biodata questionnaire items that clustered together in the factor analysis.

As the above discussion shows, the development of biodata forms can be characterized as typically emphasizing a combination of the criterion-related and construct-oriented validation strategies. However, it should be noted that these two strategies are not given equal weight in the biodata literature. Most biodata researchers give greater emphasis to criterion-related validation than to construct-oriented validation. This deficiency with regard to construct-oriented validation may be due in part to the lack of life history items that are oriented around core components of job performance. Such an orientation would be achieved through content-oriented validation, as discussed in the next section of this chapter.

Although job analysis data are useful in underpinning all three types of validation strategies described in the *Principles,* biodata developers have used job analysis information primarily to support the criterion-related aspect, rather than the construct-oriented aspect, of their validation efforts. Even where criterion-related validation is at issue, the job analysis information is used in identifying the job structure as represented in the right-hand side of Figure 1, but *not* in the identification of life history subgroups in the left-hand side of the figure. This should not be taken to imply that biodata developers ignore job information when writing life history items. In most cases, individuals who develop biodata forms first carry out literature searches in order to identify personal characteristics useful for selection to the particular type of job and then conduct extensive interviews with job incumbents and supervisors to obtain additional job information. However, the focus of this chapter is on the use of formal job analysis in biodata development, rather than on the less formal means of collecting job information that now prevail in the biodata literature. Whatever the extent of data collection through other means (and whatever the success of these efforts in terms of prediction achieved by biodata instruments), it is clear that job analysis information has been underutilized in the development and validation of biodata instruments.

Two examples will help to clarify how job analysis has been utilized (or underutilized) in biodata research and application, relative to less formal means of collecting job information. Brush and Owens (1979) describe the implementation and evaluation of a biodata methodology for use in making placement decisions in an oil company. They describe the individual assessment component of their model (see the left-hand side of Figure 1) as "people subgrouping," and the job structure component (see the right-hand side of Figure 1) as "job subgrouping." To accomplish the people subgrouping, Brush and Owens (1979) developed an extensive biographical inventory where the items "were chosen to reflect experiences commonly reported by employees in an industrial setting" (p. 371). Although this information came from a job study, the authors do not report having based the biographical inventory on the results of a formal job analysis. By comparison, the authors held that a job analysis was necessary if a meaningful job family structure was to be identified. A large number of office and clerical jobs were analyzed in terms of the kinds of activities performed on the job (using a variant of FJA) and minimal human characteristics required in each job. In other words, job analysis was directed to the criterion side of the biodata model represented in Figure 1 (i.e., to the development of the job structure), but not to the predictor side of the model (i.e., to the development of the individual assessment instrument).

This basic asymmetry in the use of job analysis is reflected in another application of biodata to placement decisions as described by Morrison (1977). On the individual assessment side, he describes the development of a BIB where most items were taken from *A Catalog of Life History Items* (Glennon, Albright, & Owens, 1966), with the remainder constructed to "reflect the uniqueness of the plant location, jobs, and broad labor market" (p. 272). Morrison (1977) does not mention the use of job analysis information in constructing his BIB. On the job structure side, however, job analysis again figures prominently. Job analysis data was used to rationally cluster jobs into two families based on similar psychological or worker requirements. In this second example, job analysis information is again directed toward the criterion, and not predictor, side of the criterion-related validation process.

In summary, traditional BIB development and validation has emphasized the criterion-related/construct-oriented validation approach, with a marked preference for criterion-related validation, but has deemphasized the role of job analysis. The only point at which formal job analysis has had an appreciable impact is in the identification of job families on the criterion side within the biodata model as represented in Figure 1. However, other researchers have developed biodata-type predictors by relying primarily on a content validation strategy. In these efforts, job analysis was used to a somewhat greater extent. It is to these predictors that we will now turn.

CONTENT-ORIENTED VALIDATION

As Gatewood and Feild (1987) point out, there are differences of opinion as to what should be called biodata. They define biodata as consisting of questions asked of applicants, usually in multiple-choice format, concerning their personal backgrounds and life experiences. Often these questions cover general background variables of life experiences that are temporally or behaviorally far removed from the job criteria predicted by the BIB. This type of BIB has already been described in the previous section. However, if one considers instruments that are designed to assess a narrower set of background variables of life experiences similar to the job situation being predicted, then a number of additional biodata-type predictors become relevant. These predictors generally rely heavily on a content-oriented validation strategy. We will now turn to a brief description of two such predictors.

Myers and Fine (1985) developed a preemployment experience questionnaire (PEQ) to order job candidates on the extent of the match between their backgrounds and job requirements. The initial phase of the project was comprised of a review of job analysis data, including information collected by FJA, for seven job families. Then three types of items were developed from the job analysis data. The first type of item assessed specific experiences closely matching the behaviors required on the job (e.g., the technical job family: "installed, repaired, or replaced any type of PBX or telephone switching equipment"). The second type consisted of generalized experiences that corresponded to tasks performed on the job (which were in turn identified through job analysis). The third type of item concerned adaptive skills required by the job that could be learned at any time throughout the total range of life experience. The items were reviewed by job experts who rated them for their relevancy to particular families. The items surviving this review (i.e., the "highly relevant" and occasionally the "moderately relevant" items) were retained for inclusion in the PEQ.

The development process for the PEQ is primarily driven by the content-oriented strategy of predictor validation. In other words, Myers and Fine (1985) wanted to establish that the PEQ items were recognizable as being closely related to the content of the job as represented by the job analysis. Importantly, in the words of Myers and Fine (1985), "content validity considerations needed to include not only the tasks and requirements of the job, but the life experiences and adaptations that would appear to dispose incumbents to perform effectively" (p. 52). The job analysis information served as a framework for writing the PEQ items and as a key input to the judgments made by the job experts as to which PEQ items to retain in the final instrument. This extensive reliance on job analysis for item development and retention is markedly different from the usual procedure for BIB item development described in the previous section.

The second example of a content-oriented validation strategy for biodata-type predictors is taken from Hough, Keyes, and Dunnette (1983). These researchers used job analysis information to develop three job-content–oriented predictor inventories. One measure, called the *Accomplishment Record Inventory*, showed criterion-related evidence of validity in predicting job performance. In this method, job incumbents were asked to describe their major accomplishments in job areas previously identified by a critical incidents job analysis (Flanagan, 1954). These responses were compared to scoring guidelines developed with the assistance of job experts who had evaluated the level of competence reflected in a representative sample of these accomplishment protocols. Hough et al. (1983) state that "this development of a method for evaluating objectively an attorney's personal record of achievement according to dimensions of performance derived through thorough job analysis constitutes the essence of a content-oriented validation strategy" (p. 274).

These two examples of the application of content-oriented validation to biodata-type predictors point to a more central role for job analysis than does the criterion-related/construct-oriented validation approach typically undertaken by developers of traditional BIBs. Interestingly, this reliance on the content-oriented validation strategy produces an instrument that is focused on a relatively narrow range of directly job-related behaviors or accomplishments as compared to the general personal background and life history items comprising the bulk of more traditional biodata instruments.

RECOMMENDATIONS FOR THE USE OF JOB ANALYSIS

Cronshaw (1991) outlines two central roles for industrial psychologists: (a) improving organizational productivity and (b) ensuring compliance with equal employment opportunity legislation. With respect to the first role, industrial psychologists can reasonably expect that when appropriate procedures are followed, biodata is predictive of future job behavior. This conclusion has been reached by independent reviews of the biodata literature (Asher & Sciarrino, 1974; Reilly & Chao, 1982). With respect to the second role, serious concerns have been raised about the traditional methods of developing and validating biodata measures. Pace and Schoenfeldt (1977) point out that although weighted applications are generally valid in predicting job behavior, the empirical approach to development of such measures (as illustrated by the criterion-related/ construct-oriented strategy described earlier in this chapter) may not prove convincing to legal authorities. Given the similarities of weighted applications to biodata, the same concerns hold with biodata predictors. Pace and Schoenfeldt (1977) recommend the use of alternative methods to ensure the job relevance of the biodata development and validation through reliance on job analysis information. This approach would "inject the hand of reason" into the process of biodata development and validation in order to ensure job-relatedness of biodata in the legal sense as well as its validity.

The recommendation by Pace and Schoenfeldt (1977) concerning the need for greater reliance on job analysis is well placed, but they do not offer specific guidance on what job analysis information should be collected or how it should be used. This more specific guidance will be offered here, using the 1987 *Principles* as the major authority on how job analysis should be conducted in support of the validation and use of biodata as a selection predictor. As a starting point, we will assume, following the arguments made earlier, that content-oriented validation should be emphasized to a greater extent in BIB construction and validation than has usually been the case in the past. BIB developers should therefore utilize all three validation strategies recommended in the *Principles* and *Standards,* including content-oriented validation, although the relative emphasis on the respective strategies may vary, depending on the specifics of the selection program.

The application of the *Principles* to the problem of developing and validating biodata yields the following recommendations regarding how job analysis should be used under each validation strategy.

Job Analysis and Criterion-related Validation

A systematic job analysis must be conducted so that the psychologist can make "good judgments about predictors" (*Principles,* p. 5). When choosing or developing BIB items reflecting personal background of life history, the psychologist is identifying what the *Principles* call "worker specifications." The *Principles* state that such inferences about worker specifications are made by "combining knowledge of the work performed and what workers have to do to perform this work" (p. 6). This job information is obtained through job analysis. According to the *Principles,* "it is...vital that the choice of both predictors and criteria be made with great care" (p. 6). Job analysis is an important contributor providing essential data for such careful decision making.

Job Analysis and Construct-oriented Validation

The *Principles* provide the following guidance regarding the role of job analysis in construct-oriented validation:

> This view of constructs and construct validity implies two aspects of a construct-related strategy for developing evidence to judge the job relatedness of a selection procedure. The first is evidence that the construct is indeed important for job performance—that is, evidence must be grounded in a thorough knowledge of the job. Ordinarily, a job analysis can provide a part of the basis for identifying and defining psychological constructs which are important to job performance. Clarity of the articulation of the meaning and the nature of the construct, and well-informed expert judgment that a logical relationship exists between the nature of the construct and identifiable demands of the job is essential. (p. 24)

As the previous discussion about the traditional development and validation of biodata shows, psychologists should conduct the formal job analyses required to forge a logical link between BIB and the "demands of the job." The use of job analysis for this purpose is clearly called for in the *Principles* in order to support construct-oriented validation.

Job Analysis and Content-oriented Validation

The *Principles* restrict the term "content-oriented validation" to refer to "situations in which a job domain is defined through job analysis by identifying important tasks, behaviors, or knowledge drawn from the domain" (p. 19). The content sampling referred to above follows from the professional judgment of the psychologist. As applied to the development of biodata questionnaires, this requires that the content of the measure be rationally linked through professional judgment to the content of the job as identified by job analysis. For example, the behavior implied by a life history item on the biodata questionnaire would have to be demonstrably related in a logical rather than empirical manner to important behaviors or performances required on the job. Importantly, the psychologist undertaking content-oriented validation must carefully define the job content to be sampled, after describing the whole job as a part of job analysis.

The *Principles* directly address the content-oriented validation of biodata items in the following way:

> Requirements for or evaluation of personal history variables, such as specific prior training, experience, or achievement can be justified on the basis of the relationship between the content of the personal history experience and the content of the job for which they are evaluated or required. To justify such relationships, more than a superficial resemblance between the content of the personal history variables and the content of the job is required.... The critical consideration is the similarity between the behaviors, products, knowledges, skills, or abilities demonstrated in the personal history variable and the behaviors, products, knowledges, skills, or abilities required on the job, whether or not there is a close resemblance between the given personal history variable as a whole and the job as a whole. (p. 22)

Again, the match between the domain of BIB items and job requirements should be established through job analysis.

JOB ANALYSIS APPROACHES TO BIODATA DEVELOPMENT AND VALIDATION

If the proposal that job analysis should play an extensive role in the development and validation of BIBs is to be followed, then the issue becomes: Which job analysis method? Can each method equally serve the "critical consideration" stated in the *Principles* (p. 22)? Can each equally provide for establishing "the similarity between the behaviors, products, knowledges, skills, or abilities demonstrated in the personal history variable, and the behaviors, products, knowledges, skills, or abilities required on the job, whether or not there is a close resemblance between the given personal history variable as a whole and the job as a whole"? Can each ensure equally well that rational as well as empirical considerations influence the development and validation of a BIB?

It is not possible here to examine all or even several job analysis methods in detail with these questions in mind. Instead, we will concentrate most of our attention on a single method, functional job analysis (FJA), which has been applied to BIB development (Brush & Owens, 1979). In doing so, we are proposing a model that is primarily content- and construct-driven, thereby reflecting the more extensive use of job analysis and overcoming its underutilization. This model will be offered as a supplement to Schoenfeldt's criterion-driven model. After examining how FJA can be used in BIB research and application, we will examine the suitability of several other job analysis methods to biodata item development.

Functional Job Analysis

It is probably no accident that when the *Principles* speak of establishing similarity between job requirements and the personal history variable, they refer to "behaviors, products, knowledges, skills, or abilities." These, then, are the most likely elements for establishing both a source and a bridge between job analysis and BIBs. The job analysis method we must look to should speak in the language that can easily be related to an individual's background. FJA is expressed in that kind of language and, in addition, provides a frame of reference for understanding nonwork activities in a person's biography (Fine, 1986, 1988).

Functional job analysis grew out of a 10-year (1950–1959) research project at the United States Employment Service (Fine, 1988, p. 1020). This project resulted in the occupational classification system in the third and fourth editions of the *Dictionary of Occupational Titles* (DOT; U.S. Department of Labor, 1965, 1977). Table 1, showing the components of this research according to Ash's (1982) classification, indicates how the FJA method measured elements from all three sources of data.

Four thousand jobs, an 18 percent sample of the job definitions in the second edition of the DOT, were independently rated for each of these components by separate raters. Their ratings were guided by benchmarks in manuals that had been developed in earlier research. All of the ratings required consensus among raters.

In the final analysis, the Things, Data, and People profiles (each job receiving a rating on all three factors) proved to be the key component in bringing together jobs that were similar in interest, aptitudes, and training

TABLE 1   Components for the Functional Occupational Classification Project

Task-based	Attribute-based	Behavior-based
Working conditions—6 factors	Aptitudes—11 factors	Worker functions: what workers do
	Interests—10 factors	
Work functions: what gets done—indefinite	Temperaments—12 factors	Things—3 levels
	Physical demands—7 factors	Data—6 levels
	Reasoning—6 levels	People—6 levels
	Math—5 levels	
	Language—6 levels	
	Specific vocational preparation—9 levels	

time (reasoning, language, and specific vocational preparation). Tempera-
ments and physical demands played a negligible role in establishing
similarity. Working conditions and what got done (process, technology)
remained largely independent of the Things, Data, and People groupings.

In 1960, a Worker Instructions scale was added to the existing scales
(Fine, 1988, p. 1032) and refined to reflect the prescription/discretion
dimension developed by Jacques (1964). According to Jacques and his
sponsor, Wilfred Brown, skill is a function of the amount of time that
elapses between the inception of a job and the output. Thus, low skilled
jobs have very short time spans, whereas highly skilled jobs have very long
time spans that run into months and years. The Worker Instructions scale
proved to be a critically important behavior scale—not only useful in the
analysis of an important content element of jobs but also in pointing to a
more profound understanding of the skill requirements of the job.

The insight gained concerning the nature of skills and, hence, the
enlargement of the job analysis was that effective job performance was
the blending of three types of skills, namely: functional, specific content,
and adaptive (Fine, 1988). These three types of skills were defined as
follows:

> *Functional skills* are those competencies that enable an individual to relate to
> things, data, and people in some combination according to personal preferences
> and level of abilities (reasoning, math, language, physical, and interpersonal
> capabilities). They are represented by the behaviors listed in the Things, Data,
> and People taxonomy.

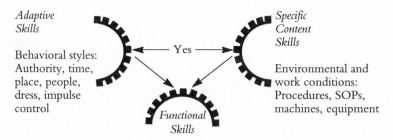

Adaptive Skills

Behavioral styles: Authority, time, place, people, dress, impulse control

— Yes →

Specific Content Skills

Environmental and work conditions: Procedures, SOPs, machines, equipment

Functional Skills

Mental, interpersonal, and physical capacities: Data, people, things

FIGURE 2   Choice Process for Effective Performance

Specific content skills are those competencies that enable an individual to perform a specific job according to standards required to satisfy the market. They are represented by work done verbs that reflect specific technological content, e.g., machining, welding, carpentering, programming, managing, sewing, typing.

Adaptive skills are those competencies that enable an individual to manage the demands for conformity and/or change in relation to physical, interpersonal, organizational, and working conditions in which a job exists. They are indirectly suggested by worker instructions and performance standards. In general, the adaptive skill requirements can be determined by asking the questions, What are the conditions (physical, social, and interpersonal) in which you must perform this task? and What are the instructions that need to be followed in order to attain the specific standards? (p. 1024)

Once these three different types of skills were defined, a fundamental dynamic associated with the individual choice process became apparent. This choice process, which has significant implications for BIBs, is represented in Figure 2. In effect, the figure suggests that individuals screen the specific content of prospective jobs (their technical demands, working conditions, pay, opportunities) through both conscious and unconscious screens of awareness of their own personal styles (e.g., preferences for kinds of instructions, authority, hours of work, place of work), typically guessing how the prospective position will be for them and then making a decision. If the decision is no, they must start over again, screening new positions. If the decision is yes, their hypothesis is that the fit is reasonably suitable. At this point, their functional skills shift into gear and they give the job a chance. If this works out as hypothesized—that is, if their adaptive skills are being fulfilled—they give the job their best shot through the exercise of their functional skills. If the job does not turn out to be suitable to their adaptive skills, their willingness to give the job their best deteriorates. They

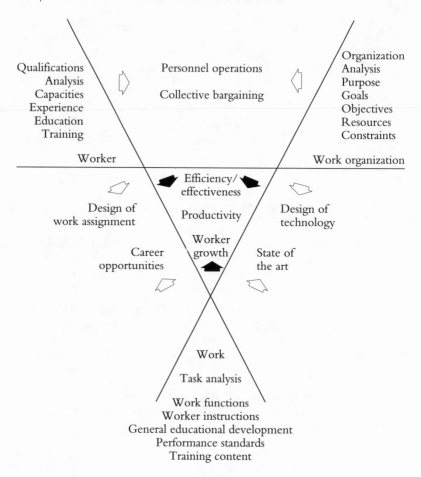

Qualifications
Analysis
Capacities
Experience
Education
Training

Personnel operations

Collective bargaining

Organization
Analysis
Purpose
Goals
Objectives
Resources
Constraints

Worker

Work organization

Efficiency/
effectiveness

Design of
work assignment

Productivity

Design of
technology

Career
opportunities

Worker
growth

State of
the art

Work

Task analysis

Work functions
Worker instructions
General educational development
Performance standards
Training content

FIGURE 3   A Systems Concept of Work Performance

drag their feet, they are absent, their functional skills are exercised at a minimum of efficiency, and, finally, they begin to look elsewhere for a new position.

Functional job analysis points to a job analysis that comprehends something beyond what comes into immediate focus when seeking a success criterion for a BIB. In the immediate focus is the task statement, but it is conceived as a systems module and therefore reaches out beyond itself, beyond the work, to the organization and the worker, as represented by Figure 3.

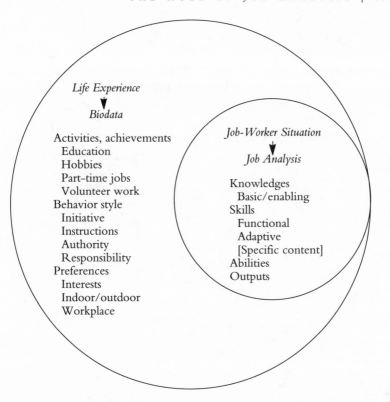

FIGURE 4   Job Analysis as a Focal Source for Criterion, Construct, and Content Items for a Biodata Instrument

This view of the nature of skills and their dynamics in the individual choice process argues for a somewhat different assessment–classification model than that of Schoenfeldt, perhaps one represented by Figure 4.

According to this model, the structure and dynamics occurring in the job-worker situation are a part of the activities of life experience. The job-worker situation, in some instances, clearly reflects and even illuminates the salient forces in life experiences. Stokes, Mumford, and Owens (1989) make the following observation that would seem to be consistent with the alternative model proposed above.

Individuals over time create a niche, which is an organized sub-environment composed of interrelated activities. Furthermore, the niche is associated with

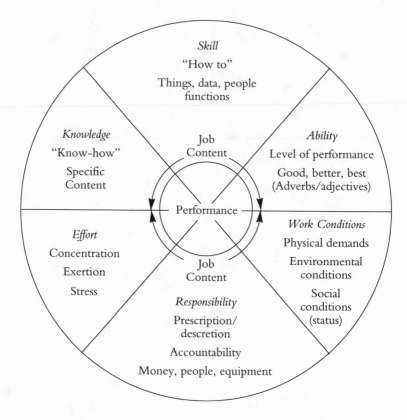

FIGURE 5   A Holistic Concept of Performance Skill Requirements

a complex constellation of differential characteristics which represent the individual's adaptive style. The adaptive style is developed to enhance adaptation to the niche created by the individual. Because the individual's niche and adaptive style influence the selection of future activities, an interpretable self-propagating developmental trajectory is made possible. (p. 542)

Depending on the vocational preparation and varieties of life experience, the job experience may develop into a systematic career that is consistent, logical, and coherent (in short, rational), or is a miscellany of trial and error or something in between (e.g., a job and a consuming hobby). Actually, despite involvement in a job–worker situation, even one that has all the aspects of a consistent career, the enveloping life experience goes on for each individual.

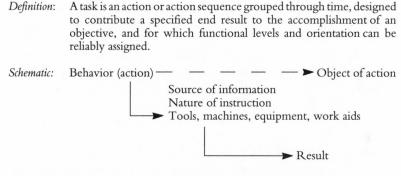

Definition: A task is an action or action sequence grouped through time, designed to contribute a specified end result to the accomplishment of an objective, and for which functional levels and orientation can be reliably assigned.

FIGURE 6   Definition and Schematic of an FJA Task Statement

The proposed model is not one of matching relatively homogeneous life groups on the basis of demographic data to job families by empirical means, but rather one of comprehending behavioral styles that allow for considerable flexibility in the occupational directions pursued. For example, the model encompasses the following situation: Two children grow up in the same household, with one parent a lawyer and the other a social worker; both obtain a good education through college; both work at summer jobs easily available in the office of the lawyer parent; both are exposed at home to an ambience of rational thought and aesthetic appreciation; yet one individual chooses a career as a lawyer and the other as an artist/painter. What motivates one is a life of structure, an attachment to precedents, order, and the ideal value of justice. What motivates the other is the need for greater expression of individual discretion, taking off in new directions, and not following precedents.

The proposed model argues for job analysis that reaches far beyond the immediate knowledge, skill, and abilities of a particular task focused on functional and specific content skills. It proposes to bring into the analysis the context of the task—the adaptive skills that encompass the effort, responsibility, and working conditions in which the tasks occur, as shown in Figure 5. To obtain these data, FJA works with the model of a task shown in Figure 6.

The result and the technology used relate the task to the objectives of the organization. The instructions and the knowledge requirement relate the task to the way the job is structured and its level of responsibility. The behavior relates the task to the level in the FJA functional scales (Fine, 1988, p. 1021) and, in effect, to the experience and training required of the worker. The FJA task contains behavior, knowledge, skill, and ability requirements that are recognizable in the activity background of an individual. The very fact that the main focus is the functional and specific content skills, with only the instructions touching upon context, points to the need to further explore the variables of context—the effort requirements (e.g., overtime requirements) and the working conditions (e.g., the physical, social, and interpersonal environment) in which the instruction/ responsibility must be exercised. At this point, we can begin to see the full range of possibilities of the job analysis as a source of items for the BIB.

Sample Biodata Items Using Functional Job Analysis

The above understanding of job analysis could lead to biodata items such as the following:

- When you were a student during your teens, you preferred homework assignments that were:
  (a) Detailed and explicit as to what was expected
  (b) Fairly specific but with a fair amount of leeway in following procedural instructions
  (c) Quite general and open-ended, allowing you to follow the instructions according to your own understanding
- When you were a young adult starting up on the first rung of your career ladder, you preferred assignment instructions that were:
  (a) Detailed and explicit as to what was expected
  (b) Fairly specific but with a fair amount of leeway in following procedural instructions
  (c) Quite general and open-ended allowing you to follow the instructions according to your own understanding
- In general, in the matter of work assignments, you prefer:
  (a) More prescription (specification) than discretion
  (b) More discretion (judgment) than prescription
  (c) About an equal division between the two
- In your leisure time, you prefer to be involved with:
  (a) Reading
  (b) Social activities
  (c) Making things in your own workroom
  (d) Sports
  (e) None of the above
- When engaged in a project, whether associated with school or a voluntary activity, the part you like best is:
  (a) Planning it
  (b) Carrying out the specified tasks
  (c) Working out unexpected problems
  (d) Showing the finished product

The above types of items draw on the functional behavioral background of the individual. They are consistent with situations the individual will encounter in the world of work. They are not concerned with *how* the individual came to have the particular proclivities and preferences displayed, as might be evident in the responses to items such as the following:

- How many books were around your house when you were growing up?
- Relative to your friends, how much time did you spend with your father during high school?
- In high school, how often did your parents criticize you?

This information could be quite interesting, as would the answers to a myriad of such questions that could be asked about a person's background. But how are they to be interpreted from a content or construct point of view? In their methodology review of background data measures, Mumford and Owens (1987) called attention to a communication by Buel to Tyler suggesting that background data items phrased in a historical context, capturing the values, attitude, and beliefs *related to performance* (our emphasis), will tend to be more effective predictors than demographic items. This finding, Buel continued, may reflect the fact that the values, attitudes, and beliefs that individuals carry with them from past situational exposures are the characteristics most likely to determine future behavior and experience. In the language of functional job analysis, what Buel is referring to are an individual's adaptive skills.

What, then, are the advantages in using the FJA approach for the development of BIBs? Three seem to have considerable value.

- The functions of FJA are behaviors reflecting skills that are continuous with all of life experience, including education, leisure time activities, and part-time jobs, thus providing a single language for describing jobs and backgrounds. By distinguishing between function, specific content, and adaptive skills, FJA can enhance both the content and construct understanding of a BIB instrument.
- BIB items can be constructed that are directly interpretable to task and performance in job-worker situations.
- FJA focuses on *doing,* not on *being.* Functions reflect activity and behavior data, not circumstantial data requiring statistical manipulation and inference to give them meaning. In the universe of indicators of individual differences, the functions of FJA are integrations of human experience that are "meaningful, cohesive, description(s) of the similarities and differences among individuals" (Stokes, Mumford, & Owens, 1989, p. 510).

OTHER JOB ANALYSIS METHODS

Ash (1982) has classified the major methods of job analysis as task-based, attribute-based, and behavior-based by referring to the elements used in each of the methods to analyze and describe the job. The first is represented by task inventories, such as the Comprehensive Occupational Data Analysis Program (CODAP; Christal & Weissmuller, 1988). An example of the attribute-based method is Fleishman's Ability Requirement Scales (Fleishman & Mumford, 1988). The Critical Incident Technique devised by Flanagan illustrates the behavior-based method (Bownas & Bernardin, 1988).

The significance of the above classification is that it is indicative of the kinds of information generated by job analyses that can be used in constructing a BIB. In the BIB, this information shows up as work experience, educational achievement, and ability and as behavioral styles such as preference for one or another type of work, ways of working, recreation, or social situations. All of these elements in an individual's background are clues to an understanding of the kind of work in which he or she is most likely to thrive.

Not all information generated by job analysis is equally useful or practical as an item source for a BIB. This principle is illustrated in Table 2. The seven job analysis methods studied by Levine, Ash, Hall, and Sistrunk (1988) are listed along the left-hand side of this table. All seven of these methods are widely accepted for use in business, industry, and government. Along the top of the table are listed the types of information required by the Division 14 *Principles* for establishing the relevance of personal history items. The entries in Table 2 (indicated by an X) show the type of information collected through each job analysis method. For example, Job Elements Analysis involves the collection of information about job incumbent behaviors, knowledges, skills, and abilities, but not about products.[2]

The results in Table 2 show that most of the seven job analysis methods generate job information that only incompletely covers the domain needed for the development of biodata items. Only FJA covers the entire job domain recommended in the *Principles* for this purpose. As a consequence, biodata developers using job analysis methods other than FJA must collect data over and above the original job analysis information in order to develop valid and defensible biodata items. Of course, the amount of additional information that must be collected depends on the job analysis method initially used. For example, use of the Ability Requirements Scales

TABLE 2   Comparison of Major Job Analysis Methods to Requirements for Constructing Biodata Items

| Method | Job Information Provided by Method | | | | |
	Behaviors	Products	Knowledges	Skills	Abilities
Job Element Analysis (Primoff & Eyde, 1988)	X		X	X	X
Position Analysis Questionnaire (McCormick & Jeanneret, 1988)	X		X	X	X
Threshold Traits Analysis (Lopez, 1988)			X	X	X
Ability Requirement Scales(Fleishman & Mumford, 1988)					X
Functional Job Analysis (Fine, 1988)	X	X	X	X	X
Job-Task Inventory Analysis/CODAP (Christal &Weissmuller, 1988)	X				
Critical Incident Technique (Bownas & Bernardin, 1988)	X				

would require considerable augmentation through other forms of job information before a full set of biodata items could be generated.

The results in Table 2 are suggestive of why biodata developers have underutilized formal job analysis. Many job analysis methods do not generate the full range of job information required for life history items and have thus proven to be of limited use for this purpose. Biodata developers may be responding to the shortcomings inherent in many job analysis methods by relying less on formal job analysis to collect job information and more on other means, including extensive literature searches and interviews with job incumbents or supervisors. The way out of this dilemma for biodata developers is to rely on job analysis methods that are as high as possible in the generality of obtained job information (Cronshaw, 1991). At present, FJA is one of the few job analysis methods available that is sufficiently high in generality of job information to fully support biodata item development.

CONCLUSIONS AND FUTURE DIRECTIONS
FOR RESEARCH AND APPLICATION

At the beginning of the chapter, a review of the biodata literature showed that researchers and practitioners in the area have tended to emphasize the criterion-related and construct-oriented strategies of predictor validation. In this chapter, an alternative approach to validating BIBs was presented, where the use of job analysis data in developing content- and construct-valid BIB items was emphasized as an alternative to the empirical approaches followed by many biodata developers in the past. The specific job analysis method proposed was FJA. Although FJA does place a heavy emphasis on content validation of BIB items, this method also assists in the construct validation, and possibly the criterion-related validation, of BIB instruments as well. Many of the job analysis methods presently available lack the generality of coverage needed to generate biodata items.

The particular advantages of FJA over the empirical approach to the BIB development should be noted. The first advantage is one of theoretical elegance that derives from the use of FJA. The theoretical understanding afforded by FJA of how people come to choose jobs and why they perform well or poorly in them should provide considerable assistance to researchers or practitioners who develop the BIB instruments intended to differentiate between good and poor job performers. The second advantage is one of economy. A large number of life experiences are judgmentally "filtered" through the screening criteria represented by FJA data, thus highlighting a much smaller set of life experience variables for inclusion in the BIB. These BIB items are by definition content valid, as they represent the activities of life experience that overlap with the activities of the present job. The development process is efficient, as well as "injecting the hand of reason" into the process. When evaluated against the *Principles* (SIOP, 1987), the FJA approach described in this chapter addresses the following validation concerns:

- *Using a criterion-related strategy to validate a BIB.* Using the FJA approach, BIB items are developed by combining knowledge of the work performed and what workers have to do to perform the work. As a result, the BIB developer can have additional confidence that the statistics generated in the criterion-related validation are meaningful and interpretable. In addition, the magnitude of the empirical relationship between the BIB predictor and the job performance criterion might be enhanced over approaches to biodata development that rely on less formal means for determining which items should be included in the final questionnaire (even if these items are further culled through empirical methods).

- *Using a construct-oriented strategy to validate a BIB.* The nature of BIB items, qua operational definitions of underlying constructs, is more interpretable when the items are based on a theoretical model of job analysis such as FJA. The logical relationship between the nature of the construct and the identifiable demands of the job is established through FJA as well (as is clearly seen in Figure 4).
- *Using a content-oriented strategy to validate a BIB.* The content of the BIB instrument is rationally linked through professional judgment to the specific content of the job, even though the life history items in the BIB come from the more general domain of life experience beyond the job-worker situation. As a consequence, even though the job-worker situation assessed by FJA is "of a piece" with the activities of life experience and is not synonymous with those experiences, the BIB items developed from the FJA data represent the broader life experiences of greatest relevance to performance on the immediate job. This selective and systematic "filtering" of life experiences through the FJA data derived from the immediate job-worker situation is the essence of content validation.

As can be seen, the approach to biodata development advocated here meets the major concerns expressed in the *Principles.*

The implications of FJA for biodata application are fairly obvious. Since the FJA approach deemphasizes raw empiricism in the development of biodata instruments, biodata developers should be able to create BIB instruments more economically and with less reliance on large validation samples and complex statistical analyses. Although practitioners can collect criterion-related evidence of validity for biodata scores by correlating them with job performance criteria, or collect construct-oriented evidence of validity by conducting factor analyses on sets of BIB items, considerable evidence of validity already exists from content-oriented validation strategies followed in BIB item development. The overall validity inference should be strengthened because validation data is available from all three sources described in the *Principles* (i.e., criterion-related, construct-oriented, and content-oriented).

There are also implications for research into biodata instruments. In particular, FJA offers a theoretical basis for making specific predictions concerning how life experiences will be related to occupational choice and performance. For example, prospective employees will tend to choose jobs matching their personal styles (e.g., for kinds of instructions and authority). Research testing these predictions would add understanding as to why and how life experience influences worker behavior on the job. Such findings would augment important work describing how people develop within life paths over long periods of time (e.g., Stokes, Mumford, & Owens, 1989). On a more routine level, researchers might compare the prediction achievable from BIBs developed using the empirical and rational approaches. One would expect to achieve better prediction from a rationally developed BIB, as compared to an empirically developed one, but research directed to this question is required before we can arrive at a firm answer.[3]

NOTES

1. The term functional job analysis (FJA) in this chapter refers to a system of job analysis developed by S. A. Fine and first described in a paper presented to the American Psychological Association in 1951: a pilot study to develop a functional classification structure of occupations. The study described was directed and carried out by Fine at the United States Employment Service from 1950 through 1959. The implications of the research for job analysis were first elaborated in an article entitled "Functional Job Analysis," which appeared in *Personnel Administration and Industrial Relations* in the spring of 1955. FJA is a unique methodology, not a generic approach to job analysis.

2. It should be noted that extra job information may be obtained after one of these job analysis methods is applied (e.g., human resource staff who have analyzed a job using job-task inventory analysis may use an add-on procedure to obtain ratings of the knowledges, skills, and abilities required to perform the tasks identified in the original job analysis). However, in this chapter we will restrict our attention to the range of job information that can be obtained by using only the seven methods in Table 2, exclusive of add-on procedures needed to collect extra data for biodata purposes.

3. Empirical evidence for the superiority of rationally developed over empirically developed biodata keys is equivocal. The few extant studies in this area, reported by Mumford and Owens (1987) in their methodology review of background data measures, suggest that rational and empirical keys yield similar predictive efficiency. However, Mumford and Owens (1987) also point out that more research is needed on the predictive efficiency of rational keys.

REFERENCES

American Educational Research Association, American Psychological Association, & National Council on Measurement in Education. (1985). *Standards for educational and psychological testing.* Washington, DC: American Psychological Association.

Ash, R. A. (1982). Job elements for task clusters: Arguments for using multi methodological approaches to job analysis and demonstration of their ability. *Public Personnel Management Journal, 11,* 80–90.

Asher, J. J., & Sciarrino, J. A. (1974). Realistic work sample tests: A review. *Personnel Psychology, 27,* 519–533.

Bownas, D. A., & Bernardin, J. J. (1988). Critical incident technique. In S. Gael (Ed.), *The job analysis handbook for business, industry and government* (pp. 1121–1137). New York: Wiley.

Brush, D. H., & Owens, W. A. (1979). Implementation and evaluation of an assessment classification model for manpower utilization. *Personnel Psychology, 32*, 369–383.

Christal, R. E., & Weissmuller, J. J. (1988). Job task inventory. In S. Gael (Ed.), *The job analysis handbook for business, industry and government* (pp. 1036-1050). New York: Wiley.

Cronshaw, S. F. (1991). *Industrial psychology in Canada.* Waterloo, Ontario: North Waterloo Press.

Fine, S. A. (1986). *Job analysis.* In R. Berk (Ed.), *Performance assessment: Methods and applications* (pp. 53–81). Baltimore: The Johns Hopkins University Press.

Fine, S. A. (1988). *Functional job analysis.* In S. Gael (Ed.), *The job analysis handbook for business, industry and government* (pp. 1010–1035). New York: Wiley.

Flanagan, J. C. (1954). The critical incident technique. *Psychological Bulletin, 51*, 327–358.

Fleishman, E. A., & Mumford, M. D. (1988). Ability requirement scales. In S. Gael (Ed.), *The job analysis handbook for business, industry and government* (pp. 917–935). New York: Wiley.

Gatewood, R. D., & Feild, H. S. (1987). *Human resource selection.* New York: The Dryden Press.

Glennon, J. R., Albright, L. E., & Owens, W. A. (1966). *A catalog of life history items.* Greensboro, NC: Richardson Foundation.

Hough, L. M., Keyes, M. A., & Dunnette, M. D. (1983). An evaluation of three "alternative" selection procedures. *Personnel Psychology, 36*, 261–276.

Jacques, E. (1964). *Time-span handbook.* London: Heineman Educational Books.

Levine, E. L., Ash, R. A., Hall, H., & Sistrunk, F. (1988). Evaluation of job analysis methods by experienced job analysts. *Academy of Management Journal, 26*, 339–348.

Lopez, F. M. (1988). Threshold Traits Analysis System. In S. Gael (Ed.), *The job analysis handbook for business, industry and government* (pp. 880–901). New York: Wiley.

McCormick, E. J., & Jeanneret, P. R. (1988). Position Analysis Questionnaire (PAQ). In S. Gael (Ed.), *The job analysis handbook for business, industry and government* (pp. 825–842). New York: Wiley.

Morrison, R. F. (1977). A multivariate model for the occupational placement decision. *Journal of Applied Psychology, 62*, 271–277.

Mumford, M. D., & Owens, W. A. (1987). Methodology review: Principles, procedures, and findings in the application of background data measures. *Applied Psychological Measurement, 11*, 1–31.

Myers, D. C., & Fine, S. A. (1985). Development of a methodology to obtain and assess applicant experiences for employment. *Public Personnel Management, 14*(1), 51–64.

Owens, W. A. (1976). Background data. In M. Dunnette (Ed.), *The handbook of industrial and organizational psychology* (pp. 609–644). Chicago: Rand-McNally.

Pace, L. A., & Schoenfeldt, L. F. (1977). Legal concerns in the use of weighted applications. *Personnel Psychology, 30*, 159–166.

Primoff, E. S., & Eyde, L. D. (1988). Job element analysis. In S. Gael (Ed.), *The job analysis handbook for business, industry and government* (pp. 807–824). New York: Wiley.

Reilly, R., & Chao, G. (1982). Validity and fairness of some alternative employee selection procedures. *Personnel Psychology, 35*, 1–62.

Schoenfeldt, L. F. (1974). Utilization of manpower: Development and evaluation of an assessment-classification model for matching individuals with jobs. *Journal of Applied Psychology, 59*, 583–595.

Society for Industrial and Organizational Psychology, Inc. (1987). *Principles for the validation and use of personnel selection procedures* (3d ed.). College Park, MD: Author.

Stokes, G. S., Mumford, M. D., & Owens, W. A. (1989). Life history prototypes in the study of human individuality. *Journal of Personality, 57*, 509–545.

U.S. Department of Labor. (1965). *Dictionary of occupational titles* (3d ed.). Washington, DC: U.S. Government Printing Office.

U.S. Department of Labor. (1977). *Dictionary of occupational titles* (4th ed.). Washington, DC: U.S. Government Printing Office.

SCALING OF BIODATA MEASURES

Once items are developed using any of the several possible approaches, the next major issues to be addressed involve questions of methods of scaling. It is not always easy to divorce item development issues from scaling issues because some item development methods may be more consistent with some scaling techniques than with others. However, it is important to describe the different scaling methods separately in order to adequately understand the different perspectives. The four chapters in this section address four general approaches to scaling: empirical, rational, factor analytic, and subgrouping. What will be apparent to readers as they review these chapters is that the line between the different techniques is not always clear. In fact, these techniques are often combined to develop a final biodata scale.

The first chapter in this section focuses on the oldest set of techniques for scoring biodata. Hogan reviews the long history of empirical scaling techniques. He describes the most popular procedures for scaling items and selecting final items in a biodata key. General operational procedures and specific techniques are reviewed. He notes that, regardless of the particular empirical keying method used, differential performance measurement is essential. He discusses the stability of various procedures and briefly reviews the reliability and validity of empirical keys. Issues of concern, such as generalizability of keys, decrease in validity over time, faking, and bias related to race, ethnicity, or gender are discussed.

In sharp contrast to the empirical approaches are the rational approaches to biodata scaling. Hough and Paullin focus specifically on the construct-oriented scale construction approach. The authors review briefly three approaches: the *external* (empirical) approach, the *inductive* (internal) approach, and the *deductive* (rational, intuitive, or theoretical) approach, and they discuss the strengths and weaknesses of each. They then compare each approach in terms of item- and scale-level validities. They summarize results obtained from a large number of studies and conclude that none of the methods is clearly superior in terms of its criterion-related validities. Moreover, they review commonly held beliefs regarding the strengths and weaknesses of each method, and they conclude that many of these common beliefs are not well supported by the data. They then provide specifics for construct-oriented scale construction, summarizing both item and scale characteristics and focusing on the importance of delineating the performance domain and identifying and defining the relevant individual difference constructs.

Schoenfeldt and Mendoza describe the development and use of biodata scales that are based on factor analytic techniques. They provide the reader with a brief overview of factor analysis, distinguishing among the different methods for deriving factors. They describe studies that represent various factor analytic approaches, and they examine the issues of generalizability across populations and factor stability across time. They then describe the use of confirmatory factor analysis in a few studies. The validities of factor analytic scales compared to biodata scales developed using other methods are compared. What is clear from their chapter is the significant contribution of factor analysis to our understanding of the dimensions of life experiences, but equally obvious is that more attention needs to be directed toward those dimensions that reflect performance-relevant constructs.

The last chapter in this section describes the subgrouping approach, which is a scaling approach unlike the traditional methods covered in the previous three chapters because it involves the clustering of individuals rather than the clustering of variables or items. Hein and Wesley describe the use of subgrouping as a scaling technique, and they differentiate it from the other approaches. They describe situations where subgrouping may or may not be appropriate. They detail the methodology used in subgrouping, including item selection procedures, the need for data reduction, and techniques for identifying groups. Hein and Wesley's detailed specification of the steps to be taken in conducting a subgrouping study are an important contribution to the biodata literature. Finally, they discuss subpopulation differences and methods for using subgroups in organizations, suggesting new directions for applying subgrouping techniques to provide valuable tools to organizations.

Empirical Keying of Background Data Measures

James B. Hogan
University of Georgia

The origin of the empirical keying approach for developing background data measures may be traced back to the early part of this century and to research sponsored in large part by the life insurance industry to improve the selection of sales agents. Use of an empirically keyed application blank, or personal history record, for selecting insurance sales agents represented a natural extension for an industry steeped in a tradition of actuarial risk analysis. Application of statistical analysis for developing an empirically based scoring key was recognized as early as 1915 by Edward A. Woods, president of the National Association of Life Underwriters and an industry leader in the movement to improve the selection and training of sales agents (Ferguson, 1961). Woods attempted a statistical analysis of the application blank item responses of successful and unsuccessful sales agents based on what was surely a familiar concept within the insurance business—the principle that the only items of predictive value are those that can be shown statistically to differentiate risk groups.

In 1916, Woods and several business associates sponsored the founding of the Bureau of Salesmanship Research at the Carnegie Institute of Technology, which in 1919 became the Bureau of Personnel Research (Ferguson, 1961). Research on empirical keying at the bureau from 1916 to 1921 provided the basis for the first published report in the applied psychology literature of a study demonstrating the potential of empirical keying for scoring a personal history blank. The study was authored by Dorothy B. Goldsmith of the Guardian Life Insurance Company of America and was published in 1922 in the *Journal of Applied Psychology*.

According to Goldsmith (1922),

> this study was made to determine whether the items of a personal history blank could be used to predict the success or failure of a salesman. That is, whether a weighted, quantitative score could be given to the answers to questions upon a history blank, in order that it might be used as an elimination test. (p. 149)

Fifty personal history blanks provided the initial item weighting sample, having been randomly selected from a total of 502 blanks completed by sales agents employed by the Guardian Life Insurance Company. Utilizing a contrasting criterion groups approach, nine items were identified that significantly differentiated upper, middle, and lower performing groups based on a criterion of first-year insurance sales. Significant items included age, marital status, education, previous occupation, life insurance personally held, service commitment, club memberships, confidence, and previous sales experience. Unit weights were assigned to item responses based on observed relationships with the performance of agents in the criterion groups. Subsequently, this empirically derived scoring key was applied to the total population of 502 personal history blanks, where it was found that

> for a life insurance company, the score on the personal history blank bears a positive relationship to the applicants future success, and that on this blank a lower critical score may be set, below which it would not be worthwhile to license an applicant. (Goldsmith, 1922, p. 155)

This line of research set the stage for what was to become the most popular method of scoring background data measures.

During the 70 years since the publication of the Goldsmith study, the empirical keying approach has been the most widely employed method for scaling background data measures subsequently used for screening job applicants in a wide variety of personnel selection contexts. Success, however, has not been without its price. The empirical keying approach has frequently been criticized for its "dust bowl empiricism" and for the consequent lost opportunities to advance knowledge and understanding of important biographical constructs and, of course, theory development. The success of the empirical keying approach in numerous settings, however, has surely promoted widespread interest and important research into background data. Research programs are under way that promise to provide for background data users a strong and theoretically sound basis for both understanding behavior and predicting future behavior (e.g., Mumford & Nichels, 1990). Indeed, promising results of recent research suggest the utility of a hybrid approach that combines the distinctive advantages of empirical and factorial scaling approaches for maximizing prediction while at the same time contributing to the understanding of important background and experience antecedents (Dalessio & Crosby, 1991).

As a relatively straightforward method, empirical keying offers a practical scaling approach for practitioners and researchers alike and has, to date, resulted in many useful background data measures, both for applied prediction purposes and for numerous research studies comparing alternative scaling techniques. This chapter covers (a) the basic intent and assumptions underlying empirical keying, (b) general operational procedures and specific techniques for empirical keying, (c) reliability and validity of empirically keyed measures, and (d) important research issues and concerns in the development of empirically keyed background data measures.

BASIC INTENT AND UNDERLYING ASSUMPTIONS

As an approach for developing valid background data measures, empirical keying seems to have proven itself. Several reviews indicate that empirically keyed background data measures are among the best available predictors of training and job performance criteria (Asher, 1972; Ghiselli, 1973; Owens, 1976; Reilly & Chao, 1982). Empirical keying generally involves the computation of a composite score from a background data measure. The composite score is usually computed as a weighted linear combination of some subset of items comprising the measure. The item weights constitute the scoring key, and their development is based on a statistical analysis of item-criterion relationships observed for a particular sample. Most empirical keying methods involve statistical techniques for generating differential item weights and rely on variance maximizing procedures. These procedures are frequently designed to achieve maximum separation of important criterion groups comprising the sample. For example, empirical keying procedures are typically used to select and weight items on the basis of their ability to differentiate membership in upper and lower performing criterion groups.

The empirical keying approach appears to be the most commonly employed scoring method when the primary purpose is to maximize prediction of an external criterion (Guion, 1965). Understanding of underlying relationships or constructs accounting for the prediction is not typically emphasized. Meaningfulness is established through demonstrated prediction of criterion performance without reference to broader theory (Mumford & Stokes, 1992). Thus, any meaning ascribed to empirically derived scores is generally limited to an assessment of predictive efficiency. Indeed, because item weights are statistically derived based on their ability to predict criteria that are frequently complex and poorly understood, resulting empirical keys are generally considered to be complex and lacking in psychological meaningfulness (Guion, 1965). Although resulting back-ground data measures may be high in criterion-related validity, support for content- and construct-related validity is seldomly pursued. Despite this apparent limitation, several researchers have observed that systematic specification and development of background data items, as well as criterion specification and development, play an important role in estab-lishing a basis for content and construct validity (Mumford & Stokes, 1992; Thayer, 1977).

Ultimately, the utility of an empirically keyed background data measure is typically judged in terms of its ability to predict criterion performance within independent samples drawn from the reference group of interest (Mumford & Stokes, 1992). Within the context of personnel selection, typical criteria include turnover, production, and performance ratings. Typical reference groups include job applicants and job incumbents. Thus, a concurrent empirical key might be developed to discriminate high from low performers within a sample of job incumbents for subsequent use in predicting the performance of job applicants (the reference group). The ultimate question is that of the generality of the empirical key, derived using a particular sample and criterion measure, for predicting performance potential within the reference group. This statement has two very impor-tant implications for the background data user.

First, the effectiveness of an empirical key will depend on the adequacy of the criterion measure used as a representation of the performance of ultimate interest (Thayer, 1977). That is, the generality of the empirical key will depend, in large part, on careful development of the criterion measure. Second, the effectiveness of an empirical key will depend on the appropri-ateness of the sample used in its development. The generality and, therefore, utility of the resulting empirically keyed measure will be diminished to the extent that the sample inadequately represents the reference group to which generalization is sought. For example, the predictive validity of a concurrently developed empirical key could be expected to suffer restrictions typical of measures developed using a sample that differs in important ways from the reference group of interest (e.g., job incumbents versus job applicants). Again, the generality of the empirical key will depend on the careful definition of the reference group and samples employed for key development.

EMPIRICAL KEYING PROCEDURES AND TECHNIQUES

Three techniques appear to be the most frequently employed for develop-ing empirically keyed background data measures, though several other strategies are described in the literature. By far the most commonly cited approach is England's (1961, 1971) weighted application blank approach (e.g., Anastasi, 1979; Cascio, 1987; Gatewood & Feild, 1990). Two other common methods are the correlational method (Lecznar & Dailey, 1950) and the differential regression method (Malone, 1978). Additional methods described in the literature include the horizontal percent method (Stead & Shartle, 1940), the deviant response technique (Malloy, 1955; Webb, 1960), and the rare response technique (Telenson, Alexander, & Barrett, 1983). Although the empirical keying methods differ somewhat with respect to how keyed items are selected and weighted, all methods share a common set of basic operational procedures. These procedures are most easily explained in relation to the weighted application blank method (England, 1971; Gatewood & Feild, 1990) and involve seven major steps: (a) choosing or developing the criterion, (b) identifying criterion groups, (c) selecting items to be analyzed, (d) specifying item response alternatives, (e) weighting items, (f) cross-validating, and (g) developing cutoff scores. Each of these steps will be described.

CRITERION DEVELOPMENT

As mentioned previously, the effectiveness of an empirical key depends on the adequacy of the operational criterion measure employed as a representation of the performance of ultimate interest (Thayer, 1977). Criterion research and development is widely viewed as a most pressing problem for personnel researchers, particularly in the context of criterion-related validation research (Cascio, 1987). Much of the concern expressed regarding the "blind empiricism" of many background data predictors may reflect a more fundamental need to better understand the psychological, experiential, and behavioral antecedents of the performance to be predicted. Yet, it is often the case that researchers resort to the most readily available or most expedient criterion measure rather than devote more effort to developing a better understanding of the performance of interest and better operational measures of that performance (Cascio, 1987).

Thayer (1977) has argued that more attention should be given to criterion development when deriving empirical keys. He noted that the empirical keying approach, as frequently applied, assumes that the available criterion adequately represents the ultimate criterion of interest. While such assumptions about the adequacy of criterion development are not unique to the development of background data measures, it is worthwhile to recognize that interpretations of observed validity coefficients will necessarily depend on the quality of the criterion measure employed during key development. Unfortunately, few studies in the background data literature have addressed criterion development issues (Mumford & Owens, 1987). Generally, criteria employed have been relatively simple (e.g., turnover, absenteeism) and have not been developed on the basis of substantive research. However, studies by Malloy (1955), Laurent (1962), and Klein and Owens (1965) suggest that empirical keys formulated on the basis of well-developed criterion measures afford greater predictive efficiency.

Cascio (1987) notes that as much effort needs to be devoted to the development of relevant, reliable, and practical criterion measures as is typically devoted to the development of written and performance tests. The first step in the development of any predictor measure involves defining the performance domain, or conceptual criterion, of interest. Ultimately, development of an operational criterion measure that is relevant hinges on this definition. Simply stated, it is essential that researchers understand the behaviors involved in the performance of interest, including specification of behaviors required for adequate perfor- mance and behaviors that distinguish the successful from the unsuccessful performer (Stokes & Reddy, 1992). In personnel selection research, the recommended method for defining the performance domain, deriving an operational criterion measure, and judging the relevance of that measure is job analysis (Gatewood & Feild, 1990). Relevance reduces to the judged correspondence between the criterion measure and the performance domain identified through an appropriate analysis of the job.

In the development of empirically keyed background data predictors, formal job analysis methods have been infrequently cited as a basis for defining the performance domain or for identifying important constructs underlying performance (see Fine & Cronshaw in this volume). It appears that the basis for criterion measures has all too often received little consideration in the development of empirically keyed background data predictors. Typically, readily available objective measures, such as turnover and productivity, are employed as criteria. More subjective measures, such as those embodied in various performance rating scales, appear to be very popular as well (Hunter & Hunter, 1984; Schmitt, Gooding, Noe, & Kirsch, 1984).

While the extent to which formal job analysis methods may actually have been used is difficult to estimate, several background data studies have successfully employed job analysis methods for defining the performance domain, identifying constructs underlying criterion performance, and generating hypotheses about prior behaviors and experiences that may condition performance. Hough (1984) employed the critical incident technique (Flanagan, 1954) in the development of an accomplishment record inventory described by the author as "a new type of biodata/

maximum performance/self-report instrument that appears to tap a component of an individual's history that is not measured by typical biodata inventories" (p. 144). Pannone (1984) and Levine and Zachert (1951) relied on task analysis (Christal & Weissmuller, 1988) to develop background data measures targeted directly at the requirements of the jobs under study. The potential usefulness of Fleishman's (1972) ability requirements scale for identifying underlying constructs that may lead to good and poor performance has also been noted (Stokes & Reddy, 1992). Fine and Cronshaw (this volume) have proposed the use of functional job analysis (Fine & Wiley, 1971) as a foundation for developing background data measures. Finally, less structured approaches such as incumbent interviews, individual biographies, and essay techniques may add important insights into those constructs underlying the performance domain and antecedent life history constructs that influence performance (Howe, 1982; Russell & Domm, 1990).

The ultimate goal when defining the performance domain for developing background data predictors lies in the identification of life history constructs that give rise to specific hypotheses about life history correlates of performance. In turn, background data items are selected or developed to test those hypotheses (Mumford & Owens, 1987; Stokes & Reddy, 1992). Mumford and Owens (1987) suggest that for a truly comprehensive domain definition, descriptive information should be drawn from multiple sources. Further, they suggest that some attention be given to variables that may likely influence performance, such as environmental conditions (e.g., organizational structures) and demographic attributes (e.g., age, previous work experience). Regardless of the methods and information sources used to define the performance domain, the purpose is to identify those criterion constructs underlying performance so that an adequate criterion measure may be developed and, at the same time, background data items that are hypothesized or demonstrated to be related to criterion performance may be selected or developed (Stokes & Reddy, 1992).

The development of an adequate and appropriate criterion for measuring performance is essential to the development of an empirically keyed background data predictor. The adequacy and appropriateness of a criterion may be evaluated against several important yardsticks. In addition to the relevance of the criterion measure for the identified performance domain, the criterion measure should be free from contamination and should be sensitive to differences in performance levels (Cascio, 1987). A criterion measure should be selected or developed that captures only those aspects of behavior judged as relevant and logically related to the criterion domain. Thus, adequate criterion performance must be clearly defined, specifying what should be both included and excluded from consideration.

Only by clearly specifying the nature of adequate criterion performance may a criterion measure be selected or developed that is neither deficient (fails to capture important elements of performance) nor contaminated. Contamination is a pervasive problem in criterion development and frequently results from influences that lie beyond the individual's control (e.g, productivity measures that fail to anticipate systematic differences in individual circumstances affecting performance). Finally, the criterion must be sensitive, that is, capable of discriminating between effective and ineffective performance.

Criterion measures commonly cited in the development of empirically keyed background data measures include job tenure (or turnover), attendance (absenteeism, tardiness), training program success (achievement, grades), advancement (promotions, salary increases), supervisory ratings, and production indices (Gatewood & Feild, 1990). Generally, objective measures (e.g., tenure, turnover, and productivity) appear to be employed more often than less objective measures (e.g., performance ratings) in the development of background data measures (Hunter & Hunter, 1984; Schmitt et al., 1984), and this trend may be even more pronounced for empirically keyed measures. Although the literature contains numerous recommendations from researchers concerning the relative merits of less objective ("soft") criterion measures versus more objective ("hard") measures, several major reviews have attempted to summarize the validity of background data measures in predicting several different criteria (Hunter & Hunter, 1984; Reilly & Chao, 1982; Schmitt et al., 1984). Taken together, results of these reviews suggest that background data measures may be somewhat less effective predictors of "hard" criteria (e.g., turnover) than of "soft" criteria (e.g., performance ratings). However, no systematic study has been undertaken to date to discover the relative predictive efficiencies of a number of different background data scale construction techniques (to include alternative empirical keying strategies) across a broad array of criterion measures.

IDENTIFYING CRITERION GROUPS

Empirical keys are frequently, but not always, developed on the basis of their effectiveness in predicting membership in criterion groups, often representing two distinct performance levels. Indeed, using the weighted application blank method, individuals may be assigned to two groups on the basis of their observed performance on the criterion (e.g., effective and ineffective, successful and unsuccessful, short tenure and long tenure). This contrasting groups method is most appropriate when the criterion measure is truly dichotomous (e.g., pass-fail). However, the common procedure for forming dichotomous criterion groups when performance is measured as a multistep, continuous variable (such as amount of sales in dollars) is to take the upper and lower 27 percent of performers (Ghiselli, Campbell, & Zedeck, 1981). Thus, in a sample of 1,000 sales agents, extreme groups would be composed of 270 high performers and 270 low performers. The goal in selecting 27 percent of the total sample is to maximize the difference between the two criterion groups while maintaining large sample sizes in both groups. The confidence that the upper group is superior to the lower group is greatest when 27 percent of the total is used to form extreme groups (Kelley, 1939). The effectiveness of an empirically keyed measure in predicting criterion group membership hinges on the appropriate identification of the criterion groups. Whether using the weighted application blank method with a dichotomous criterion or empirical keying methods that may utilize continuous criteria, differential performance measurement is critical to the development of an effective empirically keyed background data measure.

An important consideration in empirical key development is the size of the total sample that constitutes the development (or weighting) group. Adequate samples help to ensure that criterion group membership will be accurately identified and/or performance will be accurately differentiated based on non-chance differences in observed performance. As with any analysis that strives to optimize some function of the data at hand, empirical key development employs statistics that tend to capitalize on chance factors operating within the selected sample (i.e., sampling error). Since the opportunities to take advantage of chance are related positively to the number of predictors (i.e., items or response options) included in the analysis and negatively to the number of persons in the sample, the goal should be to maximize the ratio of persons to predictors. Conservative minimum ratios range from 5:1 to 10:1 (Nunnally, 1978). For methods such as the weighted application blank that derive weights for the response options associated with each item, it should be remembered that the total number of predictors included in the analysis equals the total number of response options across all background data items. (Thus, in developing a weighted application blank, the ratio of persons to predictors will be a function of the total number of response options across items.) For correlational and differential regression methods, sampling error is an even greater threat; these methods require larger sample sizes to assure the stability of resulting empirical keys. Given that the length of some background data measures approaches 100 or more predictors (items or response options), minimum recommended development or weighting samples may become quite large (e.g., 500 to 1,000 persons). Moreover, it is highly recommended that a second sample (ideally of similar size and drawn independently from the same population) be used for empirical cross-validation of the scoring key. Such large sample requirements for empirical keying efforts underscore the need for large-scale cooperative studies.

SELECTING ITEMS

The first step in developing an empirical key is the selection or development of items to be scored. Generally, the background data measure consists of a large pool of items hypothesized or demonstrated to be related to criterion performance. Given the numerous behavioral and experiential antecedents of typical criteria for which prediction is sought, as well as the inherent difficulty in discerning potential predictive relationships, a large pool of items is usually generated to ensure comprehensive coverage of potentially important behavioral and experiential antecedents of criterion performance. It is not unusual for a background data measure to include 100 or more items. Through the empirical keying process, a subset of the most predictive items is identified and each item weighted to reflect its observed relationship with the criterion of interest.

Until more recently, little guidance was available regarding background data item development. Indeed, most recommendations focused more on item formats and specifics of item construction than on methods for specifying item content (Stokes & Reddy, 1992). Asher (1972) proposed a taxonomy of background data items that categorizes items along eight dimensions: verifiable–unverifiable, historical–futuristic, actual behavior–hypothetical behavior, memory–conjecture, factual–interpretive, specific–general, response–response tendency, and external event–internal event. Although these are not mutually exclusive categories, they may provide helpful insights when developing a background data measure.

Based on a recent review of the literature, Mael (1991) presented a more comprehensive taxonomy for background data items that consists of 10 core attributes that fall into three categories. The first category contains a single attribute, historical-future/hypothetical, described as the only necessary defining attribute of background data items. The second category consists of five attributes—external-internal, objective-subjective, firsthand-secondhand, discrete-summative, and verifiable-nonverifiable—described as forming a continuum and helping to ensure the accuracy of self-report measures. The third category consists of four attributes—controllable-noncontrollable, equal access-nonequal access, job relevant-not job relevant, and noninvasive-invasive—that reflect legal or moral concerns that arise when background data for personnel selection are used. Mael (1991) points out that the nine nondefining attributes involve tradeoffs between satisfying legal constraints, minimizing faking, and maintaining a pool of usable items to cover adequately the content domain of interest. Mael (1991) calls for research that addresses the practical benefits of these attributes; additionally, he calls for the establishment of a clearinghouse that will document the validity of background data items as well as their relationship to criteria of interest. The author describes several important benefits that might result from a clearinghouse, including an enlightened "rainforest empiricism." According to Mael,

> rainforest empiricism would use the cumulative efforts of multiple iterations of empirical keying, theory development based on all aspects of a behavior rather than a single a priori construct, and the findings of other psychological disciplines to develop a solid foundation of knowledge in this realm, and to reduce the shrinkage that has plagued empirically keyed biodata. (p. 787)

Mumford and Owens (1987) have suggested a number of item content and formatting recommendations. With respect to item content, these researchers recommend the following:

- Items should principally deal with past behavior and experiences.
- Items dealing with family relationships are usually viewed as offensive.
- Specificity and brevity of items and response options are desirable.
- Items dealing with past and present behaviors and with opinions, attitudes, and values are generally acceptable.

Beyond these, few guidelines exist in the literature on developing content for background data items. As mentioned previously in the context of criterion development, job analysis information should be helpful for defining the job performance domain, which in turn may be used both for developing adequate criterion measures and for suggesting differential background and experience attributes that may be related to criterion performance. That is, definition of the job performance domain will likely suggest numerous hypotheses that relate background and experience attributes to performance potential. Items may then be developed that seek to capture those background and experience attributes hypothesized to be related to job performance. In addition to job analysis data, Mumford and Owens (1987) have identified several additional sources that might be used to guide domain definition, the development of hypotheses concerning life history influences related to job performance, and item development. These sources include the developmental psychology literature, life history interviews with incumbents, and known predictive characteristics of specific background data items. Additional approaches to item development have included the use of essay techniques (Russell & Domm, 1990; Siegel, 1956) and individual biographies (Howe, 1982).

The importance of forming meaningful hypotheses in developing item pool specifications has received increasing attention by researchers (e.g., see Russell in this volume). Mumford and Owens (1987) note that the quality of the item pool used will influence the utility of a strict empirical keying strategy. They suggest that when the item pool is deficient, contaminated, or biased, an empirical key will yield poor prediction and misleading inferences concerning individual performance, regardless of overall predictive power. For example, an item asking "How far do you live from work?" might be generally predictive of turnover behavior among job incumbents. Yet an individual applicant might be rejected not because of actual turnover risk, but because of a current inability to afford housing in the immediate area of the desired job. Thus, in the individual case, socioeconomic factors serve to exclude a job applicant who would otherwise relocate if a good job offer were extended. Mumford and Owens (1987) have framed this as a concern for adequate item specification in the development of background data measures.

Specifying Item Response Alternatives

Generally, the multiple-choice format has been recommended for background data items, with item response options lying along a continuum that approximates interval scale measurement (Mumford & Owens, 1987). After generating basic item content, appropriate response alternatives or options for each item should be designed. These alternatives serve as a means for scoring responses to the items. When initially designing the response options, the investigator may use a rational approach, informed by the results of previous research. Mumford and Owens (1987) provided a number of recommendations for formatting response options, including the following:

- Items having continuous options or alternatives should be ordered.
- Where possible, response options should form a continuum.
- All possible response options or an "escape" option should be given.
- Item options should carry a neutral or pleasant connotation.

Response options should be designed to cover all possible responses and produce an item response distribution that is at least approximately uniform. For continuous variables, response options may be defined along a continuum using equal intervals (or at least along a continuum assumed to approximate equal intervals). Whether the underlying measurement scale is continuous or discontinuous in nature, it may be desirable to transform the resulting data to facilitate scoring. For example, when inspection of an item response distribution reveals a "thin-split" (e.g., a nonuniform distribution having an infrequently endorsed response), the infrequent response option might best be eliminated or combined with a response option from a similar (perhaps adjacent) category, thereby producing a more uniform item response distribution possessing fewer response categories. Having fewer categories may simplify the subsequent weighting and scoring of these items. Where possible, England (1961) recommends transforming continuous variables using the method of equal frequency classes, where approximately equal numbers of respondents are placed in each response category. Another method is to use trial and error to determine the categorization that best brings out differences between criterion groups. This approach, however, maximizes the probability that chance differences present in the development sample will influence the weighting of items. Finally, when discontinuous response categories are employed and item weights are developed using a correlational or regression approach, it may be necessary to use appropriate dummy coding procedures to transform the data prior to analysis (Pedhazur, 1982). Thus, an item that has five discontinuous response alternatives might be coded to produce a number of separate variables for subsequent analysis.

ITEM WEIGHTING

The weighting of items lies at the very heart of empirical keying. As previously noted, most empirical keying methods involve strategies for generating differential item weights using variance maximizing procedures, frequently designed to achieve maximum criterion group separation. It should be noted, however, that unit weighting of items may be preferable in many applications (Dawes, 1971). Much may depend on the availability of adequate sample sizes necessary for developing stable differential weights. Differential weighting strategies rely on the identification of significant statistical relationships between background data item responses and performance on a criterion measure. The stability of differential weights based on these relationships depends on the availability of a large development (weighting) sample (Schmidt, 1972). A conservative recommendation is that the development sample be composed of at least 5 to 10 persons per predictor (item or response option, depending on the weighting strategy adopted; Nunnally, 1978). Beyond considerations of sample size, differential item weighting may be most profitable when the intercorrelations among items are low and when relatively few items are in use (Guilford, 1954). Additionally, lower reliabilities of individual items may limit the stability of resulting differential weights.

Empirical key development requires administration of the background data measure to a representative sample of individuals taken from the reference group of interest. In general, weights are developed by comparing item responses to criterion performance and by weighting items to reflect the degree of observed relationship with the criterion. Several methods are available for developing item weights. These methods differ primarily in terms of how items are selected and/or weighted for inclusion on the final scoring key. The differences between methods may be explained in terms of the following: (a) how items are scored (e.g., each item alternative scored; overall item scored where alternatives are viewed as positions lying along an ordinal continuum), (b) how criterion performance is measured (e.g., dichotomous criterion group membership; performance ratings or rankings), (c) how item scores are related to criterion scores (e.g., comparison of differential response rates for each item alternative against the criterion; correlation of item scores with the criterion), and (d) how item weights are statistically derived. Indeed, choice of a particular empirical keying method may be guided primarily by the nature of the items comprising the background data measure (e.g., categorical or continuum type), the nature and measurement properties of the criterion data (e.g., scale of measurement, distribution form), and the size of the available sample (e.g., relatively large or small).

The frequently cited weighted application blank (or vertical percent) method (England, 1961) involves weighting alternative response options on the basis of differences in option endorsement rates observed for contrasting criterion groups. Needless to say, criterion groups that are well differentiated in terms of criterion performance levels are needed to produce differential weights. For smaller samples, it may be difficult to form contrasting groups having sufficient persons in each group to yield stable weights, but this may also be influenced by the measurement properties of the criterion data. While truly dichotomous criterion data are most amenable to this method, continuous data may be dichotomized as necessary to form the needed contrasting groups. Care should be exercised when forming contrasting criterion groups to ensure that they are sufficiently large and, ideally, approximately equal in size.

In a classic empirical keying study that used England's (1961) weighted application blank method, McGrath (1960) developed a background data measure to distinguish between high and low credit risk groups. McGrath (1960) identified 24 out of 62 credit application and loan contract items that significantly discriminated 100 good credit risk customers from 100 poor credit risk customers. Importantly, the measure was cross-validated in a separate sample of 100 good risk and 69 poor risk customers using two different empirical keys. One key was developed to have differential item weights (based on degree of statistical significance), and the other was developed to have unit weights. Although the cross-validity obtained for each key was significant, no significant difference was found between the cross-validities for the differentially and unit weighted keys. The cross-validity for the unit weighted key was somewhat larger than it was for the differentially weighted key ($r = .58$. vs. $r = .54$). Even though the availability of high-speed computers and sophisticated statistical programs makes differential weighting as easy today as unit weighting, this modest study serves well to illustrate the comparability, if not superiority, of unit weighting found in many actual applications.

The weighted application blank method, based on item analysis procedures described by Strong (1926), involves first calculating item response rates (percentages) observed for upper and lower criterion groups. Differences in percentages between upper and lower criterion groups are calculated for each response option and a "net weight" for each response option is obtained using Strong's Tables of Net Weights for Differences in Percents (England, 1971; Stead & Shartle, 1940). These net weights were derived by Strong (1926) as a shortcut method for assigning weights without having to compute the hundreds of phi coefficients (and associated exact Type 1 error probabilities) typically required in item weighting efforts. (Research by Clark and Margolis [1971] indicates very high correlations between Strong's net weights and either t values or associated Type 1 error probabilities.) As an example, suppose that to the item "Amount of Previous Sales Experience," 35 percent of the upper criterion group and only 10 percent of the lower criterion group responded "more than 5 years." Based on this 25 percent difference in response rates, reference to Strong's Tables indicates a net weight of +6 for this alternative, which is then converted to an assigned weight of +2, as recommended by England (1961) to simplify scoring and to decrease the weighting of chance differences between criterion groups. Finally, alternatives that fail to discriminate criterion groups (no percent differences in response) are eliminated, and responses that are associated more with low than high criterion performance are assigned a low or zero weight. Thus, the weighted application blank method attempts to capture differences in patterns of responses to items by contrasting criterion groups. As such, nonlinear item–criterion relationships may be identified and appropriately reflected in the resulting weights for response alternatives.

Two other methods are frequently used for empirical keying of background data measures: the correlational method (Lecznar & Dailey, 1950) and the differential regression method (Malone, 1978). These methods are most appropriate for background data measures composed of items having continuous underlying response properties. Moreover, item–criterion relationships should be approximately linear in form. Researchers are cautioned to check for possible nonlinear relationships (Anastasi, 1979). While occurrences of nonlinearity may be tolerated when they are neither large nor numerous, researchers may want to pursue alternative empirical keying methods that emphasize response patterns if numerous and significant nonlinear trends are suspected or identified. Rather than scoring and weighting responses for each item alternative as is done in the weighted application blank method, the correlational and regression methods score items as a whole, and a single weight is assigned to each item based on the magnitude and direction of the observed correlation between the item and the criterion. Assigned item weights may be the actual correlation coefficients computed for items or, better, unit weights based on the presence or absence of statistical significance (e.g., depending on direction, ± 1 for $p < .05$). In this regard, Clark and Gee (1954) and Nach (1965) showed that the weighting of items showing weak, though significant, discrimination results in a disproportionate increase in error variance and an overall loss in reliability and predictive validity. Ideally, the magnitude of observed correlations should be evaluated in light of effect size considerations when deciding how (or if) to assign nonzero item weights. As a general rule of thumb, however, a minimum correlation of .10 to .15 has been suggested (Mumford & Owens, 1987).

Similar to the correlational method, the differential regression method uses least squares regression analysis procedures to develop a regression model that maximizes explained criterion variance. Using one of several regression procedures, items may be selected and weighted, based on the increment in criterion variance accounted for over and above that which is explained using those items already in the model (Malone, 1978). Variance maximizing procedures are apt to capitalize heavily on chance, making cross-validation that much more important. Obviously, large sample sizes are recommended for developing stable item regression weights. Given the large number of items in many background data measures and the limited sample sizes often available, some method of reducing the number of items for subsequent analysis may be needed to achieve an appropriate ratio of subjects to predictors. As an initial screen, items failing to demonstrate zero-order correlations significant at the .05 level might be eliminated from further consideration. When the number of items surviving any initial screen exceeds about two dozen, stepwise regression procedures may provide an efficient method for selecting and weighting items, though the resulting regression model will not necessarily be optimal in a least squares sense (see Gandy, Dye, & MacLane in this volume).

Several alternative weighting strategies have also appeared in the literature. One of these is a variant on the weighted application blank method and is referred to as the horizontal percent method (Stead & Shartle, 1940). With this technique, each item alternative is weighted by the ratio of the number of upper criterion group members choosing the response option to the total group. Another alternative is the deviant response method (Malloy, 1955; Webb, 1960), which employs a correlational or weighted application blank strategy to develop item weights for criterion groups consisting of individuals above or below the regression line after first partialing out the variance attributable to an initial predictor set. A variation of the deviant response method is the rare response method, which weights item responses on the basis of how few individuals select a given response. This method has been used primarily in developing clinical diagnostic instruments and is based on the proposition that rare responses have considerable informational value for describing individual differences on important psychological constructs (Berg, 1967). Weights are developed for alternatives by computing the percentage of respondents choosing each response. Item responses chosen by 15 percent or less of the sample are assigned two points, those chosen by 15.1 percent to 30 percent are assigned one point, and those chosen by more than 30 percent are assigned no points. The only known application of this method for empirical keying of background data was reported by Telenson et al. (1983), who found this method superior to the percent methods.

Very little research has been conducted comparing the various empirical keying methods. England (1971) suggested that the percent scoring methods should generally yield more stable weights than the available alternatives. However, studies by Lecznar and Dailey (1950) and Malone (1978) suggest that, although the weighted application blank procedure may initially yield higher validities, the correlational and regression methods will yield equal or somewhat better cross-validated coefficients and produce less shrinkage in cross-validation given sufficient sample sizes. Since these studies did not systematically vary sample size, it is difficult to evaluate the relative effectiveness of these techniques (Mumford & Owens, 1987). Studies by Webb (1960) and Malloy (1955) contrasted variants on the weighted application blank approach with the deviant response procedure. They found that the deviant response procedure in the initial keying sample added more to prediction than a standard empirical key. However, the Webb (1960) study suggested that the predictive power of deviant response keys may not hold up under cross-validation due to the poor reliability of residual scores.

Finally, Telenson et al. (1983) reported that, based on predictive efficiency, the rare response weighting technique was superior to the vertical (weighted application blank) and horizontal percent approaches. In a related study, Aamodt and Pierce (1987) compared the weighted application blank method to the rare response method using five different samples. These authors noted several limitations of the Telenson et al. (1983) study, including small sample sizes, inconsistent cross-validation procedures employed across keying methods, and failure to test for significant differences between validity coefficients obtained using different methods. Although the samples employed in the Aamodt and Pierce (1987) study were too small to permit empirical cross-validation, the vertical percent validity coefficients obtained were significantly higher than the rare response coefficients in three of the five samples. Aamodt and Pierce (1987) argued against the use of the rare response method for keying background data, suggesting that the technique is more appropriate for assessing conventionality and is probably inappropriate for developing a background data measure keyed to predict job performance.

Cross Validation

The importance of cross-validation in the development of any predictor measure is a well-accepted measurement principle. Cross-validation is especially important in developing empirically keyed background data measures owing to the strictly empirical procedure used to develop the item weights constituting the scoring key. Scoring weights developed on a sample will, to some extent, capitalize on sample-specific factors operating in the sample and will result in spuriously high validity estimates. It is critical that the weights developed on a sample be cross-validated. Empirical cross-validation using an independent sample is typically recommended, though frequently a single sample is randomly split into development and cross-validation (or "holdout") groups. Although recommendations vary, England (1961) suggests that one-third more individuals be included in the development sample compared to the cross-validation sample. The empirical key is applied to the cross-validation sample to obtain the "shrunken" R-square, which is a better estimate of the key's actual predictive power. When empirical cross-validation is conducted using a holdout sample, it has been recommended that a final key be developed using the total sample (development and holdout groups combined) to enhance the stability of the scoring weights developed (Pedhazur, 1982).

More recently, some researchers have advocated the use of cross-validation formula estimates as accurate, more practical, and even superior alternatives to empirical cross-validation in selection contexts (Cascio, 1982; Murphy, 1983, 1984). In a comparison of formula-based estimates with empirical cross-validity estimates for both rationally derived and empirically keyed background data measures, Mitchell and Klimoski (1986) found that formulas overestimated shrinkage for rationally derived inventories and underestimated shrinkage for empirically derived inventories. Additionally, these authors noted that the use of formula estimates may be inappropriate for empirical derivation procedures involving criterion-related selection of predictors from a larger pool of variables (e.g., through stepwise regression), which is a frequent practice in the development of empirical scoring keys (Cattin, 1980; Dorans & Drasgow, 1980; Murphy, 1984).

Cutoff Score Development

When used for selection or classification, the final step after developing an empirical key often is to establish a minimum score (the cutoff score) on the background data measure that maximizes the number of persons correctly classified in terms of predicted criterion performance. For example, if criterion performance is defined in terms of membership in high and low criterion groups, a cutoff score may be selected that separates the high from the low criterion group with minimum error and maximum group differentiation. The cutoff score may be identified by inspecting the distributions of predicted scores for the high and low criterion groups and selecting the point where the least overlap is apparent. England (1961) described a maximum differentiation procedure that employs a table for comparing the percentage of each group scoring at or above each possible total score on the background data measure. The point at which the difference between the percentages is greatest is the optimal cutoff score. Cascio (1982) recommends that external factors, such as labor market supply and the costs of classification errors, also be considered when establishing an appropriate cutoff score.

RELIABILITY AND VALIDITY OF EMPIRICAL KEYS

Due to the heterogeneity of items included in most background data measures, individual items typically show low intercorrelations (Kavanagh & York, 1972; Owens, 1976; Siegel, 1956). Consequently, lower estimates of internal consistency reliability are usually obtained. Though few studies appear in the literature, most studies report test–retest reliabilities in the range of .60 to .90. The Life Insurance Marketing and Research Association (LIMRA, 1979) reported a retest reliability (over a five-day period) of .90 on samples of 5,000 job applicants. Erwin and Herring (1977) reported retest reliabilities of .91 and .85 for biodata forms consisting of 67 and 36 items, respectively, within a sample of army recruits who were surveyed during enlistment processing and several weeks following induction. The Institute for Behavioral Research in Creativity (IBRIC, 1968) reported retest reliabilities for an empirically keyed biodata form of .82 to .88 in a sample of North Carolina high school students. Finally, Chaney and Owens (1964) reported a retest reliability (over a 19-month period) of .85 for an 82-item measure administered to a sample of 49 male college students.

Several large-scale reviews have been conducted for the purpose of examining the criterion-related validity of background data. Ghiselli's (1966) comprehensive review of occupational predictors is often cited for its showing that the biographical data method was the most effective predictor of job proficiency and training success criteria when it was averaged across occupations. Several other large-scale reviews have appeared in the literature, including those by Asher (1972), Dunnette (1962), England (1961, 1971), Hough (1986), Hunter and Hunter (1984), Owens (1976), Reilly and Chao (1982), Schmitt et al. (1984), and Schuh (1967). It is clear from these reviews that empirically keyed background data measures are among the best available predictors of job performance and training criteria, with most coefficients lying between .30 and .50 (Mumford & Owens, 1987).

Very little research has been reported in the literature comparing the validity of empirically keyed background data measures developed using alternative scaling methods. A handful of studies have compared the predictive efficiency of the empirical approach with that of factorial and rational-scaling approaches. Factorial and rational approaches have been presented as methodologies that may facilitate the interpretation of the historical antecedents of criterion performance, as well as provide more stable prediction across samples, without significant losses in predictive efficiency. Briefly, in the factorial approach, factor analysis is employed to derive homogenous factors, or life history dimensions. Scores on each of several dimensions are then weighted through multiple regression and used to predict criterion performance. Rational approaches (e.g., the indirect approach described by Mumford and Owens, 1987) require considerable knowledge and understanding of background and experience characteristics considered important for successful job performance. This information is then used to define critical psychological constructs thought to underlie successful job performance.

Mitchell and Klimoski (1982) reported the results of a study that compared the predictive validity of an empirically keyed biographical data inventory with the validity obtained for the same inventory based on a factorial approach. England's (1971) weighted application blank method was compared with a factor-analytic approach for predicting a real estate sales criterion for a sample of 698 prospective real estate sales agents. These authors hypothesized that (a) the derivation validity would be higher for the empirical approach, (b) the factor-analytic approach would produce a validity that would suffer less shrinkage on cross-validation, and (c) the cross-validities of the factor-analytic versus empirical methods would not be substantially different. Derivation validities were .59 and .36 for the empirical and factor-analytic approaches, respectively. The cross-validity obtained for the empirical approach dropped to .46, while that for the factor-analytic approach remained at .36. The resulting difference in these cross-validities favoring the empirical approach was significant at the .01 level. Thus, the first two hypotheses were confirmed, whereas the third was not. The authors recommended the empirical approach when the purpose is one of maximizing prediction of an external criterion.

Fuentes, Sawyer, and Greener (1989) compared the predictive effi-ciency of the empirical approach to that of factorial and rational-scaling methods. Based on a sample of 656 airline pilots, this study found a superior cross-validity for the empirical approach ($r = .31$) compared to that observed for the factorial approach ($r = .27$; $z = .51$, n.s.), and both cross-validities were significantly greater than that obtained for the rational key ($r = .16$). (The relatively poor performance of the rational key, as explained by the authors, may be attributable to its prior development on the basis of a different criterion employed in a previous study.) Although shrinkage was not statistically significant for either the factorial key (.02) or the rational key (.08), significant shrinkage was observed for the empirical key (.13). This finding is consistent with the Mitchell and Klimoski (1982) finding.

Finally, Dalessio and Crosby (1991) compared the predictive efficiency of the empirical and factor-analytic approaches to that of a method that combined aspects of both approaches. In this hybrid approach, items were first empirically keyed using the weighted application blank method, and then the item weights were factor-analyzed. According to the authors, this approach produces "life history dimensions or subscores that *explain* the empirically derived overall rating...without sacrificing the predictive efficiency gained from the empirical keying technique" (p. 3). Based on a sample of 9,078 life insurance sales representative applicants, predictive validities (using a sales production criterion) for each of the three methods were obtained in both development ($n = 6,056$) and cross-validation ($n = 3,022$) samples. No significant difference was observed in the cross-validities obtained for the empirical ($r = .16$) and factor-analytic ($r = .15$) approaches, although shrinkage observed for the empirical approach (.07) was significant while that observed for the factor-analytic (.04) was not. Results for the hybrid approach were very similar to those obtained for the empirical approach. The cross-validity obtained for the hybrid method ($r = .18$) was comparable to that obtained for the empirical method and, like the empirical method, showed significant shrinkage upon cross-validation (.06). The hybrid method, however, produced six interpretable dimensions (e.g., financial and career growth, knowledge of life insurance products, employment stability). Dalessio and Crosby (1991) noted the relatively small difference between the empirical and factorial cross-validities observed in their study compared to differences observed in previous research. They attribute this discrepancy to the large sample size available for their study—a sample approximately 14 times larger than the samples in either the Mitchell and Klimoski (1982) or Fuentes et al. (1989) studies. Such large samples may be expected to yield much more stable population parameter estimates. Dalessio and Crosby (1991) recommended the hybrid method as an approach that capitalizes on the strengths of both empirical and factorial methods, offering maximum predictive efficiency and, at the same time, explanatory dimensional information.

While much more research is needed that directly compares the alternative scaling methods, results to date continue to recommend the empirical approach over alternative approaches when the objective is to maximize prediction of a specific criterion. When the objective is to advance understanding of background and experience constructs and theory development, results of several studies suggest the profitability of the alternative approaches. Although the empirical and factor-analytic approaches may differ in both aim and assumptions, they hold considerable promise when combined in a complementary fashion for the development of an effective background data measure.

ADDITIONAL VALIDITY CONCERNS

Three issues related to the validity of empirically keyed background data measures deserve mentioning. One important concern with the use of the empirical keying approach is the tendency for the validity of the resulting background data measure to decay over time. A second issue relates to threats posed by the presence of self-presentation response biases, particularly respondent "faking," on the accuracy of empirically keyed background data measures. A third issue concerns the possible differential validity of empirical keys within race and gender subgroups.

Hughes, Dunn, and Baxter (1956) were among the first to report observing a steady decline in the validity of a weighted application blank over a three-year period. Dunnette, Kirchner, Erickson, and Banas (1960) reported a dramatic decline in the validity of a weighted application blank from .74 to .38 over a three-year period. Wernimont (1962) reported that the validity for the same form had dropped to .07 after five years. These results have led many researchers to recommend periodic reassessment of the cross-validity of empirical keys and reweighting when necessary (e.g., every two or three years; Reilly & Chao, 1982; Thayer, 1977).

Several reasons have been identified for the observed decreases in the validity of empirical keys across time (Mumford & Owens, 1987). First, the nature of the external criterion used during initial keying may change. Second, shifts in the nature of the target population (or reference group) may occur over time, rendering the key increasingly less effective. Third, organizational and extraorganizational changes may occur, such as changing labor market conditions, compensation arrangements, management reorganization, personnel policies, and so forth (Roach, 1971). These factors should be reviewed periodically along with a reassessment of the validity of the empirical key.

Finally, several factors may result in range restriction on either the background data predictor or the performance criterion over time, leading to reductions in observed validity. When a background data measure is used for personnel selection, hiring decisions inevitably result in restrictions in range on the criterion and reductions in estimates of concurrent validity. Also, job performance expectations for applicants may be either diminished or heightened when scores are available to managers. Score results may then be used in making decisions to provide (or withhold) additional training and support for employees, thereby narrowing job performance differences observed among those hired (producing criterion range restriction; Brown, 1978; Brumback, 1969). Additionally, the security of the scoring key can become compromised over time and, consequently, its predictive validity can be undermined. This problem has been observed in several larger scale applications where hiring managers, under pressure to fill job vacancies quickly, employ creative methods for increasing recruiting successes (Mitchell, 1987). Examples include coaching applicants through the screening process, maintaining a file of acceptable answer sheets to recycle for future applicants, and trial-and-error efforts to decipher the answer key (background data success profile), such as submitting bogus answer sheets until a success profile is discovered. Hughes et al. (1956) considered these kinds of manipulations by managers as the principle reason for the decreases in validity reported in their study.

A notable exception to the above finding was reported by Brown (1978), who found little decrease in the validity of a weighted application blank over a 38-year period despite labor market, economic, and job changes. Brown (1978) attributed this result, in large part, to maintaining the confidentiality of the scoring key and the large sample available for empirical key development. Hunter and Hunter (1984) suggest, however, that Brown (1978) evaluated the statistical significance of observed validities across time and that an examination of actual validity coefficients indicates a decay similar to that found in other studies.

Although the validity of background data measures is widely recognized, concern over response accuracy exists owing to a reliance on self-reports of past behaviors and experiences. Self-presentation response bias is a particular concern in selection contexts where individuals may be motivated to appear in a favorable light. Research results on the vulnerability of background data measures to response biases have been mixed. While some researchers have reported finding little or no evidence of response bias (e.g., Cascio, 1975; Colquitt & Becker, 1989; Keating, Paterson, & Stone, 1950; Mosel & Cozan, 1952), others have found evidence of considerable response bias (Goldstein, 1971; Hogan & Stokes, 1989). While some researchers have speculated that inconsistent research findings may be related to differences in the empirical keying strategies employed (Mumford & Owens, 1987), little systematic research has been conducted comparing the influence of response bias on background data measures developed using different empirical keying methods.

A study by Kluger, Reilly, and Russell (1991) investigated the influence of response biases on the accuracy of background data measures. These researchers compared the potential inflationary effects of a socially desirable responding (SDR) bias on background data scores derived from two empirical keying approaches: item keying and option keying. Their item-keying approach employed a correlational empirical keying method to develop differential weights for 25 Likert-type items comprising the background data measure used in the study. Their option-keying approach employed the weighted application blank method to develop unit weights for the response options associated with each of the same 25 items. This laboratory study employed a sample of 85 graduate students and instructional set manipulations designed to promote a self-presentation response motivation similar to that experienced by actual job applicants being screened for employment. It was hypothesized that option-keyed items would present a much more difficult challenge for a respondent who wished to "fake good." This hypothesis appears to have been predicated on the assumption that items bearing nonlinear relationships with the criterion are less transparent (or less "fakeable") to individuals motivated to select response options that are less candid but presumed to promote a more favorable impression. That is, the most predictive options and, therefore, the options most heavily weighted would be much more difficult to intuit owing to the complex, nonlinear empirical relationship of the item to the criterion. Thus, for this type of item, a change from an honest response to a response presumed to be more favorable (and more heavily weighted) could decrease, inflate, or leave unchanged the resultant option-keyed score. On the other hand, items keyed as a whole using the correlational method were hypothesized as being more transparent (or more "fakeable"), given that a respondent need only intuit the direction of item validity to select the response option most likely to inflate the resultant item-keyed score. Kluger et al. (1991) hypothesized that the option-keying approach would be less vulnerable to inflated item scores, and the item-keyed approach more vulnerable, when respondents attempt to distort responses in a direction perceived as more favorable.

This study's within-subjects instructional set manipulation (honest vs. simulated applicant responding) resulted in significantly higher scores for the item-keyed instrument in the simulated applicant condition compared to the honest condition. No significant differences were found for the option-keyed instrument. In fact, scores for the option-keyed instrument actually decreased from honest to simulated applicant conditions. Based on these results, Kluger et al. (1991) suggest that the type of empirical keying strategy adopted may offer an effective approach for controlling score inflation due to response bias, with option-keyed instruments less vulnerable to score inflation than item-keyed instruments. It would seem, however, that this advantage would hold primarily when item–criterion relationships are significantly nonlinear. As previously noted, in the interest of predictive efficiency, researchers are well advised to use an option-keyed empirical keying method (e.g., the weighted application blank method) when significant nonlinear item–criterion relationships are suspected or demonstrated. When item–criterion relationships are essentially linear, use of option-keyed methods would seem to offer little real advantage as a means for controlling score inflation and could have important implications for sample size requirements, given the larger number of parameters usually developed when individual options are weighted.

Little research evidence exists for the differential validity of empirical keys for race and gender groups. Several investigations have shown approximately equal empirical validities for minority and nonminority groups. Cascio (1976) reported validities of .58 and .56 for minorities and nonminorities, respectively. Similarly, results of studies conducted by LIMRA (1979) of the *Aptitude Index Battery* showed comparable validities across race groups, though their key had been rescaled for minorities. Frank and Erwin's (1978) investigation of early attrition from the army also showed no significant differences in observed validities across minority and nonminority groups. Reilly and Chao (1982) summarized the results of some studies reporting race differences. They concluded that the validity and fairness of biodata can be expected to hold across race groups. They caution, however, that the "blind empirical" approach makes it possible to select items highly correlated with race (or gender) for inclusion on the empirical key. This was illustrated by Pace and Schoenfeldt (1977), who cite a study in which having a Detroit address was predictive of the criterion. Because more minorities than nonminorities lived in the city than in the suburbs, this particular item was more likely to produce group differences. Similarly, Travers (1951) reported the results of a study to identify life history predictors of research scientists' success as administrators using job performance ratings as the criterion. Life history variables related to success included having a rural background and coming from a family of skilled craftspersons. Correlated negatively with success was having a large city background and coming from a retail-merchant family. Further research indicated that urban-reared scientists were Jewish and that performance ratings were anti-Semitically biased. Thus, application of a blind empirical approach produced a "valid" empirical key that helped to perpetuate this bias. Although identifying and eliminating criterion contamination is a difficult problem, Owens (1976) has noted that rational screening of items should be undertaken as one way of addressing this concern.

Several reviewers, noting differences in empirical validities across gender groups, have suggested that different keys may be needed for males and females (Hough, 1986; Reilly & Chao, 1982). In Ritchie and Boehm's (1977) study of management potential, a significantly higher ($p < .01$) mean validity coefficient was found for females than males. A study of navy hospital corps trainees conducted by Webster, Booth, Graham, and Alf (1978) found that males scored significantly higher on five of eleven key items, whereas females scored higher on two items. Research reported by LIMRA (1979) showed little differential validity by gender, though this was apparently achieved through rescaling of the predictor for females. Nevo (1976) reported that different items were valid for men and women in a study investigating success in the army. Validity coefficients of .36 and .18 were reported for men and women, respectively. These differences, however, may have been the result of differential range restriction operating within each subgroup (Hough, 1986). Considering gender differences that have been found at the factor level (Eberhardt & Muchinsky, 1982; Owens & Schoenfeldt, 1979) and subgroup level (Brush & Owens, 1979; Owens & Schoenfeldt, 1979), different empirical keys may be needed to achieve comparable validities for men and women (Mumford & Stokes, 1992; Reilly & Chao, 1982).

RESEARCH ISSUES, CAUTIONS, AND CONCERNS

The empirical approach for scaling background data measures has been criticized, to be sure. The approach has been most frequently criticized for its "dust bowl" or "blind" empiricism. Although empirical keying may provide superior criterion prediction, it has been argued that this prediction comes with little understanding of underlying relationships or constructs accounting for the prediction. For example, finding that the number of books an applicant reports having in the home as a child, or the amount of education attained, or the amount of life insurance owned may be related to criterion performance, but this does little to explain why this is so or why other variables are found to be unrelated. Empirical prediction has been criticized for lacking broad interpretability as well as restricting advances in conceptual understanding and theory development (Dunnette, 1962). As noted by Henry (1966), lack of understanding may ultimately limit the predictive power of background data measures. Such criticisms have led to research over the years on alternative scaling methodologies (e.g., factorial, rational, and subgrouping methodologies), with the goal of facilitating understanding of the historical antecedents of criterion performance (e.g., Baehr & Williams, 1967; Loevinger, Gleser, & DuBois, 1953; Matteson, 1978; Morrison, Owens, Glennon, & Albright, 1962; Mumford & Stokes, 1992; Owens & Schoenfeldt, 1979).

A related criticism of the empirical approach concerns the generalizability of the resulting background data measure. Because empirical keys are usually developed for a specific criterion using a specific sample, prediction is likely to capitalize on sample-specific factors. Research by Dunnette et al. (1960), Wernimont (1962), and Schwab and Oliver (1974) suggested that the empirical approach may yield unstable measures of limited general value due to capitalization on idiosyncratic factors operating in a particular sample. Thus, a background data measure keyed for a specific criterion and sample may not generalize well to other settings.

The larger matter of population, or reference group, definition has received little attention in the literature. As noted by Mumford and Owens (1987), the generality of the reference group will in part determine the generality of an empirical key, as will changes in the target population, which will lead to changes in the predictive efficiency of an empirical key. If the reference group is not a reasonably well-defined and homogenous group, extreme variation within this group will make it difficult to produce the significant group differences required in any empirical keying effort. The validities of empirically keyed background data measures are widely believed to be situationally specific. For example, Hunter and Hunter

(1984) stated that "there is evidence to suggest that biodata keys are not transportable" (p. 89). Thayer (1977) suggested that background data validities may be moderated by many factors, such as age, organizational variables, the criterion measure employed, and changes in the job over time.

A few studies have examined the generalizability of empirically keyed background data measures across organizations. Schmidt, Hunter, and Caplan (1981) found that a background data measure did not generalize across two petroleum industry jobs. In contrast, Brown (1981) examined the situational specificity of a background data inventory in a sample of life insurance salespersons. Data from more than 12,000 agents contracted by 12 companies were examined. Although the keys were generalizable, Brown (1981) concluded that as much as 38 percent of the variability in validity coefficients could be due to differences in the 12 companies. Similar results were obtained by Levine and Zachert (1951). Finally, a large-scale study by Rothstein, Schmidt, Erwin, Owens, and Sparks (1990) investigated the generalizability of empirically keyed background data validities across a variety of potential moderators, including organization, age, sex, education, experience, and tenure. This was a consortium-based study involving 79 organizations and included an empirical keying development sample of 10,697 incumbent supervisors and a concurrent cross-validation sample of over 11,000 supervisors.

Rothstein et al. (1990) developed a 41-item background data measure using the weighted application blank method. Based on performance rating data, contrasting criterion groups were formed. Successful versus unsuccessful job performance was measured in several ways, yielding dichotomous, trichotomous, and multistep criterion variables. A series of item analyses were conducted to select and weight items for inclusion on the final instrument. Importantly, items had to satisfy a rational job-relatedness check as well. The resulting empirically keyed form was cross-validated into multiple validity generalization samples; resulting cross-validities were then meta-analyzed across organizations, age levels, sex, and levels of education, supervisory experience, and company tenure.

Rothstein et al. (1990) reported that, in all cases, validities were generalizable, stable across time, and appeared to be uninfluenced by knowledge, skills, or abilities gained through job experience. Although certainly unusual in terms of its large scale, attention to criterion development, and hypothesis-based item selection, results of this study demonstrated that empirically keyed background data measures are not intrinsically situationally specific, as some researchers have asserted. This study demonstrated how proper attention to criterion and reference group definitions may play a critical role in determining the generality and utility of an empirically keyed background data measure.

Cross-cultural studies of empirical key validities have demonstrated the generalizability of background data measures across different cultures. Laurent (1970) demonstrated that a composite criterion of management success could be predicted from a background data measure for managers in the United States, Denmark, the Netherlands, and Norway. The reported validities were similar in all samples, ranging from .44 in the United States to .61 in Denmark. Hinrichs, Haanpera, and Sonkin (1976) found some cross-cultural consistency on an empirical key developed in Finland for predicting sales success. Coefficients ranged from .38 to .72 in samples obtained from the United States, Sweden, Portugal, Norway, and France. These results suggest that empirically keyed background data display some generality in the same occupation across Western cultures.

The potential difference in validities obtained for empirical keys developed from concurrent (e.g., incumbent) versus predictive (e.g., applicant) validation studies has been a long-standing concern in the development of noncognitive predictors (Guion, 1965; Guion & Cranny, 1982). One reason for this relates to a hypothesis concerning job experience differences between job applicants and incumbents. Accordingly, it has been hypothesized that the validity of concurrently derived keys may stem from the measurement of knowledge acquired from job experience. Thus, the validity of concurrent measures may result from individual differences in job experience. As pointed out by Rothstein et al. (1990), if this hypothesis is correct, concurrent validities should generally be larger than predictive validities. Furthermore, as variability in job experience among incumbents increases, concurrent validities could be expected to also increase.

Some evidence exists supporting the hypothesized influence of job experience on concurrent validities of background data measures. Some researchers have identified a tendency for concurrent validities to exceed predictive validities for background data measures. For example, Hough (1986) analyzed over 100 validity studies according to type of criterion employed. Her review indicated that median concurrent validities exceeded median predictive validities across all criterion categories except for training, where the median concurrent validity was based on a single validity study. Resulting concurrent/predictive median validities were .38/.18 for ranking and rating criteria (26 studies), .42/.20 for production criteria (10 studies), .33/.25 for absenteeism and turnover criteria (15 studies), .56/.31 for tenure criteria (18 studies), and .33/.14 for delinquency criteria (3 studies). A similar finding was reported by Hogan (1988), who analyzed 191 background data validities previously compiled and summarized by Schmitt et al. (1984). Hogan (1988) found weighted mean validities of .36 for 81 concurrent studies (average sample size of 189), .24 for 27 predictive studies (average sample of 539), and .22 for 83 predictive studies that employed the background data measure for applicant selection (average sample size of 692). Thus, a trend in mean validities revealed by Schmitt et al. (1984) when cumulating across all predictors became much more distinct when the analysis was restricted to studies that employed only background data predictors. Indeed, both simple and weighted mean validities for concurrent studies were found to exceed those for predictive studies.

Other researchers, however, have reported experimental evidence that the validity of background data may not be an artifact of individual differences in job experience. For example, Rothstein et al. (1990) conducted a meta-analysis that investigated job experience as a potential moderator of the validity of their concurrently developed background data measure. Each validity coefficient in this meta-analysis was computed on incumbents with the same number of years of supervisory experience (i.e., job experience was held constant). Nevertheless, resulting mean validities across job experience levels did not decline, suggesting to the authors that increasing job experience probably does not produce increases in concurrent validities, as could be expected if validity stemmed largely from job experience.

As pointed out by Rothstein et al. (1990), job experience is only one possible hypothesis that might predict differences between concurrent and predictive background data validities. A second hypothesis relates to motivational differences between job applicants and incumbents that may produce greater response distortion (socially desirable responding or "faking") among job applicants. Such differences in reference groups, if substantial, could produce substantial differences in the nature of the resulting empirical key. This was demonstrated by Hogan and Stokes (1989), who reported the results of a study comparing the influence of socially desirable responding (SDR) on a background data measure empirically keyed using both predictive and concurrent strategies. Predicting a turnover criterion among sales representatives within the same company, a predictive key developed on a sample of applicants ($N = 555$) differed almost completely in content from a concurrent key developed on a sample of incumbents ($N = 810$). The concurrent key failed to predict turnover in the applicant sample. Correlations of .36 ($p < .01$) and .28 ($p < .01$) were obtained between a measure of SDR and background data scores using predictive and concurrent keys, respectively. Additionally, it was found that rated item social desirability was significantly correlated with empirically derived item weight for the predictive key ($r = .66$, $p <$ .05) but not for the concurrent key ($r = -.27$, n.s.). Based on these results, the authors suggested that the differences in the scoring keys resulting from predictive and concurrent empirical keying strategies could be largely explained by the presence of greater applicant socially desirable responding to items that were characterized as more socially desirable.

When making employment decisions, and especially in personnel selection, users of background data measures should be sensitive to equal employment issues and potential legal challenges arising out of their usage (Gatewood & Feild, 1990). Background data measures are subject to provisions contained in the *Uniform Guidelines on Employee Selection Procedures* (Equal Employment Opportunity Commission, 1978) requiring that any employment procedure having an adverse impact on protected groups be demonstrably job-related. Because of the empirical procedures used to develop the measure, the scoring key may include items that bear no obvious relationship to the job or criterion of interest, even though such items are statistically related to criterion performance. Whether the presence of a statistical relationship will satisfy a requirement of job-relatedness is debatable. Practitioners faced with potential legal challenges may prefer to simply reduce or eliminate adverse impact by selectively eliminating or replacing objectionable items. Alternatively, development of separate scoring keys for each group may be considered (though separate scoring keys may well be challenged on constitutional or statutory grounds; e.g., see Civil Rights Act of 1991, especially Section 106). Thayer (1977) reported that the score distribution on the *Aptitude Index Battery,* a life insurance biodata form, was slightly lower for minorities and women, but, through rescaling, adverse impact was reduced or eliminated with modest effects on validity.

Although a showing of criterion-related validity is one method of demonstrating job-relatedness (typically, the preferred method), legal defensibility may require that items having adverse impact be shown to be manifestly job-related (e.g., through content validation; Fine & Cronshaw, this volume; Pace & Schoenfeldt, 1977). Indeed, Pace and Schoenfeldt (1977) have recommended that job analysis information be integrated into the development of background data measures to help ensure job-relatedness. Job analysis information provides a method for developing a background data item pool that adequately reflects the experiential and success dimensions of the job. Items so developed would likely lead to measures that are legally defensible, demonstrably job-related (having both criterion-related as well as content validity), and more acceptable to applicants and employers alike.

SUMMARY

This chapter began by reviewing the basic intent and assumptions under-lying empirically keyed background data measures. The empirical keying approach appears to be the most commonly employed scoring method when the primary purpose is to maximize prediction of an external criterion. Empirical keying involves the computation of a score for a background data measure through the application of a statistically derived scoring key. Item weights comprising the key are developed based on a statistical analysis of item–criterion relationships using variance maximizing procedures. When developing an empirical key, the ultimate question is that of its generality for predicting performance potential within the reference group of interest. The generality of the empirical key will depend on the careful identification of the reference group and samples employed for key development.

General operational procedures and specific techniques for empirical keying were also covered. All empirical keying methods share a common core of basic operational procedures, including criterion development, item development, item weighting, and cross-validation of the resulting empirical key. Criterion and item development rely on thoroughly defining the job performance domain. Job analysis methods may be used to define the performance domain, derive an operational criterion mea-sure, and judge the relevance of that measure. The ultimate goal when defining the performance domain is to identify important criterion constructs underlying performance so that an adequate criterion measure may be developed and, at the same time, background data items hypoth-esized to be related to criterion performance may be developed. Regardless of the particular empirical keying method used, differential performance measurement is critical to the development of an effective empirically keyed background data measure.

Three techniques appear to be the most frequently employed for developing empirically keyed background data measures. The most com-monly cited approach is England's (1961, 1971) weighted application blank method. Two other common methods are the correlational and differential regression methods. These methods differ primarily in terms of how items are selected and/or weighted for inclusion on the final scoring key. Differential weighting strategies rely on the identification of signifi-cant item–criterion relationships. The stability of differential weights based on these relationships depends on an adequately large developmental sample (e.g., 5 to 10 times as many subjects as predictors). The weighted application blank method involves weighting alternative response options on the basis of differences in option endorsement rates observed for contrasting criterion groups. This method captures differences in patterns of responses. As such, nonlinear item–criterion relationships may be reflected in the resulting empirical key. Using the correlational method, a single weight is developed for each item based on the magnitude and direction of the observed item-criterion correlation. The differential regression method uses least squares regression analysis to develop a regression model that maximizes explained criterion variance. Regardless of the method employed, cross-validation is especially important in developing empirically keyed background data measures owing to the strictly empirical procedure used to develop the scoring key.

The reliability and validity of empirically keyed background data measures were briefly reviewed. Although few studies appear in the literature, most studies report test-retest reliabilities in the range of .60 to .90. Several literature reviews clearly show that empirically keyed background data measures are among the best available predictors of both job performance and training criteria, with most coefficients lying between .30 and .50. Very little research has been conducted comparing the validity of empirically keyed background data measures with alternative scaling methods. Although more research is needed, results to date continue to recommend the empirical approach over alternative approaches when the objective is to maximize prediction of a specific criterion. Results of several studies, however, suggest the profitability of alternative approaches when the objective is to advance understanding of background and experience constructs and theory development.

Several important issues having implications for the development of empirically keyed background data measures were discussed. An important issue concerns a decline in empirical key validity across time. Many researchers recommend periodic reassessment (e.g., every two to three years) of the cross-validity of empirical keys and reweighting whenever necessary. A second issue concerns the potential for controlling response bias (or "faking") through empirical keying strategies. Little systematic research has been conducted examining the influence of response bias on background data measures developed using different empirical keying methods. Some researchers have suggested that option-keyed instruments may be less vulnerable to score inflation than item-keyed instruments. A third issue concerns possible differences in empirical key validity across race and gender groups. Although little research evidence exists for differential validity, several reviewers have noted differences in empirical validities across gender groups and have suggested that different keys may be needed for males and females. Several investigations have shown approximately equal empirical validities for minority and nonminority groups.

This chapter was concluded by reviewing several important research issues and concerns in the development of empirically keyed background data measures. The empirical keying approach has been frequently criticized for its "dust bowl" or "blind" empiricism. That is, while empirical keying may provide superior criterion prediction, it has been argued that this prediction comes with little understanding of underlying relationships or constructs accounting for the prediction. Although such criticisms have certain merit, recent research efforts have been directed at addressing this deficiency through combining a strict criterion-related approach with content and construct validation approaches. Further, the validities of empirically keyed background data measures are widely believed to be situationally specific. Studies examining the generality of empirically keyed background data measures across organizations have generally found that validities are generalizable when proper attention is given to item and criterion development. Additionally, evidence has been mixed concerning the equivalence of background data validities for concurrent versus predictive empirical keys. More research on job experience and motivational variables as potential moderators of these validities is clearly needed. Finally, for personnel selection, users of background data measures should be sensitive to equal employment issues arising from their usage.

REFERENCES

Aamodt, M. G., & Pierce, W. L., Jr. (1987). Comparison of the rare response and vertical percent methods for scoring the biographical information blank. *Educational and Psychological Measurement, 47,* 505–511.

Anastasi, A. (1979). *Fields of applied psychology* (2d ed.). New York: McGraw-Hill.

Asher, J. J. (1972). The biographical item: Can it be improved? *Personnel Psychology, 25,* 251–269.

Baehr, M., & Williams, G. B. (1967). Underlying dimensions of personal background data and their relationship to occupational classification. *Journal of Applied Psychology, 51,* 481–490.

Berg, I. A. (1967). *Response set in personality assessment.* Chicago: Aldine.

Brown, S. H. (1978). Long-term validity of a personal history item scoring procedure. *Journal of Applied Psychology, 63,* 673–676.

Brown, S. H. (1981). Validity generalization and situational moderation in the life insurance industry. *Journal of Applied Psychology, 66,* 664–670.

Brumback, G. B. (1969). A note on criterion contamination in the validation of biographical data. *Educational and Psychological Measurement, 29,* 439–443.

Brush, D. H., & Owens, W. A. (1979). Implementation and evaluation of an assessment classification model for manpower utilization. *Personnel Psychology, 32,* 369–383.

Cascio, W. F. (1975). Accuracy of verifiable biographical information blank responses. *Journal of Applied Psychology, 60,* 767–769.

Cascio, W. F. (1976). Turnover, biographical data, and fair employment practice. *Journal of Applied Psychology, 61,* 576–580.

Cascio, W. F. (1982). *Applied psychology in personnel management.* Reston, VA: Reston.

Cascio, W. F. (1987). *Applied psychology in personnel management* (3d ed.). Englewood Cliffs, NJ: Prentice-Hall.

Cattin, P. (1980). Estimation of the predictive power of a regression model. *Journal of Applied Psychology, 65,* 407–414.

Chaney, F. B., & Owens, W. A. (1964). Life history antecedents of sales, research, and general engineering interest. *Journal of Applied Psychology, 48,* 101–105.

Christal, R. E., & Weissmuller, J. J. (1988). Job-task inventory analysis. In S. Gael (Ed.), *The job analysis handbook for business, industry, and government.* New York: Wiley.

Civil Rights Act of 1991, P. L. 102–166, 105 STAT. 1071 (1992).

Clark, K. E., & Gee, H. (1954). Selecting items for interest inventory keys. *Journal of Applied Psychology, 38,* 12–17.

Clark, W. H., & Margolis, B. L. (1971). A revised procedure for the analysis of biographical information. *Educational and Psychological Measurement, 31,* 461–464.

Colquitt, A. L., & Becker, T. E. (1989, April). *Faking of a biodata form in use: A field study.* Paper presented at the 4th annual conference of the Society for Industrial and Organizational Psychology, Boston.

Dalessio, A. T., & Crosby, M. M. (1991, April). *Validity or understanding: A comparison of three biodata scoring methods.* Paper presented at the 6th annual conference of the Society for Industrial and Organizational Psychology, St. Louis.

Dawes, R. (1971). The robust beauty of improper linear models in decision making. *American Psychologist, 34,* 571–582.

Dorans, N. J., & Drasgow, F. (1980). A note on cross-validating prediction equations. *Journal of Applied Psychology, 65,* 728–730.

Dunnette, M. D. (1962). Personnel management. *Annual Review of Psychology, 13,* 285–314.

Dunnette, M. D., Kirchner, W. K., Erickson, J., & Banas, P. (1960). Predicting turnover among female office workers. *Personnel Administration, 23,* 45–50.

Eberhardt, B. J., & Muchinsky, P. M. (1982). An empirical investigation of the factor stability of Owens' biographical questionnaire. *Journal of Applied Psychology, 67,* 138–145.

England, G. W. (1961). *Development and use of weighted application blanks.* Dubuque, IA: Brown.

England, G. W. (1971). *Development and use of weighted application blanks* (Bulletin No. 55). Minneapolis: University of Minnesota, Industrial Relations Center.

Equal Employment Opportunity Commission. (1978). Uniform guidelines on employee selection procedures. *Federal Register, 43,* 38290–38315.

Erwin, F. W., & Herring, J. W. (1977, August). *The feasibility of the use of autobiographical information as a predictor of early Army attrition* (Tech. Rep. No. TR-77-A6). Alexandria, VA: U. S. Army Institute for Behavioral and Social Sciences.

Ferguson, L. W. (1961). The development of industrial psychology. In B. V. Gilmer (Ed.), *Industrial psychology.* New York: McGraw-Hill.

Fine, S. A., & Wiley, W. (1971). *An introduction to functional job analysis: Methods for Manpower Analysis.* Kalamazoo, MI: Upjohn Institute for Employment Research.

Flanagan, J. C. (1954). The critical incident technique. *Psychological Bulletin, 51,* 327–358.

Fleishman, E. A. (1972). On the relation between abilities, learning, and human performance. *American Psychologist, 27,* 1017–1032.

Frank, B. A., & Irwin, F. W. (1978). *The prediction of early Army attrition through use of autobiographical information qustionnaires* (Tech. Rep. No. TR-78–A11). Alexandria, VA: U.S. Army Research Institute.

Fuentes, R. R., Sawyer, J. E., & Greener, J. M. (1989, August). *Comparison of the predictive characteristics of three biodata scaling methods.* Paper presented at the 97th annual convention of the American Psychological Association, New Orleans.

Gatewood, R. D., & Feild, H. S. (1990). *Human resource selection* (2d ed.). Chicago: Dryden Press.

Ghiselli, E. E. (1966). *The validity of occupational aptitude tests.* New York: Wiley.

Ghiselli, E. E. (1973). The validity of aptitude tests in personnel selection. *Personnel Psychology, 26,* 461–477.

Ghiselli, E. E., Campbell, J. P., & Zedeck, S. (1981). *Measurement theory for the behavioral sciences.* San Francisco: Freeman.

Goldsmith, D. B. (1922). The use of a personal history blank as a salesmanship test. *Journal of Applied Psychology, 6,* 149–155.

Goldstein, I. L. (1971). The application blank: How honest are the responses? *Journal of Applied Psychology, 55,* 491–492.

Guilford, J. P. (1954). *Psychometric methods* (2d ed.). New York: McGraw-Hill.

Guion, R. M. (1965). *Personnel testing.* New York: McGraw-Hill.

Guion, R. M., & Cranny, C. J. (1982). A note on concurrent and predictive validity designs: A critical reanalysis. *Journal of Applied Psychology, 67,* 239–244.

Henry, E. R. (1966). *Research conference on the use of autobiographical data as psychological predictors.* Greensboro, NC: Creativity Research Institute.

Hinrichs, J. R., Haanpera, S., & Sonkin, L. (1976). Validity of a biographical information blank across national boundaries. *Personnel Psychology, 29,* 417–421.

Hogan, J. B. (1988). *The influence of socially desirable responding on biographical data of applicant versus incumbent samples: Implications for predictive and concurrent research designs.* Unpublished doctoral dissertation, University of Georgia, Athens.

Hogan, J. B., & Stokes, G. S. (1989, April). *The influence of socially desirable responding on biographical data of applicant versus incumbent samples: Implications for predictive and concurrent research designs.* Paper presented at the 4th annual meeting of the Society of Industrial and Organizational Psychology, Boston.

Hough, L. M. (1984). Development and evaluation of the "accomplishment record" method of selecting and promoting professionals. *Journal of Applied Psychology, 69,* 135–146.

Hough, L. (1986). *Utility of temperament, biodata, and interest assessment for predicting job performance: A review and integration of the literature* (PDRI Rep. No. 145). Minneapolis: Personnel Decisions Research Institute.

Howe, M. J. A. (1982). Biographical evidence and the development of outstanding individuals. *American Psychologist, 37,* 1071–1081.

Hughes, J. F., Dunn, J. F., & Baxter, B. (1956). The validity of selection instruments under operating conditions. *Personnel Psychology, 9,* 321–324.

Hunter, J. E., & Hunter, R. F. (1984). Validity and utility of alternative predictors of job performance. *Psychological Bulletin, 96,* 72–98.

Institute for Behavioral Research in Creativity (IBRIC). (1968). *Manual for Alpha biographical inventory.* Greensboro, NC: Predictions Press.

Kavanagh, M. J., & York, D. R. (1972). Biographical correlates of middle managers' performance. *Personnel Psychology, 25,* 319–332.

Keating, E., Paterson, D. G., & Stone, C. H. (1950). Validity of work histories obtained by interview. *Journal of Applied Psychology, 34,* 1–5.

Kelly, T. L. (1939). The selection of upper and lower groups for the validation of test items. *Journal of Educational Psychology, 30,* 17–24.

Klein, S. P., & Owens, W. A. (1965). Faking of a scored life history as a function of criterion objectivity. *Journal of Applied Psychology, 49,* 451–454.

Kluger, A. N., Reilly, R. R., & Russell, C. J. (1991). Faking biodata tests: Are option-keyed instruments more resistant? *Journal of Applied Psychology, 76,* 889–896.

Laurent, H. (1962). Early identification of management talent. *Management Record, 24,* 33–38.

Laurent, H. (1970). Cross-cultural cross-validation of empirically validated tests. *Journal of Applied Psychology, 54,* 417–423.

Lecznar, W. B., & Dailey, J. T. (1950). Keying biographical inventories in classification test batteries. *American Psychologist, 5,* 279.

Levine, A. S., & Zachert, V. (1951). Use of a biographical inventory in the air force classification program. *Journal of Applied Psychology, 35,* 241–244.

Life Insurance Marketing and Research Association, Inc. (LIMRA). (1979). *Agent selection research questionnaire.* Hartford, CT: LIMRA.

Loevinger, J., Gleser, G. C., & DuBois, P. H. (1953). Maximizing the discriminating power of a multiple-score set. *Psychometrika, 18,* 309–317.

Mael, F. A. (1991). A conceptual rationale for the domain and attributes of biodata items. *Personnel Psychology, 44,* 763–792.

Malloy, J. (1955). The prediction of college achievement with the life experience inventory. *Educational and Psychological Measurement, 15,* 170–180.

Malone, M. P. (1978). *Predictive efficiency and discriminatory impact of verifiable biographical data as a function of data analysis procedure.* Unpublished doctoral dissertation, University of Minnesota, Minneapolis.

Matteson, M. T. (1978). An alternative approach to using biographical data for predicting job success. *Journal of Occupational Psychology, 51,* 155–162.

McGrath, J. J. (1960). Improving credit evaluation with a weighted application blank. *Journal of Applied Psychology, 44,* 325–328.

Mitchell, T. W. (1987, September). *Electronic mechanisms for controlling false biodata in computerized selection testing.* Paper presented at the 95th annual convention of the American Psychological Association, New York.

Mitchell, T. W., & Klimoski, R. J. (1982). Is it rational to be empirical? A test of methods for scoring biographical data. *Journal of Applied Psychology, 67,* 411–418.

Mitchell, T. W., & Klimoski, R. J. (1986). Estimating the validity of cross-validity estimation. *Journal of Applied Psychology, 71*, 311–317.

Morrison, R. F., Owens, W. A., Glennon, J. R., & Albright, L. E. (1962). Factored life history antecedents of industrial research performance. *Journal of Applied Psychology, 46*, 281–284.

Mosel, J. L., & Cozan, L. W. (1952). The accuracy of application blank work histories. *Journal of Applied Psychology, 36*, 365–369.

Mumford, M. D., & Nichels, B. J. (1990). *Applying principles of content and construct validity to background data.* Paper presented at the 5th annual meeting of the Society of Industrial and Organizational Psychology, Miami.

Mumford, M. D., & Owens, W. A. (1987). Methodology review: Principles, procedures, and findings in the application of background data measures. *Applied Psychological Measurement, 11*, 1–31.

Mumford, M. D., & Stokes, G. S. (1992). Developmental determinants of individual action: Theory and practice in applying background measures. In M. D. Dunnette & L. M. Hough (Eds.), *Handbook of industrial and organizational psychology,* (2d ed., vol. 3, pp. 61–138). Palo Alto, CA: Consulting Psychologists Press.

Murphy, K. R. (1983). Fooling yourself with cross-validation: Single sample designs. *Personnel Psychology, 36*, 111–118.

Murphy, K. R. (1984). Cost-benefit considerations in choosing among cross-validation methods. *Personnel Psychology, 37*, 15–22.

Nach, A. N. (1965). A study of item weights and scale length for the SVIB. *Journal of Applied Psychology, 49*, 12–17.

Nevo, B. (1976). Using biographical information to predict success of men and women in the army. *Journal of Applied Psychology, 47*, 106–108.

Nunnally, J. C. (1978). *Psychometric theory.* New York: McGraw-Hill.

O'Leary, L. R. (1973). Fair employment, sound psychometric practices, and reality. *American Psychologist, 28*, 147–150.

Owens, W. A. (1976). Background data. In M. D. Dunnette (Ed.), *Handbook of industrial and organizational psychology* (pp. 609–644). New York: Rand McNally.

Owens, W. A., & Schoenfeldt, L. F. (1979). Toward a classification of persons. *Journal of Applied Psychology, 64*, 569–607.

Pace, L. A., & Schoenfeldt, L. F. (1977). Legal concerns in the use of weighted applications. *Personnel Psychology, 30*, 159–166.

Pannone, R. D. (1984). Predicting test performance: A content valid approach to screening applicants. *Personnel Psychology, 37*, 507–514.

Pedhazur, E. J. (1982). *Multiple regression in behavioral research.* New York: Holt, Rinehart & Winston.

Reilly, R. R., & Chao, G. T. (1982). Validity and fairness of some alternative employee selection procedures. *Personnel Psychology, 35*, 1–63.

Ritchie, R. J., & Boehm, V. R. (1977). Biographical data as a predictor of women's and men's management potential. *Journal of Vocational Behavior, 11*, 363–368.

Roach, D. E. (1971). Double cross-validation of a weighted application blank over time. *Journal of Applied Psychology, 55*, 157–160.

Rothstein, H. R., Schmidt, F. L., Erwin, F. W., Owens, W. A., & Sparks, C. P. (1990). Biographical data in employment selection: Can validities be made generalizable? *Journal of Applied Psychology, 75,* 175–184.

Russell, C. J., & Domm, D. R. (1990). *On the construct validity of biographical information: Evaluation of a theory based method of item generation.* Unpublished manuscript, Department of Industrial Relations and Human Resources, Rutgers, New Brunswick, NJ.

Schmidt, F. L. (1972). The reliability of differences between linear regression weights in applied differential psychology. *Educational and Psychological Measurement, 32,* 879–886.

Schmidt, F. L., Hunter, J. E., & Caplan, J. R. (1981). Validity generalization results for two job groups in the petroleum industry. *Journal of Applied Psychology, 66,* 261–273.

Schmitt, N., Gooding, R. Z., Noe, R. A., & Kirsch, M. (1984). Metaanalyses of validity studies published between 1964 and 1982 and the investigation of study characteristics. *Personnel Psychology, 37,* 407–422.

Schuh, A. L. (1967). The predictability of employee tenure: A review of the literature. *Personnel Psychology, 20,* 133–152.

Schwab, D. P., & Oliver, R. L. (1974). Predicting tenure with biographical data: Exhuming buried evidence. *Personnel Psychology, 27,* 125–128.

Siegel, L. A. (1956). A biographical inventory for students: Construction and standardization of the instrument. *Journal of Applied Psychology, 40,* 5–10.

Stead, N. H., & Shartle, C. L. (1940). *Occupational counseling techniques.* New York: American Book.

Stokes, G. S., & Reddy, S. (1992). Use of background data in organizational decisions. In C. L. Cooper & I. T. Robertson (Eds.), *International review of applied psychology* (Vol. 7). Sussex, England: Wiley.

Strong, E. K. (1926). An interest test for personnel managers. *Journal of Personnel Research, 5,* 194–203.

Telenson, P. A., Alexander, R. A., & Barrett, G. V. (1983). Scoring the biographical information blank: A comparison of three weighting techniques. *Applied Psychological Measurement, 7,* 73–80.

Thayer, P. W. (1977). Somethings old, somethings new. *Personnel Psychology, 30,* 513–524.

Travers, R. M. (1951). Rational hypotheses in the construction of tests. *Educational and Psychological Measurement, 11,* 128–137.

Webb, S. C. (1960). The comparative validity of two biographical inventory keys. *Journal of Applied Psychology, 44,* 177–183.

Webster, E. G., Booth, R. F., Graham, W. K., & Alf, E. F. (1978). A sex comparison of factors related to success in Naval Hospital Corps School. *Personnel Psychology, 31,* 95–106.

Wernimont, P. F. (1962). Reevaluation of a weighted application blank for office personnel. *Journal of Applied Psychology, 46,* 417–419.

5

Construct-oriented Scale Construction

The Rational Approach

Leaetta Hough
Cheryl Paullin
Personnel Decisions Research Institutes, Inc.

Measurement of individual difference variables is an important activity for psychologists. Not surprisingly, strategies for constructing scales to measure individual difference variables have proliferated. These strategies have been divided into three main types of scale or inventory construction methods. The three strategies[1] are the *external* approach (also called empirical), the *inductive* approach (also called internal), and the *deductive* approach (also called rational, intuitive, or theoretical). Controversy regarding the relative merits of these scale construction methods began in the 1940s and continues today. Each approach has had highly articulate, even revered, advocates.

A strategy of scale construction may be defined as a systematic procedure for grouping and keying item responses to form a composite score. Thus, there are two major dimensions along which scale construction strategies differ. They are (a) item selection and (b) item weighting. The pure form of the external method of scale construction makes both decisions empirically—that is, items are selected and weighted based on observed differences both on item responses and on the criterion (criterion scores or criterion-group membership). The pure form of the inductive method makes both decisions based on item analyses of the item pool. The pure form of the deductive method makes both decisions rationally based on expert opinion—that is, theory or hypotheses.

Once definitions of the methods of scale construction have been explicated, it becomes apparent that it is often difficult to classify scales unequivocally into one of the three methods. In practice, few researchers have utilized a pure form of scale construction. Instead, most have developed and utilized elements of more than one scale construction strategy. Nevertheless, it is instructive to examine the assumptions, criticisms, and advantages of each of these three strategies.

In this chapter, we describe each of the three strategies of scale/inventory construction and assess their relative effectiveness. We also describe a construct-oriented strategy of scale construction, an updated variation of the deductive approach, and argue that it is the most appropriate strategy of scale construction.

DESCRIPTION OF SCALE CONSTRUCTION STRATEGIES

EXTERNAL APPROACH

The external or empirical scale construction strategy selects and weights items according to empirical evidence that the items differentiate between people on a criterion. Several different external methods exist to identify and weight items. (See Devlin, Abrahams, & Edwards, 1992, for a description and evaluation of nine external scale construction strategies.) Often, though not always, the external or empirical approach assumes that people can be classified into groups: people who are bright or dull, people who have succeeded or failed, people who graduate versus those who drop out, people who are criminals versus those who are not, people in occupational groups such as secretaries, engineers, or artists. In this contrasted-group approach, the responses of one group are compared to the responses of the other group. Not all external methods, however, require separate groups. Methods that use correlation or regression analyses, for example, do not necessarily require separate groups. Regardless of the particular strategy, item retention and weights are determined by the empirical congruences between the responses to the predictor items and scores on the criterion.

An empirically developed scale requires cross-validation to estimate the accuracy of differentiation among people on the criterion. That is, sample-specific variance artificially inflates the relationship between test scores and criterion scores when the correlation is based on the sample for which the scale was developed. Such a fold-back correlation does indicate the success of the scale for differentiating people on the criterion in the original/

developmental sample. Usually, however, the objective is to construct a scale that can be used to predict a person's standing on a criterion when criterion information is unavailable. Cross-validation, or an estimate of it, is thus mandatory if an externally developed scale is to be used for prediction.

The most important variable that affects the magnitude of the shrinkage of the fold-back coefficient is the size of the developmental sample. The larger the developmental sample, the more stable the results, and, thus, the lower the amount of shrinkage upon cross-validation.

Well-known proponents of this strategy of scale construction, at least early in their careers, have included Alfred Binet, William England, Harrison Gough, Starke Hathaway, Paul Meehl, William Owens, and E. K. Strong, Jr. During the 1940s, the "Minnesota Point of View" (all but Binet and Strong spent either formative years or most if not all of their careers at the University of Minnesota) dominated the field.

In a seminal article, Meehl (1945) distinguished between a priori (rational) and empirical scale construction methods for developing "structured" tests. He said that "the relative uselessness of most structured personality tests is due more to a priori item construction than to the fact of their being structured" (p. 297). An important strength of the empirical approach, according to Meehl, is that subtle items—items for which the underlying construct is not apparent or the relationship of the item to the criterion is not apparent—are discovered.

One of the most frequent criticisms of this "dust bowl" empiricism is its inability to enhance scientific understanding. Ideally, items selected using this approach correlate maximally with the criterion and minimally with each other. Thus, internal consistency is low; no common theme or factor exists among the items. Indeed, the external method of scale construction results in a polyglot group of items. Interpretation of an underlying dimension is speculative at best. It's even difficult, if not impossible, to develop a true alternate form, much less an equivalent form. As a result, little understanding is gained about why a set of items predicts a criterion. The ability to generalize to another setting or criterion is limited.

INDUCTIVE APPROACH

The inductive (internal) scale construction strategy assumes that some basic structure of individual differences exists and that this structure can be discovered through factor or cluster analysis (Burisch, 1984a). The structure is thus induced. Cattell (1962), for example, views factor analysis as an essential tool for revealing psychological reality. Factor analysis has become the typical analytic strategy of scale developers using this approach to individual differences measurement.

The internal structure of the item pool is the sole determiner of an item's scale membership and its direction of keying. Both the *number* and *nature* of the resulting scales are a product of internal data analysis (Burisch, 1984a). The emphasis is on internally consistent or homogeneous scales.

This strategy has become quite popular over the years among biodata researchers interested in understanding the pattern of correlations between biodata items and between biodata and criteria. Correlations between items and between biodata factors and criteria are computed to provide insight into the structure of biodata and its correlates.

Unidimensional scaling of items enables researchers to use psychometric analytic techniques that can provide evaluation of measurement operations and theoretical insight. Drasgow and Miller (1982), for example, presented a strategy for evaluating the extent to which a measurement obtained with a scale corresponds to the underlying theoretical construct of interest. They use the term *fidelity* to refer to correspondence. They define fidelity of a scale as "the correlation between the scale and the factor that it measures" (Drasgow & Miller, 1982, p. 269), and they provide a procedure for estimating scale–factor correlations.

The inductive strategy does indeed produce homogeneous scales and, thus, opportunity for contributing to our scientific body of knowledge. However, a fundamental question remains: Is factor analysis the most appropriate approach for discovering the basic structure of individual differences? Exploratory factor analysis is subject to many criticisms. As Loevinger, Gleser, and DuBois (1953) point out, estimating the communalities to determine the number of factors to extract is less than rigorous. Although using Kaiser's criterion (Kaiser, 1958) or the scree test to help determine the number of factors to rotate gives the appearance of scientific propriety, anyone who has used factor analysis knows the selection of a solution is as much art as science. Equally important, the resulting factors are dependent upon the composition of the original item pool.

Many of the limitations of the exploratory factor model have been overcome by the development of the confirmatory factor model (Jöreskog, 1969). However, the researcher has then moved into a deductive scale construction strategy.

Fruchter (1954), author of *Introduction to Factor Analysis*, noted that differences in item extremeness can cause problems in factor analysis resulting in spurious factors or loss of important items. An examination of the amount of variance accounted for by a factor solution of biodata items suggests that significant loss of variance is typical. Owens and Schoenfeldt (1979), in developing the University of Georgia *Biographical Questionnaire*

(BQ), factor analyzed (principal component analysis) the items and found that 19 components accounted for 36 percent and 38 percent of the total variance for men and women, respectively. When rotated, they found that 13 components for men and 15 components for women were sizable and interpretable (Owens & Schoenfeldt, 1979). Eberhardt and Muchinsky (1982) investigated the factor structure of the BQ utilizing students from Iowa State University. Lautenschlager and Shaffer (1987) reanalyzed the Eberhardt and Muchinsky data and found that in the male sample, 13 components accounted for 45.6 percent of the total variance in the BQ, while in the female sample, 15 components accounted for 49.6 percent of the total variance in the BQ. In their own data set, Lautenschlager and Shaffer (1987) found that in the male sample, 13 components accounted for 39.7 percent of the total variance in the BQ; in the female sample, 15 components accounted for 46.4 percent of the total variance in the BQ. Klimoski (1973) also used principal component analysis to develop a set of biodata factor scales. His 10-factor rotated solution accounted for 33.7 percent of the total variance. Schoenfeldt (1989) also used principal component analysis to develop a set of factor scales. His 10-factor solution accounted for only 19 percent of the total variance. Baehr and Williams (1967) conducted a series of three principal factor analyses, successively excluding duplicate, ambiguous, or nonrelevant items. The resulting factor solution accounted for 43.3 percent of the common variance (Baehr & Williams, 1967). Clearly, biodata factor scales typically ignore large amounts of variance.

Is it important information that is lost? Richard Gorsuch (1991), author of *Factor Analysis* (Gorsuch, 1983), argues that it is. He and a colleague (Mershon & Gorsuch, 1988) used factor analysis to revise an original set of scales and demonstrated that the factor scales accounted for significantly less of the criterion variance than did the original scales.

Hough (1992) makes a similar point. She argues that the Big Five taxonomy of personality factors, discovered and confirmed through factor analysis, provides too crude a taxonomy and thus obscures important predictor–criterion construct relationships. Criterion-related validities are attenuated when personality variables are reduced to only five factors.

While it is true that the inductive method of scale construction does result in homogeneous scales and thus does provide greater understanding about the underlying characteristic being measured, factor analysis is not likely to lead to an adequate taxonomy of individual difference variables. One can only imagine what the field of chemistry would be like if Mendeleyev had used exploratory factor analysis to develop the taxonomy of elements in the periodic table. Equally interesting would be the results of a confirmatory factory analysis of the structure of the periodic table.

DEDUCTIVE APPROACH

This approach is also known as the rational, intuitive, or theoretical approach. In its original form, it relied solely on the test developer (or experts) for judgments regarding the suitability of an item for inclusion in the scale as well as the weighting of response alternatives. The test developer first identified and defined an individual difference variable of interest. The test developer then wrote questions (items) to elicit information regarding the manifestation of the characteristic. Item inclusion was based on the presumed relevance of the item to the underlying characteristic or trait. In short, the method assumes a one-to-one correspondence (or at least a probabilistic correspondence) of verbal reports to underlying constructs (Buchwald, 1961).

Perhaps the earliest pure form of this strategy of scale development was Woodworth's Personal Data Sheet (Woodworth, 1917). It was this early form of the deductive method of scale construction against which Meehl (1945) forcefully argued. Indeed, as Wiggins (1973) pointed out, behaviorism arose in part as a protest to the fallibility of this type of measurement and the assumptions on which it was based.

One of the criticisms of the deductive approach is that the sole criterion for item inclusion is the presumed relevance of the item to the underlying characteristic or construct. The psychologist or test developer must have insight about the item and its relationship to the underlying characteristic. As a result, subtle items—items for which the underlying construct is not apparent and/or the direction of scoring is counterintuitive—rarely appear in deductive or intuitive scales. The identification of subtle items is, however, a likely outcome with empirically developed scales.

The one-to-one correspondence between item and underlying characteristic that the deductive method of scale construction assumes may limit its ability to produce valid measures of some constructs. Meehl (1945) suggested that persons high on a particular characteristic might respond to an item in a way that is opposite to what an objective assessment of the individual would indicate. He provided examples of questions to which a psychopathic deviate typically responds in a way that is counterintuitive to what an outside observer would say is true about the individual. An example of one subtle item in the Psychopathic Deviate scale of the *Minnesota Multiphasic Personality Inventory* (MMPI) is "My parents and family find more fault with me than they should." Psychopaths answer this question "true" more often than normal individuals do (Meehl, 1945). According to Meehl (1945), only the empirical scale construction strategy can identify such examples. A good theory, however, might suggest this as part of the syndrome.[2]

Meehl (1945) and Wiggins (1973) criticized the deductive approach for several reasons. Meehl's (1945) major criticism of this approach is that it assumes that the test developer has sufficient insight and knowledge about the relationship between a test item and the underlying characteristic or construct to develop a measure of the characteristic without the benefit of data. In addition, both Meehl (1945) and Wiggins (1973) assert that this approach assumes and requires accurate introspection and accurate self-reporting for valid measurement. Though all of the assumptions and criticisms are relevant when "soft" or self-rating-type items are used, only the assumptions about test developer insight and accurate self-reporting are relevant to factual biodata-type items. Accurate introspection is not an assumption or criticism that is relevant to factual biodata-type items.

These assumptions and the implications of these assumptions are addressed below. The first section deals with criterion-related validities obtained using different scale construction methods. The second section deals with accuracy of introspection or self-assessment and accuracy of self-report.

COMPARISON OF SCALE CONSTRUCTION METHODS

CRITERION-RELATED VALIDITIES

Item-level Validity

Douglas Jackson (1971) hypothesized that subtle items, items for which the underlying characteristic is nonobvious, were simply mistakes, fortuitous and nonvalid products of the characteristics of the specific comparison groups used in scale construction. Several studies have investigated the validity of subtle and obvious items, and they support Jackson's view.

One type of research design examines the magnitude of the validities of subscales made up of obvious versus subtle items. For example, Wiener (1948) subdivided each of five scales into subscales of subtle and obvious items and compared the criterion-related validities of the scales. He found that the subtle subscales were less valid (median $r_{pb} = -.08$) than the obvious subscales (median $r_{pb} = .24$). Similarly, McCall (1958) found the point–biserial correlation was .03 for subtle items and .26 for obvious items.

A second research design examines the correlation between subtlety of an item and its criterion-related validity. Duff (1965) used this approach. He correlated the subtlety of items with their validity and obtained negative correlations ranging from −.22 to −.48. Similarly, Holden and Jackson (1979) found negative correlations ranging from −.20 to −.44 between subtlety scores of items and empirical validities. Using a somewhat different research design, Worthington and Schlottman (1986) found that scales that included subtle items did not retain their significance when the variance of the obvious items was partialed out.

Gynther and Burkhart (1983) compared subtle, neutral, and obvious items from four MMPI scales and found that subtle items enhanced overall validity for two scales, Psychopathic Deviate and Mania. The research design of this study, however, may limit its generalizability. Gynther and Burkhart (1983) used other self-report test data as criteria. Thus, these results may not hold up when the criteria are objective or others' ratings. These two scales, however, may be examples of constructs for which people high on a characteristic respond to certain questions in a way that suggests inaccurate introspection. Both the external and deductive scale construction (i.e., a good theory) might identify such items.

These findings taken together suggest that subtle items, often considered a unique virtue of external scale construction, are often less valid than obvious items. Indeed, subtle items may actually reduce scale validity in most instances.

Scale-level Validity

Meehl (1945) enunciated the now classic argument that external scales should be more criterion-valid than purely rational scales. Twenty-six years later, Jackson (1971) argued that although Meehl's 1945 position was defensible at the time, understanding gained through research had provided the basis for maximally valid scales developed purely through rational scale construction. Going further, Jackson challenged the most sophisticated external methods to match the criterion-related validity that could be produced by skilled, or perhaps even inexperienced, item writers operating on a purely rational basis. These two major position papers highlight a history of controversy over the relative criterion-related validity of scales constructed by different methods.

Several researchers have compared the effectiveness of different scale construction methods. Indeed, at least 39 separate articles appear in the literature in which the author(s) compared the effectiveness of scale construction methods in terms of criterion-related validity. Many of these studies are summarized below.

A review of the 39 studies revealed that not all of them were appropriate for inclusion in the present review, and some were then eliminated from further consideration. There were several reasons for eliminating studies. First, studies were eliminated if the criterion or criteria were based on self-report or self-ratings. That is, we included only studies that utilized objective criteria or others' ratings of the individual. The following studies were eliminated because the criterion or criteria were either self-report or self-rating: Borgen (1972); Butt and Fiske (1968); Clifton, Costanza, Reiter-Palmon, and Mumford (1991); Connelly, Clifton, and Mumford (1991); Reilly and Echternacht (1979); and Uhlman, Reiter-Palmon, and Connelly (1990). Second, studies were eliminated if they lacked cross-validation of empirically keyed scales and sufficient information to estimate the cross-validity. The following studies were eliminated for this reason: Crewe (1967) and Klingler, Johnson, Giannetti, and Williams (1977). Third, studies were eliminated if they lacked sufficient information to convert the results into correlation coefficients. The following study was eliminated for this reason: Hedlund, Cho, and Wood (1977). Fourth, studies were eliminated if comparisons were between variations of the same broad class of scale development strategy. For example, studies that compared only variants of the external method of scale construction were excluded. The following studies were eliminated for this reason: Aamodt and Pierce (1987); Devlin, Abrahams, and Edwards (1992); Hermans (1969); Lecznar and Dailey (1950); Malloy (1955); McGrath (1960); Schaie (1963); Scollay (1956); and Telenson, Alexander, and Barrett (1983).

Information from the 21 studies that met our criteria for inclusion in this analysis appears in Table 1. Summarizing the information was not entirely straightforward. An important consideration was the statistic to use to compare across studies.

The first statistic we considered was the correlation coefficient. Unfortunately, the correlation coefficient is not appropriate for the present purpose. First, an important observation about the 21 studies shown in Table 1 is that only a few studies compared all three construction strategies. A second important observation is that criterion variables differ from study to study.

These two observations would not generally give us pause. However, Goldberg (1972), when examining the relative effectiveness of the different scale strategies, found a strategy-by-criterion interaction. He found that the intuitive and deductive scale construction methods predicted "predictable" criterion measures very well, whereas the external (empirical) construction strategy attained only moderate levels of validity for such criteria. When the predictability of the criterion measure was low, the external (empirical) method of scale construction strategy outperformed the inductive and deductive scale construction methods. Though additional research is required to replicate this finding, we nevertheless concluded that it was inappropriate to compute an average validity coefficient across studies for each type of scale construction strategy and then compare the magnitude of that coefficient to a similarly computed validity coefficient for another scale construction strategy. Such a summary

TABLE 1 Comparison of Criterion-related Validities of Different Scale Construction Strategies

Study	Sample Size[1]	Subjects	Criterion	Validity External (empirical)	Inductive (internal)	Deductive (rational)
Alumbaugh, Davis, & Sweney (1969)	73	57 male alcoholics and 16 male neurotics	Correctly classified as alcoholic	.06[2] .11[4] .07[5] .11[7] $\bar{x}=.09$	.07[3] .12[6] $\bar{x}=.10$	
	85	37 female alcoholics and 48[8] female neurotics	Correctly classified as alcoholic	.13[2] .06[4] .09[5] .12[7] $\bar{x}=.10$	.15[3] .13[6] $\bar{x}=.14$	
Ashton & Goldberg (1973)	168	Female college students	Peer ratings of target constructs	.27[14]	.26[12]	.29[9] .18[10] .29[11] .35[13] $\bar{x}=.28$
Berkeley (1953)[15]	306; 302 337; 332	Male air force officer candidates	Final grade Military grade Academic grade Pass/fail	.22 .17 .30 .17 $\bar{x}=.22$	.15 .26 .16 .22 $\bar{x}=.16$	

TABLE 1 Comparison of Criterion-related Validities of Different Scale Construction Strategies (continued)

Study	Sample Size[1]	Subjects	Criterion	Validity External (empirical)	Validity Inductive (internal)	Validity Deductive (rational)
Burisch (1978)	138	Female college students	Peer ratings of target constructs		.39[16] .41[18]	.39[17]
	69			.43[19]		
	69			.36[19]		
				$\bar{x} = .40$	$\bar{x} = .40$	
Burisch (1984b)	135	College students	Peer ratings of target constructs		.48[22]	.51[20] .54[21] .45[23] .49[24]
						$\bar{x} = .50$
	101	College students	Peer ratings of target constructs		.35[22]	.38[23] .45[25]
						$\bar{x} = .42$
	31	Outpatients at a psychiatric clinic[26]	Psychiatrists' global ratings of target construct		.56[22]	.70[23] .77[25] .60[27] .58[28]
						$\bar{x} = .66$
Dalessio & Crosby (1991)	3022	Life insurance sales representatives (inventory completed as applicants)	Sales production	.16	.15	

TABLE 1 Comparison of Criterion-related Validities of Different Scale Construction Strategies (continued)

Study	Sample Size[1]	Subjects	Criterion	External (empirical)	Inductive (internal)	Deductive (rational)
					Validity	
Fuentes, Sawyer, & Greener (1989)	212	Airline pilots	Ground school grades	.32	.27	.16
Goldberg (1972)	152	Female college freshmen	Peer ratings and other non-self-report criteria[29]	.27	.28[30] .22[31]	.32[32] .30[33]
					$\bar{x} = .25$	$\bar{x} = .31$
Hamilton (1971)[34]	70	Male college students	Peer ratings of target construct	.39	.41	
Hase & Goldberg (1967)	201	Female college freshmen	Peer ratings and other non-self-report criteria[29]	.27[35]	.26[36]	.30[37] .29[38]
						$\bar{x} = .30$
Heilbrun (1962)	166	College students	Number of friends	.13	.08	
Hornick, James, & Jones (1977)	398	Male fire fighters	Supervisors' ratings of job performance	.46	.49[39]	
Jackson (1975)[40]	116	Female college students	Roommates' ratings of sociability	.07[41]	.29[42] .34[43]	
						$\bar{x} = .32$
Knudson & Golding (1974)	64	High school seniors	Peer ratings of target constructs[29]	.08[44]	.35[45] .22[46] .17[47]	
						$\bar{x} = .25$

TABLE 1 Comparison of Criterion-related Validities of Different Scale Construction Strategies (continued)

Study	Sample Size[1]	Subjects	Criterion	External (empirical)	Inductive (internal)	Deductive (rational)
					Validity	
Matteson (1978)	168	Male refinery operator employees	Score on a battery of four cognitive tests[48]	.33[49]	.31[50]	
Mezzich, Damarin, & Erickson (1974)	223	Psychiatric inpatients	Psychologists' clinical diagnoses	.36	.18	.26
Mitchell & Klimoski (1982)	359	Real estate students	Real estate license	.46	.36[39]	
Overall (1974)	926	126 psychiatric outpatients and 800 normal adults	Correct classification	.29[51]	.24[51]	
Schrader (1975)[52]	753	Employees of a petro-chemical company	Composite of job grade and supervisors' ratings and other miscellaneous criteria	.44 .43 .41 .44	.44[53] .41[53] .38[53] .41[53]	.39 .50 .50 .43
				$\bar{x} = .43$	$\bar{x} = .41$	$\bar{x} = .46$
Schoenfeldt (1989)[54]	252	Customer service employees	Supervisors' ratings of customer service	.04	.25	.25
			Supervisors' ratings of overall performance	.10	.16	.22
			Times absent	.35	.37	.41
			Days absent	.05	.17	.18
			Days tardy	.15	.23	.37
				$\bar{x} = .14$	$\bar{x} = .24$	$\bar{x} = .29$

TABLE 1 Comparison of Criterion-related Validities of Different Scale Construction Strategies (continued)

Study	Sample Size[1]	Subjects	Criterion	Validity		
				External (empirical)	Inductive (internal)	Deductive (rational)
Taylor, Ellison, & Tucker (1965)	148	NASA scientists	Supervisors' ratings of creativity	.49		.48
			Number of publications	.55		.40
			Number of patents	.22		.28
				$\bar{x} = .42$		$\bar{x} = .39$
	152	NASA scientists	Supervisors' ratings of creativity	.43		.46
			Number of publications	.55		.47
			Number of patents	.09		.19
				$\bar{x} = .36$		$\bar{x} = .37$

1. When the sample sizes of the correlations differ for the different scale construction strategies, the sample sizes are presented in the following order: external, inductive, then deductive.
2. The external scale construction method was correlation ranking. The 20 items with the highest correlation with the criterion in the developmental sample were included in the equation.
3. Items that loaded .35 or higher on the alcoholism factor in the developmental sample were included in the equation.
4. Stepwise regression in the developmental sample was used to form the equation.
5. The same procedure described in footnote 2 was used, except the initial item pool consisted only of items for which the endorsement frequency differed by at least plus or minus six.
6. The same procedure described in footnote 3 was used, except the initial item pool consisted only of items for which the endorsement frequency differed by at least plus or minus six.
7. The same procedure described in footnote 4 was used, except the initial item pool consisted only of items for which the endorsement frequency differed by at least plus or minus six.
8. The number of females included in the study is 48, not 45, as reported in the text of the study.
9. Value represents the average validity of 15 rational scales developed by 15 psychology graduate students. Three different constructs were measured.

10. Value represents the average validity of 15 rational scales developed by 15 individuals with no training in psychology. The same three constructs referred to in footnotes 9, 11, 12, 13, and 14 were measured.

11. Value represents the average validity of three theoretically developed scales using *California Psychological Inventory* (CPI) items. The same three constructs referred to in footnotes 9, 10, 12, 13, and 14 were measured.

12. Value represents the average validity of three factor-analytically derived scales using CPI items. (See Hase and Goldberg, 1967, for a description of the procedures used to derive these scales.) The same three constructs referred to in footnotes 9, 10, 11, 13 and 14 were measured.

13. Value represents the average of three of Jackson's *Personality Research Form* (PRF) scales. These scales were developed using a construct-oriented scale construction strategy in which data relevant to the internal consistency of the scales were used to refine scales. Factor analysis was not, however, used to identify the set of constructs. The same three constructs referred to in footnotes 9, 10, 11, 12, and 14 were measured.

14. Value represents the average validity of three CPI empirically developed scales. The same three constructs referred to in footnotes 9, 10, 11, 12, and 13 were measured.

15. Homogeneous keys were developed on airmen and validated on officer candidates. The empirical keys were developed on officer candidates in Officer Candidate School.

16. Value represents the average validity of the *Freiburger Persönlichteitsinventar* scales, which were factor-analytically derived.

17. Value represents the average validity of eight rationally formed scales from the *Freiburger Persönlichteitsinventar* item pool.

18. The items making up the item pool referred to in footnote 17 were factor analyzed. The value in the table represents the average validity of those factor scales.

19. The sample of 138 was divided in half to provide two development and two cross-validity samples—that is, a double cross-validation approach. This value represents the cross-validity of the equation developed in the other half of the sample.

20. Value represents the average validity of *Hamburger Depressions-Skala*.

21. Value represents the average validity of a shortened version (i.e., 9 items rationally chosen) of the *Hamburger Depressions-Skala* inventory referred to in footnote 20.

22. Value represents the average validity of scale 3 of the *Freiburger Persönlichteitsinventar*, a factor-analytically derived scale.

23. Value represents the average validity of a shortened form (eight items rationally chosen) of scale 3 of the *Freiburger Persönlichteitsinventar*.

24. Value represents the average validity of a five-item rationally developed scale that took about one hour to develop.

25. Value represents the average validity of a five-item rationally developed scale, a revised version of the scale referred to in footnote 24.

26. Group A in Study 3 is not reported in this table. Only rationally developed scales were administered to Group A; thus, comparisons with other scale methods was impossible for Group A.

27. Value represents the validity of the nine-item *Erlanger Depressions-Skala*.

28. Value represents the validity of the 16-item *Depressivitäts-Skala*.

29. Validities for self-report criteria, which were reported in the study, are not reported in this table.

30. Principal component analysis was used to develop these inductive scales.

31. Multiple scalogram analysis was used to develop these inductive scales.

32. A theoretical approach based on Murray's "manifest needs" was used to develop several of Gough's "folk concepts."

33. These scales were rationally constructed to measure several of Gough's "folk concepts."

34. The comparisons for the flexibility scales are not reported in this table because the author incorrectly classified the *California Psychological Inventory* (CPI) Flexibility scale as an empirical scale. Gough (1968) describes the Flexibility scale as rationally developed. A comparison between scale construction methods is thus not possible for the flexibility scales. The comparisons for the self-esteem scales are also not reported in this table. The author combined two rationally developed CPI scales to form a CPI self-esteem scale. (See Gough, 1968, for a description of CPI scales and their development.) Such a scale is not an empirically developed scale. Thus, a comparison between scale construction methods for the self-esteem scales is also not possible.

TABLE 1   Comparison of Criterion-related Validities of Different Scale Construction Strategies (continued)

35. Value represents the average validity of 11 empirically developed *California Psychological Inventory* scales.

36. Value represents the average validity of 11 factor-analytically derived (using the BC TRY System for multidimensional analysis) scales using *California Psychological Inventory* items.

37. Three advanced clinical psychology graduate students developed 11 theoretical scales by agreeing upon the relevance of each *California Psychological Inventory* item for measuring 11 of Murray's theoretical "manifest needs." The value represents the average validity of these 11 scales.

38. Value represents the average validity of four of the rationally developed *California Psychological Inventory* scales as well as seven scales rationally developed by Harold Hase for the study.

39. The authors label all the scales rational. However, the scales were developed using principal component analysis and are thus classified in our table as an inductive method of scale construction.

40. Only the results for the sociability construct are reported here. The author incorrectly classified two of the *California Psychological Inventory* scales (Social Presence and Tolerance) as empirically developed. According to Gough (1968), they were not empirically developed; thus, a comparison between scale construction methods is not possible for two of the three constructs.

41. Value represents the validity of the empirically developed *California Psychological Inventory* Sociability scale.

42. Value represents the average validity for scales developed rationally by undergraduate psychology students.

43. Value represents the validity of the Affiliation scale of the *Personality Research Form* developed by Douglas Jackson.

44. Value represents the average validity of the *Schedule of Interpersonal Response* scales that were derived using principal component analysis.

45. Value represents the average validity of the *Personality Research Form* developed by Douglas Jackson.

46. Value represents the average validity of the *Interpersonal Check List* scales developed by R. LaForge and R. Suczek.

47. Value represents the average validity of a set of rationally developed scales intended to measure the theoretical octants of T. Leary's interpersonal behavior circle.

48. Only correlations with the score on the battery of four cognitive tests are reported in this table because that was the only criterion that both types of scales were intended to predict.

49. The empirical scale was developed on two prior samples; the value thus represents a cross-validity.

50. The author reported only a fold-back coefficient (i.e., correlation that is not cross-validated). The value reported here is the estimated cross-validity using Wherry's (1931) formula for estimating the cross-validity of a multiple correlation coefficient. (Only the two homogeneous scales that were most highly correlated with the criterion were included in the multiple regression equation.)

51. The author reported only fold-back coefficients (i.e., correlations that are not cross-validated). The value reported here is the estimated validity using Wherry's (1931) formula for estimating the cross-validity of a multiple correlation coefficient.

52. Only three (i.e., rational, empirical, and empirical–empirical) of the five types of scales are reported in this table because the other two methods were combinations of rational and empirical approaches.

53. The authors label this scale as empirical. It is, however, formed on the basis of cluster analysis and thus is classified in this table as an inductive scale construction strategy.

54. The author also developed a post hoc scale that was based on a factor analysis of the valid a priori rational scale items. It is unclear where this type of scale should be classified in the present table and it is thus not reported.

statistic would confound predictability of criterion with effectiveness of scale construction strategy.

The difficulty associated with summarizing correlation coefficients across studies does not apply to averaging correlation coefficients within a study. This is important because studies differed in the number of correlations that were computed within study, and we preferred to weight the results based on the number of subjects in a study rather than the number of criteria—that is, correlations computed—in a study. Thus, in Table 1, when more than one validity coefficient for a scale construction type is reported for a study, we computed the average criterion-related validity of that scale construction strategy for that study. These values appear in Table 1 at the end of each study in the "Validity" column.

We could not, however, simply weight these within-study correlation coefficients by their sample size and compute the average validity for each scale construction strategy. As we have described, such a summary would confound predictability of criterion with effectiveness of scale construction strategy. Instead, for each study we computed the difference between the average validity of one scale construction method and the average validity of each other scale construction method examined in the study.

This produced three separate distributions of differences in average validities (averages computed within study). That is, one distribution consists of the differences in average validities between external and inductive scale construction strategies. The second distribution consists of the differences in average validities between external and deductive scale construction strategies. The third distribution consists of the differences in average validities between inductive and deductive scale construction strategies.

Table 2 shows the distribution of differences in average validities for the deductive and external methods of scale construction. Table 2 also shows the sample size for each difference, the median difference in average validity, and the weighted (by sample size) mean difference in average validity. Table 3 shows this same information for the comparisons between deductive and inductive scale construction strategies. Table 4 shows the same information for the comparisons between external and inductive scale construction strategies.

The comparisons indicate that no method has a clear superiority over any other method in terms of criterion-related validity. The criterion-related validities obtained with the deductive method are, on average, .01 correlation points higher than those obtained with the external method and .05 correlation points higher than those obtained with the inductive method. The criterion-related validities with the external method are, on average, .02 correlation points higher than those obtained with the

TABLE 2 Summary of Criterion-related Validities:
Deductive Versus External Scale Construction Methods

	Difference in Validity[*]	Sample Size
	+.25	116
	+.15	252
	+.04	152
	+.03	201
	+.03	753
	+.02	70
	+.01	152
	+.01	168
	−.01	92
	−.03	148
	−.05	166
	−.10	223
	−.16	212
Median difference in validity	+.01	
Weighted mean difference in validity	+.01	
Standard deviation	.06	

[*]A positive sign indicates deductive scale construction strategy average validity (within study) is higher than the external scale construction average validity.

inductive method. The deductive method and the external method produce similar results. The deductive method, however, appears to be somewhat better than the inductive method in terms of criterion-related validity.

ACCURACY OF INTROSPECTION, SELF-ASSESSMENT, AND SELF-REPORT (FAKING)

Meehl (1945) and Wiggins (1973) criticized the deductive method of scale development for several reasons. One area of criticism related to the need for accurate introspection, self-assessment, and self-report. Meehl argued that empirically developed scales were immune to such requirements and, hence, criticisms.

Subtle Versus Obvious Items

One touted virtue of subtle items (often considered a virtue unique to the external scale construction method) is that respondents are unable to intuit what the "correct" answer is and are thus unable to intentionally distort their responses. Holden and Jackson (1981) examined the relative

TABLE 3   Summary of Criterion-related Validities:
Deductive Versus Inductive Scale Construction Methods

	Difference in Validity*	Sample Size
	+.18	223
	+.17	64
	+.10	31
	+.07	101
	+.06	152
	+.05	252
	+.05	753
	+.04	201
	+.03	168
	+.02	135
	−.01	138
	−.11	212
Median difference in validity	+.05	
Weighted mean difference in validity	+.05	
Standard deviation	.01	

*A positive sign indicates deductive scale construction strategy average validity (within study) is higher than the inductive scale construction average validity.

TABLE 4   Summary of Criterion-related Validities:
External Versus Inductive Scale Construction Methods

	Difference in Validity*	Sample Size
	+.18	223
	+.10	359
	+.06	312
	+.05	926
	+.05	212
	+.02	753
	+.02	168
	+.02	152
	+.01	201
	+.01	168
	+.01	3,022
	.00	104
	−.01	73
	−.03	398
	−.04	85
	−.10	252
Median difference in validity	+.02	
Weighted mean difference in validity	+.02	
Standard deviation	.03	

*A positive sign indicates external scale construction strategy average validity (within study) is higher than the inductive scale construction average validity.

usefulness of subtle and obvious scales in instances in which respondents were motivated to distort their responses. They found no evidence that subtle scales were superior. On the other hand, Burkhart, Christian, and Gynther (1978) found that endorsement of obvious items was a direct function of instructional set (i.e., to fake), whereas endorsement of subtle items was inversely related to instructional set. However, they also concluded that "subtle items did not appear to measure the constructs for which they had been originally intended" (Burkhart, Christian, & Gynther, 1978, p. 76).

Of course, not all items in empirically developed scales are subtle. A thorough analysis of the argument that empirically developed scales are immune to intentional distortion must also address the issue at the scale level as well as at the item level.

Several research studies document the conclusion that empirically developed scales can be faked. Some examples are Doll (1971); Haymaker and Erwin (1980); Klein and Owens (1965); Lautenschlager and Atwater (1986); Meehl and Hathaway (1946); Mock (1947); Schrader and Osburn (1977); Thornton and Gierasch (1980); Trent, Atwater, and Abrahams (1986); and Walker (1985). The argument that empirically developed scales are immune to intentional distortion is simply not supported by research. The evidence for all types of scale construction methods is clear: Respondents are able to distort their responses when instructed to do so.

Response Option Desirability

Closely linked to the obvious/subtle controversy is the criticism that deductive scales are more subject to distortion because the social desirability of the response is obvious. Fundamental to the criticism is the assumption that distortion in the direction of greater endorsement of socially desirable response options reduces the validity of the self-report.

Hogan and Stokes (1989) examined this assumption and found the opposite was true. They found that "response desirability was *positively* related to *both* predictive and concurrent item validities" (Hogan & Stokes, 1989, p. 8).

This does not appear to be an isolated finding. Ruch and Ruch (1967) found that a scale designed to measure intentional distortion correlated with sales success. Similarly, Hough et al. (1993) found positive correlations between a scale measuring social desirability of response and job performance for several different nonmanagement job families. Instead of attenuating criterion-related validity, socially desirable responding appears to be positively correlated with the criterion.

In a similar line of research, Hough, Eaton, Dunnette, Kamp, and McCloy (1990) found that criterion-related validities of deductive scales do not appear to be adversely affected by socially desirable responding. Other research (Dunnette, McCartney, Carlson, & Kirchner, 1962) suggests, however, that criterion-related validity of self-report instruments may be reduced when job applicants distort their self-descriptions and the information from the content scales is used for personnel decisions.

Objective Versus Subjective Items

Another common assumption is that objective items are resistant to faking. However, research on the accuracy of objective or verifiable responses has produced mixed results. Goldstein (1971) and Weiss and Dawis (1960), for example, found substantial disagreement between self-reported information and the truth for objective items. Cascio (1975), Keating, Paterson, and Stone (1950), and Mosel and Cozan (1952), on the other hand, found substantial agreement between self-reported information and the truth for objective items.

Regardless of such inconsistencies for objective items, it is assumed that objective items are more accurately reported and more resistant to distortion than are subjective items. However, the evidence is mixed for subjective items as well. On the one hand, Shaffer, Saunders, and Owens (1986) found that inductive scales made up of objective items were more accurately reported than factor scales made up of subjective items. In a faking experiment, Doll (1971) found that when participants were instructed to look as good as possible for a research position, significantly greater distortion occurred on objective items than on subjective items.

Mabe and West (1982) conducted a meta-analysis of studies examining the validity of self-evaluations of ability. They concluded that "gross generalizations concerning people's tendency to overestimate their abilities are unwarranted and that self-enhancing, accurate, or modest reports may be found, depending on certain conditions" (Mabe & West, 1982, p. 287).

They found that certain measurement conditions affect the likelihood of accurate self-evaluation and reporting. The three measurement conditions relevant to the present discussion are (a) anonymity of self-evaluation, (b) instructions emphasizing comparison with others, and (c) an expectation that the self-evaluation will be compared with criterion measures (i.e., verified). Each of these conditions produced more accurate self-reports than the counterpart condition. That is, (a) when the name of the respondent is requested, the self-report is less accurate; b) when items are worded in absolute terms rather than comparative terms, the self-report is less accurate; and (c) when there is no expectation that information will be verified, the self-report is less accurate.

Anonymity is obviously not possible when self-report inventories are used for personnel decisions. Thus, one conclusion from the Mabe and West meta-analysis is that self-distortion is likely to occur when self-report inventories are used as part of a hiring process.

Assuming that response distortion is likely in a personnel selection setting, the Mabe and West (1982) conclusions imply three strategies that may reduce distortion. Strategy one: Items should be written such that respondents are asked to compare and rate themselves relative to other people they know. Strategy two: Instructions should inform respondents that a check of the accuracy of the information will be performed. This check could be in the form of actually checking other records for accuracy of the self-report. Strategy three: A *lie-detection* scale could be developed to identify people who are presenting themselves in an overly desirable way.

One might infer from strategy two that objective items would be preferable to subjective items because they are more verifiable. Thus, strategies one and two would result in opposite type items. That is, objective, verifiable items are generally stated in absolute terms. For example, the question

How often do you exercise?
a. 1 or 2 days a week
b. 3 or 4 days a week
c. 5 or 6 days a week
d. 7 days a week

is more objective and thus more verifiable than a question that asks for a comparison between self and others. A question that asks for a comparison is usually stated in relative terms. For example, the item

How often do you exercise?
a. more often than your friends
b. about as often as your friends
c. not quite as often as your friends

is more subjective and less verifiable than the previous item. Mabe and West found that questions that required comparisons with other people resulted in more accurate self-reports than questions that did not require such comparisons. A contradiction thus results when Mabe and West's results are extended to item characteristics that are effective in reducing distortion in self-reports. Strategy one suggests that subjective items are more resistant to distortion, whereas strategy two suggests that objective items—that is, verifiable items—are more resistant to distortion.

Doll (1971) conducted a study that bears directly on the issue of measurement conditions effective in reducing distortion on objective and subjective items. He set up four experimental conditions. One condition was the honest condition. A second condition instructed participants to respond to the inventory as though they were applying for a research position and wanted to look good, but that there would be an interview in which they would have to defend their answers. A third condition instructed participants to respond to the inventory as though they were applying for a research position and wanted to look good, but to keep in mind that the inventory included a lie scale that would identify people who exaggerated. A fourth condition instructed participants to respond to the inventory as though they were applying for a research position and wanted to look as good as possible.

He found that in the "look as good as possible" condition, objective items were distorted significantly more often than subjective items. In fact, 97 percent of the objective items were distorted, whereas 81 percent of the subjective items were distorted. Clearly, though, both types of items were faked.

The expectation that responses would need to be defended reduced the faking dramatically. Only 17 percent of the objective items were distorted in the "defend in interview" condition, compared to 97 percent in the "look as good as possible" condition. Thirty-five percent of the subjective items were distorted in the "defend in interview" condition, compared to 81 percent in the "look as good as possible" condition. Clearly, informing respondents of a consequence affected the amount of distortion in their self-reports.

The only condition in which the level of faking on subjective and objective items was not different from the honest condition (not statistically significant) was the "lie scale" condition. Moreover, the amount of distortion in the "lie scale" condition was similar to the lowest level of distortion in the entire study, which was obtained for objective items in the "defend in interview" condition. This study suggests that one effective strategy for reducing distortion is to develop a lie scale and inform respondents of its existence.

Other studies have also found that informing respondents of detection methods and verification procedures, as well as warning them of negative consequences of distorting their responses, reduces distortion in self-descriptions. Mock (1947), Nias (1972), Schrader and Osburn (1977), Haymaker and Erwin (1980), Lautenschlager and Atwater (1986), and Trent, Atwater, and Abrahams (1986), for example, investigated the effects of such warnings. All concluded that warnings do reduce the amount of intentional distortion in self-report questionnaires.

SUMMARY OF COMPARISONS BETWEEN
SCALE CONSTRUCTION METHODS

The data suggest that the deductive and external methods of scale construction do not differ from each other in terms of the criterion-related validities that are obtained. Moreover, the data suggest that subtle items appear to decrease the validity of a scale. Thus, one of the supposed advantages of the empirical method of scale construction evaporates, ironically, when data relevant to the issue are examined.

The data also suggest that if and when accuracy of self-report is an issue, it is an issue for all three methods of scale construction. Given the concern about intentional distortion in applied settings where anonymity is not possible, the data suggest that developing a lie detection scale and informing respondents of its existence has considerable merit.

CONSTRUCT-ORIENTED SCALE CONSTRUCTION

Over the years, the deductive method has become associated with hypothesis testing, theory building, and construct validation. Indeed, construct-oriented scale construction is simply an updated variation of the deductive approach.

The specifics of this strategy can and will take many forms. However, two principles or requirements are essential to the programmatic development of construct-valid scales. The first requirement is a psychological theory that includes a taxonomic structure of relevant individual difference variables. The second requirement is data. Data are required to develop and revise the scales to ensure scale homogeneity, convergent and discriminant validity, and generalizability. These are the central requirements of a construct-oriented scale construction strategy, and they are based on the classic works of Cronbach and Meehl (1955), Loevinger (1957), D. T. Campbell and Fiske (1959), Cronbach, Rajaratnam, and Gleser (1963), and Jackson (1970).

One of the important strengths of this approach is its usefulness for hypothesis testing and, thus, scientific understanding. Landy (1986) and Binning and Barrett (1989) have provided a much-needed description and explanation of construct validation for psychologists conducting personnel selection research. It is within this context that we describe the development of construct-valid scales. In the sections that follow, we will first describe the process of identifying the individual difference constructs that are relevant to developing and testing a theory of job performance. Then we will describe the item and scale characteristics of construct-valid measures.

IDENTIFYING CONSTRUCTS TO MEASURE

Within the applied prediction setting of predicting differences in individual job performance, two sets of constructs need to be defined: job performance constructs and individual difference constructs. Both are discussed in the sections that follow.

Delineating the Performance Domain

Performance is a commonly used criterion in selection settings and is used as if it has a commonly accepted meaning (J. P. Campbell, 1990b). Yet job performance can be many things. Borman and Motowidlo (1993), for example, define job performance in behavioral terms. They categorize job performance as task performance and contextual performance. They define *task performance* as proficiency at performing activities that are formally recognized as part of the job. They define *contextual performance* as proficiency at performing activities that support the organizational, social, and psychological environment of the organization but that are not a formal part of the job. Contextual performance includes behaviors such as volunteering to perform tasks or duties that are not normally part of the job, helping and cooperating with others, following organizational rules and procedures even when they are personally inconvenient, and endorsing, supporting, and defending organizational objectives. This point of view conceptualizes job performance in terms of behaviors that are categorized into dimensions. Other authors emphasize the outcome or results of job performance. Kane's (1986) approach to job performance measurement typifies this point of view. The results, or outcome approach, emphasize the importance of goal attainment.

Regardless of how the performance domain is conceptualized, it is important to understand that the job performance domain is a set of constructs (Binning & Barrett, 1989; Smith, 1976). An important part of the job analysis is to specify and define the domain of performance constructs that make up job performance.

Identifying and Defining the Relevant Individual Difference Constructs

The job analysis should also result in a set of carefully defined individual difference constructs that are hypothesized to account for differences in the job performance constructs. In addition, construct validation requires that the nomological network of relationships between individual difference constructs, measures of those constructs, job performance constructs, and measures of those constructs be specified. It is this set of hypotheses or theory of job performance that criterion-related validation efforts confirm or disconfirm. A good theory about the individual differences that account for differences in job performance will depend on the quality of the job analysis and the quality of the review of prior relevant research, both of which are needed to develop a good theory or model of job performance.

Construct validation assumes that constructs relate differentially to each other. Indeed, the nomological network is a specification of these different relationships. In personnel selection research, this means that individual difference constructs relate differentially to each other and to job performance constructs. The pattern of these relationships—the nomological net—constitutes the set of hypotheses that criterion-related validation strategies investigate. Only when both predictor space and criterion space are fully defined and measured is it possible for evidence of convergent and discriminant validity to emerge.

One of the most notable construct validation efforts was Project A, funded during the 1980s by the Army Research Institutes for the Behavioral and Social Sciences. This project was noteworthy for a variety of reasons, one of which was the extensive effort to develop a taxonomy of individual difference constructs and a taxonomy of performance constructs. Both cognitive and noncognitive individual difference constructs were measured, as well as a wide spectrum of performance constructs. (The extensiveness of predictor and criterion construct specification, measurement, and validation is documented in a special issue of *Personnel Psychology*. See especially C. H. Campbell et al., 1990; J. P. Campbell, 1990a; J. P. Campbell, McHenry, & Wise, 1990; McHenry, Hough, Toquam, Hanson, & Ashworth, 1990; and Peterson et al., 1990.)

In that project, individual difference constructs show different patterns of relationships with other individual difference constructs and with job performance constructs. That is, when the full array of correlations between individual difference constructs, between performance constructs, and between individual difference constructs and performance constructs is examined, the pattern of relationships for each construct differs. In this construct-oriented study, the patterns of relationships reveal meaningful convergent and discriminant validity.

Other personnel selection research that has been construct oriented has also demonstrated convergent and discriminant validity. For example, Pulakos, Borman, and Hough (1988) demonstrated in two different samples that measures of predictor constructs have predictably different patterns of correlations with different criteria. Hough (1992) also demonstrated that when personality scales are grouped into constructs and criterion measures are grouped into constructs, different patterns of correlations between personality constructs and criterion constructs emerge. Both articles highlight the importance of defining and developing both predictor and criterion constructs. Both articles also demonstrate that when the pattern of correlations between construct-oriented measures of predictor and criterion constructs is examined, the pattern is meaningful and predictable. Both articles demonstrate the value of construct-oriented test validation for scientific understanding.

ITEM CHARACTERISTICS OF CONSTRUCT-VALID MEASURES

Face Validity

It is probably obvious by now that we believe most items in a construct-valid scale are face valid. This is not to say that the item has face validity for the job in question for which the scale may be used to select employees. Rather, the item should be face valid in terms of the psychological construct being measured.

The review of the criterion-related validities of obvious versus subtle items in the "Item-level Validity" section of this chapter suggests that obvious items typically contribute greater criterion-related validity than do subtle items. While some psychological constructs may be so poorly understood that subtle items are useful, in the area of personnel selection, the relevant constructs are not constructs for which subtle items or items with counterintuitive keying are necessary or desirable.

Objective/Subjective Items

Research suggests that subjective or nonverifiable items may be as criterion valid as, and perhaps even more criterion valid than, verifiable or objective items. Hogan and Stokes (1989), for example, used a self-report questionnaire that asked about such issues as interests, motivations, preferences, and personal characteristics, and obtained cross-validities consistent with those that Schmitt, Gooding, Noe, and Kirsch (1984) reported in their meta-analysis of validity studies. The items, with possibly one exception, were subjective and unverifiable.

Similarly, Taylor and his colleagues, using an a priori key, obtained validities in the .30s and .40s for predicting scientific creativity and productivity (Taylor, Ellison, & Tucker, 1965). The best scale across a variety of settings and samples was Professional Self-Confidence (Taylor & Ellison, 1967), a scale made up of "soft," subjective items. One of the most effective items in the scale and in the entire inventory was the following:

What do you consider to be your capacity or ability to succeed in research?
a. superior
b. above average
c. about average
d. slightly below average
e. does not apply

This item is both an obvious item and a subjective item. It is our opinion that items in construct-valid scales can be either objective or subjective.

Item Response Weights

Unit weighting is typically used for construct-oriented scales. A variety of evidence supports the use of unit weighting.

Empirical evidence suggests unit weights are as good as empirically derived weights. McGrath (1960) compared three methods of item weighting. One method weighted each response category according to its degree of significance in discriminating between two criterion groups in a developmental sample. The second method was unit weighting of options. The third method was a combination of the first and second methods. The cross-validated validities were .54, .58, and .52 for scoring methods one, two, and three, respectively. All of the coefficients were significantly different from zero, and none of the differences was significantly different from the others. The presence of sampling error with the inevitable shrinkage in predictive efficiency that characterizes empirical weighting strategies results in unit weights doing as well as and, when developmental samples are small, probably better than empirical weights. Moreover, Burt (1950), Gulliksen (1950), Lawshe and Schucker (1959), and Wilks (1938) all conclude that the more variables there are in a composite, the more the weights can differ markedly from a least-squares solution without negatively affecting the correlation between the composite and the criterion.

Another reason for differentially weighting response options or items is to reflect the importance of the specific content area to the construct domain. However, as Lawshe and Schucker (1959) note, "nothing is to be gained by differentially weighting items in a long test" (p. 104). Furthermore, the higher the intercorrelation among the items or components, the less differential weighting will affect the correlation between the scale score and a criterion (Lawshe & Schucker, 1959).

Social Desirability

The evidence suggests that intentional distortion in self-report questionnaires is a concern in a personnel selection setting, and, unfortunately, most items can be intentionally distorted. Therefore, we recommend addressing the issue of social desirability at both the item level and scale level.

One promising strategy at the item level involves removing the variance associated with social desirability. Jackson and Messick (Jackson, 1967) proposed a Differential Reliability Index that provides an estimate of the reliable item variance remaining after subtracting desirability variance. As

Neill and Jackson (1970) demonstrate, this index does aid in selecting items that are lower in desirability bias while maintaining scale homogeneity. Thus, a purer measure of the construct results.

Attention to social desirability only at the item level, however, is insufficient. Attention to social desirability at the scale level is also important. Scales that measure the extent of intentional distortion in self-report questionnaires can provide valuable information and can be an important deterrent to distortion in self-report measures.

SCALE CHARACTERISTICS OF CONSTRUCT-VALID MEASURES

Construct-valid scales are homogeneous scales. Ideally, coefficient alpha should be approximately .80, perhaps higher. Items that do not show good item–total scale correlations should be deleted. Data are thus critically important for revising a scale to ensure that homogeneity is a characteristic of the scale.

A construct-valid scale should be content valid as well. We use the term *content valid* to mean that the items in the scale faithfully represent or map the domain of the individual difference construct. We do not use the term *content validity* to mean that the items bear a veridical relationship to the job performance domain.

The nomological network of relationships hypothesized during the job analysis must be empirically tested. Construct-valid scales should show a pattern of both convergent and discriminant validity between predictor measures and between predictor and criterion measures. (See D. T. Campbell & Fiske, 1959, for a description of the pattern of correlations in a multi-trait, multi-method matrix that demonstrates convergent and discriminant validity.) Many of the coefficients will be in the form of criterion-related validities, and the pattern of these correlations should demonstrate predictable convergent and discriminant validity.

SUMMARY

The criticisms of the deductive method of scale construction are unfounded. We have demonstrated that deductive scales (rationally developed scales) correlate with criteria as well as scales developed via the external (empirical), and correlate as well as, if not somewhat better than, inductive (internal) methods of scale construction. We also have demonstrated that subtle items are not more useful than obvious items. Indeed, obvious items are typically more criterion valid than subtle items are, and both subtle and obvious items are fakeable. When self-report information is gathered and respondents provide their names, lie detection scales and warnings about consequences of distortion are effective in reducing distortion.

Construct-oriented scale development is a variant of the deductive method of scale construction. However, construct-oriented scale construction requires both theory and data. That is, development of construct-valid scales involves theory building and hypothesis testing. Data are required for refining the items in the scale as well as for confirming or disconfirming the pattern of hypothesized correlations between the construct and other constructs (both criterion constructs and other predictor constructs). Evidence of construct validity of a scale rests on data demonstrating that the internal structure of the scale is homogeneous and data demonstrating that the measure of the construct relates to other variables as hypothesized. Construct-valid scales are a necessity if scientific understanding is desired.

NOTES

1. Subgrouping is not included as a scale development strategy because it groups people rather than items and is thus not a method for measuring individual difference variables.

2. Indeed, Meehl later softened his position. He, along with Cronbach (Cronbach & Meehl, 1955), provided the classic description of construct validation and its role in theory building and hypothesis testing.

REFERENCES

Aamodt, M. G., & Pierce, W. L., Jr. (1987). Comparison of the rate response and vertical percent methods for scoring the biographical information blank. *Educational and Psychological Measurement, 47,* 505–511.

Alumbaugh, R. V., Davis, H. G., & Sweney, A. B. (1969). A comparison of methods for constructing predictive instruments. *Educational and Psychological Measurement, 29,* 639–651.

Ashton, S. G., & Goldberg, L. R. (1973). In response to Jackson's challenge: The comparative validity of personality scales constructed by the external (empirical) strategy and scales developed intuitively by experts, novices, and laymen. *Journal of Research in Personality, 7,* 1–20.

Baehr, M. E., & Williams, G. B. (1967). Underlying dimensions of personal background data and their relationship to occupational classification. *Journal of Applied Psychology, 51,* 481–490.

Berkeley, M. H. (1953). *A comparison between the empirical and rational approaches for keying a heterogeneous test* (Research Bulletin No. 53-24). Lackland Air Force Base, TX: United States Air Force, Air Research and Development Command, Human Resources Research Center (DTIC No. 19091).

Binning, J. F., & Barrett, G. V. (1989). Validity of personnel decisions: A conceptual analysis of the inferential and evidential bases. *Journal of Applied Psychology, 74,* 478–494.

Borgen, F. H. (1972). Predicting career choices of able college men from occupational and basic interest scales of the Strong Vocational Interest Blank. *Journal of Counseling Psychology, 19,* 202–211.

Borman, W. C., & Motowidlo, S. J. (1993). Expanding the criterion domain to include elements of contextual performance. In N. Schmitt & W. C. Borman (Eds.), *Personnel selection* (pp. 71–98). San Francisco: Jossey-Bass.

Buchwald, A. M. (1961). Verbal utterances as data. In H. Feigl & G. Maxwell (Eds.), *Current issues in the philosophy of science* (pp. 461–468). New York: Holt, Rinehart and Winston.

Burisch, M. (1978). Construction strategies for multiscale personality inventories. *Applied Psychological Measurement, 2,* 97–111.

Burisch, M. (1984a). Approaches to personality inventory construction: A comparison of merits. *American Psychologist, 39,* 214–227.

Burisch, M. (1984b). You don't always get what you pay for: Measuring depression with short and simple versus long and sophisticated scales. *Journal of Research in Personality, 18,* 81–98.

Burkhart, B. R., Christian, W. L., & Gynther, M. D. (1978). Item subtlety and faking on the MMPI: A paradoxical relationship. *Journal of Personality Assessment, 42,* 76–80.

Burt, C. (1950). The influence of differential weighting. *British Journal of Psychology, Statistical Section, 3,* 124–125.

Butt, D. S., & Fiske, D. W. (1968). Comparison of strategies in developing scales for dominance. *Psychological Bulletin, 70,* 505–519.

Campbell, C. H., Ford, P., Rumsey, M. G., Pulakos, E. D., Borman, W. C., Felker, D. B., deVera, M. V., & Riegelhaupt, B. J. (1990). Development of multiple job performance measures in a representative sample of jobs. *Personnel Psychology, 43,* 277–300.

Campbell, D. T., & Fiske, D. W. (1959). Convergent and discriminant validation by multitrait-multimethod matrix. *Psychological Bulletin, 56,* 81–105.

Campbell, J. P. (1990a). An overview of the army selection and classification project (Project A). *Personnel Psychology, 43,* 231–239.

Campbell, J. P. (1990b). The role of theory in industrial and organizational psychology. In M. D. Dunnette & L. M. Hough (Eds.), *Handbook of industrial and organizational psychology* (2d ed., vol. 1, pp. 39–73). Palo Alto, CA: Consulting Psychologists Press.

Campbell, J. P., McHenry, J. J., & Wise, L. L. (1990). Modeling job performance in a population of jobs. *Personnel Psychology, 43,* 313–333.

Cascio, W. F. (1975). Accuracy of verifiable biographical information blank responses. *Journal of Applied Psychology, 60,* 576–580.

Cattell, R. B. (1962). Personality assessment based upon functionally unitary personality traits, factor analytically demonstrated. In G. S. Nielsen (Ed.), *Personality research: Proceedings of the XIV international congress of applied psychology* (Vol. 2, pp. 198–219). Copenhagen: Musksgaard.

Clifton, T. C., Costanza, D. P., Reiter-Palmon, R., & Mumford, M. D. (1991, June). *Development of background data rational scales for positive and negative emotionality.* Paper presented at the meeting of the American Psychological Society, Washington, DC.

Connelly, M. S., Clifton, T. C., & Mumford, M. D. (1991, June). *Contrasting theory based background data scaling procedures.* Paper presented at the meeting of the American Psychological Society, Washington, DC.

Crewe, N. M. (1967). Comparison of factor analytic and empirical scales. *Proceedings of the 7th Annual Convention of the American Psychological Association, 2,* 367–368.

Cronbach, L. J., & Meehl, P. E. (1955). Construct validity in psychological tests. *Psychological Bulletin, 52,* 281–302.

Cronbach, L. J., Rajaratnam, N., & Gleser, G. C. (1963). Theory of generalizability: A liberalization of reliability theory. *British Journal of Statistical Psychology, 16,* 137–163.

Dalessio, A. T., & Crosby, M. M. (1991, April). *Validity or understanding: A comparison of three biodata scoring methods.* Paper presented at the annual meeting of the Society for Industrial and Organizational Psychology, St. Louis.

Devlin, S. E., Abrahams, N. M., & Edwards, J. E. (1992). Empirical keying of biographical data: Cross validity as a function of scaling procedure and sample size. *Military Psychology, 4,* 119–136.

Doll, R. E. (1971). Item susceptibility to attempted faking as related to item characteristics and adopted fake set. *Journal of Psychology, 77,* 9–16.

Drasgow, F., & Miller, H. E. (1982). Psychometric and substantive issues in scale construction and validation. *Journal of Applied Psychology, 67,* 268–279.

Duff, F. L. (1965). Item subtlety in personality inventory scales. *Journal of Consulting Psychology, 29,* 565–570.

Dunnette, M. D., McCartney, J., Carlson, H. C., & Kirchner, W. K. (1962). A study of faking behavior on a forced-choice self-description checklist. *Personnel Psychology, 15,* 13–24.

Eberhardt, B. J., & Muchinsky, P. M. (1982). An empirical investigation of the factor stability of Owens' biographical questionnaire. *Journal of Applied Psychology, 67,* 138–145.

Fruchter, B. (1954). *Introduction to factor analysis.* Princeton, NJ: Van Nostrand.

Fuentes, R. R., Sawyer, J. E., & Greener, J. M. (1989, August). *Comparison of the predictive characteristics of three biodata scaling methods.* Paper presented at the annual meeting of the American Psychological Association, New Orleans.

Goldberg, L. R. (1972). Parameters of personality inventory construction and utilization: A comparison of prediction strategies and tactics. *Multivariate Behavioral Research Monograph,* No. 72–2.

Goldstein, I. L. (1971). The application blank: How honest are the responses? *Journal of Applied Psychology, 55,* 491–492.

Gorsuch, R. L. (1983). *Factor analysis* (2d ed.). Hillsdale, NJ: Erlbaum.

Gorsuch, R. L. (1991, August). On the predictive power of higher order factors. In S. N. Strack (Chair), *The big five*. Symposium conducted at the annual meeting of the American Psychological Association, San Francisco.

Gough, H. G. (1968). An interpreter's syllabus for the California Psychological Inventory. In P. McReynolds (Ed.), *Advances in psychological assessment* (Vol. 1, pp. 55–79). Palo Alto, CA: Science and Behavior Books.

Gulliksen, H. (1950). *Theory of mental tests*. New York: Wiley.

Gynther, M. D., & Burkhart, B. R. (1983). Are subtle MMPI items expendable? In J. N. Butcher & C. D. Spielberger (Eds.), *Advances in personality assessment* (Vol. 2). Hillsdale, NJ: Erlbaum.

Hamilton, D. L. (1971). A comparative study of five methods of assessing self-esteem, dominance, and dogmatism. *Educational and Psychological Measurement, 31,* 441–452.

Hase, H. D., & Goldberg, L. R. (1967). Comparative validity of different strategies of constructing personality inventory scales. *Psychological Bulletin, 67,* 231–248.

Haymaker, J. C., & Erwin, F. W. (1980). *Investigation of applicant responses and falsification detection procedures for the Military Applicant Profile* (Final Project Report, Work Unit No. DA644520). Alexandria, VA: U.S. Army Research Institute for the Behavioral and Social Sciences.

Hedlund, J. L., Cho, D. W., & Wood, J. B. (1977). Comparative validity of MMPI-168 factors and clinical scales. *Journal of Multivariate Behavioral Research, 12,* 827–329.

Heilbrun, A. B. (1962). A comparison of empirical derivation and rational derivation of an affiliation scale. *Journal of Clinical Psychology, 18,* 101–102.

Hermans, H. J. M. (1969). The validity of different strategies of scale construction in predicting academic achievement. *Educational and Psychological Measurement, 29,* 877–883.

Hogan, J. B., & Stokes, G. S. (1989, April). *The influence of socially desirable responding on biographical data of applicant versus incumbent samples: Implications for predictive and concurrent research designs*. Paper presented at the annual meeting of the Society for Industrial and Organizational Psychology, Boston.

Holden, R. R., & Jackson, D. N. (1979). Item subtlety and face validity in personality assessment. *Journal of Consulting and Clinical Psychology, 47,* 459–468.

Holden, R. R., & Jackson, D. N. (1981). Subtlety, information, and faking effects in personality assessment. *Journal of Clinical Psychology, 37,* 379–386.

Hornick, C. W., James, L. R., & Jones, A. P. (1977). Empirical item keying versus a rational approach to analyzing a psychological climate questionnaire. *Applied Psychological Measurement, 1,* 489–500.

Hough, L. M. (1992). The "big five" personality variables—construct confusion: Description versus prediction. *Human Performance, 5,* 139–155.

Hough, L. M., Carter, G. W., Dohm, T. E., Nelson, L. C., & Dunnette, M. D. (1993). *Development and validation of the Universal Test Battery: A computerized selection system for non-management employees at Bell Atlantic* (Institute Report No. 219). Minneapolis: Personnel Decisions Research Institutes.

Hough, L. M., Eaton, N. K., Dunnette, M. D., Kamp, J. D., & McCloy, R. A. (1990). Criterion-related validities of personality constructs and the effect of response distortion on those validities [Monograph]. *Journal of Applied Psychology, 75,* 581–595.

Jackson, D. N. (1967). *Personality research form.* Goshen, NY: Research Psychologists Press.

Jackson, D. N. (1970). A sequential system for personality scale development. In C. D. Spielberger (Ed.), *Current topics in clinical and community psychology* (Vol. 2, pp. 61–96). New York: Academic Press.

Jackson, D. N. (1971). The dynamics of structured personality tests: 1971. *Psychological Review, 78,* 229–248.

Jackson, D. N. (1975). The relative validity of scales prepared by naive item writers and those based on empirical methods of personality scale construction. *Educational and Psychological Measurement, 35,* 361–370.

Jöreskog, K. G. (1969). A general approach to confirmatory maximum likelihood factor analysis. *Psychometrika, 34,* 183–202.

Kaiser, H. F. (1958). The varimax criterion for analytic rotation in factor analysis. *Psychometrika, 23,* 187–200.

Kane, J. S. (1986). Performance distribution assessment. In R. A. Berk (Ed.), *Performance assessment: Methods and applications* (pp. 237–273). Baltimore: Johns Hopkins University Press.

Keating, E., Paterson, D. G., & Stone, C. H. (1950). Validity of work histories obtained by interview. *Journal of Applied Psychology, 34,* 1–5.

Klein, S. P., & Owens, W. A. (1965). Faking of a scored life history blank as a function of criterion objectivity. *Journal of Applied Psychology, 49,* 452–454.

Klimoski, R. J. (1973). A biographical data analysis of career patterns in engineering. *Journal of Vocational Behavior, 3,* 103–113.

Klingler, D. E., Johnson, J. H., Giannetti, R. A., & Williams, T. A. (1977). Comparison of the clinical utility of the MMPI basic scales and specific MMPI state-trait scales: A test of Dahlstrom's hypothesis. *Journal of Consulting and Clinical Psychology, 45,* 1086–1092.

Knudson, R. M., & Golding, S. L. (1974). Comparative validity of traditional versus S-R format inventories of interpersonal behavior. *Journal of Research in Personality, 8,* 111–127.

Landy, F. J. (1986). Stamp collecting versus science: Validation as hypothesis testing. *American Psychologist, 41,* 1183–1192.

Lautenschlager, G. J., & Atwater, D. C. (1986). *Controlling response distortion on an empirically keyed biodata questionnaire.* Unpublished manuscript.

Lautenschlager, G. J., & Shaffer, G. S. (1987). Reexamining the component stability of Owens' biographical questionnaire. *Journal of Applied Psychology, 72,* 149–152.

Lawshe, C. H., & Schucker, R. E. (1959). The relative efficiency of four test weight methods in multiple prediction. *Educational and Psychological Measurement, 19,* 103–114.

Lecznar, W. B., & Dailey, J. T. (1950). Keying biographical inventories in classification test batteries. *American Psychologist, 5,* 279.

Loevinger, J. (1957). Objective tests as instruments of psychological theory [Monograph]. *Psychological Reports, 3,* 635–694.

Loevinger, J., Gleser, G. C., & DuBois, P. H. (1953). Maximizing the discriminating power of a multiple-score test. *Psychometrika, 18,* 309–317.

Mabe, P. A., III., & West, S. G. (1982). Validity of self-evaluation of ability: A review and meta-analysis. *Journal of Applied Psychology, 67,* 280–296.

Malloy, J. (1955). The prediction of college achievement with the life experience inventory. *Educational and Psychological Measurement, 15,* 170–180.

Matteson, M. T. (1978). An alternative approach to using biographical data for predicting job success. *Journal of Occupational Psychology, 51,* 155–162.

McCall, R. J. (1958). Face validity in the D scale of the MMPI. *Journal of Clinical Psychology, 14,* 77–80.

McGrath, J. J. (1960). Improving credit evaluation with a weighted application blank. *Journal of Applied Psychology, 44,* 325–328.

McHenry, J. J., Hough, L. M., Toquam, J. L., Hanson, M. A., & Ashworth, S. (1990). Project A validity results: The relationship between predictor and criterion domains. *Personnel Psychology, 43,* 335–354.

Meehl, P. E. (1945). The dynamics of "structured" personality tests. *Journal of Clinical Psychology, 1,* 296–303.

Meehl, P. E., & Hathaway, S. R. (1946). The K factor as a suppressor variable in the MMPI. *Journal of Applied Psychology, 30,* 525–564.

Mershon, B., & Gorsuch, R. L. (1988). Number of factors in the personality sphere: Does increase in factors increase predictability of real-life criteria? *Journal of Personality and Social Psychology, 55,* 675–680.

Mezzich, J. E., Damarin, F. L., & Erickson, J. R. (1974). Comparative validity of strategies and indices for differential diagnosis of depressive states from other psychiatric conditions using the MMPI. *Journal of Consulting and Clinical Psychology, 42,* 691–698.

Mitchell, T. W., & Klimoski, R. J. (1982). Is it rational to be empirical? A test of methods for scoring biographical data. *Journal of Applied Psychology, 67,* 411–418.

Mock, S. J. (1947). Biographical data. In J. P. Guilford & J. I. Lacey (Eds.), *Printed classification tests* (Research Rep. No. 5, pp. 767–795). Army Air Forces Aviation Psychology Program.

Mosel, J. L., & Cozan, L. W. (1952). The accuracy of application blank work histories. *Journal of Applied Psychology, 36,* 365–369.

Neill, J. A., & Jackson, D. N. (1970). An evaluation of item selection strategies in personality scale construction. *Educational and Psychological Measurement, 30,* 647–661.

Nias, D. K. B. (1972). The effects of providing a warning about the lie scale in a personality inventory. *British Journal of Educational Psychology, 42* (3), 308–312.

Overall, J. E. (1974). Validity of the psychological screening inventory for psychiatric screening. *Journal of Consulting and Clinical Psychology, 42,* 717–719.

Owens, W. A., & Schoenfeldt, L. F. (1979). Toward a classification of persons [Monograph]. *Journal of Applied Psychology, 68,* 569–607.

Peterson, N. G., Hough, L. M., Dunnette, M. D., Rosse, R. L., Houston, J. S., Toquam, J. L., & Wing, H. (1990). Project A: Specification of the predictor domain and development of new selection/classification tests. *Personnel Psychology, 43,* 247–276.

Pulakos, E. D., Borman, W. C., & Hough, L. M. (1988). Test validation for scientific understanding: Two demonstrations of an approach to studying predictor-criterion linkages. *Personnel Psychology, 41,* 703–716.

Reilly, R. R., & Echternacht, G. J. (1979). Validation and comparison of homogeneous and occupational interest scales. *Applied Psychological Measurement, 3,* 177–185.

Ruch, F. L., & Ruch, W. W. (1967). The K Factor as a (validity) suppressor variable in predicting success in selling. *Journal of Applied Psychology, 51,* 201–204.

Schaie, K. W. (1963). Scaling the scales: Use of expert judgment in improving the validity of questionnaire scales. *Journal of Consulting Psychology, 27,* 350–357.

Schmitt, N., Gooding, R. Z., Noe, R. A., & Kirsch, M. (1984). Meta-analyses of validity studies published between 1964 and 1982 and the investigation of study characteristics. *Personnel Psychology, 37,* 407–422.

Schoenfeldt, L. F. (1989, August). *Biographical data as the new frontier in employee selection research.* Division 5 Presidential address at the annual meeting of the American Psychological Association, New Orleans.

Schrader, A. (1975). *A comparison of the relative utility of several rational and empirical strategies for forming biodata dimensions.* Unpublished doctoral dissertation, University of Houston.

Schrader, A. D., & Osburn, H. G. (1977). Biodata faking: Effects of induced subtlety and position specificity. *Personnel Psychology, 30,* 395–404.

Scollay, R. W. (1956). Validation of personal history items against a salary increase criterion. *Personnel Psychology, 9,* 325–335.

Shaffer, G. S., Saunders, V., & Owens, W. A. (1986). Additional evidence for the accuracy of biographical data: Long-term retest and observer ratings. *Personnel Psychology, 39,* 791– 809.

Smith, P. C. (1976). Behaviors, results, and organizational effectiveness: The problem of criteria. In M. D. Dunnette (Ed.), *Handbook of industrial and organizational psychology* (pp. 745–775). Chicago: Rand McNally.

Taylor, C. W., & Ellison, R. L. (1967). Biographical predictors of scientific performance. *Science, 155,* 1075–1080.

Taylor, C. W., Ellison, R. L., & Tucker, M. F. (1965). *Biographical information and the prediction of multiple criteria of success in science.* Greensboro, NC: Creativity Research Institute of the Richardson Foundation.

Telenson, P. A., Alexander, R. A., & Barrett, G. V. (1983). Scoring the biographical information blank: A comparison of three weighting techniques. *Applied Psychological Measurement, 7,* 73–80.

Thornton, G. C., III, & Gierasch, P. F., III. (1980). Fakability of an empirically derived selection instrument. *Journal of Personality Assessment, 44,* 48–51.

Trent, T. T., Atwater, D. C., & Abrahams, N. M. (1986, April). Biographical screening of military applicants: Experimental assessment of item response distortion. In G. E. Lee (Ed.), *Proceedings of the Tenth Annual Symposium of Psychology in the Department of Defense* (pp. 96–100). Colorado Springs, CO: U.S. Air Force Academy, Department of Behavioral Sciences and Leadership.

Uhlman, C. E., Reiter-Palmon, R., & Connelly, M. S. (1990, April). *A comparison and integration of empirical keying and rational scaling of biographical data items.* Paper presented at the meeting of the Southeastern Psychological Association, Atlanta.

Walker, C. B. (1985, February). *The fakability of the Army's Military Applicant Profile (MAP).* Paper presented at the annual meeting of the Human Resources Management and Organizational Behavior Association, Denver.

Weiss, D. J., & Dawis, R. V. (1960). An objective validation of factual interview data. *Journal of Applied Psychology, 44,* 381–385.

Wherry, R. J., Sr. (1931). A new formula for predicting the shrinkage of the coefficient of multiple correlation. *Annals of Mathematical Statistics, 2,* 440–457.

Wiener, D. N. (1948). Subtle and obvious keys for the Minnesota Multiphasic Personality Inventory. *Journal of Consulting Psychology, 12,* 164–170.

Wiggins, J. S. (1973). *Personality and prediction: Principles of personality assessment.* Reading, MA: Addison-Wesley.

Wilks, S. S. (1938). Weighting systems for linear functions of correlated variables when there is no dependent variable. *Psychometrika, 3,* 23–40.

Woodworth, R. S., (1917). *Personal data sheet.* Chicago: Stoelting.

Worthington, D. L., & Schlottman, R. S. (1986). The predictive validity of subtle and obvious empirically derived psychological test items under faking conditions. *Journal of Personality Assessment, 50,* 171–181.

Developing and Using Factorially Derived Biographical Scales

Lyle F. Schoenfeldt
Texas A & M University

Jorge L. Mendoza
University of Oklahoma

The history of the biographical questionnaire for prediction and selection coincides with the chronology of empirical keying. The empirical keying approach traditionally associated with biographical data is founded on item–criterion relationships, and it is intended to maximize the accuracy of the prediction of external criteria (Guion, 1965). With a history extending almost a century, the results of using empirically keyed biographical items have been impressive and have marked biographical data as one of the best predictors of career and organizational criteria (Asher, 1972; Henry, 1966; Mitchell & Klimoski, 1982; Owens, 1976; Reilly & Chao, 1982; Schuh, 1967).

As noted by Mumford and Owens (1987), "While the predictive power of...empirically keyed background data measures is undoubted...the very success of this technique has become something of a liability" (p. 2). Put simply, the downside of empirical keying is the unscientific nature of the process. For example, Korman (1968) objected to the "brute empirical approach, where items are utilized according to the specific situation, rather than to the meaningfulness of the variables and the possible psychological constructs which could lead to an effective theory" (p. 308).

The desire to retain predictive power while at the same time assuring scientific integrity has led to the development of other item-scaling procedures for use with biographical data. These other procedures have included both rational and factorial approaches and combinations of the two. In particular, factor analysis represents a logical means of going from item responses to dimensions, and for this reason has been used extensively with biographical information. In fact, the presence of factorial dimensions of biographical items has been instrumental in opening up the important lines of research exemplified by the seminal work of Owens (1968, 1971, 1976; Owens & Schoenfeldt, 1979) and his collaborators, including Schoenfeldt (1974) and Mumford (1988; Mumford & Nickels, 1989; Nickels & Mumford, 1989). More than anything else, it is the application of the factorial approach to biographical items that represents the new frontier in personnel selection research noted by Fleishman (1988). Specifically, Fleishman noted three trends that indicate this frontier: (a) the refining of the traditional empirical keying, (b) explorations of the potential value of background data in performance prediction, and (c) research of background data as the basis for a general descriptive system.

The purpose of this review is to consider (a) the origin of the factorial approach, (b) the validity of biographical factors, (c) factor analytic methods that have been used with biographic data, and (d) potential applications of the factorial approach.

ORIGINS AND LOGIC UNDERLYING FACTORIAL SCALING OF BIOGRAPHICAL DATA ITEMS

ORIGINS OF FACTOR ANALYSIS

From a historical perspective, the original application of factor analysis has been associated with the measurement of intellect (Guion, 1965). Spearman (1904), Thurstone (1938), and Guilford (1956, 1967), to name a few, proposed various models of human aptitudes and abilities based on their respective factor analytic work. These researchers, along with others using factor analytic methods, administered batteries of intellective tests and observed relationships (correlations) among the various measures. Also, the researchers knew that each test measured constructs common to some of the remaining battery, as well as a construct unique to that particular test. Factor analysis was an attempt to identify the common constructs in a large number of tests. These common constructs were called *factors*.

In pursuing the identification of the common factors, these researchers discovered that the factor analytic solution is not unique. That is, two researchers factor-analyzing the same data set could arrive at different solutions that are equally defensible. This problem is partly due to the rotational process that a researcher engages in to interpret the factors. The issue of factor rotation will be discussed later. In the meantime, it is important to keep this indeterminacy in mind as the applications of factor analysis are discussed.

GOALS OF FACTOR ANALYSIS

Factor analysis can help the researcher organize test results in two ways (Weiss, 1976). First, factor analysis can be useful in achieving parsimony—that is, in reducing a large number of tests into a smaller set of measurements. For example, through factor analysis a researcher with a battery of 20 tests might find that 99 percent of the domain being assessed could be defined with a much smaller set of tests. Clearly, patterns of individual differences could be more easily perceived and understood from a smaller set of independent measures. Results of this nature would lead to a great deal of savings.

Second, factor analysis can be useful in gaining understanding of interrelationships among tests. In using factor analysis, the investigator is concerned with the structure of a set of variables as a means of generating or refuting hypotheses about this structure.

The factor analytic goals of parsimony and understanding are not mutually exclusive, and both are important. Understanding the structure of a domain can assist with the goal of defining a smaller test battery.

Related to the two applications, parsimony and understanding, is the distinction between factor analysis and component analysis. Component analysis is more typically associated with data reduction because a component is an observable linear combination of the original set of variables. Thus, there are no common and unique unobservable factors in the component model, as there are in the factor analysis model. Generally, the goal in data reduction is a reduced set of variables on which individuals can be scored. On the other hand, a factor is a hypothetical, unobserved variable or construct. A common factor is an unobserved, hypothetical construct that contributes to the variance of at least two of the original variables. A unique factor is an unobserved, hypothetical variable that contributes to the variance of only one of the observed variables. Thus, factor analysis in which the common variances are set to one and the unique variances are set to zero is by definition a component analysis.

Factor analysis was originally developed to study the structure of cognitive abilities and, as exemplified by the work of Guilford (1956, 1967), Vernon (1961), and Humphreys (1981), to name a few, continues as an important research technique in the cognitive domain. Additionally, there have been important advances in the noncognitive domains, including personality and biographical data. These latter applications of factor analysis will be discussed next.

FACTOR ANALYSIS AS APPLIED
TO PERSONALITY INVENTORIES

Best known are the applications of factorial methods to measures of personality. Typical personality inventories have many items, sometimes several hundred. It is desirable to use factor analytic procedures with such data, both for data reduction and to understand the constructs being measured.

Well-known examples of personality tests built on a factor analytic foundation include the *16-PF* (Cattell & Stice, 1957) and the *Guilford-Zimmerman Temperament Survey* (Guilford, Zimmerman, & Guilford, 1976). For these personality instruments, item responses of examinees are scored on factorially defined dimensions. The factor scores then define each individual's personality profile.

Factor analytic work of personality tests over a 45-year period has resulted in the derivation of what are called the Big Five personality dimensions: Extroversion, Agreeableness, Conscientiousness, Emotional Stability (versus Neuroticism), and Culture, or Intellect (Digman, 1990; Goldberg, 1993). The domains incorporate hundreds of traits and personality constructs researched over the years and provide what Goldberg (1993) has termed "a scientifically compelling framework in which to organize the myriad individual differences that characterize humankind" (p. 27). These dimensions have been repeatedly replicated in many different populations, languages, and age groups, using a variety of approaches to assessment (Hogan, 1991).

Of even greater significance, distillation of the Big Five has served to focus research and application in a variety of areas. For example, important reviews of the literature have concluded that personality measures, when classified with the Big Five schemata, are systematically related to a variety of job performance criteria (Barrick & Mount, 1991; Tett, Jackson, & Rothstein, 1991).

FACTOR ANALYSIS AS APPLIED
TO BIOGRAPHICAL DATA

As indicated previously, applications of biographical data historically have been synonymous with empirical prediction. Biographical items, and in some cases alternatives to biographical items, have been treated as independent predictors and have been differentially weighted to predict criteria of interest.

Credit for first use of biographical data, in the form of a weighted application, dates back to 1884 and is given to T. L. Peters of the Washington Life Insurance Company (Atlanta, Georgia) for the selection of life insurance sales agents (Ferguson, 1962). There were a number of pre- and post-World War I extensions of this early research, including studies by Goldsmith (1922) and Russell and Cope (1925). By the time of World War II, the military need had transformed the biographical questionnaire into the multiple-choice form that is most used today (Owens, 1976). By the 1950s, biographical data had come to encompass a broad range of information, including verifiable items similar to those on an application blank (e.g., type of previous job) and those associated with typical behavior (e.g., extent of participation in team sports, extent of watching TV) and attitudes and beliefs (e.g., favorite subject in school, extent to which you feel dress is important to success). The one thing common to this early history of biographical data was a reliance on empirical scoring. In this context, there was little need for factor analysis. The empirical procedure produced the desired results.

Applying factor analysis to biographical data originated almost exclusively in a desire to reduce data. As with personality measures, biographical questionnaires frequently involve many items, possibly several hundred. Even when empirically scored, it may be desirable to factor-analyze items to understand better the dimensions being measured. Early rational and factorial approaches were undertaken by Berkeley (1953), Morrison, Owens, Glennon, and Albright (1962), Baehr and Williams (1967, 1968), and Matteson, Osburn, and Sparks (1969).

FACTOR ANALYTIC METHODS AS APPLIED
TO BIOGRAPHICAL ITEMS

PRINCIPAL COMPONENTS FACTOR ANALYSIS

Virtually all of the factor analytic applications with biographical data have been principal components analysis. As indicated, the primary aim of principal components analysis is to develop a new set of dimensions or components from an original set of items. Whereas the items are intercorrelated, the dimensions can be made orthogonal. It is desirable that the new dimensions account for as much of the nonerror variance in the original set of variables as possible.

The fact that principal components analysis is often used to identify a smaller number of components that account for a relatively large percentage of the total variance of the original variables makes it a natural for use with biographical items. This result is because biographical questionnaires always have a large number of items, frequently several hundred, that are known to represent a circumscribed set of components.

Component analysis solutions, however, tend to have more factors than those from factor analyses. This result is due to the difference between the two models. As mentioned, in the factor analysis model each original variable is a linear combination of common factors and a single unique factor. These common and unique factors are unobservable. In factor analysis, the researcher is only interested in analyzing the covariation between the common factors; whereas in the principal component analysis, the researcher is interested in the covariation between the variables. But parsimony comes at a price in factor analysis. Because the variance of each common factor is unknown and the number of common factors is also unknown, there is a basic indeterminancy in the factor analysis model. That is, to determine the number of common factors, one must know the common variances, but to determine the common variances it is necessary to know the number of factors. Although there are ways to get around this problem, this fact is a serious nuisance of the common exploratory factor analytic model. In practice, however, principal components analysis and factor analysis often yield similar solutions.

One central issue in component and factor analyses is the interpretation of factors. Generally, factors are identified with the loadings. The loadings tell how the variables are associated with the factors. Under an orthogonal rotation, the loading is the correlation between the variable and the factor. In practice, after an initial factor analytic solution is obtained, the factor axes are rotated to enhance interpretation. By rotating the factors, it is possible to change the loadings, thus making the identification of factors easier. Thurstone (1947) proposed the criterion of *simple structure* to aid in the identification of factors. When one rotates to simple structure, one is trying to generate factors that have high loadings on certain variables but not on others.

There are two general ways in which factor axes can be rotated: orthogonal and oblique. The most common procedure is called an *orthogonal rotation*. This rotation preserves the original orientation of the axes so that they remain perpendicular. The other method is called an *oblique rotation*. In this rotation the axes are rotated independently with no regard to orthogonality. Three of the most popular rotation procedures are the varimax, quartimax, and equimax. Simply, the procedures differ in their definition of simple structure. The varimax procedure is perhaps the most widely used.

Three popular oblique rotation procedures are the oblimax, oblimin, and promax. One advantage of the orthogonal solution is that the factor scores are uncorrelated. However, this should not be the sole guideline in deciding between an orthogonal or an oblique solution. Usually both solutions should be obtained, and the researcher should choose the one that makes the most theoretical sense. With this background, it is now possible to review the literature dealing with the application of component and factor analyses to biographical items.

Factor Content

Mumford and Owens (1987) reported that 21 studies using factor and principal components analyses of background data items were found in the literature. They identified the content of each dimension, concluding that the 26 dimensions shown in Table 1 best summarized the factor analysis results. As can be seen, dimensions concerned with Adjustment, Academic Achievement, Introversion, Intellectual/Cultural Pursuits, Social Leadership, and Maturity emerged most frequently.

It is important to note that the results shown in Table 1 are, to some extent, a function of the items involved. Owens and his colleagues have undertaken the bulk of the factor analytic work, using items of a general development nature constructed for administration to a college-age population. The factors that emerged tended to reflect this orientation.

The results of a study by this chapter's authors (Schoenfeldt, 1989; Schoenfeldt, Varca, & Mendoza, 1992) provide an example of similarity and differences in factors that emerge when the items have a different orientation than those of Owens. A 137-item biographical questionnaire was constructed to measure background, interests, and attitudes indicative of customer service orientation. Specifically, the questionnaire covered 16 aspects of service delivery identified through an extensive job analysis. The 16 a priori dimensions, divided into four overall categories, are shown in Table 2.

The questionnaire was completed by over 867 service employees, along with a large number of applicants. Most of the 137 biographic items were continuous—that is, with options in ascending or descending order. Several items were noncontinuous, and several of these asked respondents to mark more than one option. The separate options of noncontinuous

TABLE 1   Factor Analytic Dimensions Identified by Various Studies ($N = 21$)

Dimension	Number of Studies
1. Adjustment	18
2. Academic Achievement	16
3. Intellectual/Cultural Pursuits	13
4. Introversion versus Extroversion	13
5. Social Leadership	12
6. Maturity	11
7. Career Development	10
8. Religious Involvement	9
9. Athletic Pursuits	8
10. Independence	8
11. Parental Socioeconomic Status	8
12. Social Conformity	8
13. Achievement Motivation	7
14. Parental Warmth	7
15. Profession Skills	7
16. Scientific/Engineering Pursuits	7
17. Self-esteem	7
18. Organizational Commitment	6
19. Parental Control	6
20. Personal Conservatism	6
21. Trade Skills	5
22. Family Commitment	4
23. Work Values	4
24. Health	3
25. Sibling Relationships	3
26. Urban/Rural Background	1

From "Methodology Review: Principles, Procedures and Findings in the Application of Background Data Measures" by M. D. Mumford and W. A. Owens, 1987, *Applied Psychological Measurement, 11*, pp. 1–31. Copyright 1987 by Applied Psychological Measurement, Inc. Adapted by permission.

items were treated as individual items, each with a yes–no response. Following these conversions were a total of 240 scorable biographic items.

As part of the research, the item responses were factor-analyzed. The 240 items were included in a principal components factor analysis. Ten factors accounting for 19 percent of the total variance were rotated using a promax procedure. The 10 factors, along with an example item from each, are shown in Table 3.

Of note is the fact that the factors tend to reflect the a priori dimensions (Table 2) more than those from other studies (Table 1). At least 7 of the 10 dimensions from Table 3 are directly analogous to the a priori dimensions, the exceptions being Group Membership Participation (2), Male Orientation (7), and Accomplishments (9). At the same time, the fit

TABLE 2   A Priori Dimensions

Scale	Example Item
Dealing With People	
1. Sociability	Volunteer with service groups
2. Agreeableness/Cooperation	Argue a lot compared with others
3. Tolerant	Response to people breaking rules
4. Good Impression	What a person wears is important
Outlook	
5. Calmness	Often in a hurry
6. Resistance to Stress	Time to recover from disappointments
7. Optimism	Think there is some good in everyone
Responsibility/Dependability	
8. Responsibility	Supervision in previous jobs
9. Concentration	Importance of quiet surroundings at work
10. Work Ethic	Percent of spending money earned in high school
Other	
11. Satisfaction with Life	How happy in general
12. Need for Achievement	Ranking in previous job
13. Parental Influence	Mother worked outside home when respondent was young
14. Educational History	Grades in math
15. Job History	Likes/dislikes in previous job
16. Demographic	Number in family

of the 10 factorial dimensions from the service orientation study with the 26 general dimensions of Table 1 is less obvious. While it is possible to see how the Parental Interest dimension from Table 3 might fit the Parental Warmth dimension from Table 1 or the Family Orientation (Table 3) would relate to Family Commitment (Table 1), the comparability is less obvious for most of the remaining dimensions. Although it is possible to look at factors emerging across studies (Table 1), most biographic factors are going to be most related to the item pool from which they emerge (Tables 2 and 3) than from some general conceptualization of biographic factor structure.

Factor Generalizability

There have been a small number of studies examining the generalizability across subpopulations of factors resulting from biographic items. Mumford et al. (1983) compared the dimensional structure obtained in three item pools when male and female item responses were factored separately and

TABLE 3 Factor Scales

Dimension	No. Items	Alpha Reliability	Example Item
1. Sociability	10	0.77	Introduce oneself to strangers
2. Group Membership Participation	10	0.79	Volunteer with service groups
3. Impatience	10	0.76	Upset while waiting
4. Parental Interest	10	0.66	Parents taught hobby
5. Previous Employment	10	0.78	Number of sales jobs
6. Work Ethic	10	0.63	Distracted by family problems at work
7. Male Orientation	11	0.68	Response to competition
8. Work Responsibility	10	0.64	How often late for class in high school
9. Hurry/Accomplishments	11	0.45	Earned major purchase in high school
10. Family Orientation	8	0.36	Assisted with care of family

together. Their results suggested that although there are similarities, preserving separate structures led to more interpretable results.

Gonter (1979) compared the dimensional structures resulting from a comparison of black and white females and found them to be similar. Cassens (1966) factor-analyzed a 62-item biographical questionnaire in samples of managers from a number of different countries. He found that of the 10 factors identified, nine were generalizable across cultures. As noted by Mumford and Owens (1987), these findings suggest that cultural groups having similar life histories are likely to result in similar biographic structures.

Factor Stability

Several studies have examined the stability of dimensional structures over time, samples, and age groups. Owens and Schoenfeldt (1979) looked at the predictive characteristics of orthogonal principal components derived from large samples of college students tested over a period of several years. More specifically, they were predicting an array of criteria, including such things as academic performance, choice of major, and participation in activities for successive groups of students. They noted that the results were sufficiently stable to be maintained in independent samples, with almost no loss in predictive power.

Corroborating this, Mumford and Owens (1984) found generalizability of results in the biographic factors derived from looking at three background questionnaires administered to seven cohorts over a 10-year interval. These results suggest dimensions derived from biographic items generalize to similar independent samples.

Excellent information exists to suggest that the dimensional structures obtained from background data items are stable over substantial periods of time. Eberhardt and Muchinsky (1982) readministered the Owens and Schoenfeldt (1979) 118-item background questionnaire to a sample of midwestern first-year college students some 10 years later. The factorial dimensions obtained for males were substantially similar to those of Owens and Schoenfeldt (1979), but those for females were markedly different. Interestingly, the nature of the shifts indicated increasing similarity among men and women, suggesting a possible shift in the role of women over the decade interval. Lautenschlager and Shaffer (1987) reanalyzed the data from both studies, and their findings suggest that the instability of the factor structure for women resulted from shortening the background questionnaire from 389 items to 118 items, rather than from shifts in women's roles. When only the 118 items were factor-analyzed for men and women in the earlier sample, the two solutions, obtained 10 years apart, were virtually identical.

Other studies examined age effects on the dimensionality of background data inventories. Mumford, Shaffer, Ames, and Owens (1983) examined the stability of the male and female dimensional structures produced by a common item pool in two age groups known to be facing different developmental tasks associated with their postcollege job and career status. Highly different dimensional structures were obtained in these two age groups for both men and women. This conclusion was supported in a separate study by Mumford (1986), who found that very different kinds of background data dimensions emerged from item pools tailored to capture developmentally significant behaviors and experiences occurring in adolescence, youth, and young adulthood. The common theme from these several studies is the observation that when individuals representing different age groups have shifts in the nature of their experiences, different dimensional structures will be required to capture the variance in responses to background items.

CONFIRMATORY FACTOR ANALYSIS

Confirmatory factor analysis (CFA) has received considerable attention in recent years. This technique has been made possible through the existence of distributional theory in maximum likelihood factor analysis that allows for specific model testing in the form of confirmatory factor analysis (Jöreskog, 1969; Jöreskog & Sörbom, 1981).

As described by Bobko (1991), the logic associated with confirmatory factor analysis is straightforward, though the statistical estimation procedures are complex. On the basis of theory or prior empirical results, a researcher may have an explicit hypothesis about the underlying factor structure of a particular domain. For example, a set of biographic items may be constructed to represent several preconceived dimensions. After administration of the items to a suitable sample, it would be possible to confirm the hypothesized structure from the responses to items by establishing a hypothesized pattern of factor loadings and/or factor correlations. These hypothesized parameters are fixed in advance such that the maximum likelihood estimation of the remaining parameters is made conditional on the fixed values (Bobko, 1991). The fit of the resultant model can be tested using the chi-square test. If the hypothesized model is not rejected, it is possible to conclude that the model is an "acceptable candidate" for consideration as the theoretical structure that fits the data (Bobko, 1991, p. 668). Thus, theoretically, the indeterminacies found in exploratory factor analysis are not present in CFA. However, care has to be taken in specifying a model that is identified. If the model is not identified, a unique solution cannot be obtained, and the estimation of the factor loadings is not possible.

There have been few examples using confirmatory procedures with biographic data. Schoenfeldt and Mendoza (1988) developed a biographic questionnaire designed to measure managerial effectiveness. The 209 items were written to measure the 10 dimensions (representing 3 general constructs) of the conceptualization of the managerial role suggested by Steger, Manner, Bernstein, and May (1975). The final questionnaire was administered over a three-year period to approximately 1,500 students attending summer orientation conferences.

For the confirmatory factor model, the hypothesis matrix consisted of the 10 dimensions of the conceptualization of the managerial role, 6 competency dimensions or functions (administration, technical-professional, influence-control, sales, training-development, forecasting-planning), 3 roles (evaluator, motivator, director), and a managerial style dimension. Biographic items were hypothesized to have a loading of 1.00 on the dimension they were written to measure and a loading of zero on the remaining 9 dimensions. Not all of the 209 items were hypothesized to load on 1 of the dimensions.

LISREL VI was used to develop dimensions that replicate the model. The LISREL procedure confirmed the existence of most, but not all, of the dimensions. Because previous research (Schoenfeldt, 1979) suggested that the six functions and three roles of the management model collapse into two major dimensions, the first primarily interpersonal (e.g., sales, influence-control, motivation) and the second primarily substantive (e.g., administration, technical-professional, forecasting-planning), a LISREL model with two dimensions was explored. These two major dimensions were confirmed in the LISREL analysis.

Although not involving confirmatory factor analysis per se, the study by Hansen (1989) used a procedure related to CFA and illustrates the model testing procedure. Hansen (1989) proposed a causal model of the industrial accident process, and he used LISREL VI to test the model with data gathered on 362 chemical industry workers. The model proposed that social traits (maladjustment), some characteristics of neurosis, cognitive ability, employee age, and job experience would have independent causal effects on the accident criterion. The results showed the social maladjustment and distractibility variables to be significant causal parameters of accidents. Further, the data provided a reasonable fit to the model, although there was much variance in the criterion not explained by the model.

One reason for the scarcity of research using confirmatory factor analysis with biographic data has to do with the large number of parameters that need to be estimated in conjunction with the procedure. Specific model testing using a hypothesized factor theory to guide the analysis requires reliable measurement vehicles and understanding of the data. While biographic scales tend to be reliable, relying on separate items does not produce sufficient stability to obtain the needed goodness of fit between the items and the hypothesized model. For those desiring to use biographic data with confirmatory factor analysis, the solution is to combine multiple items into mini-homogenous scales. These scales will then provide a reliable basis for the model testing.

THE VALIDITY OF BIOGRAPHICAL DATA FACTORS

Validity is defined as the accuracy of inferences made from scores. In some cases, these inferences have to do with future events, and the logical test is a correlation between test scores and criterion measures. In other applications, these inferences have to do with the constructs being measured and the degree to which they contribute to understanding. Here, the test of validity is more elusive and relates to the sustained value of the theory engendered.

PREDICTIVE VALIDITY

Factorial Prediction

As summarized by Mumford and Owens (1987), several studies have demonstrated the predictive validity of biographical factors. Morrison, Owens, Glennon, and Albright (1962) factored 3 criteria and 75 biographical items that had been administered to 418 petroleum research scientists. They found that 5 factors yielded significant prediction of creativity and performance. In a related study, Morrison (1977) used 8 background factors to predict performance of a sample of 250 processing and heavy equipment operators. Cross-validated multiple Rs of 0.35 and 0.53 were obtained from a weighted combination of scores on these scales.

In a series of studies, Vandeventer, Taylor, Collins, and Boone (1983) found that scores on background data factors would predict success in air traffic controller's school. In another study, Engdahl (1980) found that biographical factors predicted occupational values.

A series of studies by Owens and his colleagues found that scores on background data factors derived in earlier developmental periods would predict scores on background data factors derived in later development periods (Lucchesi, 1984; Mumford, 1986; Neiner & Owens, 1982). Neiner and Owens (1985) were successful in using biographical factors to predict single-item job choice criteria among college graduates six years after the original biographical data were collected. These studies have important implications for the predictive value of factors derived from biographical data items.

Empirical Prediction

A major review of empirical prediction using biographical data was undertaken by Reilly and Chao (1982). Their report summarized 44 studies involving a total of over 11,000 subjects. Each of these studies used empirical item weighting to predict a criterion of interest and, in addition, employed a cross-validation of results. The average cross-validated criterion correlation was a respectable 0.35.

At least two studies have examined the cross-cultural generalizability of biodata items. Hinrichs, Haanpera, and Sonkin (1976) developed a 21-item biographical key to predict sales success in Finland and Sweden. Validity in the Finnish and Swedish samples was 0.72. The empirical key was then cross-validated in Sweden ($r = 0.42$), Norway ($r = 0.56$), the United States ($r = 0.33$), Portugal ($r = .0.38$), and France ($r = 0.24$). Results were significant for Sweden, Norway, and the United States, but did not reach significance for Portugal or France. The authors concluded that the general pattern, including those that did not reach statistical significance, suggested that there is some cross-national validity of significant biographical patterns related to success in the sales occupation under study.

In another study, Brown, Corrigan, Stout, and Dalessio (1987) also demonstrated that empirical keys can generalize across cultures. Biographical keys to predict survival and production of life insurance sales representatives were developed using samples from the United States, Canada, and South Africa. These keys were then cross-validated in each of the other countries and on two smaller groups from Great Britain and Australia. The three keys (United States, Canada, and South Africa) were similar, with an average intercorrelation of 0.76. Validities with the three keys ranged from 0.11 to 0.36, and averaged 0.20. Only one of the validities, which resulted from using the South African key to predict in Australia ($r = 0.11$), was not statistically significant. The results suggest that the same biographical items, scaled in the same way, predict life insurance sales success across these English-speaking cultures.

Empirical Versus Factorial Prediction

Although there are a number of studies in which biographical factors have been developed, few studies have compared the predictiveness of factors with the predictiveness of empirical keys using the same items (Mitchell & Klimoski, 1982). Studies by Hornick, James, and Jones (1977) and Berkeley (1953) used both procedures, but neither study reported differences between cross-validities for the two scoring methods (Mitchell & Klimoski, 1982).

One of the few studies to compare empirically and factorially derived keys was that of Mitchell and Klimoski (1982). They developed 88 biographic items for administration to potential real estate sales associates, the criterion being license attainment. A total of 689 real estate students completed the questionnaire. Empirical keys were developed using a cross-tabulation procedure to develop weights.

Items were continuous and were factor-analyzed using a component model to form the rational scales. Six principal-axis factors, accounting for 31.5 percent of the total variance, were rotated using an orthogonal (varimax) procedure. Factor scores were computed and related to the licensure criterion using a multiple regression procedure.

TABLE 4 Obtained Validity Coefficients

Scoring Method	Derivation ($n = 266$)	Cross-validation ($n = 359$)
Rational (component)	.355	.362
Empirical (weighted application blank)	.592	.462

The Mitchell and Klimoski (1982) results are shown in Table 4. Both procedures produced significant results, with the empirical prediction being significantly higher using the empirical approach. In terms of obtained criterion variance accounted for by the cross-validities, an 8.2 percent improvement occurs in favor of the empirical ($r^2 = .213$) over the rational ($r^2 = .131$) approach. The procedures were also compared using a hits/misses frequency tabulation. The rational approach correctly classified 232 persons, whereas the empirical approach correctly classified 245 persons, for a net gain of 13 persons and a 5.6 percent improvement in favor of the empirical approach. These results led Mitchell and Klimoski (1982, p. 416) to conclude that "the practical differences between the two approaches appear to be modest," with the empirical approach offering at least some benefit beyond that obtained by the rational approach.

The Mitchell and Klimoski (1982) results are in line with conventional wisdom, namely, that empirical procedures will have greater shrinkage following cross-validation, but they will result in greater predictive validity. What is unknown is the extent to which factorial scales will show greater generalizability and stability. As was noted by Mumford and Owens (1987), this conclusion finds some support in a comparison of the results obtained in the Morrison et al. (1962) factorial study of innovation among petroleum scientists with the results obtained in the Smith, Albright, Glennon, and Owens (1961) study of empirical keys in predicting the same criteria in the same sample.

CONSTRUCT VALIDITY

Although further research may demonstrate the value of biographic factors in direct prediction, we have already seen that the real gain in employing biographic factors is through alternate models of prediction. The seminal work along these lines was that of Owens (1968, 1971). In this conceptualization, Owens (1971) proposed biographic factors as the basis for understanding individual differences, and he used these factors to form subgroups such that individuals with similar backgrounds (vis-à-vis the biographic factors) would be grouped together. The idea was to develop a more general descriptive system formulated by identifying modal patterns of individual development without reference to a particular criterion measure.

The basic methodology outlined by Owens (1971) and adapted for the person–job match by Schoenfeldt (1974) envisioned the following series of steps:

1. Designing a biographic questionnaire measuring the major developmental experiences of the target group
2. Administering the biographic questionnaire to a large sample
3. Summarizing item responses through principal components factor analysis (in most cases, separate factor analyses would be undertaken for major population groups, such as men and women)
4. Scoring individuals on the biographic dimensions so as to form a profile of scores for each individual
5. Calculating an intersubject similarity matrix (e.g., D^2 by Cronbach and Gleser, 1953) to assess the similarity between each person's profile and those of all other members of the sample
6. Subgrouping using a clustering procedure (e.g., Ward & Hook, 1963) to identify subgroups of similar individuals (Feild & Schoenfeldt, 1975)
7. Summarizing mean differences between subgroup members and the sample as a whole on background data items and factor scores to describe each subgroup

This procedure was used in a series of over 50 studies, the results of which were summarized by Owens and Schoenfeldt (1979). Overall, the research indicated that membership in background data subgroups, defined from factorially derived biographical items, was an effective predictor of a variety of criteria. In addition, the model proposed by Owens (1971) resulted in a far-reaching understanding of how background characteristics related to future events.

POTENTIAL APPLICATIONS
AND SPECIAL MERITS

The study by Schoenfeldt (1989; Schoenfeldt, Varca, & Mendoza, 1992) is exemplary of the applications of factorial methodology with biographical data. The study illustrated a procedure for the development of a biographical inventory around the results of a job analysis. Key dimensions affecting the behavior of interests were identified, then the items were built to represent the dimensions. Later the inventory was factor-analyzed to see if the dimensions were captured by the items and to gain further understanding of the dimensions themselves. The investigators used factor analysis instead of confirmatory factor analysis because little was known about the dimensions. If more had been known about the dimensions, a confirmatory factor analysis could have been performed, given adequate item reliability. Clearly, a task for researchers is the one of generating biographical items that measure the dimension of interest while keeping the scale as unidimensional as possible. Perhaps, as we gain more understanding of the important dimensions in biodata and their relation to performance, the chore of generating items to measure specific dimensions will become more efficient.

POTENTIAL AVENUES FOR FUTURE RESEARCH

One challenge for future generations of researchers is to establish developmental biographical dimensions that can be measured consistently across studies and that are related to the performance of different tasks. As is implied in this chapter, this is not an easy task and is one that still is in its infancy. But such advancement would allow for a variety of developments in the use and understanding of biographical data not yet possible. For one, it is possible to envision a computerized approach to the construction of biographical inventories in which items are selected from a large calibrated pool of items. The approach could be similar to the one now used in computerized adaptive testing for cognitive tests. After establishing a subject's age and sex, and the purpose of the inventory, a number of preliminary questions could be asked of the subject. On the basis of the subject's responses to these items, the computer would select a number of additional items, one at a time, to measure the dimension or dimensions of interest. Clearly, such a system would be difficult to design and implement, in that it would involve the integration and compilation of many well-designed factor analytic studies and developmental research. In theory, however, the task seems attainable and worth pursuing.

SUMMARY

Factor analysis has made important contributions to the development and understanding of biographical data. Many of the factor analytic studies have shown similarities in factor content. These results are summarized in Table 1.

Although the results were consistent to a degree across different item pools, each factor analysis also tended to reflect the item pool from which it originated. The factors were not only stable over time in the prediction of job performance, but in many cases the factors generalized across different populations.

The role of confirmatory factor analysis in the development of biographical inventories was also examined. Confirmatory factor analysis consisted of developing the biographical questionnaire around a set of target dimensions that had been identified by a job analysis or through other means. The role of the confirmatory factor analysis was one of verifying that, indeed, those dimensions were captured by the inventory. So rather than developing an all-encompassing biographical questionnaire, the aim was to construct a questionnaire that reflected a set of a priori dimensions. Such an a priori approach is more likely to lead to theory development.

REFERENCES

Asher, J. J. (1972). The biographical item: Can it be improved? *Personnel Psychology, 25,* 251–269.

Baehr, M. E., & Williams, G. B. (1967). Underlying dimensions of personal background data and their relationship to occupational classification. *Journal of Applied Psychology, 51,* 481–490.

Baehr, M. E., & Williams, G. B. (1968). Prediction of sales success from factorially determined dimensions of personal background data. *Journal of Applied Psychology, 63,* 98–103.

Barrick, M. R., & Mount, M. K. (1991). The Big Five personality dimensions and job performance: A meta-analysis. *Personnel Psychology, 44,* 1–26.

Berkeley, M. H. (1953, July). *A comparison between the empirical and rational approaches for keying a heterogeneous test* (Research Bulletin 53-24). Lackland Air Force Base, TX: 6570th Personnel Research Laboratory Human Resources Research Center.

Bobko, P. (1991). Multivariate correlational analysis. In M. D. Dunnette & L. M. Hough (Eds.), *Handbook of industrial and organizational psychology* (2d ed., vol. 1, pp. 637–686). Palo Alto, CA: Consulting Psychologists Press.

Brown, S. H., Corrigan, J. E., Stout, J. D., & Dalessio, A. T. (1987, August). *The transportability of biodata keys across English-speaking cultures.* Paper presented at the annual meeting of the American Psychological Association, New York.

Cassens, F. P. (1966). *Cross-cultural dimensions of executive life history antecedents.* Greensboro, NC: Creativity Research Institute, The Richardson Foundation.

Cattell, R. B., & Stice, G. F. (1957). *Handbook for the Sixteen Personality Factor Questionnaire.* Champaign, IL: Institute of Personality and Ability Testing.

Cronbach, L. J., & Gleser, G. (1953). Assessing similarity between profiles. *Psychological Bulletin, 50,* 456–473.

Digman, J. M. (1990). Personality structure: Emergence of the five-factor model. *Annual Review of Psychology, 41,* 417–440.

Eberhardt, B. J., & Muchinsky, P. M. (1982). An empirical investigation of the factor stability of Owens's Biographical Questionnaire. *Journal of Applied Psychology, 67,* 714–727.

Engdahl, B. E. (1980). *The structure of biographical data and its relationship to needs and values.* Unpublished doctoral dissertation, University of Minnesota, Minneapolis.

Feild, H. S., & Schoenfeldt, L. F. (1975). Ward and Hook revisited: A two-part procedure for overcoming a deficiency in the grouping of persons. *Educational and Psychological Measurement, 35,* 171–173.

Ferguson, L. W. (1962). *The heritage of industrial psychology.* Hartford, CT: Author.

Fleishman, E. A. (1988). Some new frontiers in personnel selection research. *Personnel Psychology, 41,* 679–701.

Goldberg, L. R. (1993). The structure of phenotypic personality traits. *American Psychologist, 48,* 26–34.

Goldsmith, D. B. (1922). The use of personal history blanks as a salesmanship test. *Journal of Applied Psychology, 6,* 149–155.

Gonter, D. (1979). *Comparison of blacks and whites on background data measures.* Athens, GA: Institute for Behavioral Research.

Guilford, J. P. (1956). The structure of intellect. *Psychological Bulletin, 53,* 267–293.

Guilford, J. P. (1967). *The nature of human intelligence.* New York: McGraw-Hill.

Guilford, J. S., Zimmerman, W., & Guilford, J. P. (1976). *The Guilford-Zimmerman Temperament Survey handbook.* Palo Alto, CA: Consulting Psychologists Press.

Guion, R. M. (1965). *Personnel testing.* New York: McGraw-Hill.

Hansen, C. P. (1989). A causal model of the relationship among accidents, biodata, personality, and cognitive factors. *Journal of Applied Psychology, 74,* 81–90.

Henry, E. (1966). Conference on the use of biographical data in psychology. *American Psychologist, 21,* 247–249.

Hinrichs, J. R., Haanpera, S., & Sonkin, L. (1976). Validity of a biographical information blank across national boundaries. *Personnel Psychology, 29,* 417–421.

Hogan, R. T. (1991). Personality and personality measurement. In M. D. Dunnette & L. M. Hough (Eds.), *Handbook of industrial and organizational psychology* (2d ed., vol. 2, pp. 753–831). Palo Alto, CA: Consulting Psychologists Press.

Hornick, C. W., James, L. R., & Jones, A. P. (1977). Empirical item keying versus a rational approach to analyzing a psychological climate questionnaire. *Applied Psychological Measurement, 1,* 489–500.

Humphreys, L. G. (1981). The primary mental abilities. In M. P. Friedman, J. P. Das, & N. O'Connor (Eds.), *Intelligence and learning*. New York: Plenum.

Jöreskog, K. (1969). A general approach to confirmatory maximum likelihood factor analysis. *Psychometrika, 34,* 183–202.

Jöreskog, K., & Sörbom, D. (1981). *LISREL VI: Analysis of linear structural relations by maximum likelihood and least square methods*. Chicago: National Educational Resources.

Korman, A. K. (1968). The prediction of managerial performance: A review. *Personnel Psychology, 21,* 295–322.

Lautenschlager, G. J., & Shaffer, G. S. (1987). Reexamining the component stability of Owens's Biographical Questionnaire. *Journal of Applied Psychology, 72,* 149–152.

Lucchesi, C. Y. (1984). *The prediction of job satisfaction, life satisfaction and job level from autobiographical dimensions: A longitudinal application of structural equation modeling*. Unpublished doctoral dissertation, University of Georgia, Athens.

Matteson, M. G., Osburn, H. G., & Sparks, C. P. (1969). *A computer-based methodology for constructing homogeneous keys with applications to biographical data* (Report No.1). Houston, TX: University of Houston, Personnel Psychology Services Center.

Mitchell, T. W., & Klimoski, R. J. (1982). Is it rational to be empirical? A test of methods for scoring biographical data. *Journal of Applied Psychology, 67,* 411–418.

Morrison, R. F. (1977). A multivariate model for the occupational placement decision. *Journal of Applied Psychology, 62,* 271–277.

Morrison, R. F., Owens, W. A., Glennon, J. R., & Albright, L. E. (1962). Factored life history antecedents of industrial research performance. *Journal of Applied Psychology, 46,* 281–284.

Mumford, M. D. (1986). *The description of individual differences in development: Cross-time versus point-in-time summarizations*. (Available from Michael D. Mumford, Department of Psychology, George Mason University, 4400 University Drive, Fairfax, VA 22030).

Mumford, M. D. (1988, April). *Validating background data measures: Some thoughts on constructs, content, and criteria*. Paper presented at the annual meeting of the Society for Industrial and Organizational Psychology, Dallas.

Mumford, M. D., & Nickels, B. J. (1989). *Making sense of people's lives: Applying principles of content and construct validity to background data*. (Available from Michael D. Mumford, Department of Psychology, George Mason University, 4400 University Drive, Fairfax, VA 22030).

Mumford, M. D., & Owens, W. A. (1984). Individuality in a developmental context: Some empirical and theoretical considerations. *Human Development, 27,* 84–108.

Mumford, M. D., & Owens, W. A. (1987). Methodology review: Principles, procedures, and findings in the application of background data measures. *Applied Psychological Measurement, 11,* 1–31.

Mumford, M. D., Shaffer, G. S., Ames, S. D., & Owens, W. A. (1983). *Analysis of PCEI responses over time*. Athens, GA: Institute for Behavioral Research.

Mumford, M. D., Shaffer, G. S., Jackson, K. E., Neiner, A., Denning, D., & Owens, W. A. (1983). *Male-female differences in the structure of background data measures*. Athens, GA: Institute for Behavioral Research.

Neiner, A. G., & Owens, W. A. (1985). Using biodata to predict job choice among college graduates. *Journal of Applied Psychology, 70,* 127–136.

Nickels, B. J., & Mumford, M. D. (1989). *Exploring the structure of background data measures: Implications for item development and scale validation.* (Available from Michael D. Mumford, Department of Psychology, George Mason University, 4400 University Drive, Fairfax, VA 22030).

Owens, W. A. (1968). Toward one discipline of scientific psychology. *American Psychologist, 23,* 782–785.

Owens, W. A. (1971). A quasi-actuarial basis for individual assessment. *American Psychologist, 26,* 992–999.

Owens, W. A. (1976). Background data. In M. D. Dunnette (Ed.), *Handbook of industrial and organizational psychology.* New York: Rand McNally.

Owens, W. A., & Schoenfeldt, L. F. (1979). Toward a classification of persons. *Journal of Applied Psychology, 64,* 569–607.

Reilly, R. R., & Chao, G. T. (1982). Validity and fairness of some alternative employee selection procedures. *Personnel Psychology, 35,* 1–62.

Russell, W., & Cope, G. V. (1925). Method of rating the history of achievements of applicants. *Publication of Personnel Studies, 3,* 202–219.

Schoenfeldt, L. F. (1974). Utilization of manpower: Development and evaluation of an assessment-classification model for matching individuals with jobs. *Journal of Applied Psychology, 59,* 583–595.

Schoenfeldt, L. F. (1989, August). *Biographical data as the new frontier in employee selection research.* Paper presented at the annual meeting of the American Psychological Association, New Orleans.

Schoenfeldt, L. F., & Mendoza, J. L. (1988, August). *The content and construct validation of a biographical questionnaire.* Paper presented at the annual meeting of the American Psychology Association, Atlanta.

Schoenfeldt, L. F., Varca, P., & Mendoza, J. L. (1992, January). *Selecting customer service oriented employees: New applications of biographical data.* (Available from L. Schoenfeldt, Department of Management, Texas A&M University, College Station, TX 77843-4221).

Schuh, A. L. (1967). The predictability of employee tenure: A review of the literature. *Personnel Psychology, 20,* 133–152.

Smith, W. J., Albright, L. E., Glennon, J. R., & Owens, W. A. (1961). The prediction of research competence and creativity from personal history. *Journal of Applied Psychology, 45,* 59–62.

Spearman, C. (1904). "General intelligence" objectively determined and measured. *American Journal of Psychology, 15,* 201–293.

Steger, J. A., Manners, G., Bernstein, A. J., & May, R. (1975). The three dimensions of the R & D manager's job. *Research Management, 18*(3), 32–37.

Tett, R. P., Jackson, D. N., & Rothstein, M. (1991). Personality measures as predictors of job performance: A meta-analytic review. *Personnel Psychology, 44,* 703–742.

Thurstone, L. L. (1938). Primary mental abilities. *Psychometric Monographs, 4.*

Thurstone, L. L. (1947). *Multiple factor analysis.* Chicago: University of Chicago Press.

Vandeventer, A. D., Taylor, D. K., Collins, W. E., & Boone, J. O. (1983). *Three studies of biographical factors associated with success in air traffic control specialist screening/training at the FAA Academy*. Washington, DC: Federal Aviation Administration.

Vernon, P. E. (1961). *The structure of human abilities*. New York: Wiley.

Ward, J. H., & Hook, M. E. (1963). Application of an hierarchical grouping procedure to a problem of subgrouping profiles. *Educational and Psychological Measurement, 23*, 69–81.

Weiss, D. J. (1976). Multivariate procedures. In M. D. Dunnette (Ed.), *Handbook of industrial and organizational psychology*. New York: Rand McNally.

Scaling Biodata Through Subgrouping

Michael Hein
Middle Tennessee State University

Scott Wesley
Educational Testing Service

DESCRIPTION

Although the predictive power of well-developed empirically keyed background data scales is documented (Asher, 1974; Ghiselli, 1973; Mumford & Owens, 1987; Mumford & Stokes, 1992), questions have been raised concerning the efficiency and substantive meaningfulness of these scales (Dunnette, 1962; Guilford, 1959; Korman, 1968; O'Leary, 1973; Owens, 1976; Pace & Schoenfeldt, 1977). The most salient criticism revolves around the specificity of empirical keys to the criterion and sample at hand (Thayer, 1977). Because empirical keys are constructed by contrasting the responses of an applicant group with the responses of incumbents, such as high performers, the predictive power of the measure is somewhat contingent on the characteristics of the applicants (Dunnette, 1962; Dunnette, Kirchner, Erickson, & Banas, 1960; Wernimont, 1962) and the particular criterion measure used in performance assessment (Owens, 1976; Thayer, 1977). Although this does not necessarily preclude stability and validity generalization (Brown, 1981; Richardson, Bellows, Henry, & Co., 1984), it does make it difficult to develop keys that will predict multiple criteria.

When investigators must predict performance on multiple criteria across a variety of situations and populations, the need to develop separate keys becomes burdensome. Recognition of this problem led Owens (1968, 1971, 1976) to recommend the construction of descriptive systems with greater generality. This may be accomplished by identifying modal patterns of individual development. Unlike empirical keys, the developmental patterns are based on communalities of life experiences and behaviors rather than on empirical relationships to criteria.

In Owens' work, subgrouping emerged as an attempt to develop general descriptive systems. In developing these systems, subgrouping also contributes to an integration of the idiographic and nomothetic approaches in psychology (Cronbach, 1957, 1975; Mumford, Snell, & Hein, in press). The idiographic approach holds that understanding may be derived from examining each individual's unique pattern of life history experiences (e.g., Pervin, 1984). This approach lacks both theoretical parsimony and practical utility when attempting to predict criteria for a large number of individuals. In contrast, the nomothetic approach, which searches for laws of general behavior, provides little in the way of explaining a particular individual's behavior. Subgrouping procedures identify groups of individuals whose prior behavior and experiences are similar enough to be summarized with little loss in information about individual group members.

Background data prediction is based on the general premise that the best predictor of what an individual will do in the future is what he or she has done in the past (Owens, 1976). The basis of subgrouping is a logical extension of this premise: That is, individuals who have behaved one way in the past will behave similarly in the future. Subgrouping is viable because of the interrelated nature of human differences and the communality of many life experiences to which individuals within a given age and culture are exposed. With a limited number of relevant individual differences and experiences within a culture or subculture, it is likely that a relatively small number of patterns may be descriptive of a majority of individuals' life experiences (Mumford, Stokes, & Owens, 1990).

Subgrouping techniques, therefore, identify modal patterns of life history experiences. These modal patterns can be used to understand the developmental history of an individual and to predict future behavior based on his or her subgroup's pattern of past experiences and behavior. This allows for greater parsimony than an idiographic approach and more detail than a nomothetic one.

Scaling biographical items through a subgrouping procedure is a pattern- or person-oriented approach. It is differentiated from rational and factorial scaling techniques, which represent variable-oriented, nomothetic approaches. Within the variable-oriented approaches, one attempts to measure an individual's standing on a specific construct or set of constructs through the assessment of past behavior and experiences related to the development of the constructs. The investigator then assesses the degree of linear relationship between these constructs and criterion performance. Obviously, as the number of predictors or criteria increases, the complexity involved in assessing predictor–criterion relationships increases.

When multiple criteria are of interest, subgrouping has much to offer. First, it permits the quantification of general patterns of behavior and experience, which should yield better prediction of criteria than less behaviorally and experientially comprehensive predictors. Second, it allows for the prediction of criterion performance through multiple patterns. A basic concept here is adapted from the literature on aggregation bias, which holds that aggregation is an inappropriate summarization of data when the data are highly variable (James, 1982). In contrast, aggregating the data of subgroup members who share similar behaviors and experiences is an appropriate use of aggregation. It follows that when individuals can achieve criterion success through different mechanisms, identifying the mechanisms or predictive patterns of the mechanisms should yield greater prediction of criterion performance. Third, subgrouping methodology, as alluded to earlier, produces a more general predictive system by defining common developmental patterns appearing in the population that are not empirically constrained to a specific criterion measure. These general patterns of differential development can be used to predict multiple criteria in multiple settings (Brush & Owens, 1979; Schoenfeldt, 1974).

We must mention, however, that subgrouping is not appropriate for all situations. In particular, use of a subgrouping technique is limited by the fact that a rather large sample size ($N = 300$ to $1,000$) is necessary to assure that the resulting subgroups are adequately large ($N > 15$). Further, when developing a classification system, it is necessary to use both a derivation and holdout (cross-validation) sample. Subgrouping also requires a well-defined set of descriptor variables in order to obtain accurate classifications of individuals. Subgrouping, therefore, may not be an appropriate scaling technique with which to make personnel decisions when important job dimensions are not well defined or tapped by the item pool. Table 1 summarizes questions to be answered when considering the use of subgrouping.

TABLE 1   Determining When Subgrouping Is Appropriate

Are multiple criteria of interest?
Does job performance consist of many distinct dimensions?
Are individuals being placed into one of several possible alternative jobs?

Is the sample large enough?
To identify subgroups, enough individuals of the relevant types need to be
present in the applicant pool. A typical subgrouping study may require 300
to 1,000 individuals.

*Will criterion prediction be enhanced by capturing nonadditive moderator relationships
among the predictor set?*
If straightforward linear relationships between predictors and criteria are
anticipated, then another scaling technique is more appropriate. If, however,
different patterns of abilities are capable of contributing to successful criterion
performance (e.g., more than one type of person is capable of effective
performance), then subgrouping is a viable approach.

METHODOLOGY

ITEMS

Subgroups are defined by the items in the analysis through the application
of profile similarity measures (e.g., distances and correlations) and clustering algorithms. Therefore, the psychometric properties of items that enter
into the analyses should be appropriate for these techniques. Specifically,
items should be ordinal level or higher and should, as often as possible, be
measured on the same scale. Large differences in the scale of items, in
particular the number of alternatives, will affect item weighting. If large-
scale differences in items are unavoidable, items can be standardized before
the analysis. Standardization, however, may affect the discriminatory
power of variables and reduce the chance of detecting subgroup differences
(Matthews, 1979).

Item Selection

To ensure the most effective use of subgrouping methodology for
prediction, items should be selected or generated on the basis of domain
coverage. If the item pool is not broad and general, then general developmental patterns will not emerge in the subgroups. Good pattern definition
requires that items measure a wide range of situations and developmentally
significant, or salient, behavior and experiences. Items selected on the basis
of a theoretical rationale are more likely to yield separable and interpretable
subgroups than items selected on a purely empirical basis (Aldenderfer &
Blashfield, 1984). If subgrouping is being used to develop a predictive

classification system, then the first step is to identify developmental dimensions that the investigator hypothesizes are related to the criteria. Then items should be selected and/or generated that are thought to measure these developmental dimensions or to differentiate subgroups of individuals on these dimensions.

Data Reduction

Once the item set has been obtained, it is necessary to decide whether item data should be aggregated or scaled in any way before the cluster analysis. The data should be reliable over time and relatively independent. When combined, they should provide a good summarization of the individual or some specific aspect of the individual. Most studies of biodata subgroups conducted to date have used principal axes or principal components analysis to form scales from the life history items (Brush & Owens, 1979; Mumford & Owens, 1984; Owens & Schoenfeldt, 1979). These studies clustered individuals based on factor scores. Wesley (1989) grouped individuals directly from item data, citing the reliability and independence of the items and a desire to avoid aggregation across groups (Baehr & Williams, 1967; Shaffer, Saunders, & Owens, 1986). Of course, any form of aggregation results in some loss of information. Clustering on factor scores will result in some loss of distinction between groups that are not well separated in the cluster space and in possible loss of discriminating information (Rohlf, 1970). Clustering on item data, however, will result in highly correlated items acting as a weighting of the dimension being measured by those items (Aldenderfer & Blashfield, 1984). Therefore, if descriptor sets are constructed so that the number of items measuring a dimension are representative of the weights that would be desired for those dimensions, then the optimal approach is to subgroup individuals using item-level data. Additionally, if one wishes to maintain fine distinctions among clusters or if items are relatively independent of each other, as is often the case with biodata, then the use of item data is recommended. If, however, a weighting of dimensions by the number of items is not desired and the investigator is mainly concerned with clusters that are well separated in the cluster space, factor analysis or rational scale formation are feasible data reduction techniques. Thus, the recommendation to use item or scale scores is dependent on the investigator's overall objective and hypotheses about the data. It should be pointed out, however, that differences in the assignment of individuals to subgroups or the characteristics of resulting subgroups as a consequence of scaling technique have yet to be assessed directly.

Tesser and Lissitz (1973) and Lissitz and Schoenfeldt (1974) have argued that the predictive utility of subgrouping stems from its ability to capture nonadditive moderator relationships between predictors and criteria by other items or dimensions in the descriptor set. One influence on the decision to use item or scale scores may be the level at which the investigator believes these moderator relationships are occurring. In other words, if scale formation would eliminate single items that may act as moderators of other items, then subgrouping on item data may be necessary to capture the full relationship. If moderator effects are hypothesized at the scale level, however, factor analysis or rational scaling techniques could be employed without undue loss of information. This would result in a more reliable and, often, more easily interpretable set of subgroups. Once again, this is very likely to be influenced by the characteristics of the item pool (e.g., Are there enough items covering each relevant dimension to form a scale for that dimension?). Thus, we cannot overemphasize the need for careful construction of the initial item pool and development of a priori hypotheses about the relationships between variables in the predictor and criterion sets.

IDENTIFYING SUBGROUPS: CLUSTER ANALYSIS

The idea of empirically clustering entities was first proposed over 50 years ago by Zubin (1938) and Tryon (1939). The procedure, however, attracted little attention until the early 1960s, when the advent of computers made the procedure considerably less difficult and time-consuming (Blashfield, 1976). Two biologists, Robert Sokal and Peter Sneath, increased interest in the procedure with their seminal work, *Principles of Numerical Taxonomy* (Sokal & Sneath, 1963). Since then, the use of cluster analysis has expanded into several fields, including psychology, psychiatry, sociology, geography, and zoology.

Increased interest and use of the methodology has led to a proliferation of clustering algorithms. In 1979, Edelbrock estimated the number of algorithms at well over 100. It is beyond the scope of this chapter to review these procedures. The interested reader is referred to reviews by Aldenderfer and Blashfield (1984), Anderberg (1973), Everitt (1974), and Hartigan (1975).

Cluster analysis involves the use of statistical procedures and algorithms to create a classification system or taxonomy. In using a clustering procedure, information about the entities in a data set is reorganized into relatively homogeneous groups or "clusters." In work with biodata, the entities refer to individuals.

Similarity Measures
The raw data for a cluster analysis consists of N cases (individuals) measured on P variables. The similarity of each case's variable profile to the

profile of each other case is calculated and the result is an $N \times N$ similarity matrix. There are many ways to measure similarity or proximity. In the social sciences, the two most frequently used measures are correlation coefficients and distance measures (Aldenderfer & Blashfield, 1984; Garwood, Anderson, & Greengart, 1991). As noted by Cronbach and Gleser (1953), similarity between profiles can be based on *shape* (the pattern dips and rises across the variables), *scatter* (the dispersion of the scores around their average), and *elevation* (the mean score of the case over all the variables). Correlation coefficients are shape measurements. Distance measures are responsive to both elevation and shape, but elevation differences generally are the critical factor in generating the cluster solution (Aldenderfer & Blashfield, 1984).

The decision between correlational or distance measures should be based on whether the investigator wishes to focus on profile shape or elevation. Because life history items tend to be scaled along quantitative continua (e.g., On the average, how many hours per week of homework did you do in high school? In high school, how many close female friends did you have?), we look for differences in elevation and therefore use distance measures. We often use the squared Euclidean distance metric (d^2) because it provides a particularly effective index of distance (Rounds, Dawis, & Lofquist, 1987) and because it is sensitive to shape and scatter as well as elevation (Hamer & Cunningham, 1981).

CLUSTERING TECHNIQUES

Hierarchical Clustering

The most popular cluster analysis methods are the agglomerative hierarchical methods (Blashfield & Aldenderfer, 1978). These methods start with a search through the $N \times N$ similarity matrix. At each step in the clustering, the two clusters that are most similar are merged. Here, *cluster* refers to both individuals and to sets of individuals who had been merged at earlier steps.

The various agglomerative hierarchical methods differ only in their merger rules. For example, under the merger rule for single linkage, the clusters containing the two most similar individuals at a step are joined. Thus, only a single link between two individual cluster members is required for two clusters to join (Aldenderfer & Blashfield, 1984).

A frequently used hierarchical method is the Ward and Hook algorithm (Ward, 1963; Ward & Hook, 1963). This algorithm is designed to generate clusters in such a way that the variance within clusters is minimized. The method is based on the assumption that the loss of information about the individual at any clustering stage can be measured in terms of the total sum of squared deviations of every point from the centroid of the cluster to which the individual belongs. The algorithm is designed to join those clusters whose joining minimizes an increase in this error sum of squares. A solution is obtained based on its utility in maximizing between-cluster variance while minimizing within-cluster variance. It is of note that this procedure has demonstrated higher accuracy than other hierarchical procedures in classifying known populations from contrived sets of data (Blashfield, 1976; Blashfield & Morey, 1980; Kuiper & Fisher, 1975; Mojena, 1977).

Least Squares Clustering

With the Ward and Hook procedure it is advisable to control for the drift away from early assignees (Feild & Schoenfeldt, 1975; Gustafson, 1987; Lissitz & Schoenfeldt, 1974; Mumford & Owens, 1984; Owens & Schoenfeldt, 1979; Zimmerman, Jacobs, & Farr, 1982). Once assigned to a subgroup, the individual remains in that subgroup. As additional subjects are added, the profile of the subgroup may shift, leaving the early assignees on the periphery. Therefore, we use the Ward and Hook procedure to determine the number of subgroups to be formed, and a second clustering algorithm to allocate individuals to subgroups. For this, we typically use the nonhierarchical k-means analysis (MacQueen, 1967).* This procedure involves (a) dividing the data into a prespecified number of clusters (as determined from the Ward and Hook analysis); (b) computing the centroid of each of k cluster "seeds," which are the first k entities encountered; (c) assigning the remaining entities to the cluster with the centroid closest to the entity's profile; (d) computing new centroids for each cluster; (e) using these new centroid seeds for another assignment pass through the data; (f) recomputing centroids based on the second iteration; and (g) continuing iterations until no further reassignments occur (Anderberg, 1973).

---

* Feild and Schoenfeldt (1975) have recommended a similar two-step approach involving (a) an affirmation program that compares the profile of each subject to the profile of every subgroup and either affirms membership in the assigned subgroup or removes the individual from it, and (b) a discriminant analysis to reclassify poorly fitting individuals. Both methods attempt to correct for drift through the application of a least squares approach. The k-means procedure, however, uses a strict least squares algorithm, whereas the discriminant analysis is based on a weighted least squares approach, with variables being weighted to allow for the maximum discrimination among groups. To our knowledge, the degree to which the two procedures would result in different solutions for a real data set remains an empirical question.

TABLE 2   Ward and Hook Sample Output

Stage	Clusters	ESS*	Δ in ESS
283	20	5,436	77
284	19	5,514	78
285	18	5,593	79
286	17	5,674	81
287	16	5,759	85
288	15	5,846	87
289	14	5,941	95
290	13	6,043	102
291	12	6,147	104
292	11	6,253	106
293	10	6,371	118
294	9	6,491	120
295	8	6,630	139
296	7	6,782	152
297	6	6,970	188
298	5	7,177	207
299	4	7,503	326
300	3	7,947	444
301	2	8,745	798
302	1	11,552	2,807

* Error (within-subgroup) sum of squares

Determining the Number of Underlying Clusters

Because cluster analysis is used to generate homogeneous groups within a data set, determining the optimal number of groups is critical. Similarly, iterative procedures require the user to specify the number of groups thought to be present in the data prior to the creation of these groups by the procedure. Unfortunately, there are no satisfactory methods for determining the number of underlying clusters (Everitt, 1979). If anything, the number-of-clusters problem is more difficult than the familiar number-of-factors problem in factor analysis.

One method for estimating the number of underlying clusters in a data set is to observe the total error sum of squares (ESS) within clusters, after the clusters have been joined. Table 2 provides some sample output from a Ward and Hook procedure. The data set is 303 individuals measured on 25 variables. Each variable is measured on a five-point scale. The table provides the clustering stage, the number of clusters in the stage, the ESS of the joining clusters, and the change in the ESS (Δ_{ESS}) from the previous stage. To determine the appropriate number of underlying clusters, the

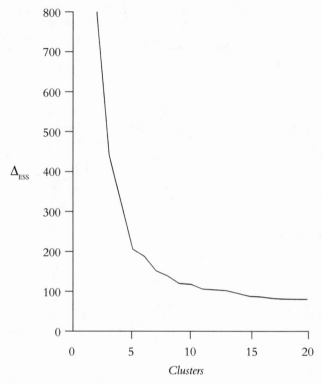

Δ_{ESS}

Clusters

Note: Δ_{ESS} associated with clusters 2 through 20 are plotted

FIGURE 1   Scree Plot for Determining the Number of Clusters

investigator can plot the Δ_{ESS} as a scree and look for a sharp jump between stages (see Figure 1). In Table 2, going from 11 groups to 10 groups results in a Δ_{ESS} of 118, an increase of 12 units over the previous change. Combining groups previous to this stage had resulted in minor Δ_{ESS} (i.e., 2 units). This suggests that 11 is a possible break point and that 11 groups may be a more accurate representation than 10 groups. Note that going from 10 to 9 only results in a 2-unit increase in change, while going from 9 to 8 results in a further 19-unit increase. This suggests that 9 groups may be a viable solution. As with factor analysis, the decision regarding the number of groups is partially influenced by the investigator's desired degree of parsimony. Going from 5 groups to 4 groups results in a very large Δ_{ESS}

(119 units). Thus, it seems unwise to consider a solution of fewer than 5 groups.

Whenever people are classified into a limited set of categories, the possibility exists that some people will not fit. These individuals have been referred to as *isolates* or, collectively, the *residue* (Bergman, 1988). When forming subgroups on background data, these individuals might represent truly rare patterns of life history events and/or measurement error. Bergman recommends retesting isolates in order to eliminate the possibility that the rare pattern is a result of measurement error. While retesting may be impractical or may not reclassify the individual into an existing subgroup, human resource management might, nevertheless, require that these individuals be classified in some way. Mumford et al. (1990) have suggested that these individuals be allowed partial classification in multiple subgroups based on their probability of membership in each subgroup. This is one method of handling rare patterns. Of course, if a pattern has been undersampled, it is likely that, over time, enough individuals with this pattern would be sampled to allow for the formation of a subgroup.

This raises the question of how many individuals are needed to determine that a subgroup exists. A subgroup of two individuals may represent a stable and legitimate pattern; however, decisions based on samples of less than 15 to 20 are unlikely to be accurate. Subgroups of less than 15 individuals should be examined closely to see if they can reasonably be combined with another subgroup based on the distances between the centroids of the clusters. Otherwise, until a sufficient sample of these individuals has been obtained, it may be necessary to treat them as partial members of two or more subgroups, as suggested by Mumford et al. (1990).

Developing Clusters Within or Across Gender

The evidence regarding the generality of biographical data for males and females is inconclusive. Ritchie and Boehm (1977) found that an empirical key developed on female managers was predictive for males, albeit with lower mean scores for the males. Nevo (1976) found higher validity coefficients for separate sex samples when attempting to predict military success, suggesting that the criterion for success was different for the two sexes. Mumford et al. (1983) obtained more interpretable subgroups with separate sex solutions than same sex solutions. Mumford, Snell, and Hein (in press), however, combined subgroups of different sexes to explain religious involvement. If the developmental patterns leading to successful performance or the definition of successful performance are expected to be substantially different for males and females, then the subgrouping should be done for each sex separately. Otherwise, it might be advisable to compare separate sex solutions with a combined sex solution and choose the solution that yields the clearest assignment of individuals to groups and the most interpretable subgroups.

Probability of Subgroup Membership

Once assignments are made with the clustering procedure, we verify them with a discriminant analysis. In this procedure, subgroup assignment is used as a classification variable, and the background data are used as predictors. Discriminant functions are generated, as well as each individual's probability of belonging to each subgroup. Individuals are assigned to the subgroup for which their probability of belonging is highest. A comparison of the assignments generated by the cluster analysis versus those made by the discriminant analysis may give some evidence of a good solution.

Assigning New Individuals to Clusters

New individuals (e.g., those from a holdout sample) may be classified by applying the discriminant functions generated on the derivation sample to the new individuals' responses to the biodata items. If the probabilities of subgroup membership show little shrinkage from the derivation sample to the holdout sample, then there is some evidence for the stability of the solutions (Owens & Schoenfeldt, 1979).

One advantage of subgrouping is that the solutions should be more stable than those generated through empirical keying. Stability of a subgrouping solution raises the question of how long a subgroup assignment will be valid for a given individual. A follow-up question concerns how long one can expect the solution to remain valid for the applicant population. The answers to these questions will depend, to some extent, on the characteristics of the item pool. If the pool captures major developmental dimensions and a wide range of job-relevant dimensions, then the subgrouping solution should have greater stability for the individual and the group. Subgroup assignment for the individual can change when the individual either passes through life experiences that are not covered by the items or has a critical experience that shifts the individual to another subgroup (Mumford, Wesley, & Shaffer, 1987). There are three conditions that can affect the subgrouping solution for a group of individuals: (a) a sociological or cultural change causes the developmental experiences of the current applicant group to be markedly different than the experiences of the derivation sample; (b) there is a major change in the demands of the job; or (c) there is a major change in the type of individual applying for the job (e.g., recessionary times bring on an influx of overqualified applicants).

GENERATING SUBGROUP DESCRIPTIONS

Differences Within Biodata Items

To appraise the characteristics and generate descriptions of the subgroups, we typically conduct a series of tests of mean differences. Here, each subgroup's mean scores on the descriptor items are contrasted with the mean scores of the group as a whole or minus the subgroup's data. Traditional significance tests do not apply here because the multivariate normality assumption has been violated (Aldenderfer & Blashfield, 1984). All differences greater than a predetermined amount (e.g., a quarter of a standard deviation) are considered relevant for interpretation purposes. This analysis is carried out separately for members of the derivation and holdout samples to appraise the stability of the observed differences. It may also be useful to conduct certain pairwise comparisons of subgroups to better understand pattern differences. Important differences and similarities may be masked when a subgroup is compared to the whole group. Further, the group mean may be an inappropriate use of aggregation (James, 1982).

The content of items yielding relevant and stable differences are then reviewed in order to formulate a developmentally oriented theory accounting for the origin of these differences and a brief consensual label to summarize them. These initial labels and interpretations are then reviewed by colleagues. As an example, Table 3 contains labels and descriptions of a few of the subgroups obtained by Wesley (1989).

Differences in Relationship to Reference Variables

The external validity of the interpretations can be assessed using a set of independent reference or marker variables. These variables might include measures of personality, cognitive style, vocational interest, and/or academic achievement. Based on the nature of the measures and the interpretations generated for each subgroup, hypotheses are formulated in terms of which of the subgroups will exhibit differential behavior on each reference measure. The extent of differential behavior that will indicate a meaningful difference is predetermined. As with the biodata items, we have used a quarter standard deviation difference from the overall mean as an indication of a meaningful difference.

VERIFYING SUBGROUPS: RELIABILITY AND VALIDITY

Two distinct assessments of reliability are relevant to the use of subgrouping techniques as a method of scaling life history items: (a) the reliability of the descriptors or items and (b) the reliability of the resultant classification

TABLE 3   Sample Labels and Descriptions of Subgroups

Label	Description

Female Subgroups

Competitive Extroverts	Individuals of this subgroup tended to be raised in warm, supportive, middle-class families. The major characteristic of the subgroup was its high degree of involvement in athletics and physical activities. In high school they dated frequently, had many friends, and exhibited some facility for leadership. They enjoyed school, perhaps more for social aspects than academic reasons, as they showed only sample-typical achievement in their courses. In college these females tended to join social groups, like sororities, and continued to show involvement with athletics. They also showed higher than average religious involvement. They tended not to spend spare time reading or attending cultural events.
Social Liberal	These individuals tended to come from upper- and upper-middle-class families (i.e., 82% as compared to 52% for the sample). As adolescents they reported considerable parental latitude. During high school they tended to be unsuccessful in academics but socially and athletically involved. In college they led a rather nontraditional life-style. For example, 70 percent reported they had at some time lived with a member of the opposite sex in contrast to only 24 percent of the total sample. Also, twice as many subgroup members had demonstrated for a political or social cause as had the sample (51% to 24%). College years for this group were also marked by low religious involvement, an interest in art and literature, and high social activity.
Collegiate Explorers	One of the smaller and more complicated subgroups, the Collegiate Explorers expressed high interests in somewhat nontraditional areas during high school (e.g., they repaired things, they read business and sports magazines, and they were active in hobby clubs). They tended to come from lower-middle-class, restrictive families. Conflict with parents and siblings was apparent. Academically, this group was not successful (e.g., on an item concerning class standing, this group was more than a standard deviation below the overall group mean). In college there was an increase in social contact and interest in cultural activities. These females were much more typical of the other subgroups in college than in high school.

TABLE 3   Sample Labels and Descriptions of Subgroups (continued)

Label	Description
Male Subgroups	
Constricted Athletes	Individuals of this subgroup were raised in warm, supportive, middle- and upper-middle-class families. They tended to have very good relationships with their parents, particularly their fathers. The major characteristic of this subgroup was its very high involvement in athletics. Seven items related to physical activity and sports yielded a mean difference of at least a half standard deviation from the total sample. As a whole, the subgroup was gregarious, popular, and confident. Academically, they were about average. In college these males maintained a high level of activity in sports and did not pursue other activities, such as cultural events, religion, reading, or student government. They tended to be more conservative than other subgroups. A reasonably high percentage (33%) were married before graduation.
Disadvantaged Pragmatists	These individuals were raised by lower-middle- and middle-class parents with relatively little education. Their fathers tended to have lower-level occupations. In high school they were athletically active, but rather withdrawn socially and in other extracurricular areas. Outside interests in college were limited to athletics and religion. They tended to be more conservative than other subgroups. Many subgroup members worked and/or borrowed their way through school and only 5 of 78 (6%) planned to continue their education after college, compared to 15 percent of the total sample.
Adjusted Social Achievers	Typically, males in this subgroup were raised in warm and supportive upper-middle-class families. In high school they were successful in their courses (e.g., 63% graduated in the top 10% of their high school class, compared to 35% for the sample). They were popular, participated in clubs and student government, and were active in the church. In college they tended to join social groups like fraternities and to date frequently. Many subgroup members continued their involvement in student government.

From "Background Data Measures and Career Outcomes: Some Developmental Influences on Person-Job Matching" by S. Wesley, 1989, unpublished doctoral dissertation, Georgia Institute of Technology, Atlanta. Copyright 1989 by S. Wesley.

system. The relative independence of background data items generally precludes the use of internal consistency measures as a means of assessing item reliability. Retest reliability studies have, however, generally obtained coefficients in the .60 to .80 range, indicating impressive stability of responses, even over relatively long intervals (Mumford & Owens, 1987; Wesley, 1989).

Assessing the reliability of the obtained classification system is not as straightforward a proposition and, generally, has not been attempted. Assessment of stability across items, however, has been addressed by Hein and Mumford (1988). They examined profile stability by rationally dividing the descriptor set in half, essentially creating parallel forms. Split-half reliability coefficients around .75 were obtained when the resultant profiles of dimension mean scores were correlated within preestablished subgroups. Stability of the structure has also been assessed by comparing solutions obtained across multiple samples (Anderson, 1972; Johnson, 1972; Owens & Schoenfeldt, 1979). Obtaining similar subgroup solutions across multiple samples provides evidence for the generality of the classification system.

When addressing the assessment of the validity of the subgrouping solution, it is useful to think both in terms of the internal validity and the external validity of the solution (Cook & Campbell, 1979; Fleishman & Mumford, 1991). Internal validity refers to the clarity of the subgrouping solution (e.g., Does the solution identify meaningful differences between groups of individuals?). Some indicators of internal validity are the proportion of people who can be unambiguously classified into a subgroup, the ratio of between-cluster distances to within-cluster distances, and the degree to which the resultant classification system lends itself to psychological interpretation. The first two indicators of internal validity can be statistically assessed via discriminant analysis and multivariate analysis of variance. Although use of these techniques for descriptive purposes is feasible, once again one must bear in mind that after a cluster analysis has been used to identify subgroups, traditional tests of statistical significance with other multivariate techniques are not appropriate, as the assumption of multivariate normality is not met (Aldenderfer & Blashfield, 1984). A number of statistical indices for internal validity have been proposed in the clustering literature. Milligan (1981) empirically examined 30 of these indices and identified 6 that seemed to be valid measures of the degree of true cluster recovery in a data set. Of the 6, Baker and Hubert's (1972) gamma index performed best in most situations. The use of these measures, however, depends on the identification of an appropriate null distribution. Further, these internal statistical indices do not seem to be readily comparable across levels of hierarchical clustering solutions. Thus, although statistical heuristics can be developed, assessment of internal validity remains a largely subjective procedure.

Examination of the external validity of the classification system is inherent in the use of subgroups for predictive purposes. External validation of a predictive system is an assessment of the ability of the classification structure to differentiate individuals on relevant criterion variables. Several statistical methods, including discriminant analysis, chi-square tests, multivariate analysis of variance, and canonical correlation analysis, have been used to assess the external validity of subgrouping procedures for a variety of criterion variables.

As previously mentioned, cross-validation of the subgroup structure can be achieved by applying discriminant functions derived from the original classification sample to the biodata responses of unclassified individuals. If the majority of new individuals can be successfully classified into the existing structure, then there is some evidence of the reliability, internal validity, and domain coverage of the system. However, cross-validation of the subgroup structure is not evidence for the external validity of the classification system. Evidence for external validity is provided by a cross-validation of the relationship of the subgroup structure to the criterion variables. A holdout, cross-validation, or double-cross-validation sampling strategy could be used for this purpose.

APPLYING SUBGROUPS

Although the number of empirical investigations employing subgroups is limited due to the relatively recent emergence of the technique, background data subgroups have been successfully applied to the prediction of educational and job choice, educational and job performance, and social adjustment (Mumford & Stokes, 1992). Additionally, Mumford et al. (1990) have developed an approach to the use of subgroups for individual prediction based on the probability of subgroup membership and the probability that a member of a subgroup will exhibit satisfactory performance on the criterion. Undoubtedly, the most common use of biographical information has been for selection purposes. The application of the probability approach to selection purposes is rather straightforward. Once the probability of an individual's belonging to a given subgroup and the probability that a member of the subgroup will exhibit acceptable performance on the criterion of interest have been established, then the probability that the individual will exhibit acceptable criterion performance is the product of the two probabilities. This probability of acceptable performance for an individual can function as his or her predicted criterion

TABLE 4   Steps for Developing Background Data Subgroups for Selection

1. Conduct a thorough job analysis that includes an examination of the job-relevant KSAOs.

2. Select or develop items to measure life history experiences that are hypothesized to lead to the development of the job-relevant KSAOs. Include items designed to measure possible moderating experiences.

3. Decide on the level of data that is most appropriate (i.e., item data or factor scores).

4. Cluster the data to form subgroups.

5. Assess the reliability of the subgrouping solution.

6. Collect criterion data.

7. Determine the probability of each subgroup exhibiting acceptable performance on the criteria. Use only those individuals who have at least a .80 probability of belonging to one subgroup.

8. Calculate a predicted criterion score for each individual by multiplying the probability that he or she belongs to a subgroup by the probability of that subgroup exhibiting acceptable criterion performance.

9. Compute the initial validity estimate for the subgrouping procedure by correlating the predicted criterion score with the actual performance.

10. Cross-validate the procedure by using a discriminant analysis to assign a new set of applicants to existing subgroups. Calculate their predicted score as above.

---

score. Predicted criterion scores are then correlated with actual criterion scores to provide an estimate of the validity coefficient. It is recommended that the initial probabilities of subgroup members achieving acceptable criterion performance be calculated using only those individuals who have at least a .80 probability of assignment to one subgroup and that the predictive system be cross-validated before being used for decision making in an organization. Table 4 summarizes these steps. Mumford et al. (1990) provide a description of how to adapt this approach to multiple criteria and for individuals with probabilities of being in more than one subgroup.

Although existing studies indicate that subgrouping background data may provide unique predictive information, selection is only one possible use for the differential information provided by subgroups. Through the application of Schoenfeldt's (1974) assessment-classification model, subgroups are a viable approach to employee placement, career development, and succession planning. The differential information provided by subgroups may also provide a natural means for tailoring training programs to subpopulations, consistent with the recommendations of Cronbach and Snow (1977) concerning the interactions of instructional techniques and individual aptitudes.

Additionally, subgrouping has implications for job analysis, job design, and performance appraisal. Many jobs, especially those requiring social and interpersonal skills, allow for more than one method of achieving effective criterion performance. For example, a salesperson may achieve or exceed quota by making frequent "cold calls." In contrast, another salesperson may make an equal number of sales by making fewer but more thoroughly researched calls. Both methods may be equally valid ways of achieving high performance. Nevertheless, current methods of job analysis, job design, and performance appraisal would treat both methods as dimensions or factors. For example, a job description developed by aggregating across individuals who employ different techniques will be mixed and not adequately capture any of the methods of achieving successful performance (Hein & Mumford, 1988). Person-oriented approaches to job analysis, job design, and performance appraisal might include multiple sets of knowledge, skill, and ability descriptions that could be tailored to different subgroups. Multiple sets of task statements (e.g., in a job description) are not needed if they are written in terms of desired end states or objectives rather than processes.

SUBPOPULATION DIFFERENCES AND VALIDITY GENERALIZATION

The evidence concerning the degree to which a subgrouping solution may be transportable from one situation to another is limited and inconclusive. Owens and Schoenfeldt (1979) examined the degree to which a solution was stable on samples drawn from the same basic population at different points in time and found strong evidence of stability. This situation would be analogous to a single employer drawing from a stable geographic and educational subpopulation. Anderson (1972) was able to form a single set of subgroups using the same questionnaire at three U.S. universities, two in the Southeast and one in the Midwest. Subjects from the southeastern schools overlapped extensively in their subgroup memberships, whereas students from the midwestern school overlapped the other two much less. Johnson (1972) was unable to replicate the subgroup structure of Owens and Schoenfeldt (1979) in a southern junior college using the same questionnaire, citing substantial differences in the prior experiences of the two samples. Therefore, a subgrouping solution appears to generalize when the life histories of the individuals in the samples are reasonably similar. Although further research may identify parameters of subpopulations that could be used to make transportability decisions, the mixed nature of the validity generalization evidence at this point indicates a need for extreme caution.

EQUAL EMPLOYMENT OPPORTUNITY CONSIDERATIONS

Subgrouping as a human resource management tool has some specific equal employment opportunity considerations. Subgrouping is essentially a method of tailoring the predictive key to empirically derived groups of people in order to obtain more exact prediction than in the aggregate. If subgroups are not roughly equivalent for protected and nonprotected groups, then subgrouping may be seen as an application of different and potentially discriminatory selection standards. Although this is possible, it is also possible that subgrouping can be an effective way of combating discrimination by capturing different paths to successful criterion performance. If protected class members are achieving successful performance through the application of different resources, the resources may be identified through a subgrouping procedure rather than being lost or diluted in the aggregate.

Subgrouping also offers advantages as a social research tool. It allows for the identification of patterns of life history experiences that can contribute to the development of social and work-related resources. Patterns of experience that do not contribute to the development of successful resources can be identified and remediation steps (e.g., training, coaching, counseling) can be taken. If we do not collect such information out of a fear of potential discrimination, then the sources that contribute to successful personal development may not be identified and understood.

NEW DIRECTIONS

It may be premature to discuss new directions for a technique that has such limited empirical testing. Nevertheless, we will take the liberty of discussing the possible implications of some relatively recent studies involving the subgrouping technique.

Meaning Differences

Although subgrouping may identify groups of individuals who have systematically different patterns of life history, some differences in patterns are often irrelevant to the criterion variables of interest. One might expect differences in the pattern of relationships whenever the criterion has substantially different meaning for subsets of individuals. For example, job satisfaction may be determined by factors such as skill variety, task significance, and task identity for some individuals and by recognition and reward structures for others.

Mumford et al. (in press) have demonstrated that it is possible to aggregate subgroups based on the degree to which they hold a common meaning for the criterion. Here, *common meaning* is defined as a common causal system or nomothetic net. Essentially, this technique involves an extra step after the initial clustering solution. The initial subgroups are clustered based on the pattern of relationships between the criterion variable and a set of reference or marker variables that make up the nomothetic net. This set of variables is hypothesized to be differentially related to criterion variables for different sets of subgroups. Subgroups that display a common set of relationships with these reference variables are combined. Predictive systems are then constructed within each of these aggregate subgroups. Simple subgrouping may capture these differences, but cluster analysis may divide people into subgroups that display differences on variables that are not directly relevant to the criterion variables. For example, if job performance is a construct that displays differential predictive systems for subsets of individuals, variation in job performance may be more precisely modeled if predictive systems are constructed within groups of individuals for whom job performance has similar meaning. This procedure has been demonstrated to yield aggregate subgroups that are qualitatively different from those obtained from a higher-order clustering (Mumford et al., in press).

An additional prediction approach can be used based on the meaning differences logic outlined above. If the predictor variables have been carefully selected due to hypothesized relationships with the criterion, then it may be possible to aggregate subgroups based on the pattern of correlations between the predictors and the criterion within subgroups. Essentially, the investigator would combine subgroups that show similar patterns of relationships with the criterion variable. To the best of our knowledge, this method of aggregation has not yet been empirically evaluated.

Crystallization of Developmental Patterns

Another avenue of investigation relevant to the use of subgrouping procedures is the question of when an individual's subgroup status stabilizes or crystallizes. In an initial investigation of pattern crystallization, Mumford et al. (1987) used background data items administered in adolescence, college, and postcollege to determine when individuals could first be unambiguously assigned to one of a set of preexisting developmental patterns. After the individuals who crystallized (i.e., came to clearly express a pattern) in any of the three periods had been identified, a series of discriminant analyses were conducted to identify the characteristics associated with early and late crystallization. It was found that different patterns tended to crystallize in different developmental periods. Further, these differences in timing appeared to be reasonably systematic and consistent with the subgroups' interpretations and opportunities. For example, early crystallizers stabilized in somewhat traditional patterns that are reinforced during early adulthood.

The differences in the timing of crystallization are of some interest with respect to Holland's (1963, 1985) notion that people tend to enter occupations congruent with their broader pattern of prior behavior and experiences. More specifically, crystallized individuals should have a firm idea of what they want in an occupation and firm standards for evaluating what they are actually getting. Thus, crystallized individuals should show strong reactions to good and poor matches between the demands made by the occupation they enter and their broader pattern of prior behavior and experiences. Uncrystallized individuals, on the other hand, are likely to be uncommitted to a particular pattern while engaging in ongoing exploration. As a result, they should view good and poor matches with relative equanimity. Wesley (1989) found support for this interaction in subgroups of young adult males.

CONCLUSION

In this chapter we have attempted to provide a description of subgrouping and a brief overview of the subgrouping methodology that is used when scaling biodata responses. The technique is relatively new in psychology, but nevertheless has great potential for both success and frustration. On the positive side, it can predict multiple criteria and permits successful performance to be achieved through alternate routes. Further, the use of subgrouping in human resource management activities such as training and development, placement, job design, and succession planning has great potential. On the negative side, subgrouping is a demanding and resource-intensive technique. It requires a large number of subjects and a large amount of data. Most of our studies are based on at least 2,000 subjects and 300 variables. This obviously requires quite a bit of time for both the computer and the investigator.

The authors made roughly equal contributions to this manuscript. Therefore, order of authorship was decided based on the toss of a coin.

We would like to thank Richard Tannenbaum for his insightful comments concerning an earlier draft of this manuscript.

REFERENCES

Aldenderfer, M. S., & Blashfield, R. K. (1984). *Cluster analysis*. Beverly Hills, CA: Sage.

Anderberg, M. R. (1973). *Cluster analysis for applications*. New York: Academic Press.

Anderson, B. B. (1972). *An inter-institutional comparison on dimensions of student development: A step toward the goal of a comprehensive developmental integrative model of human behavior*. Unpublished doctoral dissertation, University of Georgia, Athens.

Asher, J. J. (1974). The biographical item: Can it be improved? *Personnel Psychology, 25,* 251–269.

Baehr, M., & Williams, G. B. (1967). Underlying dimensions of personal background data and their relationship to occupational classification. *Journal of Applied Psychology, 51,* 481–490.

Baker, F. B., & Hubert, L. J. (1972). Measuring the power of hierarchical cluster analysis. *Journal of the American Statistical Association, 70,* 31–38.

Bergman, L. R. (1988). You can't classify all of the people all of the time. *Multivariate Behavioral Research, 23,* 425–441.

Blashfield, R. K. (1976). Mixture model tests of cluster analysis: Accuracy of four agglomerative hierarchical methods. *Psychological Bulletin, 83,* 377–388.

Blashfield, R. K., & Aldenderfer, M. S. (1978). The literature on cluster analysis. *Multivariate Behavioral Research, 13,* 271–295.

Blashfield, R., & Morey, J. (1980). A Monte Carlo study of four subgrouping algorithms. *Applied Psychological Measurement, 4,* 329–336.

Brown, S. H. (1981). Validity generalization and situational moderation in the life insurance industry. *Journal of Applied Psychology, 66,* 664–670.

Brush, D. H., & Owens, W. A. (1979). Implementation and evaluation of an assessment classification model for manpower allocation. *Personnel Psychology, 3,* 369–383.

Cook, T. D., & Campbell, P. T. (1979). *Quasi-experimentation: Design and analysis in field settings.* Boston: Houghton Mifflin.

Cronbach, L. J. (1957). The two disciplines in scientific psychology. *American Psychologist, 12,* 671–684.

Cronbach, L. J. (1975). Beyond the two disciplines of scientific psychology. *American Psychologist, 30,* 116–127.

Cronbach, L. J., & Gleser, G. C. (1953). Assessing similarity between profiles. *Psychological Bulletin, 50,* 456–473.

Cronbach, L. J., & Snow, R. E. (1977). *Aptitudes and instructional methods.* New York: Irvington.

Dunnette, M. D. (1962). Personnel management. *Annual Review of Psychology, 1,* 285–314.

Dunnette, M. D., Kirchner, W. K., Erickson, J., & Banas, P. (1960). Predicting turnover among female office workers. *Personnel Administration, 23,* 45–50.

Edelbrock, C. (1979). Mixture model tests of hierarchical clustering algorithms: The problem of classifying everybody. *Multivariate Behavioral Research, 14,* 367–384.

Everitt, B. S. (1974). *Cluster analysis.* London: Heineman.

Everitt, B. S. (1979). Unresolved problems in cluster analysis. *Biometrics, 35,* 169–181.

Feild, H. S., & Schoenfeldt, L. F. (1975). Ward and Hook revisited: A two-part procedure for overcoming a deficiency in the grouping of persons. *Educational and Psychological Measurement, 35,* 171–173.

Fleishman, E. A., & Mumford, M. D. (1991). Evaluating classifications of job behavior: A construct validation of the ability requirements scale. *Personnel Psychology, 44,* 523–575.

Garwood, M. K., Anderson, L. E., & Greengart, B. J. (1991). Determining job groups: Application of hierarchical agglomerative cluster analysis in different job analysis situations. *Personnel Psychology, 44,* 743–762.

Ghiselli, E.E. (1973). The validity of aptitude tests in personnel selection. *Personnel Psychology, 26,* 461–467.

Guilford, J. P. (1959). *Personality.* New York: McGraw-Hill.

Gustafson, S. B. (1987). *Person and situation subgroup membership as a predictor of job performance and perceptions.* Unpublished doctoral dissertation, Georgia Institute of Technology, Atlanta.

Hamer, R. M., & Cunningham, J. W. (1981). Cluster analyzing profile data confounded with interrater differences: A comparison of profile association measures. *Applied Psychological Measurement, 5,* 63–72.

Hartigan, J. A. (1975). *Clustering algorithms.* New York: Wiley.

Hein, M., & Mumford, M. D. (1988, August). *Continuity and change: An integration of nomothetic and idiographic perspectives.* Poster presented at the American Psychological Association, Atlanta.

Holland, J. L. (1963). Explorations of a theory of vocational choice and achievement: II. A four-year prediction study. *Psychological Reports, 12,* 547–594.

Holland, J. L. (1985). *Making vocational choices: A theory of vocational personalities and work environments.* Englewood Cliffs, NJ: Prentice-Hall.

James, L. R. (1982). Aggregation bias in estimates of perceptual agreement. *Journal of Applied Psychology, 67,* 214–229.

Johnson, R. (1972). *Homogeneous subgroups based on biographical data as predictors of educational success in a junior college.* Unpublished doctoral dissertation, University of Georgia, Athens.

Korman, A. K. (1968). The prediction of managerial performance: A review. *Personnel Psychology, 21,* 295–322.

Kuiper, F. K., & Fisher, L. A. (1975). A Monte Carlo comparison of six clustering procedures. *Biometrics, 31,* 777–783.

Lissitz, R. W., & Schoenfeldt. L. F. (1974). Moderator subgroups for the estimation of educational performance. *American Educational Research Journal, 11,* 63–75.

MacQueen, J. (1967). Some methods for classification and analysis of multivariate observations. In J. Neyman (Ed.), *Proceedings of the Fifth Berkeley Symposium on*

Mathematical Statistics and Probability (Vol. 1). Berkeley: University of California Press.

Matthews, A. (1979). Standardization of measures prior to clustering. *Biometrics, 35,* 892.

Milligan, G. W. (1981). A Monte Carlo study of thirty internal criterion measures for cluster analysis. *Psychometrika, 46,* 187–199.

Mojena, R. (1977). Hierarchical grouping methods and stopping rules: An evaluation. *Computer Journal, 20,* 359–363.

Mumford, M. D., & Owens, W. A. (1984). Individuality in a developmental context: Some empirical and theoretical considerations. *Human Development, 27,* 84–108.

Mumford, M. D., & Owens, W. A. (1987). Methodology review: Principles, procedures, and findings in the application of background data measures. *Applied Psychological Measurement, 11,* 1–31.

Mumford, M. D., Shaffer, G. S., Jackson, K. E., Neiner, A., Denning, D., & Owens, W. A. (1983). *Male-female differences in the structure of background data measures.* Athens, GA: Institute for Behavioral Research.

Mumford, M. D., Snell, A., & Hein, M. B. (in press). Varieties of religious experience: Person influences on continuity and change in religious involvement. *Journal of Personality.*

Mumford, M. D., & Stokes, G. S. (1992). Developmental determinants of individual action: Theory and practice in applying background measures. In M. D. Dunnette (Ed.), *Handbook of industrial and organizational psychology* (2d ed., vol. 3, pp. 61–138). Palo Alto, CA: Consulting Psychologists Press.

Mumford, M. D., Stokes, G. S., & Owens, W. A. (1990). *Patterns of life adaptation: The ecology of human individuality.* Hillsdale, NJ: Erlbaum.

Mumford, M. D., Wesley, S. S., & Shaffer, G. S. (1987). Individuality in a developmental context II: The crystallization of developmental trajectories. *Human Development, 30,* 291–321.

Nevo, B. (1976). Using biographical information to predict success of men and women in the army. *Journal of Applied Psychology, 61,* 106–108.

O'Leary, L. R. (1973). Fair employment, sound psychometric practice, and reality. *American Psychologist, 28,* 147–149.

Owens, W. A. (1968). Toward one discipline of scientific psychology. *American Psychologist, 23,* 782–785.

Owens, W. A. (1971). A quasi-actuarial basis for individual assessment. *American Psychologist, 26,* 992–997.

Owens, W. A. (1976). Background data. In M. D. Dunnette (Ed.), *Handbook of industrial and organizational psychology* (pp. 609–644). Chicago: Rand McNally.

Owens, W. A., & Schoenfeldt, L. F. (1979). Toward a classification of persons. *Journal of Applied Psychology, 64,* 596–607.

Pace, L. A., & Schoenfeldt, L. F. (1977). Legal concerns in the use of weighted application blanks. *Personnel Psychology, 3,* 159–166.

Pervin, L. A. (1984). Idiographic approaches to personality. In N. Endler & J. Hunt (Eds.), *Personality and the behavioral disorders* (2d ed., vol. 1). New York: Wiley.

Richardson, Bellows, Henry, & Co. (1984). *Executive summary: The manager profile record*. Washington, DC: Author.

Ritchie, R. J., & Boehm, V. R. (1977). Biographical data as a predictor of women's and men's management potential. *Journal of Vocational Behavior, 11*, 363–368.

Rohlf, F. J. (1970). Adaptive hierarchical clustering schemes. *Systematic Zoology, 19*, 58–82.

Rounds, J. B., Dawis, R. V., & Lofquist, L. H. (1987). Measurement of person environment fit and prediction of satisfaction in the theory of work adjustment. *Journal of Vocational Behavior, 31*, 362–371.

Schoenfeldt, L. F. (1974). Utilization of manpower: Development and evaluation of an assessment classification model for matching individuals and jobs. *Journal of Applied Psychology, 5*, 583–585.

Shaffer, G. S., Saunders, V., & Owens, W. A. (1986). Additional evidence for the accuracy of biographical data: Long-term retest and observer ratings. *Personnel Psychology, 3*, 791–807.

Sokal, R., & Sneath, P. (1963). *Principles of numerical taxonomy*. San Francisco: Freeman.

Tesser, A. & Lissitz, R. W. (1973). On an assumption underlying the use of homogeneous subgroups in prediction. *Catalog of Selected Documents in Psychology, 3*, 38.

Thayer, P. W. (1977). Somethings old, somethings new. *Personnel Psychology, 3*, 513–524.

Tryon, R. C. (1939). *Cluster analysis*. Ann Arbor, MI: Edwards Brothers.

Ward, J. J. (1963). Hierarchical grouping to optimize an objective function. *Journal of the American Statistical Association, 58*, 236–244.

Ward, J. J., & Hook, M. E. (1963). Application of a hierarchical grouping procedure to the problem of grouping profiles. *Educational and Psychological Measurement, 23*, 69–81.

Wernimont, P. F. (1962). Reevaluation of a weighted application blank for office personnel. *Journal of Applied Psychology, 4*, 417–419.

Wesley, S. S. (1989). *Background data measures and career outcomes: Some developmental influences on person–job matching*. Unpublished doctoral dissertation, Georgia Institute of Technology, Atlanta.

Zimmerman, R., Jacobs, R., & Farr, J. (1982). A comparison of the accuracy of four methods of clustering jobs. *Applied Psychological Measurement, 6*, 353–366.

Zubin, J. A. (1938). A technique for measuring like-mindedness. *Journal of Abnormal and Social Psychology, 33*, 508–516.

ISSUES IN VALIDATION AND APPLICATION

In this section a number of important issues related to the validation and the implementation of biodata forms in selection systems are addressed. Brown's chapter, the first in this section, is a general overview of many of the important decisions faced when validating a biodata inventory. He begins by reviewing how to plan a validation study, and he discusses the strengths and weaknesses associated with a number of approaches. His in-depth discussion of a number of techniques, such as different methods for configural scaling, provides the reader with a great deal of information about both old and new approaches to scaling biodata inventories. He makes a number of practical recommendations for individuals attempting the use of the techniques, including warnings of the pitfalls associated with them.

Next, Schmidt and Rothstein address an important and sometimes controversial issue with respect to biodata research: the extent to which biodata inventories can be expected to generalize across jobs and organizations. Though validity generalization is generally accepted for cognitive ability tests, Schmidt and Rothstein provide evidence that the notion that

197

biodata are less generalizable may not be an accurate one. They provide data to demonstrate that biodata forms can be developed that are generalizable.

Two chapters in this section focus on biodata form development issues in different contexts. Pannone's chapter specifically reviews selection studies that have been conducted in skilled, semiskilled, and unskilled jobs. Issues that are specific to selection in such jobs, such as reading levels and unionization of employees, are discussed. In another context, Gandy, Dye, and MacLane report on an extensive biodata form development project conducted at OPM with entry-level nonsupervisory positions in professional and administrative occupations across most federal agencies. After describing the development of the biodata form, they examine its construct validity, including the use of confirmatory factor analysis.

Stokes and Cooper more generally address the development and use of biodata inventories, focusing on both the typical and atypical criteria that have been used in previous biodata studies, including turnover, adjustment, accidents, job satisfaction, and team performance. They then tackle the issue of the generalizability of biodata across occupational categories, summarizing research on the comparability of items and factors across a number of occupations.

Sharf's chapter provides an excellent description of legal issues and EEO issues in the use of biodata inventories. In his chapter, the various regulations, including such areas as privacy invasion, Title VII and the Civil Rights Act, and the ADA, are evaluated, and recommendations for biodata form development are included. His chapter cautions us to be cognizant of the burgeoning regulation and public attention devoted to test items.

The possibility that applicants might fake their responses to a biodata form has been of considerable interest to those who use biodata for selection purposes. Lautenschlager provides an extensive review of the literature on accuracy and faking of biodata inventories. He distinguishes between three different ways to operationally define accuracy and the implications of the different definitions. He summarizes the results of previous studies, noting situations in which distortion may be more likely to occur. He recommends techniques for assessing distortion and makes general recommendations both for practice and for future research.

Validating Biodata

Steven H. Brown
LIMRA International

Gaining insight into the usefulness of a biodata measure requires the consideration of a number of issues and procedures. Discussions of purposes for validating biodata, situational constraints and issues, and item scaling and validation designs make up the heart of this chapter. Unfortunately, space does not allow in-depth treatment of all issues; therefore, wherever possible, sources that provide more in-depth treatment of procedures or issues are noted. A few other caveats need to be made explicit. First, this chapter will not deal with the extremely important item generation step that is key to the majority of biodata validation efforts. Biodata measures are valid only to the extent that they adequately tap relevant life experiences. Item generation procedures are discussed by Russell (see Chapter 2 of this volume). Second, criterion development is important in any validation effort. However, in most cases, the issues of criterion development for biodata measures differ little from those for the validation of other types of predictors. Hence, this chapter will devote little explicit attention to the development of criteria. When particular item scaling and validation strategies do require particular criterion characteristics, these concerns are noted but not elaborated upon. Nevertheless, appropriate measures of performance and/or other relevant criteria are as important as, if not more important than, the biodata items and scaling results themselves. Unlike many other types of measures of individual differences, biodata item scaling and validation are often inseparable. The more frequently used scaling techniques are an integral part of the validation process. Thus, this chapter will deal with item scaling techniques as a component of validation. Beyond issues of item scaling, the validation procedures for biodata differ little from those of other tests.

PLANNING BIODATA VALIDATION STUDIES

The success of any validation effort is directly proportional to the care and effort devoted to planning the study. The planning must begin with a careful consideration of the study's purpose. What is the major goal of the validation study? What behaviors or performances are to be predicted? Too often, researchers give these questions far less attention than they need and conduct studies that are ineffective. The selection of a scaling and validation strategy requires careful attention to the questions the researcher wishes to answer.

PURPOSE OF STUDY

Conceptually, the development of biodata measures serves one or more of five general purposes: performance prediction, placement, needs analysis, theory testing, and theory building. Historically and most frequently, performance prediction has been the primary goal of biodata measure developers.

Predictions of future job performance have been focal. In making selection decisions, biodata measures have a well-documented history of success. Reviews by Asher (1972), Barge and Hough (1976), Hunter and Hunter (1984), Mumford and Owens (1987), Owens (1976), Reilly and Chao (1982), Reilly and Warech (1988), and Schmidt, Gooding, Noe, and Kirsch (1984) have documented this success for a wide range of jobs and criteria.

Studies of *placement decisions* made through biodata measures have rarely appeared in the literature. Work by Brush and Owens (1979), Eberhardt and Muchinsky (1984), Morrison (1977), Neiner and Owens (1985), and Schoenfeldt (1974) has shown the relationship of biodata factors or biodata-based subgroup membership to later occupational and vocational choice. Demographic trends suggest a future scarce labor pool for professional-level positions because of the aging of the population. As this unfolds, pure selection will decrease in importance. Placement decisions will dominate. Biodata applications would benefit from increased research directed at improving placement decisions.

The use of biodata measures for training needs analysis has not yet appeared in the literature. However, one study of managerial selection currently being conducted by the Life Insurance Marketing and Research Association (LIMRA) has this as a secondary goal. Through a series of biodata scales developed to measure experiences and attitudes indicative of characteristics related to key managerial behaviors, reseachers expect to identify key developmental needs. As labor pools become increasingly tight, the development of existing employees to fill voids in an organization's human resource requirements will take on increasing emphasis. Hence, placement and training needs analysis are likely to become increasingly important purposes for biodata measures.

Theory testing as the primary purpose in developing biodata measures begins with a rather explicit theory of behavior. In this case, a biodata measure would be developed as an operationalization of a central construct or constructs of the theory. Once the measure was developed, the researcher would subject the measure to a series of studies to build evidence for the construct and its nomological network. In practice, programs evaluating biodata measures in this way are lacking. The closest examples involve loosely defined theories built through job-analytic work and operationalized as a biodata tool (Goldberg, 1972; Stricker, 1989). Unfortunately, such efforts have typically involved little exploration of the nomological network other than to assess whether such scales predict performance on the job. Theory testing requires a carefully planned series of studies.

The development of the *Biographical Questionnaire* (BQ) by Owens and his colleagues, along with many studies investigating it in differing situations, are among the best examples of the use of biodata for theory building. These are based on Owens' (1968, 1976) premise that the identification of modal patterns of individual development will lead to biodata tools with more generalizability. Subgrouping is the cornerstone of this program of study. The theory built in this way is beginning to yield the predictive system that Owens envisioned. Mumford and Owens' (1987) review of this research concludes that membership in background data subgroups is an effective predictor of a variety of educational and occupational criteria.

ITEM SCALING STRATEGIES

The purpose of the validity study will limit, to a large extent, the biodata item scaling procedures available. Before discussing specific techniques with purposes for which each is well suited, a brief definition of the major groupings of strategies is in order. Each will be explored more fully later. Figure 1 depicts two broad groups of keying methods—those that are externally based (often called empirical) and those that are internally based.

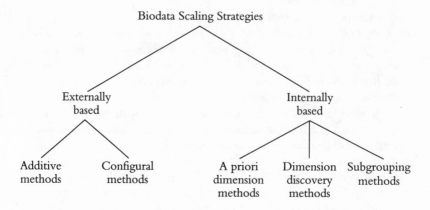

FIGURE 1 Strategies for Scaling Biodata Items

Externally Based Approaches

Externally based strategies look at individual item–criterion relationships and then select and weight items to maximally discriminate between levels of criterion performance. Historically, this family of approaches forms the foundation of biodata validation efforts. As early as 1935, Long and Sandiford (cited in Mitchell & Klimoski, 1986) reviewed 23 different empirical scaling methods. Two major groups of empirical approaches exist: those that assume additive item–criterion relationships and those that assume a contingent relationship between items and look at item profiles to classify individuals into predictor groups. Each predictor group has an associated predicted level of success for the criterion.

Additive keying methods look at individual item–criterion relationships and then select and weight items (and/or item response alternatives) to maximally discriminate between levels of criterion performance or group membership. The biodata score is a linear composite of those item responses and items that are assigned weights.

Configural keying methods reject the additive model for an interactive one. Additive models obtain a total score through a variety of patterns of item responses. Configural techniques, on the other hand, place individuals into a predictor class only when the same pattern of responses to key items matches those of every other individual in the class. Thus, configural methods treat predictors as configurations (interactively), expecting to find improved predictability.

Internally Based Approaches

Internally based strategies, as a group, scale biodata items on the basis of their internal relationships. These can be based on targeted or a priori dimensions or can be more exploratory in scope and attempt to discover the dimensionality of a given set of biodata items. A third approach, subgrouping, is based not so much on the dimensionality of items, but on similarities in the way people respond to them. The internally based strategies separate item scaling and test construction from empirical validation. Concerns of content and construct validity can be quite important in the scaling phase. Criterion-related and further construct validation follow.

A priori dimension methods begin with a definition of key behaviors or psychological constructs believed to be related to the criteria of interest. Items are explicitly written to capture an individual's past behaviors that indicate the focal a priori behaviors or constructs. Item selection for scale inclusion are based on expert judgment, internal consistency analyses, or both. Scale scores are then related to criteria measures in criterion-related validation analyses.

Dimension discovery methods subject items to factor, component, or cluster analysis to identify some small number of dimensions that account for a significant proportion of the item variance and have a degree of psychological meaningfulness. For validation work, dimension scores are then related to the criteria of interest.

Subgrouping methods are best exemplified by the work of Owens (1976) and Owens and Schoenfeldt (1979). Items are factor-analyzed as in the dimension discovery approach, individuals are profiled on their resulting factor scores, and these profiles are clustered into subgroups. Individuals within the subgroups are described by their mean profile. Criterion-related validation looks at subgroup similarities and differences on the criteria of interest.

VALIDATION STUDY CONSTRAINTS AND RELATED ISSUES

Beyond purpose, biodata developers need to consider their particular situation before making a decision on the validation and scaling approach. Specifically, we must ask how the results of the biodata measures are to be communicated. If the use is purely for prediction, a score that simply reflects a predicted criterion standing may be enough. If, on the other hand, results need to be understood by those who complete the measure, multiple scores with some psychological or behavioral meaning may be required.

204 | ISSUES IN VALIDATION AND APPLICATION

Who will receive the score? What is the user's level of sophistication with test interpretation? How will the results be used? Answers to these questions depend not only on the measure's purposes but also on the applied situation. An empirically developed measure that maximally predicts some criterion of interest will be useless if lay users do not believe in it because it holds no psychological meaning to them. In cases such as these, improved understanding and acceptance is worth some loss of predictive power.

The criteria will influence the choice of scaling approach, particularly when choosing among externally based techniques. Some techniques require dichotomous or dichotomized criteria, others need continuous criteria, and still others work with categorical criteria or criterion groups. Further, the number of criteria may dictate that particular scaling methods are or are not appropriate.

Future generalization needs must also be considered when planning the validation study. To what extent are available validation samples similar to samples that are later targets for using the biodata tool? As generalizability increases in importance, an externally based approach may be less desirable. Related to the generalizability question is the nature of the validation sample. In an employment setting, the availability of an applicant sample, a new employee sample, and/or a cross-section of existing employees affects how keys can be developed, the timing of the development, and the generalizability of results. An applicant sample may be desirable or even necessary for the development of internally based scales, rational scales, or subgroups; however, this sample alone will not be useful for empirical key development.

Other concerns are the numbers of cases available and the time allotted for the study. A priori key development approaches require fewer cases than do dimension discovery approaches. Externally based techniques require large samples of several hundred or more, and subgrouping approaches may need even more cases to yield stable, reliable results.

The available time affects keying decisions to some extent. More importantly in combination with the type of samples available, the time frame limits the range of validation paradigms that are feasible. For example, predictive studies are not possible unless some—often significant—time can be allotted for criterion maturation.

In summary, many issues need to be considered in planning a validation study for a biodata measure. The goals of the biodata development effort guide the selection of an item scaling technique. Once the goals are delineated, other concerns further define the scaling technique decision and the selection of a validation strategy. The nine considerations for validation and the key levels of each are listed in Table 1. These

TABLE 1   Important Considerations in Validating Biodata Measures

Validation Consideration	Key Levels or Categories
Primary purpose	Prediction, placement, training needs analysis, theory building, theory testing
Secondary purpose	Prediction, placement, training needs analysis, theory building, theory testing
Feedback of results	Decision making only, understanding, program placement
Type of criteria	Dichotomous or dichotomized, continuous categorical (groups)
Number of criteria	One, two, or more
Generalization needs	No need to extend results, wish to apply to varying situations
Type of sample	Applicant, newly selected, cross-section of previously selected group
Sample size	Less than 200, moderate, large (1,000 or more)
Time frame available	Short (1 to 6 months) Moderate (6 months to 1 year) Long (longer than 1 year)

considerations and levels lead to some 24,000 potential combinations of options. We cannot deal explicitly with each of these. However, the following sections will make a choice of techniques and strategies easier by detailing the strengths, weaknesses, and constraints of each major scaling procedure.

SPECIFIC BIODATA SCALING METHODS

We have briefly mentioned five general categories of item scaling procedures. Each of these has several alternative approaches that may be appropriate to particular situations. Here we will take a look at one of the individual methods and discuss the characteristics, constraints, and assumptions underlying it. Other scaling methods will be briefly noted and references provided. Several of these methods have received considerable attention in the literature; others are rarely mentioned but appear to hold some potential for successful application to biodata. Figure 2 lists the methods to be discussed.

ADDITIVE METHODS

The Weighted Application Blank Procedure

RATIONALE: The weighted application blank (WAB) procedure identifies individual item responses that differentiate between desirable and undesirable criterion groups. By determining the predictive power of each item response, it is possible to assign weights to each possible item response. These weights are then totaled and used as a predictor of criterion group membership. Specific procedures are well documented by England (1971).

REQUIREMENTS AND ASSUMPTIONS: When using WAB scaling, researchers make several assumptions about the items and the criterion. First, item responses must be categorical or categorized. If the items are categorized, England (1971) recommends that each grouping of alternatives be of a roughly equal frequency. Second, the WAB requires one dichotomous or dichotomized criterion. If the criterion is dichotomized, extreme criterion groups can be used. To be effective, the desirable group must truly represent the type of individuals desired in the future, and the undesirable group must represent the type one wishes to avoid (England, 1961). Extreme criterion groups may be quite useful for the prediction of very strong or very weak performance. Unfortunately, this approach requires large samples within the extreme groups and appears to have received little rigorous assessment in the literature.

Item–criterion relationships need not be linear. The technique is based on the relationship of individual alternative endorsement rates to criterion group membership. However, in that correlational techniques are used to assess the validity of the instrument, a linear total score–criterion score relationship is assumed.

As an externally based technique, the WAB procedure requires a sample for which criterion data exist in order to develop a weighting scheme. Further, the reference groups should be as similar as possible to the group to which the key will later be applied. The key maximally differentiates between the desirable and undesirable groups on which it was developed. When applied to groups that vary from these groups, the key will lose predictive power.

In making no assumptions about item–criterion relationships and basing weighting on percentage differences, the technique capitalizes on chance.

Additive Methods	Configural Methods	A Priori Dimension Methods	Dimension Discovery Methods	Subgrouping Methods
Weighted application blank	Reductive approaches Dual pattern approaches Cumulative approaches	Theoretical approach Homogeneous scaling	Factor analysis Principal components analysis	Developmental-integrative model
Horizontal percentile method	AID THAID CHAID		Cluster analysis	
Item/criterion regression	CART			
Deviate keying	Neural networking approaches			

FIGURE 2 Specific Biodata Scaling Methods

Development samples yield inflated predictor–criterion correlations. The use of large sample sizes for key development reduces this capitalization. Despite England's recommendation of 150 as adequate, key development samples of 500 or more are much more likely to yield relatively stable response weights.

RELIABILITY CONCERNS: For the WAB method, test–retest is the most important measure of reliability to be considered. The few studies that report test–retest reliabilities describe values ranging from .60 to .96, with the level being somewhat dependent on time between testing and item type (Brush, 1974; Chaney, 1964; McManus & Mitchell, 1987).

VALIDATION DESIGN ISSUES: Successful application of the WAB technique requires a large sample of cases representative of the group to which the resulting keys will be applied. Thus, a predictive validity study represents the best paradigm. Ideally, this would be a study in which the item responses are collected but not used in the making of selection decisions. Criterion data are collected at an appropriate later point and a key is developed. Concurrent designs are also applicable, but care must be taken to assure that responses represent the subjects' experiences before they become members of the selected group.

A cross-validational design is required; a double or triple cross-validation design is preferred. In a triple design, the sample is split into thirds, and three keys are developed using a differing set of two groups each time. The keys are then crossed on the appropriate third group that was not in the development sample for that particular key. The average total score–criterion cross-validity across the three keys represents the reported validity. The key to be used in the future is developed using all of the cases. This represents the best estimates of the item or item alternative weights for the population (Campbell, 1974). Shrinkage formulae, though quite valuable in much cross-validation work, are not directly applicable in the WAB methodology.

STRENGTHS: The WAB approach is easy to apply and tends to yield empirical validity estimates that, when properly constructed and cross-validated, are high—often higher than those resulting from other approaches (Asher, 1972; Henry, 1966; Mumford & Owens, 1987; Owens, 1976; Reilly & Chao, 1982; Schuh, 1967).

LIMITATIONS: Unfortunately, the WAB approach yields little understanding of the predictor–criterion relationship under study. As Mumford and Owens (1987) state, "Because empirical keys select items solely on the basis of their ability to predict complex criterion performance, item content tends to be complex and lack psychological meaningfulness" (p. 15).

Also, the keys that are developed are closely tied to the specific sample and criteria employed in key development. This limitation can, however, be overcome when care is taken in assuring large development samples that are representative of the jobs for which the measure will be used. Additive keys have successfully been generalized across organizations with similar jobs (Brown, 1981; Rothstein, Schmidt, Erwin, Owens, & Sparks, 1990) and across cultures with similar jobs (Hinrichs, Haanpera, & Sonkin, 1976; Laurent, 1970; Levine & Zachert, 1951; Strong, 1926).

Pace and Schoenfeldt (1977) warn that the "raw empiricism" of the WAB approach make it particularly vulnerable to legal inquiries. They further argue that this approach would be hard to defend if adverse impact on a protected group were found.

Other Additive Methods

HORIZONTAL PERCENTILE: Proposed by Stead and Shartle (1940), horizontal scaling takes its name from the method used to generate response weights. For each item response alternative, the total number of high-criterion group responders is divided by the total number who responded to the alternative regardless of criterion group membership. This percentage value, or some rounded multiple of it, becomes the response weight (Telenson, Alexander, & Barrett, 1983). Except for the scale development step, the scaling comments made about the WAB approach hold true for the horizontal approach. This approach has been only occasionally used in scaling biodata. When used, the results are mixed at best (Telenson, Alexander, & Barrett, 1983).

ITEM/CRITERION REGRESSION: While very similar to the previous two empirical approaches, the item–criterion regression approach derives not item alternative weights, but simply item weights. This approach assumes that item alternatives have a natural or theoretical continuum and that alternatives can be ordered and assigned numbers. Further, this scaling technique takes advantage of a continuous criterion. Item weights are derived directly from the item–criterion correlation coefficients or other applicable measures of covariation. Typically, the developer retains those items that meet some level of statistical significance. A simple summing of the item scores (chosen response categories times the item weight) or the application of a weighting procedure such as multiple regression result in the total biodata score (Gandy, Outerbridge, Sharf, & Dye, 1989; Lecznar & Dailey, 1950; & Malone, 1978). When the criterion is categorical, multiple discriminant analysis can be used. Again, the more detailed comments about the WAB approach apply to item–criterion regression scaling.

DEVIATE KEYING: Neidt and Malloy (1954) suggest an approach for adding new test items to a test battery already in use. The deviate keying technique uses criterion groups defined by the distance above or below the regression line between the existing predictor and the criterion. Criterion scores for developing item weights are the differences between actual and predicted criterion scores. Item weights are derived by any of the additive approaches. The deviate keying approach suffers from this rather convoluted and logically deficient approach to criterion score development.

Studies of this technique report very mixed results (Meyers & Schultz, 1950; Schultz & Green, 1953; Malloy, 1955; and Webb, 1960). Webb (1960) found that the deviate key outperformed an external criterion key in the developmental sample but found little difference in the cross-validation sample. Further analyses of these data suggested that the greater drop in validity for the deviate key resulted from the higher instability of the item weights related to extreme response frequency. Like other empirical methods, the deviate keying approach needs large ns and must be cross-validated. Criterion unreliability further compounds the shrinkage problem.

Recommendations

Additive external keying methods in general, and more specifically the WAB approach, are appropriate when performance prediction is a very major or the only concern. When generalization is of little importance or is expected to be to situations and populations that are relatively similar to the development situation, the WAB is an effective item-scaling approach. Multiple keys can be developed for multiple criteria and for placement or needs analysis situations. However, multiple keys can be burdensome to create, validate, and use. Further, convincing users of their utility may be quite difficult when no psychological meaningfulness exists.

Some degree of understanding of the keying results may be achieved through factor analyses of keyed items using the weight of the item alternatives as derived through the WAB. LIMRA successfully applied this approach with a life insurance agent selection questionnaire in the United Kingdom and Republic of Ireland (Crosby, Dalessio, & McManus, 1990). Unfortunately, this approach, too, yields little in the way of construct explication.

Using 275 cases, Malloy (1955) compared the WAB approach with two regression-based approaches. Generally, comparable cross-validities were found for a tenure criterion; for absenteeism, the validity of the WAB shrank significantly, more than did the validity for the regression approaches. Similarly, Lecznar and Dailey (1950) compared the WAB approach with an item–criterion regression approach and found equal developmental validity and less shrinkage for the item regression approach. Well-controlled studies of several of the additive methods are needed. Appropriate independent variables include sample size, population validity, number and type of items, and type of criterion.

CONFIGURAL METHODS

Configural methods assume that predictive information is contained in the pattern of responses to a set of items, even when the responses, taken singly, contain no useful information (Meehl, 1950). McQuitty (1957) breaks configural approaches into three classes: reductive approaches, dual pattern approaches, and cumulative approaches.

Reductive Approaches

Reductive approaches begin with an individual's response pattern across all items. Analytic procedures reduce the total response pattern to one or more patterns of less than all the items. In so doing, these approaches isolate the major response patterns that are unique to each criterion group of subjects. McQuitty (1957) defines a major response pattern as a pattern of item responses that includes the maximal number of items that are endorsed by a specific minimum number of subjects from one criterion group but are endorsed by no subjects from other criterion groups. McQuitty's (1957) reduction techniques assume a single criterion variable and are potentially useful in developing typologies. These procedures typically yield many molar types, with only a few individuals representing each. The techniques were developed prior to the ready availability of computers, are computationally burdensome, and have been largely forgotten. McQuitty's (1957) limited research suggests that the results can compare favorably to other empirical item-scaling approaches. While the procedures do ignore item content during the scaling, the resulting reduced patterns are claimed to be interpretable and can yield a degree of understanding.

Dual Pattern Approaches

Dual pattern approaches first classify individuals into groups on the basis of scores on multiple criteria. Using a pattern approach, each criterion pattern of scores is represented by a class of subjects. Next, the technique determines the pattern of responses to predictor items that characterize each criterion class of subjects. Thus, a predictor item response pattern is associated with each criterion pattern. The predictor response patterns are then cross-validated as predictors of criterion patterns on a holdout sample (McQuitty, 1957). Thus, the dual-pattern analytic technique yields core types—empirically derived types of individuals. Core types are empirically defined, are relatively few, and can be broken into the molar types seen in reductive techniques. Unfortunately, like the reduction strategies, dual-pattern analysis appears to have not been applied to biodata scaling problems.

Cumulative Approaches: Automatic Interaction Detector (AID)

The third class of configural scaling techniques is cumulative in nature. Rather than beginning with response patterns across all items, these approaches begin with the one item that best differentiates criterion groups or levels and pairs it with all others until the best pair of items is found. This continues until new items yield no further improvement in predictability (Lubin & Osburn, 1957). Refinements of this cumulative approach have been applied to developing biodata tools. Perhaps the best known application of this general approach are the automative interaction detection (AID) procedures (Sonquist, 1970; Sonquist, Baker, & Morgan, 1973; Sonquist & Morgan, 1964).

RATIONALE: The AID methodology is based on the cumulative approach to contingency data analysis. Specifically, the AID approach employs a nonsymmetrical branching process based on variance analysis techniques. This process subdivides subjects into a series of subgroups that maximize the prediction of either dichotomous or continuous criterion. The AID approach to the problem of item scaling is to construct prediction rules based on binary decision trees (Sonquist & Morgan, 1964). The procedure begins with one item and splits the sample into two groups based on endorsed item alternatives. Various item-alternative-based splits are evaluated until the one that best differentiates on the criterion is found. After evaluating each item in this way, the procedure retains the item whose split differentiates best. Two new groups are formed based on responses to this best discriminating item. The two new groups are then split in the same manner. Thus, the basic idea is to select each split of subjects such that the cases going to each new subset are more homogeneous on the criteria than was the original subset. This process continues until further splitting yields no benefit.

REQUIREMENTS AND ASSUMPTIONS: The AID methodology makes no assumptions of linearity or additivity of item–criterion relationships. Items can be ordered or categorical. Continuous variables can be used, but if the number of possible values is large, grouping will be required. The criterion must be either dichotomous or continuous. Categorical criteria cannot be analyzed with AID or its relatives. AID selects splitting rules that maximize criterion differentiation and, therefore, capitalizes on chance. Thus, very large sample sizes, in the thousands, should be used in developing and cross-validating AID trees. As the number of items and item splits increase, the sample size needs increase rapidly.

RELIABILITY CONCERNS: Reliability takes on a particularly important role at the item level with AID approaches. Specifically, the branches are based on item responses. Thus, an unreliable item near the top of the tree can severely influence prediction of the criterion. Another reliability concern has to do with the reproducibility of the trees on new samples. Two samples with the same items and criteria will not necessarily produce identical trees. This becomes less of a problem as sample size and item reliability increases and as the number of predictors and number of potential splits per predictor decrease. More important, however, is whether the results of final nodes of the AID process are similar. Thus, the proper focus should be on the composition of the final groups and on the interpretation of the combinations of item responses they represent.

VALIDATION DESIGN ISSUES: AID models are developed using criterion values; hence, an empirical study is a minimum requirement. Further, the capitalization on chance that is built into the model makes a cross-validation design a requirement. The triple cross-validation approach suggested for the WAB is equally applicable to AID models. With AID models, cross-validation takes the form of running each hold-out subject down the decision tree and assigning the subject to a final group. The predicted value for each group member is the group's mean criterion value as computed in the development analysis. Predicted and actual criterion scores are correlated to assess the cross-validity of the model.

STRENGTHS: The AID approach yields binary prediction trees that are potentially valid predictors of future behavior. AID takes into account the configural relationships of items with the criteria and yields some understanding of how the predictor and criterion are related. The process makes few assumptions about the predictors, the criterion, or the form of relationship between the two.

LIMITATIONS: The major weakness in the AID approach is in the large sample size needed in order to produce stable results. As with other empirical approaches, item content does not play a role in developing predictions. Thus, the approach is inappropriate for theory testing, but may be quite useful for theory generation. AID relies heavily on individual items; therefore, item reliability is vitally important. While probably not a problem for the more objective forms of biodata items, more subjective items may not be suitable to this type of analysis. Finally, the technique is relatively untested for biodata usage. Three studies (Sorenson, 1964; Tanofsky, Shepps, & O'Neill, 1969; Woodruff, Robins, Taibleson, Reich, Schwin, & Frost, 1973) suggest potential, but the approach is far too unresearched to form any firm conclusions.

Other Cumulative Approaches

In addition to AID, other procedures that are available for cumulative configural analysis include THAID (Morgan & Messinger, 1973), CHAID (Perreault & Barksdale, 1980), and CART (Breiman, Friedman, Olshen, & Stone, 1984). These methods differ from AID primarily in the decision rules applied in judging splits, as well as in the types of predictors and criteria that can be handled.

Neural Networking Approaches

A promising new approach uses a rapidly expanding segment of the artificial intelligence field known as *neural network technology*. Neural nets emulate the way a human brain functions by intricately link-ing many processing elements or nodes into patterns similar to those existing between neurons in the brain. Construction begins with supervised learning in which known inputs (biodata items) are paired with known outputs (criterion levels). Training occurs as the neural net finds a way to map mathematically the inputs onto the known outputs. Particularly intriguing is a second learning process known as *un-supervised learning*. Here, the net identifies "natural" clusterings of in-put data and provides insight into the nature of complex problems. Further, neural nets have the ability to generalize relationships for inputs and outputs they have never seen. Thus, neural nets can accommodate input–output relationships that change gradually over time (Rochester, 1990).

As might be expected, neural net construction does require large samples (15 cases per attribute under study) and cross-validation. Current applications include reviewing patterns of credit card fraud to identify suspicious card usage and evaluating patterns of thermal neutron activity to detect baggage containing terrorist bombs. In both applications, neural nets outperformed more conventional techniques (Ver Duin, 1990).

Recommendations

With newer, potentially more efficient methodologies for contingency data analysis, configural procedures should be seriously evaluated for their ability to combine item-based information in configural ways. The CART methodology of Breiman, Friedman, Olshen, and Stone (1984) appears to hold promise, as does neural networking. The current lack of experience in using these models with biodata makes it difficult to assess their predictive efficacy when compared with other techniques. With large samples of appropriate items, the validities could rival those of additive empirical approaches.

One potential use of the AID type algorithms has yet to be explored. Specifically, rather than using individual items as predictors, configural models based on biodata dimensions or factors may prove useful not only in improved predictions but also in improved interpretability.

A PRIORI DIMENSION METHODS

This internally based approach to biodata scaling begins with a determination by the test developer that particular psychological constructs are to be measured. Typically the constructs chosen are those believed (often as the result of job-analytic research) to underlie job performance or other criteria of relevance to the developer. Biodata items are then written or chosen from existing item pools, based on the belief that they tap one of the constructs of interest. This strategy, like others already discussed, has been operationalized in several different ways.

Theoretical Approach

The theoretical approach (Goldberg, 1972) selects items to measure particular constructs based solely on the judgment of one or more experts. While steps may be taken to purify the resulting scales by having a new group of experts re-sort the items into scales, no other item analysis steps are taken. Item alternative weights (if necessary) are assigned by experts, and scale scores are arrived at through a simple summing.

Homogeneous Scaling

A second approach to scale construction has its roots in the work of Dubois, Loevinger, and Gleser (1952) and Jackson (1970). Using the method of homogeneous scaling or rational scaling (Goldberg, 1972; Hornick, James, & Jones, 1977), a group of experts first sorts items into targeted psychological constructs. Items are then administered to subjects, and scales are purified through internal consistency analyses.

RATIONALE: The basic rationale behind homogeneous scale construction is that homogeneous measures of psychological constructs can be developed through internal consistency analyses. It is then assumed that if the constructs were appropriately selected, the resulting scales will be predictive of the criteria of interest and will provide considerable psychological insight as well. Homogeneous scale development can take a number of forms. Illustrative approaches are described by Stricker (1989) and Jackson (1970).

REQUIREMENTS AND ASSUMPTIONS: Compared with other approaches, the homogeneous scaling procedure makes few assumptions. The major assumptions are that the psychological constructs identified as being important really are important and that experts can write and evaluate an item's ability to tap the targeted constructs. When item correlations are applied, we assume that items are linearly related to the construct being measured. This is probably not a major concern, since items are written or chosen explicitly for their relationship to the construct. Use of acquiescence and/or social desirability scales in the item analysis procedures also assumes that relevant measures of these concepts are available or can be written.

RELIABILITY CONCERNS: Internal consistency reliability is a major concern in the development of homogeneous scales. The item analysis procedure was developed to yield scales with high internal consistency reliability. Evidence suggests that the process works relatively well. Stricker's (1989) final five biodata-based personality scales yielded coefficient alpha reliability estimates of .66 to .78. These scales were made up of 8 to 22 items. Using a similar procedure with personality items, Hase and Goldberg (1967) found internal consistency reliability values for 22 homogeneously developed scales ranging from .48 to .88 (mean = .74). For 11 theoretically developed scales the range was .25 to .85 (mean = .64). Siegel (1956) used a process that started with a priori item clusters, but allowed dimensions to be created and redefined throughout an interactive item analysis procedure. He reported split-half test reliabilities for 10 scales that ranged from between .41 and .78 (mean = .65).

VALIDATION DESIGN ISSUES: The homogeneous scaling technique requires a developmental sample of subjects who are as similar as possible to those for whom the test is intended. In an employment situation, this should be an applicant sample. However, unlike externally based strategies, the sample sizes need not be extremely large. Rather, all that is necessary is a sample large enough to derive relatively stable item statistics.

Validation, at a minimum, will require showing that the scale scores are related to the criteria of interest. This could be either a predictive or concurrent study. Through these criterion-related studies, predictive effectiveness can be shown. However, if understanding is important, some form of construct validation is needed. Better understanding comes through studying the relationship of the developed scales to measures with known meaning. Homogeneous scaling maximizes the internal consistency of scales. This does not necessarily assure that the scale is measuring the targeted construct, nor does it assume that the targeted construct actually underlies criterion performance. Thus, unless further explorations of the nomological network are made, psychological interpretations of scale scores could be misleading.

STRENGTHS: Several advantages of the homogeneous scaling approach are noteworthy. First, when carefully conducted, the process yields scales that can be tied directly to an analysis of the criteria of interest. Content validity can be expected to be strong, and because of the direct attempt to measure meaningful psychological constructs, there is real potential for showing evidence of construct validity and, therefore, increased understanding. Further, because the technique does not utilize maximization or covariation techniques, sample size requirements are much less than for alternative approaches. Validation study samples can be smaller because cross-validation will be unnecessary (unless scale scores are combined through a multiple regression or other technique that capitalizes on chance). The validities of homogeneous scale scores should shrink little in cross-validation.

LIMITATIONS: While the potential for increased understanding is inherent in the method, it is not by any means guaranteed. The items must be written or chosen such that they clearly measure the targeted domain. Otherwise, the constructs we have measured may be quite different from those we think we have measured. So, too, must good judgment guide the item analysis. Core items could easily be dropped early in the process and result in less salient items driving the scale.

A final limitation is the scarcity of published biodata development efforts using this technique. Of particular concern is the difficulty of assessing how well biodata scales that are developed through homogeneous techniques predict key criteria, especially when compared to keys developed in other ways.

Recommendations
Evidence for or against the use of a priori dimension strategies is weak. Homogeneous scales with satisfactory internal consistency reliabilities can

be generated. The homogeneous scaling approach also yields some level of predictive effectiveness. Hase and Goldberg (1967) compared the empirical validities of principal factors, empirical group discriminative scaling, homogenous scaling, and theoretical scaling and found that the four approaches were equivalent in their validity across 13 diverse criteria. In a less successful application of a priori dimension techniques, Mitchell and Klimoski (1986) found little predictability for scales developed using the theoretical approach. Similarly, Stricker (1989) found that only one of five homogeneous scales showed even modest validities in predicting leadership potential.

Unfortunately, little exploration of the nomological networks for targeted constructs has been reported. The homogeneous scaling techniques offer hope for understanding biodata–criterion relationships, but that hope is far from being realized.

In general, there is little to recommend in the theoretical approach to biodata scaling when performance prediction is a major concern; however, homogenous scaling does offer promise. When theory testing is our primary or even a strong secondary goal, only this approach appears feasible. Of the many current approaches to scaling biodata items, only this approach builds scales to measure important a priori constructs. For placement and training needs analysis, homogeneous scales, when well explored and defined, hold potential.

DIMENSION DISCOVERY METHODS

The dimension discovery methods are based on a test developer's desire to identify some small number of dimensions or factors being measured by the biodata items of interest. Three general approaches have been used for this purpose: factor analysis of items, component analysis of items, and cluster analysis of items. In each case, the result is a reduced number of new variables underlying the full set of items. We will focus on factor analytic approaches and specifically on factor extraction through the principal factors technique.

Factor Analysis

RATIONALE: The primary goal in the factor analytic approach to biodata construction is to develop meaningful dimensions or factors based on a current set of items. Thus, for this approach to be useful, the resulting dimensions must be interpretable to the test user. For without improved meaningfulness, the factorial approach is simply an empirical approach based on factors or clusters of items rather than on the items themselves.

Procedures for employing the factor analytic approach are documented by Baehr and Williams (1967), Childs and Klimoski (1986), Klimoski (1973), and Mitchell and Klimoski (1982).

REQUIREMENTS AND ASSUMPTIONS: In using a principal factors approach to scaling biodata, several important assumptions are made. First, the item alternatives must be ordered along some continuum. While on the surface this seems very reasonable, biodata items often do not have a natural order. For example, if an item asks, "What is your occupation?", there is no natural order of occupations. However, depending on the criterion of interest or the dimension one wishes to measure, an ordering can be defined. Another potential solution to this problem is through dummy-coding the item alternatives. This, however, could lead to concerns over factoring dichotomous items.

A second assumption when using a principal factors approach is that the common variance among items is more important than the unique variance. Thus, in predicting future events, we are willing to base decisions on information based solely on the resulting dimension structure. Evidence to date suggests that biodata items, as currently written and used, hold much unique variance. Mumford and Owens (1987) report that retained factor solutions typically account for only 30 to 50 percent of the total item variance. This is fine if that common variance is the variance that is predictive. Unfortunately, we have no studies available to suggest or confirm that this necessarily is the case.

A third assumption made when using the principal factors approach to biodata scaling and validation is that the relationship between the item as scaled and the criterion is linear. Even when alternatives are ordered along some natural continuum, the relationship of the alternatives to the criterion is often nonlinear. Experience suggests that there are a number of items for which the linear relationship is strong, up to a point. The item–criterion regression lines tend to flatten out at the upper end of the item alternative range. Beyond a certain response level on the item, the criterion level does not increase. To the extent that such item criterion relationships are in the item pool, the validity of factorial scales is likely to be less than optimal.

The principal factors analysis approach also assumes that both items and subjects represent populations. Theoretically, in applying this technique, attempts to generalize beyond the current set of items and subjects should not be made (Weiss, 1976). Further discussion of this will be made later when discussing alternative dimension discovery approaches.

RELIABILITY CONCERNS: With factorial approaches, internally consistent dimensions are expected and thus should be evaluated. Results of internal consistency analyses by Baehr and Williams (1967) and Owens (1976) suggest that dimension reliabilities in the .70s can be expected. Thus, given enough items per dimension (five to six minimum), acceptable levels of internal consistency reliability are likely. Related to reliability is concern over the stability and generalizability of factor structures when applied to new samples. Little or no stability investigation has been conducted with principal factors solutions to biodata items. However, based on factors resulting from principal components analyses, Owens and his colleagues suggest that the component stability across similar samples of subjects and over time is generally satisfactory, particularly when the Owens' *Biographical Questionnaire* or *Biographical Information Blank* is used (Ames, 1983; Eberhardt & Muchinsky, 1982; Lautenschlager & Shaffer, 1987; Mumford & Owens, 1987; Owens & Schoenfeldt, 1979). When sex and age effects are studied, evidence using Owens' (1976) items suggests that different factor structures are likely for men and women and that different structures are likely to emerge by age group (Mumford, Shaffer, Ames, & Owens, 1983; Mumford, Shaffer, Jackson, Neiner, Denning, & Owens, 1983). Given these differences, we might also expect different races and ethnic origins to yield different factor structures. Such results could be problematic in applied selection settings.

VALIDATION DESIGN ISSUES: One immediate concern in developing and validating factorial scales for use in performance prediction is the need for an applicant sample. While not explicitly addressed in the literature, factor structures may vary between applicant and employee samples. Basing development effort solely on an employee (concurrent) sample could yield dimensions that are appropriate only for current employees (or other preselected referent groups). This becomes increasingly serious as the employee sample becomes increasingly restricted.

At a minimum, an empirical validation study is needed to link the dimensions to the criterion. If dimension scores are unit weighted to create a total score or are used individually, a cross-validation design may be unnecessary. A concurrent design may be feasible, although care must be taken to assure that the items are relatively unbiased when answered by the restricted group (typically employees).

STRENGTHS: The factorial approach to biodata scales offers several important advantages. The method can yield dimensions that have the potential for conveying psychological meaning. Empirical validities can be substantial, though typically somewhat below those of empirical approaches (Fuentes, Sawyer, & Greener, 1989; Mitchell & Klimoski, 1982; Mumford & Owens, 1987). The development of such scales does not appreciably capitalize on chance, and items are not individually keyed. There-fore, large empirical validation samples are generally not needed. Still, vali-dation samples of 100 or more would seem prudent. Because this approach can yield meaningful dimensions, it has the potential of being very useful in making placement decisions and in identifying training needs.

LIMITATIONS: The problem of item uniqueness is one limitation of the factorial approach. By focusing on common variance, the factorial ap-proach throws out the unique variance. The question that needs to be addressed is how predictive is the unique variance and, if it is predictive, can we develop additional items that will make more of it common? This can be accomplished, but at what price?

The factor analytic approach also requires a large sample of subjects in the factoring process. Stable factor solutions typically require in the neigh-borhood of 10 subjects per item (Nunnally, 1978). Hence, to factor a 200-item questionnaire, 2,000 subjects would be needed. In many cases, this is not feasible.

The final shortcoming of the factorial approach may be the difficulties involved in building psychologically meaningful dimensions. Developing meaningful dimensionality requires substantial construct validation work. The developer must explicitly define a nomological network and investi-gate the focal dimensions under a number of circumstances. The process requires substantial time as well as many targeted subjects willing to participate in the evaluation process. To date, this programmatic research has not appeared in the literature.

Other Dimension Discovery Techniques

While the principal factors approach is probably the most common form of covariation analysis applied to biodata keying, others are available and, in some circumstances, are quite appropriate. Within factor analytic techniques, the choice of methods should be based on the assumptions made as to whether subjects or items represent samples or populations. Strictly speaking, principal factors analysis is appropriate only when both subjects and items are assumed to represent the population. Generalizing beyond those variables or the development group of subjects should not be attempted. More often, the goal is to generalize to a broader population of subjects. Canonical factor analysis is designed to yield a set of factor scores for individuals that maximizes prediction of factor scores from responses to the original items. This, however, creates a new problem, in that the canonical method requires that the number of factors be known in advance (Weiss, 1976). No application of this method to biodata scaling could be found.

When the covariation analysis focuses not on the common item variance but on the total item variance, principal components analysis and cluster analysis methods may be applicable. While principal components analysis has been used to reduce an initial set of biodata items to a smaller set of underlying factors, this total item variance approach does tend to analyze some unreliable item variance. Further, the solution provided by this method often capitalizes on that unreliability (Weiss, 1976). This method was applied by Morrison, Owens, Glennon, and Albright (1962) when 75 valid personal history items were factored into five dimensions. Those dimensions accounted for only 23 percent of the total item variance. Eberhardt and Muchinsky (1982), Lautenschlager and Shaffer (1987), Owens and Schoenfeldt (1979), and Schmuckler (1966) are among those who have employed principal components analysis with biodata items.

Cluster analysis is a third item covariation methodology that can be applied in order to group items into meaningful subgroups. Cluster analyses yield clusters that classify items in relation to each other. The grouping is based not on common variance but on the total item variance. Thus, item variance is not partitioned across clusters. Cluster analysis is appropriate when the data violate the assumptions of factor analysis and the goal is to develop an item taxonomy or classification scheme (Weiss, 1976). By keeping all of an item's variance intact, clustering approaches can potentially group items into a smaller meaningful set of clusters. The predictability in the item uniqueness can be maintained. Actual application of this technique to biodata items could not be found. It is a worthy topic for future investigation.

Recommendations

The dimension discovery approach to biodata scaling is particularly appropriate when interpretation and prediction are both important. Thus, covariation techniques are well suited to the development of biodata for placement and training needs analysis. While typically not as empirically valid as empirical methods, the covariation analysis techniques do yield valid predictions. When the goal is theory building, covariation techniques, if carefully applied, offer some real potential. If maximal prediction of performance is the sole goal, these techniques are cumbersome and yield less than optimal predictive power. The WAB approach continues to offer greater potential here.

SUBGROUPING METHODS

This final general approach to biodata keying stems from the belief that people, grouped on the basis of the pattern of their prior experiences, will behave similarly in the future. Thus, the goal of subgrouping strategies is to identify coherent, meaningful groups of people, groups that are based on responses to biodata items. The key proponents of this approach, Owens and his colleagues, have amassed a large body of evidence attesting to the efficacy of this developmental-integrative model.

The Developmental-Integrative Model

RATIONALE: The developmental-integrative model as operationalized by Owens (1968, 1971, 1976) and Owens and Schoenfeldt (1979) proposes the subgrouping of subjects based on similarities in the patterns of prior experiences. Groups of people who have behaved in a similar way in the past can be expected to behave similarly in the future. The general procedure begins with the development of an item pool of biodata experiences covering a broad spectrum of situations. Items are administered to a large sample of individuals, and a principal components analysis is carried out. This analysis yields dimensions that are then used to profile individuals. Next, profiles are entered into a cluster analyses procedure to identify subgroups of individuals with similar profiles. Cluster centroids are used to describe and label each cluster or subgroup.

REQUIREMENTS AND ASSUMPTIONS: Owens' subgrouping approach, as laid out in the previous discussion, assumes that item–dimension relationships are linear, that item alternatives are ordered along some continuum, and that item uniqueness is expendable. The approach also assumes that items can be written that are, on the one hand, broad enough to be applicable to a relatively general population and, on the other hand, tap information that is predictive in targeted situations.

RELIABILITY CONCERNS: Cluster analysis results will only be stable if the measures that are clustered are reliable. Hence, if profiles of individual items are to be clustered, item reliabilities become a concern; similarly, when clustering is based on dimension scores, the reliability of the dimensions should be assessed. Also of concern are the stability and generalizability of the resulting subgroups of interest, the changing subgroup membership that may occur over time and experience, and the reproducibility of the subgroups in a new setting with similar subjects as well as with a different population of subject. Research reported in Mumford and Owens (1987) suggests relatively positive results for this large-scale biodata research program.

VALIDATION DESIGN NEEDS: The process of validating subgrouping approaches is quite different from that of other approaches. The value of the approach is directly related to its ability to capture meaningful developmental patterns that go beyond those embodied in the biodata variables used for defining the subgroups. To this end, Owens and Schoenfeldt (1979) administered a number of standard psychological tests and observed the results of these in relation to subgroup definitions. Further research (reported in Mumford & Owens, 1987) has shown subgroup status to be an effective predictor of performance in some 80 to 90 percent of the studies conducted. Performance areas studied included academic achievement (overachievement and underachievement), vocational interests, drug use, personality, social behavior, and motivation.

STRENGTHS: The potential benefits of subgrouping are substantial. The results of the few studies using external occupational criteria are promising. Successful salespeople clustered into three of nine subgroups identified by Taylor (1968) and Pinto (1970) used subgroups to successfully predict sales performance. Criterion information is not used in developing subgroups, so shrinkage of coefficients is not expected. The process, when developed with a broad sample of items and subjects, can apply across a wide range of situations. Further, subgrouping is claimed to be dynamic in the sense that as further information is gathered about subgroups, it can be used to improve future predictions.

LIMITATIONS: Large sample sizes are required to perform the component analysis step for subgrouping strategies. Large samples also improve the stability of clustering solutions. Because different approaches to clustering can yield quite different results, two researchers working with identical data sets are likely to generate different cluster solutions. These and related variations in results should be examined before a subgrouping solution is accepted (Weiss, 1976). A further shortcoming associated with the use of cluster analysis is the problem of outliers and overlaps. Owens and Schoenfeldt (1979) were unable to classify 27 percent of the individuals entering the cluster analysis. In a theory-generation environment, this may not be a major problem. It is untenable in an applied situation, such as when selection decisions are to be made. From a purely practical point of view, users of the selection questionnaire would be quite disgruntled if no prediction could be made for as many as one-quarter of the individuals tested. From a pure criterion prediction point of view, these unclassified cases could be predicted to be average, but little can be done to realize such information associated with knowing group membership. Loosening group classification criteria could also yield less dictinct and interpretable groups.

Recommendations

One of the major positive results of the subgrouping approach to biodata is the large program of theory-building research that Owens and his colleagues have generated. The study of biodata has been advanced by the interest in understanding what is being measured by a particular biographical questionnaire and the resulting subgroups of individuals. The focus of this series of studies has primarily been on college experiences. This needs to be broadened. Perhaps a broader, adult-oriented biodata reference questionnaire would be a first step.

Subgrouping holds promise for prediction. Unfortunately, with very few selection studies to recommend it, we cannot judge how well biodata-based subgroups will predict job performance in particular situations. Empirical approaches need to be directly challenged by subgrouping strategies. Subgrouping also holds potential for improving placement decisions. Studies by Brush and Owens (1979), Neiner and Owens (1985), Eberhardt and Muchinsky (1984), and Mecham, Stokes, and Owens (in press) provide preliminary evidence that occupational choice is related to subgroup membership.

Subgrouping techniques may also help evaluate training needs of existing employees. In this context, however, the items would have to be more specific and probably narrower in scope. Theory testing is possible through subgrouping if the dimensions are built through an a priori, homogeneous scaling approach. Further, it may be possible to define subgroups a priori, empirically confirm them, and then explore the theory.

COMBINING SCALING STRATEGIES

Many scaling strategies and techniques can be applied to the development of biodata tools. Each has particular strengths and limitations. Moreover, many of the various approaches can easily be combined. One general approach might be to develop the tool using an additive externally based approach and to follow that up with a dimension discovery approach. The latter step will aid in understanding the dimensionality of the predictive items as keyed to the specific criterion. This approach has been successfully applied by Crosby, Dalessio, and McManus (1990).

Alternately, one could develop the instrument through a theoretical a priori dimension approach and subsequently develop scaling through an externally based strategy. Predictions developed through an additive externally based approach could be used in conjunction with those developed configurally. Dimension scores, whether developed through a priori techniques or discovery techniques, might also be combined configurally or through subgrouping, as demonstrated by Owens and Schoenfeldt (1979).

One potentially useful approach is to follow a dimension discovery construction effort with an item-response-theory-based analysis. Multiple response models can potentially accommodate biographical items. Further, IRT procedures have been applied to identify items that are biased toward particular groups of respondents (Hulin, Drasgow, & Parsons, 1983). An application of these analyses to biodata scales is likely in the near future.

With careful attention to technique assumptions, restrictions, strengths, and limitations, the sequential combining of scaling strategies may yield biodata tools that capitalize on the strengths of each technique and minimize the limitations. Research is needed to assess this potential.

VALIDATION DESIGNS
AND VALIDITY IMPLICATIONS

As noted earlier, efforts to validate biodata begin with an examination of the purposes for developing the instrument and an understanding of the various situational constraints to be addressed. Externally based scaling strategies require criterion data in the scaling phase. Internally based strategies do not.

Space does not permit an in-depth review of validation design strategies and their implications. Substantive discussions can be found in Barrett, Phillips, and Alexander (1981), Cook and Campbell (1976, 1979), Guion and Cranny (1982), Landy (1986), Messick (1981), and Sussmann and Robertson (1986). When we discuss validation designs, the issues that are important to ability tests or personality inventories are usually applicable to biodata instruments. In each case, validation seeks to confer substantive meaning on inferences that can be drawn from test scores. Messick (1981) discusses three perspectives on the mediation of test and nontest behaviors and examines their implications for psychological measurement. These realist, constructivist, and constructive-realist views of the test–nontest relationships are important considerations in the development and validation of biodata instruments, as well as for personality and cognitive measures. Further, Messick points out several pitfalls in validation design that lead to confusion in score interpretation. Sussmann and Robertson (1986) assess 11 common criterion-related validation designs based on Cook and Campbell's (1976) four types of validity: statistical conclusion validity, internal validity, construct validity, and external validity. Their evaluation suggests that none of the 11 designs can be considered the most appropriate design for all purposes. Each has a different pattern of vulnerability to threats to these four types of validity. In validating biodata, regardless of whether an externally based or an internally based strategy is used, care must be taken to understand the potential threats to validity, and the ways in which various designs deal with the threats. Sussmann and Robertson (1986) argue convincingly that understanding can only come through programmatic research based on a series of studies using different designs.

Several recent biodata research have gone beyond the typical single, criterion-oriented study approach to validating biodata. Mumford and Nickels (1990) have argued that in order to contribute to understanding, biodata measures need to be tied to psychological constructs. Evidence for content and construct validity will build as these constructs are specified, adequately sampled through previous behaviors and experiences, and related to later performance. To this end, two general kinds of biodata constructs are proposed to predict performance. The first set of constructs focuses on the resources individuals need to perform. The second set centers on the constructs that condition an individual's willingness to use the resource constructs. Mumford and Nickels (1990) discuss various strategies for assessing biodata measures based on this transactional resources allocation model.

Schoenfeldt and Mendoza (1988) relate an effort to build a biodata instrument to test Schoenfeldt's (1979) four-dimension models of managerial effectiveness. This model drove a content-oriented biodata questionnaire development effort using the theoretical a priori dimension technique. Construct validation used a confirmatory factor model with some mixed success. As an example of the theory testing use of biodata, the study suggests a first step in construct validation. Later steps should expand to include alternative measures of the construct and some examination of how the constructs relate to managerial performance.

A third recent development effort looks at the construct validity of the *Individual Achievement Record* (IAR), a biodata instrument developed and validated as an aid in the selection for entry-level federal professional and administrative positions (see Chapter 11 of this volume). Gandy, Outerbridge, Sharf, and Dye (1989) developed the IAR by applying an externally based item–criterion regression technique to items selected to tap four content areas. The construct validity of the IAR is now being assessed. The four factors measured by the IAR are general self-esteem, scholastic achievement, academic achievement, and social leadership. Other measures included in the construct validation efforts include ability and aptitude measures, temperament and personality measures, work values, and vocational interests. Dye (1990) has proposed several models relating the biodata scores to outside measures, and is currently conducting the necessary analyses to evaluate the models.

The Life Insurance Marketing and Research Association (LIMRA) has developed, implemented, and maintained biodata instruments for over 50 years and for more than 10 million job candidates. Developed in the 1930s to select life insurance agents in the United States, the current measure, the *Career Profile,* has a long history of research (Thayer, 1977).

Originally, the *Career Profile* consisted of 10 biographical questions keyed against success as an agent and was moderated by groupings of candidates (Life Insurance Sales Research Bureau, 1937). Brown (1978) applied the original key to data collected nearly 40 years later and observed little loss in predictive power. *Career Profile* research has examined issues related to revalidating and revising a test that is in use (Brown, 1979; Brown, Stout, Dalessio, & Crosby, 1989; Crosby, 1990; McManus, 1989b; Peterson & Wallace, 1966) and has looked closely at the whole issue of identifying and discouraging faking and response manipulation (Baratta & Stout, 1989; McManus, 1989a, 1989b).

SOME FINAL COMMENTS

The validation of biodata measures cannot be neatly summarized in a cookbook format. In all validation efforts, many issues, goals, and constraints directly influence the direction of our efforts. Of primary concern must be a careful delineation of our primary goals in developing a biodata questionnaire. In many cases, for better or for worse, our only goal is to make better predictions of performance. There is nothing wrong with this as a sole purpose. With better prediction come other outcomes that are quite worthy—greater profits for the company, better service to the public, and fewer personnel frustrations that result from less accurate decisions. The future suggests that demographic changes in the next decades will cause labor shortages. If so, we can clearly expect a deemphasis of selection and an increased emphasis on placement and training needs analysis. Purely empirical approaches are likely to become less useful.

Those who decry the empiricism that has yielded the biodata scoring keys that most often improve predictions do make a very worthwhile point. The raw empiricism of the pure externally based scaling strategies does little to advance the discipline of industrial and organizational psychology. Unfortunately, many of the more enlightened studies are little better. Our understanding of the relationship of how prior experiences and behaviors influence future behavior will grow only with large programs of research. This research needs to focus on a core taxonomy of constructs that

TABLE 2   Item Scaling Techniques for Various Study Goals

Secondary Purpose	Primary Purpose				
	Performance Prediction	Placement	Training Needs Analysis	Theory Building	Theory Testing
Performance Prediction	Additive Configural	Additive Configural Dimension discovery	Additive Configural Dimension discovery	Dimension discovery Subgrouping	A priori dimension
Placement	Additive Configural Dimension discovery Subgrouping	Additive Dimension discovery Subgrouping	A priori dimension Dimension discovery	Dimension discovery Subgrouping	A priori dimension
Training Needs Analysis	Additive A priori dimension Configural Dimension discovery	A priori dimension Dimension discovery	A priori dimension Dimension discovery	Dimension discovery Subgrouping	A priori dimension
Theory Building	Dimension discovery Subgrouping	Dimension discovery Subgrouping	Dimension discovery Subgrouping	Dimension discovery Subgrouping	A priori dimension
Theory Testing	A priori dimension	A priori dimension	A priori dimension	A priori dimension	A prior dimension

can be measured through biodata items. The operationally defined constructs must then undergo the scrutiny of multiple studies and validation designs.

Central, too, to any discussion of validation is the development of criteria. Space prevents any in-depth comments about this subject, but that should not be interpreted as a lack of importance. Generally, good biodata measures will be constructed only after careful consideration is made of the performance that is to be predicted and the conditions under which it will occur. Campbell (1990) presents a general theory of performance that may help biodata researchers do a better job of identifying appropriate performance measures and of developing biodata items and measures that explicitly tap the targeted performance domain.

In summary, we are again drawn to the premise that all biodata instruments are developed and validated for one or two overriding purposes. Table 2 creates a grid in which the columns represent possible primary purposes and the rows represent secondary goals. Cell entries represent biodata scaling strategies that appear to offer the greatest potential for the stated goals. In some cases, these entries are research based. More often, however, they are based on educated guesses—guesses that need to be confirmed with research.

Several points are worth noting. If theory testing is either a primary or secondary goal, only the a priori dimension approach appears to hold promise. Also worth noting is that the externally based techniques, traditionally the most frequently used approach, are the clear preference only when prediction is the only goal. They may also be valuable for combined prediction and placement situations, but they are only one of several feasible approaches.

As seen from Table 2, in many cases there is no clearly preferred approach. Only comparative studies of specific scaleing techniques will lead to a more completely defined grid. Each scaling strategy has a place. Future research will allow practitioners and scientists to choose the techniques that are most likely to help them accomplish their biodata validation goals.

REFERENCES

Ames, S. D. (1983). *Prediction of research vs. applied interests in veterinarians: A biographical approach*. Unpublished master's thesis, University of Georgia, Athens, GA.

Asher, J. J. (1972). The biographical item: Can it be improved? *Personnel Psychology, 25,* 257–269.

Baehr, M. E., & Williams, G. B. (1967). Underlying dimensions of personal background data and their relationship to occupational classification. *Journal of Applied Psychology, 51,* 481–490.

Baratta, J. E., & Stout, J. D. (1989). *Fakability of a computerized biodata instrument* (Tech. Rep. No. MRR10–1989). Hartford, CT: Life Insurance Marketing and Research Association.

Barge, B. N., & Hough, L. M. (1988). Utility of biographical data for predicting job performance. In L. M. Hough (Ed.), *Utility of temperament, biodata, and interest assessment for predicting job performance: A review and integration of the literature* (ARI Research Note RN 88–02). Alexandria, VA: U.S. Army Institute for the Behavioral and Social Sciences.

Barrett, G. V., Phillips, J. S., & Alexander, R. A. (1981). Concurrent and predictive validity designs. *Journal of Applied Psychology, 66,* 1–6.

Breiman, L., Friedman, J., Olshen, R., & Stone, C. (1984). *Classification and regression trees.* New York: Wadsworth.

Brown, S. H. (1978). Long-term validity of a personal history item scoring procedure. *Journal of Applied Psychology, 63,* 673–676.

Brown, S. H. (1979). Validity distortions associated with a test in use. *Journal of Applied Psychology, 64,* 460–462.

Brown, S. H. (1981). Validity generalization and situational moderation in the life insurance industry. *Journal of Applied Psychology, 66,* 664–670.

Brown, S. H., Stout, J. D., Dalessio, A. T., & Crosby, M. M. (1989). Stability of validity indices through test scores ranges. *Journal of Applied Psychology, 73,* 736–742.

Brush, D. H. (1974). *Predicting major field of college concentration with biographical and vocational interest data: A longitudinal study.* Unpublished master's thesis, University of Georgia, Athens, GA.

Brush, D. H., & Owens, W. A. (1979). Implementation and evaluation of an assessment classification model for manpower utilization. *Personnel Psychology, 32,* 369–383.

Campbell, J. P. (1974). *Psychometric theory in industrial and organizational psychology* (Rep. No. 2001). Arlington, VA: Personnel and Training Research Programs, Office of Naval Research.

Campbell, J. P. (1990). Modeling the performance prediction problem in industrial and organizational psychology. In M. D. Dunnette & L. M. Hough (Eds.), *Handbook of industrial and organizational psychology* (2d ed., vol. 1, pp. 687–732). Palo Alto, CA: Consulting Psychologists Press.

Chaney, F. B. (1964). *The life history antecedents of selected vocational interests.* Unpublished doctoral dissertation, Purdue University, West Lafayette, IN.

Childs, A., & Klimoski, R. J. (1986). Successfully predicting career success: An application of the biographical inventory. *Journal of Applied Psychology, 71,* 3–8.

Cook, T. D., & Campbell, D. T. (1976). The design and conduct of quasi-experiments and true experiments in field settings. In M. D. Dunnette (Ed.), *Handbook of industrial and organizational psychology* (pp. 223–326). Chicago: Rand McNally.

Cook, T. D., & Campbell, D. T. (1979). *Quasi-experimentation: Design and analysis issues for field settings.* Chicago: Rand McNally.

Crosby, M. M. (1990, April). *Social desirability and biodata: Predicting sales success.* Paper presented at the annual meeting of the Society for Industrial and Organizational Psychology, Miami Beach, FL.

Crosby, M. M., Dalessio, A. T., & McManus, M. A. (1990). *Stability of biodata dimensions across English-speaking cultures: A confirmatory investigation.* Paper presented at the annual meeting of the American Psychological Association, Boston.

DuBois, P. H., Loevinger, J., & Gleser, G. C. (1952). *The construction of homogeneous keys for a biographical inventory* (USAF Human Resources Research Bulletin No. 52–18, 19p).

Dye, D. A. (1990). *Construct validity of the Individual Achievement Record.* Paper presented at the annual meeting of the Society for Industrial and Organizational Psychology, Miami Beach, FL.

Eberhardt, B. J., & Muchinsky, P. M. (1982). An empirical investigation of the factor stability of Owens' biographical questionnaire. *Journal of Applied Psychology, 67,* 138–145.

Eberhardt, B. J., & Muchinsky, P. M. (1984). Structural validation of Holland's hexagonal model: Vocational classification through the use of Holland's model. *Journal of Applied Psychology, 69,* 174–181.

England, G. W. (1971). *Development and use of weighted application blanks* (Bulletin No. 55, rev. ed.). Minneapolis: University of Minnesota, Industrial Relations Center.

Fuentes, R. R., Sawyer, J. E., & Greener, J. M. (1989). *Comparison of the predictive characteristics of three biodata scaling methods.* Paper presented at the annual meeting of the American Psychological Association, New Orleans.

Gandy, J. A., Outerbridge, A. N., Sharf, J. C., & Dye, D. A. (1989). *Development and initial validation of the Individual Achievement Record (IAR).* Washington, DC: U.S. Office of Personnel Management.

Goldberg, L. R. (1972). Parameters of personality inventory construction and utilization: A comparison of prediction strategies and tactics. *Multivariate Behavior Research Monograph* (No. 72–2).

Guion, R. M., & Cranny, C. J. (1982). A note on concurrent and predictive designs: A critical reanalysis. *Journal of Applied Psychology, 67,* 239–244.

Hase, H. D., & Goldberg, L. R. (1967). The comparative validity of different strategies of deriving personality inventory scales. *Psychological Bulletin, 67,* 231–248.

Henry, E. R. (1966). *Research conference on the use of autobiographical data as psychological predictors.* Greensboro, NC: The Creativity Research Institute, The Richardson Foundation.

Hinrichs, J. R., Haanpera, S., & Sonkin, L. (1976). Validity of a biographical information blank across national boundaries. *Personnel Psychology, 29,* 417–421.

Hornick, C. W., James, L. R., & Jones, A. P. (1977). Empirical item keying versus a rational approach to analyzing a psychological climate questionnaire. *Applied Psychological Measurement, 1,* 489–500.

Hulin, C. L., Drasgow, T., & Parsons, C. K. (1983). *Item response theory: Application to psychological measurement.* Homewood, IL: Dow Jones-Irwin.

Hunter, J. E., & Hunter, R. F. (1984). Validity and utility of alternative predictors of job performance. *Psychological Bulletin, 96,* 72–76.

Jackson, D. N. (1970). A sequential system for personality scale construction. In C. D. Spielberger (Ed.), *Current topics in clinical and community psychology* (Vol. 2, pp. 61–96). New York: Academic Press.

Klimoski, R. J. (1973). A biographical data analysis of career patterns in engineering. *Journal of Vocational Behavior, 3,* 103–113.

Landy, F. J. (1986). Stamp collecting versus science: Validation as hypothesis testing. *American Psychologist, 41,* 1183–1192.

Laurent, H. (1970). Cross-cultural cross validation of empirically validated tests. *Journal of Applied Psychology, 54,* 417–423.

Lautenschlager, G. J., & Shaffer, G. S. (1987). Reexamining the component stability of Owens' biographical questionnaire. *Journal of Applied Psychology, 72,* 149–152.

Lecznar, W. B., & Dailey, J. T. (1950). Keying biographical inventories in classification test batteries. *American Psychologist, 5,* 279.

Levine, A. S., & Zachert, V. (1951). Use of a biographical inventory in the air force classification program. *Journal of Applied Psychology, 35,* 241–244.

Life Insurance Sales Research Bureau. (1937). *Selection of agents.* Hartford, CT: Author.

Lubin, A., & Osburn, H. G. (1957). A theory of pattern analysis for the prediction of a qualitative criterion. *Psychometrika, 122,* 63–73.

Malloy, J. (1955). The prediction of college achievement with the life experience inventory. *Educational and Psychological Measurement, 15,* 170–180.

Malone, M. P. (1978). Predictive efficiency and discriminatory impact of verifiable biographical data as a function of data analysis procedures. (Doctoral dissertation, Illinois Institute of Technology). *Dissertation Abstracts International,* 4520–B.

McManus, M. A. (1989a). *Detection of faking on an empirically-based biodata instrument* (Tech. Rep. No. MRR8–1989). Hartford, CT: Life Insurance Marketing and Research Association.

McManus, M. A. (1989b). *The impact of data manipulation by recruiters on validity estimates* (Tech. Rep. No. MRR7–1989). Hartford, CT: Life Insurance Marketing and Research Association.

McManus, M. A., & Mitchell, T. W. (1987). *Test and retest reliability of the Career Profile.* Hartford, CT: Life Insurance Marketing and Research Association.

McQuitty, L. L. (1957). Isolating predictor patterns associated with major criterion patterns. *Educational and Psychological Measurement, 17,* 3–42.

Mecham, R. C., Stokes, G. S., & Owens, W. A. (in press). *The prediction of job family membership from life history subgroups.*

Meehl, P. E. (1950). Configural scoring. *Journal of Consulting Psychology, 14,* 165–171.

Messick, S. (1981). Constructs and their vicissitudes in educational and psychological measurement. *Psychological Bulletin, 89,* 575–588.

Meyers, R. C., & Schultz, D. G. (1950). Predicting academic achievement with use of a new attitude-interest questionnaire, I. *Educational and Psychological Measurement, 10,* 654–663.

Mitchell, T. W., & Klimoski, R. J. (1982). Is it rational to be empirical? *Journal of Applied Psychology, 67,* 411–418.

Mitchell, T. W., & Klimoski, R. J. (1986). Estimating the validity of cross-validity estimation. *Journal of Applied Psychology, 71,* 311–317.

Morgan, J. N., & Messinger, R. C. (1973). *THAID: A sequential search program for the analysis of nominal scale dependent variables.* Ann Arbor, MI: Institute for Social Research, University of Michigan.

Morrison, R. F. (1977). A multivariate model for the occupational placement decision. *Journal of Applied Psychology, 62,* 271–277.

Morrison, R. F., Owens, W. A., Glennon, J. R., & Albright, L. E. (1962). Factored life history antecedents of industrial research performance. *Journal of Applied Psychology, 46,* 281–284.

Mumford, M. D., & Nickels, B. J. (1990). *Applying principles of contact and construct validity to background data.* Paper presented at the annual meeting of the Society for Industrial and Organizational Psychology, Miami Beach, FL.

Mumford, M. D., & Owens, W. A. (1987). Methodological review: Principles, procedures, and findings in the application of background data measures. *Applied Psychological Measurement, 11,* 1–31.

Mumford, M. D., Shaffer, G. S., Ames, S. D., & Owens, W. A. (1983). *Analysis of PCE1 responses over time.* Athens, GA: Institute for Behavioral Research.

Mumford, M. D., Shaffer, G. S., Jackson, K. E., Neiner, A., Denning, D., & Owens, W. A. (1983). *Male-female differences in the structure of background data measures.* Athens, GA: Institute for Behavioral Research.

Neidt, C. O., & Malloy, J. P. (1954). A technique for keying items of an inventory to be added to an existing test battery. *Journal of Applied Psychology, 38,* 308–312.

Neiner, A. G., & Owens, W. A. (1985). Using biodata to predict job choice among college graduates. *Journal of Applied Psychology, 70,* 127–136.

Nunnally, J. C. (1978). *Psychometric theory* (2d ed.). New York: McGraw-Hill.

Owens, W. A. (1968). Toward one discipline of scientific psychology. *American Psychologist, 23,* 782–785.

Owens, W. A. (1971). A quasi-actuarial prospect for individual assessment. *American Psychologist, 26,* 992–999.

Owens, W. A. (1976). Background data. In M. D. Dunnette (Ed.), *Handbook of industrial and organizational psychology* (pp. 609–644). Chicago: Rand McNally.

Owens, W. A., & Schoenfeldt, L. F. (1979). Toward a classification of persons [Monograph]. *Journal of Applied Psychology, 65,* 569–607.

Pace, L. A., & Schoenfeldt, L. F. (1977). Legal concerns in the use of weighted applications. *Personnel Psychology, 30,* 159–166.

Peterson, D. A., & Wallace, S. R. (1966). Validation and revision of a test in use. *Journal of Applied Psychology, 50,* 13–17.

Perrault, W. D., & Barksdale, H. C., Jr. (1980). A model-free approach for analysis of complex contingency data in survey research. *Journal of Marketing Research, 17,* 503–515.

Pinto, P. R. (1970). *Subgrouping in prediction: A comparison of moderator and actuarial approaches.* Unpublished doctoral dissertation, University of Georgia, Athens.

Reilly, R. R., & Chao, G. T. (1982). Validity and fairness or some alternative employee selection procedures. *Personnel Psychology, 35,* 1–62.

Reilly, R. R., & Warech, M. A. (1988). *The validity and fairness of alternative predictors of occupational performance.* Unpublished manuscript, Stevens Institute of Technology, Hoboken, NJ.

Rochester, J. B. (1990). New business uses for neuro-computing. *I/S Analyzer, 28,* 1–16.

Rothstein, H. R., Schmidt, F. L., Erwin, F. W., Owens, W. A., & Sparks, P. P. (1990). Biographical data in employment selection: Can validities be made generalizable? *Journal of Applied Psychology, 75,* 175–184.

Schmidt, N., Gooding, R. Z., Noe, R. A., & Kirsch, M. (1984). Meta-analyses of validity studies published between 1964 and 1982 and the investigation of study characteristics. *Personnel Psychology, 37,* 407–422.

Schmuckler, E. (1966). *Age differences in biographical inventories: A factor analytic study.* Greensboro, NC: The Creativity Research Institute, The Richardson Foundation.

Schoenfeldt, L. F. (1974). Utilization of manpower: Development and evaluation of an assessment-classification model for matching individuals with jobs. *Journal of Applied Psychology, 59,* 583–595.

Schoenfeldt, L. F. (1979). Some possible applications for knowledge of the manager's role. In P. Pinto (Chair), *Analyzing managerial work requirements.* Symposium conducted at the annual meeting of the American Psychological Association, New York.

Schoenfeldt, L. F., & Mendoza, J. L. (1988). *The content and constant validation of a biographical questionnaire.* Paper presented at the annual meeting of the American Psychological Association, Atlanta.

Schuh, A. L. (1967). The predictability of employee tenure: A review of the literature. *Personnel Psychology, 20,* 133–152.

Schultz, D. G., & Green, B. F., Jr. (1953). Predicting academic achievement with the use of a new attitude-interest questionnaire, II. *Educational and Psychological Measurement, 13,* 54–64.

Siegel, L. A. (1956). A biographical inventory for students: I. Construction and standardization of the instrument. *Journal of Applied Psychology, 40,* 5–10.

Sonquist, J. A. (1970). Multivariate model building. In *The Validation of a Search Procedure.* Ann Arbor, MI: University of Michigan, Survey Research Center.

Sonquist, J. A., Baker, E. L., & Morgan, J. N. (1973). *Searching for structure* (rev. ed.). Ann Arbor, MI: University of Michigan, Institute for Social Research.

Sonquist, J. R., & Morgan, J. N. (1964). *The detection of interaction effects* (University of Michigan Survey Research Center Monograph No. 35). Ann Arbor, MI: University of Michigan Press.

Sorenson, W. W. (1964). *Configural scoring of biographical terms for predicting sales success.* Unpublished doctoral dissertation, University of Minnesota, Minneapolis.

Stead, N. H., & Shaartle, C. L. (1940). *Occupational counseling techniques.* New York: American Book.

Stricker, L. J. (1989). *Assessing leadership potential at the naval academy with a biographical measure* (Research Rep. No. RR 89–14). Princeton, NJ: Education Testing Service.

Strong, E. K. (1926). An interest test for personnel managers. *Journal of Personnel Research, 5,* 194–203.

Sussmann, M., & Robertson, D. U. (1986). The validity of validity: An analysis of validation study designs. *Journal of Applied Psychology, 71,* 461–468.

Tanofsky, R., Shepps, R. R., & O'Neill, P. J. (1969). Pattern analysis of biographical predictors of success as an insurance salesman. *Journal of Applied Psychology, 53,* 136–139.

Taylor, L. R. (1968). *A quasi-actuarial approach to assessment.* Unpublished doctoral dissertation, Purdue University, Lafayette, IN.

Telenson, P. A., Alexander, R. A., & Barrett, G. V. (1983). Scoring the biographical information blank: A comparison of three weighting techniques. *Applied Psychological Measurement, 7,* 73–80.

Thayer, P. W. (1977). Something old, something new. *Personnel Psychology, 30,* 513–524.

Ver Duin, W. (1990). Neural nets: Software that learns by example. *Computer-Aided Engineering,* pp. 62–66.

Webb, S. C. (1960). The comparative validity of two biographical inventory keys. *Journal of Applied Psychology, 44,* 177–183.

Weiss, D. J. (1976). Multivariate procedures. In M. D. Dunette (Ed.), *Handbook of industrial and organizational psychology* (pp. 327–362). Chicago: Rand McNally.

Woodruff, R. A., Jr., Robins, L. N., Taibleson, M., Reich, T., Schwin, R., & Frost, N. (1973). A computer assisted derivation of a screening interview for hysteria. *Archives of General Psychiatry, 29,* 450–454.

Application of Validity Generalization to Biodata Scales in Employment Selection

Frank L. Schmidt
University of Iowa

Hannah R. Rothstein
Baruch College

Validity generalization (VG) research consists of the application of meta-analysis methods to validity data for employment tests of aptitude and ability. This research has resulted in strong conclusions that the validities of such instruments are generalizable across settings, organizations, geographical areas, time periods, and even across different jobs (e.g., Dunnette et al., 1982; Hunter, 1983; Pearlman, Schmidt, & Hunter, 1980; Schmitt, Gooding, Noe, & Kirsch, 1984; Schmidt, Hunter, & Pearlman, 1981; see also Hartigan & Wigdor, 1989; and Schmidt, 1988b). At first glance it might appear that such research and such conclusions would be equally possible in the case of empirically constructed biodata scales used in employment selection. A considerable number of biodata validity studies have been conducted over the years, and meta-analysis has been presented as a general methodology for integrating research findings in any area (Hunter & Schmidt, 1990; Hunter, Schmidt, & Jackson, 1982).

However, closer examination reveals important differences in these two areas of application. In the usual application of VG methods, the validity data base to be used is produced by searching the published and unpublished research literature for all available studies addressing a given test type and job category (e.g., Hirsh, Northrop, & Schmidt, 1986; Pearlman et al., 1980; Schmidt, Gast-Rosenberg, & Hunter, 1980). This is in contrast to a more limited VG analysis in which data from only a single organization (e.g., Schmidt, Hunter, Pearlman, & Caplan, 1981) or specified group of organizations (e.g., Schmidt, Hunter, & Caplan, 1981) are included. It is also in contrast to the case in which validity data only on a single predictor instrument (e.g., the *General Aptitude Test Battery*; Hunter, 1983) are included. In the aptitude and ability areas, sufficient studies are often available to allow such more focused studies. In the biodata area, this is rarely the case. The relevant body of literature is smaller, and there are not typically sufficient studies to focus on a specific occupation or instrument. This places a greater evidential burden on broad VG studies drawn from the entire research literature. But in the biodata area, such broad VG studies encounter problems that do not occur in the aptitude and ability area.

ABILITY VERSUS BIODATA: SIX IMPORTANT DIFFERENCES

There are at least six conceptual and methodological differences between application of VG methods to typical validity studies of aptitude and ability measures and application to those of typical biodata scales. These differences are important in determining the proper interpretation of the VG results in the two areas.

THE CONSTRUCT MEASURED

In the abilities domain, all tests included in a VG analysis measure the same construct, and the nature of the construct is relatively well known. For example, the construct may be verbal ability. All the tests of verbal ability included in the meta-analysis measure this construct, and so there is no variability across studies in the construct measured. Different verbal ability tests may emphasize slightly different aspects or manifestations of verbal ability, but these different measures are known to correlate very highly (controlling for random measurement error) and thus are known to measure essentially the same construct. Further, the nature of the construct is reasonably well known from the psychometric and differential psychology literatures. That is, we not only know that the construct is constant across studies, but we also know something about the meaning (construct validity) of that construct.

In contrast, the objective of most biodata scales is to measure multiple constructs. In addition, different biodata scales may measure different constructs or different combinations of constructs. Further, the nature of constructs measured by various biodata scales is not well defined. Since correlations among different biodata scales are rarely known, it is difficult to assess their equivalence. Thus, when VG analyses of biodata validities from the general literature are conducted, it is the validity of the general *method* of biodata scale construction, not the validity of a specific *construct,* that is being assessed. The same is true for VG studies of employment interviews and assessment centers.

STANDARDIZATION OF MEASUREMENT PROCEDURES

In the abilities area, the predictors used are usually commercially developed tests with standardized instructions, time limits, and conditions of measurement. In the biodata area, because scales are developed in a single organization, this is less likely to be true, potentially creating variation in the method employed. This problem is likely to be more severe for employment interviews and assessment centers than for biodata scales. However, it may be of some consequence for biodata studies.

HOMOGENEITY OF OCCUPATIONS

In the abilities area, because many studies have been available, it has been possible to conduct initial VG analyses on very homogenous job groups, that is, single job titles. For example, Pearlman et al. (1980) conducted separate VG analyses on each of five specific clerical job families; Schmidt et al. (1980) conducted an analysis specifically for computer programmers. As is now well known, it was later found that task differences per se between jobs do not moderate validities of aptitude and ability tests (Schmidt, Hunter, & Pearlman, 1981), making it possible to pool studies across wider job groups. It was then possible to apply VG analyses to job groups heterogeneous in task composition but relatively homogeneous in level of cognitive demands (e.g., Hunter, 1983, 1986). Level of cognitive demand *was* found to moderate validity levels. This subsequent analysis was possible because of the large number of studies available.

We cannot, on the basis of present evidence, generalize these findings about the effect of job content on validities from the cognitive domain to biodata or other noncognitive measures. The theory developed to explain the findings in the cognitive domain (e.g., see Hunter, 1986) does not appear to be applicable to noncognitive domains. Thus, research on potential job content moderators of validity should be conducted specifically for biodata scales. But at the present time this is not possible, because sufficient single-job validity studies do not exist. In the biodata area, VG analyses are usually possible only if studies are pooled across a wide variety of jobs. The same is true for the assessment center and the employment interview, as we will discuss later.

HOMOGENEITY OF CRITERION TYPE

Validity may be different for different criterion types. The most frequently made distinction is between measures of performance in training programs and overall performance on the job. In the abilities domain, there have usually been sufficient studies to allow separate VG analyses for these two criterion measures. The initial general finding was that cognitive abilities predict performance in training better than they predict performance on the job—although validities are substantial and generalizable for both (e.g., see Pearlman et al., 1980; Schmidt, Hunter, & Pearlman, 1981; Schmidt, Hunter, Pearlman, & Hirsh, 1985). However, it was later found than when job performance is measured using job sample measures rather than supervisory ratings, mean validity for job performance was just as high as for training performance (Hunter, 1983; Nathan & Alexander, 1988; Schmidt, Hunter, & Outerbridge, 1986). The lower validities for performance on the job are a function of the use of supervisory ratings as criterion measures.*

In the biodata area, after studies from the general literature are separated by type of criterion measure (e.g., overall job performance, absenteeism, turnover, sales, etc.), there are typically not sufficient studies in most of the categories to allow highly dependable VG analyses. On the other hand, pooling across different criterion types could make clear interpretation of the results difficult.

ESTIMATING ARTIFACT MEANS AND VARIANCES

Most VG meta-analyses are conducted using distributions of artifacts—predictor reliabilities, criterion reliabilities, and range restriction levels.

---

* The proper interpretation of this finding is as yet uncertain. It may mean that supervisory ratings contain substantial elements of construct invalidity. Or it may mean that supervisory ratings reflect real variance in job performance—due to individual differences in motivation—that job sample measures do not capture.

If complete artifact information is available for each observed validity, then each coefficient can be corrected individually, and the meta-analysis can be performed on the corrected correlations. Although this does occur (Pearlman, 1982; Stern, 1987), it is unusual for individual studies to contain complete artifact information. Thus, most VG studies are conducted using artifact distribution meta-analysis methods (Hunter & Schmidt, 1990, chap. 4). Although the artifact distributions can sometimes be compiled from the studies in the VG analysis (see Hirsh et al., 1986; and Schmidt, Hunter, & Caplan, 1981, for examples), the artifact distributions used are usually those based on the employment test validation literature as a whole (Pearlman et al., 1980; Schmidt & Hunter, 1977; Schmidt, Hunter, Pearlman, & Shane, 1979). Because this literature is so vast, it has successfully formed the basis of estimated artifact distributions that were later shown empirically to be quite accurate (Alexander, Carson, Alliger, & Cronshaw, 1989; Schmidt, Hunter, Pearlman, & Hirsch, 1985). This consideration is important because, except for the correction for sampling error variance, artifact distributions determine all the corrections made to the validity data. For example, the mean level of the range restriction artifact determines the mean size of the range restriction correction made.

In the biodata area, extensive information on these artifacts is not available in the general literature, making it more difficult to have confidence in the artifact distributions that are employed. The alternative of not correcting for these artifacts—for example, making no corrections for criterion unreliability or range restriction—is not viable. Failure to correct for these two artifacts leads to large downward biases in the final validity estimates.

No correction is made for attenuation due to *predictor* unreliability, but variance across studies in observed validities that is due to *variability* in predictor unreliability should be corrected for. But in the case of biodata scales, it is less clear what form of reliability coefficient is appropriate for the predictor. In the aptitude and abilities domains, equivalent forms reliability estimates are appropriate, and these are known empirically to be reasonably closely estimated by KR-20 reliabilities and other similar internally based estimates of equivalent forms reliability. In the biodata domain, coefficient alpha or other estimates of the coefficient of equivalence (i.e., internally based estimates of equivalent forms reliability) are questionable because the scale is usually not designed or intended to measure a single homogeneous construct. Reliability of heterogeneous scales of this sort is usually assessed using test-retest reliability. But this form of reliability treats item-specific variance as true variance, further emphasizing the fact that each biodata scale—and, indeed, each item in each scale—may measure a different construct.

SECOND-ORDER SAMPLING ERROR

If a VG study (or any other meta-analysis) is conducted on a large number of representative studies, the results will be quite accurate and stable. That is, the results will not be dependent on possible idiosyncratic characteristics of the group of studies that happened to be available. We can be fairly confident that if the VG analysis were repeated on another such large group of studies, the results would be very similar. But if the number of studies in the VG analysis is small, and especially if the sample sizes within those studies are small, stability is not assured. This phenomenon is called *second-order sampling error* (Hunter & Schmidt, 1990, chap. 9; Schmidt, Hunter, Pearlman, & Hirsh, 1985). In the abilities domain, second-order sampling error is usually not a serious problem, because the number of studies in the VG analysis is typically quite large (at least 50 to 100 studies, and sometimes several hundred). For example, Pearlman et al. (1980) found 882 studies relating perceptual speed measures to performance on the job of clerical workers. A VG analysis based on a large number of studies allows confidence in the stability of the findings. It also provides a standard against which to interpret VG analyses in the cognitive (aptitudes and abilities) domain that are *not* based on substantial numbers of studies. If such VG analyses are very discrepant from those based on large numbers of studies, then their results are called into question. Also, in the cognitive domain, because there are many different VG analyses that have been conducted, it is possible to combine findings across meta-analyses. Such an analysis is called a *second-order meta-analysis*. Second-order meta-analysis provides additional assurance against second-order sampling error (Hunter & Schmidt, 1990, chap. 9).

In the biodata area, second-order sampling error is potentially a much greater problem, for three reasons. First, the number of studies in a given VG analysis is likely to be relatively small. Second, there will rarely be even one large-scale VG analysis that can serve as a standard for evaluating the results of smaller VG analyses. Third, second-order meta-analyses will rarely be possible or appropriate.

CAN THESE PROBLEMS BE CIRCUMVENTED?

The discussion thus far may make it appear that there is little value in using VG methods to cumulate biodata studies. Actually, the difficulties in biodata applications may in general be no greater than those for applications to assessment centers (Gaugler, Rosenthal, Thornton, & Bentson, 1987), the interview (McDaniel, Whetzel, Schmidt, Hunter, Maurer, & Russell,

1988), and evaluations of education and experience (McDaniel, Schmidt, & Hunter, 1988). Applications of VG methods to data on these three selection procedures have made significant contributions to the knowledge base for selection procedure validity. One finding in these meta-analyses has been that despite potential variability across studies in constructs measured and in degree of standardization of measurement, and despite the heterogeneity of occupations studied, the variance remaining in observed validities after artifactual variance is controlled is quite small—and, in fact, generally no greater than for cognitive ability tests. Under these conditions, this finding strengthens rather than weakens the conclusions of generalizable validities. The finding of limited true validity variance also strongly suggests that there are not large moderators of validity for these predictors. Thus, these VG studies have provided valuable information about the validities of assessment centers, interviews, and ratings of education and experience. Therefore, similar applications of VG methods to the general biodata validity literature may also have value.

Four studies that have included diverse jobs, organizations, and instruments have reported results for biodata validities. Two studies were not meta-analyses but did report mean observed validities. Dunnette (1972) included 115 biodata validities from jobs in the petroleum industry and reported an average validity of .34. Reilly and Chao (1982) included 44 biodata validities and found an average validity of .35. The first meta-analysis (Hunter & Hunter, 1984) included only biodata scales that were cross-validated against supervisory ratings of job performance; this study reported an average validity of .37 for 12 correlations, with an estimated true standard deviation of validity of .10. For 29 studies using a supervisory ratings criterion, Schmitt et al. (1984) reported an average observed validity of .32, with an estimated true standard deviation of .09. Brown (1981) meta-analyzed a single biodata instrument used by 12 life insurance companies and reported an estimated mean true validity of .26, which was generalizable across the companies in his study. The results of these studies suggest that well-constructed biodata instruments have substantial validity; unfortunately, for the reasons outlined earlier, they cannot comprehensively address the generalizability of a specific biodata scale.

The ideal VG analysis of biodata would be one in which the six difficulties discussed above could be avoided or circumvented. Such an analysis would provide the most accurate possible picture of the potential for validity generalizability inherent in biodata. Recently, we were fortunate to participate in conducting such a VG analysis of biodata (Rothstein, Schmidt, Erwin, Owens, & Sparks, 1990). The several VG analyses in this research were conducted on numerous studies of the validity of a single biodata scale, the biodata subscale of the *Supervisory Profile Record*

(SPR; Richardson, Bellows, Henry, & Co., 1981). The SPR is used in the selection of first-line supervisors. Only items that showed validity across different organizations were retained in the development of this scale. Rothstein et al. (1990) described in detail the development and validation of this biodata key. The studies included in the VG analysis were cross-validation studies and were not used in the development of the key. Let us now examine how each of the six problems discussed above is avoided in this VG study.

The Construct Measured

The same instrument (i.e., the same biodata key) was used in all studies conducted in 79 different organizations. Therefore, the construct or constructs measured were the same in all studies. Thus, there was no need for concern about "mixing apples and oranges" in measures of the independent variable. But what was the construct that was measured? The biodata key used scored items from two rationally clustered subscales: (a) present self-concept evaluation and (b) present work values orientation.

For an individual to score high on the present self-concept evaluation scale, he or she would have a pervasive feeling of self-worth and confidence, believe that he or she works better and faster than others in his or her area of specialization, be recognized for accomplishments, be outgoing, be a good communicator, be a person who takes clear positions, and feel healthy and satisfied with current life situations.

The following are two items from that scale:

The amount of recognition which I usually receive for my accomplishments is:
a. none at all
b. occasional recognition, but not much
c. about as much as deserved
d. as much as deserved
e. sometimes more than deserved

Of the following statements, the one which describes me best is:
a. much more talker than listener
b. somewhat more talker than listener
c. about as much talker as listener
d. somewhat more listener than talker
e. much more listener than talker

An individual scoring high on present work values orientation is one who prefers to work independently and who values hard work, drive, organization of time, and work planning. This person works well under pressure, is comfortable working on more than one thing at a time, and views him or herself as making progress and expects to continue to do so. The following are two items from that scale:

The kind of supervision I like best is:
a. very close supervision
b. fairly close supervision
c. moderate supervision
d. minimal supervision
e. no supervision

My work habits are such that I prefer:
a. to work on one thing at a time
b. to work on several things at a time
c. to work on many things at a time

Thus, there is some knowledge of what the constructs are. However, more research is needed on the construct validity of biodata scales. Such research is now being conducted at the U.S. Office of Personnel Management in connection with the development of the *Individual Achievement Record* (Gandy, Outerbridge, Sharf, & Dye, 1990). Research that explicates the psychological meaning of biodata items predictive of success at work would be of considerable value. One question of particular significance to VG analyses is whether the constructs underlying various valid biodata scales are similar. If so, VG analyses of these scales would create cumulative knowledge not only about the validity of biodata inventories as a selection tool but also about the meaning of the constructs measured.

STANDARDIZATION OF MEASUREMENT PROCEDURES

Instructions and conditions of administration were carefully developed and were held constant in the 79 organizations in which studies were conducted (Richardson, Bellows, Henry, & Co., 1981). Thus, measurement procedures were standardized.

HOMOGENEITY OF OCCUPATIONS

All study participants were first-line supervisors. Both white and blue collar supervisors were included, and it was possible to show that this difference did not affect (moderate) scale validities. Thus, all validities were for a single job, and the possibility that occupational differences might constitute an undetected moderator was ruled out.

HOMOGENEITY OF CRITERION TYPE

In all studies the criterion measures were ratings by two different supervisors on the same carefully developed multiscale rating instrument. There were two types of instruments in each study: ratings of *ability* to perform the job duties and ratings of *actual performance* of job duties. VG analyses were conducted separately for each type of rating; results were essentially identical. Thus, there was no mixing of criterion types that could complicate interpretation of results.

ESTIMATING ARTIFACT MEANS AND VARIANCES

Complete artifact information was available for each observed validity. That is, for each observed validity coefficient there was an associated criterion reliability and index of range restriction. Predictor reliability was also known, but because the predictor was always the same scale, the reliability was constant across studies, and thus there was no need to correct for the effects of differences between studies in predictor reliability (see Schmidt, Hunter, Pearlman, & Hirsh, 1985, Q&A 31). Therefore it was possible to (a) correct each observed validity individually for criterion unreliability and range restriction and (b) perform the meta-analysis on the corrected correlations. The final correction in this form of meta-analysis is the correction for the sampling error variance of the *corrected* correlations. However, it should be noted that the earlier correction of each observed validity for criterion unreliability and range restriction corrects for validity differences between studies due to variations in these two artifacts. This method of meta-analysis is more exact than the more commonly used method that employs distributions of artifacts, the values of which are not associated with specific observed coefficients. Further details are given in Hunter, Schmidt, and Jackson (1982, chap. 3) and in Hunter and Schmidt (1990, chap. 4).

Although individual correction and subsequent analysis of corrected correlations is the preferred method of meta-analysis, it had not at that time been applied in a published study because the necessary information had not been available. Two unpublished dissertations based on military data (Pearlman, 1982; Stern, 1987) have used this method. Brown (1981) did correct each coefficient individually and computed the mean of the corrected correlations; however, his variance corrections were made using artifact distribution-based meta-analysis (although these distributions were derived from the data set analyzed). At that time there were no published descriptions of methods of meta-analysis for individually corrected correlations. Thus, this VG analysis was methodologically unique: It came from a major civilian job family in a large number of organizations; it contained complete artifact information on every validity coefficient; it corrected each coefficient individually; and the full meta-analysis was performed on the corrected correlations.

Ratings of each individual in the sample were made by the immediate supervisor (Rater 1) and by an additional evaluator who knew the subject's performance well enough to rate it (Rater 2). Duty and ability composites consisted of the average rating across all rated elements. The duty and ability rating composites were then averaged separately across the two raters. The average of the two raters' average ratings, for duty and ability, respectively, served as the validation criteria. Reliability estimates for each of the criteria—the mean of two raters' ratings—were calculated by correlating the respective Rater 1 and Rater 2 averages and then adjusting this figure using the Spearman-Brown formula for two raters. This average reliability was .69 for the ability ratings and .64 for the duty ratings. The corrections for criterion unreliability were made before the corrections for range restriction because the reliabilities were computed directly on the groups being studied (Hunter et al., 1982); that is, the criterion reliability estimates were for the restricted group. The applicant standard deviation was 4.72, a value that is almost the same as the average incumbent (restricted) value (mean restricted $sd = 4.68$). The applicant SD was based on 17,962 recent candidates for promotion to first-line supervisor in a number of organizations using the SPR as part of the selection process. Candidates are typically nominated by their supervisors and must successfully meet several other prescreening requirements before being allowed to take the SPR. Thus, candidates are a somewhat homogenous group, but these processes accurately reflect how applicant pools are created in organizations. The incumbents in the validity studies, on the other hand, were often older, less educated, and entered their supervisory positions at a time when selection standards were lower. Thus, they were typically about as variable on the biodata scale as current applicants.

SECOND-ORDER SAMPLING ERROR

The number of observed validity coefficients was large enough in the VG analysis across organizations (79) that second-order sampling error was not a major concern. In addition, the average number of subjects per study was relatively large ($N = 143$) in comparison with VG studies of aptitudes and abilities. The total number of supervisors was over 11,000. In other VG analyses conducted, the number of validities was smaller, but the N per validity was larger. For example, in the analysis by years of supervisory experience, there were 22 observed validities; however, the N per observed validity was larger: 464. Finally, the pattern of results across the eight VG analyses (by organization, race, sex, education, white vs. blue collar, company service, supervisory experience, and age) was consistent and very similar, further obviating any concerns about second-order sampling error.

CONCLUSION

Thus, this application of VG methods to biodata was able to avoid all of the usual difficulties that detract from the interpretability of the results. It is therefore instructive to examine the findings and conclusions in this study because they demonstrate the degree of generalizability of validity that is possible for biodata scales under the best of circumstances. Although biodata data bases of this sort will never be common, we are aware of three similar data bases compiled by the same firm. These are data bases for the Managerial Profile Record (for managers), the Candidate Profile Record (for clerical workers), and the Law Enforcement Profile Record (for police). VG analyses are now under way for these scales; we expect that the pattern of results they produce will corroborate our findings for the SPR. Preliminary findings for the Managerial Profile Record, using a criterion of job level attained, appear consistent with those for the SPR; currently, however, complete results are available only for the SPR.

THE GENERALIZABILITY OF BIODATA VALIDITIES

NEED BIODATA VALIDITY BE SITUATIONALLY SPECIFIC?

It is widely believed that the validities of empirically keyed biographical data scales are situationally specific. For example, Hunter and Hunter (1984) state that "there is evidence to suggest that biodata keys are not transportable" (p. 89). Thayer (1977) argues that biodata validity is moderated by such factors as age, organizational practices and procedures, the criterion used, and temporal changes in the nature of the job. Dreher and Sackett (1983) have commented that despite sizable validities, the use of organizational-specific (and subgroup-specific) items and keys precludes the possibility of generalized validities in the case of biodata. In our experience, many researchers have expressed the belief that organizationally specific validities are inevitable in the case of biodata. Therefore, the key VG analysis in our study was the one across organizations. Results were calculated separately for the two kinds of ratings. The key findings are summarized below:

Ratings	ρ	SD_ρ	90% C.V.	No. rs
Ability to perform	.36	.082	.26	79
Performance on duties	.34	.104	.20	79

Since the results are similar for the two types of job performance ratings scales, we will focus our discussion on only one set of figures—those for the ability ratings. These show a mean true validity of .36 and a standard deviation of true validities of .082. The 90 percent credibility value is .26. Thus, across organizations, 90 percent of true validities can be expected to be at least .26 or larger. Clearly, these findings show that biodata scales with generalizable validities can be constructed. Biodata validities need not be specific to particular organizations, contrary to currently prevailing belief. An interesting question for future research is whether biodata-assessed constructs other than the two measured here will show the same degree of generalizability under the same research conditions. Although interorganizational generalizability is probably the most important finding, this research also shows that the biodata scale validities generalized across other variables frequently hypothesized as moderators: race, sex, educational levels, years of company service, years of supervisory experience, and age. In fact, the average SD_ρ value for these eight VG analyses was much smaller than that for the VG analysis across organizations; the mean SD_ρ value was .012. Further, for two of these hypothesized moderators—years of company service and years of supervisory service—the SD_ρ value was zero. The largest value of SD_ρ among these potential moderators was for sex, yet this value (.033) was still very small. Mean true validities in these eight VG analyses ranged from .32 to .34. Hence, the evidence for the generalizability of these biodata validities is even greater for these variables than it is for generalization across organizations. Nevertheless, because of the strong prevailing traditional belief that biodata validities are inherently specific to particular organizations, we view the finding of generalizability across organizations as having greater practical significance. We therefore return to the evaluation of this finding.

First, consider the mean level of true validity across organizations: .36. This value is very similar to average values found in previous biodata research using a criterion of supervisory ratings of job performance. As mentioned earlier, Schmitt et al. (1984) found an average uncorrected biodata validity of .32; Hunter and Hunter (1984) reported an average cross-validated biodata scale validity of .37 (corrected for criterion unreliability only); Reilly and Chao (1982) found a mean uncorrected validity of .35. Other studies, such as those by Dunnette (1972) and Asher (1972), reported similar values. The critical difference between these studies and ours is that all of these authors concluded that biodata validities were not generalizable, that they were specific to particular organizations. Our data and results indicated that, at least under the conditions in our study, biodata validity can be generalizable.

COMPARISON WITH COGNITIVE TEST VALIDITIES: MEAN VALIDITY

How does our mean value of .36 compare to mean (generalizable) true validities for cognitive tests? Schmidt, Hunter, Pearlman, and Shane (1979) reported VG analyses for three cognitive tests specifically for first-line supervisors (see their Table 6, p. 273). Mean true validities were .64 for general mental ability (75 studies), .48 for mechanical comprehension (36 studies), and .43 for spatial ability (18 studies). All values are larger than our .36. As shown by Hunter (1986), mechanical comprehension, spatial ability, and other specific aptitudes probably derive their validity from the fact that they are in part measures of general mental ability. Thus, the most relevant figure is the .64 for general mental ability. This value is 1.78 times as large as our value of .36. However, we can also compare our results to those of Hunter (1983). Based on validity studies of the *General Aptitude Test Battery* (GATB) of the U.S. Employment Service, Hunter (1983) found a mean true validity of .51 for the job family (job complexity category No. 3) to which the job of first-line supervisor belongs. This figure is 1.42 times as large as our figure of .36. Thus, while the mean true validity of the biodata scale is substantial and is apt to yield large practical utility for employing organizations (Hunter & Schmidt, 1982a, 1982b; Schmidt, 1988; Schmidt, Hunter, McKenzie, & Muldrow, 1979), the validity and utility of general mental ability is greater. The validity of an optimally weighted combination of both would, of course, be expected to be higher than either alone. Finally, we note that our biodata scale assessed

TABLE 1   Comparison of True Standard Deviations for Biodata
(Ability Ratings Criteria) and Cognitive Abilities Meta-analyses

Sample Study	Average SD_p	Number of Meta-analyses Summarized	Number of Validities	Mean Sample Size
1. Current study— organizations	.082	1	79	142
2. Current study— all variables	.023	8	227	765
3. Pearlman et al. (1980)—individual job families across predictors	.143	32	2,162	62
4. Lilienthal & Pearlman (1982)— combined aide/ technician group across predictors	.170	8	357	104

only two constructs, as described earlier. It is possible that a biodata scale measuring different constructs or more constructs could have higher validity. However, based on the results of the various reviews of biodata validity cited earlier, it would not appear that such biodata scales are very common.

COMPARISON WITH COGNITIVE TEST VALIDITIES: STANDARD DEVIATION OF VALIDITIES

The key question in connection with biodata, however, was never its mean level of validity, but rather the generalizability of that validity. The critical index of generalizability is SD_p, the standard deviation of true validities. Small SD_p values mean extensive generalizability, and vice versa. The SD_p values in our biodata VG study can be compared to a representative sample of estimated true standard deviations from meta-analyses of a variety of cognitive abilities tests using job proficiency criteria taken from Pearlman et al. (1980) and Lilienthal and Pearlman (1983). These are shown in Table 1. The estimated true standard deviations from the biodata meta-analyses are considerably smaller than those yielded by meta-analyses of cognitive ability tests. The biodata true standard deviations range from 57 to 14 percent as large as the values for cognitive abilities. In particular, the SD_p across organizations is only 52 percent as large as the average of the two comparable values for cognitive tests (.143 and .170; average = .1565); this finding suggests that these biodata validities may be *more*—rather than less—generalizable across organizations than cognitive ability tests. These comparisons are with clerical jobs (Pearlman et al., 1980) and aide and technician jobs (Lilienthal & Pearlman, 1983). We can also make a comparison with exactly the same job. The value of SD_p for general mental ability for first-line supervisors in Schmidt, Hunter, Pearlman, and Shane (1979, Table 6) is .23. Our obtained SD_p value of .082 is only 36 percent as large, again indicating *greater* generalizability for the biodata scale than for a cognitive ability. However, one might argue that use of a single measure of general mental ability (versus a variety of tests) combined with use of a single rating scale format for the criterion measure would yield smaller SD_p values for cognitive tests. That is, one could argue that under circumstances similar to those in our biodata VG study, SD_p for cognitive tests would be much smaller. This suggests a comparison with Hunter's (1983) results. In that study, general mental ability was measured in all studies using the same instrument (the *GATB*), and the job performance rating scale used was the same in all studies. The SD_p value for job family No. 3 (in which first-line supervisors are included) is .15, thus supporting this hypothesis. The SD_p values in job families 1 through 5 were .03, .15, .15, .03, and .06, respectively, yielding an average of .084. Although the .15 figure is still larger than our value of .082 (by 82%), we must remember that the job complexity categories (job families) are of necessity quite broad, and, therefore, that job family No. 3 contains some jobs of considerably lower complexity than the job of first-line supervisor. On that basis, we would expect a larger SD_p value than that for first-line supervisors alone. On the other hand, the average SD_p value of .084 across the five job families is nearly identical to the biodata value of .082 for ability ratings, and is a little smaller than the .104 value of SD_p for the duty ratings. Thus, on balance it would appear that the degree of generalizability of validity of the biodata score and general mental ability is very similar. Both types of validity show a very high degree of generalizability.

This similarity of degree of validity generalizability provides the basis for hypothesizing that the validity of this biodata scale is actually *constant* across organizations and other hypothesized potential moderators. In the case of cognitive abilities, including general mental ability, there is now substantial evidence that the true value of SD_p is actually zero (Hunter & Schmidt, 1990, chaps. 4, 5, & 9; Schmidt, Hunter, Pearlman, & Hirsh, 1985; Schmidt & Hunter, 1984; Schmidt, Ocasio, Hillery, & Hunter,

1985). That is, the evidence indicates that obtained nonzero estimates of SD_p stem from failure to correct validity variance for all artifactual sources of variance. The fact that validities of the SPR biodata scale appear to have levels of generalizability very similar to that of general mental ability suggests that it may be possible to create biodata scales with fully constant validities. If so, then the actual state of nature would be maximally discrepant with prevailing conventional beliefs. We shall return to this point later.

The results of our study (Rothstein et al., 1990) contraindicate the currently dominant belief that biodata validities are intrinsically specific to particular organizations. They also present strong counterevidence to the hypothesis that biodata validities are necessarily moderated by age, sex, race, education, tenure, or previous experience. The 90 percent credibility values are on average only .03 lower than the mean true validity, providing strong support for validity generalization; the magnitudes of these values indicate that the generalized validity is substantial. These results do not indicate that this level of generalizability can always be expected from biodata. Given conventional methods of biodata instrument construction and validation, these results probably represent the exception rather than the rule. *The point is that biodata instruments can be constructed and validated in a way that will lead to validity generalizability.* Our findings show that large sample sizes, multiple organizations, and cross-organizational keying of the biodata scale can yield generalizable validities. Thus, the current findings also point out the advantages of consortium-based, multiple-organization biodata research.

OTHER ISSUES

DECAY OF VALIDITY OVER TIME

It is a common finding that the validity of biodata keys decays over time, resulting in a requirement for rekeying (Hunter & Hunter, 1984; Thayer, 1977). Our research did not directly examine the question of temporal specificity or stability, but it does offer some indirect evidence bearing on this issue. Because the data from the first consortium of studies was gathered in 1974 and the data for the last was gathered in 1985, a time span of over 10 years was covered. This was a time span in which many social changes were taking place. Nevertheless, a key composed of items keyed in the developmental samples yielded substantial validities in the cross-validation sample up to 11 years later. This suggests that methods of biodata scale construction and validation based on large samples and successive replications produce validities that generalize across organizations and across other potential moderator variables, *as well as* validities that tend to be stable over fairly long periods of time. That is, generalizability and temporal stability of biodata validities may both depend on the same processes of scale construction.

JOB EXPERIENCE AND BIODATA VALIDITY

Our findings bear on another hypothesis important to the use of biodata in selection: the hypothesis that biodata validity in concurrent studies stems from the measurement of knowledge acquired from job experience. If this hypothesis were correct, then concurrent validities would typically be much larger than the corresponding predictive validities. This would be a serious problem because predictive validities are the basis for selection utility. If this hypothesis were correct, then concurrent validities should be much smaller when experience on the job is held constant. That is, this hypothesis holds that it is differences between individuals in job experience that create individual differences in biodata scores and therefore cause the validity of biodata scores. In the meta-analyses of years of supervisory experience, each validity coefficient was computed on individuals with the same number of years of experience on the job; that is, job experience was held nearly constant. Yet mean validity did not decline for either ability or duty ratings. Thus, biodata validity does not appear to be an artifact of individual differences in job experience.

It should be noted, however, that the question of whether biodata validities are created by individual differences in job experience is not the same as the question of whether concurrent validities are the same as predictive validities, nor does it address whether validities for data collected under research conditions are the same as validities for data collected for operational use. All validities in our VG analysis were concurrent, and the data were collected for research purposes only. The job experience hypothesis, which our data contraindicate, is only one possible hypothesis that might predict differences between validities from different research designs. For example, greater response distortion on the part of job applicants compared with incumbents is another such hypothesis. The literature on the faking of biodata responses indicates that biodata responses can be faked, but that faking does not necessarily affect validity (Baratta & Stout, 1990; Colquitt & Becker, 1989; Klein & Owens, 1965). We do know that for cognitive tests, concurrent and predictive validities are very similar (American Psychological Association, 1987; Schmitt et al., 1984), but we cannot assume that these findings for measures of maximum performance will hold true for measures of typical performance, such as biodata scales. Similarly, the issue of faking answers is not relevant to studies of cognitive ability measures, but it is potentially quite relevant to self-report measures such as biodata instruments. We believe, therefore, that research comparing predictive and concurrent validities, as well as research comparing validities for data collected under research and operational conditions for the same biodata scale, would be quite useful.

SITUATIONAL SPECIFICITY AND NONCOGNITIVE PREDICTORS

Finally, the findings of this study bear on an hypothesis that is important for personnel selection in general: the hypothesis of situational specificity of validities (Schmidt, Hunter, Pearlman, & Hirsh, 1985). In many individual validity generalization studies, the findings indicate that the presence of validity can be generalized, but statistical artifacts do not appear to explain *all* the variability in validities. In the case of cognitive ability tests, as noted earlier, there is substantial evidence that the remaining variability in validities is also due to artifacts for which one cannot correct (Hunter & Schmidt, 1990, chaps. 4 & 5; Schmidt & Hunter, 1984; Schmidt, Hunter, Pearlman, & Hirsh, 1985; Schmidt, Ocasio, Hillery, & Hunter, 1985). Some have proposed that in the case of noncognitive predictors, this remaining amount of validity variability can be expected to be considerably larger than in the case of cognitive ability tests (Sackett, Schmitt, Tenopyr, Kehoe, & Zedeck, 1985; Schmitt & Schneider, 1983). Although biodata responses may reflect in part the expression of abilities in life activities, biodata is generally regarded as a noncognitive predictor. In the case of noncognitive predictors, it is expected that such factors as organizational value systems, management philosophies, leadership styles, and organizational cultures will be major determinants of what kinds of people are successful in the organization (Schmitt & Schneider, 1983), and thus major moderators of the validities of noncognitive selection procedures. This moderating effect is expected to be much larger than in the case of cognitive abilities, and thus noncognitive predictors become a critical test for the situational specificity hypothesis.

The findings of this study refute this hypothesis for an important noncognitive predictor. Across 79 varied organizations, the standard deviation of biodata validities for the scale studied was only .082 for ability ratings and .104 for the duty ratings. As illustrated in our earlier discussion, a comparison of these values with corresponding values from the abilities domain indicates that situational specificity is no more in evidence in the biodata domain than in the abilities domain. Thus, these findings are further strong evidence against the situational specificity hypothesis: The evidence against situational specificity now extends into the noncognitive domain.

From a psychological point of view, these findings indicate that biodata questionnaires are capable of measuring characteristics of people that are conducive to success or failure on the job in a wide variety of settings, organizational climates, and technologies. This has been the premise of Owens' research, particularly his assessment-classification model (Owens, 1968, 1976; Owens & Schoenfeldt, 1979; Schoenfeldt, 1974). The study described here focused on the major job family of first-line supervisors; similar studies are now under way for managers, clerical workers, and law enforcement personnel. What is needed next is research that explicates the psychological meaning of biodata items predictive of success at work. VG analyses of studies of this type would create cumulative knowledge not only about the validity generalizability of the biographical inventory as a method of employee selection but also about the constructs underlying the relationship between biodata scale scores and work performance.

SUMMARY

Many difficulties stand in the way of informative application of VG methods to biodata validities drawn from the general literature on selection procedure validity. These difficulties appear to be considerably more severe than in the case of employment tests of aptitudes and abilities. However, studies that successfully circumvent these difficulties can, if they are large enough in number, reveal the potential inherent in biodata for generalizable validity. Such biodata data bases will probably never be common, and the studies in question may not appear in the general archival literature. The validity data base for the biodata component of the Supervisory Profile Record was the basis for the research described here. This research avoided the usual problems to be expected in the application of VG methods to biodata validities. The results of this research demonstrate that the validity of this carefully developed biodata questionnaire for the job of first-line supervisor generalizes across a wide variety of different organizations, showing that biodata validity need not be organizationally specific. Validity was also found to generalize across such previously hypothesized moderators as race, sex, educational level, years of company service, years of supervisory experience, and age. Validity was also found to be temporally stable, and there was evidence that the validity did not stem from measurement of knowledge and skills acquired on the job. Finally, the results provide additional evidence against the general hypothesis of situational specificity of validities; the findings disconfirm that hypothesis in an important noncognitive domain. This is significant, because it has been hypothesized that situational specificity can be expected to be greater in noncognitive than in cognitive domains.

REFERENCES

Alexander, R. A., Carson, K. P., Alliger, G. M., & Cronshaw, S. F. (1989). Empirical distributions of range restricted SD_x in validity studies. *Journal of Applied Psychology, 74,* 253–258.

American Psychological Association, Society for Industrial and Organizational Psychology, Inc. (Division 14). (1987). *Principles for the validation and use of personnel selection procedures* (3d ed.). College Park, MD: Author.

Asher, J. J. (1972). The biographical item: Can it be improved? *Personnel Psychology, 25,* 251–269.

Baratta, J. E., & Stout, J. D. (1990). *Fakability of a computerized biodata instrument.* Paper presented at the annual meeting of the Society for Industrial and Organizational Psychology, Miami Beach.

Brown, S. H. (1981). Validity generalization and situational moderation in the life insurance industry. *Journal of Applied Psychology, 66,* 664–670.

Brown, S. H. (1978). Long term validity of a personnel history item scoring procedure. *Journal of Applied Psychology, 63,* 673–676.

Colquitt, A., & Becker, T. (1989). *Faking of a biodata form in use: A field study.* Paper presented at the annual meeting of the Society for Industrial and Organizational Psychology, Boston.

Dreher, G. F., & Sackett, P. R. (1983). *Perspectives on staffing and selection.* Homewood, IL: Irwin.

Dunnette, M. D. (1972). *Validity study results for jobs relevant to the petroleum refining industry.* Washington, DC: American Petroleum Institute.

Dunnette, M. D., Rosse, R., Houston, J. S., Hough, L. M., Toquam, J., Lammlein, S., King, K., Bosshardt, M. J., & Keyes, M. (1982). *Development and validation of an industry-wide electric power plant operator selection system.* Minneapolis: Personnel Decisions Research Institute.

Gandy, J. A., Outerbridge, A. N., Sharf, J. C., & Dye, D. A. (1990). *Development and initial validation of the Individual Achievement Record (IAR).* Washington, DC: U.S. Office of Personnel Management.

Gaugler, B. B., Rosenthal, D. B., Thornton, G. C., & Bentson, C. (1987). Meta-analysis of assessment center validity. *Journal of Applied Psychology, 72,* 493–511.

Hartigan, J. A., & Wigdor, A. K. (1989). *Fairness in employment testing: Validity generalization, minority issues, and the General Aptitude Test Battery.* Washington, DC: National Academy Press.

Hirsh, H. R., Northrop, L. C., & Schmidt, F. L. (1986). Validity generalization results for law enforcement occupations. *Personnel Psychology, 39*, 399–420.

Hunter, J. E. (1983). *Test validation for 12,000 jobs: An application of job classification and validity generalization analysis to the General Aptitude Test Battery (GATB; Test Research Rep. No. 45).* Washington, DC: U.S. Employment Service, U.S. Department of Labor.

Hunter, J. E. (1986). Cognitive ability, cognitive aptitudes, job knowledge, and job performance. *Journal of Vocational Behavior, 29*, 340–362.

Hunter, J. E., & Hunter, R. F. (1984). Validity and utility of alternative predictors of job performance. *Psychological Bulletin, 96*, 72–98.

Hunter, J. E., & Schmidt, F. L. (1982a). Fitting people to jobs: Implications of personnel selection for national productivity. In E. A. Fleishman & M. D. Dunnette (Eds.), *Human performance and productivity: Vol. 1. Human capability assessment* (pp. 233–284). Hillsdale, NJ: Erlbaum.

Hunter, J. E., & Schmidt, F. L. (1982b). Ability tests: Economic benefits versus the issue of fairness. *Industrial Relations, 21*(3), 293–308.

Hunter, J. E., & Schmidt, F. L. (1990). *Methods of meta-analysis: Correcting error and bias in research findings.* Beverly Hills, CA: Sage.

Hunter, J. E., Schmidt, F. L., & Jackson, G. B. (1982). *Meta-analysis: Cumulating research findings across studies.* Beverly Hills, CA: Sage.

Klein, S. P., & Owens, W. A. (1965). Faking of a scored life history blank as a function of criterion objectivity. *Journal of Applied Psychology, 49*, 452–454.

Laurent, H. (1970). Cross-cultural validation of empirically validated tests. *Journal of Applied Psychology, 54*, 417–423.

Lilienthal, R. A., & Pearlman, K. (1983). *The validity of federal selection tests for aid/technicians in the health, science, and engineering fields.* Washington, DC: U.S. Office of Personnel Management, Office of Personnel Research and Development.

McDaniel, M. A., Schmidt, F. L., & Hunter, J. E. (1988). A meta-analysis of the validity of training and experience ratings in personnel selection. *Personnel Psychology, 41*, 283–314.

McDaniel, M. A., Whetzel, D. L., Schmidt, F. L., Hunter, J. E., Maurer, S., & Russell, J. (1988). *The validity of employment interviews: A review and meta-analysis.* Unpublished manuscript.

Nathan, B. R., & Alexander, R. A. (1988). A comparison of criteria for test validation: A meta-analytic investigation. *Personnel Psychology, 41*, 517–535.

Owens, W. A. (1968). Toward one discipline of scientific psychology. *American Psychologist, 23*, 782–785.

Owens, W. A. (1976). Background data. In M. D. Dunnette (Ed.), *Handbook of industrial and organizational psychology* (1st ed., pp. 609–644). Chicago: Rand McNally.

Owens, W. A., & Schoenfeldt, L. F. (1979). Toward a classification of persons. *Journal of Applied Psychology, 63*, 569–607.

Pearlman, K. (1980). Job families: A review and discussion of their implications for personnel selection. *Psychological Bulletin, 87*, 1–28.

Pearlman, K. (1982). *The Bayesian approach to validity generalization: A systematic examination of the robustness of procedures and conclusions.* Unpublished doctoral dissertation, Department of Psychology, George Washington University, Washington, DC.

Pearlman, K., Schmidt, F. L., & Hunter, J. E. (1980). Validity generalization results for tests used to predict job proficiency and training success in clerical occupations. *Journal of Applied Psychology, 65,* 373–406.

Reilly, R. R., & Chao, G. T. (1982). Validity and fairness of some alternative employee selection procedures. *Personnel Psychology, 35,* 1–62.

Richardson, Bellows, Henry, & Co. (1981). *Supervisory Profile Record technical reports* (Vols. 1–3). Washington, DC: Author.

Rothstein, H. R., Schmidt, F. L., Erwin, F. W., Owens, W. A., & Sparks, C. P. (1990). Biographical data in employment selection: Can the validities be made generalizable? *Journal of Applied Psychology, 74,* 175–184.

Sackett, P. R., Schmitt, N., Tenopyr, M. L., Kehoe, J., & Zedeck, S. (1985). Commentary on forty questions about validity generalization and meta-analysis. *Personnel Psychology, 38,* 697–798.

Schmidt, F. L. (1988a). The problem of group differences in ability test scores in employment selection. *Journal of Vocational Behavior, 33,* 272–292.

Schmidt, F. L. (1988b). Validity generalization and the future of criterion-related validity. In H. Wainer & H. Braun (Eds.), *Test validity* (pp. 173–189). Hillsdale, NJ: Erlbaum.

Schmidt, F. L., Gast-Rosenberg, I., & Hunter, J. E. (1980). Validity generalization results for computer programmers. *Journal of Applied Psychology, 65,* 643–661.

Schmidt, F. L., & Hunter, J. E. (1977). Development of a general solution to the problem of validity generalization. *Journal of Applied Psychology, 62,* 529–540.

Schmidt, F. L., & Hunter, J. E. (1978). Moderator research and the law of small numbers. *Personnel Psychology, 31,* 215–232.

Schmidt, F. L., & Hunter, J. E. (1984). A within setting test of the situational specificity hypothesis in personnel selection. *Personnel Psychology, 37,* 317–326.

Schmidt, F. L., Hunter, J. E., & Caplan, J. R. (1981). Validity generalization results for two job groups in the petroleum industry. *Journal of Applied Psychology, 66,* 261–273.

Schmidt, F. L., Hunter, J. E., McKenzie, R. C., & Muldrow, T. W. (1979). The impact of valid selection procedures on work-force productivity. *Journal of Applied Psychology, 64,* 609–626.

Schmidt, F. L., Hunter, J. E., & Outerbridge, A. N. (1986). Impact of job experience and ability on job knowledge, work sample performance, and supervisory ratings of job performance. *Journal of Applied Psychology, 71,* 432–439.

Schmidt, F. L., Hunter, J. E., & Pearlman, K. (1981). Task differences and validity of aptitude tests in selection: A red herring. *Journal of Applied Psychology, 66,* 166–185.

Schmidt, F. L., Hunter, J. E., Pearlman, K., & Caplan, J. R. (1981). *Validity generalization results for three occupations in Sears, Roebuck and Company.* Chicago: Sears, Roebuck.

Schmidt, F. L., Hunter, J. E., Pearlman, K., & Hirsh, H. R. (1985). Forty questions about validity generalization and meta-analysis. *Personnel Psychology, 38,* 697–798.

Schmidt, F. L., Hunter, J. E., Pearlman, K., & Shane, G. S. (1979). Further tests of the Schmidt-Hunter Bayesian validity generalization procedure. *Personnel Psychology, 32,* 257–381.

Schmidt, F. L., Ocasio, B. P., Hillery, J. M., & Hunter, J. E. (1985). Further within-setting empirical tests of the situational specificity hypothesis in personnel selection. *Personnel Psychology, 38,* 509–524.

Schmitt, N., Gooding, R. Z., Noe, R. A., & Kirsch, M. (1984). Meta-analysis of validity studies published between 1964 and 1982 and the investigation of study characteristics. *Personnel Psychology, 37,* 407–422.

Schmitt, N., & Schneider, B. (1983). Current issues in personnel selection. In K. M. Rowland & G. R. Ferris (Eds.), *Research in personnel and human resources management* (Vol. 1). Greenwich, CT: JAI.

Schoenfeldt, L. F. (1974). Utilization of manpower: Development and evaluation of an assessment-classification model for matching individuals with jobs. *Journal of Applied Psychology, 59,* 583–594.

Stern, B. (1987). *Job complexity as a moderator of the validity of the Armed Services Vocational Aptitude Battery.* Unpublished doctoral dissertation, George Washington University, Washington, DC.

Thayer, P. W. (1977). Somethings old, somethings new. *Personnel Psychology, 30,* 513–524.

Blue Collar Selection

Ronald Pannone
Port Authority of New York and New Jersey

INTRODUCTION

The use of background data in hiring decisions predates any documented scientific applications. When an individual considers another person for employment purposes, the nature of that situation, either an interview or review of an employment application, imposes an evaluative function on the decision maker with reference to some criteria of interest. This process, for the most part, involves judgments about the applicant and his or her past and typically includes predictions about the future. Although many assume that the employment interview is the most frequently used personnel selection technique, Levine and Flory (1975) have pointed out that the background data provided on applications and résumés are typically evaluated before or as part of the interview process. Therefore, background data may be used more frequently than interviews in hiring.

Given the extent to which background characteristics are important in employment decision making, the development of structured approaches with background data in employment decision making was an inevitable outgrowth. The ever increasing costs associated with the development and operation of testing programs have forced many employers to explore a variety of approaches to evaluating applicants' qualifications. Whereas many employers have reduced their testing programs, others, such as public sector employers, have drifted from traditional testing approaches to self-report measures such as background data.

The use of background data as predictors is not surprising, since re-search evidence has supported a widely accepted cliché in psychology that the best predictor of future behavior is past behavior. Reviews of the literature on background data have consistently demonstrated that bio-graphical questionnaires are effective predictors of a wide variety of criteria (Asher, 1972; Asher & Sciarrino, 1974; England, 1967; Mumford & Owens, 1987; Owens, 1976; Reilly & Chao, 1982; van Rijn, 1980). However, these reviews have also revealed that, compared to the total number of studies published on background data, the studies that involve blue collar occupations are surprisingly few. Background data appear to have been underutilized and underreported in the blue collar area, especially considering the following:

- Use of background data predictors has advantages, including pro-viding a standardized approach to evaluating applicants' suitability (Owens, 1976).
- Administration and scoring of background data items is relatively easy, especially when items are presented in checklist or multiple choice formats (Mosel & Wade, 1951).
- Use of background data for selection has proven to be cost effective, especially when compared to the cost of the employment interview (Blumenfeld, 1973; Lee & Booth, 1974; Super, 1960).

BLUE COLLAR WORK
AND BLUE COLLAR WORKERS

Blue collar occupations, although difficult to precisely define, typically include hourly workers involved in the manufacturing, maintenance, and repair of machinery, equipment, and building structures, as well as construction trade- and craft-related occupations and a variety of unskilled laborer positions. Typical blue collar occupations include jobs such as carpenter, auto mechanic, assembly line worker, electrician, laborer, machine operator, painter, printer, and welder. These positions are markedly different from the types of positions typically included in published background data research, such as research scientist and sales, management, clerical, administrative, and data processing personnel.

The term *blue collar* has historically been applied to the type of positions in which work is performed in rough, protective clothing, and some degree of heavy manual labor is involved. Typical blue collar work involves installing components, repairing and fabricating parts, and maintaining and erecting buildings, roadways, equipment, mechanical systems, and motors.

The blue collar worker uses hand tools, power tools, stationary and mobile equipment, and physical strength to perform the work. The work itself is often performed under a variety of environmental conditions, with workers required to stand and bend for prolonged periods, often in uncomfortably hot and cold environments that are noisy, dusty, and dirty.

The nature of the functions performed by the blue collar worker are generally more narrow in range than professional and technical occupations, and the workers themselves typically have less discretion in how the work is to be done. Blue collar work is often prescribed in specifications, blueprints, safety codes, and general trade and organizational practices.

The skills required to perform blue collar work are infrequently acquired through formal instruction. Instead, the skills generally are developed through on-the-job training, structured experience requirements, or apprenticeship programs. As a result, educational levels and reading levels may not equal those of professional and technical personnel.

As would be expected with this type of population, face validity is a crucial concern that influences the type of background data strategy employed. To maintain applicant motivation, background data items must appear to be job related. Therefore, life history items linked to personality traits or motivational criteria generate suspicion in applicants and supervisors alike. Given the criteria in question, life history items may be appropriate for prediction purposes but inappropriate in terms of applicant acceptance. From a face validity perspective, content valid questionnaire development strategies may be most appropriate for blue collar populations. However, due to the small sample sizes generally found in blue collar work groups that are organized by function, content valid approaches limit the types of scoring techniques available.

With the exception of blue collar work forces in the largest organizations, most blue collar work is performed by individuals in small crews with clear boundaries and responsibilities. As such, blue collar work is often performed by unionized workers, which can severely restrict the type of criteria available for prediction studies. Whereas much of the published research on background data utilizes criteria such as supervisory ratings of performance and proficiency, contractual issues with labor unions may preclude such ratings from being generated on union members. As a result, criteria are more difficult to obtain, and they are usually highly suspect due to issues of trade loyalty, crew loyalty, and a general unwillingness of first-line supervisors of unionized workers to treat them differentially for any purpose. This characteristic of blue collar work is further complicated by a trend in many large organizations toward contracting outside the organization for the types of services these workers supply.

BLUE COLLAR BACKGROUND DATA RESEARCH

As with other types of populations, background data have been used with blue collar occupations to predict a variety of criteria, including tenure, supervisory performance ratings, test performance, and training performance. Also, background data models reported in the literature include weighted application blanks, life history questionnaires, and training and experience evaluations scored with both unit weighting and regression approaches. These studies are reported below.

TENURE

The use of a weighted application blank for hiring seasonal unskilled blue collar employees was reported in 1955 (Dunnette & Maetzold, 1955). An interesting aspect of this study was that the weighted application blank, used to predict tenure, was applied to the selection of employees doing different kinds of jobs. Using a weighted application blank scoring system (England, 1967), a number of items were utilized that effectively differentiated long tenure and short tenure employees. Upon cross-validation, only 16 percent of the short tenure employees reached or exceeded the median score of the long tenure employees, and only 18 percent of the long tenure employees fell below the median score of the short tenure employees. In other cross-validations, the scoring system was applied to applicants at other plant locations and was found to be an effective predictor of tenure.

In a similar study, a weighted application blank was constructed to select permanently employed unskilled blue collar workers doing different kinds of work (Scott & Johnson, 1967). Upon cross-validation, the weighted application blank (WAB) correctly classified 72 percent of the holdout group into short-term or long-term employees. In addition, the correlation between the weighted application blank scores and months on the job was .45 ($p < .01$). Also, using a multiple regression equation with the significant items, the percentage of correct classifications was slightly reduced when applied to the holdout group (70% instead of 72% for the WAB), and the correlation between WAB scores and months on the job was reduced from .41 to .31. A number of possibilities were cited for the results found related to the multiple regression approach, including a small sample size relative to the number of predictors and a nonlinear relationship between the criterion and some predictors.

JOB PERFORMANCE

One of the first reported applications of background data in blue collar hiring occurred in 1932 with taxi cab drivers (Viteles, 1932; cited in Owens, 1976). A scoring procedure that was applied to an employment application form resulted in substantial hiring improvements when cross-validated. At the cutting score, the process resulted in the elimination of 60 percent of the poorest earners while retaining 78 percent of the highest earners.

Mosel (1952) researched the relationship between education and experience background data and supervisory ratings of job performance for 13 skilled trades in the federal work force. Of the thirteen correlation coefficients reported, only two, painter and auto mechanic, correlated significantly (.26 and .27, respectively). Mosel also reported that the average correlation across all trades was .09 and concluded that very little to no relationship exists between rationally developed background data and supervisory performance ratings. In a similar study, Primoff (1958) found that months of experience and years of education were not predictive of on-the-job performance ratings. Also, a validity study in the United States Civil Service Commission (1947) for teletype repairmen demonstrated a correlation of .05 between education and experience ratings and supervisory ratings of job performance.

In 10 studies conducted with skilled craftsmen applicants at the Standard Oil Company (1962), a biodata form demonstrated a median validity of .45 with a criterion consisting of multiple alternation rankings on overall job performance.

TRAINING PERFORMANCE

In a unique study, Helmreich, Bakeman, and Radloff (1973) used a life history questionnaire to predict the performance of navy divers in training. Important aspects of successful completion of training included factors such as their ability to work effectively underwater, to get along effectively with fellow teammates, and to adapt to a stressful, isolated, and confined environment (1973, p. 148). The life history questionnaire was correlated with a pass-fail criterion and class rank for those successfully completing training. Using 10 predictors, a multiple regression analysis yielded cross-validated multiple correlations of .58 with the pass-fail criterion and .59 with performance criteria in the form of class rank. The authors also reported a nonsignificant correlation of −.11 between scores on the *Navy*

General Classification Test, a general ability measure, and the pass-fail criterion, indicating that success in training was more related to achievement motivation than academic intelligence.

TEST PERFORMANCE

Background data have also been used in blue collar settings as screening devices for testing programs utilizing both aptitude and general ability measures, as well as content valid selection tests. Sparks (1971) researched the relationship between scores on a life history questionnaire and scores on an aptitude battery for refinery technicians in an attempt to reduce the number of failures participating in an extensive testing process. In the weighting group, measures of nonverbal reasoning, chemical comprehension, reading ability, math ability, and learning ability correlated .52, .69, .62, .44, and .64 with background scores, respectively. Sparks (1971) reported a correlation of .85 between the background scores and the pass-fail criterion. In the cross-validation sample, the background scores correlated .52 , .65, .57, .43, and .56 with a slightly different battery of aptitude measures, and correlated .61 with the pass-fail criterion.

In a similar study with electricians and a content valid testing program, Pannone (1984) found a correlation of .42 between biographical questionnaire scores designed to measure very specific aspects of related training and experience and test scores. He reported that only 20 percent of the failures reached or exceeded the median score of the passers, and only 11 percent of the passers fell below the median score for the failures. At a certain cutting score, 59 percent of the failures would have been screened out with only 13 percent of the passers. Of particular interest, Pannone was able to demonstrate the effects of faking on validity coefficients. By including statements on the training and experience evaluation form that referred to experience maintaining nonexistent electrical equipment, Pannone was able to separate the sample into fakers and nonfakers. When separated into subgroups, the correlations between background scores and test scores was .55 for the nonfakers and .26 for the fakers, indicating that faking introduced error variance that moderated the validity coefficients.

SPECIAL ISSUES IN BLUE COLLAR
BACKGROUND DATA RESEARCH

The research cited above suggests a number of issues that merit consideration with the use of background data in blue collar areas. With the relatively small number of published studies in this area, it is clear that background data with blue collar applications are probably underreported and/or underutilized. Regardless, a number of lessons can be learned and used to focus future thinking in this area.

SCALE CONSTRUCTION AND SCORING

The reported research on blue collar applications of biodata have used life history questionnaires, weighted application blanks that collect standard applicant data, and very specific items regarding previous training and work experience. As with background data in general, the advice of Owens (1976) still holds true: "The moral seems clear; although one may include some items because they have priorly demonstrated validity in reasonably similar circumstances, biodata items are much more likely to be validated if they are knowledgeably beamed at a specific target" (p. 614).

Life history questionnaires, by their very nature, are typically designed to capture the most broad and complex aspects of human behavior. As a result, scale construction and item generation are typically based on the researcher's hypotheses concerning the relationship between the life experience represented and the criteria of interest. These complexities imply the need for scoring procedures that account for the many relationships among life history items and the criteria. As a result, multiple correlation techniques have been used with individual items and factors to predict criteria such as performance on aptitude batteries, training performance, and tenure. Regarding blue collar applications, the construction and scoring of background data is not unlike white collar applications.

The items used with weighted application blanks in blue collar applications have been somewhat narrower in scope than the typical item on a life history questionnaire, for the most part, using data found in the common employment application form. The scoring procedures described by England (1967) have been applied with considerable success, with some authors reporting validities equal to or greater than those obtained utilizing more complex multiple regression scoring systems (Scott & Johnson, 1967). Once again, weighted application blanks in blue collar studies have not differed substantially from other studies with different groups.

Background data forms consisting of items that relate to very specific aspects of prior training and work experience have a face validity quality that is particularly appealing in the blue collar area. Based on content validity models, training and experience evaluations have been used almost as extensively as written tests (Saso & Tanis, 1974). Unlike multiple regression approaches and weighted application blank scoring systems that assign weights based on the relationship between the item and the criteria, training experience evaluations typically have predetermined standards by which responses are evaluated. The use of training and experience evaluations as predictors assumes that knowledge, skills, and abilities acquired in previous experience will be transferred to the present situation. However, a major criticism is that, although they delineate what an applicant has done in the past, training and experience evaluations say little about an applicant's level of skill or proficiency. A number of types of training and experience evaluations have been used (Ash, 1981), and in a recent meta-analysis of validity, McDaniel, Schmidt, and Hunter (1988) found validities ranging from .45 to .11, depending on the training and experience methodology utilized.

Unfortunately, training and experience evaluation validation studies have not been published nearly as widely as they have been used. As McDaniel, Schmidt, and Hunter (1988) have described,

> despite the fact that training and experience evaluations are frequently used personnel selection methods, particularly in the public sector, personnel psychologists have conducted relatively little research on the validity of training and experience evaluations, and most of this research has not been published. (p. 284)

The major appeals of the use of content validity models in blue collar applications are face validity and job relatedness. These concerns are particularly important from an employee relations perspective. When the training and experience evaluation form items are closely linked to a job analysis, job relatedness is virtually assured. For example, to predict scores on a content valid written test, Pannone (1984) utilized the actual job analysis task statements as background data items. Items of this sort embrace the behavioral consistency model proposed by Wernimont and Campbell (1968) that emphasizes an evaluation of previous achievement on activities that are as similar to the actual criteria as possible. Although some researchers have reported very promising validities with test performance (Pannone, 1984; Sparks, 1971) and performance criteria (McDaniel, Schmidt, & Hunter, 1988), others have been less successful (Mosel, 1952; Primoff, 1958; U.S. Civil Service Commission, 1947), depending on the criterion of interest.

In terms of predictive utility, previous research in blue collar settings suggests that motivational criteria are best predicted by life history items using regression scoring procedures. Test performance and training performance have been effectively predicted by both rationally developed and empirically developed life history questionnaires and training and experience evaluations. However, regardless of the method of scale construction and scoring model utilized, the prediction of job performance in blue collar occupations has been inconsistent. This is most likely attributable to the variety of issues surrounding the nature of supervisory ratings, including range restriction, lack of reliability, and labor union issues. Hopefully, future research will utilize other types of performance criteria beyond supervisory ratings, such as the frequency of certain types of errors, complaints, disciplinary actions or grievances, injuries, policy infractions, and a variety of production records. These components of performance are underutilized as criteria in the literature.

FAKING

Because it is suggested that face validity may be more important to the acceptance of biodata forms among blue collar workers than among professional personnel, who may be more accustomed to broad-based testing procedures, the issue of faking is very important. Face-valid biodata forms are more easily faked. But research concerning the effects of faking on rationally developed biographical questionnaires such as training and experience evaluations has been scant. Pannone (1984) found that faking on a rationally developed biographical questionnaire under selection conditions clearly introduced a source of error variance that tended to reduce validity coefficients. In addition, Anderson, Warner, and Spencer (1981) found that through the use of a lie scale, 45 percent of all applicants indicated that they had observed or performed one or more nonexistent tasks. In this volume, Lautenschlager (chapter 14) has made a number of suggestions for reducing faking that may be useful in controlling distortion in forms developed for blue collar occupations. Lie scales and the use of verifiable items, along with threats to verify responses, are among the potentially useful approaches. These issues need further exploration among blue collar employees.

SUBGROUP FAIRNESS AND ADVERSE IMPACT

When used as a selection device, background data forms are subject to all of the scrutiny that is directed to tests. Many of the items included in life history forms or training and experience evaluations can be related to gender, age, socioeconomic status, or race. Therefore, as with any selection device, questions of unfairness with EEOC protected groups should be examined.

An Exxon, U.S.A. study (1973) found subgroup differences on the items of a background survey that used scores on a mechanical comprehension test as a criterion. The greatest item differences were on the items referring to family background. Findings such as these could be particularly problematic from an EEO perspective if the items were scored empirically. For example, such an empirical scoring system could inadvertently be designed to maximize subgroup differences, even though items demonstrating the strongest correlation with the criterion may show a very logical content relationship.

In two earlier studies for refinery workers, Sparks (1965a, 1965b) found no subgroup differences for blacks and whites on validity coefficients with test battery scores as the criterion. However, subsequent research on data from Sparks' studies (Moore, 1968) found significant mean differences in criterion scores. Also, by analyzing individual items, Moore was able to delete a number of items to reduce adverse impact with only a minimal effect on the validities.

Reilly and Chao (1982) reviewed 11 background data studies that reported ethnic subgroup data and found significant mean differences in only three cases. They concluded that for empirically keyed forms, a relationship exists between criterion mean differences and background data mean differences. Where criterion differences are large, adverse impact will exist, but background mean differences will be smaller where criterion mean differences are smaller. They also concluded that "the validity and fairness of biodata can be expected to hold for minority and majority groups, but different keys may be needed for males and females" (p. 13).

Issues of unfairness to protected groups with training and experience evaluations or other types of rationally developed background questionnaires have not been reported in the literature. Also, no studies were found that reported ethnic or gender subgroup means with performance criteria or tenure in blue collar settings.

DISCUSSION

A number of broad recommendations can be offered regarding the use of background data in blue collar settings. Given the wide range of theoretical orientations, form and item types, scoring procedures, and criteria that have been used, it is clear that background data have been successfully utilized in a number of instances with validities equal to or greater than those typically associated with tests. Recognizing the ease of collecting background data, as well as the benefits of standardization, it is safe to say that background data forms are viable alternatives to traditional testing programs.

As with testing programs, a number of areas deserve special attention. The sample sizes required to develop fully cross-validated empirically keyed forms are particularly difficult in the blue collar area. Many organizations do not have the staff numbers or hiring volume that are required for empirical keying. The organizations that do have adequate staffing are typically represented by labor unions and, as a result, are often precluded from generating performance criteria. Consortium research holds promise for smaller employers in this area and should be encouraged.

Since face validity is a crucial concern in blue collar samples, content-oriented strategies scored rationally or empirically that capture key prior experiences hold promise. This would guard against the researcher's tendency to use a blindly empirical approach instead of developing forms and items based on job analyses or hypotheses regarding the job and its performance requirements. Regarding empirical keying, Mumford and Owens (1987) appropriately state, "the very success of this technique has become something of a liability.... In their satisfaction with the resulting validity coefficients, investigators have often lost sight of the psychological principles underlying the development and application of background data measures" (p. 2). Items and background data forms developed from job analyses are targeted directly to job requirements, an aspect of the life history approach that is particularly problematic from an EEO perspective. However, it has also been shown that properly developed and researched empirical forms actually can be helpful in reducing adverse impact while maintaining reasonable validity (Moore, 1968).

Training and experience evaluations seem to merit additional research. While meta-analysis has shown validity for certain types of training and experience evaluations (McDaniel, Schmidt, & Hunter, 1988), a number of researchers have demonstrated that broad measures of amounts of education and experience are less useful as predictors (Mosel, 1952; Pannone, 1984; Primoff, 1958). This research suggests that, where training and experience evaluations are used, they should measure very specific aspects of training and experience as identified in a thorough job analysis. Also, the effects and extent of faking should be closely examined, and methods for controlling faking should be considered (see Lautenschlager's chapter in this volume).

A number of areas deserve attention in future blue collar background data research. Regarding performance criteria, researchers should attempt to use a variety of indices other than supervisory ratings. Criteria such as production records, frequency of errors, and quality control statistics may provide the needed measures. Training is a crucial concern in many organizations, and the cost of training increases as the complexity of jobs continues to increase. Background data may offer organizations an effective means of selection for training that is more cost effective than aptitude test batteries, and background data forms may be more acceptable to applicants. This notion should be more thoroughly explored. Also, for blue collar positions where adaptability to difficult or unusual environmental conditions is important, such as underwater diver, background data may prove to be particularly effective predictors.

Finally, as organizations continue to become more complex social systems, background data will continue to be used as predictors of complex criteria. For example, the trend toward team-based structures within organizations suggests the need for highly developed social and interpersonal skills. In such organizations, the ability to work effectively as a member of a team is often as important as technical skills. Life history items would most likely be a viable research technique to predict success and to increase our understanding of the development and structure of related skills and attributes. Since researchers have found background data to have utility in many traditional areas of interest, such as job performance, training performance, tenure, and test performance, future research will hopefully involve a variety of higher order applications.

REFERENCES

Anderson, C. D., Warner, J. C., & Spencer, C. C. (1981). Inflation bias in self-assessment examinations: Implications for valid employee selection. *Journal of Applied Psychology, 69,* 574–580.

Ash, R. A. (1981). Comparison of four approaches to the evaluation of job applicant training and work experience. *Dissertation Abstracts International, 42,* 4606b.

Asher, J. J. (1972). The biographical item: Can it be improved? *Personnel Psychology, 25,* 251–269.

Asher, J. J., & Sciarrino, J. A. (1974). Realistic work sample tests: A review. *Personnel Psychology, 27,* 519–533.

Blumenfeld, W. S. (1973, May–June). Application, application. *Atlanta Economic Review,* 8–13.

Dunnette, M. D., & Maetzold, J. (1955). Use of the weighted application blank in hiring seasonal employees. *Journal of Applied Psychology, 39,* 308–310.

England, G. W. (1967). *Development and use of weighted application blanks.* Dubuque, IA: Brown.

Exxon Company, U.S.A. (1973, April). Background factors associated with mechanical comprehension test scores. *Personnel Research,* 73–76.

Hassler, H. W., Myers, J. H., & Seldin, M. (1963). Payment history as a predictor of credit risk. *Journal of Applied Psychology, 47*(6), 383–385.

Helmreich, R., Bakeman, R., & Radloff, R. (1973). The life history questionnaire as a predictor of performance in navy diver training. *Journal of Applied Psychology, 57*(2), 148–153.

Lee, R., & Booth, J. M. (1974). A utility analysis of a weighted application blank designed to predict turnover for clerical employees. *Journal of Applied Psychology, 4,* 516–518.

Levine, E. L., & Flory, A., III. (1975). Evaluation of job applicants: A conceptual framework. *Public Personnel Management, 4,* 378–385.

McDaniel, M. A., Schmidt, F. L., & Hunter, J. E. (1988). A meta-analysis of the validity of methods for rating training and experience in personnel selection. *Personnel Psychology, 41,* 283–313.

Moore, C. L. (1968). *Ethnic differences as measured by a biographical inventory questionnaire.* Greensboro, NC: The Creativity Research Institute of the Smith Richardson Foundation.

Mosel, J. N. (1952). The validity of rational ratings of experience and training. *Personnel Psychology, 5,* 1–9.

Mosel, J. N., & Wade, R. R. (1951). A weighted application blank for the reduction of turnover in department store sales clerks. *Personnel Psychology, 4,* 177–184.

Mumford, M. D., & Owens, W. A. (1987). Methodology reviews: Principles, procedures, and findings in the application of background data measures. *Applied Psychological Measurement, 2*(1), 1–31.

Owens, W. A. (1976). Background data. In M. D. Dunnette (Ed.), *Handbook of industrial and organizational psychology* (1st ed.). Chicago: Rand McNally.

Pannone, R. D. (1984). Predicting test performance: A constant valid approach to screening applicants. *Personnel Psychology, 37,* 507–514.

Primoff, E. S. (1958, April). *Report on validation of examination for electrical repairer, McClellan Field, CA.* Washington, DC: Personnel Research and Development Center.

Reilly, R. R., & Chao, G. T. (1982). Validity and fairness of some alternative employee selection procedures. *Personnel Psychology, 35,* 1–62.

Saso, E. D., & Tanis, E. P. (1974). *Selection and certification of eligibles: A survey of policies and practices.* Chicago: International Personnel Management Association.

Scott, R. D., & Johnson, R. W. (1967). Use of the weighted application blank in selecting unskilled employees. *Journal of Applied Psychology, 51*(5), 393–395.

Sparks, C. P. (1971, June). *Using life history items to predict cognitive test scores.* Humble Oil and Refinery Company, Experimental Publication System, 12, Ms. No. 477–2.

Sparks, C. P. (1965a). *Prediction of cognitive test scores by life history items: Comparison across different ethnic groups.* Houston: Author.

Sparks, C. P. (1965b). *Using life history items to predict cognitive test scores.* Houston: Author.

Standard Oil Company, NJ. (1962). *Social science research reports: Selection and placement* (Vol. II). New York: Author.

Super, D. E. (1960). The biographical inventory as a method for describing adjustment and predicting success. *Bulletin of the International Association of Applied Psychology, 9,* 19–39.

United States Civil Service Commission (1947, June). *Validity study of examination for semi-automatic teletype writer repairman.* Examining and Placement Division, Policy and Test Development Section, Washington, DC.

van Rijn, P. (1980, December). *Biographical questionnaires and scored application blanks in personnel selection.* Washington, DC: Office of Personnel Management.

Wernimont, P. F., & Campbell, J. P. (1968). Signs, samples, and criteria. *Journal of Applied Psychology, 52*(5), 372–376.

Federal Government Selection
The Individual Achievement Record

Jay A. Gandy
Cooperative Personnel Services

David A. Dye
Charles N. MacLane
U.S. Office of Personnel Management

This chapter describes the first major application of biodata in the U.S. civil service and a program of continuing research relating to its use.[*] The primary focus is on the *Individual Achievement Record* (IAR; Gandy, Outerbridge, Sharf, & Dye, 1989), a biodata form used as a component of a nationwide selection program for entry-level nonsupervisory positions in over one hundred professional and administrative occupations across most federal agencies.

The IAR is an example of a large-scale application of biodata. Perhaps more importantly, it is a research vehicle for improving both understanding and practice relating to the use of biodata, particularly in the context of personnel selection. The research program thus reflects conditions, generally subscribed to but less widely observed, in which theory, research, and applications can be mutually informed in a relatively immediate manner.

The chapter has three main sections. First, the development of the IAR is described, including item development, empirical keying and concurrent cross-validation, fairness analysis, and validity generalization analysis

---

[*] The opinions expressed in this chapter are the authors' and do not necessarily represent the official policy of the U.S. Office of Personnel Management.

(described in more detail in Gandy et al., 1989). Second, the construct validity of the IAR is discussed, including the results of research relating the IAR to other measures in a confirmatory factor model. Third, the results to date of research relating to several methodology issues are described, including innovations in biodata scoring and evaluative comparisons of job performance criteria.

BACKGROUND

The history of biodata use in U.S. civil service selection programs is a short one, if biodata are defined in terms of empirically keyed questionnaires. In a more general sense, evaluations of biographical information on the education, training, and experience of job applicants have been a mainstay of civil service examinations for many decades. Typically developed on the basis of content validity, such evaluation procedures have assumed a wide variety of forms with varying degrees of criterion-related support (Lyons, 1989). It is important to note, however, that traditional evaluations of education and experience focus on specialized occupational skill, knowledge, and achievement and thus have little applicability to entry-level positions in which highly specialized capabilities are not expected.

A major impetus for use of biodata was the perceived need to better tap the developmental antecedents of effective job performance (e.g., Mumford & Owens, 1987). Empirically keyed instruments covering a broad array of general experiences and achievements were seen as a potentially effective means of capturing the extent to which individuals have taken advantage of the various opportunities available to them. Biodata prediction was seen to have potential in expanding the scope of measurement beyond written ability tests while reducing the impact on minorities typically found with ability tests (Reilly & Warech, 1988).

There are several reasons for limited use of biodata measures, including privacy (particularly in the governmental employment context), content and construct validity, stability of empirical validities over time, and occupation- and situation-specific validities (McKillip & Clark, 1974; van Rijn, 1980). A fresh look at these issues in 1986 and 1987 led to optimism that they were surmountable. For example, items could be developed with attention to content and job relevance and screened to avoid invasion of privacy without, we hoped, compromising the validity. Stability of validity could be increased by using large samples for item keying and validation. Both stability and generalizability could be enhanced by basing item keying on broadly based samples and by using a broadly applicable measure of job performance. These considerations were included in a rational-empirical framework.

DEVELOPMENT AND CRITERION-RELATED VALIDATION

METHOD

Item Development

Development of an item inventory began with three preparatory activities: (a) review of job analysis information on federal nonsupervisory professional and administrative occupations (McKillip, Trattner, Corts, & Wing, 1977), (b) review of available taxonomies of past behavior items (England, 1971; Glennon, Albright, & Owens, 1966), and (c) establishment of criteria for the acceptability of biodata for public-sector use. To be acceptable, items had to deal with events generally perceived as being substantially under individual control, have potential relevance to job performance, be verifiable in principle, avoid invasion of personal privacy, and avoid stereotyping by race, sex, or national origin. Although this screening process eliminated many of the traditional categories of background data, the remaining acceptable domains included school and educational experience, work history, skills, and interpersonal relations. A pool of 148 (with 5 alternative) multiple-choice items was developed in these areas. Examples are shown in Figure 1.

A formal test plan was not used for item development. In general, items were constructed to reflect loosely formed hypotheses that differences in applicants in the school, work, and interpersonal areas tapped by the items would be related to differences in job performance. This intuitive and judgmental process was aided by familiarity with (a) job analysis information and job requirements (skills, knowledge, abilities, and other characteristics) and (b) general characteristics of the applicant population in terms of the range of sources and types of prior experience. Thus, a concerted effort was made to cover life experiences, choices, and outcomes that are mediated by a wide range of motivational, interpersonal, and cognitive constructs.

Basically, two types of items were constructed: One reported facts and relatively objective information; the other reported perceptions of personal skills, knowledge, and abilities from the perspectives of others (e.g., peers, teachers, and former supervisors). The latter items were closely linked to job analysis information but more susceptible to distortion; the former were more broadly related to general developmental success and were believed to be more resistant to distortion.

Most items were designed with response alternatives on a continuum, although some (about 10%) were categorical (e.g., courses of study, sources of information, reasons for choice or action). Escape options were typically

1. My *high school* teachers would most likely describe my *self-discipline* as:
   a. superior
   b. above average
   c. average
   d. below average
   e. don't know

2. The number of *high school* clubs and organized activities (such as band, sports, newspaper, etc.) in which I participated was:
   a. 4 or more
   b. 3
   c. 2
   d. 1
   e. didn't participate

3. My grade point average in my *college major* was:
   a. I did not go to college or went less than two years
   b. less than 2.90
   c. 2.90–3.19
   d. 3.20–3.49
   e. 3.50 or higher

4. In the past three years, the number of different paying jobs I have held for more than two weeks is:
   a. 7 or more
   b. 5–6
   c. 3–4
   d. 1–2
   e. none

5. My previous supervisors (or teachers if not previously employed) would most likely describe my *problem-solving skills* as:
   a. superior
   b. above average
   c. average
   d. below average
   e. don't know

FIGURE 1   Examples of Biodata Items

written for both types of items to allow for "don't know" and inapplicability responses.

Criterion

A confidential supervisory performance appraisal, based on the *Descriptive Rating Scale* (DRS) used extensively by the U.S. Employment Service (U.S. Department of Labor, 1974), was chosen as the criterion for the initial validation study. The DRS reflects a "job-generic" appraisal designed to be applicable to performance in a broad spectrum of occupations (see Figure 2 for an example). This appraisal includes five-level performance

How much does the employee know about the job? (Employee's understanding of the principles, equipment, materials, and methods that have to do directly or indirectly with the work.)

a. Has very limited knowledge. Does not know enough to do the job adequately.
b. Has little knowledge. Knows enough to get by.
c. Has acceptable amount of knowledge. Knows enough to do good work.
d. Has very broad knowledge. Knows enough to do very good work.
e. Has complete knowledge. Knows enough to perform all work extremely well.

FIGURE 2   Example Item From the Six-item Performance Appraisal Form Used as the Job Performance Criterion

descriptions for each of the following performance dimensions: quantity of work, quality of work, accuracy, job knowledge, and efficiency in handling multiple activities, plus a summary appraisal. The criterion score was the average rating across all scales. Criterion reliability is unknown but estimated at .60 based on typical expectations of reliability of supervisory appraisals (Schmidt & Hunter, 1977).

The criterion was selected to measure job-related success and was not intended to reflect a general measure of social adjustment or life success.

Research Sample

Research materials were prepared for distribution to all external hires at the entry level (GS 5 to 7) for professional and (nonclerical) administrative career occupations through all appointment authorities for calendar years 1983 through 1986 who were still employed in the same occupation ($N = 13,000$), plus a weighted random sample ($N = 2,300$) of inservice placements based on population size by occupation. External hires were proportionally overrepresented, since the intended use of the biodata form was for external hiring. Appraisal forms were distributed to the supervisors of sample members. Matched returns of completed biodata forms and supervisory appraisals were obtained for 6,300 employees. Comparisons against central personnel data files showed the sample to be reasonably representative of both external and internal hires with respect to gender, race and national origin, occupations, and agencies.

Procedure

Research materials were delivered to sampled employees and supervisors nationwide through approximately 900 servicing personnel offices of 35 agencies. Supervisors were requested to allow time on the job for completion of the questionnaire. All participants were assured of confidentiality, and completed materials were mailed directly to the Office of Personnel Management in preaddressed envelopes.

Validation Method

A double cross-validation design was used entailing the following steps: (a) dividing the total sample into random halves, (b) developing a scoring key (described below) on each half, (c) applying the key developed on each half to the other half, (d) correlating the resulting scores with job performance, and (e) evaluating the degree of correlation "shrinkage" when a key is applied to a sample other than the one on which it was developed. The final key was developed on the total sample.

Item Keying and Scoring

Scoring keys were developed based on point-biserial correlations between item responses and the criterion. A minimum correlation of .042 ($p < .001$ for total sample; $p < .05$ for split-half) and unit weights ($-1, 0, +1$) were applied in keying response choices. Additionally, rational decision rules were developed to avoid illogical keying in exceptional situations of low response rates to extreme response choices. Keying was done independently by two psychologists, and differences—due almost exclusively to clerical error—were jointly resolved.

Several items that met the statistical standard were rejected based on further evaluation against the policy criteria discussed above and were not included in validity analyses.

Subgroup Analyses

Separate validity analyses were conducted by source of entry (external hire and inservice placement), age, sex, and race/national origin subgroups having n values of 200 or larger. Fairness analyses (Cleary, 1968) were carried out by testing for differences in standard errors, regression slopes, and intercepts (Gulliksen & Wilks, 1950).

Validity Generalization

Five separate meta-analyses were conducted to evaluate whether the validity of a common scoring key was moderated by differences in occupations, occupational families, occupation sample size, and agency setting. To carry out the meta-analyses, validity coefficients were computed, respectively, for each of 105 occupations, 6 occupational families, 98 occupations represented by small samples ($n < 200$), 7 occupations with large samples ($n = 200+$), and 28 agencies. Conservative procedures were followed, in which no corrections to validity coefficients were made and only the effect of sampling error on variance in validities was taken into account. Thus, each meta-analysis consisted of computing the mean validity, weighted by sample size; the standard deviation (and variance) of the validity distribution; the standard deviation (and variance) expected statistically due to sampling error; the remaining variance after subtracting sampling error; and the lower limit of the 90 percent confidence interval.

RESULTS AND DISCUSSION

Score and Criterion Distributions

The score distribution was approximately normal. The criterion distribution was skewed toward higher ratings, as is typical of performance appraisals, but had adequate variance to support planned analyses.

Cross-validation

The critical cross-correlations were .33 and .32—that is, the predictor–criterion correlations that resulted from the application of the scoring keys developed on each sample half to the independent half. Little shrinkage occurred in validity coefficients in the cross-comparisons (.34 to .33 and .34 to .32), providing strong support for the robustness of keys developed on large samples. For the total sample, the validity of the *total* key with the total sample was .33 (.43 when corrected for criterion reliability estimated at .60). The observed validity of the *total* key with each sample half was also .33.

Subgroup Analyses, Instrument Modification, and Fairness Analyses

Subgroup analyses were conducted using 84 items and the item response weights found to be valid based on the *total* key. The upper section of Table 1 shows comparative data on predictor performance and validity by race/ ethnic group, gender, age, and source of hire. Little difference in predictor scores was found by age (32 and under versus over 32) or source of hire (internal versus external). Females averaged higher scores (−.26 SD), and whites averaged higher scores relative to African-Americans (.35 SD) and Hispanics (.20 SD). The differences in score levels found between whites and minority groups are small relative to those typically found on ability tests (Reilly & Warech, 1988).

To reduce intergroup mean scores differences, 20 items were deleted that reflected relatively lower validities for minorities in conjunction with adverse impact. This procedure was reasonably successful, as may be seen in the lower section of Table 1. Effect size differences narrowed considerably, while overall validity of the modified (64-item) instrument changed minimally from $r = .33$ to .32 (.43 to .41 when corrected for criterion reliability).

TABLE 1 Results by Subgroup Before and After Selected Item Deletions

Subgroup	N	Mean	SD	Effect Size	Validity
		Before item deletions			
Whites	4,842	50.66 (2.80)	9.97 (19.31)		.33
Blacks	916	47.24 (−3.82)	9.61 (18.60)	.35	.28
Hispanics	310	48.67 (−1.05)	10.12 (19.60)	.20	.30
Males	3,535	48.86 (−0.67)	9.80 (18.97)		.33
Females	2,757	51.46 (4.35)	10.07 (19.49)	−.26	.32
32 or under	3,130	49.86 (1.26)	9.97 (19.30)		.32
Over 32	3,162	50.14 (1.79)	10.03 (19.42)	−.03	.34
Internal appointment	1,015	50.55 (2.59)	9.74 (18.86)		.34
External appointment	5,277	49.89 (1.32)	10.05 (19.45)	.07	.33
Total sample	6,292	50.00 (1.53)	10.00 (19.36)		.33
		After item deletions			
Whites	4,842	50.47 (4.59)	9.93 (15.70)		.32
Blacks	916	47.83 (0.43)	9.92 (15.67)	.27	.29
Hispanics	310	49.67 (3.33)	10.50 (16.60)	.08	.29
Males	3,535	49.35 (2.83)	10.03 (15.86)		.32
Females	2,757	50.83 (5.17)	9.89 (15.64)	−.15	.32
32 or under	3,130	49.76 (3.48)	9.71 (15.34)		.32
Over 32	3,162	50.24 (4.23)	10.28 (16.25)	−.05	.33
Internal appointment	1,015	50.50 (4.64)	10.18 (16.10)		.32
External appointment	5,277	49.50 (3.70)	9.96 (20.99)	.06	.32
Total sample	6,292	50.00 (3.85)	10.00 (15.81)		.32

Note: Effect size = $\dfrac{Mean_{group\,1} - Mean_{group\,2}}{SD_{within\,group}}$

Means and SDs shown in parentheses are based on raw scores.

No statistically significant differences in subgroup validities were found before or after the item deletions. Also, comparisons of subgroup standard errors, regression slopes, and intercepts failed to indicate any unfairness to minorities and gender groups either before or after instrument modification. Differences in intercepts indicated a small but statistically significant ($p < .01$) degree of overprediction for African-Americans and Hispanics from the use of the common regression line; that is, levels of job performance predicted by scores tended to be slightly higher than measured job performance.

META-ANALYSES: The results of five separate meta-analyses (shown in Table 2) supported the generalizability of a common scoring key across occupations and agency settings. Sample-size-weighted mean observed validities across 105 occupations, 6 job families, 98 occupations with small samples, 7 occupations with large samples, and 28 agencies were all within the narrow range of .29 to .31. The 90 percent credibility values (CV)—indicating the level above which 90 percent of validities would be expected to fall—ranged from .19 (for small sample occupations) to .30 (for agencies). In the agency meta-analysis (in which each validity coefficient was computed using all employees in the agency sample combined across occupations), 100 percent of the variance in validities across agencies could be accounted for by sampling error. The results from the analysis across agencies were interpreted as a strong indication that the criterion-related validity of the common scoring key was not moderated by differences in agency settings, such as mission, organizational culture, rating tendencies, and mix of occupations. The analyses on occupational groupings indicate that validities generalize well across occupations, but they also suggest that limited potential exists for enhancing validity through the development of occupation-specific keys. For example, after subtracting variance expected from sampling error, the estimated true standard deviation for observed (uncorrected) validities across the six occupational families was less than .03. This small variation in validities suggests limited room for improvement—at least through traditional keying methods.

OPERATIONAL FORM: An operational form of the IAR was prepared consisting of 112 items, 64 of which are scored. The additional items were included for research purposes, including identification of possible faking. Predictive criterion-related validation studies of the IAR and written tests are planned when technically feasible, based on hiring volume and criterion maturity.

TABLE 2   Meta-analyses of Validity by Occupations and Agencies

Variables	Number of rs	Total N	Mean r	Observed SD_r	SD_e	90% CV
Occupations	105	6,295	.30	.13	.11	.21
Occupational families	6	5,917	.30	.04	.03	.26
Occupational sample ($n = 200+$)	7	2,906	.31	.07	.04	.23
Occupational sample ($n < 200$)	98	3,389	.29	.17	.14	.19
Agencies	28	6,293	.30	.06	.06	.30

CONSTRUCT VALIDITY

The previous section demonstrated that the IAR is a valid predictor of job performance and is a promising tool for promoting fairness in selection. These findings are consistent with the objectives of our federal hiring program and with biodata research in general. To complement the empirical validity evidence, this section presents findings of a study to improve our understanding of the construct base of the IAR.

We recognize that the content of the IAR is somewhat unique and that this may limit conclusions we can derive for biodata in general. Certain principles were followed during item development to restrict the use of many traditional biodata areas considered inappropriate for a merit system environment. Still, the IAR was developed to tap individual qualities associated with accomplishments and experiences that are common to many biodata inventories. In particular, we anticipate that the IAR assesses attributes that go beyond the measurement of cognitive reasoning abilities to include aspects of achievement and work motivation. Our study had three objectives:

- To identify underlying factors measured by the IAR through exploratory factor analysis
- To assess the adequacy of the identified factors and clarify their meaning in terms of underlying characteristics and individual qualities
- To discuss how the specific content and characteristics of the items used in the IAR may lead to a greater understanding of biodata

METHOD

The study was conducted in three phases. In Phase 1, an exploratory factor analysis identified a set of preliminary dimensions. In Phase 2, a confirmatory factor model was developed and cross-validated to establish an appropriate factor structure. Confirmatory factor methods (Hayduk, 1987; Long, 1983) were used to minimize the amount of "raw empiricism" typically used to evaluate biodata instruments. In Phase 3, the constructs represented were clarified by comparing the factors in the model to reference measures selected from well-known measurement domains. All analyses were performed using PC-LISREL Version VI (Jöreskog & Sörbom, 1986).

Samples

Two samples of federal government employees were used. The first sample, used in phases 1 and 2, consisted of the original group of 6,300 employees discussed in the previous section. The second sample, used in phases 2 and 3, consisted of 1,841 employees who were administered the IAR plus a series of reference measures. For the second sample, the typical participant was 32 years old, had a college degree, and had been on the job for slightly less than one year. Employees in both samples were given time on the job to participate in the study and were assured that the scores would not affect their job standing.

Instruments

Both samples completed the 112-item version of the IAR. The second sample was also administered a set of reference measures that included four entire instruments, each covering one of four major measurement domains. Six individual subscales measuring finer aspects of achievement were also administered because they were considered important for clarifying the divergent or unique nature of the factors. A description of the instruments and scales within the major domains follows.

- *Cognitive ability.* A 60-item, multiple-choice, written ability test developed by the U.S. Office of Personnel Management was used to represent this domain (Northrop, Nester, Diané, & Colberg, 1989). It yields two subscores, verbal ability and quantitative reasoning ability. For this study, the two subscores were combined into a single overall score.
- *Temperament/personality.* The most recent version of the *NEO Personality Inventory* (Costa & McCrae, 1985), modeled after the popular five-factor theory of personality, was given. The NEO

contains 200 scorable items. For each item, respondents are asked to indicate their level of agreement on a five-point scale, ranging from "strongly disagree" to "strongly agree." The inventory yields five major domain scores: Neuroticism, Extraversion, Openness, Agreeableness, and Conscientiousness.

Four individual subscales from the *California Psychological Inventory* (CPI; Gough, 1987)—Capacity for Status, Achievement via Conformance, Achievement via Independence, and Work Orientation—were used to assess various aspects of achievement. The Locus of Control scale (Rotter, 1966) and Janis-Field self-esteem scale (Robinson & Shraver, 1973) were also used.

- *Vocational interests.* The *Self-Directed Search* (SDS; Holland, 1985), based on Holland's typology of personality, was selected to represent this domain. The SDS was developed based on research indicating that vocational choice is determined by several characteristics. In the SDS, these characteristics include competencies, preferred activities, and self-ratings of various skills and abilities. Based on the answers given in the SDS, respondents are categorized into one of six personality types: Realistic, Investigative, Artistic, Social, Enterprising, and Conventional. The six types provide an indication of one's preference for given vocational areas.

- *Work values.* The *Comparative Emphasis Scale* (CES; Ravlin & Meglino, 1986) was used to represent the domain of work values. The CES is a 24-item forced-choice measure yielding four scores. For each item, respondents are presented with a pair of statements, with each statement representing one of four values: Achievement/Working Hard, Concern for/Helping Others, Fairness, and Honesty/Integrity. Respondents are given one point for each value every time a statement representing that value is chosen from the pair. Because of the forced-choice format, the CES is an *ipsative* measure. This means that scores for the four scales are not independent; that is, respondents score higher on one scale at the expense of the others.

Phase 1: Exploratory Analysis

A principal factors analysis, placing squared multiple correlations on the diagonal, was performed. To assist in determining an appropriate number of factors to represent best the content of the IAR, the Kaiser criterion of eigenvalues greater than 1.0 was used. Scree plots showing the amount of variance explained by the extracted factors were also reviewed. To assist in choosing a preferred factor solution, solutions consisting of three to six factors were rotated for better interpretability and examined. An oblique rotation was preferred, since it was believed that the underlying factors were correlated.

Phase 2: Factor Model Development

In this phase, a confirmatory factor model was developed using items from the IAR only. The goal was to derive an acceptable model (in terms of statistical fit) that describes the content of the IAR in substantive terms.

The specification of a confirmatory factor model requires performing at least the following three steps: (a) specifying a proposed number of factors, (b) determining what items should serve as "observed indicators" of the factors, and (c) specifying which model parameters (i.e., item factor loadings and factor intercorrelations) should be fixed and which should be set free to be estimated. Performing these steps means that a priori hypotheses are made about the nature of the underlying factor structure.

Based on the factors identified in the exploratory analysis, an initial model containing four common factors was specified. Twelve rationally formed item composites, three per factor, were posited as observed indicators of the factors. In the initial model, the item composites were allowed to load on a single factor only. An illustration of the initial factor model is shown in Figure 3.

The adequacy of the initial model was evaluated by means of a specification search (MacCallum, 1986). A specification search is a sequential process of modifying a factor model to improve fit and meaning. Ways to improve model fit include (a) adjusting the proposed number of factors, (b) altering the assignment of observed indicators to the factors, and (c) changing the pattern of fixed and free parameters to be estimated. From the initial model, the specification search called for two of the item composites to load on more than one factor. In the final analysis, the revised model allowed for the academic skills and academic evaluations composites to load on both the work competency and high school achievement factors. These changes were considered reasonable on substantive grounds.

Because the specification search had the potential for capitalizing on chance factors in the first sample, the model was cross-validated on the second sample. Cross-validation is highly recommended to confirm the stability of factor models (Cudeck & Browne, 1983; Long, 1983; MacCallum, 1986). For this analysis, the multisample feature of LISREL VI was used to test the hypothesis that the model holds in both samples simultaneously.

Phase 3: Extension of Factor Model to Reference Measures

The purpose of this phase was to define and explicate the constructs represented by the factors derived in Phase 2 using the set of reference measures. All analyses were performed on the second sample.

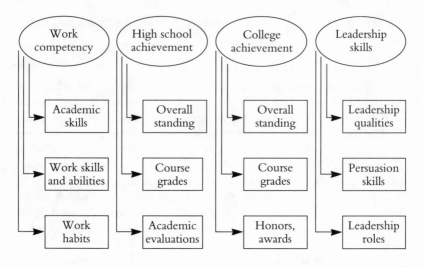

FIGURE 3   Initial Factor Model Specification

First, factor scores based on the assigned IAR composites were computed. Correlations were then computed between the factor scores and the entire set of reference measures. Next, to clarify further the divergent nature of the factors, a joint factor analysis was performed containing the IAR item composites and the reference measures from the cognitive, temperament, and vocational interest domains. In this analysis, factor loadings for the IAR composites were fixed to those that were obtained in Phase 2, whereas the reference measures were allowed to load freely on all factors.

RESULTS

Phase 1
The exploratory analysis suggests that the IAR measures four underlying factors:

- *Work competency:* self-assessments of various skills, abilities, and work habits applicable to the work setting
- *High school achievement:* self-reports of academic achievement and self-discipline in the classroom setting

- *College achievement:* self-reports of academic performance, honors, and awards in the college environment
- *Leadership skills:* self-assessments of various leadership roles, skills, and experiences in work and social settings

Phase 2

The results from the specification search are given in Table 3. The table presents the factor loadings and intercorrelations for the final model. Note that the two additional loadings for the composites resulting from the specification search are much smaller than the loadings from the initial model. Still, all the loadings in the table are highly significant. The pattern of intercorrelations is informative. Not surprisingly, the two academic factors are correlated; also, the Work Competency and Leadership Skills factors are highly correlated. It is interesting that the academic factors and Leadership Skills are virtually unrelated.

An advantage of confirmatory factor analysis is that it allows one to determine the acceptability of the fit of a model to the data. The chi-square statistic, a traditional measure of overall fit of the model, was not heavily relied upon here. This is because it is well known that chi-square is inflated by large sample sizes (e.g., >500), making its value not very meaningful. Instead, the goodness-of-fit index (GFI) and the root mean square residual (RMSR) were used as stand-alone indices of fit (Jöreskog & Sörbom, 1986). The values for these fit indices were .97 and .03, respectively. Comparing these figures to a Monte Carlo study conducted by Anderson and Gerbing (1984), we concluded that the model fits the data very well.

The results of the cross-validation analysis provided strong evidence that the structure of the factor model is stable. As one comparison, the GFI and RMSR in the second sample were identical to the first sample, .97 and .03, indicating the same degree of fit. Under the multi-sample analysis, a comparison was made to evaluate the similarity between the factor solutions of the first and second samples. Here, the principal interest was to determine if the overall *pattern* of factor loadings and intercorrelations was the same in both samples. Using a chi-square difference test comparing nested models (i.e., similar patterns of loadings versus exact loadings), the hypothesis of similar patterns of factor solutions was supported, $\chi^2 (20, N = 4,821) = 30.12$, $p = .05$. Finally, the factor loadings and intercorrelations derived for the second sample were compared to those presented in Table 3. The largest difference in corresponding factor loadings between the two samples was .01. The largest absolute difference in corresponding factor intercorrelations was .03.

TABLE 3   Confirmatory Factor Model Loadings and Intercorrelations

Factor/Item Composite	Work Competency	High School Achievement	College Achievement	Leadership Skills
Work competency				
Academic skills	.62	.23		
Work skill/abilities	.96			
Work habits	.79			
High school achievement				
Overall standing		.90		
Course grades		.88		
Academic evaluations	.22	.72		
College achievement				
Overall standing			.89	
Course grades			.79	
Honors/awards			.75	
Leadership skills				
Leadership qualities				.80
Persuasion skills				.73
Leadership roles				.39

	Factor Intercorrelations			
	1	2	3	4
1. Work competency	—	.20	.24	.63
2. High school achievement		—	.44	−.02
3. College achievement			—	.09
4. Leadership skills				—

Note: All factor loadings are statistically significant, $p < .01$.

Phase 3

The correlations between the IAR factors and the full set of reference measures are given in Table 4. Because of the large samples used, most of the correlations in the table are statistically significant. Therefore, to assist in explicating the nature of the constructs represented by the factors, it is more informative to focus on the patterns of the correlations.

With the exception of the work values domain, it can be seen that each major domain shows some relationship to the factors. Of interest is what

TABLE 4 Correlations Between Four Factors and Reference Measures

Major Domain/ Measure	Factor[a]			
	Work Competency	High School Achievement	College Achievement	Leadership Skills
Cognitive ability				
OPM ability test	.12***	.36***	.33***	−.08***
Temperament/personality				
NEO:Neuroticism	−.37***	−.03	−.04	−.40***
NEO:Extraversion	.34***	.07*	.03	.57***
NEO:Openness	.23***	.14***	.16***	.25***
NEO:Agreeableness	.10**	.09**	.04	−.06
NEO:Conscientiousness	.43***	.14***	.15***	.41***
Locus of Control	−.17***	.02	−.02	−.20***
CPI:Achievement via Conformity	.28***	.26***	.24***	.25***
CPI:Achievement via Independence	.19***	.11**	.18***	.16***
CPI:Work Orientation	.20***	.08**	.10**	.15***
CPI:Capacity for Status	.29***	.08**	.12***	.40***
Janis Self-esteem	.41***	.03	.04	.57***
Vocational interest				
SDS:Realistic	.15***	−.14***	−.10**	.16***
SDS:Investigative	.19***	.15***	.13***	.11**
SDS:Artistic	.15***	.11**	.09**	.18***
SDS:Social	.22***	.03	.06	.35***
SDS:Enterprising	.31***	−.04	−.04	.51***
SDS:Conventional	.00	−.03	−.07*	.02
Work values				
CES: Achievement/Working Hard	.03	−.04	−.08*	.09**
CES:Helping/Concern for Others	−.12***	.01	−.03	−.16***
CES:Fairness	.08*	.02	.10**	.02
CES:Honesty/Integrity	.02	.01	.02	.04

Note: [a]*ns* range from 841 to 954.
*p < .05; **p < .01; ***p < .001.

the four factors have in common with one another. All four factors share similar relationships to the NEO Openness, CPI Achievement via Conformance, CPI Achievement via Independence, and SDS Investigative scales. Taken together, this suggests that all the factors measure an individual's drive to succeed and an openness to new situations, beliefs, and ideas. This finding is consistent with the anticipation that the IAR generally assesses aspects related to the work motivation and achievement of the individual.

To assess the divergent nature of the factors, it is of interest to consider how the factors relate differently to the reference measures. A pattern emerges if the two academic factors are considered separately from the work-oriented factors (i.e., Work Competency and Leadership Skills). The academic factors show the greatest relationship with the cognitive ability domain and share little relationship with the noncognitive domains. The CPI achievement scales are an exception to this rule. This suggests that the academic factors are more closely associated with measuring one's reasoning abilities, but that they still measure a strong drive to do well.

It was expected that the Achievement Via Conformance scale would show a greater relationship with the high school factor, as evidence suggests that it measures a preference for working in clearly defined settings (Gough, 1964); also, that the Achievement Via Independence scale, which is designed to assess a preference for working in settings involving freedom and individual initiative, would be more related to college achievement (Gough & Lanning, 1986). However, neither of these expectations was well supported.

The pattern for the work-oriented factors is the reverse of the academic ones, where the greatest relationships are with the temperament/personality and vocational interest domains. In particular, the highest relationships are with the NEO Conscientiousness and Extraversion, Janis-Field Self-esteem, and the SDS Social and Enterprising scales. This suggests that these two factors are measuring motivational aspects dealing with working hard, striving to get ahead, self-confidence, and an interest in occupations emphasizing leadership and interpersonal skills.

To clarify the conceptual differences among the factors, the joint factor analysis is presented in Table 5. This analysis gives a clearer idea of how the two academic factors differ from one another, and how the two work-oriented factors differ from one another. For this analysis, the work values instrument and the specific subscales in the temperament/personality domain were removed.

Both academic factors are related positively to the cognitive ability test and to the NEO Openness scale, which measures the level of appreciation for intellectually stimulating situations. This pattern supports the cognitive emphasis of the factors discussed earlier. Because the loadings for the remaining reference measures are not high, differences between the two academic factors in terms of their achievement emphasis are not clear. Still, High School Achievement is positively related to NEO Extraversion and

TABLE 5   Joint Factor Analysis: IAR Item Composites
and Reference Measures

External Domain/ Scale	Factor[a]			
	Work Competency	High School Achievement	College Achievement	Leadership Skills
Cognitive ability				
OPM ability test	.24**	.30**	.17**	−.21**
Temperament/personality				
NEO:Neuroticism	−.10*	.04	−.03	−.38**
NEO:Extraversion	−.24**	.09*	−.01	.87**
NEO:Openness	−.06	.12**	.11**	.41**
NEO:Agreeableness	.00	.03	.04	.03
NEO:Conscientiousness	.15**	.02	.07*	.35**
Vocational interest				
SDS:Realistic	.08	−.09*	−.09*	.21**
SDS:Investigative	.09*	.19**	.00	.19**
SDS:Artistic	−.14**	.14**	.03	.46**
SDS:Social	−.25**	.08*	.01	.77**
SDS:Enterprising	−.20**	.09**	−.11**	.87**
SDS:Conventional	−.17**	.11*	−.14**	.29**

Note: IAR item composite loadings were fixed to those in Phase 1 and are not shown.
[a]$n = 1,015$; *$p < .05$.

five of the six vocational interest scales. On the other hand, College Achievement is related to NEO Conscientiousness and shows little or negative relationships with all of the scales in the vocational interest domain.

Taken together, this suggests that the difference between High School Achievement and College Achievement may be characterized in terms of a social emphasis. That is, success during high school may be more associated with social interaction, outgoing behavior, and a general enthusiasm for many areas; college success appears to be more a function of hard work and self-discipline, with little expression of interest for certain career paths.

The divergent nature of the Work Competency and Leadership Skills factors is much more apparent. First, the pattern of relationships to cognitive ability and NEO Extraversion are the opposite. Work Competency is related positively to the cognitive ability test and related negatively to NEO Extraversion; Leadership Skills is related negatively to the cognitive ability test and is very highly related positively to the NEO

Extraversion scale. Second, Leadership Skills is related to NEO Openness and all of the vocational interest scales, especially SDS Social and SDS Enterprising; Work Competency shows little or negative relationships with the vocational interest domain.

These findings suggest that the achievement emphasis of these two factors can also be differentiated in terms of a social emphasis, particularly with respect to the influence of other people. Work Competency can be characterized in terms of achievements that require reasoning ability and little social interaction; Leadership Skills is characterized better in terms of achievements involving ascendant behavior, social interaction, an openness to new and possibly risky situations, and little reasoning ability.

DISCUSSION

Derived Factor Model for the IAR

The specification search used to develop the factor model confirmed the legitimacy of the proposed factor structure of the IAR. Because the model held up under cross-validation, the factor structure appears to be stable across samples. This is consistent with the anticipation that the IAR measures constructs that are generally important in the prediction of job success. Because some biodata literature indicates that the meaning of factors may change after a period of years (Eberhardt & Muchinsky, 1982), further work to assess the stability of the IAR factor structure over time would be of interest.

A note can be made about the use of confirmatory factor analysis and structural equation modeling in general. It was our intent in this study to utilize confirmatory methods as a means to reduce the empiricism that has characterized biodata research. Still, the full potential of these techniques was not utilized. To improve the conceptual understanding of biodata, researchers should continue to take advantage of these techniques to formulate and test specific hypotheses.

Improved Understanding of the IAR

Our research provided a clearer understanding of the IAR as a predictor of job performance. It is evident that the IAR is complex factorially, sharing relationships to cognitive and noncognitive domains. The four identified factors, which portray the content of the IAR well, show that the IAR measures individual achievements in academic, work, and interpersonal settings (Gandy et al., 1989). In a broader sense, the findings of this research confirm the anticipation that the IAR moves beyond an assessment of general reasoning ability to measure attitudes, self-esteem, and interests, particularly those associated with work motivation and achievement.

It was surprising that the IAR showed little relationship to the work values domain, especially with the Achievement scale of the CES. Certainly the IAR does measure aspects of achieving and working hard. While the reason for this finding is not clear, it may be that the ipsative nature of the CES interfered with observing its true relationship to the IAR. In other words, because the instrument forced respondents to make decisions about their Achievement value in competition with other values, the construct validity of the Achievement scale may have been mitigated.

Biodata as a Predictor of Job Performance

A finding of great interest was the pattern that the academic and work-oriented factors exhibited with the cognitive and noncognitive domains. While the observed relationships may not be very surprising, what may be informative is the reason. The items contained in the two work-oriented factors require a fair amount of self-assessment regarding one's skills, abilities, and behaviors. The items contained in the two academic factors generally require much less introspection and instead ask for self-reports that are fairly factual and easily verifiable. It may be that the difference in the way that the items were phrased was partly responsible for the pattern of results. If that is the case, it could mean that developers of biodata would be able to exercise greater control in what biodata measures just by how items are worded.

METHODOLOGICAL RESEARCH: SCORING INNOVATIONS AND CRITERION COMPARISONS

Unlike many methods of measurement, the development of biodata instruments for use in applied contexts has not, to a great degree, been an outgrowth of theory; and the evolution of theory has not, in general, been energized by the results of operational use. Rather, the two have proceeded independently: Theory-building has depended on internal (factor and cluster) analyses (e.g., Owens & Schoenfeldt, 1979), while applications have been derived from external analyses in which items have been chosen blindly, based on their statistical relationships with an outside criterion (e.g., Rothstein, Schmitt, Erwin, Owens, & Sparks, 1990).

This separation has led to suggestions by researchers (e.g., Mumford & Owens, 1987) that content be a central part of the development of biodata selection procedures. Products developed from this hypothesis have shown promise (e.g., Nickels, 1989). However, Ostroff and Schmidt (1987) found that ratings of the content validity of in-basket items did not agree with their criterion-related validities. Mitchell and Klimoski (1982) reported that the criterion-related validities of biographical information question-naires developed by an empirical strategy were higher than those developed with a rational strategy even after cross-validation. In addition, the stability of the few existing biodata selection procedures that have a broad base of empirical support across occupations, such as the procedure used in the life insurance industry and studied by Brown (1981), argues for underlying areas of meaning that are unlikely, in our present state of knowledge, to be tapped completely by direct methods of item specification based on raters' judgments.

This evidence suggests that innovation in empirical biodata develop-ment strategies could be rewarding. It could lead to increased understand-ing of the bases of relationships between biodata and external criteria and in even more effective measurement products. In contrast with written cognitive ability tests, there has been little applied research of this type.

A primary reason for this apparent deficiency is the need for very large sample sizes in order to (a) do analyses of sufficient power at the (biodata) item level and to (b) conduct exploratory analyses among the large number of data points found in the typical biodata instrument. The proper use of exploratory data analysis is to suggest theories that can then be the basis for further data collection and/or analyses. Unless sample sizes are very large, error in the data will suggest theories that will not be supported subse-quently (Cohen & Cohen, 1983).

The sizes of the research samples on which the IAR was developed and tested made it feasible to conduct several empirically oriented studies. These studies focused on (a) item weighting based on least squares regression, (b) configural scoring (Meehl, 1954), and (c) criterion selection.

STUDY 1: LEAST SQUARES REGRESSION WEIGHTING

Although multiple regression techniques are statistically optimal for deter-mining predictor–criterion relationships, equal weights have been declared preferable for many applications (Dawes, 1971). Schmidt (1972) has shown that differences between regression weights do not, in general, become reliable enough to be preferred over unit weights until sample sizes reach 500. In addition, regression analyses would not be considered for indi-vidual items in a test because they are usually not considered reliable enough as single measures of a defined construct. Biographical information items, however, to the extent that they are fact-based and tied to a specific referent, are likely to be relatively reliable. They are candidates for a variance maximizing procedure if the sample size is large enough. The samples involved in Office of Personnel Management research appeared to be ideal for such analysis. The goals of the analyses were (a) to determine whether the predictive power of biodata items could be increased and redundant items eliminated in a research setting and (b) to evaluate the content of such a reduced predictor set as a basis for clarifying the underlying components of criterion-related validity.

Method

The first sample for this analysis included 5,277 federal employees, a subset of the IAR development sample described previously, who were hired from outside the government. Their responses to 139 items from the original IAR research instrument were taken for analysis. The external criterion for this sample was the average of the research job performance ratings, previously discussed. The second sample was composed of 1,641 newly hired federal law enforcement officers who were in training. They responded to the same 139 items as did the first sample, plus 10 new items hypothesized to predict law enforcement officer performance. The external criterion for the law enforcement sample was the final training grade, reflecting class test scores and the instructor's evaluation.

Analysis

The regression analyses of each sample's responses were conducted in two stages. Initially, 76 of the 139 items were selected for analysis because they represented continua of behavior and because they appeared to be representative of the areas of education and experience that might be relevant to federal government work in general or to law enforcement in particular. The statistical properties of the items were not considered.

With this many predictors, some method of selecting predictors based on their explained unique variance in the criterion was needed. Stepwise regression methods will select items but will capitalize heavily on chance to the extent that sample size is small. Cohen and Cohen (1983, p. 125) recommend a ratio of subjects to predictors of 40 to 1. For the first sample, this ratio was about 70 to 1 and, for the second sample, about 20 to 1. The results of the analysis of the second sample must be viewed, therefore, with more caution. Stepwise regression was useful in the first stage for reducing the number of items to a computationally manageable number. Stepwise regression selects and deletes predictors based on a significance test but does not guarantee that the optimally valid combination of predictors will be chosen.

In the second stage, a regression analysis that seeks to maximize the shrunken multiple R squared (R^2) was performed on the items that met a

.15 significance level. This analysis guarantees that the optimal combination of predictors will be found because it examines every combination of predictors for every specified number of predictors. That is, the best single predictor is found, the best two predictors are found, and so on. For each model, or set, of predictors, the program tried out every possible subset contained in the set.

Results

For the first sample, the stepwise regression analysis for job performance regressed on development sample responses identified 31 items for further analysis. The 21 items attaining the highest significance levels were entered in the R^2 analysis. An asymptote in the adjusted R^2 was reached as the predictor group with 18 predictors was entered. It was possible for the six best predictors to not include all, or any, of the five best predictors, but the variables in this analysis generally remained in the model once they were entered. The first six always remained after they were entered.

The shrunken R^2 is .157 ($r = .40$) for the 18 optimal predictors, but it is based on only these preselected variables. A double cross-validation was performed on randomly selected halves of the sample, each having 2,638 cases. The regression weights developed on each randomly chosen half were applied to the other half. The R^2 estimate obtained from random sample A was .138 ($r = .37$), and the estimate from random sample B was .143 ($r = .38$). Thus, .38 is a conservative shrunken validity estimate—conservative because split-half shrinkage estimates tend to underestimate validity (Cattin, 1980).

Descriptions of the 18 optimal (in a regression sense) items are listed in Table 6. The items are listed in the order in which they entered the models accounting for variance in the criterion. Because of error, it is highly likely that this order only approximates the population order. Each description summarizes the nature of the experience or achievement on which the item is focused. If the item is based on the judgments of peers or a supervisor, this is noted in parentheses. Otherwise, the item is based on facts presumed to be documented. A striking balance was found between those items based on supervisor judgments, those based on peer judgments, and those based on documentation: There are six items each based on peer and supervisor judgments and five based on documentation. There is also a balance between items in which relationships or social competencies are involved (affiliative) versus those focusing on cognitive competencies (intellective). In Table 6, 13 of the 18 primary items that can be clearly assigned to one of these two categories are identified. There are six affiliative items and seven intellective items.

TABLE 6   Optimal Predictor Set: Job Performance Criterion

1. *Giving advice (peers)*	10. Forced job resignations
2. **Speed of work (supervisor)**	11. **Simultaneous multitask performance (supervisor)**
3. **College achievement**	
4. *Organizational achievement*	12. *Verbal communications (peers)*
5. *Leadership (peers)*	13. *Status (peers)*
6. **High school achievement**	14. Time since college
7. Supervision needed (supervisor)	15. **Mastery of assignments (supervisor)**
8. *High school leadership (peers)*	16. Language skills (peers)
	17. **Efficiency (supervisor)**
9. **Past work performance (supervisor)**	18. Suggestions made on job

Note: Affiliative items are italicized; intellective items are in bold letters.

For the law enforcement sample, the stepwise regression analysis for training scores regressed on the item responses identified 44 items for further analysis. The 28 items attaining the highest significance levels were entered in the R^2 analysis. An asymptote in the adjusted R^2 was reached with a group of 21 predictors. The shrunken R^2 was .218 ($r = .47$) for the 21 optimal predictors. Again, a double cross-validation on randomly selected halves of the sample, each having 820 cases, was performed. The R^2 estimate obtained from random sample A, with weights from random sample B, was .1901 ($r = .44$), and the estimate from random sample B was .1866 ($r = .43$).

Descriptions of the 21 optimal law enforcement biodata items are listed in Table 7 approximately in the order in which they account for variance. One would expect that items related to academic accomplishment would be more highly predictive of what is largely classroom training. In fact, six of the intellective items deal with grades, academic potential, or graduate school experience. Compared to the first sample (Table 6), there were more academically oriented items. Strikingly, no affiliative items were common to the lists in Tables 6 and 7. The items in Table 7 focus on control (items 3, 5, and 7) and socially conforming types of participative behavior

TABLE 7   Optimal Predictor Set: Training Grade Criterion

1. **College achievement**	12. High school sports achievement
2. **High school science achievement**	13. **Efficiency (supervisor)**
3. *Patience with co-workers (peers)*	14. Suggestions made on job (supervisor)
4. Graduate education	15. Earnings record
5. *Aggressiveness (peers)*	16. Decision to become law enforcement officer (peers)
6. **High school achievement**	17. **Speed of work (supervisor)**
7. *High school discipline (teachers)*	18. **High school academic potential (teachers)**
8. **College achievement**	19. *High school social relations (peers)*
9. Sources of job information	
10. Chosen for committees (supervisor)	20. Employment during college
11. *Social participation (peers)*	21. Military law enforcement experience

Note: Affiliative items are italicized; intellective items are in bold letters.

(items 11 and 19). Thus, a post hoc content analysis of the psychometrically salient items appears consistent with both a classroom setting and a law enforcement orientation. It appears doubtful, however, that the nonintellective items would have been selected over other apparently relevant items by even a theoretically sophisticated researcher prior to the analysis. This is evidenced by the relative lack of success of items that were written to be job related. Of these 10, only 3—items 9, 16, and 21—proved to explain substantial independent variance.

Comparative Analyses

The validities for the 139 items answered by the developmental sample and the 149 items answered by the law enforcement trainee sample were also determined by another standard procedure that was a variation of the correlational method (Mumford & Owens, 1987). The biserial correlation between each option of each biodata item and the criterion was determined and corrected for attenuation due to uneven response splits by multiplying by a correction factor of .7978 as recommended by Kemery, Dunlap, and Griffeth (1989). Each score on each option that correlated positively with the criterion at least at the .05 level of significance was weighted with that correlation, while those that did not reach significance were not weighted. The item scores were totaled and correlated with the criterion.

For the first sample, the total sample correlation was .35, and the random sample cross-validities were .33 and .32. These cross-validities were identical to those found by applying unit weighting in the initial IAR validation, discussed previously. For the second (law enforcement) sample, the total sample correlation was .41 and the cross-validities were .37 and .37. Least squares differential weighting of biodata items thus produced conservative gains of between .05 and .06 validity points in each of the analyses.

We also found that, whereas some biodata items proved to be generalizable, others appeared to be situationally specific. In fact, special care should be used in choosing a criterion for biodata instrument development. For example, training and job performance criteria should not be used interchangeably, as they often have been in validation of cognitive ability tests. It should be possible to write items for specific jobs and criteria, but it pays, apparently, to write large numbers of items and use a quasi-empirical item selection process. Of course, sample sizes should be large. The practical gain, from a utility point of view, can be substantial. Given the several thousand hires expected each year under the new examination of which the IAR is a part, the potential savings is in the order of hundreds of thousands of dollars each year.

STUDY 2: CONFIGURAL SCORING

Owens and his colleagues have developed and carried out work directed toward finding psychologically meaningful groups of individuals formed on the basis of relationships among biodata items. They have been able to demonstrate both temporal stability and stability across groups (Mumford & Owens, 1987). One approach that could result in the formation of groups based on an external criterion was proposed by Meehl (1954). He notes the desirability of identifying variables (he focuses on clinical diagnostic variables) for which the rate of change of the slope with respect to the criterion is dependent on other predictor variables. He termed this approach *configural* (Meehl, 1954, p. 134). This approach is particularly interesting for the analysis of biodata because it introduces a developmental component in the empirical scoring of biodata items. If it can be demonstrated that individuals' responses are made in patterns, these patterns may have the property of reflecting "broad complex processes emerging over time rather than content homogeneity" (Mumford & Owens, 1987, p. 4).

Method

This study was carried out with the 5,277-member subset of the development sample described previously. Members' responses to the original 139 items formed the data base for these analyses.

Analysis

Configural scoring is based on an interaction between two or more variables in which their validities are jointly dependent. Hierarchical regression analysis (Cohen & Cohen, 1983) can be used to detect joint dependence—that is, interaction. In this model of regression analysis, the items and their products, which are the interactions, are entered sequentially. If significant variance is found to be explained by the interaction terms after the variance associated with the items themselves has been removed, then a configural system has been defined.

The significance of this approach goes beyond increases in validity. Champoux and Peters (1980) have applied the hierarchical regression analysis to job design research. They point out that a significant interaction term, even though it adds to the R^2 by as little as .002, can have value in theory building. By looking at selected levels of both variables, it is possible to see how both change and to possibly understand, in the case of biodata, the nature of the biodata variable itself.

Analyses were made of possible interactions among the items thought to have joint theoretical relevance. Only 45 of the thousands of possible products of two and three items were tested. The approach followed was the hierarchical regression analysis outlined by Cohen and Cohen (1983). The individual variables are entered first in a hierarchical fashion in the regression equation, followed by the products of these variables that carry the interaction. Because of the size of the sample, a number of the interaction (product) terms entered significantly in the regression equation. Only those for which the adjusted R^2 was at least .002 were considered for further analysis, to attempt to ensure that interactions with substantive as well as statistical meaning were studied.

Results

Although some three-item interactions had a higher adjusted R^2, the example focused on here involves only two items for ease in understanding the process. These two items—A and B—measured high school math achievement and high school science achievement, respectively. The

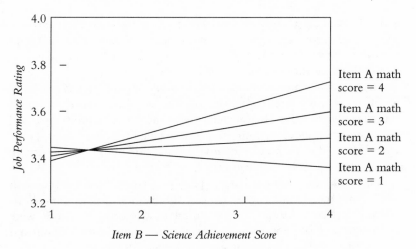

FIGURE 4 Relationships of Job Performance Ratings and Science Achievement Scores as a Function of Math Achievement Scores

products of scores on these items (among others) tested the hypothesis that predictable variance in job and academic skills might depend on the possession of presumably more basic abilities such as mathematical and verbal ability. The adjusted R^2 for items A and B was .0157; and with the interaction term, the R^2 was .0184. The difference between these is .0027. The equation for the regression of the job performance criterion on the two items and the interaction term is:

$$y = 3.5412 - .0649 \text{ (item A)} - .0758 \text{ (item B)} + .0467 \text{ (item A} \times \text{item B)}$$

The changes in the relationship between scores on item B and ratings are dependent on changes in scores on item A and illustrate a true interaction effect. The nature of the interaction effect is more easily seen as a series of curves in Figure 4. Here it is clear that the relationship between science scores and job performance ratings changes from being slightly negative for those with low math scores to successively more positive.

STUDY 3: RESEARCH RATINGS VERSUS ADMINISTRATIVE RATING AS CRITERIA

Do supervisors rate employees differently under open administrative conditions versus confidential (research) conditions? If so, do the differences impact criterion-related validity of biodata or the characteristics of individuals likely to be selected? These questions have received little research attention (Dickinson, Hassett, & Tannenbaum, 1986) but have both theoretical and practical importance for empirical keying and validation of biodata. From theoretical standpoints, given empirical keying of items against the criterion, biodata scores would appear likely to mirror, in a policy-capturing sense, systematic differences or preferences related to employee characteristics that are reflected by the criterion. From a practical standpoint, the additional time and costs entailed in collection of special appraisals need to be justified relative to those for administrative ratings, which are frequently readily available.

This study was conducted in two phases: (a) Characteristics of research and administrative ratings were compared across four job tenure cohorts (Gandy & Mann, 1991); and (b) characteristics of high scorers were compared on biodata instruments keyed from administrative ratings and research ratings (Gandy, Mann, & Outerbridge, 1990).

Method

In Phase 1, the sample of 7,358 employees included those from IAR development (described earlier) plus 1,058 employees who received research ratings but did not complete the biodata questionnaire. Administrative summary ratings were obtained from central personnel data files; these ratings were on a five-point scale conceptually similar to the research ratings and were made within approximately six months of the research ratings. Four tenure groups (n = 875 to 2,604) were defined corresponding to one to four years since hire. In Phase 2, scoring keys were developed against administrative performance appraisals, using the same item pool, sample, and methodology as that for IAR development, discussed earlier.

Results and Discussion

The distributions of research and administrative ratings were virtually identical in terms of means and standard deviations (M = 3.55 and 3.53, SD = .72 and .72). These similarities, however, could be misleading: A correlation of .40 between the ratings indicated that individuals ranked somewhat differently. Also, when rating under research conditions, supervisors made greater use of the full scale. Perhaps surprisingly, the research ratings were more lenient at the highest two rating levels (51% versus 41%), suggesting the influence of informal pressures to hold down administrative ratings.

An interaction of ratings and tenure was found ($p < .01$), such that administrative ratings were lower than research ratings for newer hires (tenure of 1 to 2 years) and higher than research ratings for those with three to four years tenure. Also, under administrative conditions, supervisors tended to give substantially higher ratings to employees having prior work experience (p < .001), whether job-related or not. If we assume greater verity in the research ratings, the administrative ratings could lead to both Type I and II errors. Higher administrative ratings, for example, were associated (p < .01) with having worked previously in another federal position; research ratings showed no such relationship. Conversely, administrative ratings for employees with up to two years of job tenure were unrelated to several measures of academic achievement, while research ratings showed correlations of .11 to .15 (p < .01) with those measures.

In Phase 2, given the moderate correlation between the types of ratings, differences were expected in validities of instruments keyed to each criterion. Large differences were not evident in cross-validation, however, where the cross-validities were .28 and .30 for administrative rating keys, versus .32 and .33 for the research rating keys.

Apart from level of validity, a critical question was the extent to which the different instruments and keys would tend to select individuals having different characteristics. Similarities were stronger in some respects than expected. The respective biodata score distributions correlated .82, had an 81 percent overlap of individuals in the upper halves, and reflected virtually identical percentages of individuals with "superior" abilities (based on self-reports of supervisor/peer appraisal), such as logical reasoning, planning and organizing, and attention to detail.

On the other hand, there were important differences. The instrument based on research ratings would select more college graduates (70% versus 59% in the upper half), more individuals age 30 or younger (49% versus 37%), and more individuals with high levels of academic achievement in high school and college. The instrument based on administrative ratings appeared to give inflated weight to experience and gave virtually no weight to educational achievement, consistent with the findings in Phase 1.

We concluded that research appraisals are to be preferred over administrative appraisals as biodata criteria, but also that the inclusion of a wide range of job relevant biodata items appears to facilitate stable empirical keying and to offer some protection against variations in criteria that may reflect systematic biases.

CONCLUSION

Research findings were supportive of the usefulness of empirically weighted biographical information for personnel selection within a public sector environment. In conjunction with a number of controls in the design, development, and keying of biodata, (a) a highly useful level of empirical validity was obtained, (b) fairness both to minorities and gender groups was indicated, and (c) validity of a common scoring key generalized quite well across different occupations and job settings. Confirmation of these findings, which were based on entry-level professional hires measured in a concurrent design after one to four years tenure, will be sought in a predictive design when technically feasible.

Confirmatory factor analysis was found to be a useful means for furthering the understanding of biodata. Construct validity studies found that the IAR measures several important aspects of individual performance. Factors dealing with past achievements in academic settings were most related to cognitive (reasoning) ability, but they also indicated a general desire to succeed. Self-assessment factors dealing with work competencies and leadership skills were more indicative of qualities associated with motivational behavior, such as conscientiousness, working hard, and striving to get ahead.

While our research supports the presence of four factors to represent the IAR, an alternative interpretation is that there may be a certain pervasive similarity in what all four of the factors measure. Because the IAR content was designed to assess accomplishments over an extended period of time in a variety of academic, work, and social situations, it may be that all of the factors measure, to some degree, a general appraisal of one's ability to adjust to personal circumstances and to succeed in life. Still, the construct analyses indicated that the IAR clearly is not a personality test. Rather, these analyses indicated that cognitive and noncognitive characteristics contribute, in a remarkably balanced way, to broader biodata indicators of work competency, achievement, and interpersonal skills. The scoring and criterion analyses, moreover, suggest that the balance in construct under-pinnings contributes to compensatory characteristics such that biodata scores reflect a variety of developmental patterns related to job success.

Specific findings pointed to potential practical gains in biodata useful-ness and to promising avenues for further research:

- Scoring methodology analyses indicated that least squares differential weighting can increase validity substantially—and do so with a smaller number of items.
- Although validity generalized as hypothesized across almost 100 occupations, validity of noncognitive biodata items was found to vary substantially when applied to a different job family.
- An initial exploration into the complex area of response pattern–criterion relationships suggests that configural scoring may have implications for both increased understanding and validity. (In preliminary analyses not reported here, there are indications that response inflation, that is, faking, can be more accurately iden-tified in a configural scoring framework.)

Criterion issues are particularly germane to biodata research and applications. In comparisons of administrative and research (confidential) ratings as criteria for biodata, we concluded that research ratings are probably well worth the extra effort. Even though similar levels of predictor–criterion correlation were obtained, biodata scoring based on administrative ratings appeared to undervalue some characteristics, such as academic achievement, and overvalue others, such as length of work history. Administrative ratings appear responsive to a variety of expectations and pressures in the operational setting that do not necessarily correlate strongly with effective job performance, and the reflection of such factors in biodata scoring is probably undesirable.

Several areas of criterion research may be fruitful, including further attention to extending and expanding concepts of what we should be predicting. Beyond identifying major factors that describe effective performance, which is of major importance in itself, we need to investigate approaches for better person–job matching and factors that jointly predict both retention and performance.

REFERENCES

Anderson, J. C., & Gerbing, D. W. (1984). The effect of sampling error on convergence, improper solutions, and goodness-of-fit indices for maximum likelihood confirmatory factor analysis. *Psychometrika, 49,* 155–173.

Brown, S. H. (1981). Validity generalization in the life insurance industry. *Journal of Applied Psychology, 66,* 664–670.

Cattin, P. (1980). Estimation of the predictive power of a regression model. *Journal of Applied Psychology, 65,* 407–414.

Champoux, J. L., & Peters, W. S. (1980). Applications of moderated regression in job design research. *Personnel Psychology, 30,* 47–54.

Cleary, T. A. (1968). Test bias: Prediction of grades of negro and white students in integrated colleges. *Journal of Educational Measurement, 5,* 115–124.

Cohen, J., & Cohen, P. (1983). *Applied multiple regression/correlation analysis for the behavioral sciences.* Hillsdale, NJ: Erlbaum.

Costa, P. T., & McCrae, R. R. (1985). *The NEO Personality Inventory manual.* Odessa, FL: Psychological Assessment Resources.

Cudeck, R., & Browne, M. W. (1983). Cross-validation of covariance structures. *Multivariate Behavioral Research, 18,* 147–167.

Dawes, R. (1971). The robust beauty of improper linear models in decision making. *American Psychologist, 34,* 571–582.

Dickinson, T. L., Hassett, C. E., & Tannenbaum, S. I. (1986). *Work performance ratings: A meta-analysis of multitrait-multimethod studies* (AFHRL Tech. Rep. No. 86–32). Brooks AFB, TX: Training Systems Division, Air Force Human Resources Laboratory.

Eberhardt, B. J., & Muchinsky, P. M. (1982). An empirical investigation of the factor stability of Owens' Biographical Questionnaire. *Journal of Applied Psychology, 67,* 138–145.

England, G. W. (1971). *Development and use of weighted application blanks* (rev. ed.). Minneapolis: University of Minnesota, Industrial Relations Center.

Gandy, J. A., & Mann, W. G. (1991, April). Performance appraisals: Some systematic differences in administrative and research ratings. In A. Kluger (Chair), *Performance appraisal, decision making, and training.* Poster session at the annual meeting of the Society for Industrial and Organizational Psychology, St. Louis, MO.

Gandy, J. A., Mann, W. G., & Outerbridge, A. N. (1990, April). Job performance criteria and biodata validity: Comparisons and considerations. In J. C. Sharf (Chair), *Innovative research on the IAR: The first federal-wide biodata form.* Symposium conducted at the annual meeting of the Society for Industrial and Organizational Psychology, Miami Beach, FL.

Gandy, J. A., Outerbridge, A. N., Sharf, J. C., & Dye, D. A. (1989). *Development and initial validation of the Individual Achievement Record* (IAR; OPRD Report). Washington, DC: U.S. Office of Personnel Management.

Glennon, J. R., Albright, L. E., & Owens, W. A. (1966). *A catalog of life history items.* Prepared for the American Psychological Association—Division 14. Reproduced by The Creativity Research Institute of The Richardson Foundation.

Gough, H. G. (1964). Academic achievement in high school as predicted from the California Psychological Inventory. *Educational and Psychological Measurement, 55,* 174–180.

Gough, H. G. (1987). *Manual for the California Psychological Inventory.* Palo Alto, CA: Consulting Psychologists Press.

Gough, H. G., & Lanning, K. (1986). Predicting grades in college from the California Psychological Inventory. *Educational and Psychological Measurement, 46,* 205–213.

Gulliksen, H., & Wilks, S. S. (1950). Regression tests for several samples. *Psychometrika, 15*(2), 91–114.

Hayduk, L. A. (1987). *Structural equation modeling with LISREL: Essentials and advances.* Baltimore: Johns Hopkins University Press.

Holland, J. L. (1985). *The Self-directed Search.* Odessa, FL: Psychological Assessment Resources.

Jöreskog, K. G., & Sörbom, D. (1986). *LISREL VI user's guide* (4th ed.). Mooresville, IN: Scientific Software.

Kemery, E. R., Dunlap, W. P., & Griffeth, R. W. (1989). Correction for variance restriction in point-biserial correlations. *Journal of Applied Psychology, 73,* 688–690.

Long, J. S. (1983). *Confirmatory factor analysis: A preface to LISREL.* Beverly Hills, CA: Sage.

Lyons, T. J. (1989). *Validity of education and experience measures in traditional rating schedule procedures: A review of the literature.* Washington, DC: U.S. Office of Personnel Management.

MacCallum, R. (1986). Specification searches in covariance structure modeling. *Psychological Bulletin, 100,* 107–120.

McKillip, R. H., & Clark, C. L. (1974). *Biographical data and job performance* (Tech. Rep. No. TM–74–1). Washington, DC: Office of Personnel Management.

McKillip, R. H., Trattner, M. H., Corts, D. B., & Wing, H. (1977). *The professional and administrative career examination: Research and development* (PRR–77–1). Washington, DC: U.S. Service Commission.

Meehl, P. (1954). *Clinical vs. statistical prediction.* Minneapolis: Colwell Press.

Mitchell, T. W., & Klimoski, R. J. (1982). Is it rational to be empirical? A test of methods for scoring biographical data. *Journal of Applied Psychology, 67,* 411–418.

Mumford, M. D., & Owens, W. A. (1987). Methodology review: Principles, procedures, and findings in the application of background data measures. *Applied Psychological Measurement, 11,* 1–31.

Nickels, B. J. (1989). *Exploring the structure of background data measures: Implications for item development and scale validation.* Unpublished doctoral dissertation, Georgia Institute of Technology, Atlanta.

Northrop, L. C., Nester, M. A., Diané, C., & Colberg, M. (1989). *Development of tests for job families.* Washington, DC: Office of Personnel Management.

Ostroff, C., & Schmitt, N. (1987). *The relationship between content and criterion-related validity indices: An empirical investigation.* Paper presented at the annual meeting of the Society for Industrial and Organizational Psychology, Boston.

Owens, W. A., & Schoenfeldt, L. F. (1979). Toward a classification of persons. *Journal of Applied Psychology, 64,* 569–607.

Ravlin, E. C., & Meglino, B. M. (1986). *Comparative Emphasis Scale.* Columbia, SC: University of South Carolina, Riegel and Emory Center.

Reilly, R. R., & Warech, M. A. (1988). *The validity and fairness of alternative predictors of occupational performance.* Unpublished manuscript, Stevens Institute of Technology, Hoboken, NY.

Robinson, J. R., & Shraver, P. R. (1973). *Measures of social psychological attitudes.* Ann Arbor, MI: Institute for Social Research.

Rothstein, H. R., Schmidt, F. L., Erwin, F. W., Owens, W. A., & Sparks, C. P. (1990). Biographical data in employment selection: Can validities be made generalizable? *Journal of Applied Psychology, 75,* 175–184.

Rotter, J. B. (1966). Generalized expectancies for internal versus external control of reinforcement. *Psychological Monographs, 80* (1 Whole No. 609).

Schmidt, F. L. (1972). The reliability of differences between linear regression weights in applied differential psychology. *Educational and Psychological Measurement, 32,* 879–886.

Schmidt, F. L., & Hunter, J. E. (1977). Development of a general solution to the problem of validity generalization. *Journal of Applied Psychology, 62,* 529–540.

U.S. Department of Labor. (1974). *Descriptive rating scale* (Form MA–7–66, Rev. 3–74). Washington, DC: U.S. Dept. of Labor, Manpower Administration.

van Rijn, P. (1980). *Biographical questionnaires and scored application blanks in personnel selection* (PRR–80–31). Washington, DC: U.S. Office of Personnel Management.

Selection Using Biodata
Old Notions Revisited

Garnett S. Stokes
Lisa A. Cooper
University of Georgia

The predictiveness of biodata measures is generally unquestioned, and biodata have been shown to have utility across a wide range of jobs and criteria. Many other chapters in this book focus on special topics related to the development and use of biodata measures. In this chapter, we will examine some of the jobs and the criteria for which biodata have been found to be useful. Our focus will be primarily on special criteria for which biodata are promising, but for which only limited, if any, data are available in the literature. We will make no attempt to thoroughly review the literature. Instead, our goal is to suggest some additional uses of biodata not mentioned in other chapters and, we hope, to generate applied research in these areas.

TYPICAL AND ATYPICAL CRITERIA

Biodata forms have been used to predict a wide range of criterion variables. Table 1 provides a summary of validity coefficients for several categories of criteria based on data provided from Reilly and Chao (1982), Barge and Hough (1986), Hunter and Hunter (1984), and Schmitt, Gooding, Noe, and Kirsch (1984). From the results in the table, it appears that biodata forms are particularly useful for predicting training success, proficiency ratings, and wages, criteria that are commonly predicted by biodata

TABLE 1   Criterion Categories

	Reilly & Chao (1982)		Barge & Hough (1986)		Hunter & Hunter (1984)		Schmitt et al. (1984)	
	r_{xy}	N	r_{xy}	N	r_{xy}	N	r_{xy}	N
Training success	.39	3	.25	18	.30	11		
Absenteeism and turnover			.25	15			.21	28
Tenure	.32	13	.32	18	.26	23		
Proficiency ratings	.36	15	.32	26	.37	12	.32	29
Production data	.46	6	.31	10			.21	19
Substance abuse			.26	1				
Delinquency			.20	3				
Unfavorable discharge			.27	2				
Promotion					.26	17		
Achievement/ grades							.23	9
Status change							.33	6
Wages	.34	7					.53	7

researchers in industry. Biodata appear less useful for predicting absenteeism and turnover, other common criterion variables.

TURNOVER

Although turnover is frequently the criterion variable of interest to biodata form developers, from Table 1 it is apparent that the validity coefficients tend to be lower than those found for other criteria. These lower coefficients may result because absenteeism has been inappropriately combined with turnover in assessing the studies. Even so, sophisticated measures of turnover often are not developed for validation studies. Instead, the focus has been primarily on predicting a dichotomous variable reflecting who has left within some period of time and who has remained, and sometimes there is not a distinction between voluntary and involuntary turnover (e.g., Stokes, Hogan, & Snell, 1993). More careful development of turnover criterion measures is warranted. In addition, because the causes of turnover are multiple and complex (Campion, 1991), a wide range of literature needs to be consulted in developing biodata forms, including the literature on job choice and job change.

Two recent studies focused on factors that may influence turnover. Both studies identified job changers—that is, those individuals who leave their jobs to pursue positions in different career areas. The first study, conducted by Palmer (1992), examined the early adolescent experiences (measured at age 18) and adult background experiences (measured in 1980) of long-term managers (those who were employed in management positions in 1980 and 1989) and early-exit managers (those who were in management positions at the first assessment in 1980, but who left management prior to 1989, at the second assessment). She found that it was possible to identify the early-exit managers at a better than chance rate. The early adolescent experiences that distinguished the two groups from each other were Social Introversion, Religious Activity, Intellectualism, and Social Desirability, with the early-exit managers having higher scores on Social Introversion and Social Desirability and lower scores on Intellectualism and Religious Activity than the long-term managers. Measures taken in early adulthood of Job Satisfaction, Nonwork Satisfaction, and Occupational Status were expected to differentiate the two groups of managers from each other, but this was not supported. The factors that distinguished male managers in general from individuals in all other occupations in the sample were the very ones on which early-exit managers scored differently, suggesting that it should be possible to use some of these factors in predicting turnover among managers.

Allison (1992) examined job change, or *occupational discontinuity*, a term applied to pursuit of a career in a completely different field or profession. Individuals who had changed by moving from one of eight occupational groups to another were compared to those who had remained in the same occupational group since completing college. She found that adolescent experiences predicted occupational discontinuity for women but not for men. The women who experienced occupational discontinuity had better parental relationships, came from families with higher socioeconomic status, and experienced more friction with their siblings. Young adult life experiences (collected six to eight years after college graduation) were found to be predictive for males who had experienced occupational discontinuity, but they were not predictive for females. Males who experienced occupational discontinuity were socially inactive, felt that college did not prepare them for life, were unsure of what they were looking for in a job, and were not likely to have found the job they wanted after college. Allison's findings suggest the importance of including biodata items that reflect life experiences across different time periods of adult development in order to capture potentially useful information for predicting job tenure.

Both of these studies suggest the complexity of predicting turnover in an organization. Poor initial person–job fit is only one possible factor. Both voluntary and involuntary turnover may be the result of many factors. Regardless of the theoretical model on which one might rely for investigating turnover, it is essential that biodata form developers are cognizant of the research literature in developing a model for predicting tenure in organizations.

ADJUSTMENT

Biodata may be useful for predicting a range of adjustment criteria, such as substance abuse, delinquency, and unfavorable discharge (Barge & Hough, 1986). The validity coefficients for these criteria have ranged from .20 to .27 (see Table 1). Increasingly, researchers have been interested in identifying potential "problem employees" using biodata. Some examples of recent research include those of Haymaker (1986) and McDaniel (1989). Haymaker used biodata to predict employee integrity. He obtained a cross-validated $r = .32$ using a polygraph as a criterion measure. McDaniel used background investigation data to predict discharge from military service within 30 months for "failure to meet minimum behavioral or performance criteria" (pp. 965–966). Individuals receiving this discharge experienced drug and alcohol problems, desertion, imprisonment, or discipline problems, as well as dismissal from military training. He factor-analyzed his 93-item background investigation form and identified seven factors. Two factors, School Suspension and Quitting School, yielded the highest validities (rs = .14 and .17, respectively, corrected for range restriction). The factor reflecting Grades and School Clubs was negatively related to the criterion, whereas the Legal System Contacts factor was positively related.

The increasing interest of organizations in predicting employee integrity and the use of biodata forms to solve this problem will be offset by the intense scrutiny of biodata form content by the government and by agencies concerned with privacy invasion issues (for more information, see the chapter by Sharf in this book). Researchers in this area must be cautious in developing biodata forms to screen for adjustment or integrity, though one can see the value of providing employers with information to screen problem employees. Biodata forms may be less invasive than some of the traditional personality measures used, such as the *Minnesota Multiphasic Personality Inventory* (MMPI), but the criteria used in this area may be problematic (Sackett, Burris, & Callahan, 1989). Industrial and organizational psychologists need to be involved in this research in order to provide their expertise in the development of sound criterion measures.

McDaniel (1989) pointed out other limitations inherent in using self-report measures to obtain information usually gathered through background investigations. When inquiring about illegal acts and socially undesirable behaviors, one can expect applicants to tend to respond in a socially desirable way. Low test–retest reliabilities for his Drug Use and Legal System Contact scales support the notion that some distortion of responses has occurred. Also, respondents may answer differently depending on whether or not they feel their responses will be verified through information collected from other sources (see the chapter by Lautenschlager in this book for a thorough review). Although both of these limitations are frequently a concern in the development and use of biodata forms, these problems become more critical with instruments designed to measure undesirable behaviors. The infrequency of many dishonest or harmful acts also makes prediction particularly difficult. This problem is further confounded when one considers that items that are verifiable through other sources (such as criminal and motor vehicle records, credit reports, and personal references) only identify those who engaged in the undesirable behavior and were caught. Researchers need to keep these problems in mind in designing their biodata instruments.

In consideration of these difficulties, we need a better understanding of the antecedents of undesirable behaviors in order to develop measures that can adequately predict them. Though not without problems in interpretation, conducting a study using background data to predict specific MMPI profiles or other measures of psychopathology might be useful for developing an understanding of antecedent behaviors. In the meantime, for predicting adjustment or integrity criteria, a clinical psychologist may need to be consulted to assist in determining the content of a biodata form.

ACCIDENTS/WORKERS' COMPENSATION

The rising costs associated with health care have led organizations to try many avenues for reducing their costs. Job-related injuries cost American employers enormous sums in workers' compensation. Increasingly, it has become popular for organizations to seek ways to identify the "accident prone" applicants so they can deny them employment or provide special training (Barge, 1991; Hansen, 1988). Industrial and organizational psychologists need to be involved in this critical area of concern to organizations.

Research investigating personal factors associated with accidents has a long history in psychology (Hansen, 1988, 1989), and there has been some evidence that biodata variables may be useful for predicting accidents. For example, relationships with parents frequently have been found to relate to accidents (Adams, 1970; Harano, Peck, & McBride, 1975; McGuire, 1976). One comprehensive study reported by Denning (1983) investigated the role of biodata in predicting accidents. In her study, individuals who had been involved in an OSHA-recordable accident (medical treatment, restricted workday, or lost workday) during the previous two years were included in one group ($n = 247$), and a random sample of individuals not involved in an accident ($n = 251$) during the same period were included as a second group. Self and supervisory ratings of safety performance were also obtained for each member of the sample. A biodata form was rationally developed to measure 15 factors identified from past literature as predictive of accidents. The 15 factors are listed in Table 2. In addition to the biodata factors, measures of personality, values, and perceptual ability were collected. Personality was measured through a series of tests, including *Gordon's Personal Profile* (Gordon, 1963), *Gordon's Personal Inventory* (Gordon, 1963), *Rotter's Locus of Control* (Rotter, 1966), and *Crowne-Marlowe Social Desirability* (Crowne & Marlowe, 1964). The *Survey of Interpersonal Values* (Gordon, 1960) was used to assess six different values. Perceptual abilities were measured using the *Flanagan Industrial Tests Components* (Flanagan, 1960) and *Precision* (King, 1957), as well as with a number-checking test. Overall, the biodata factors were the best predictors of who would be involved in an accident. Those who were involved in accidents differed in terms of Socioeconomic Status, Manual Labor, Sociability, Sensation/Excitement Seeking, Competitiveness, Emotionality, Responsibility, and Initiative.

Unexpectedly, the factors that predicted accidents differed somewhat from those that predicted safety performance ratings obtained from the employees and from their first- and second-line supervisors. For example, the accident group was more sociable, more competitive, more responsible, less emotional, more experienced with manual labor, and demonstrated more initiative than the randomly selected no-accident group. Yet those identified as unsafe performers through self and supervisory ratings were opposite on these dimensions, and this pattern was consistent with predictions based on previous research. To investigate this discrepancy in the findings, individuals who had experienced accidents during the

TABLE 2 Rationally Developed Factors Used to Predict
Accidents and Safety Performance

1. *Socioeconomic Status:* Five items describing parental educational level, occupational level, and income

2. *Parental Relations:* Three items measuring parental involvement and closeness

3. *Mobility:* Six items measuring number of times moved prior to age 18, travel distances, and number of times changed jobs

4. *Manual Labor:* Six items measuring involvement in mechanical work, repairs, and yard and garden work or work on a farm

5. *Health:* Seven items measuring physical conditioning, activity level, and smoking habits

6. *Sociability:* Eight items measuring liking of parties, number of times spent going out, desire to work with others, and ease of meeting and talking with strangers

7. *Sensation/Excitement Seeking:* Seven items measuring age when getting first car, alcohol consumption, smoking, and risk taking

8. *Conventional:* Three items measuring appropriateness of behavior expected by parents and attempts to conform

9. *Competitiveness:* Three items measuring comparing self to others and aggressiveness

10. *Emotionality:* Six items measuring reactions to criticism and to people who attempt to upset the respondent, dealing with practical jokes, and working under pressure

11. *Impulsivity:* Eleven items measuring care in making decisions, speed of work, tolerance for routine, repetitive activities, and planning for future events

12. *Responsibility:* Ten items measuring age started earning money, life insurance policies, working at jobs at early age, number of dependents, savings, responses to emergency situations, and sense of responsibility

13. *Initiative:* Seven items measuring suggestions to supervisor, attempts to do one's best, persistence in doing difficult tasks, and drive

14. *Persistence:* Seven items measuring procrastination, perseverance when distractions are around, and leaving jobs unfinished

15. *Attitude toward work:* Nine items measuring feelings about work schedules, impact of work on nonwork, problems with red tape on the job, ease of work, and reasons for taking current job

two-year period were subgrouped on the basis of their biodata profiles using a Ward and Hook (1963) hierarchical clustering procedure. Two subgroups of injured employees were identified, and their profiles provided two very different portraits of employees. One subgroup characterized the typical accident prone employee described in the literature: low socioeconomic status, poor parental relations, low sociability, low conventionality, high emotionality, low initiative, low persistence, high impulsivity, and a poor attitude toward work. The second, larger cluster of individuals involved in accidents were very similar to the random sample of no-accident employees.

In part, these findings explained the contradictions between results of the accident/no-accident comparisons, but they also demonstrated another important consideration in doing biodata research predicting accidents: The criteria used may influence the conclusions drawn in the study. The use of accident criteria alone may be problematic due to their infrequent nature and to the fact that accidents have multiple causes. Safety ratings by supervisors may not be an adequate substitute, however. Until we understand more about the relationship between accidents and safety performance, perhaps both types of data should be gathered. Of course, it is a good idea to obtain accident measures over a long period of time to increase the reliability of the information. In addition, data that are available related to cause, intensity, and conditions are useful in classifying accidents more accurately.

JOB SATISFACTION

Job satisfaction is another criterion variable of interest to organizations, but very few studies exist relating background data to satisfaction. In their extensive review of the literature, Barge and Hough (1986) did not find any studies that addressed this relationship. Yet early researchers in the area of job satisfaction recognized the importance of individual differences in determining satisfaction (Fisher & Hanna, 1931; Friend & Haggard, 1948). In fact, family background was considered an important determinant in these early studies. Yet extensive research in the field has focused on the specific situations that influence satisfaction, though some researchers have investigated an interactional model between person and situation variables (Dawis & Lofquist, 1984; Holland, 1973, 1985). Schneider's (1987) attraction–selection–attrition framework provides a dynamic interactional model in which both persons and their environments are shaped by each other. Arvey, Carter, and Buerkley (1991) reviewed some of the evidence regarding dispositional and situational influences on job satisfaction. They concluded that "it is obvious that both factors associated with the individual and facets of the job environment are important determinants of job satisfaction" (p. 376), though they also conclude that it is difficult to form precise estimates of the importance of each factor. They advise that person variables need to be chosen on a theoretical basis, using variables with well-established nomological nets (Weiss & Adler, 1984; cited in Arvey et al., 1991).

Life experiences would be an excellent vehicle for examining differences in job satisfaction and for determining organizational rewards that could be applied to subsets of individuals. A handful of studies, most of them unpublished, have investigated the relationship of life experiences to job satisfaction.

Stiles (1983) investigated the ability of Owens' *Biographical Questionnaire* (BQ) to predict job satisfaction eight years following college graduation. The research participants were 313 men and 157 women who had been working full-time in their jobs for at least six months. Factors derived from the BQ (Mumford, Stokes, & Owens, 1990; Owens & Schoenfeldt, 1979) were used in regression analysis to predict an 11-item index of job satisfaction (coefficient alpha = .83 for men and .79 for women). For men it was found that Socioeconomic Status, Warmth of Parental Relationship, and Social Introversion predicted job satisfaction 12 years later (R squared = .07). For women, Positive Academic Attitude and Adjustment significantly predicted job satisfaction (R squared = .06). Predictive keys were developed for both men and women using item correlations of the 118 items of the BQ. A 10-item biodata key produced a cross-validated r = .32 for men, and a 6-item biodata key produced a cross-validated r = .34 for women. Thus, it appears that biodata may be very useful for this purpose.

Lucchesi (1983) applied structural equation modeling to the longitudinal prediction of work and nonwork satisfaction and job level using biodata factors derived from Owens' BQ (Owens & Schoenfeldt, 1979). Her sample included 313 males who took the BQ in 1968 and who reported their satisfaction and job level in 1980. The cross-validation sample consisted of 307 males who took the BQ in 1970 and reported their satisfaction in 1980 as well. Her results were not as impressive as those obtained by Stiles. She examined five biodata factors: SES, Maladjustment, Parental Warmth, Assertiveness, and Academic Achievement. Though her factors were not identical to those used by Owens and Schoenfeldt, there was some similarity. Some paths changed signs upon cross-validation, indicating instability in the model. Only assertiveness was a consistent, though weak, predictor of job satisfaction 12 years later.

Examining both work and nonwork satisfaction and using the Ward and Hook (1963) hierarchical clustering procedure, Shaffer (1987) identified patterns of work and nonwork satisfaction in a sample of college graduates six to eight years following college graduation. Twenty items from Owens' *Post College Experience Inventory* (PCEI; Mumford, Stokes, & Owens, 1990) were used to assess work and nonwork satisfaction. Factors derived from these 20 items served as variables in the clustering procedure. Five subgroups were identified for men and six subgroups were identified for women, each reflecting significantly different satisfaction profiles. The largest group for both men and women were those who were generally satisfied on all work and nonwork factors. A smaller but still significant group for both men and women were those who were generally dissatisfied on all work and nonwork satisfaction factors. The remaining groups consisted of individuals who were satisfied with some aspects of their lives and dissatisfied with others. The findings in this study suggest that distinct satisfaction profiles exist.

Life experiences measured with Owens' BQ were used to distinguish between the groups. It was found that parental relationships during adolescence distinguished between those who were generally satisfied and those who were not. In addition, adolescent socioeconomic status, sports participation, and social activities distinguished among the groups. Thus, life events and experiences were related to significant occupational criteria years later.

The three studies just discussed investigating satisfaction were longitudinal in design, with a time lag between data collections of 12 years. There was overlap in the data sets used for the three studies, so they are not independent, but the results provide some promise that biodata may be useful for predicting job satisfaction and other motivationally laden criteria in organizations. Moreover, the finding that patterns of satisfaction can be identified and that the different groups of people display differences in past histories is consistent with the notion that some aspects of satisfaction are dispositional. This suggests that organizations may be able to use biodata to determine strategies for dealing with their employees in ways that are more specific to their needs rather than targeting organizational interventions at the average employee.

Team Performance

In 1976, Owens stated, "If subjects with similar biodata-defined backgrounds are of greater than average compatibility, then the efficiency of the work force may depend to a very important extent on discovering who should work with whom" (p. 640). The burgeoning use of work teams makes such comparisons imperative. Whether individuals are working in designated work teams or not, Campbell (1992) has suggested that teamwork is one of eight general performance dimensions. Yet the actual composition of work teams has received relatively little study compared to other areas of team research (Levine & Moreland, 1990; Sundstrom, DeMeuse, & Futrell, 1990).

Biodata would seem to have some potential as a vehicle for composing work teams, as suggested by Owens. Buel (1989) conducted a study in which he used biodata factors to predict peer evaluations of team performance on three aspects of cooperative behavior: information, schedule, and work sharing; personal performance and adaptability; and teamwork. He found several dozen items that were predictive, measuring the favorability of the individual's self-perceptions, involvement in activities that require cooperation, such as sports, and motivation to contribute to group efforts.

Mitchell (1992) also has developed a biodata form to predict effective teamwork. His biodata form was developed a priori to predict a number of criteria in a sample of 117 maintenance mechanics, technicians, and inspectors. His definition of the criterion dimension was "cooperative work behavior for effective teamwork: participating, volunteering, sharing, helping, and contributing toward team activities; enjoying and working with others; accepting feedback and working to improve team performance, putting the welfare of the group above personal gain" (p. 7). Fifteen biodata items were devised to predict teamwork. They were constructed to measure (a) previous conflicts with supervisors or co-workers, (b) preference for working alone versus in teams, (c) style for resolving conflicts, (d) reactions to criticisms, (e) tendency to blame others, (f) adjustments to change or interruptions, (g) willingness to compromise, (h) sensitivity to the needs of others, (i) task versus people orientation, and (j) competitiveness and individualistic goal orientation. The biodata key, uncorrected for attenuation or range restriction, was correlated $r = .27$, $p < .01$ with the criterion measure.

Thus, it appears that a biodata form may be useful for predicting team performance. However, the research conducted thus far does not address the issue of composing optimal work teams for different purposes. Much of the research that has been done on composing work teams has focused on ability, personality, and demographic variables. Tziner and Eden (1985) found that military tank crews composed of high-ability individuals performed better than expected, whereas crews composed of low-ability persons performed worse than expected. The effects of the personalities of group members have typically been investigated in the context of appropriate groups for therapy. Unfortunately, there are no consistent recommendations from this literature regarding effective group compositions

(Levine & Moreland, 1990). George (1990) found that both negative and positive affect were related to behavior in work groups, a finding that is useful for understanding the impact of personality characteristics on work team performance. Yet investigation of these variables separately fails to provide the comprehensive assessment of individuals required for mixing and matching members of work teams.

Biodata-based subgroups may provide such a comprehensive assessment mechanism for forming effective work teams. Owens and Schoenfeldt (1979) reported the results of a large number of studies which demonstrated that biodata-based subgroups are internally similar and externally distinct on factors relevant to team performance, such as ability, leadership, decision making, creativity, and personality. Knowledge of biodata-subgroup membership might be an excellent tool for determining placement into a preexisting work team or for determining the combination of individuals who might best work together, depending on the type of task required of the group.

We have begun investigating this possibility in a laboratory study. In our preliminary work we have attempted to demonstrate that biodata-based subgroups perform differently when working together, in spite of their similarity in terms of past experience, age, and sex, which, based on past research, should lead to cohesion and good performance in all groups (Levine & Moreland, 1990). Using subgroups formed on the basis of adolescent and college life experiences (Wesley, 1989), work groups were assembled that had been defined as statistically good fits within a single subgroup. Teams consisted of members from the same biodata-based subgroup. Participants were involved in an ice-breaking exercise prior to beginning the group task, which consisted of the identification of new student government officers. Trained observers recorded the behavior of the group, and individual participants were asked to complete a series of ratings on other group members following the group exercise.

Specific predictions were made about the performance of different subgroups based on their biodata profiles and the research literature on group behavior. For example, subgroups that were high in terms of past social activities were predicted to be more sociable and cooperative than those subgroups with low sociability in the past, and subgroups with past histories of leadership activities were predicted to be the most decisive and effective groups. Thus far, we have sufficient data for analysis of only four male and four female subgroups. Many of our predictions were supported, though our results are clearly preliminary. We are continuing with data collection in order to enlarge the number of groups for identifying the most effective and ineffective teams. We have begun to mix effective and ineffective teams to determine the best combination of subgroup members for achieving specific goals. We are encouraged that biodata subgroup membership might be useful in organizations for identifying team members.

The research results in this area, then, suggest that biodata might be useful in two ways. First, biodata may be useful for selecting individuals more suited for teamwork when the organization or the nature of the job requires team effectiveness. Second, biodata-based subgroups may eventually provide a great deal of information regarding the optimal mix of individuals to use in forming work teams composed for different purposes.

SUMMARY OF CRITERIA

We have discussed the validity of biodata for predicting a large number of criteria. It is apparent that biodata have great utility for predicting criteria not often well predicted by ability measures, such as adjustment, turnover, satisfaction, team performance, and safety performance. Biodata may provide an alternative to cognitive ability tests as general selection procedures, or they may effectively be used to provide incremental validity beyond that found with a cognitive ability selection battery. An important issue in assessing the utility of biodata, however, is whether biodata forms are as generalizable as standard cognitive ability tests.

GENERALIZABILITY OF BIODATA ACROSS OCCUPATIONAL CATEGORIES

A primary concern of decision makers interested in implementing biodata forms as selection tools is the degree to which biodata keys are generalizable across organizations and jobs (Stokes & Reddy, 1992). We shall next address some of the evidence to date and review some of the nagging research questions.

Biodata forms have been validated in a wide range of jobs. Tables 3 and 4 provide summaries of studies obtained from Barge and Hough (1986) and Mumford and Owens (1987), respectively. From these tables, it is clear that biodata forms have been used successfully in many occupational groups. Validity coefficients from the two tables range from .10 for unskilled workers to .54 for supervisors.

Until recently, the notion pervading the literature had been that biodata keys cannot be generalized from job to job or organization to organization (Dreher & Sackett, 1983; Hunter & Hunter, 1984). Some studies have

TABLE 3   Summary of Barge and Hough (1986) Results

Job Category	Number of Studies	Median Validity	Range
Supervisors	3	.54	.41–.60
Sales	4	.36	.20–.42
Science/engineers	10	.49	.22–.70
Managers	2	.38	.35–.40
Skilled workers	5	.11	.05–.45
Unskilled workers	8	.10	.05–.53
Clerical	15	.42	.10–.74
Military			
Officers or candidates	5	.17	.07–.20
Drill instructors	4	.27	.16–.38
Enlistees	23	.24	.09–.57
Other	4	.28	.10–.40
Miscellaneous	9	.41	.06–.60

TABLE 4   Validity Summary from Mumford and Owens (1987)

	Average	
	r	n
Performance of managers	.35	21
Sales success	.35	17
Factory jobs (including skilled craftspersons)	.46	14
Clerical performance	.48	13
Military	.34	13
Overall*	.42	112

*Includes validity coefficients in addition to those listed in the table

From "Methodology Review: Principles, Procedures and Findings in the Application of Background Data Measures" by M. D. Mumford & W. A. Owens, 1987, *Applied Psychological Measurement, 11*, pp. 1–31. Copyright 1987 by Applied Psychological Measurement, Inc. Reprinted by permission.

contradicted this common assumption. Buel, Albright, and Glennon (1966) applied a 33-item scoring key originally developed and validated for researchers in the petroleum industry to research personnel in a pharmaceutical company. The validity coefficients were highly similar across four criteria. Campbell, Dunnette, Lawler, and Weick (1970) discussed the development of a biodata questionnaire to identify future managers at the Standard Oil of New Jersey. A strong emphasis in the study had been placed on the core activities across functional areas in five affiliate companies. Thus, the unique functions across specialty areas were ignored. Their biodata form was found to generalize. Similarly, Rothstein, Schmidt, Erwin, Owens, and Sparks (1990) developed and validated a biodata form for selection of approximately 11,000 first-line supervisors in 79 different organizations. Items were selected for the form that performed well across organizations. Consequently, the final form was generalizable. Work has continued with the generalizability of biodata forms developed for selecting managers and for selecting clerical personnel in three job families (teller/customer service, processing/verifying, and secretarial/clerical). These results look promising thus far, making it clear that it is possible to develop biodata forms that can generalize across jobs and across organizations.

Left unanswered is the question of the best methods for enhancing the generalizability of biodata across organizations. One study used the strategy of focusing on common job dimensions for development of the biodata form; another study simply included only those items that were correlated in all organizations for which the final form was developed. Because empirical keys focus on item-level or option-level relationships with the criterion, there would seem to be greater chance for sample-specific findings than when rationally developed dimensions are used, yet this has not been tested. Moreover, we do not know how widely biodata dimensions or empirical keys might generalize.

Buel, Albright, and Glennon (1962) noted that empirical keys were of limited use beyond the purpose for which they were developed and that the "general and scientific utility" would not be improved until we have gained a better understanding of their complex factorial structure. They also suggested that researchers with applied interests would benefit from having a resource of items that would not need to be analyzed in each different setting. Thirty years later we still are not much closer to understanding the factor structure of empirical keys or the generalizability of items and/or factors. We reviewed some of the literature on both items and factors identified in biodata research, and what follows is a summary of our findings.

SUMMARY OF PREDICTIVE BIODATA ITEMS

In an attempt to assess the generalizability of biodata items, we reviewed the literature to determine the comparability of items that were predictive across a variety of jobs. As might be expected, this proved to be a difficult task, since studies that show the predictive ability of empirically keyed biodata inventories generally do not include a listing of the most predictive items. The studies that were identified exhibit some of the common criticisms associated with empirical keys, but they also show evidence of similar predictive ability for some items in different circumstances. Most of the studies that reported predictive biographical items were not very extensive and primarily included demographic variables such as age and experience (see Table 5). Although it may be useful to know that older and more experienced applicants are better performers, these types of predictor–criterion relationships provide little insight about the predictive ability of biodata items. Two more extensive studies were identified that examined a variety of biographical items that appear to assess attitudes, interests, self-evaluations, work preferences, and relationships with others, in addition to more demographic items.

In the first study, Kavanagh and York (1972) examined the biographical correlates of department heads in a large midwestern manufacturing company. Performance ratings were obtained from plant managers, who were the department heads' immediate supervisors, and from their most effective and least effective subordinates. The department heads completed a 41-item biographical inventory, and the significant relationships between the items and performance ratings are reported in Table 6. A second study that examined staff nurse performance identified a number of biographical items that distinguished between high and low performers (Dyer, Monson, & Van Drimmelen, 1975). Table 7 shows the significant relationships between the biographical items and several measures of quality of patient care and performance that were obtained from both trained observers and the nurses' supervisors, subordinates, and peers. An official performance rating (proficiency) was obtained from hospital records.

Although the review of predictive biodata items provided in Tables 5, 6, and 7 was not exhaustive, and the results are somewhat dated, they provide some examples of issues related to empirically keyed biodata inventories. Several items in the Dyer et al. (1975; Table 7) study predicted differently depending on which criterion variable was used. For example, "feeling responsible for work assignment deadlines to a *great* extent" was predictive for high performance scores from staff nurses' second-level

TABLE 5 Biographical Items Predictive of Performance Criteria

Study	Job Category	N	Predictive Items	Criterion
Tanofsky, Shepps, & O'Neill (1969)	Insurance salespersons	1,525	High prior income More than two dependents	Average sales
Azen, Snibbe, & Montgomery (1973)	Law enforcement officers	95	Age Height	Job type Number of auto accidents
Johnson, Newton, & Peek (1979)*	Clerical workers	162	Age at first job Age at application Average job tenure Number of previous jobs(–) Reason for leaving previous job(–) Salary of last job(–)	Tenure
Hoiberg & Pugh (1978)*	Navy (across 7 occupational groups)	7,923	Age at enlistment Education School expulsions and suspensions(–) Arrests(–)	Performance effectiveness[1]
Booth, McNally, & Berry (1978)*	Navy hospital ($N = 2,835$) corpsmen and dental technicians ($N = 848$)	3,683	Age at enlistment Years of school Difficulties with school authorities(–)	Performance effectiveness[2]

TABLE 5 Biographical Items Predictive of Performance Criteria (continued)

Study	Job Category	N	Predictive Items	Criterion
Umeda & Frey (1974)	Ministers	92	Age when career choice made(-) Percentage of college expenses earned	Self-ratings and objective performance measures[3]

Note: (-) indicates a negative relationship between the predictor and criterion.
* indicates that study results were successfully cross-validated.

[1] Measured by discharge from the navy, demotion or unauthorized absence, incarceration in a military or civilian correctional facility, and highest pay grade level achieved during the post two-year follow-up period

[2] Measured by completion of training, remaining on job for at least two years, and advancement beyond apprenticeship level during post-training

[3] A bid system was used to develop a weighted multiple criterion composed of self-ratings of job satisfaction, job success, human relations skills, public speaking ability, and counseling skills, and objective measures such as number of baptisms per year, congregation size, status of job title, number of paid supervisees, and time devoted to professional reading.

TABLE 6 Significant Relationships Between Biographical Items
and Performance Ratings for Department Heads Reported
by Kavanagh and York (1972)

Biographical Item	Performance Rating Dimension
Happiness of childhood family	Planning (FM+), Achievement Orientation (FM+)
Highest educational level attained	Representing (PM), Finances (PM), Intellectual (PM)
Age at time of high school graduation	Human Relations (FM+), Concern for Quality (FM+)
Size of high school attended	Coordinating (PM)
Hours per week averaged on part-time paid jobs during last couple of years of high school	Achievement Orientation (PM)
Personal evaluation of executive ability or potential executive ability in terms of percentage-wise location	Finances (PM), Markets (PM), Achievement Orientation (PM)
Speed of work activity in terms of slower, faster, or very much faster than others	Investigating (PM), Leadership Orientation (PM), Independence (PM), Achievement Orientation (PM)
Assessment of highest supervisory level attainable by respondent	Planning (PM), Investigating (PM), Evaluating (PM), Staffing (PM), Finances (PM), Intellectual (PM), Independence (PM), Achievement Orientation (PM)
Supervisory level at which respondent would best like to work	Finances (PM)
Rate of physical growth during teens compared to others of same sex	Achievement Orientation (PM)
Evaluation of present physical condition	Finances (PM), Independence (PM), Achievement Orientation (PM), Markets (FM-)
Economic level of immediate family when respondent was young person	Representing (FM-), Personnel (FM-), Leadership Orientation (FM-)
Economic level of family compared to high school classmates	Evaluating (FM+)
Leadership of conversation at social affairs compared with others	Representing (PM)

TABLE 6   Significant Relationships Between Biographical Items
           and Performance Ratings for Department Heads Reported
           by Kavanagh and York (1972) (continued)

Biographical Item	Performance Rating Dimension
Evaluation of skill in driving a car compared to others	Coordinating (FM+), Supervising (FM+), Staffing (FM+), Negotiating (FM+), Methods (FM+), Equipment (FM+), Leadership Orientatio (FM+)
Evaluation of job ability relative to a list of 100 typical people— response in terms of percentage location	Planning (PM), Evaluation (PM), Finances (PM), Markets (PM), Intellectual (PM), Independence Location (PM), Achievement Orientation (PM)
Size of undergraduate school	Representing (PM), Finances (PM), Intellectual (PM), Coordinating (FM-)
Type and size of community in which undergraduate school was located	Representing (PM), Finances (PM)
Type and size of community preferred by respondent in which to have attended undergraduate school	Finances (PM)
Hours per week spent in study outside class during last year of college	Representing (PM), Finances (PM)
Scholastic standing at college graduation	Finances (PM)
Bachelor's degree hours	Intellectual (PM)
Number of part-time jobs during college	Finances (PM), Negotiating (FM-)
Number of hours per week on part-time jobs during last couple of years in college	Finances (PM), Intellectual (PM)

Note: PM = Plant manager (department head's supervisor)
    FM+ = Foreman (department head's most effective subordinate)
    FM- = Foreman (department head's least effective subordinate)
    Data were analyzed with a modified ANOVA technique using the 60 ratings (20 each from PM, FM+, and FM-) as the dependent variables and the 41 biographical items as the independent variables. Items reported were significantly related to performance ratings at $p < .01$.

From "Biographical Correlates of Middle Managers' Performance " by M. J. Kavanagh & D. R. York, 1972, *Personnel Psychology, 25*, pp. 319–332. Copyright 1972 by Personnel Psychology, Inc. Reprinted by permission.

TABLE 7   Biographical Items That Predict Quality of Patient Care and
Performance of Staff Nurses Reported by Dyer et al. (1975)

High Scorers	Low Scorers	Criterion[*]
Liked clearly specified assignments about half the time	Liked clearly specified assignments most of the time	1
Encouraged associates to continue their education most of the time	Rarely encouraged associates to continue their education	1
Felt that classmates came to them for assistance only rarely	Felt that classmates came for assistance less than half of the time	1
Felt they express themselves orally to a great extent	Felt they express themselves orally to a considerable extent	1
Indicated that people were most important, when completing a word-ranking task	Indicated that learning was most important	1, 2, 3
Enjoyed filling out the questionnaire	Found the questionnaire neither interesting nor too distasteful	1
Enjoyed what they do on the job most of the time	Enjoyed what they do on the job less than half the time	4, 5
Possess teaching ability to a great extent	Possess teaching ability to a moderate extent	4
Felt they expressed themselves in writing to a limited extent	Felt they expressed themselves in writing to a considerable extent	3, 4, 5
Felt they have considerable ability to organize	Felt they have a limited ability to organize	4
Felt proud of their work to a great extent	Felt proud of their work to a moderate extent	4
Felt responsible for work assignment deadlines to a great extent	Felt responsible for work assignment deadlines to a considerable extent	4, 7 (reversed)
Have not participated in community organizations	Have participated in community organizations for 7–10 years	2
Have a diploma in nursing	Have an associate degree	2

TABLE 7   Biographical Items That Predict Quality of Patient Care and
           Performance of Staff Nurses Reported by Dyer et al. (1975)
           (continued)

High Scorers	Low Scorers	Criterion*
Felt people misunderstood them little if at all	Felt misunderstood to a moderate extent	5
Worked as a staff nurse 11 or more years	Worked as a staff nurse 2 years or less	5
Had 11 years or more experience as a surgical staff nurse	Had no experience as a surgical staff nurse	5
Had 3–6 years experience as an operating room staff nurse	Had 2 years or less experience as an operating room staff nurse	5
Had 19 years or more experience	Had less than 2 years experience	5
Wanted to be all-around American girls in high school	Wanted to be humorous and witty	4, 5
Had 2 years or less experience as a head nurse	Had 7–10 years experience as a head nurse	6
Entered nursing on advice of parents, relatives, or counselors	Made plans on their own	3, 6, 7
Education was very important, practically imperative in their childhood home	Education was important but not imperative	6
Had 2 years or less professional experience	Had 19 years or more professional experience	6
Enjoyed directing the work of others to a moderate extent	Enjoyed directing the work of others to a considerable extent	3 (reversed), 7
Worked as supervisor 3–6 years	Had never supervised others	4
Surpassed 90 percent of their classmates in high school	Surpassed 80 percent of their high school classmates	4
Actively led the discussion in a group	Led the discussion an average amount	4
Felt somewhat comfortable talking with patients who complain about care	Felt very comfortable talking with patients who complain about care	4

TABLE 7   Biographical Items That Predict Quality of Patient Care and
Performance of Staff Nurses Reported by Dyer et al. (1975)
(continued)

High Scorers	Low Scorers	Criterion*
Derived greatest satisfaction from working with and through others	Derived greatest satisfaction from personally doing things for patients	3, 4
Liked to pursue thoughts less than half the time	Liked to pursue thoughts half the time	3
Encouraged associates to continue their education about half the time	Encouraged associates to continue their education all the time	3
Evaluated their thoughts most of the time	Evaluated their thoughts all of the time	3
Liked to work alone to a limited extent	Liked to work alone to a moderate extent	3

*Criterion Key:

1. Wayne State scale scores
2. Performance score from head nurse
3. Composite—derived by averaging scores from the various raters
4. Performance score—second-level supervisors
5. Official ratings—proficiency rating obtained from hospital records
6. Patient-care scores from peers
7. Patient-care scores from subordinates

Note: Only items that were correlated at the $p < .05$ level in one direction for high scorers and the opposite direction for low scores were reported. Sample size ranged from $N = 258$ to $N = 310$. Results were not cross-validated.

From "What Are the Relationships of Quality of Patient Care to Nurses' Performance, Biographical and Personality Variables?" by E. D. Dyer, M. A. Monson, & J. B. Van Primmelen, 1975, *Psychological Reports, 36*, pp. 255–266. Copyright 1975 by *Psychological Reports*. Reprinted by permission.

supervisors, whereas low scorers "felt responsible for work assignment deadlines to a *considerable* extent." This same item predicted in a reverse manner when the criterion was patient-care scores obtained from the nurses' subordinates, which demonstrates the predictor's dependence on the criterion.

Very often, the causal relationship between the item and the criterion is explained by the item's ability to predict for that particular job in that particular situation rather than by any theoretical relationship between the predictor and the criterion. In other words, the best explanation has generally been that past behavior is the best predictor of future behavior.

For instance, a plausible explanation is not readily apparent for the relationship between "wanting to be an all-around American girl in high school" and high proficiency scores for staff nurses, while "wanting to be humorous and witty" predicts low scorers. With other items, the logical relationship may not be readily apparent, although further examination usually reveals an explanation for the predictor–criterion relationship. For instance, "having more than two dependents" probably provides the motivation for insurance salespersons to be high performers.

For other items, the relationship between the predictor and criterion are more apparent, and underlying dimensions or factor structures may be identified. There appears to be an academic achievement factor underlying the items that predict middle management performance (see Table 6). Education is also important to predicting effective performers in the navy (Hoiberg & Pugh, 1978) and among staff nurses (Dyer et al., 1975). Items related to education may generalize across different jobs, although one could expect the relationships to vary depending on both the criterion and the job for which the inventory is being validated. Hoiberg and Pugh (1978) and Booth, McNally, and Berry (1978) both found number of arrests to be negatively related to effective performance in the navy. Other similarities between the items, such as age or experience, are of less interest, since they represent common demographic variables rather than life experience variables. Although this compilation of items might provide a useful starting point for the development of a biodata inventory, no additional evidence of the generalizability of empirical keys was obtained.

SUMMARY OF BIODATA FACTORS

The technique of using exploratory factor analysis or principal components analysis to develop scales for keying has yielded some evidence of improved generalizability over empirical keying solutions. Mitchell and Klimoski (1982) contrasted the predictive ability of these two methods and found that empirical keys predicted better than a weighted combination of six factorial scales in both the validation and cross-validation samples. The factorial scales showed less shrinkage in cross-validation, suggesting that these scales may display greater generality and stability.

Although factorial scales may not be as predictive as empirical keys, they do have the additional benefit of providing meaningful descriptive dimensions. Mumford and Owens (1987) reviewed the literature and found that there were 21 factor and principal components analyses of background data. They reviewed the content of each factor and made a judgment as to which of 26 generic, conceptual dimensions each could be assigned. In some cases a factor may have been assigned to more than one of the generic categories if it appeared to capture significant elements of both. Table 8 shows the results of their analysis. As can be seen from the results, a number of these generic dimensions appear to emerge in factor analysis more frequently than others, particularly those dimensions concerned with adjustment, maturity, academic achievement, intellectual/cultural pursuits, introversion versus extroversion, social leadership, and career development. Mumford and Owens suggest that further examination of the predictive capabilities of factorial scales is needed, particularly since it was readily apparent that the content and construct validity of the scales has received little attention.

Factorial scales have displayed some evidence of criterion-related validity; unfortunately, Mumford and Owens did not include criterion information from most of the studies they reviewed, in large part because such criterion information was not available. Knowledge of the applied situations in which factor scales have been found to be predictive would help formulate a better understanding of the potential for improved generalizability of factorial scales. We reviewed the literature in order to identify studies that related factor scales to performance criteria. Table 9 shows the factors that were identified and the criteria for which they were predictive (when available). Studies that did not utilize performance-type criteria were excluded from consideration.

The methods used in the studies to investigate the relationships between the factor scales and the criteria varied. Usually, scores on the factor scales were entered into a multiple regression equation, and the regression weights were used as an indicator of the importance of a factor to the criterion. Only two of the studies—McDaniel (1989) and Stokes, Gore, Eastman, and Morris (1992)—directly computed validity coefficients for each of the factor scales. The validity coefficients for the factors were relatively low, with the highest validity coefficient of $r = .15$ ($p < .001$) found by McDaniel and of $r = .25$ ($p < .01$) found by Stokes et al. Russell, Mattson, Devlin, and Atwater (1990) computed the cross-validities between the five criterion measures and the empirically keyed scale scores for the five-factor solution. Morrison, Owens, Glennon, and Albright (1962) used the profiles of the criterion factor loadings on each of the five identified dimensions to interpret the relationship between the factors and the criteria.

An examination of Table 9 reveals that Academic Achievement factors were common across most of the studies. The results of the search conducted by Mumford and Owens (1987) suggested that Academic Achievement should have been one of the most frequently observed

TABLE 8 Number of Factor Analytic Studies (*N* = 21) Identifying Generic Dimensions Reported by Mumford and Owens (1987)

Dimension	Number
1. Introversion versus Extroversion	13
2. Social leadership	12
3. Independence	8
4. Self-esteem	7
5. Achievement motivation	7
6. Social conformity	8
7. Personal conservatism	6
8. Maturity	11
9. Adjustment	18
10. Academic achievement	16
11. Parental warmth	7
12. Parental control	6
13. Parental social economic status	8
14. Sibling relationships	3
15. Religious involvement	9
16. Family commitment	4
17. Urban/rural background	1
18. Health	3
19. Athletic pursuits	8
20. Scientific/engineering pursuits	7
21. Intellectual/cultural pursuits	13
22. Work values	4
23. Organizational commitment	6
24. Professional skills	7
25. Trade skills	5
26. Career development	10

From "Methodology Review: Principles, Procedures and Findings in the Application of Background Data Measures" by M. D. Mumford and W. A. Owens, 1987, *Applied Psychological Measurement, 11,* pp. 1–31. Copyright 1987 by Applied Psychological Measurement, Inc. Reprinted by permission.

TABLE 9 Biographical Factors and Their Predictive Relationship to Various Performance Criteria

Study	Samples	Factors	Criterion Measures
Morrison, Owens, Glennon, & Albright (1962)[a]	Petroleum research scientists N = 418	1. Favorable Self-perception (P & CR) 2. Inquisitive, Professional Orientation (PD) 3. Utilitarian Drive (P & CR) 4. Tolerance for Ambiguity (PD) 5. General Adjustment (P & CR)	Performance and creativity ratings (P & CR) Patent disclosures (PD)
Baehr & Williams (1968)[b]	Salespersons N = 210	1. Financial Responsibility (PR, MSVR, and MaxSVR) 2. Stability (MSVR & MaxSVR) 3. Leadership & Group Participation (PR) 4. Parental Family Adjustment (−PR, −MaxSVR) 5. Early Family Responsibility (−TN, PR, MaxSVR, −RTD) 6. School Achievement (PR, MSVR) 7. Drive (RTD) 8. Educational-Vocational Consistency (RTD) 9. General Health (−RTD) 10. Vocational Satisfaction (−TN) 11. Vocational Decisions (TN)	Performance rating (PR) Mean sales volume rank (MSVR) Maximum sales volume rank (MaxSVR) Tenure (TN) Route difficulty (RTD)
LaRocco, Ryman, & Biersner (1977)[b*]	Navy recruits in basic training N = 1,292	1. Antisocial Behavior (DIS) 2. Family Characteristics 3. Social Participation (−DIS)	Discharge prior to graduation (DIS)

TABLE 9 Biographical Factors and Their Predictive Relationship to Various Performance Criteria (continued)

Study	Samples	Factors	Criterion Measures
Baehr (1978)[b]	Bank officers, salespersons, police patrol, officers and state police N = not reported	1. School Achievement 2. School Activities 3. Higher Educational Achievement (PR) 4. Drive (PR) 5. Leadership and Group Participation (PR) 6. Financial Responsibility (PR) 7. Early Family Responsibility (PR) 8. Parental Family Adjustment (PR) 9. Successful Professional Parents 10. Job and Personal Stability (PR)	Performance ratings (PR)
Matteson (1978)[b]	Operating jobs at a U.S. refinery N = 2,590	1. Academic Ability (TN2) 2. Scientific Interests (TN2) 3. Mechanical-Electrical Orientation 4. Athletic Involvement (−TN2, −TN10) 5. Paternal Blue Collar Background (TN2, TN6, TN10) 6. Maternal Employment History 7. Rural Background 8. Risk-taking behavior (TN6, TN10) 9. Social Activeness 10. Upper Middle Class Background (TN6) 11. Parental Permissiveness (−TN6,−TN10) 12. Favorable Self-Perception (−TN6)	Tenure at 2 months (TN2) Tenure at 6 months (TN6) Tenure at 10 months (TN10)

TABLE 9 Biographical Factors and Their Predictive Relationship to Various Performance Criteria (continued)

Study	Samples	Factors	Criterion Measures
Childs & Klimoski (1986)[b]	Diverse occupations $N = 555$	1. Social Orientation (JS, PS, & CS) 2. Economic Stability (CS) 3. Work Ethic Orientation (CS) 4. Educational Achievement (JS & CS) 5. Interpersonal Confidence (JS, PS, & CS)	Job success (JS), personal success (PS), and career success (CS)
Haymaker (1986)[c]	Applicants for positions at two supermarkets $N = 12,046$	1. Educational Adjustment 2. Self-Concept 3. Attitudinal Factor	Integrity (IN) Turnover (TO)
McDaniel (1989)[d]	Military recruits $N = 9,336$	1. School Suspension (UNDIS) 2. Drug Use 3. Quitting School (UNDIS) 4. Employment Experience 5. Grades and School Clubs 6. Legal System Contacts 7. Socioeconomic Status	Unsuitability discharge (UNDIS)
Russell, Matteson, Devlin, & Atwater (1990)[e]	First-year students at the Naval Academy $N = 917$	1. Life Problems and Difficulties (LDP, MQPR) 2. Aspects of Task Performance (AQPR) 3. Work Ethic/Self-discipline (MPR, AQPR, MQPR) 4. Assistance From Others 5. Extraordinary Goals or Effort	Leadership (LDR), military quality point rating (MQPR), academic quality point ratio (AQPR), military performance rating (MPR)

TABLE 9 Biographical Factors and Their Predictive Relationship to Various Performance Criteria (continued)

Study	Samples	Factors	Criterion Measures
Gandy, Dye, & MacLane (in this volume)[c]	Entry-level non-supervisory positions in professional and administratrive occupations across most federal agencies $N = 8,141$	1. Work Competency 2. High School Achievement 3. College Achievement 4. Leadership Skills	Supervisory performance apppraisal (SPA)
Stokes, Gore, Eastman, & Morris (1992)[c]	Craftspersons and assembly-line positions at a manufacturing company $N = 163$	1. Working With Others 2. Agreeableness (INTACT, PHYS & PROC) 3. Impulsiveness/Distractibility 4. Respect From Others 5. Health/Physical Fitness (COMM) 6. Mechanical Interest and Ability (PHYS, TECH, & TROAB) 7. Work Motivation (INMOT, COMM, TECH) 8. Approval Seeking 9. Math and Science Achievement	Interaction/motivation (INMOT), interaction with others (INTACT), oral/written communication (COMM), physical ability (PHYS), technical expertise (TECH), troubleshooting ability (TROAB), quality/thoroughness of work (QTW), reliability/dependability (REL), judgment/decision making (JUD), following rules/procedures (PROC)

Note: Methods used to assess relationship between the predictor and criteria varied and are as follows:

a = Profiles of criteria factor loadings on each of the five dimensions

b = Weights obtained from regression equation

c = Factor analysis of an empirically keyed inventory

d = Correlation of the biodata factors to the criteria

e = Cross-validation between the five criterion measures and the empirically keyed scale scores for the five factor solution

(criteria) following a factor indicates a significant predictive relationship between the factor and the criteria in parentheses.

(-criteria) indicates a negative relationship between the factor and criteria.

* indicates results were cross-validated.

factors. This was also evident in our search of biodata items, which revealed a number of studies in which education was predictive of the criteria. Academic Achievement factors included measures of grades in school (high school and college), awards and honors, a general liking and adjustment to the school environment, participation in school clubs and extracurricular activities, higher education achievement, and a feeling that school was successful and stimulating. Exceptions were the School Achievement and School Activities factors examined by Baehr in 1978, which were not related to any of the performance criteria. Academic Achievement and related factors were predictive of performance for salespersons, bank officers, military recruits, and operators at a U.S. refinery.

Other factors frequently common across the studies are those that measure family background and relationships. The factors considered to be in this category include background factors such as Family Characteristics, Socioeconomic Status, Paternal Blue Collar Background, Maternal Employment History, Upper-middle-class Background, and Rural Background, as well as relationship factors such as Parental Permissiveness and Parental Family Adjustment. The jobs for which these factors were predictive include salespersons, police patrol officers, state police, and operators jobs at a U.S. refinery. Several of the family background factors were not related to the performance criteria in the studies in which they were examined. In LaRocco, Ryman, and Biersner (1977), the Family Characteristics factor, which measured mother's education, number of brothers and sisters, and number of older brother and sisters, did not exhibit any predictive relationship with the criterion. Successful Professional Parents (Baehr, 1978), Maternal Employment History, Rural Background (Matteson, 1978), and Socioeconomic Status (McDaniel, 1989) were also not found to predict the performance criteria under investigation.

Several other factors proved to be predictive in different situations. Economic Stability and Financial Responsibility, factors that were measures of respondent's ability to manage personal economics of defined proportions through earning, accumulating, saving, and investing, were shown to be predictive of the performance of salespersons and bank officers (Baehr, 1978; Baehr & Williams, 1968). These factors were also predictive of career success (Childs & Klimoski, 1986). McDaniel (1989) and LaRocco et al. (1977) both found that measures of antisocial behavior, such as running away from home, playing hooky, being expelled/suspended/quitting school, drug use, and arrest records were all predictive of the discharge of military recruits. Factors that measured interpersonal confidence and favorable self-perceptions were predictive of performance and creativity ratings for research scientists (Morrison, Owens, Glennon,

& Albright, 1962) and tenure of refinery workers (Matteson, 1978). Childs and Klimoski (1986) also found that an interpersonal confidence factor predicted job, personal, and career success. Baehr and Williams (1968) and Baehr (1978) used essentially the same factors in their studies and found them to have similar predictive capabilities. Leadership and Group Participation, Drive, and Early Family Responsibility were found to be valid predictors in both studies, although the performance criteria and jobs were different. Baehr (1978) also found that the factor of Job and Personal Stability was predictive for both police officers and state police officers.

The remaining factors were either not examined in other studies or were found to be predictive only for the situations in which they were examined. Social Orientation, Work Ethic Orientation, Risk-taking Behavior, General Health, Scientific Interests, Athletic Involvement, Educational-Vocational Consistency, Vocational Satisfaction, Vocational Decisiveness, Inquisitive Professional Orientation, Utilitarian Drive, Tolerance for Ambiguity, and General Adjustment were all shown to have some degree of predictive validity in the studies in which they were examined.

These results help to demonstrate the improved generalizability of factor scales over item-level analyses. In particular, factors that measure academic achievement and aspects of parental background and relationships show evidence of generalizability across a wide range of jobs. Other factors may also generalize, but it was difficult to determine the extent to which they may be applied in different situations due to the lack of consistency among the studies.

Studies that employ factorial scale methods often fall into the same empirical trap as studies that use empirical keying methods. Both methods include items that were considered to be predictive of the criteria, usually without any theoretical justification for including them. The theoretical explanation is generally obtained from the factor analysis, which identifies the dimensions underlying the predictive items. However, factors are only as good as the items that are entered into the analysis. Items that are thrown together without rhyme or reason may result in factors that are not easily interpreted. This also may result in lower correlation coefficients that are frequently found in studies that use factor scale keys. The combination of empirical items into factors may gloss over the predictive ability of the items that are highly correlated with the criterion through combining them into a scale with fewer predictive items. Since validity coefficients for factor scale keys appear to have more potential for generalizability than validity coefficients for empirical keys, development of factors on some theoretical basis may improve their predictive ability and their usefulness.

EXTENT OF GENERALITY OF BIODATA

The generalizability of ability tests across broadly defined job families is well established (Schmidt et al., 1993). However, some researchers have argued that job families are more likely to moderate validities for biodata and for personality tests than for cognitive ability measures (Sackett, Schmitt, Tenopyr, Kehoe, & Zedeck, 1985). In fact, Schneider's attraction-selection-attrition (ASA) model (Schneider, 1987) is consistent with this notion. In reviewing the item and factor relationships obtained with biodata, it is apparent that ability factors are among those that appear consistently across a variety of jobs, suggesting that to the extent biodata forms assess ability, they may be as generalizable as cognitive ability tests. However, variables other than ability emerge consistently as well, and there is no literature to shed light on the extent of their generalizability. Moreover, we do not know what type of job information leads to the development of job families that enhance the validity and generalizability of biodata. An organization attempting to develop entry-level screening procedures that incorporate both cognitive ability tests and biodata measures has very little information to be used in determining the best method for forming job families. For the cognitive ability tests, the job families may be broadly defined in terms of general work dimensions. For the purpose of developing and validating biodata measures, more specificity in the job definitions may be important (see the chapter by Fine and Cronshaw in this volume for a discussion of the utility of job analysis techniques in the development of biodata forms). Clearly, job families are formed for different purposes, and for an organization it would be most convenient to use the same job families for the development of selection and promotion procedures, whether the selection procedure is an ability test or a biodata form. Extensive work is needed in this area if biodata are to be used extensively as selection procedures. Taxonomic work related to both biodata factors and work dimensions is essential.

We have preliminary information to suggest that biodata scores are related to specific job dimensions. Stokes, Mecham, Block, and Hogan (1989) presented the relationship between Owens' factors from the BQ (Owens & Schoenfeldt, 1979) and dimensions derived from the *Position Analysis Questionnaire* (PAQ; McCormick, Jeanneret, & Mecham, 1972) using canonical correlation analysis. Two functions each were derived for men and women, accounting for 2 and 3 percent of the variance, respectively. The results suggested a small relationship between the biodata factors and job dimensions, but the canonical functions were difficult to interpret. More recently, Stokes and Mecham (1992) used factors from the

TABLE 10   Biodata Factors as Predictors of Work Dimensions Derived From
the Position Analysis Questionnaire (PAQ)

PAQ Dimensions		Biodata Factors Predictive in Model	Beta	Adjusted R^2
Performing clerical and/or related activities	Males:	Academic Achievement	-.14	
		Socioeconomic Status	-.20	.07
		Positive Academic Attitude	-.12	
		Religious Activity	-.17	
	Females:	Social Leadership	-.12	
		Parental Control versus Freedom	.11	
		Feelings of Social Inadequacy	-.14	.05
		Popularity With Opposite Sex	.13	
		Social Maturity	-.12	
Engaging in physical activities	Males:	Socioeconomic Status	-.14	.01
	Females:	Cultural Literary Interests	-.17	
		Athletic Participation	.14	
		Popularity With Opposite Sex	.12	.07
		Adjustment	-.11	
Having decision, communicating and general responsibilities	Males:	Academic Achievement	.14	
		Positive Academic Attitude	.14	.04
	Females:	Warmth of Maternal Relationship	.12	
		Parental Control Versus Freedom	-.12	.03
		Adjustment	-.14	

Note: Biodata factors used are those described in Owens and Schoenfeldt (1979). Only a subset of analyses are presented. Complete results may be obtained by contacting first author.

BQ to predict specific dimensions on the PAQ using a series of multiple regression analyses. Several work dimensions were successfully predicted by adolescent life experiences (BQ factors). A subset of results appears in Table 10. These results suggest the promise of eventually obtaining a taxonomy of biodata factors that are related to specific work dimensions. Ultimately, organizations could apply biodata forms measuring specific dimensions to the jobs in their organization based on job analysis information, such as that obtained from the PAQ. Researchers are currently investigating the dimensionality of work (Harvey, 1992) and work performance (Borman, 1992; Campbell, 1992), and their findings should enhance the search for a taxonomy of biodata factors predictive of performance in established job families.

CONCLUSION

We have reviewed much of the literature related to the criteria for which biodata are predictive and the generality of biodata items and factors across occupational categories. Much work remains to be done to establish the utility of biodata forms as alternative selection procedures. If we can see biodata inventories as comprehensive assessments of individuals' life histories (as they are applicable to work performance) rather than as forms developed to predict for a specific purpose (e.g., turnover among clerical workers), we might begin to achieve the development of construct-valid instruments with broad applications in organizations. Moreover, biodata forms should have widespread applicability in a society that increasingly moves toward maximizing the classification of individuals in organizations rather than toward maximizing prediction of performance in specific occupations (Tyler, 1986). Changes in the work force may make such transitions in our approach to selection imperative. A taxonomy of biodata factors and relevant work performance dimensions would be a great asset in making the transition from prediction to classification. Recent research into the construct validation of biodata factors and into the generalizability of biodata provide a useful framework for future research.

REFERENCES

Adams, J. P. (1970). Psychosocial aspects of highway accidents. *Behavioral Research in Highway Safety, 1,* 3–18.

Allison, I. E. (1992). *Biodata as a predictor of occupational discontinuity.* Unpublished doctoral dissertation, University of Georgia, Athens.

Arvey, R. P., Carter, G. W., & Buerkley, P. K. (1991). Job satisfaction: Dispositional and situational influences. In C. L. Cooper & I. T. Robertson (Eds.), *International review of industrial and organizational psychology* (Vol. 6, 359–383). London: Wiley.

Azen, S. P., Snibbe, H. M., & Montgomery, H. R. (1973). A longitudinal predictive study of success and performance of law enforcement officers. *Journal of Applied Psychology, 57*(2), 190–192.

Baehr, M. E. (1978, August). *Underlying dimensions of personal background data for occupational level and sex subgroups and their application for the management of human resources*. Paper presented at the International Congress of Applied Psychology, Munich, Germany.

Baehr, M. E., & Williams, G. B. (1968). Predictors of sales success from factorially determined dimensions of personal background data. *Journal of Applied Psychology, 52*(2), 98–103.

Barge, B. N. (1991, April). *Controlling employee health costs: A new frontier for applied psychology*. Paper presented at the annual meeting of the Society of Industrial and Organizational Psychology, St. Louis, MO.

Barge, B. N., & Hough, L. M. (1986). Utility of biographical data for predicting job performance. In L. M. Hough (Ed.), *Utility of temperament, biodata, and interest assessment for predicting job performance: A review of the literature* (ARI Research Note No. 88-02, pp. 91-130). Alexandria, VA: U.S. Army Research Institute.

Booth, R. F., McNally, M. S., & Berry, N. H. (1978). Predicting performance effectiveness in paramedical occupations. *Personnel Psychology, 31,* 581–593.

Borman, W. C. (1992). Job behavior, performance, and effectiveness. In M. D. Dunnette & L. M. Hough (Eds.), *Handbook of industrial and organizational psychology* (Vol. 2, pp. 271–326). Palo Alto, CA: Consulting Psychologists Press.

Buel, W. D. (1989). *A biographical study of teamwork*. Tampa, FL: Byron, Harless, Reid, & Associates.

Buel, W. D., Albright, L. E., & Glennon, J. R. (1966). A note on the generality and cross-validity of personal history for identifying creative research scientists. *Journal of Applied Psychology, 50,* 217–219.

Campbell, J. P. (1992). Modeling the performance prediction problem in industrial and organizational psychology. In M. D. Dunnette & L. M. Hough (Eds.), *Handbook of industrial and organizational psychology* (Vol. 1, pp. 687–732). Palo Alto, CA: Consulting Psychologists Press.

Campbell, J. P., Dunnette, M. D., Lawler, E. E., & Weick, K. (1970). *Managerial behavior and performance effectiveness*. New York: McGraw-Hill.

Campion, M. A. (1991). Meaning and measurement of turnover: Comparison of alternative measures and recommendations for research. *Journal of Applied Psychology, 76,* 199–212.

Childs, A., & Klimoski, R. J. (1986). Successfully predicting career success: An application of the biographical inventory. *Journal of Applied Psychology, 71,* 3–8.

Crowne, D. P., & Marlowe, D. (1964). *The approval motive: Studies in evaluative dependence*. New York: Wiley.

Dawis, R.V., & Lofquist, L. H. (1984). *A psychological theory of work adjustment*. Minneapolis: University of Minnesota Press.

Denning, D. (1983, March). *Correlates of employee safety performance*. Paper presented at the Southeastern Industrial and Organizational Psychology Association Meeting, Atlanta, GA.

Dreher, G. F., & Sackett, P. R. (1983). *Perspectives on staffing and selection*. Homewood, IL: Irwin.

Dyer, E. D., Monson, M. A., & Van Drimmelen, J. B. (1975). What are the relationships of quality of patient care to nurses' performance, biographical and personality variables? *Psychological Reports, 36,* 255–266.

Fisher, V. E., & Hanna, J. V. (1931). *The dissatisfied worker.* New York: Macmillan.

Flanagan, J. C. (1960). *Flanagan Industrial Tests: Components.* Chicago: SRA.

Friend, J. G., & Haggard, E. A. (1948). Work adjustment in relation to family background. *Applied Psychological Monographs, 16.* Stanford, CA: Stanford California Press.

George, J. M. (1990). Personality, affect, and behavior in groups. *Journal of Applied Psychology, 75,* 107–116.

Gordon, L. V. (1963). *Gordon Personal Inventory.* New York: Harcourt Brace Jovanovich.

Gordon, L. V. (1963). *Gordon Personal Profile.* New York: Harcourt Brace Jovanovich.

Gordon, L. V. (1960). *Survey of Interpersonal Values.* New York: Harcourt Brace Jovanovich.

Hansen, C. P. (1988). Personality characteristics of the accident involved employee. *Journal of Business and Psychology, 2,* 346–365.

Hansen, C. P. (1989). A causal model of the relationship among accidents, biodata, personality, and cognitive factors. *Journal of Applied Psychology, 74,* 81–90.

Harano, R. M., Peck, R. G., & McBride, R. S. (1975). The prediction of accident liability through biographical data and psychometric tests. *Journal of Safety Research, 7,* 16–52.

Harvey, R. J. (1992). Job analysis. In M. D. Dunnette & L. M. Hough (Eds.), *Handbook of industrial and organizational psychology* (Vol. 2, pp. 71–163). Palo Alto, CA: Consulting Psychologists Press.

Haymaker, J. C. (1986, August). *Biodata as a predictor of employee integrity and turnover.* Paper presented at the annual meeting of the American Psychological Association, Washington, DC.

Hoiberg, A., & Pugh, W. A. (1978). Predicting navy effectiveness: Expectations, motivation, personality, aptitude, and background variables. *Personnel Psychology, 31,* 841–852.

Holland, J. L. (1973). *Making vocational choices: A theory of careers.* Englewood Cliffs, NJ: Prentice-Hall.

Holland, J. L. (1985). *Making vocational choices: A theory of careers.* (2d ed.). Englewood Cliffs, NJ: Prentice-Hall.

Hunter, J. E., & Hunter, R. F. (1984). Validity and utility of alternative predictors of job performance. *Psychological Bulletin, 96,* 72–98.

Johnson, D. A., Newton, N. A., & Peek, L. A. (1979, May–June). Predicting tenure of municipal clerical employees: A multiple regression analysis. *Public Personnel Management,* 182–190.

Kavanagh, M. J., & York, D. R. (1972). Biographical correlates of middle managers' performance. *Personnel Psychology, 25,* 319–332.

King, J. E. (1957). *Precision.* New York: Industrial Psychology, Inc.

LaRocco, J. M., Ryman, D. H., & Biersner, R. J. (1977). Life history and mood as predictors of adjustment in navy recruit training. *Journal of Community Psychology, 5,* 46–51.

Levine, J. M., & Moreland, R. L. (1990). Progress in small group research. *Annual Review of Psychology, 41,* 585–634.

Lucchesi, C. Y. (1983). *The prediction of job satisfaction, life satisfaction, and job level from autobiographical dimensions: A longitudinal application of structural equation modeling.* Unpublished doctoral dissertation, University of Georgia, Athens.

Matteson, M. T. (1978). An alternative approach to using biographical data for predicting job success. *Journal of Occupational Psychology, 51,* 155–162.

McCormick, E. J., Jeanneret, P. R., & Mecham, R. C. (1972). A study of job characteristics and job dimensions as based on the Position Analysis Questionnaire (PAQ). *Journal of Applied Psychology, 56,* 347–368.

McDaniel, M. A. (1989). Biographical constructs for predicting employee suitability. *Journal of Applied Psychology, 74,* 964–970.

McGuire, F. L. (1976). Personality factors in highway accidents. *Human Factors, 18,* 433–442.

Mitchell, T. W. (1992, May). *A priori biodata to predict teamwork, learning rate, and retention.* Paper presented at the annual meeting of the Society of Industrial and Organizational Psychology, Montreal.

Mitchell, T. W., & Klimoski, R. J. (1982). Is it rational to be empirical? A test of methods for scoring biographical data. *Journal of Applied Psychology, 67,* 411–418.

Morrison, R. F., Owens, W. A., Glennon, J. R., & Albright, L. E. (1962). Factored life history antecedents of industrial research performance. *Journal of Applied Psychology, 46*(4), 281–284.

Mumford, M. D., & Owens, W. A. (1982). Life history and vocational interests. *Journal of Vocational Behavior, 21,* 330–348.

Mumford, M. D., & Owens, W. A. (1987). Methodology review: Principles, procedures, and findings in the application of background data measures. *Applied Psychological Measurement, 11*(1), 1–31.

Mumford, M. D., Stokes, G. S., & Owens, W. A. (1990). *Patterns of life history: The ecology of human individuality.* Hillsdale, NJ: Erlbaum.

Owens, W. A., & Schoenfeldt, L. F. (1979). Toward a classification of persons [Monograph]. *Journal of Applied Psychology, 63,* 569–607.

Palmer, H. T. (1992). *An examination of individuals in managerial and nonmanagerial positions using biodata.* Unpublished doctoral dissertation, University of Georgia, Athens.

Reilly, R. R., & Chao, G. T. (1982). Validity and fairness of some alternative employee selection procedures. *Personnel Psychology, 35,* 1–62.

Rothstein, H. R., Schmidt, F. L., Erwin, F. W., Owens, W. A., & Sparks, C. P. (1990). Biographical data in employment selection: Can validities be made generalizable? *Journal of Applied Psychology, 75,* 175–184.

Rotter, J. B. (1966). Generalized expectancies for internal versus external control of reinforcement. *Psychology Monographs, 80* (Whole No. a609).

Russell, C. J., Mattson, J., Devlin, S. E., & Atwater, D. (1990). Predictive validity of biodata items generated from retrospective life experience essays. *Journal of Applied Psychology, 75*(5), 569–580.

Sackett, P. R., Burris, L. R., & Callahan, C. (1989). Integrity testing for personnel selection: An update. *Personnel Psychology, 42,* 491–529.

Sackett, P. R., Schmitt, N., Tenopyr, M. L., Kehoe, J., & Zedeck, S. (1985). Commentary on forty questions about validity generalization and meta-analysis. *Personnel Psychology, 38,* 697–798.

Schmidt, F. L., Law, K., Hunter, J. E., Rothstein, H. R., Pearlman, K., & McDaniel, M. (1993). Refinements in validity generalization methods: Implications for the situational specificity hypothesis. *Journal of Applied Psychology, 78,* 3–12.

Schmitt, N., Gooding, R. Z., Noe, R. A., & Kirsch, M. (1984). Meta-analyses of validity studies published between 1964 and 1982 and the investigation of study characteristics. *Personnel Psychology, 37,* 407–422.

Schneider, B. (1987). The people make the place. *Personnel Psychology, 40,* 437–453.

Shaffer, G. S. (1987). Patterns of work and nonwork satisfaction. *Journal of Applied Psychology, 72,* 115–124.

Stiles, P. M. (1983). *Biographical predictors of job satisfaction.* Unpublished masters thesis, University of Georgia, Athens.

Stokes, G. S., Gore, B. A., Eastman, L., & Morris, D. (1992). *Report on the validation of a test battery to select machine adjusters and craftsmen.* Boston: Scientific Management Techniques.

Stokes, G. S., Hogan, J. B., & Snell, A. F. (in press). Comparability of applicant and incumbent samples for the development of biodata keys: The influence of social desirability. *Personnel Psychology.*

Stokes, G. S., & Mecham, R. C. (1992). *Adolescent life experiences as predictors of work dimensions based on the Position Analysis Questionnaire.* Athens: University of Georgia.

Stokes, G. S., Mecham, R. C., Block, L. K., & Hogan, J. E. (1989, April). *Classification of persons and jobs.* Poster presented at the meeting of the Society for Industrial and Organizational Psychology, Boston.

Stokes, G. S., & Reddy, S. (1992). Use of biographical data in organizational decisions. In C. L. Cooper & I. T. Robertson (Eds.), *International review of industrial and organizational Psychology.* London: Wiley.

Sundstrom, E., DeMeuse, K. P., & Futrell, D. (1990). Work teams: Applications and effectiveness. *American Psychologist, 45,* 120–133.

Tanofsky, R., Shepps, R. R., & O'Neill, P. J. (1969). Pattern analysis of biographical predictors of success as an insurance salesman. *Journal of Applied Psychology, 53*(2),136–139.

Tyler, L. E. (1986). Back to Spearman? *Journal of Vocational Behavior, 29,* 445–450.

Tziner, A., & Eden, D. (1985). Effects of crew composition on crew performance: Does the whole equal the sum of its parts? *Journal of Applied Psychology, 70,* 85–93.

Umeda, J. K., & Frey, D. H. (1974). Life history correlates of ministerial success. *Journal of Vocational Behavior, 4,* 319–324.

Ward, J. J., & Hook, M. E. (1963). Application of an hierarchical grouping procedure to the problem of grouping profiles. *Educational and Psychological Measurement, 23,* 69–81.

Wesley, S. S. (1989). *Background data subgroups and career outcomes: Some developmental influences on person–job matching.* Unpublished doctoral dissertation, Georgia Institute of Technology, Atlanta.

The Impact of Legal and Equal Employment Opportunity Issues on Personal History Inquiries

James C. Sharf

George Washington University

It has been estimated that falsification of credentials among job candidates across the board occurs in about 30 percent of all applications and 15 percent of applications from candidates for high-level positions, with higher incidences during uncertain economic times (Kandel, 1983). In light of this estimate, the issue addressed in this chapter is to what extent may an employer legally use objective selection procedures that probe an applicant's personal history.

First of all, questions perceived as intrusive can result in defamation, invasion of privacy, and infliction of emotional distress tort claims and/or statutory violations brought under federal, state, and local legislation (Kandel, 1990). The most general protection emanates from the U.S. Constitution and a number of state constitutions that protect individuals from governmental invasions of privacy. By contrast, state laws generally apply to inquiries made by private employers.[1]

Although admittedly complex, the legal constraints on the use of objective employment selection procedures have been thoroughly described in a number of sources (Arvey & Farley, 1988; Ballew, 1987; Bersoff, 1981; Booth & Mackay, 1980; Bureau of National Affairs, 1982; "Comment," 1987; Gold, 1985; Gottfredson & Sharf, 1988; Landy, 1986; Ledvinka, 1982; Ledvinka & Schoenfeldt, 1978; Lerner, 1979;

Potter, 1986; Schlei & Grossman, 1983; Schmidt & Hunter, 1981; Sharf, 1988, 1991; Tenopyr, 1981; Thompson & Thompson, 1982; and Wunder & Sparks, 1991). This chapter is more narrowly focused on that aspect of employment testing that Owens (1976) refers to as the objective measurement of prior experience in the form of scored autobiographical questions.

Such autobiographical personal history questions are referred to as *biodata*. In identifying the legal and EEO constraints on the use of personal history questions for employment selection purposes, one necessarily needs to address the most basic question of just what selection procedures are included under the rubric of biodata.

In the most basic sense, biodata describe the many ways in which the behavior of an individual can be said to be similar to, or different from, the behavior of all other individuals. At its most abstract level, Mumford, Stokes, and Owens (1990) discuss biodata as follows:

> A legitimate indicator of individuality exists whenever variance among individuals exceeds that attributable to random measurement error. Thus, the sheer number of behaviors that could be legitimate indicators of individuality prohibits a comprehensive description of every person in terms of all their discrete behaviors. Consequently, a perennial problem entails determining how information derived from various indicators of individuality across persons may be summarized in a viable description of the individual. (p. 4)

Thus, an obvious starting point in addressing the legality of using biodata for employment selection purposes is to take a look at how the data universe of discrete personal history questions may be reduced to a more manageable form.

Over the years, some researchers have focused on organizing the universe of discrete personal history questions into a series of taxonomies (Fleishman & Quaintance, 1984; Landy & Farr, 1983; Mumford & Owens, 1984; Mumford et al., 1990). Among the earliest efforts to develop biodata taxonomies organized around categories of personal history questions are those of Glennon, Albright, and Owens (1961), shown in Appendix A, and England (1971), shown in Appendix B. Other biodata taxonomies include the research of Morrison, Owens, Glennon, and Albright (1962); Owens (1968, 1971, 1976); Owens and Schoenfeldt (1979); and Schoenfeldt (1974).

These biodata taxonomies provide an economical way of getting a handle on biodata by elevating the focus from the data universe level of specific personal history questions to the information level of categories of behavior. As can be seen in Appendices A and B, the behavioral categories used in each taxonomy reveal a substantial level of agreement between taxonomic categories, even though there is not a perfect match of discrete personal history questions within specific categories.

Although the focus of this chapter will be on legal constraints affecting the use of discrete personal history questions for employment selection purposes, efforts will be made to draw more general conclusions about those behavioral categories identified in the biodata taxonomies in Appendices A and B that have been found to be predictive of job success.

RIGHT TO PRIVACY ISSUES

Privacy is hardly a new issue facing behavioral scientists (Executive Office of the President, 1967; Harris & Westin, 1979; Jones, Ash, & Soto, 1989; National Association of Attorneys General, 1976). In addition to the Constitution, the principal legal constraint at the federal level is the Privacy Act of 1974. Although the 1974 Privacy Act provided relatively few specifics regarding prohibited categories of personal history information, there was an appreciation for the larger public policy responsibility that is borne by the federal government. Congress was aware that employers were able to have data bases swept to obtain information such as an applicant's financial condition, criminal and driving records, arrests, and workers' compensation filings. As Rothfeder (1990) put it, "for employers, it's far easier to scan a list and read a report than to step through the legal mine fields posed by a fac-to-face talk" (p. 128).

In passing the Privacy Act of 1974, Congress took notice that "the right to privacy is a personal and fundamental right protected by the Constitution of the United States" (P.I. 93-579, Sec. 2(b)4). Under the Privacy Act of 1974, Congress directed federal agencies to "collect information to the greatest extent practicable directly from the subject individual when the information may result in adverse determinations about an individual's rights, benefits, and privileges under federal programs" (5 U.S.C. 552(e)(2)).

Thus the Privacy Act of 1974 did not discourage federal use of personal history information, as long as it is collected directly from the individual— as is generally the case with objectively scored biodata questionnaires.

More recently, the Office of Technology Assessment (OTA; 1990), a research arm of the U.S. Congress, issued a report that gave additional guidance to biodata users with regard to privacy rights. The report focused on pencil-and-paper integrity testing for preemployment screening but spoke to the more general issue of a job applicant's privacy rights:

> In 1967, the Office of Science and Technology of the Executive Office of the President established a panel to examine the issue of privacy and behavioral research [which] defined the right to privacy as "the right of the individual to decide for himself how much he will share with others his thoughts, his feelings, and the facts of his personal life." (p. 71)

> Perhaps the central reason that the privacy debate is difficult to unravel is that although privacy is a fundamental value in our society, it is not well conceptualized and is difficult to define. Three central aspects of privacy do recur,

however...: First, there is the notion that certain types of information are inherently private. Second is the concept of a boundary between the individual and others; people should know the boundary between themselves and others and understand what information is crossing it. The third conceptual issue is the responsibility of organizations with regard to personal information. (p. 73)

An applicant may believe that his or her answers to a question or series of questions is legitimate, but if the answers are then interpreted to make specific conclusions about propensity for future behavior, the applicant may feel that his or her privacy has been invaded. (p. 73)

Even a valid psychological reason must be weighed along with social and ethical concerns to determine the appropriate balance between the individual's right to privacy and the employer's right (or need) to choose employees who will not commit certain acts. (p. 71)

By the nature of the personal history questions asked, integrity testing may be more intrusive of personal privacy, but biodata users need to be sensitized to these same issues. Although the OTA report focused on integrity testing, the report also makes the following points regarding the precedent of case law as of the fall of 1990 when the report was completed:

To date, there has not been a published negligent hiring case in which an employer's defense rested on the use of paper-and-pencil integrity tests....(p. 30)

Evidence on the precise role of test scores in hiring does not exist in the aggregate, and there have been no individual cases decided in which plaintiffs argue that an integrity test per se was the basis of discrimination. (p. 70)

TRENDS IN LITIGATION

Recent litigation reveals that employers have become increasingly wary of lawsuits charging libel, defamation of character, or invasion of privacy by former employees who are turned down for a new job because of remarks made by a former employer (Minuti, 1988; Walker, 1984). A recent survey by the National Association of Corporate and Professional Recruiters shows that an overwhelming majority of the companies surveyed—81 percent—try to check references before a job offer is made. At the same time, however, nearly half of all companies contacted now have a policy against giving references to current or former employees ("Privacy," 1988, p. 64).

Even though inquiries directed to a candidate's former employers are likely to go unanswered, an employer may be liable for an employee's conduct for *not* asking about the candidate's personal history. Under "negligent hiring" doctrine, employers may be liable for the wrongful action of their employees, even if the action occurred outside the scope of employment, if employers do not exercise reasonable care in selecting and retaining competent and safe employees. If an employee injures a third party as a result of the employer's failure to ascertain and deal with "dangerous proclivities" that should have been known, then tort liability may befall the employer (Kandel, 1990, p. 83). This legal double bind finds the employer unwilling to release personal history information regarding former employees and at the same time pursuing the very same personal history information about candidates for employment.

The scope of employers' concerns with privacy issues was the subject of cover stories in *Business Week* ("Privacy," 1988), which forecasted that "privacy may be the most important social issue in the 1990s."

More recently, *Business Week* ("Is Your Boss," 1990) wrote of the litigation brought under the California State Constitution (*Soroka v. Dayton-Hudson Corporation*) resulting from an employer's use of the MMPI, which asked about the individual's sexual preferences, bladder function, and religious convictions:

> It isn't information that most people volunteer [and] employees can sue for invasion of privacy. But to win damages, judges have said, workers must prove that their "reasonable expectations of privacy" outweigh the company's reasons for spying. That dispute over work place privacy highlights what will be "the hottest employment-law topic of the 1990s." (p. 74)

Reilly and Warech (in press) make much the same point with regard to personal privacy sensitivities in using biodata:

> Because of their atheoretical nature, biodata scores have poor face validity and it is difficult to give candidates meaningful feedback on their performance. This may lead to some perception of unfairness on the part of job applicants. Secondly, applicants may object to some biodata questions as invasive of their privacy.

AN INCREASINGLY CONFOUNDED STATE AND LOCAL REGULATORY WEB

Wholly aside from privacy issues becoming "the hottest employment-law topic of the 1990s" ("Is Your Boss," 1990), private sector employers with employees in more than one political jurisdiction will be increasingly confounded by the regulatory web of state and local laws, regulations, and guidelines (Gerstner, 1990). Included within this web are prohibitions against asking specific personal history questions in the employment context (Ash, 1989, 1991; Gibbons, 1980; Greenwalt, 1975; Kandel, 1989). For example, section 1 of the California State Constitution describes the "inalienable right" of citizens to privacy in matters such as the right to control what information is collected about a person and how such information is kept and used, as well as the right to inspect any information collected to correct errors it may contain.

States are already being pressured to address genetic screening, perhaps the most intrusive of all personal history inquiries. For example, several states, including Iowa, Wisconsin, and Oregon, have passed laws barring employers from using genetic screening that discriminates against "at risk" candidates such as carriers of sickle cell anemia. As of the summer of 1993, however, there have been few workplace discriminations resulting from genetic screening. A 1989 survey of the nation's 500 largest companies by the congressional Office of Technology Assessment found that fewer than five percent had conducted some form of genetic screening. "But some geneticists expect that to change as the costs drop and a wider variety of diseases can be diagnosed....At least half the states are debating this issue" ("Biotech Debate," 1992, H1).

Ash (1989, 1991) has compiled a listing of specific personal history questions (see Appendix C) that are prohibited by statute, regulation, and guidelines at the various state and local levels of government. Thus, state and local jurisdictions may prohibit practices not prohibited by federal law, but they may not authorize employment practices that would violate federal law. This point will become even more germane in the context of EEO laws where state laws have in several instances exceeded the Federal Title VII burden of proof.

Perhaps even more confounding is Mitchell's (1989) compilation of specific personal history questions (see Appendix D), each of which has been shown empirically to predict sales success but has nonetheless been specifically prohibited by state preemployment inquiry laws, regulations, and guidelines.

Some of the personal history questions identified by Ash in Appendix C and Mitchell in Appendix D that are prohibited by one or more state or local jurisdictions are also noted in the Glennon and England biodata taxonomies in Appendices A and B. Inspecting those behavioral categories that include prohibited questions reveals a consistent pattern. Prohibited personal history questions are found in the taxonomic categories of classification/personal data (such as marital status), health, money, and socioeconomic level/financial status.

An inspection of Appendices A and B will reveal, however, that the majority of categories of personal history questions have not been affected by state and local prohibitions. Nevertheless, based on the likelihood that the right to privacy will become an increasingly sensitive issue, it is reasonable to expect that state and local jurisdictions will continue to expand the prohibitions against employers asking specific personal history questions. Accordingly, biodata users should view the classic biodata taxonomies in Appendices A and B as a contemporary "score card" for anticipating and avoiding the ever more confounded state and local regulatory web.

TITLE VII OF THE CIVIL RIGHTS ACTS OF 1964 AND 1991

Since biodata items are objective measures of prior experiences in the form of scored autobiographical questions (Owens, 1976), the starting point for understanding the EEO laws is to define the legal standard by which employers are held accountable for using any objective selection procedures. Objective employment selection procedures have been successfully challenged under the disparate impact (adverse impact) theory of discrimination under Title VII of the Civil Rights Act of 1964 (Lee, 1988).

The disparate impact definition of discrimination has now been codified in Sec. 105(a) of the Civil Rights Act of 1991, under which an employer has the *burden of persuasion* in defending any selection procedure, including biodata, which adversely affects candidates on the basis of race, color, religion, sex, and national origin. The employer must "demonstrate that the challenged practice is job related for the position in question and consistent with business necessity." Upon such a demonstration, a charging party could still prevail, however, by demonstrating that there is an "alternative employment practice" with less adverse impact "and the respondent refuses to adopt such alternative employment practice."

Biodata will become increasingly attractive as an "alternative selection procedure" under Title VII because empirically keyed, valid biodata instruments generally have comparable validity to more generalizable cognitive ability measures but have less adverse impact (Reilly & Warech, in press):

> Research has demonstrated that empirically keyed biodata instruments have validities approaching, and sometimes exceeding, that of cognitive ability tests for a wide variety of job-related behavior.

> The available research suggests that biodata may have less adverse impact than tests and appears to meet the standard definition of fairness to minorities.

Sec. 105(b) of the Civil Rights Act of 1991 stipulates that the concepts of *job relatedness* and *business necessity* are to be interpreted in light of the precedent of Supreme Court decisions prior to *Wards Cove Packing Co. v. Atonio.* Because the Act does not further define these critical terms other than to defer to the precedent of Supreme Court decisions, litigation again becomes the consequence of Congress' unwillingness to make the hard legislative decisions (Sharf, 1988). Interestingly enough, however, in the quarter century since the Civil Rights Act of 1964 became law, a search of the precedent of Title VII case law reveals no challenges to biodata but does show that the Justice Department recommended use of a biodata instrument in a public sector consent decree ("Las Vegas Police," 1987).[2]

CHALLENGING BIODATA ITEMS AS COMPONENTS OF SELECTION PROCEDURES

One of the most problematic implications of Title VII case law involves determining whether plaintiffs' discovery will be permitted to be pursued to the item level.[3] Although employers may not keep discrete information on *each component* of the overall selection decision, which generally includes combining both objective and subjective information, a potential problem arises from the fact that discrete item analysis information is available. Discrete item analysis is a requisite step in empirically keying biodata questions at the item or item alternative level. In other words, much in the same vein as Willy Sutton's defense that the reason he robbed banks is because that was where the money was, biodata items may become vulnerable to challenge because discrete item analysis information is a matter of record and, therefore, likely to attract adversarial attention (in the same way, incidently, that validation studies did as a consequence of *Griggs*).

Two Title VII decisions have addressed the issue of plaintiffs advocating that objective selection procedures be defended at the subtest/item level rather than at the level of the total test.[4] In *Kirkland v. New York Department of Corrections,* the trial court held:

> Any...approach (other than scrutinizing the overall examination procedure) conflicts with the dictates of common sense. Achieving at least a passing score on the examination in its entirety determines eligibility for appointment, regardless of performance on individual subtests. Accordingly, plaintiffs' case stands or falls on comparative pass rates alone.

The Sixth Circuit's reasoning was similar in *Smith v. Troyan* in rejecting plaintiffs' advocacy that the employer defend "subtests":

> That blacks fare less well than whites on the..."subtest" in the process of hiring East Cleveland police officers is insufficient in itself to require defendants to

justify the [subtest] as being job-related. Carried to its logical extreme, such a criterion would require the elimination of individual questions marked by poorer performance by a racial group, on the ground that such a question was a "subtest" of the "subtest."

GENERALLY ACCEPTED PRINCIPLES
REGARDING ITEM DISCLOSURE

The American Psychological Association (APA, 1990) has drafted a statement on the Disclosure of Test Scores, Test Items, and Test Protocols, which undoubtedly will come into play if Title VII litigation is pursued to the item level. In this statement, it is proposed that

APA strongly opposes the release of...test items....

First,...appropriate use can not be ensured if...test items...are released to individuals who are not professionally qualified to interpret them because they lack the technical knowledge and training....

Second, interpretations and recommendations which are derived from assessment should be based on the individual's performance on one or more complete assessment techniques...not responses to individual items....

Third, disclosure of test items or test protocols containing individual items to unqualified persons may decrease the test's validity....

Finally, disclosure of test items and test protocols may constitute an infringement of Section 117 of the copyright law.

In legal proceedings, should a court persist in requiring release of...test items...psychologists should request: (1) the court issue a protective order prohibiting parties from making copies of these materials;...(3) materials not be publicly available as part of the case record; (4) testimony on specific items and responses be sealed and not included in the record; and (5) pleadings and other documents filed should not, unless absolutely necessary, reference individual items and responses, and any portion of any document that does so should be sealed.

Several years earlier, the APA (1988) had adopted a policy regarding proposed legislation based on the "Golden Rule" settlement that would have required the discarding of test items with response rates that differed when comparing minorities to nonminorities. Again in the context of possible Title VII challenges to biodata items, the position of the APA (1988) with regard to item deletion challenges is worth noting:

The "Golden Rule" refers to a settlement agreement between the Golden Rule Insurance Company and the Educational Testing Service (ETS) concerning tests developed by ETS for the Illinois Insurance licensing examinations. The most frequently quoted aspect of the settlement concerns the use of test items for which majority and minority groups have differential correct response rates....There is considerable concern that scientific judgments may be compromised by legal and political considerations promulgated as a result of the Golden Rule agreement....When any bias reduction technique is designated in legislation, the following issues must be considered.

First, the mere existence of differences between groups is not an accurate indication of bias....Differences between groups also may reflect valid behavioral differences....Specifying arbitrary values for correct response rates for items and arbitrary value differences between groups is not a sound practice.

Second, selective elimination of items is not acceptable if it results in the removal or underrepresentation of content areas that upon careful consideration are viewed as relevant.

Third, procedures that require choosing items on the basis of considerations other than those leading to optimal measurement of the relevant construct are likely to lower the psychometric quality of the test....The inclusion of items with relatively lower reliability and validity for the sole purpose of reducing group differences could likely result in poorer tests.

Fourth, the elimination of difficult items actually may not reduce potential differences in mean test scores between minority and non-minority groups. Its results actually are unpredictable. It either may enlarge or reduce differences between groups.

There is no scientific justification for the prescription of any single technique of items bias detection in the test construction process.

In summary, with regard to Federal EEO laws, Title VII precedent may be read to favor the adoption of biodata as a "suitable alternative" selection procedure having validity comparable to more generalizable cognitive ability tests but with substantially less adverse impact. Discrete personal history questions may be scrutinized, however, as "components" of selection procedures having adverse impact, even though lower courts have previously ruled against defending subtests and test items. The profession is clearly opposed either to disclosing test items generally or to discarding valid test items because of group differences, although it should be noted that the decision of whether to key a biodata item with empirical validity may consider differences in response rates across subgroups covered by Title VII. Just how far Title VII will be litigated in pursuit of "components" of selection procedures having adverse impact may be of considerable concern to all employment test users, but especially to users of biodata because of the availability of item analysis data as a matter of record.

THE AMERICANS WITH DISABILITIES ACT OF 1990

The Americans With Disabilities Act (ADA) of 1990 became effective July, 1992, and covers 43 million disabled Americans of whom 67 percent are unemployed ("Small Business," 1989). The ADA was reported by *The New York Times* as

> amount[ing] to a bill of rights...culminat[ing] more than two decades of efforts by the handicapped to gain recognition as an oppressed minority....Said Senator Edward M. Kennedy..."This legislation will go down as one of the most important accomplishments in the history of the Congress." (Rasky, 1989, p. E–5)

The ADA does not merely prohibit discrimination against the disabled (as Title VII prohibits discrimination against minorities and women), but imposes an affirmative obligation on employers to "reasonably accommodate" each disabled individual. The ADA does not preempt any existing federal or state law. Thus, a single violation can subject an employer to actions under the ADA, the Rehabilitation Act of 1973, and/or state and local discrimination laws and various tort causes of action.

Title 1 of the ADA deals with employment and is modeled on Section 504 of the Rehabilitation Act of 1973, which imposes nondiscrimination obligations on the recipients of federal grants. Efforts have been made to investigate the effects of nonstandardized test administration on the handicapped (Nester, 1984), but the research findings in the academic context have not been particularly encouraging for employment testing. Those verbal, quantitative, and reasoning skills that are generally predictive of job performance are the very skills required for academic performance (Willingham et al., 1988).

Indeed, with regard to the testing of handicapped persons as required by the Rehabilitation Act of 1973, the National Research Council in 1982 noted: "Industrial psychologists have serious doubts as to whether compliance with the regulations concerning testing of the handicapped is possible" (Sherman & Robinson, 1982, p. 982).

DEFINITIONS

The definition of *disability* in the ADA is quite comprehensive and covers 900 different conditions, actual or perceived:

> The term "disability" means, with respect to an individual (a) a physical or mental impairment that substantially limits one or more of the major life activities of such individual; (b) a record of such an impairment; or (c) being regarded as having such an impairment. (ADA, Section 3)

What is meant by "substantially limits one or more major life activities" will necessarily be determined in case-by-case litigation, since Congress chose not to define this term in the ADA.

Under Title 1: Employment, an employer may not deny an employment opportunity to a "qualified individual with a disability" if the denial is based on the need to make "reasonable accommodation" for the physical or mental impairment of the individual so that he or she can perform an "essential function" of the job, unless to do so "would impose an undue hardship on the operation of the business" (see Appendix E).

IMPLICATIONS

First of all, Sec. 102(b)(1) of the ADA refers to an "adverse impact" trigger to create a prima facie presumption of discrimination. The most basic question, therefore, becomes whether a statistical disparity alone will be sufficient under the ADA to create a prima facie presumption of discrimination and thus shift the burden of proof to the employer to demonstrate that the selection procedure is "job-related and consistent with business necessity, and such performance cannot be accomplished by reasonable accommodation" (see Sec. 103, Appendix E). The fact that the accommodation is necessary cannot be an adverse factor in the employment decision. Furthermore, a plaintiff need not prove that the alleged discrimination was based solely on a disability. Instead, "a violation occurs where discrimination on the basis of disability is a 'factor.' "

The Supreme Court has addressed the use of statistical disparities as prima facie evidence of discrimination under Section 504 of the Rehabilitation Act of 1973 upon which the ADA was modeled. The unanimous Supreme Court in 1985 in *Alexander v. Choate* decided against use of the statistical disparity definition of "adverse impact" to establish a Section 504 prima facie case. (See Appendix F for court reasoning.)

Choate stood for the proposition that the Rehabilitation Act of 1973 was meant to open the doors of opportunity in terms of equal treatment but did not validate the use of statistical disparities to establish a prima facie adverse impact presumption of discrimination.

The regulatory and judicial interpretation of Sec. 102(b) (6) will be of considerable consequence to industrial and organizational psychologists as the precedent of case law under the ADA is established. If courts interpret the ADA as Section 504 of the Rehabilitation Act of 1973 was interpreted by the Supreme Court in *Choate,* an individual claim will not automatically be established on the statistical "disparate impact" ("adverse impact") theory of discrimination but more likely on the "disparate treatment" theory.[5] Should courts *not* follow *Choate's* lack of enthusiasm for statistical "disparate impact" arguments, use of virtually any objective employment standard would create a prima facie liability under the ADA. Thus, this aspect of case law will be of considerable consequence.

Second, with regard to the reference in Sec. 101(8) to the performance of "essential functions," a Senate Labor Committee report states that *essential functions* are "job tasks that are fundamental and not marginal," which one attorney has described as "defining the obscure by the vague" (Lindsay, 1989).

> What is clear is that in determining whether a person can carry out the essential functions of a job, job tasks will have to be evaluated in some detail, as will the nature and extent of the claimant's impairment.
>
> "Individualized" inquiry will preclude employers from obtaining a speedy disposition of most claims. In *Hall v. U.S. Postal Service*, 857 F.2d 1073 (6th Cir. 1988), a federal appeals court denied an employer summary judgment even though the job description for the position in question specified that an employee "must be able to lift 70 pounds," and the claimant conceded she "could not lift that much." The court concluded there was a "genuine factual dispute regarding the essential functions of the...position" based on an affidavit from the claimant that she never observed any employees in the position "doing any heavy lifting." Significantly, the decision in *Hall* was cited with approval by the Senate Labor Committee report. This detailed review of job duties may also require many employers to quantify the time that is actually spent on essential tasks by each employee. In *Ackerman v. Western Electric Company*, 643 F. Supp. 836 (N.D. Cal. 1986), aff'd, 860 F.2d 1514 (9th Cir. 1988), the court, in applying a California statute very similar to the ADA, stated that the employer could not successfully defend a claim brought by an asthmatic telecommunications equipment installer by showing that certain tasks were essential functions for installers "as a group," because these tasks were "not essential to any particular individual's performance of the job." The court then examined how much time the claimant spent on tasks that might interfere with her asthma and, finding that about 12 percent of her time was spent on such tasks, concluded that these tasks were "proportionately so insignificant that (they) cannot be considered an essential function of her position." Use of this proportionality test raises the question: What proportion would have been significant? 20 percent? 30 percent?

Third, defining what is meant by "appropriate adjustment or modifications of examinations, training materials, or policies" (Sec. 101(9)) raises the most basic question of how the ADA will influence an employer's use of any standardized, objective selection procedure. (See Appendix G for the APA's statement in its *Standards for Educational and Psychological Testing* (1985) with regard to the "adjustment or modification" language in Sec. 101(9) (B) of the ADA.)

Fourth, the ADA's definition of employment discrimination may have a negative impact on the use of personal history questions, since under Sec. 102(b)(7), an otherwise valid selection procedure should not reflect a sensory, manual, or speaking impairment unless it is intended to measure such skills. Obviously the critical issue is whether the ADA is interpreted under the "disparate treatment" or "disparate impact" theory of discrimination. If statistical disparities are sufficient under the ADA to establish a prima facie presumption of discrimination under the "disparate impact" interpretation, then the most basic question in reviewing the taxonomies in Appendices A and B becomes whether there are any categories of behavior that would not indirectly reflect a disabled individual's sensory, manual, or speaking impairment (Potter & Reesman, 1990).

Should statistical disparities alone be sufficient to establish a prima facie presumption of discrimination under the ADA, then Sec. 102(b) (7) could be construed to favor content validity ("where such skills are the factors that the test purports to measure") over other types of validity evidence. Support for this interpretation can be found in the legislative history of the ADA, where Sec. 102(b) (6) is referred to as providing the "framework for employment selection procedures which is designed to assure that persons with disabilities are not excluded from job opportunities *unless they are actually unable to do the job"* (emphasis added; *House Labor Report* at 71; *Senate Report* at 37). On the other hand, if the "disparate treatment" theory prevails under the ADA, use of a standardized, job-related employment procedure would be likely to prevail no matter what line(s) of validity evidence were developed. Of course, if a selection procedure is designed to measure "skills...that the test purports to measure," then Sec. 102(b) (7) does not require any modification. Such a stipulation, however, is of little comfort to users of biodata since biodata frequently describes *signs* rather than *samples* of prior behavior (Wernimont & Campbell, 1968).

Additionally, with regard to personal history questions, Sec. 102(c) of the ADA categorically prohibits inquiries regarding an applicant's physical or mental condition. As is shown below, the employer may inquire only about the ability to perform job-related functions:

Sec. 102(c) Medical examinations and inquiries.
(2) Preemployment.
(A) Prohibited examination or inquiry. (An employer)...shall not...make inquiries of a job applicant as to whether such applicant is an individual with a disability or as to the nature or severity of such disability.
(B) Acceptable inquiry. (An employer) may make preemployment inquiries into the ability of an applicant to perform job-related functions.

Literally applied, Sec. 102(c) (2) (A) would preclude personal history questions that were signs of an individual's disability in the sense of indirectly identifying that disabled person's condition, such as not having participated in team sports, debating society, or cheerleading, to give but a few obvious examples.

Finally, as is frequently the case when Congress chooses not to define basic terms in sweeping legislative enactments, what is meant by "undue hardship" under the ADA will ultimately be left up to the courts. The situationally specific criteria defining "undue hardship" guarantee that there will be extensive litigation over many years before the precedent of case law defining "reasonable accommodation" can be generalized to a new situation. This could be one of the reasons that the *Wall Street Journal* editorial ("The Lawyer's," 1989) referred to the ADA as "The Lawyer's Employment Act: Like so much recent federal law-making, the bill is a swamp of imprecise language: it will mostly benefit lawyers who will cash in on the litigation that will force judges to, in effect, write the real law" (p. A–18).

More surprising was the position taken by the *New York Times* ("Blank Check," 1989) in an editorial that the ADA was a "blank check for the disabled":

> Predictions about the bill's projected benefits are obviously speculative. Worse, nobody has even tried to speculate about its costs....No one wishes to stint on helping the disabled. It requires little legislative skill, however, to write blank checks for worthy causes with other people's money. (p. A-24)

ENFORCEMENT

The Equal Employment Opportunity Commission issued ADA regulations in July, 1991, fleshing out their first regulatory suggestion of what the ADA is to mean in practice. It is likely that the EEOC will advocate in both regulations and in court what it intends the ADA to mean, and it is not unrealistic to expect that the special interests of 43 million disabled Americans will also be advocated in amicus briefs directed to the trial courts and, in all eventuality, to the Supreme Court. Undoubtedly, considerable attention on both sides of the table will be given to just what it means "to discriminate" under the ADA.

Should the courts interpret the ADA under a "disparate impact" theory, the most problematic aspect of the ADA with regard to standardized use of valid biodata instruments will be whether the employer "discriminates" in failing to modify a standardized set of questions in response to a disabled individual's request to obtain "reasonable accommodation" by dropping certain questions. The employer will be burdened to argue that non-standardized administration would constitute an "undue hardship" on account of the loss of validity since modification of a standardized instrument influences validity in unknown ways (AERA, APA, & NCME, 1985).

In other words, the employer could be burdened to defend why exceptions should not be made for specific biodata items, the modification or removal of which would afford "reasonable accommodation," which is defined in the ADA to include "appropriate adjustments or modifications of examinations." For an employer successfully to defend an ADA challenge to a discrete personal history question within a standardized instrument successfully, a detailed, fact-specific, individualized inquiry of whether such accommodation would impose an "undue hardship" is required. But even when the issue is determined, it will be unlikely to generalize readily because of the situational specificity of the precedent. If the courts interpret the ADA under the "disparate treatment" theory, however, the issue of "reasonable accommodation" may not be as likely to be sought in modifying valid, objective selection procedures (including biodata). This would be the case because all applicants would be treated the same (no "disparate treatment") and statistical disparities would *not* be sufficient to establish a prima facie presumption of discrimination.

DISCUSSION

Three legal theories influencing the use of personal history inquiries have been discussed in this chapter. First, with regard to privacy, the prudent employer and industrial and organizational psychologist would be well advised to avoid those categories of personal history questions in the biodata taxonomies found in Appendices A and B that have already been found invasive of personal privacy under an increasingly confounded regulatory web of state and local laws, regulations, and guidelines. Invasive personal history questions are largely to be found in the following categories: classification/personal data (such as marital status), health, money and socioeconomic level/financial status. Incidently, should privacy become "the issue of the 90s," the classic biodata taxonomies in Appendices A and B may provide a convenient "score card" for tracking the precedent of case law and identifying those categories of personal history questions to be avoided.

Second, with regard to Title VII, as previously mentioned, there is no precedent of case law addressing the use of biodata for employment selection purposes (although the U.S. Department of Justice has recommended use of biodata in a consent decree). What is problematic under Title VII is whether item analyses will be discoverable as "components" of selection procedures. If item analysis data were to be disclosed, researchers would be asked to explain item selection decision rules since it would become apparent that statistical significance is a necessary, but not sufficient, prerequisite to "keying" an item. The decision on whether or not to key any biodata item alternative would likely be found to entail judgmental discretion, such as considering differences in response rates between groups in classes covered by Title VII. Because large differences in item response rates result in "adverse impact," the exercising of discretion not to use such items at least partly explains why biodata typically have less "adverse impact" than cognitive ability tests. An obvious next step might be to burden the user to justify using items with *any* adverse impact.

For example, a biodata item asking about sports might show empirically that those individuals who participated in sports performed better than others on a relevant criterion measure (such as job performance), and that members of one group (race? sex? religion?) participated more frequently in sports than members of another group. Even though such a hypothetical item empirically "keys," when faced with a large disparity in response rates between groups in a class covered by Title VII, the researcher may either counterbalance such an item with an item chosen more frequently by other groups in the class or may choose not to use the item. If such judgmental discretion were to be eliminated, however, by a statutory or regulatory rule stipulating acceptable response rate differences, it would likely result in abandoning entire biodata categories such as "school" and "education."

Another liability of disclosing item selection decision rules may be described as the "perishable" nature of the biodata validity evidence. Explaining a biodata item decision rule is to identify the key that reveals how an item alternative is scored. Although a researcher may be encouraged to explain what makes a biodata instrument useful in predicting a criterion of interest, such well-intended explanations may ultimately destroy the validity of the biodata instrument. Public disclosure of an item key, or even a general explanation of what is being measured by the items, would likely invite coaching in which an applicant would be tempted (if not encouraged) to second-guess keyed alternatives rather than candidly and honestly choose the alternative most descriptive of his or her prior experience.

If most applicants were to choose a "keyed" alternative, the effect would be to give everyone credit for the item, and the item would no longer be useful for distinguishing between levels of experience. The net effect of a disclosed "key" or an explanation of what is being measured would lead to an increasing percentage of applicants who do well as the "key" becomes known. When this happens, the validity would have figuratively perished since the test would no longer be distinguishing between levels of experience but would be measuring the effectiveness of test coaching.

Should the burden of proof fall on the employer under Title VII to defend discrete personal history questions that have adverse impact, for reasons detailed below, more than empirical evidence may be required to satisfy job-relatedness and/or business necessity.

The profession's concern with the lack of understanding regarding biodata measures is hardly new and has often been characterized as "dustbowl empiricism." In 1965, the year that Title VII became the law of the land, Guion observed:

> Testing techniques can be used to reliably quantify observations or other variables which are not in themselves tests, [such as a] "score" given to responses on an application blank....What do such predictors measure? Unfortunately, one often does not know what specific traits are represented by these numbers. From a theoretical point of view, at least, such "measures" obviously leave much to be desired.
>
> The fact remains, however, that they often do correlate reliably with criteria. To the extent that the correlations are statistically significant, these predictors actually do add to the predictive effectiveness of tests more firmly based on psychological theory. It would be poor economy for a test specialist to refuse to use something he does not fully understand when it adds appreciably to the predictive validity of his test batteries. (p. 380)

Raw empiricism alone in the form of criterion-related validity evidence at the item and/or item alternative level will likely prove less and less useful in defending the job-relatedness of biodata under either Title VII or the ADA. Given today's even more complicated burden of proof, Pace and Schoenfeldt's 1977 observation was prescient:

> The criterion-related validity of weighted applications is not at issue....The standard procedure may, however, weight items bearing no rational relationship to the job in question. To quote Guion (1965): "The procedure is raw empiricism in the extreme; the 'score' is the most heterogeneous value imaginable, representing a highly complex and unusually unraveled network of information." The [authors] contend that criterion-related validity may be insufficient excuse for the continued use of an application which weights non-job-relevant items in a discriminatory manner. (p. 160)

The profession has become far more demanding of the burden to justify biodata than in the recent past. Should the Title VII burden of proof be successfully construed by the plaintiffs' bar as requiring biodata validity evidence at the item level, the American Psychological Association's amicus brief filed with the U.S. Supreme Court in 1987 in *Watson v. Fort Worth Bank and Trust Co.* will undoubtedly be cited:

> The use of past experience to make judgments about future performance...is one aspect of a recognized selection device called biographical inventory technique or, more commonly, "biodata." See Owens, Background Data in *Handbook of Industrial and Organizational Psychology* (M. Dunnette, ed., 1976). When used properly, biographical inventories which include prior experiences are "especially appropriate for assessing the qualifications of women and minority groups." See A. Anastasi *Psychological Testing* 616 (5th ed., 1982). To serve this purpose, however, *the biodata inventory must focus on "specific, job-*

relevant past achievements, rather than on the passive exposure implied by the customary education and experience records"....As with all selection devices, *the most reasonable and justifiable approach in biodata is to base the choice of items on a well-done job analysis, matching the items to the knowledge, skill and ability requirements of the job descriptions.* See Pace & Schoenfeldt, Legal Concerns in the Use of Weighted Applications, 30 *Personnel Psychology,* 159 (1977). *Past experience alone, without the careful selection of both logically and empirically justified life-history questions, is unacceptable as a selection device.* (emphasis added)

Thus it would seem that the position of the APA requiring "both logically and empirically justified life-history questions" will increasingly become the standard *if* the Title VII burden of proof is construed to reach the level of discrete biodata items.

Taxonomies will become increasingly central in addressing the question of what psychological constructs are being measured by discrete biodata items. Although the generalizability of a specific biodata instrument for the same job across organizations has been reported by Rothstein, Schmidt, Erwin, Owens, and Sparks (1990), as Reilly and Warech (in press) note:

The atheoretical, empirical nature of most biodata instruments presents special problems in assessing the generalizability of results across studies. For example, biodata instruments do not purport to measure specific constructs that might allow studies of discriminant and convergent validity. Indeed, it is difficult to obtain information from study to study that includes the types of items that might consistently predict certain types of behaviors.

The strategic use of biodata taxonomies in designing biodata research has already been anticipated by Gandy et al. (see Chapter 11 of this volume), as reported in their chapter in this handbook (see also Gandy, Outerbridge, Sharf, & Dye, 1989). Gandy's chapter reveals that decision rules were developed to consider only those categories of biodata judged to be relevant in the first instance; confirmatory factor analysis research was pursued after the validity had been established in order to understand more completely what behavior was actually being measured. If the APA's amicus position in *Watson* (cited above) is any indication of the direction in which the generally accepted principles and practices of personnel psychology is moving, Gandy et al. and Rothstein et al. (1990) can be viewed as prototypical biodata research designs, to be emulated and elaborated in the years to come.

The Americans With Disabilities Act of 1990 will require the attention of industrial and organizational psychologists. Whether the ADA will be interpreted under a "disparate treatment" or "disparate impact" theory of discrimination has considerable consequence for all users of valid, objective selection procedures.

Under a "disparate impact" theory, an employer using virtually any valid, objective selection procedure may well be challenged to provide "reasonable accommodation" by eliminating those specific test items adversely affecting an impaired individual. The same line of reasoning may burden employers to provide "reasonable accommodation" by dropping discrete personal history questions from a valid biodata instrument. Although this may seem inconsequential to a plaintiff alleging discrimination on the grounds of a disability, dropping items from a standardized instrument affects validity and established norms in an unknown way, as the APA has pointed out. Should the precedent of ADA case law develop under the "disparate impact" theory, there may be opportunities for the Society of Industrial and Organizational Psychology to advise trial courts, even the Supreme Court, as to whether confounding the validity of a valid biodata instrument by dropping an item or items constitutes an "undue hardship."

CONCLUSION

It is the author's judgment that personal history questions included in standardized biodata selection procedures henceforth will require logical as well as empirical evidence to meet the emerging consensus of what constitutes generally accepted principles and practices of personnel psychology. Empirically keyed biodata items will only be the starting point. Taxonomies will provide the logical framework for organizing such empirical data-points into more meaningful categories of information about what behavior is actually being measured. In the not-too-distant future, industrial and organizational psychologists will probably begin speaking both of taxonomic categories of organizationally effective behavior and of discrete behaviors measured by biodata items that are demonstrably contributing to organizational productivity. Thus, the challenge presented by privacy, EEO, and disability legislation is to deliver what we as professionals have been talking about for years—that is, understanding what we are measuring and articulating our knowledge candidly to the world. As research designs become more comprehensive to meet these challenges, however, industrial and organizational psychologists will be well advised to follow anticipated legal and regulatory developments closely. It is likely, for example, that the burden of proof under ADA and Title VII will become one and the same. It is the hope of the author that this chapter will aid in viewing anticipated legal and regulatory challenges as opportunities: the opportunity to explain how discrete biodata items contribute to our understanding of organizationally effective behavior, and the opportunity to pursue the goal of merit-based equality of employment.

APPENDIX A
THE GLENNON ET AL. TAXONOMY
OF PERSONAL HISTORY ITEMS FOUND
TO BE PREDICTIVE OF JOB SUCCESS

CLASSIFICATION DATA

Age, height, weight, *marital status,* age when married, number of marriages, dependents, location of early childhood, change of residence, size of community, name same as father

HABITS AND ATTITUDES

Reading habits, physical exercise, smoking, drinking, major accomplishments, food preference, use of personal time, willingness to express opinions, association with peers, church attendance, travel, confidants, childhood, social schedule, TV viewing, vacation time

HEALTH

State of health, sick leave use, disabilities, stamina, sleep habits, illness, colds, accidents

HUMAN RELATIONS

Experience with disliked co-worker, social interaction, neighbor interaction, making new friends, social ease, former friends, first impressions, interpersonal distractions, sympathy, complaints, small group preference, age of friends, immediate neighbors, close friends

MONEY

Budgeting, *debt, first mortgage, monthly credit payments,* age of car, amount of life insurance, estimated annual salary, income as teen, charitable contributions, *savings,* alumni contributions, country club membership, clothing, auto accidents, total family income, *recent amount borrowed,* car purchases, vacation costs

PARENTAL HOME, CHILDHOOD, TEENS

Geography of childhood, moving as teen, section of town, rearing, siblings, parent's education, father's occupation, parental school interest, attitude toward college, paternal support, paternal social history, paternal attitudes, paternal sibling preference, family ancestors, paternal occupational stability, maternal schooling, maternal siblings' education, maternal sibling preference, maternal aunts and uncles, family bonding, career direction, books in home, use of family car, swimming age, *present proximity to parents,* maternal employment, community employment opportunities, repair work, number of siblings, childhood distress, age voice changed, childhood happiness, family discipline, childhood recreation, workshop access, rearing experience, discipline experience, confidants, parental achievements, parental disagreements, parental leisure, parental finances, parental entertainment, relatives, freedom in evenings, academic exposure, punishment, parental influence, magazine subscriptions, friends' age, exposure to tragedy, reading habits, parental socializing, paternal professionalism, paternal work supervision, paternal uncles and aunts, maternal socializing, religious observance, peer relations, paternal weekend work habits, household responsibilities, career advice, most successful relative, use of weekends, parental extracurricular support, maternal socialization, urban/rural exposure, music lessons, family guests, parental permission, peer exposure, parental dating supervision, time with siblings, sibling arguments, time away from family, parental academic interest, family socioeconomic status, parental support, reading habits, parental concern for finances, paternal reading habits, maternal reading habits, parental discipline, parental academic interest, parental reading support, family income source, relation to peer group, extracurricular activities, team participation, teen activity count, athletic participation, scouting achievement, extracurricular high school, extracurricular junior high school, weeknights out, affiliation

PERSONAL ATTRIBUTES

Handling mistakes, forgetting ideas, creativity, risk taking, betting, willingness to make decisions, investment objectives, auto violations, decision quality, attitude toward gambling, assumption of responsibility, decision making, publications, inventions, patents

PRESENT HOME, SPOUSE AND CHILDREN

Spouse support of career, willingness to move, spouse's employment, spouse's socioeconomic status, spouse's educational attainment, time with children, child discipline, social scene, spouse problems, *home requirements*, spouse's job status, child's educational expectation, agreement with children, spouse career support, decision making in home, sibling rivalry, marital discourse, home repairs, sleeping habits, time at address

RECREATION, HOBBIES, AND INTERESTS

Use of leisure time, recreational choices, hobbies, participation in group activities, concert attendance, vacations, fiction reading, magazine subscriptions, books owned, amount of leisure time, social organization participation, social organization leadership, physical activities, degree of participation, elective offices, social organization membership

SCHOOL AND EDUCATION

Grade level attainment, educational problem solving, adequacy of secondary education, best high school subjects, type of college attended, number of secondary schools attended, success relative to peers of same sex, age at high school graduation, academic achievement in college, degree of academic challenge, elected student offices, type of college attended, characteristics of best teacher, number of college majors, percent of college expenses earned, influence in attending college, sources of educational finance, least preferred subjects, most negative school experience, most positive school experience, extent of formal education, curriculum choice retrospective, easiest high school courses, most difficult high school courses, kinds of secondary schools attended, best courses, best study conditions, part-time work during school, educational expenses earned, academic potential, class standing size of high school, size of college, time since graduation, difficulty of high school, academic recognition from teachers, preschool attendance, nursery school attendance, kindergarten attendance, age first reading, grade school library card, high school library card, strongly disliked teacher, teacher knew me personally, college expectations, curriculum choice freedom, college grading practices, class attendance attitudes, high school academic achievement, studying up to capability, homework punctuality, classroom volunteering, college course load, age at graduation, type of scholarship, easiest subjects, extracurricular leadership, main courses, rate of progress relative to sex cohort, friends in school, considered quitting college, office made me most proud, choice of meeting location with friends

SELF-IMPRESSIONS

Expectations how others feel, opportunism, athletic ability, public speaking, commitment, attention span, personal appearance, reaction to frustration, letting off anger, most difficult task, achievement relative to peers, expectations as a supervisor, sleep experience, personality self-description, evaluation of success, open mindedness, reaction to competition, productivity, conditions of peak performance, religious commitment, reaction to stress, nervousness, peer respect, friendships, artistic ability, distractions, best self-description, friends' description

VALUES, OPINIONS, AND PREFERENCES

Greatest satisfactions, willingness to travel, attitudes toward drinking, church activity participation, sources of inspiration, reading preferences, religious influence, choice of TV programs, sociability, choice of movies, closure of unfinished business, significance of religion, reading preferences, fantasies, interpersonal irritations, preferable city size, motivating force in life, music appreciation, puzzle solving, retirement expectations, social philosophy, shyness, travel enjoyment, desire for social prominence, vacation choice, source of best learning, attitude toward science, geographic choice, childhood retrospective, qualities of a woman, best judging a man, attitude towards experts, political agreement with friends, political preference, party of choice

WORK

Reason for choosing profession, age at which career chosen, problem solving, characteristics of best supervisor, least preferred work policies, recognition for good work, detail orientation, work stamina, ideal job, most important factor for promotion, primary career goal, taking work home, career achievement expectations, work speed, reason for leaving last job, origins of job problems, tolerance for uncertainty, most satisfying work, five year personal goals, greatest source of job satisfaction, enjoyment of work, most preferred supervision, most preferred aspect of work, degree of challenge of present job, prior job experience, average length of prior jobs, sources influencing choice of work, source of first full-time job, source of present job, time out of work between jobs, upward organizational influence, negative experiences of first job, competing for promotion, first boss' evaluation of work, reasons for changing jobs, time to full job competence, diversity of jobs, preferred part of country, least difficult part of work, length of present employment, self-employment history, career opportunities for recent graduates, jobs in past five years, weeks unemployed in past year, months unemployed in past five years, least preferred aspect of work, most preferred aspect of work, jobs applied for in past two years, interview rapport, preferred line of work, time in work similar to present position, different jobs in past three years, relative previous earnings, least preferred aspect of work, least preferred treatment on job, most preferred job opportunity, career handicaps, willingness to quit job, supervisory experience, preferred compensation plan, predominant career to date, performed job better way, future aspirations, importance of present job, cooperation received on present job, commuting time, income satisfaction, feelings towards duties performed, most important contribution to success, most difficult part of work, most instrumental to career progress, greatest opportunity as youth, handling sarcasm, challenge of obsolescence

Note: Personal history questions prohibited by one or more state or local jurisdictions are in italics.

From *A Catalog of Life History Items* by J. R. Glennon, L. E. Albright, & W. A. Owens, 1961, Washington, DC: The Scientific Affairs Committee of the American Psychological Association.

APPENDIX B
THE ENGLAND TAXONOMY OF PERSONAL HISTORY ITEMS FOUND TO BE PREDICTIVE OF JOB SUCCESS

PERSONAL

Age, age at hiring, *marital status,* number of years married, if have dependents, if have children, age when first child born, *physical health, recent illness/operations,* time lost from job for specified previous period, general living conditions, *domicile,* location of residence, size of home town, number of times moved in recent period, length of time at last address, nationality, birth place, weight and height, sex

GENERAL BACKGROUND

Occupation of father, occupation of mother, occupation of brothers, sisters, or other relatives, military service and rank, military discharge record, early family responsibility, parental family adjustment, professionally successful parents, stable or transient home life, wife does not work outside home

EDUCATION

Finances—extent of dependence on parents, type of course studied in grammar school, major field of study in high school, specific courses taken in high school or college, subjects liked/disliked in high school, years since leaving high school, type of school attended, college grades, scholarship level, grammar school and high school grades, graduated at early age compared with classmates

EMPLOYMENT EXPERIENCE

Educational/vocational consistency, previous occupations (general type of work), held job in high school (type of job), number of previous jobs, specific work experience, previous selling experience, previous life insurance sales experience, total length of work experience, being in business for self, previous employee of company now considering application, seniority in present employment, tenure on previous job, employment status at time of application, reason for quitting last job, length of time unemployed, previous salary earned

SKILLS

Ability to read blueprints, does repair work on own car, amount of previous training for applicant job, amount of previous training for any other job, possesses specific skills required for job, number of machines that a person can operate

SOCIOECONOMIC LEVEL—FINANCIAL STATUS

Financial responsibility, *number of creditors, number of accounts with finance companies, number of accounts with stores, amount loaned as a proportion of total income, monthly mortgage payment,* highest pay received, *debts, net worth, savings,* amount of life insurance carried, amount of other insurance carried, *kinds and number of investments, real estate owned, owns automobile, and make and age of auto owned, owns furniture,* has telephone in home, minimum current living expenses, salary requests, earnings expected

SOCIAL

Club membership (social, community, campus, high school), frequency of attendance at group meetings, offices held in clubs, experience as a group leader, church membership

INTERESTS

Prefers outside to inside labor, hobbies, number of hobbies, specific type of hobbies, leisure time activities preferred, sports, number of sports active in, most important source of entertainment

PERSONAL CHARACTERISTICS, ATTITUDES EXPRESSED

Willingness to relocate or transfer, confidence expressed by applicant, basic personality needs as expressed by applicant in reply to question on application blank, drive stated job preferences

MISCELLANEOUS

Time taken for hiring negotiations between applicant and company, former employer's estimate of applicant, interviewer's estimate of applicant's success based on health, social personality, relationships, etc., source of reference to company for job application, has relatives or acquaintances presently working for company, number of character references listed, availability for entire season of work stated, availability to start work immediately, manner of filling out application blank (time taken, method used, way information stated), restrictions on hours available for duty

Note: Personal history questions prohibited by one or more state or local jurisdictions are in italics.

From *"Taxonomy of Past Behavior"* by G. England, 1971, Minneapolis: University of Minnesota, Industrial Relations Center. Copyright 1971 by University of Minnesota. Reprinted by permission.

APPENDIX C
PERSONAL HISTORY QUESTIONS PROHIBITED BY STATUTE, REGULATION, AND GUIDELINES AT THE STATE AND LOCAL LEVELS OF JURISDICTION

Age, application falsification, arrests, birthplace/citizenship, bonding, childcare, children, convictions/court records, credit rating, dependents, economic status/bankruptcy, education, experience, family, garnishment records, health, hospitalized/doctor's care, language skills, lowest salary accepted, marital status, military service, name, national origin/ancestry, notice in case of emergency, organizations, performance ability, physical condition/handicap, physical description/photograph, political affiliation, pregnancy, race/color, references, relatives, religion, rent/own car/home, residence, residence/duration of, sex, sexual preference, special qualifications, spouse's work, widowed/divorced/separated, work schedules

APPENDIX D
PERSONAL HISTORY QUESTIONS VALID FOR THE SALES JOB FAMILY BUT UNACCEPTABLE UNDER STATE GUIDELINES

"Own or rent home"

Validation Studies	Disapproving States	
Brown (1978)	California	Rhode Island
England (1971)	Colorado	South Dakota
Mitchell & Klimoski (1982)	Idaho	Utah
Mosel (1952)	Kansas	Washington
Mosel & Wade (1951)	Minnesota	West Virginia
Thayer (1977)	Nevada	Wisconsin
Thompson (1942)	New Jersey	

"Age or date of birth"

Validation Studies	Disapproving States	
England (1971)	Alaska	New York
Goldsmith (1922)	Arizona	Ohio

Hughes (1956)	California	Rhode Island
Husband (1925)	Hawaii	South Dakota
Manson (1925)	Idaho	Utah
Merenda & Clarke (1959)	Iowa	Washington, DC
Minor (1958)	Kansas	West Virginia
Mitchell (1980)	Maine	
Mosel (1952)	Michigan	
Mosel & Wade (1951)	Minnesota	
Roach (1971)	Nevada	
Thayer (1977)	New Hampshire	
Thompson (1942)	New Jersey	
Wallace (1949)	New York	

"Marital status"*

Validation Studies	Disapproving States
England (1971)	Arizona
Goldsmith (1922)	California
Hughes (1956)	Colorado
Husband (1949)	Massachusetts
Manson (1925)	Nevada
Merenda & Clarke (1959)	New Hampshire
Mosel (1952)	New Jersey
Mosel & Wade (1951)	Utah
Otis (1941)	Washington
Porter & Steers (1973)	West Virginia
Tanofsky, Shepps,	
& O'Neill (1969)	
Thayer (1977)	
Thompson (1942)	
Wallace (1949)	

"General health or illness"

Validation Studies	Disapproving States	
Mosel (1952)	California	Ohio
Mosel & Wade (1951)	Colorado	Utah
Toole et al. (1972)	Michigan	Washington
	Nevada	

"Reside with parents or relatives"

Validation Studies	Disapproving States	
England (1971)	California	Michigan
Mitchell & Klimoski (1982)	Colorado	Nevada
Mosel (1952)	Hawaii	New Hampshire
Mosel & Wade (1951)	Indiana	New Jersey
	Maine	Utah
	Massachusetts	Washington

"Current or past assets or credit"

Validation Studies	Disapproving States
Baehr & Williams (1968)	Arizona
Baier & Dugan (1957)	California
Brown (1978)	Colorado
Goldsmith (1922)	Idaho
Harrell (1960)	Illinois
Hughes (1956)	Kansas
Husband (1949)	Minnesota
Manson (1925)	Nevada
Merenda & Clarke (1959)	New Jersey
Mitchell (1980)	Rhode Island
Mosel & Wade (1951)	Utah
Tanofsky, Shepps,	West Virginia
& O'Neill (1969)	Wisconsin
Thayer (1977)	
Thompson (1942)	
Wallace (1949)	

'A larger group of states disapproves of pre-employment inquiries regarding "number of children."

From *"Are weighted application data valid and legal?"* by T. Mitchell, 1989, paper presented at the National Assessment Conference, Minneapolis. Copyright 1989 by Personnel Decisions, Inc. Reprinted by permission.

APPENDIX E
EXCERPT FROM TITLE 1
OF THE AMERICAN DISABILITIES ACT

Title 1: Employment
Sec. 101. Definitions

(8) Qualified Individual With A Disability. The term "qualified individual with a disability" means an individual, with a disability who, with or without reasonable accommodation, can perform the essential functions of the employment position that such individual holds or desires. For the purposes of this title, consideration shall be given to the employer's judgment as to what functions of a job are essential, and if an employer has prepared a written description before advertising or interviewing applicants for the job, this description shall be considered evidence of the essential functions of the job.

(9) Reasonable Accommodation. The term "reasonable accommodation" may include...(B) job restructuring, part-time or modified work schedules, reassignment to a vacant position, acquisition or modification of

equipment or devices, *appropriate adjustment or modifications of examinations, training materials or policies,* the provision of qualified readers or interpreters, and other similar accommodations for individuals with disabilities. [emphasis added]

(10) Undue Hardship. (A) In General—The term "undue hardship" means an action requiring significant difficulty or expense, when considered in light of the factors set forth in subparagraph (B). (B) Factors to be Considered: In determining whether an accommodation would impose an undue hardship on a covered entity, factors to be considered include (i) the nature and cost of the accommodation...; (ii) the overall financial resources of the facility..; the number of persons employed at such facility;...the effect on the expenses, resources or the impact otherwise of such accommodation upon the operation of the facility; (iii) the overall financial resources of the covered entity; the overall size of the business...with respect to the number of its employees; the number, type, and location of its facilities; and (iv) the type of operation...including the composition, structure, and functions of the work force..; the geographic separateness, administrative, or fiscal relationship of the facility...in question to the covered entity.

Sec. 102 Discrimination. (b) Construction: The term "discriminate" includes

(1) limiting, segregating, or classifying a job applicant or employee in a way that adversely affects the opportunities or status of such applicant or employee because of the disability of such applicant or employee;...

(3) utilizing standards, criteria, or methods of administration (A) that have the effect of discrimination of the basis of disability;...

(5) (A) not making reasonable accommodations to the known physical or mental limitations of an otherwise qualified individual with a disability who is an applicant or employee, unless such covered entity can demonstrate that the accommodation would impose an undue hardship on the operation of the business of such covered entity; or (B) denying employment opportunities to a job applicant or employee who is an otherwise qualified individual with a disability, if such denial is based on the need of such covered entity to make reasonable accommodation to the physical or mental impairments of the employee or applicant;

(6) using qualification standards, employment tests or other selection criteria that screen out or tend to screen out an individual with a disability or a class of individuals with disabilities unless the standard, test or other

selection criteria, as used by the covered entity, is shown to be job-related for the position in question and is consistent with business necessity; and

(7) *failing to select* and administer *tests* concerning employment in the most effective manner *to ensure that,* when such test is administered to a job applicant or employee who has a disability that impairs sensory, manual or speaking skills, *such test results accurately reflect the skills aptitude, or whatever other factor of such applicant or employee that such test purports to measure, rather than reflecting the impaired sensory, manual, or speaking skills of such employee or applicant (except where such skills are the factors the test purports to measure).* [emphasis added]

Sec. 103 Defenses

(a) In General. It may be a defense to a charge of discrimination under this Act that an alleged application of qualification standards, tests, or selection criteria that screen out or tend to screen out or otherwise deny a job or benefit to an individual with a disability has been shown to be job-related and consistent with business necessity, and such performance cannot be accomplished by reasonable accommodation, as required in this title.

APPENDIX F
EXCERPT FROM SUPREME COURT
DECISION IN *ALEXANDER V. CHOATE*

All the Courts of Appeals that have addressed the issue have agreed that, at least under some circumstances, (Sec.) 504 reaches disparate-impact discrimination.

At the same time, the position urged by respondents—that we interpret (Sec.) 504 to reach all action disparately affecting the handicapped—is also troubling because the handicapped typically are not similarly situated to the non-handicapped, respondents's position would in essence require each recipient of federal funds first to evaluate the effect on the handicapped of every proposed action that might touch the interests of the handicapped, and then to consider alternatives for achieving the same objectives with less severe disadvantage to the handicapped. The formalization and policing of this process could lead to a wholly unwieldy administrative and adjudicative burden.

Just as there is reason to question whether Congress intended (Sec.) 504 to reach only intentional discrimination, there is similarly reason to question whether Congress intended (Sec.) 504 to embrace all claims of disparate-impact discrimination. Any interpretation of (Sec.) 504 must therefore be responsive to two powerful but countervailing considerations—the need to give effect to the statutory objectives and the desire to keep (Sec.) 504 within manageable bounds. Given the legitimacy of both of these goals and the tension between them, we decline the parties' invitation to decide today that one of these goals so overshadows the other as to eclipse it. While we reject the boundless notion that all disparate-impact showings constitute prima facie cases under (Sec.) 504, we assume without deciding that (Sec.) 504 reaches at least some conduct that has an unjustifiable disparate impact upon the handicapped.

APPENDIX G
STATEMENT FROM APA
REGARDING "ADJUSTMENT
OR MODIFICATION" LANGUAGE

Despite the history of attempts to modify tests for handicapped people, significant problems remain. First, there have been few empirical investigations of the effects of special accommodation on the resulting scores or on their reliability and validity. Strictly speaking, unless it has been demonstrated that the psychometric properties of a test, or type of test, are not altered significantly by some modification, the claims made for the test by its author or publisher cannot be generalized to the modified version...

Of all the aspects of testing people who have handicapping conditions, reporting test scores has created the most heated debate. Many test developers have argued that reporting scores from nonstandard test administrations without special identification (often called "flagging" of test scores) violates professional principles, misleads test users, and perhaps even harms handicapped test takers whose scores do not accurately reflect their abilities. Handicapped people, on the other hand, have generally said that to identify their scores as resulting from nonstandard administrations and in so doing to identify them as handicapped is to deny them the opportunity to compete on the same grounds as nonhandicapped test takers, that is, to treat them inequitably. Until test scores can be demonstrated to be comparable in some widely accepted sense, there is little hope of happily resolving from all perspectives the issue of reporting scores with or without special identification....

NOTES

1. Employers concerned with compensatory and punitive damages from common law claims will want to watch for the Supreme Court decision in *Pacific Mutual Life Insurance Company v. Haslip* (89-1279).

2. The single precedent in which an employer's use of biodata was at issue was a challenge under state law in which the Supreme Court of the State of Iowa upheld the City of Des Moines' use of a biodata test used by the Civil Service Commission to select police sergeants. Plaintiffs had objected to a number of specific personal history questions that were read into the court's opinion, which included the following questions among others: "Did you have sex before you were 16?" "Did you have a tattoo before you were 16?" (*Patch v. Civil Service Commission of the City of Des Moines, #64265, Supreme Court of Iowa, Aug. 27, 1980*; see also *Court v. Bristol-Myers Co.*, 431 N.E. 2nd 908 [Mass. 1982]).

3. The *Uniform Guidelines on Employee Selection Procedures* issued by the Equal Employment Opportunity Commission (29 C.F.R. 1607.1) require an employer to keep documentation of their selection procedures, including the records of the *component process* for selection procedures that may arguably have an adverse impact. EEOC general regulations require an employer (a) to retain applications and supporting material for 6 months and (b) to keep information on each applicant's race, sex and national origin in a separate file from personnel records (form 100, Employer Information Report EEO-1).

4. A Supreme Court decision frequently cited as protecting an employer from item disclosure, *Detroit Edison Co. v. National Labor Relations Board_U.S_5 Mar 79*, was not a Title VII case but rather was brought under the National Labor Relations Act (NLRA). In *Detroit Edison*, the union had argued that the employer had violated its duty to bargain collectively under the NLRA by refusing to provide tests and answer sheets to be turned over to an industrial psychologist selected by the union. The Supreme Court held:

> A person's interest in preserving the confidentiality of sensitive information contained in his personnel files has been given forceful recognition in both federal and state legislation governing the recordkeeping activities of public employers and agencies. See e.g., Privacy Act of 1974, 5 U.S.C P552a (written consent required before information in individual records may be disclosed, unless the request falls within an explicit statutory exception). Indeed, the federal Privacy Act ban on unconsented-to disclosure of employee records without written consent has been construed to provide a valid defense to a union request for certain employee personnel data made pursuant to the terms of a public employee collective-bargaining agreement.

5. The disparate treatment theory of discrimination under Title VII was spelled out by the Supreme Court in *McDonnell Douglas v. Green* (1973):

> The complainant in a Title VII trial must carry the initial burden under the statute of establishing a prima facie case of racial discrimination. This may be done by showing:

(i) that he belongs to a racial minority;

(ii) that he applied and was qualified for a job for which the employer was seeking applicants;

(iii) that, despite his qualifications, he was rejected and

(iv) that, after his rejection, the position remained open and the employer continued to seek applicants from persons of complainant's qualifications.

REFERENCES

Ackerman v. Western Electric Company, 643 F. Supp. 836 (N.D. Cal. 1986) aff'd, 860 F. 2d 1514 (9th Cira. 1988).

Alexander v. Choate, 469 U.S. 287 (Jan. 9, 1985).

American Educational Research Association, American Psychological Association, & National Council on Measurement in Education. (1985). *Standards for educational and psychological testing.* Washington, DC: American Psychological Association.

American Psychological Association. (1987, November 5). Amicus brief filed with U.S. Supreme Court in *Watson v. Fort Worth Bank & Trust Co.* In *Daily Labor Report, 213*(D1-10). Washington, DC: Author.

American Psychological Association. (1988). *Implications for test fairness of the "Golden Rule" company settlement.* Committee on Psychological Tests and Assessment. Washington, DC: Author.

American Psychological Association. (1990). *DRAFT statement on the disclosure of test scores, test items, and test protocols.* Washington, DC: Author.

Arvey, R., & Faley, R. (1988). *Fairness in selecting employees.* Reading, MA: Addison-Wesley.

Ash, P. (1989). *The legality of pre-employment inquiries: A guide to state and other jurisdictional rules and regulations.* Park Ridge, IL: London House.

Ash, P. (1991). Law and regulation of pre-employment inquiries. *Journal of Business and Psychology, 5*(3), 291–308.

Baehr, M., & Williams, G. (1986). Prediction of sales success from factorially determined dimensions of personal background data. *Journal of Applied Psychology, 52,* 98–103.

Baier, D., & Dugan, R. (1957). Factors in sales success. *Journal of Applied Psychology, 41,* 37–40.

Ballew, P. J. (1987). Courts, psychologists, and the EEOC's Uniform Guidelines: An analysis of recent trends affecting testing as a means of employee selection. *Emory Law Journal, 36,* 203.

Bersoff, D. (1981). Testing and the law. *American Psychologist, 36,* 1047.

Biotech debate: Who will read the gene maps? (1992, July 5). *Washington Post,* H1.

Blank check for the disabled? (1989, September 6). *The New York Times,* A–24.

Booth, D., & Mackay, R. (1980). Legal constraints on employment testing and evolving trends in the law. *Emory Law Journal, 29,* 121.

Brown, S. (1978). Long-term validity of a personal history item scoring procedure. *Journal of Applied Psychology, 63,* 673–676.

Bureau of National Affairs. (1982). *Fair employment practice manual*. Washington, DC: Author.

Comment. (1987). Courts, psychologists, and the EEOC's Uniform Guidelines: An analysis of recent trends affecting testing as a means of employee selection. *Emory Law Journal, 36,* 203.

Court v. Bristol-Myers Co., 431 N.E. 2nd 908 (Mass. 1982).

England, G. (1971). *Weighted application blanks*. Minneapolis: Industrial Relations Center, University of Minnesota.

Executive Office of the President, Office of Science and Technology. (1967, February). *Privacy and behavioral research*. Washington, DC: U.S. Government Printing Office.

Fleishman, E., & Quaintance, M. (1984). *Taxonomies of human performance*. New York: Academic Press.

Gandy, J., Outerbridge, A., Sharf, J., & Dye, D. (1989). *Development and initial validation of the Individual Achievement Record*. Washington, DC: U.S. Office of Personnel Management.

Gerstner, L. (1990, November 25). Untangle the state regulatory web. *The New York Times,* F–13.

Gibbons, J. (1980). *Privacy protection and personnel administration*. New York: The New York Chamber of Commerce and Industry.

Glennon, J. R., Albright, L. E., & Owens, W. A. (1961). *A catalog of life history items*. Washington, DC: The Scientific Affairs Committee of the American Psychological Association.

Gold, M. (1985). *Griggs'* folly: An essay on the theory, problems, and origin of the adverse impact definition of employment discrimination and a recommendation for reform. *Industrial Relations Law Journal, 7,* 429.

Goldsmith, D. (1922). The use of the personal history blank as a salesmanship test. *Journal of Applied Psychology, 6,* 149–155.

Gottfredson, L., & Sharf, J. (Eds). (1988, December). Fairness in employment testing. *Journal of Vocational Behavior, 33*(Whole issue), 225–477.

Greenwalt, K. (1975). *Legal protections of privacy*. Washington, DC: Office of Telecommunications Policy, Executive Office of the President.

Griggs v. Duke Power Co. 401 U.S. 424 (1971).

Guion, R. (1965). *Personnel testing*. New York: McGraw-Hill.

Hall v. U.S. Postal Service, 857 F. 2d 1073 (6th Cir. 1988).

Harrell, T. (1960). The validity of biographical data items for food company salesmen. *Journal of Applied Psychology, 44,* 31–33.

Harris, L., & Westin, A. (1979). *Dimensions of privacy: A National Opinion Research survey of attitudes toward privacy*. Stevens Point, WI: Sentry Insurance.

House Report. (1990). No. 101–485, 101st Cong., 2d Sess., Pt.2.

Hughes, J. (1956). Expressed personality needs as predictors of sales success. *Personnel Psychology, 9,* 347–357.

Husband, R. (1949). Techniques of salesman selection. *Educational & Psychological Measurement, 9,* 129–148.

Is nothing private? (1989, September 4). *Business Week,* pp. 74–82.

Is your boss spying on you? (1990, January 15). *Business Week*, pp. 74–75.

Jones, J., Ash, P., & Soto, C. (1989 draft). *Employment privacy rights and pre-employment honesty tests*. Park Ridge, IL: London House.

Kandel, W. (1983). Dissemblers and EEO. *Employee Relations Law Journal, 8*, 505.

Kandel, W. (1989). Current developments in employment litigation: *Atonio and Betts* — Burden of proof and other barriers to plaintiffs in wholesale litigation under ADEA and Title VII. *Employee Relations Law Journal, 15*(2), 267–280.

Kandel, W. (1990). Current developments in employment litigation. *Employee Relations Law Journal, 16*(1), 79–87.

Kirkland v. New York State Department of Correctional Services, 374 F.Supp. 1361, 7 FEP Cases 694 (S.D.N.Y. 1974).

Landy, F. (1986). Stamp collecting versus science: Validation as hypothesis testing. *The American Psychologist, 41*(11), 1183–1192.

Landy, R., & Farr, J. (1983). *The measurement of work performance: Method, theory and application*. New York: Academic Press.

Las Vegas police reach consent decree with Justice Dept. to settle bias charges. (1987, October 27). *Daily Labor Report, 201*(A–1).

The Lawyer's employment act. (1989, September 11). *Wall Street Journal*, A–18.

Ledvinka, J. (1982). *Federal regulation of personnel and human resource management*. Boston: Kent.

Ledvinka, J., & Schoenfeldt, L. (1978). Legal developments in employment testing: *Albemarle* and beyond. *Personnel Psychology, 31*, 1.

Lee, C. (1988). Testing makes a comeback. *Training, 25*(12), 49–59.

Lerner, B. (1979). Employment discrimination: Adverse impact, validity, and equality. 1979 *Supreme Court Review* 17.

Lindsay, R. (1989, Winter). Discrimination against the disabled: The impact of the new Federal legislation. *Employee Relations Law Journal, 15*(3), 333–345.

Manson, G. (1925). What can the application blank tell? Evaluation of items in personal history records of four thousand life insurance salesmen. *Journal of Personnel Research, 4*, 73–99.

McDonnell Douglas Corp. v. Green, 411 U.S. 792, 5 FEP 965 (1973).

Merenda, R., & Clarke, W. (1959). The predictive efficiency of temperament characteristics and personal history variables in determining success of life insurance agents. *Journal of Applied Psychology, 43*, 360–366.

Minor, F. (1958). The prediction of turnover among clerical employees. *Personnel Psychology, 11*, 393–409.

Minuti, M. (1988). Employer liability under the doctrine of negligent hiring: Suggested methods for avoiding the hiring of dangerous employees. *Delaware Journal of Corporate Law, 13*(2), 501–532.

Mitchell, T. (1980). *Theoretical biodata: An oxymoron?* Unpublished master's thesis, Ohio State University, Columbus.

Mitchell, T. (1989). *Are weighted application data valid and legal?* Paper presented at the National Assessment Conference, Minneapolis.

Mitchell, T., & Klimoski, R. (1982). Is it rational to be empirical? A test of methods for scoring biographical data. *Journal of Applied Psychology, 67*, 411–418.

Morrison, R., Owens, W., Glennon, J., & Albright, L. (1962). Factored life history antecedents of industrial research performance. *Journal of Applied Psychology, 46*(4), 281–284.

Mosel, J. (1952). Prediction of department store sales performance from personal data. *Journal of Applied Psychology, 36,* 8–10.

Mosel, J., & Wade, R. (1951). A weighted application blank for reduction of turnover in department store sales clerks. *Personnel Psychology, 4,* 177–184.

Mumford, M., & Owens, W. (1984). Individuality in a developmental context: Some empirical and theoretical considerations. *Human Development, 27,* 84–108.

Mumford, M., Stokes, G., & Owens, W. (1990). *Patterns of life history: The ecology of human individuality.* Hillsdale, NJ: Erlbaum.

National Association of Attorneys General. (1976). *Privacy: Personal data and the law.* Raleigh, NC: Author.

Nester, M. (1984). Employment testing for handicapped persons. *Public Personnel Management Journal, 13,* 417–434.

Office of Technology Assessment, U.S. Congress. (1990, September). *The use of integrity tests for pre-employment screening* (OTA-SET-442). Washington, DC: U.S. Government Printing Office.

Otis, J. (1941). Procedures for the selection of salesmen for a detergent company. *Journal of Applied Psychology, 25,* 30–40.

Owens, W. (1968). Toward one discipline of scientific psychology. *The American Psychologist, 23,* 782–785.

Owens, W. (1971). A quasi-actuarial basis for individual assessment. *The American Psychologist, 26,* 992–999.

Owens, W. (1976). Background data. In M. D. Dunnette (Ed.), *Handbook of industrial and organizational psychology.* Chicago: Rand McNally.

Owens, W., & Schoenfeldt, L. (1979). Toward a classification of persons. *Journal of Applied Psychology, 46,* 329.

Pace, R., & Schoenfeldt, L. (1977). Legal concerns in the use of weighted applications. *Personnel Psychology, 30,* 159.

Pacific Mutual Life Insurance Company v. Haslip (89–1279).

Patch v. Civil Service Commission of the City of Des Moines, #64265, Supreme Court of Iowa, Aug. 27, 1980.

Porter, L., & Steers, R. (1973). Organizational, work and personal factors in employee turnover and absenteeism. *Psychological Bulletin, 80,* 151–176.

Potter, E. (1986). *Employee selection: Legal and practical alternatives to compliance and litigation* (2d ed.). Washington, DC: National Foundation for the Study of Equal Employment Policy.

Potter, E., & Reesman, A. (1990). *The Americans With Disabilities Act: Testing and other employee selection procedures.* Washington, DC: National Foundation for the Study of Equal Employment Policy.

Privacy Act of 1974. (1974, December 31). U.S. Code 1982 Title 5, PP 552a, P.I. 93–579.

Privacy: Companies are delving further into employees' personal lives and workers are fighting harder for the right to be let alone. (1988, March 28). *Business Week,* pp. 61–68.

Rasky, S. (1989, September 17). How the disabled sold Congress on a new bill of rights. *The New York Times,* 1979, E–5.

The Rehabilitation Act of 1973, 29 U.S.C. PP 794 (Section 504).

Reilly, R., & Warech, M. (in press). The validity and fairness of alternatives to cognitive tests. In Wing, L. (Ed.), *Employment testing and public policy.* Berkeley, CA: Kluwer Press.

Roach, D. (1971). Double cross-validation of a weighted application blank over time. *Journal of Applied Psychology, 55,* 157–160.

Rothfeder, J. (1990, September 24). Looking for a job? You may be out before you go in. *Business Week,* pp. 128–130.

Rothstein, H., Schmidt, F., Erwin, F., Owens, W., & Sparks, P. (1990). Biographical data in employment selection: Can validities be made generalizable? *Journal of Applied Psychology, 75*(2), 175–184.

Schlei, B., & Grossman, P. (1983). *Employment Discrimination Law* (2d ed.). Washington, DC: Bureau of National Affairs.

Schmidt, F., & Hunter, J. (1981). Employment testing: Old theories and new research findings. *The American Psychologist, 36*(10), 1128–1137.

Schoenfeldt, L. (1974). Utilization of manpower: Development and evaluation of assessment-classification model for matching individuals with jobs. *Journal of Applied Psychology, 59,* 583.

Senate Report. (1989). No. 101-116, 101st Cong., 2d Sess.

Sharf, J. (1988). Litigating personnel measurement policy. *Journal of Vocational Behavior, 33*(Whole issue), 235–271.

Sharf, J. (1991). Employment testing and the law in the United States. *Applying psychology in business: The handbook for managers and human resource professionals.* Lexington, MA: D.C. Heath & Co.

Sherman, S., & Robinson, N. (1982). *Ability testing of handicapped people: Dilemma for government, science, and the public.* Washington, DC: National Academy Press.

Small business and local government groups question costs of Federal bill for disabled. (1989, October 31). *Daily Labor Report, 209*(C–6).

Smith v. Troyan, 10 FEP Cases 1384 (Sixth Cir., July 3, 1975).

Soroka v. Dayton-Hudson Corp. H-143579-3 (Cal. filed Nov. 24, 1989).

Tanofsky, R., Shepps, R., & O'Neil, P. (1969). Pattern analysis of biographical predictors of success as an insurance salesman. *Journal of Applied Psychology, 53,* 136–139.

Tenopyr, M. (1981). The realities of employment testing. *The American Psychologist, 36*(10), 1120–1127.

Thayer, P. (1977). Something old, something new. *Personnel Psychology, 30,* 513–524.

Thompson, C. (1942). Predicting success of Britannica salesmen. *Psychological Bulletin, 39,* 435.

Thompson, C., & Thompson, R. (1982). Court standards for job analysis in test validation. *Personnel Psychology, 35,* 865.

Toole, D., Gavin, J., Mundy, L., & Sells, S. (1972). The differential validity of personality, personal history, and aptitude data for minority and non-minority employees. *Personnel Psychology, 25,* 661–672.

Walker, S. (1984, Summer). Negligent hiring: Employer's liability for acts of an employee. *The American Journal of Trial Advocacy, 7*(3), 603–610.

Wallace, S. (1949). A note on Kahn and Hadley's "factors related to life insurance selling." *Journal of Applied Psychology, 33,* 356–358.

Wards Cove Packing Company v. Atonio, 109 S.Ct. 3115 (1989).

Watson v. Fort Worth Bank & Trust, 56 U.S.L.W. 4922 (June 29, 1988).

Wernimont, P., & Campbell, J. (1968). Signs, samples, and criteria. *Journal of Applied Psychology, 52*(5), 372–376.

Westin, A. (1970). *Privacy and freedom.* New York: Athenaeum.

Willingham, W., Ragosta, M., Bennet, R., Braun, H., Rock, D., & Powers, D. (1988). *Testing handicapped.* Boston: Allyn and Bacon.

Wunder, S., & Sparks, P. (1991). Fairness in personnel selection. In J. Jones, B. Steffy, & D. Bray (Eds.), *Applying psychology in business.* Lexington, MA: Heath.

Accuracy and Faking of Background Data

Gary J. Lautenschlager
University of Georgia

Truth does not consist in never lying but in knowing when to lie and when not to do so.—*Samuel Butler*

When an individual is confronted by an organization to reveal his innermost feelings, he has a duty to himself to give answers that serve his self-interest rather than that of The Organization. In a word, he should cheat.—*William H. Whyte, Jr.*

INTRODUCTION

Life history and background questionnaires have been used successfully for several types of personnel decisions (Asher, 1972; Guion, 1965; Owens, 1976; Schuh, 1967). The term *biodata,* as used here, will refer generically to the broad array of question types that have been employed in this area. Several authors have provided information to aid the construction and use of biodata items (Aherns, 1949; Albright, Glennon, & Smith, 1961; Asher, 1972; Mael, 1991; Mumford & Owens, 1987; Mumford & Stokes, 1992; Owens, 1976; Pannone, 1984; Stricker, 1989). Suffice it to say that biodata has referred to factual kinds of questions about life and work experiences, as well as to items involving opinions, values, beliefs, and attitudes that reflect a historical perspective. The former types of questions are common to many employment application blanks, and the latter types of questions are similar to those used in a variety of noncognitive tests.

Biodata questionnaires present respondents with the task of completing a series of items that may cover a broad or narrow range of prior life experiences. The questionnaires are comprised of items drawn to serve the purposes of the test constructor, yet the questions are answered by the test taker, and, hence, aspects of both biography and autobiography would seem to apply. Thus, although the individual's history is limited by the questions asked by the biographer(s), most often for specific purposes, the basis of the content of that biography is the self-reported set of responses.

ACCURACY AND BIAS

Researchers have noted that although biodata questionnaires have been widely used for personnel decisions, only a limited number of published studies have focused on the potential problems of accuracy and bias in answers to biodata items (Brumback, 1969; Owens, 1976; Schrader & Osburn, 1977). Perhaps investigators felt, as did Nunnally (1967), that since "biographical inventories ask the subject factual questions about his personal history... [responses to the items] are not likely to be strongly influenced by social desirability" (p. 512). However, Mock (1947) reported on research conducted during World War II that focused on the detection and control of falsification in responses to a biographical questionnaire in aviator selection.[*]

Concern over the potential problem of response dissimulation is not unique to biodata questionnaires, but is shared by a wide variety of noncognitive measures (personality, attitudes, interests, etc.) that may be used for selection or other purposes of the organization (Paulhus, 1986, 1991; Zerbe & Paulhus, 1987). The accuracy of biodata has been addressed on both a specific level—by assessing the veracity of the responses made to individual items—and at more general levels—by determining the effects on the scores obtained on empirical keys or by other scoring methods. Verification, or some comparison to an objective state of affairs, may be possible for factual items. However, for other item types there may be no means for external verification. Although the focus here is on what research has been done regarding the accuracy of biodata responses, it is useful to

---

[*] I wish to thank Larry Stricker of Educational Testing Service for calling the Mock (1947) study to my attention.

note there is an increasing concern and interest in the construct validity evidence for biodata measures (Mumford & Nickels, 1990; Mumford & Stokes, 1992; Russell & Domm, 1990; Sharf, Dye, Gandy, & MacLane, 1990). Construct validity was proffered by Cronbach and Meehl (1955) for criterion selection in test validation, and construct validity may be the most important form of validation (Cronbach, 1990; R. Hogan & Nicholson, 1988; Landy, 1986). To the extent that a measure is an accurate reflection of the intended property and free from bias, it will be a more valid representation of the desired construct.

Studies of the accuracy of biodata have been conducted in situations involving personnel decisions with actual applicants, under circumstances simulating personnel decision situations (e.g., using either job incumbents or college students role-playing as applicants), and in experiments that have been conducted for more general research purposes. Accuracy itself has been operationally defined in at least three different ways:

- *Correlational accuracy* refers to obtaining the same pattern of responses. For example, the correlation between two sets of values for responses to the same item may be examined as evidence of validity (i.e., using an external source for comparison with self-reported responses) or stability (i.e., obtaining two separate self-reported responses to the item from the same sample of subjects at different times). This definition of accuracy is sensitive to differences in the rank ordering of individuals within each of the two sets of values, but not to any constant shifts in responses between sets.
- *Level or mean differences* refers to differences either within or between groups of respondents. Here the average response computed for a group of subjects may be compared under two different administration conditions, or it may be compared to the average response of another group. This measure is independent of the correlational measure and may reflect differences in responses unrelated to pattern. For example, although the pattern may be unchanged, a constant shift in scores upward or downward could occur, indicating a change in level. Level differences at the item response level may cancel out at some aggregate level, such as when a criterion key is used.
- *Absolute accuracy* regards deviation in responses at the individual subject level as inaccurate. This index is reported in terms of the percentage agreement taken across subjects for a given item. Changes in individual responses could occur without showing any systematic changes in pattern or level at higher levels of data aggregation. Also, it may be possible for changes at the item level to have no effect on keyed scores.

These different definitions of accuracy have different implications for what is, and what is not, labeled as accurate. Some studies have made use of more than one of these indices.

Inaccurate responses may result for various reasons. They may be the result of outright dishonesty on the part of the respondent. At times the respondent's intent may not stem from dishonesty as much as from a desire to gain social approval. Inaccuracy may also result from problems associated with memory or from lack of self-knowledge. For longitudinal studies, developmental influences may alter interpretation of some life history events leading to differences in responses over time that may not be inaccurate, but just simply different. Other sources of inaccuracy may arise from problems in the items themselves and from errors in the verifying information obtained from external sources (e.g., company records).

SYNOPSIS OF PUBLISHED LITERATURE

A search of the literature focused on the topics of response distortion, faking, and accuracy of responses to biodata questions resulted in the identification of 12 published articles spanning the period from 1950 to 1990. Table 1 presents information about the characteristics of each of these studies. In addition, the results of each study are described in some detail below.

TWELVE STUDIES EXAMINING ACCURACY AND FAKING ON BIODATA QUESTIONNAIRES

Keating, Paterson, and Stone (1950)
This study reported some of the earliest quantitative evidence concerning the accuracy of self-reports of work history information. The sample consisted of 236 unemployed persons who had registered for employment at a United States Employment Service office. The personal history data were collected by interview in a job counseling context and not with a written biographical inventory. The items investigated were weekly wages, duration of employment, and job duties for jobs held in the previous year. The correlations between self-reported values and information obtained from previous employers were .90 for males and .93 for females for wages and .98 for both sexes for employment duration. For the job duties category, only percentage agreement figures were provided. Although the percent agreement was 94 percent for males and 96 percent

TABLE 1 Characteristics of Studies Examining Response Distortion to Biographical Questionnaire Items

Study	Subjects/Job Type	Situation	Focus	Measure of Distortion
Keating et al. (1950)	Unemployed workers (79 female, 157 male)	Job counseling	Verifiable items (3)	Correlation and percent agreement
Mosel & Cozan (1952)	Job applicants: sales and office (65 female, 61 male)	Selection	Verifiable items (3)	Correlation and percent agreement
Klein & Owens (1965)	Students (55) Recruiters (79)	Simulation with faking instructions	Empirical keys (2) (41 items) [a]	Transparency index: maximum possible score minus observed score
Goldstein (1971)	Job applicants: nurses aides (111)	Selection	Verifiable items (4)	Percent agreement
Doll (1971)	Aviation officer candidates (300)	Simulation with faking instructions	Mixed item types (200 items)	Changes in item option endorsement
Cohen & Lefkowitz (1974)	Job applicants: clerical, sales, supervisory (118)	Selection	Mixed item types (80 items)	Item discrimination for MMPI K-scale groups
Casio (1975)	Incumbent police officers (8 female, 104 male)	Research purposes	Verifiable items (17)	Correlation and percent agreement
Schrader & Osburn (1977)	College students (57 female, 91 male)	Simulation with faking instructic.	Empirical keys (2) (57 items)	Mean differences between fake and honest scores
Thornton & Gierasch (1980)	College students (94 male)	Simulation with faking instructions	Empirical keys (10) (no. items unspecified)	Mean differences between fake and honest scores

TABLE 1 Characteristics of Studies Examining Response Distortion to Biographical Questionnaire Items (continued)

Study	Subjects/Job Type	Situation	Focus	Measure of Distortion
Pannone (1984)	Job applicants: electricians (221)	Selection	One "fake" (verifiable) item	Between-group differences for falsifiers vs. nonfalsifiers on means and correlations
Shaffer et al. (1986)	College students (113 female, 124 male)	Research purposes	Mixed item types (118) Component scores (13 for males, 14 for females)	Test-retest correlations and mean differences at five years
	Parent(s) as observer (53 female, 56 male)	Research purposes	Mixed item types (26 for males, 22 for females) Component scores (3)	Correlation of parent (as observer) with original student response and mean differences
Hough et al. (1990)	Faking study: enlisted military (245 male)	Simulation with faking instructions	Content and response validity scores (15; 209 items)	Between-group mean differences
	Concurrent study: enlisted military (9,359; sex unspecified)	Research purposes	Content and response validity scores (15)	Moderation of criterion-related validities using response validity scale scores
	Applicant comparisons with above groups: Recent inductees (125; sex unspecified)	Selection-like context	Content and response validity scores (15)	Between-group mean differences on scales

Note: Numbers in parentheses indicate sample size for "Subjects/Job Type" or number of items/keys/scores for "Focus." Where sample sizes are given without other information, the sex of subjects was not specified.

[a] Since each key had 22 items, and at least 3 items were common to both, the total could not exceed 41 items.

for females, it is not clear exactly how such agreement was defined. It is useful to note that Keating et al. (1950, p. 8) were concerned with two types of verification errors in their study, namely, that information obtained from employers might itself be inaccurate and that interviewers may have introduced errors of their own into the data. It would seem the effects of such errors were likely minimal on the measures of accuracy employed.

Mosel and Cozan (1952)

This study replicated the study by Keating et al. (1950) in a personnel selection context. Mosel and Cozan noted that the accuracy of application blank information could set limits on the utility of such information for prediction and could be an important determinant regarding the need for independent sources of background information. Self-reported work history data were obtained from application blanks completed for sales and office positions in a single company. Although the 126 applicants were not warned that responses would be verified, the authors assumed some respondents would expect a reference check. Precautions were taken to avoid one form of bias by not informing the former employer of the applicant's claims.

The results were consistent with the Keating et al. (1950) study, with correlations between self-report and verified values in the lower .90s for wages and slightly higher for employment duration for jobs held within the year before the application for employment was made. Contrary to Keating et al. (1950), the distortion present in the applicant-supplied information was nearly all overestimation, a point that would have been lost if only the correlation coefficients were compared. The agreement for job duties was 84 percent for males and 87 percent for females, figures slightly lower than those reported by Keating et al. (1950). It is not clear whether the definition of agreement between applicant and employer reports of job duties used in these two studies may have contributed to the difference in results.

Klein and Owens (1965)

This study addressed the faking of responses to an empirically keyed life history form developed to predict scientific research creativity. The questionnaire was more comprehensive and based on a wider array of life experiences than the questions used in the studies discussed above. Scoring keys were available for both an objective and a subjective criterion of research creativity. It was not clear from the methods whether all 484 multiple-choice items from the biodata questionnaire (Smith, Albright, Glennon, & Owens, 1961) were used or only the subset of items forming the two empirical keys. The participants were college seniors and a group of college recruiters; the latter group was responsible for recruiting doctoral candidates for employment. One group of seniors ($N = 40$) completed the questionnaire twice, first under instructions to provide honest responses, and again a week later under instructions to complete the form as if they were actually applying for a job requiring a truly creative scientist. The second group of seniors ($N = 15$) completed the questionnaire once under the fake instructions. The interviewers ($N = 79$) were told to complete the questionnaire as the "typical, creative research scientist would" (p. 453).

The authors employed a transparency index as the measure of accuracy. This represented the difference between the maximum possible score and the observed score in standardized form and is effectively a level-difference measure of accuracy. The subjective key was found more susceptible to faking than the objective key for both college seniors and college recruiters. It should be noted that scores on both keys were significantly altered. Seniors who had completed an earlier administration of the questionnaire were able to fake a subsequent administration more effectively than those who were instructed to fake responses on the first attempt. Prior exposure to the questionnaire appeared to facilitate faking. The differences between keys in their susceptibility to faking were not seen as attributable to factors such as proportions of verifiable and/or socially desirable item choices.

Goldstein (1971)

This study examined the accuracy of application blank information provided by 111 applicants for a nurse's aide job. The focus was on agreement between information provided on an application blank with information obtained from previous employers. The items used inquired about whether the applicant had previously worked for the employer, marital status, previous position held, duration of employment, previous wages, and reason for leaving. The percentage of respondents for whom data on a given item matched that given by the previous employer served as the accuracy index. Distortion in the previous employer's responses was noted as a potential source of error, though it was largely dismissed based on the results obtained.

There were a substantial number of discrepancies between the responses of applicants and information obtained from previous employers. Consistent with distortion of similar information as noted in the employment interview (Blum & Naylor, 1968), the most inaccurately reported pieces of information were duration of employment and previous wages. These latter findings are in contrast to those reported by Keating et al. (1950) and Mosel and Cozan (1952). However, these earlier studies relied on the correlation measure of accuracy.

Doll (1971)

This study examined faking on individual items from a 200-item biographical inventory covering childhood experiences and activities, academic experiences, attitudes and interests, value preferences, and other self-descriptive items. The items were categorized as continuous versus noncontinuous, and as objective versus subjective. However, since the number of objective items that were also noncontinuous was very small, these two item facets were confounded.

The respondents were 300 college graduates who were receiving armed services preflight training at that time. Three different administration conditions were employed. First, all respondents completed the questionnaire after being told to respond honestly and that the responses were to be used for research purposes only. Following this, the sample was divided into three groups of 100 respondents that each completed a second administration with the intent of applying for a research position in one of the following conditions: (a) fake to look good, but be prepared to defend any answers in an interview; (b) fake to look good, but be aware there is a lie scale to identify people who exaggerate; or (c) fake to look as good as possible. The measure of faking that was employed indexed whether response-option popularity had shifted between honest and fake administrations. The results showed a greater propensity for subjective and continuous items to be faked. The greatest amount of faking occurred under instructions to fake to look as good as possible. An interesting point was that the lie scale condition produced significantly less distortion than either of the other two conditions.

Cohen and Lefkowitz (1974)

In this study, an 80-item biodata questionnaire was administered to 118 applicants for clerical, supervisory, and sales positions. Their purpose was to identify characteristics of persons likely to fake responses in a socially desirable direction. The K-scale from the MMPI was used as the index of faking in a socially desirable direction and served as the criterion for validating biodata item responses. This scale has been used to correct scores on the MMPI as a control for faking.

Groups were formed based on a dichotomization of K-scale scores at the median ($Md = 18$). Fourteen biodata items were selected to identify potential fakers based on a cross-validation study using a hold-out group method. Cohen and Lefkowitz (1974) state that those qualities portrayed in the responses to the 14 items may be taken at face value. In addition, they allowed that since only 4 out of these 14 items were verifiable, the responses to the unverifiable biodata items may also reflect the same socially desirable response set that was measured by the K-scale.

Cascio (1975)

This study examined the accuracy of responses to 17 verifiable bio-graphical items for a sample of incumbent police officers. The items were taken from a 184-item biographical questionnaire given in an experimental administration to 784 officers. A random sample of 112 of these officers was used for the study. Responses to the 17 items were compared with data from the confidential application blank that each officer had completed before employment, with this latter information having previously been verified.

The items were answerable using continuous or ordered response categories, with the possible exceptions of marital status, reason for leaving last full-time job, and type of high school attended longest. Correlations between respondents' and verified values were reported as ranging from .41 to 1.0, with a median $r = .94$. Only two items yielded correlations below .66—age at first marriage and type of high school attended longest. Although the item "the number of jobs held since leaving school but prior to present job" had an acceptable correlation (its value was not reported), one half of the respondents underreported this number. Only one item, "reason for leaving last full-time job," was comparable with earlier studies. The results for that item were viewed as consistent with Keating et al. (1950) and Mosel and Cozan (1952), but in contrast to Goldstein (1971). Although differences among studies for job types and administration conditions were noted, the results were interpreted as additional evidence that responses to verifiable items are unlikely to be distorted.

Schrader and Osburn (1977)

This study was conducted to determine whether intentional faking would alter scores on an empirically keyed biographical questionnaire. Schrader and Osburn manipulated the specificity of the position description provided to subjects, which described either a specific sales position or a general management position. Some subjects were told that there may be a lie-detection scale among the items. The 57-item biodata questionnaire contained subjective and objective items, with continuous and noncontinuous response options. The items covered background experiences, attitudes, and self-perceptions. Empirical keys, one for a sales position and the other for assessing management potential, had been developed by a large petrochemical firm.

The subjects were undergraduate college students who responded to the questionnaire under the fake conditions first ($N = 196$), and one to two weeks later completed the same inventory in an honest condition ($N = 148$). This was done to mitigate against the effect that prior exposure to the questionnaire could, by itself, enhance the amount of faking (Klein & Owens, 1965).

The results showed that the threat of lie detection reduced the amount of response distortion on keyed total scores. This was true regardless of position specificity. Contrary to the expectation that those instructed in details about a specific position would be more able to distort responses, subjects given the management position instructions did better overall on both keys. This was explained by noting that the sales position description contained duties more similar to a management position than a stereotypical sales position. There was also a substantial correlation ($r = .80$) between the two sets of keyed scores for the honest responses. The authors concluded that perhaps the stereotypes utilized by the subjects in the specific position condition interfered with effective faking.

Finally, Schrader and Osburn (1977) noted that "data collection resulted in a significant variation in the number of subjects in the cells" (p. 400). At the outset, 196 subjects were given the initial fake administration of the questionnaire. If there had been an equal number of subjects in each condition at the start, then most of the subject attrition would have occurred in the two lie scale conditions. It is not known whether differential attrition at the honest administration may have affected the results.

Thornton and Gierasch (1980)

This study also examined the susceptibility of an empirically keyed biographical inventory to faking. The inventory used had been developed for selecting and placing management trainees in a nationwide firm. Separate keys were available for predicting performance in 10 job-related areas, and the keys were based on results from a concurrent cross-validation design. The general areas covered by questions on the biodata questionnaire included childhood experiences, school and work achievements, and preferences and skills related to work and leisure. All items employed a multiple-choice format, but no mention is made of the total number of items.

Male college students ($N = 94$) participated in the study by completing the questionnaire under both an honest and a fake instructional set. The fake set was created by asking subjects to "answer the test items in such a way as to maximize the probability of obtaining a managerial job" (p. 49). Order of instructional set was counterbalanced, and only the instructional set effect, comparing honest versus faked responses, was significant. Significant score increases were reported for 7 of the 10 biodata scales under the fake conditions. The authors concluded that even empirically derived keys may be no less susceptible to faking than measures developed for more general purposes.

Pannone (1984)

Pannone developed a biographical questionnaire using a rational, behavioral consistency approach where the items were developed from job task statements, which themselves totally covered the domain of an electrician's job. The response scale simply reflected the level of experience the respondent had with each task. As such, all the items would seem to be objective, and thus potentially verifiable. No indication of the total number of items was provided. In order to assess faking on this questionnaire, a single additional item was used that asked for level of experience with a nonexistent piece of electrical equipment. Responses to that item were not included as part of the biodata score.

Over one-third of the 221 applicants for the job claimed to have some level of experience with the nonexistent piece of electrical equipment. Splitting the sample based on the response to this faking item, the biodata scores of the fakers were significantly greater than those for the honest applicants. Significant correlations were obtained between the biographical questionnaire and both a written test of job knowledge and years of work experience for the honest applicants. Although the biographical scores correlated significantly with the written test for the fakers, the correlation was substantially lower. In addition, whereas the written test correlated significantly with both years of electrical training and years of work experience for the honest applicants, similar relations were not found for the fakers. Response to the faking item was not related to the written test score.

In effect, a considerable proportion of applicants faked a response on an objective biodata item. This distortion had an effect on the validity of the total biodata questionnaire scores. Since the fakers as a group scored significantly higher on the biodata inventory, it would have been interesting to know the effect that removing the fakers would have had on the overlap of the distributions of passers and failures (Pannone, 1984, Table 2, p. 511).

Shaffer, Saunders, and Owens (1986)

This study examined the long-term stability of responses to biodata questions. Its focus was on the accuracy of biodata used in a research setting with 237 college students. Owens' 118-item biographical questionnaire was employed (Owens & Schoenfeldt, 1979). The questions cover demographics, early experiences, and attitudes believed related to personality, adjustment, and success in various life pursuits. The item format is multiple-choice with ordered response options.

Test-retest data were collected for individuals who had completed their first testing at the time of entry to college and again 5 years later. In addition, observer reports were also collected from parents of some respondents for a select subset of items from the questionnaire. Each parent was instructed to answer the items as they believed their child would have answered at the time of entering college. Data were obtained from at least one parent for about half of the respondents. Accuracy and stability were examined at both the component score and item levels for the test-retest and the observer data.

At the component score level, test-retest correlations ranged from .49 to .91 for the 13 components used for males, and from .50 to .88 for the 15 components for the females, with most values in both groups being quite respectable. Those components comprised of more objective items tended to have the highest test-retest correlations for each sex. Mean shifts in component scores from test to retest were noted on 4 of the 13 components for males, and on 6 of the 14 components for females. These mean changes were evenly split between objective and subjective factors for males, while five of the mean differences were on the more subjective components for the females.

The correlations between component scores of the subjects at initial testing (i.e., 5 years earlier) with those based on the responses of their parents showed the same pattern as noted above for the test-retest data, although the magnitudes were substantially lower. This may be expected, since such comparisons involve both source and time sampling differences. Only three components were examined for each sex, and only one component for males resulted in a mean difference. Since the scores of sons and parents were unrelated on this component (social desirability), it is unclear just what this mean difference represents.

More than 60 percent of the test-retest correlations at the item level were above .50 for both sexes. However, about 30 percent of the items for both males and females yielded significant mean differences between testings. Comparison of parents' item responses with those of their children showed generally lower correlations than the test-retest item correlations. Significant mean differences from parent responses occurred on 7 out of 26 items for males, and on 6 out of 22 items for females. For the test-retest data there were mean differences on 7 out of the 26 items for males, and on 9 out of the 22 items for females.

Shaffer et al. (1986) discuss several possible sources of inaccuracy in the item-level data. Item objectivity was cited as one source, and the authors showed that an index of item objectivity was positively related to the magnitude of the test-retest item correlations for both sexes. A second potential source of inaccuracy was the influence of social desirability on item responses. Here an index of item susceptibility to socially desirable responding was found to be negatively related to test-retest correlations for both sexes. This suggested that greater susceptibility to social desirability had led to somewhat lowered response consistency. (It would also be interesting to know the correlation between the item objectivity index and the social desirability index.) The third source of inaccuracy focused on potential confusion with the time reference in the question (i.e., not all items made specific reference to high school experiences). However, this source of inaccuracy was ruled out for both sexes.

Hough, Eaton, Dunnette, Kamp, and McCloy (1990)

In this study, various mechanisms for detecting response distortion on a 209-item rationally developed biodata questionnaire entitled *Assessment of Background and Life Experiences* (ABLE) were investigated. The scoring of the questionnaire produced values for each of ten content scales that were related to six temperament constructs; another score was based on self-reported items about physical condition; and scores on four response validity scales were also obtained (Peterson et al., 1990).

The temperament constructs had been selected based on R. Hogan's (1982) six factors that are related to the Big Five personality dimensions (Hough et al., 1990; John, 1990). The four validity scales are of special interest here, as each focuses on a problem area believed to potentially affect the accuracy of obtained scores. A separate validity scale was specifically designed to detect each of the following problems: random responding, social desirability, intentionally creating a poor impression, and lack of self-knowledge.

Hough et al. (1990) examined response distortion in several ways. First, a faking study was conducted using 245 male enlisted personnel who completed the ABLE under both honest and either fake good (i.e., be sure that the army selects you) or fake bad (i.e., be sure that the army does not select you) instructions. The order of honest and faking conditions was counterbalanced. Since significant interactions involving the order effect were obtained, responses to only the first administration of the ABLE were used in subsequent analyses. This was done to best reflect an administration similar to an applicant setting.

Significant effects were found comparing the honest and fake-good conditions across the 11 content scales. Mean scores were consistently greater for the fake good condition. A similar but opposite set of results was obtained for comparisons of the honest with the fake bad conditions, where all mean scores for the fake bad condition were consistently lower across the content scales. The effect sizes for the fake bad comparisons were uniformly larger than the fake good comparison for the same content scale, possibly indicating ceiling effects or other limitations involved with increasing scores in the fake good condition.

The response validity scales did appear effective in distinguishing the three groups from one another. The social desirability scale detected a mean difference between the fake good condition and the honest condition, with higher scores in the former group. The other three validity scales were useful in discriminating the fake bad condition from the honest condition.

Further evidence of the usefulness of the validity scales was presented showing that identification of random responding, of high rates of socially desirable responding, and of those likely to be trying to create a poor impression were all potentially useful in an operational sense. Comparisons based on large to very large sample sizes were presented that demonstrated that some concurrent validities between ABLE content scales scores and various performance criteria were moderated by these three response sets. Differences on the self-knowledge scale were not found to moderate any of the validities.

Another important aspect of the Hough et al. (1990) study was its conclusion of a sample of recent inductees who completed the ABLE in a situation that closely approximated selection. Comparisons of the means for this group with those from the honest condition for the faking study showed 7 scales where the means for inductees were lower and 4 scales where their means were higher. The magnitudes of the differences were greatest for the scales where the inductees had the lower scores. When compared to the much larger concurrent validity sample, the inductees scored lower on 6 and higher on 5 of the content scales. Here again, the magnitudes of the differences were greatest on the scales where the inductees had the lower scores. This was taken as evidence that incumbents represent a more select (restricted) group on the attributes measured.

Factors Affecting Comparisons Across Studies

Assessing the cumulative meaning of the set of studies described above is complicated by several factors. First, the contents of the biodata questionnaires are not comparable across studies, and this has also been viewed as a problem for validity generalization (Dreher & Sackett, 1983). The studies by Keating et al. (1950), Mosel and Cozan (1952), and Goldstein (1971) covered virtually the same application blank items, whereas the study by Cascio (1975) had only one such item in common with these other studies. All of these studies were focused on a relatively small number of items with verifiable responses that are typical of application blanks. The remaining studies used larger sets of items. Among these latter studies, Pannone (1984) used a narrow range of life experiences that focused on tasks of a particular job, while Hough et al. (1990) used a broad range of item content.

Another difference between studies rests with the operational definition used for accuracy. Of the studies that focused on response verification, three relied primarily on the correlation measure of accuracy and reported a high degree of accuracy (Cascio, 1975; Keating et al., 1950; Mozel & Cozan, 1952). Since Cascio's (1975) study was based on incumbent police officers, one might expect a high level of agreement. When absolute agreement was used, responses to some verifiable items were found to be inaccurate for job applicants (Goldstein, 1971; Pannone, 1984). The most frequently used measure of accuracy among the remaining studies was the mean difference measure (Hough et al., 1990; Klein & Owens, 1965; Schrader & Osburn, 1977; Shaffer et al., 1986; Thorton & Gierasch, 1980).

The studies also differ in terms of the level of analysis employed. Some studies focused on individual item responses, others on keyed scale scores, and still others on component, factorial, or rational scale scores. Although the linear combinations used at higher levels of analysis are based on item level responses, it is possible for the effects of distortion at the item level to be offset by aggregation over items and/or respondents (Furnham, 1986; Lautenschlager, 1986). However, this should not be assumed true in any given instance. For empirically keyed instruments, a response might change in an absolute sense, but be immaterial for the keyed value (i.e., both response options get keyed with the same value).

The studies reported here also differed in terms of the situation or context of measurement. As reported in Table 1, only four of the studies were conducted under selection circumstances, and one of the studies reported by Hough et al. (1990) would also seem reasonable to include here. There is some evidence that the importance of the situation (i.e., selection vs. nonselection) is minimal for faking studies that have used interest inventories (Abrahams, Neuman, & Githens, 1971), with a caveat that use of an entire inventory rather than a select set of keyed items be employed to reduce the transparency of the items (Zalinski & Abrahams, 1979). The findings of Hough et al. (1990) would suggest that inclusion of a broad array of items with item content dispersed is not likely to present serious problems of intentional distortion in operational use.

General Findings

There is evidence that objective biodata items are less susceptible to distortion than items that are more subjective. This evidence comes in several forms. Doll (1971) investigated changes in option endorsement at the item level and found more response changes on subjective items.

Shaffer et al. (1986) found that long-term stability, as indexed by both the correlational and mean difference measures of accuracy, was better for objective items. Klein and Owens (1965) found that a biodata key based on a subjective criterion was more susceptible to faking than one based on an objective criterion. The results of studies employing only verifiable items would suggest that when the correlation accuracy measure is used, the responses were accurate (Cascio, 1975; Keating et al., 1950; Mosel & Cozan, 1952), but when absolute accuracy was used, responses were less accurate (Goldstein, 1971; Pannone, 1984). Mumford and Owens (1987) state that the mixed findings from studies of verifiable biodata items may indicate a shift in level that does not affect the rank ordering of individuals and, thus, represents a general self-presentation bias.

There is also evidence that direct warnings of possible response verification may reduce intentional distortion (Doll, 1971; Schrader & Osburn, 1977). On this point there have been several unpublished studies in military testing situations that also support the use of warning statements to reduce response distortion (Haymaker & Erwin, 1980; Lautenschlager & Atwater, 1986; Trent, Atwater, & Abrahams, 1986). Mock (1947) reported the effects of different instructional sets on responses to a 65-item biodata form comprised of factual questions. He found that the strongest warning to avoid falsification of responses, which outlined the seriousness of the offense and its consequences, produced the lowest mean score on an attrition criterion key scale for a large sample of military aviator candidates. However, this warning did not improve the validity of the biodata questionnaire compared to standard instructions that requested that the subjects simply tell the truth about themselves. Instructions that encouraged laxity in responding did produce less valid responses.

It seems clear that when instructed to do so, respondents are capable of distorting their responses so as to either increase or decrease their scores as requested. This was true for both empirical keys (Klein & Owens, 1965; Schrader & Osburn, 1977; Shaffer et al., 1986; Thorton & Gierasch, 1980) and rationally developed scales (Hough et al., 1990).

DISCUSSION AND DIRECTION FOR FUTURE RESEARCH AND PRACTICE

EFFECTS ON VALIDITY

The published evidence is mixed regarding how the validity of biodata scale scores might be affected by distortion. On the one hand, Pannone (1984) found that the biodata scores of fakers were not as strongly correlated with written test scores as were those of the honest respondents, suggesting validity was affected by faking. In effect, self-presentation bias was not uniform across individuals in the total sample. Hough et al. (1990), however, reported that distortion as indexed by several response validity scales had virtually no effect on the concurrent validities for biodata scales. It is important to note that the biodata questionnaires used in these two studies were very different. Pannone's questionnaire was focused on job content for one particular type of job, and, thus, its validity may have been more easily compromised by faking. The Hough et al. (1990) questionnaire measured a broad array of temperament constructs. Also, the specificity of the position(s) involved seems an appropriate concern in comparing these studies. It seems likely that Pannone's (1984) respondents would have sensed greater competition for positions. Selection pressures, and perhaps the applicants' perceptions of competition for available positions at entry to the organization, may affect both the need and willingness to distort responses.

There is also evidence that the social desirability content of biodata items may actually increase validity for sales positions (Dunnette, McCartney, Carlson, & Kirchner, 1962; J. B. Hogan & Stokes, 1989). Hough et al. (1990) noted this and suggested that the differences with their findings and those of Dunnette et al. (1962) may be due to differences in the populations involved and to specific characteristics that may be differentiating for sales job applicants. It may be that the type of job influences the role of socially desirable responding. Zerbe and Paulhus (1987) discuss a number of points that would be useful to consider in future research in this area.

LEVEL OF ANALYSIS

Should response distortion be examined at the item level or at some aggregate level? It would seem that each level of analysis serves a purpose. Clearly, here one needs to be concerned with both detecting faking at the item level and determining the impact of faking in terms of effects on scores, however the latter are derived. In the final analysis, it is the validity of those scores that should be of most concern. The detection of faking on items may be useful in isolating potential sources of distortion. Thus, significant distortion at an aggregate level could suggest a need for examination of distortion at the item level. If the source(s) of distortion can be more precisely located, then it (they) can be removed, through either the revision or elimination of such items. The discussion presented in Nederhof (1985) and Hough et al. (1990) on the success of various methods to reduce distortion is relevant here.

Assessing Distortion

What measure of distortion should be employed? One could argue that even if response shifts occur, as long as the shift is relatively uniform across subjects (i.e., the rank order of respondents is preserved), then the faking of the item is inconsequential. A counter argument here is that if one is concerned about faking, it is generally not because one thinks it will be uniform across respondents, but rather because it can isolate select fakers. Accepting that some people will be more inclined (and perhaps have greater need) to fake, it seems reasonable to assume that rank ordering would be violated. The question is just how sensitive are the various accuracy indices to the problem of the likely low base rates of fakers in our samples of actual applicants?

What form of faking is really damaging? Regarding individual differences in the ability to consciously manipulate scores on personality inventories, R. Hogan (1991) concluded that "the ability to enhance scores on personality inventories is itself a personality variable that is also associated with good adjustment" (p.32). It is interesting to note that shortly thereafter, he also notes that better adjusted persons tend to have higher self-deception scores, that is, positively biased self-images. The distinction is that self-deception is not defined as involving a conscious effort.

Biodata Items and General Adjustment

In the final analysis, it is not an index of faking at the group level that is of interest, but rather an index that might indicate who is and, therefore, who is not, faking. The approach of controlling for the effects of social desirability by adjusting scores on noncognitive measures has been criticized as hopeless, if not mindless (Rorer, 1990). It is important to note here that some aspects of socially desirable responding are really associated with general adjustment (R. Hogan, 1991; Paulhus, 1991), and since various types of biodata items have been shown to relate to adjustment constructs (Mumford & Owens, 1987; Smernou & Lautenschlager, 1991), one may not want to remove such effects from responses to a given biodata questionnaire. A key component of the contents of many biodata items may be a natural reflection of what is, *in fact,* socially desired. Attempts at using corrections for such factors have not proven generally successful in enhancing the validity of scores (Cronbach, 1990; Rorer, 1990). Adopting the approach of developing separate response validity scales, as employed by Hough et al. (1990), would seem to hold more promise.

TYPES OF DISTORTION

Response distortion can result for different reasons. One is an outright conscious misrepresentation of facts, which may be construed as dishonesty. Another may be due to failure of memory. Yet another form may result more from a tendency to exaggerate in self-presentation, and generally this will be a matter of degree. Such exaggeration may be impression management, when consciously invoked, or may be a manifestation of self-deception (see below). In studies that have employed instructions to fake good and/or fake bad, the respondents may distort responses along lines of schemas or stereotypes they hold, which may or may not come into play outside of research testing contexts.

Paulhus (1986, 1991) discusses two types of socially desirable responding that have relevance here, and these types have been identified by others (e.g., Jackson & Messick, 1962). The first type is labeled *impression management* and represents the conscious attempt to put oneself in the best light possible. The second type has been referred to as *self-deception* and represents "a less conscious attempt to look good to oneself" (Paulhus, 1986, p. 146). There are surface similarities between these types and the measures of social desirability and self-knowledge used by Hough et al. (1990). The self-deception and self-knowledge items reflect aspects of adjustment, and research indicates that these facets of socially desirable responding should not be controlled for in other measures (R. Hogan, 1991; Paulhus, 1991). The connection between impression management and social desirability is most direct and critical to the discussion here. It would seem that the inclusion of impression management scales as part of an effort to identify potential fakers may prove useful.

In a similar vein, the use of Pannone's (1984) method for assessing distortion seems particularly appealing. However, without knowing the content of the faking item, it is not possible to assess if ambiguity in the item itself may have contributed to the extensive distortion of responses he observed. Those wishing to use a similar methodology would do well to consider how best to describe nonexistent equipment/tasks to avoid any confusion with those that do exist. Items of this type could easily be included in an operational biodata form. However, such items might be detectable by decision makers or others wishing to circumvent the system (Hughes, Dunn, & Baxter, 1956; Thayer, 1977).

Pannone (1984) examined faking in a specific context that seems very close to what honesty or integrity tests attempt to measure. Respondents may not have been trying to appear more socially desirable in an impression management sense, but more likely were deliberately falsifying experience with a nonexistent piece of equipment. Rather than attempt to review the literature on honesty testing here, which would lead the discussion too far afield, the reader is referred to reviews by Sackett and Harris (1984) and Sackett, Burris, and Callahan (1989).

ORDER EFFECTS IN EXPERIMENTAL STUDIES OF FAKING

The finding of an interaction between the order of faking and honest administrations by Hough et al. (1990) merits further consideration for research into faking. It would be useful to note the locus and nature of the interaction effects. Although Klein and Owens (1965) noted an order effect for faking versus honest administrations, Thorton and Gierasch (1980) found neither order effects nor an interaction involving order. A difference between the Hough et al. (1990) and the other studies of induced faking was the inclusion of conditions to fake bad in their design. It may be premature to abandon the use of repeated measurement methods for examining the nature of response distortion in experimental studies (Gordon & Gross, 1978; Lautenschlager, 1986), as suggested by Hough et al. (1990). However, it is not clear that studies of induced faking have any clear analog in operational testing conditions (Abrahams et al., 1971; Furnham, 1986).

THE ROLE OF AGE

Thayer (1977) cited early research by Kurtz (1941) and Kornhauser that suggested the importance of age as a moderator in the use of biographical data for selection of life insurance agents. Cohen and Lefkowitz (1974) found self-reported age, along with several other biodata items, was useful in predicting who would respond to personality items in a socially desirable direction. Pannone (1984) reported that applicants who faked responses had significantly more work experience. Assuming for the moment that this difference itself was not attributable to distortion, then experience may be a proxy for age. Kurtz (1941) found that age made a difference in how personality versus biodata items were weighted to predict success of life insurance agents. For those under 26 years of age, the personality items were weighted more than the biodata items, while scores for the older applicants were weighted with just the opposite emphasis. This may be taken as evidence that age-related factors have an impact on distortion and/ or the validity of biodata scores. It is also important to note here that some of the differences in the longitudinal study of item responses reported by Shaffer et al. (1986) may have been due to developmental changes.

ISSUES FOR PRACTICE AND RESEARCH

- We need more evidence to determine whether a true selection situation affects distortion of responses to biodata items and whether this influences validity. If there are such effects, we must consider how to reduce demands that influence the amount and type(s) of distortion present. General and local employment conditions may serve as cues to the need to attend to distortion.
- It may be useful to include items or scales designed to detect distortion. This can take several different forms: (a) the use of fake questions of the type used by Pannone (1984), (b) the use of social desirability and other response validity scales such as those used by Hough et al. (1990), or (c) the use of an impression management scale such as the one developed by Paulhus (1991). If one were following the advice of Pace and Schoenfeldt (1977), that is, using job analysis as a basis for construction of the biodata instrument, then it would seem more likely that the use of specific fake questions would fit in better with the item content. For biodata questionnaires with more broadly based item content, the inclusion of scales to assess impression management may be less obvious to the respondent, especially if such items are interspersed.
- The repetition of a few biodata items may prove a useful check on the accuracy of responses. This would be easy to implement for a computer administration of a biodata questionnaire, where respondents are not at liberty to review their previous responses. However, if subjects become aware of item repetition, this may influence responses and produce undesired consequences. On the topic of computer administration, another possibility is worth noting. McDaniel and Timm (1990) recently reported on the potential use of reaction time as a means for assessing distortion to biodata items. A key issue would be how baseline latency is determined, and such an approach would tend more toward idiographic assessment. In addition, there may be other relevant issues to consider associated with honesty measurement (Adair, 1973; Sackett et al., 1989) and computer administration of questionnaires (Lautenschlager & Flaherty, 1990; Martin & Nagao, 1989).
- Warnings regarding verification of responses may be useful where there are a number of verifiable biodata items. It is doubtful that warnings will have as much effect when the respondent has reason to question the potential for response verification. Care should be taken to ensure that the use of warnings is appropriate and does not itself lead to unintended consequences.

- Several authors have suggested criteria for constructing biodata items that may make them less prone to distortion. Without attempting to be exhaustive, such factors include a focus on factual matters that are observable (i.e., potentially verifiable) and refer to specific time periods (Asher, 1972; Mumford & Owens, 1987; Stricker, 1989).
- Care should be taken to ensure that the respondent is indeed the one providing the answers and that no coaching has taken place. Protection of the scoring key is an important consideration to avoid contamination by the coaching of would-be recruits by the recruiter on how to complete a biodata questionnaire (Brown, 1978; Peterson & Wallace, 1966). It is not unusual for a well-intentioned recruiter to try to find a particular set of responses that passes the scoring key. Once determined, a set of such answers might well be used in the coaching of job candidates the recruiter views as desirable. Here it would be useful to employ checks to determine unusual response pattern consistencies based on particular recruiters and/or testing sites. It may also be useful to determine if changes in training, policies, or procedures might help minimize the reinforcement value of such behavior on the part of recruiters.
- Once potential cases of response distortion have been identified, it would be important to seek out other corroborative information. This could take the form of response verification where feasible and warranted. Well-developed scales that detect possible distortion may eventually reduce costs associated with external response verification. However, periodic checks of continued validity would be advisable.
- Finally, for more general research purposes, it would be useful to examine the stability of biographical information through alternative research procedures. The results of biodata item and component stability obtained by Shaffer et al. (1986) are encouraging, but perhaps the assumptions used in testing for stability were a bit too restrictive. Alternative methods to consider include multiple group and multiple occasion component analysis and autoregressive and growth curve models (Kenny & Campbell, 1989; McArdle & Epstein, 1987; Millsap & Meredith, 1988).

Despite these obstacles, there seems to be considerable interest in the examination of distortion in responses to biodata questionnaires, as evidenced by the number of relevant titles of presentations at professional meetings in recent years (Baratta & Stout, 1990; Colquitt & Becker, 1989; Crosby, 1990; Hogan & Stokes, 1989; McDaniel & Timm, 1990; McManus, 1990; Stricker, et al., 1987). Given the present state of research in this area, such interest is needed and welcomed. It may well be that the concern over distortion of biodata responses is much ado about next to nothing. If so, then additional research and applications should bear this out.

CONCLUSION

In his chapter on background data, Owens (1976) noted that although biodata inventories are often good predictors of relevant criteria, "we lack longitudinal evidence ... that what the S says he did (in the past) is *really* what he did" (p. 619). More recently, Mumford and Stokes (1992) have noted that the assumption that an accurate biodata instrument is more valid than a less accurate one has not been adequately tested. To date, we are really not much closer to knowing the absolute truthfulness of the responses given to biographical data items, and it is reasonable to question whether such knowledge is obtainable, or even necessary. As noted in some studies where verifiable biodata items were involved, some of the discrepancies observed may have resulted from error in the validating (external) information itself.

Certainly, accurate knowledge of what the subject actually did would be useful in its own right. However, given the broad array of the types of questions included in many biodata questionnaires, the issue is often taken beyond what the respondent *did* in the past to what was felt, believed, preferred, and perceived. To that end, given developmental changes, the limitations of autobiographical memory, and the potential biases present in judgments (in self-reports or the observations of others), it may be too much to expect response verification or response stability in any exacting sense. At best, we can attempt to detect distortion and take such information into consideration when making decisions.

REFERENCES

Abrahams, N. M., Neuman, I., & Githens, W. H. (1971). Faking vocational interests: Simulated versus real life motivation. *Personnel Psychology, 24,* 5–12.

Adair, J. G. (1973). *The human subject: The social psychology of the psychological experiment.* Boston: Little, Brown.

Aherns, E. (1949). *Handbook of personnel forms and records.* New York: American Management Association.

Albright, L. E., Glennon, J. R., & Smith, W. J. (1961). *The use of psychological tests in industry.* Cleveland: Howard Allen.

Asher, J. J. (1972). The biographical item: Can it be improved? *Personnel Psychology, 25,* 251–269.

Atwater, D. C., & Abrahams, N. M. (1983). *Adaptability screening: Development and initial validation of the recruiting background questionnaire* (RBQ; NPRDC TR 84–11). San Diego: Navy Personnel Research and Development Center.

Baratta, J. E., & Stout, J. D. (1990, April). *Fakability of a computerized biodata instrument.* Paper presented at the annual meeting of the Society for Industrial and Organizational Psychology, Miami Beach, FL.

Blum, M. L., & Naylor, J. C. (1968). *Industrial psychology.* New York: Harper & Row.

Brown, S. H. (1978). Long-term validity of a personal history item scoring procedure. *Journal of Applied Psychology, 63,* 673–676.

Brumback, G. B. (1969). A note on criterion contamination in the validation of biographical data. *Educational and Psychological Measurement, 29,* 439–443.

Brush, D. H., & Owens, W. A. (1979). Implementation and evaluation of an assessment classification model for manpower utilization. *Personnel Psychology, 32,* 369–383.

Campbell, J. P. (1990). An overview of the army selection and classification project. *Personnel Psychology Special Issue: Project A: The U.S. Army Selection and Classification Project, 43,* 231–378.

Cascio, W. F. (1975). Accuracy of verifiable biographical information blank responses. *Journal of Applied Psychology, 60,* 767–769.

Cohen, J., & Lefkowitz, J. (1974). Development of a biographical inventory blank to predict faking on personality tests. *Journal of Applied Psychology, 59,* 404–405.

Colquitt, A. L., & Becker, T. E. (1989, April). *Faking of a biodata form in use: A field study.* Paper presented at the annual meeting of the Society for Industrial and Organizational Psychology, Boston.

Cronbach, L. J. (1990). *Essentials of psychological testing* (6th ed.). New York: Harper & Row.

Cronbach, L. J., & Gleser, G. C. (1965). *Psychological tests and personnel decisions.* Urbana: University of Illinois Press.

Cronbach, L. J., & Meehl, P. E. (1955). Construct validity in psychological tests. *Psychological Bulletin, 52,* 281–302.

Crosby, M. M. (1990, April). *Social desirability and biodata: Predicting sales success.* Paper presented at the annual meeting of the Society for Industrial and Organizational Psychology, Miami Beach, FL.

Doll, R. E. (1971). Item susceptibility to attempted faking as related to item characteristic and adopted fake set. *Journal of Psychology, 77,* 9–16.

Dreher, G. F., & Sackett, P. R. (1983). *Perspectives on employee staffing and selection.* Homewood, IL: Irwin.

Dunnette, M. D., McCartney, J., Carlson, H. C., & Kirchner, W. K. (1962). A study of faking behavior on a forced-choice self-description checklist. *Personnel Psychology, 15,* 13–24.

Furnham, A. (1986). Response bias, social desirability, and dissimulation. *Personality and Individual Differences, 7,* 385–400.

Goldstein, I. L. (1971). The application blank: How honest are the responses? *Journal of Applied Psychology, 55,* 491–492.

Gordon, M. E., & Gross, R. H. (1978). A critique of methods for operationalizing the concept of fakeability. *Educational and Psychological Measurement, 38,* 771–782.

Guion, R. M. (1965). *Personnel testing.* New York: McGraw-Hill.

Haymaker, J. C., & Erwin, F. W. (1980). *Investigation of applicant responses and falsification detection procedures for the Military Applicant Profile* (Final Project Report, Work Unit No. DA644520). Alexandria, VA: U.S. Army Reserach Institute for the Behavioral and Social Sciences.

Hogan, J. B., & Stokes, G. S. (1989, April). *Influence of socially desirable responding on empirically validated biodata keys.* Paper presented at the annual meeting of the Society for Industrial and Organizational Psychology, Boston.

Hogan, R. (1991). Personality and personality assessment. In M. Dunnette & L. M. Hough (Eds.), *Handbook of industrial and organizational psychology* (2d ed., vol. 2, pp. 873–919). Palo Alto, CA: Consulting Psychologists Press.

Hogan, R., & Nicholson, R. A. (1988). The meaning of personality test scores. *American Psychologist, 43,* 621–626.

Hough, L. M. (1989). Development of personality measures to supplement selection procedures. In B. J. Fallon, H. P. Pfister, & J. Brebner (Eds.), *Advances in industrial and organizational psychology.* Amsterdam: North Holland.

Hough, L. M., Eaton, N. K., Dunnette, M. D., Kamp, J. D., & McCloy, R. A. (1990). Criterion-related validities of personality constructs and the effect of response distortion on those validities. *Journal of Applied Psychology, 75,* 581–595.

Hughes, J. F., Dunn, J. F., & Baxter, B. (1956). The validity of selection instruments under operational conditions. *Personnel Psychology, 9,* 321–324.

Jackson, D. N., & Messick, S. (1962). Response styles on the MMPI. *Journal of Abnormal and Social Psychology, 65,* 285–289.

John, O. P. (1990). The "Big 5" factor taxonomy: Dimensions of personality in the natural language and in questionnaires. In L. A. Previn (Ed.), *Handbook of personality: Theory and research.* New York: Guilford.

Keating, E., Paterson, D. G., & Stone, C. H. (1950). Validity of work histories obtained by interview. *Journal of Applied Psychology, 34,* 6–11.

Kenny, D. A., & Campbell, D. T. (1989). On the measurement of stability in overtime data. *Journal of Personality, 57,* 445–481.

Klein, S. P., & Owens, W. A. (1965) Faking of a scored life history blank as a function of criterion objectivity. *Journal of Applied Psychology, 49,* 452–454.

Kurtz, A. K. (1941). Recent research in the selection of life insurance agents. *Journal of Applied Psychology, 25,* 11–17.

Landy, F. J. (1986). Stamp collecting versus science: Validation as hypothesis testing. *American Psychologist, 41,* 1183–1192.

Lautenschlager, G. J. (1986). Within-subject measures for the assessment of individual differences in faking. *Educational and Psychological Measurement, 46,* 309–316.

Lautenschlager, G. J., & Atwater, D. C. (1986). *Controlling response distortion on an empirically keyed biodata questionnaire.* Unpublished manuscript.

Lautenschlager, G. J., & Flaherty, V. L. (1990). Computer administration of question-naires: More desirable or more social desirability? *Journal of Applied Psychology, 75, 310–314.*

Mael, F. A. (1991). A conceptual rationale for the domain and attributes of biodata items. *Personnel Psychology, 44,* 763–792.

Martin, C. L., & Nagao, D. H. (1989). Some effects of computerized interviewing on job applicant responses. *Journal of Applied Psychology, 74,* 72–80.

McArdle, J. J., & Epstein, D. (1987). Latent growth curves within developmental structural equation models. *Child Development, 58,* 110–133.

McDaniel, M. A., & Timm, H. (1990, August). *Lying takes time: Predicting deception in biodata using response latency.* Paper presented at the annual meeting of the American Psychological Association, Boston.

McManus, M. A. (1990, April). *Detection of faking on an empirically-keyed biodata instrument.* Paper presented at the annual meeting of the Society for Industrial and Organizational Psychology, Miami Beach, FL.

Millsap, R. E., & Meredith, W. (1988). Component analysis in cross-sectional and longitudinal data. *Psychometrika, 53,* 123–134.

Mitchell, T. W., Chair, Arvey, R. D., Ashworth, S. D., Hogan, R., Hough, L. M., Pajanen, G. E., Reilly, R. R., & Schoenfeldt, L. F. (1989, April). *Biodata vs. personality: The same or different classes of individual differences.* Panel discussion presented at the annual meeting of the Society for Industrial and Organizational Psychology, Boston.

Mock, S. J. (1947). Biographical data. In J. P. Guilford & J. I. Lacey (Eds.), *Printed classification tests (Report No. 5).* Army Air Forces Aviation Psychology Program Research Reports. Washington, DC: U.S. Government Printing Office.

Mosel, J. M., & Cozan, L. W. (1952). The accuracy of application blank work histories. *Journal of Applied Psychology, 36,* 365–369.

Mumford, M. D., & Owens, W. A. (1987). Methodology review: Principles, procedures, and findings in the application of background data measures. *Applied Psychological Measurement, 11,* 1–31.

Mumford, M. D., & Nickels, B. J. (1990, April). *Applying principles of content and construct validity to background data.* Paper presented at the annual meeting of the Society for Industrial and Organizational Psychology, Miami Beach, FL.

Mumford, M. D., & Stokes, G. S. (1992). Developmental determinants of individual action: Theory and practice in applying background data measures. In M. D. Dunnette & L. M. Hough (Eds.), *Handbook of industrial and organizational psychology* (2d ed., vol. 3, pp. 61–138). Palo Alto, CA: Consulting Psychologists Press.

Nederhof, A. J. (1985). Methods of coping with social desirability bias: A review. *European Journal of Social Psychology, 15,* 263–280.

Nunnally, J. C. (1967) *Psychometric theory.* New York: McGraw-Hill.

Owens, W. A. (1976) Background data. In M. D. Dunnette (Ed.), *Handbook of industrial and organizational psychology* (1st ed., pp. 609–644). Chicago: Rand McNally.

Owens, W. A., & Schoenfeldt, L. F. (1979). Toward a classification of persons. *Journal of Applied Psychology, 65,* 569–607.

Pace, L. A., & Schoenfeldt, L. F. (1977). Legal concerns in the use of weighted applications. *Personnel Psychology, 30,* 159–166.

Pannone, R. D. (1984). Predicting test performance: A content valid approach to screening applicants. *Personnel Psychology, 37,* 507–514.

Paulhus, D. L. (1984). Two-component models of socially desirable responding. *Journal of Personality and Social Psychology, 46*(3), 598–609.

Paulhus, D. L. (1986). Self-deception and impression management in test responses. In A. Angleitner & J. S. Wiggins (Eds.), *Personality assessment via questionnaires* (pp. 143–165). Berlin: Springer-Verlag.

Paulhus, D. L. (1991). Measurement and control of response bias. In J. P. Robinson, P. R. Shaver, L. Wrightsman, & F. M. Andrews (Eds.), *Measures of personality and social-psychological attitudes.* San Diego: Academic Press.

Peterson, D. A., & Wallace, S. R. (1966). Validation of a test in use. *Journal of Applied Psychology, 50,* 13–17.

Peterson, N. G., Hough, L. M., Dunnette, M. D., Rosse, R. L., Houston, J. S., Toquam, J. L., & Wing, H. (1990). Project A: Specification of the predictor domain and development of new selection/classification tests. *Personnel Psychology, 43,* 247–276.

Rorer, L. G. (1990). Personality assessment: A conceptual survey. In L. A. Previn (Ed.), *Handbook of personality: Theory and research.* New York: Guilford.

Russell, C. J., & Domm, D. R. (1990). *On the construct validity of biographical information: Evaluation of a theory based method of item generation.* Paper presented at the annual meeting of the Society for Industrial and Organizational Psychology, Miami Beach, FL.

Sackett, P. R., Burris, L. R., & Callahan, C. (1989). Integrity testing for personnel selection: An update. *Personnel Psychology, 42,* 491–529.

Sackett, P. R., & Harris, M. M. (1984). Honesty testing for personnel selection: A review and critique. *Personnel Psychology, 37,* 221–245.

Schrader, A. D., & Osburn, H. G. (1977) Biodata faking: Effects of induced subtlety and position specificity. *Personnel Psychology, 30,* 395–404.

Schuh, A. J. (1967) Predictability of employee tenure: A review of the literature. *Personnel Psychology, 20,* 133–152.

Shaffer, G. S., Saunders, V., & Owens, W. A. (1986). Additional evidence for the accuracy of biographical data: Long-term retest and observer ratings. *Personnel Psychology, 39,* 791–809.

Sharf, J. C., Dye, D. A., Gandy, J. A., & MacLane, C. N. (1990, April). *Innovative research on the IAR: The first federal-wide biodata form.* Paper presented at the annual meeting of the Society for Industrial and Organizational Psychology, Miami Beach, FL.

Smernou, L. E., & Lautenschlager, G. J. (1991). Autobiographical antecedents and correlates of neuroticism and extraversion. *Personality and Individual Differences, 12,* 49–59.

Smith, W. J., Albright, L. E., Glennon, J. R., & Owens, W. A. (1961). The prediction of research competence and creativity from personal history. *Journal of Applied Psychology, 45,* 59–62.

Stricker, L. J. (1989). *Assessing leadership potential at the naval academy with a biographical measure* (Research Rep. No. RR–89–14). Princeton, NJ: Educational Testing Service.

Stricker, L. J. (Chair), Trent, T., Pannone, R., Vezina, P., Mitchell, T. W., & Walker, C. (1987, August). *Problems of biodata distortion in personnel selection systems.* Symposium conducted at the annual meeting of the American Psychological Association, New York.

Thayer, P. W. (1977). Somethings old, something new. *Personnel Psychology, 30,* 513–524.

Thornton, G. C., & Gierasch, P. F. (1980). Fakability of an empirically derived selection instrument. *Journal of Personality Assessment, 44,* 48–51.

Trent, T. T., Atwater, D. C., & Abrahams, N. M. (1986, April). Biographical screening of military applicants: Experimental assessment of item response distortion. In G. E. Lee (Ed.), *Proceedings of the Tenth Annual Symposium of Psychology in the Department of Defense* (pp. 96–100). Colorado Springs, CO: U.S. Air Force Academy, Department of Behavioral Sciences and Leadership.

Wesman, A. G. (1952). Faking personality test scores in a simulated employment situation. *Journal of Applied Psychology, 36,* 112–113.

Zalinski, J. S., & Abrahams, N. M. (1979). The effects of item context in faking personnel selection inventories. *Personnel Psychology, 32,* 161–166.

Zerbe, W. J., & Paulhus, D. L. (1987). Socially desirable responding in organizational behavior: A reconception. *Academy of Management Review, 12*(2), 250–264.

CONTRIBUTIONS
OF BIODATA
TO ORGANIZATIONS

Whereas the last section included chapters dealing with the specifics of validating and implementing biodata forms, this section includes chapters that provide a more general focus on uses of biodata in organizations, with a view toward the broader implications for their use. Schneider and Schneider provide an organizational framework for biodata research and theory using the attraction–selection–attrition (ASA) model. The ASA model is based on the notion that "the people make the place," or that individuals are attracted to, selected by, and stay with organizations that match their personal characteristics, and it is the characteristics of the individuals in the organization that define it. They review extensive literature in diverse areas, such as vocational interests and turnover, to provide support for their model. The authors suggest that the life history perspective applied in an organization might ultimately provide a means for specifying the kinds of experiences individuals need to have in an organization in order for the organization to be effective. Thus, life experiences can become an avenue for making changes at both the individual and organizational level.

Morrison's chapter also takes the approach that biodata information, rather than being static, can be used for growth of both the individual and the organization. Morrison provides an overview of the career development literature, then describes how biodata may be useful in setting up a career development system. He describes such a system in terms of inputs, processes, and outcomes, and he specifies where biodata can be useful in each section of the model. His chapter includes a discussion of career development among special groups, such as women and African Americans, and he concludes with areas needed for further research and important potential applications in organizations. Like Schneider's chapter, Morrison provides a still largely unexplored framework for use of biodata in a broader context.

The last chapter in this section focuses on the utility of biodata and ways of assessing utility in an organization. Mitchell's discussion revolves primarily around the selection context. With the characteristics of the work force continually evolving, alternatives to cognitive ability tests may predict important unique variance in our selection decisions. Mitchell's chapter provides the formulas for utility estimates and the rationale behind them. He offers his rules of thumb for estimating utility and reviews various threats to utility, such as inadequate validation designs and the misuse of items. Mitchell argues that biodata add to the validity and accuracy of selection and placement programs and offer a fair mechanism for decreasing the adverse impact of our selection programs as well as increasing opportunities for members of traditionally disadvantaged groups.

Biodata

An Organizational Focus

Benjamin Schneider
Jodi L. Schneider
University of Maryland at College Park

For numerous prediction purposes in industrial and organizational psychology, the scored biographical inventory demonstrates consistent validities in excess of .30, with many validities above .50 (Reilly & Chao, 1982). These validity coefficients emerge in such diverse studies as predictions of turnover, career progress, job satisfaction, job performance, and college major and for such diverse groups as college students, various military occupations, clerical workers, managers, and various scientific/engineering occupations (see Hunter & Hunter, 1984; Owens, 1976; Reilly & Chao, 1982). There is evidence to suggest that biodata can demonstrate cross-cultural stability of validity (Laurent, 1970) and that carefully developed biodata items may yield less severe adverse impact than more standard paper-and-pencil measures of cognitive ability (Reilly & Chao, 1982).

These findings do not surprise us. That is, the scored biographical inventories (hereafter simply biodata) used in these validity studies are based on prior validation against some criterion or criteria of the biographical items that are scored. Cumulating valid items *should* yield validity against the criterion of interest. What we *do* find surprising in our review of the biodata literature is that there are at least three methodological variations in the way biodata are used in prediction studies. For expository purposes, we call these variations the *individual,* the *cluster,* and the *career* methods.

In the *individual* method, biographical information is collected from individuals, and weights for that information are derived against individually based criteria. The eventual biodata measure is a scored composite of valid items in which both the predictor and the criterion are expressed in terms of individual differences. For example, in a classic biodata procedure, applicants for a job complete a biographical information blank (BIB) and one year later their turnover is assessed. Weights for valid items, those items that correlate strongly with turnover, are determined, and the score for future applicants on the BIB is a composite of the valid (weighted) items. Most studies using biodata (and the weighted application blank) as a basis for making predictions appear to be of this variety.

The biodata method we call the *cluster* method has been pioneered by Owens and his colleagues (cf. Mumford & Owens, 1987; Owens, 1976; Owens & Schoenfeldt, 1979). In this technique, BIBs are completed by college students and, on the basis of similarity in response patterns, students are placed into biodata clusters. These clusters are comprised of persons who share common life history experiences, so they are called life history subgroups. Owens and his colleagues have shown that predictions of an individual's future behavior based on that individual's cluster membership is at least as accurate as predictions based on that individual's own biodata factor scores. In fact, membership in a biodata cluster can validly predict such diverse criteria as college major, grade point average, participation in extracurricular activities, and future vocational choice (Mumford & Owens, 1987).

In the cluster method, the predictor data are not individual differences, but differences in clusters to which individuals belong. Here individuals share common life histories with members of their own cluster, and the *cluster* differs significantly from other clusters. The criteria used in Owens and his colleagues' research vary from individual differences criteria (like GPA) to membership in other clusters (like vocational choices).

The *career* method is typified by studies showing that persons who enter particular occupations or careers share common life experiences (e.g., Eberhardt & Muchinsky, 1982; Neiner & Owens, 1985). In these studies, the emphasis is on the biographical information associated with people in a career; the goal is to find similarities between persons within a career and differences between persons in different careers. *It is very important to note that in this method, one begins with the career and predicts similarity in life history experiences.* This differs from the cluster method, in which individuals are first clustered based on their life history experiences.

The career method of biodata research will be a central focus of this chapter because it is conceptually analogous to the framework we develop here. That is, in the career method, as in our own conceptualization, similarities within (a career, an organization) and differences between (careers, organizations) are the foci of interest. Thus, we strive to predict the similarity of persons in terms of their life history experiences *after* identifying the career (organization) in which they hold membership. Readers will, of course, identify the fact that what we call the career method is the strategy used by developers of various vocational and occupational interest inventories (e.g., Kuder, 1946; Strong, 1943). That is, the strategy was to find statements of interest that were shared by persons within an occupation and that differentiated persons in that occupation from persons in other occupations.

It is possible to place the three different approaches to biodata methodology on a continuum. One end of the continuum would be anchored by traditional biodata research, with its emphasis on both individual differences in biodata and individual differences in criterion behavior. The other end of the continuum would be anchored by research that explores the life history experience differences between people in different careers. In the middle of the continuum would be research that focuses on placing persons with similar life history experiences into clusters that maximize between cluster differences and, subsequently, on using cluster membership data to make both individual (e.g., GPA) and cluster membership (e.g., vocational choice) predictions.

AN ORGANIZATIONAL FRAMEWORK
FOR BIODATA RESEARCH AND THEORY

The framework outlined here borrows heavily on previous research and theory from both the biodata literature and the literature in industrial and organizational psychology and organizational behavior. From the biodata literature, we borrow the fundamental idea that persons in a *natural* cluster, (i.e., a career) tend to share life history experiences. In addition, we draw heavily on the biodata literature that focuses on the prediction of turnover. As will be noted, this latter literature becomes particularly important with respect to the current framework.

Within industrial and organizational psychology, we borrow from ideas presented by Schneider (1983a, 1983b, 1987) on the attraction–selection–attrition (ASA) cycle. The ASA cycle proposes that people are attracted to, are selected by, and stay with organizations that are in keeping with their own attributes. The ASA model predicts that people within an organization will be more similar to each other than they are to persons in other organizations. Further, it predicts that if this is not true, the dissimilar persons will leave, thus having the effect of increasing the homogeneity of the persons in the setting.

The ASA framework is based on numerous literatures that suggest that persons of similar kinds are naturally attracted to, are selected by, and stay with particular kinds of activities and endeavors. These literatures are found in such diverse areas of psychology as theoretical tests of expectancy theory (Vroom, 1966), conceptualization of careers and career environments (Holland, 1985), interpersonal attraction (Byrne, 1971), and biodata predictions of academic major and participation in extracurricular activities (Owens & Schoenfeldt, 1979). For example, the career psychology literature has demonstrated that there is homogeneity of people, in terms of personality and life history experiences, within a particular vocation. Vocations can be characterized as having different opportunities and demands that influence the types of people they attract and retain.

The root conceptualization of behavior on which the ASA process is based is interactional psychology. Interactional psychology is a subfield of personality theory that is based on the ideas that situations and persons are inseparable (Bowers, 1973; Endler & Magnusson, 1976a) and that situations are what the persons in them construe them to be (Weick, 1979). The interactional perspective has evolved from debates between personologists and situationists, the former arguing for the dominance of persons in understanding the etiology of observed behavior and the latter taking the perspective of situational determinism. Bowers (1973) and others (e.g., Epstein & O'Brien, 1985) have argued for the position that persons *constitute* the situation and thus *are* the situation for much of the behavior of interest to psychology.

Much of the research in industrial and organizational psychology and organizational behavior that may be viewed as interactional in its basic impetus has followed the person–environment (P–E) fit model. The basis of the P–E fit approach to understanding behavior is the idea that particular persons are more likely to be productive and/or satisfied in particular environments because they fit that environment (see *Journal of Vocational Behavior,* 1987, for a review). We will review some of that literature later in this chapter as it pertains particularly to organizational choice. Suffice it to say at this point that the P–E fit approach to understanding behavior is a powerful strategy for diagnosing the consequences for persons of particular settings.

In Schneider's ASA conceptualization, the nature of settings is a consequence of fit that is achieved through three mechanisms: attraction, selection, and attrition. He proposes that these three mechanisms yield increasingly homogenous environments and that this homogeneity in persons comprising environments determines the way organizations look and feel to both participants and observers (Schneider, 1987).

Schneider has suggested that the ASA process has important effects on the climate and culture of organizations. He thus proposes that the climate and culture of a setting are actually a product of the people in the setting, rather than an outcome of the structure or technology of the setting. That is, he argues that structure and technology are *outcomes* of the choices of persons in a setting and, as such, are the mediating causes of climate and culture rather than the primary causes.

Surely, there are moderators to this successive approximation process. For example, it is clear that a poor economy yields lower attrition rates in organizations. Lower attrition rates mean that people who do not fit in a setting do not leave it. Schneider argues that in such situations, the level of dissatisfaction rises, general morale in the workplace decreases, and, when the economy improves, unusually large numbers of individuals leave the organization. Another potential moderator concerns the restricted opportunities persons may have in the kinds of organizations that are available for employment. For example, in a coal-mining town, people do not have the same range of opportunities as do persons in urban areas. Schneider's model suggests that even then individual differences in predilections for employment settings emerge—some persons gravitate to blasting, others to drilling, and still others into management positions or the union hierarchy. Perhaps most interestingly, Schneider's perspective suggests that the store owners and teachers in coal-mining communities would be different from those who work in the mines and that persons unable to achieve some person–job or person–organization fit in the community would eventually leave the community entirely.

Another potential moderator of the ASA process is the quality of organizational information that is presented to applicants during the recruitment and selection process. People who do not receive complete and accurate information during the organizational choice process may join an organization, only to discover eventually that they do not fit the organization. On the other hand, applicants who are given realistic and complete information about an organization (such as with a realistic job preview; Wanous, 1980) may be better equipped to select organizations they will fit. Thus, homogeneity in life history experiences should be greater in organizations that advocate information dissemination, such as realistic job previews, than in organizations that do not—at least during the attraction and selection phases of the ASA cycle.

If Schneider is correct in his basic ASA propositions, and if biodata predictions of vocational choice and turnover are valid, it follows that life history experience data and turnover may, in fact, be useful for describing organizational membership and organizational climate or culture.

In order to make this inferential leap, we must note that researchers in the biodata and turnover literatures have emphasized both understanding and prediction of persons who leave an organization, but they have ignored those who stay. Suppose one were to study those who stay in an organization? The ASA model would predict that those persons would be similar. Indeed, we hypothesize that biodata predictions of *turnover* from an organization are also biodata predictions of *retention*. We further propose that the biodata attributes of those who stay in some organizations will differ from the biodata attributes of those who stay in other organizations. It follows that different organizations should be characterized by persons who differentially fit those organizations due to differences in their life history experiences.

To substantiate these hypotheses, we shall review, in turn, three different literatures. First, we shall present the beginning of a theory regarding life history and organizational behavior. The theory is grounded in the ASA (Schneider, 1987) and person–environment fit literatures. Second, we shall review the biodata literature on the prediction of vocational choice. Third, we shall review the biodata literature on the prediction of turnover. Finally, we shall present some conclusions and suggestions for future research.

THE VOCATION-SPECIFIC ORGANIZATION: BEGINNING OF A THEORY

We propose that organizations that are defined by specific vocations have characteristic ways of responding to their environments that are in keeping with the life history experiences of the people in those vocations. Thus, for example, we propose that professional associations—law firms, accounting firms, engineering firms, medical practices, architectural firms, and other similarly vocation-specific firms or organizations—each display characteristic ways of responding to the environments in which they exist.

We believe this follows from a special form of the person–environment fit heuristic referred to earlier as the ASA paradigm (Schneider, 1987). The ASA model was developed to explore the ways by which the choices people make—whether implicitly or explicitly—about the vocations and organizations in which they work might shed light on the nature of organizations. The model builds on interactional and career psychology, each of which suggests that people are not randomly assigned to, nor do they randomly find themselves in, particular careers or organizations (Bowers, 1973; Holland, 1985; Schneider, 1987).

A fundamental proposition of the ASA model is the nonrandom assignment of persons not only to careers but also to organizations. As noted earlier, in this chapter the model is extended to indicate a more specific consequence concerning the vocation-specific organization. Schneider and others (e.g., George, 1989) have had difficulty identifying the organizational attributes on which to focus the generic ASA model, so the concept of the professional firm (i.e., a vocation-specific organization) simultaneously capitalizes on the career literature and carries forward the notion that organizations may be characterized by particular kinds of persons (Holland, 1985; Schneider, 1987).

If persons choose particular vocations, and those vocations define organizations, *and* if persons are known to share common life history experiences, then it follows that life history similarity can be expected for people in the same vocation-specific organization.

A focus on the person–environment fit issues of organizations is certainly not new; indeed, origins of this idea may be traced back to Lewin (cf. 1935). Lewin and others (cf. Spokane, 1987, for a review of the P–E fit literature), however, presented a P–E fit model based on the idea that the environment was separate from the persons in it. Thus, the environment in essentially all P–E fit perspectives on behavior is a depersonalized, nonhuman, nonsocial environment. In contrast, Schneider's ASA model, building on Holland's perspective, emphasizes the idea that the persons in a place define it as a *human* organization. In addition, following the thinking of Bowers (1973), Bem and Allen (1974), Epstein, (1980), Kohn and Schooler (1983), and others (see Magnusson & Endler, 1977, and Endler & Magnusson, 1976b, for reviews), Schneider's framework emphasizes explicitly the concept of choice. By *choice,* he means the active choice made by persons to enter or exit situations; this is in contrast to the frequently made assumption that persons are somehow randomly assigned to situations as if they were the subjects in some grand experimental design.

The ASA framework can appear quite rational, with its emphasis on individual choices. That is, Schneider emphasizes the idea that people choose to seek employment in organizations that attract them and choose to leave organizations in which they do not fit. His use of the *choice* construct should not be construed to mean conscious or volitional choice. By *choice,* he means more of a natural tendency to seek equilibrium, where the equilibrium state is one of comfort in terms of the fit of person type to setting type. Perhaps the concept of successive approximations, borrowed from the operant learning field, is most accurate in the way Schneider conceptualizes choice. The perspective is that, over time, persons move in and out of settings so that they are increasingly able to approximate an optimal fit of themselves to the setting. This is quite similar to Holland's (1985) theory of career choice: Persons continually seek a more optimum fit of their career interests to their career environments.

In what follows, we shall first review the biodata–vocational choice literature and then the biodata–turnover literature. In both reviews we shall focus on the implications of these existing literatures for understanding vocation-specific organizations and the life history experiences of their members.

THE BIODATA–VOCATIONAL CHOICE RELATIONSHIP

We shall review the relationship between biodata and vocational choice as support for the idea that similar life history experiences lead individuals into similar organizations. Thus, organizations are likely to attract and retain specific types of people who influence the climate and culture of the organization. One way life history experiences influence the types of people who enter and remain in an organization is through the impact of life experiences on vocational choice. Similar processes may account for attraction to and retention in an organization.

For example, Bretz, Ash, and Dreher (1989) argue that the vocational choice framework is likely to have implications for organizational choice as well. Indeed, Keon, Latack, and Wanous (1982) have commented that "organizational choice can be seen as the first step a person takes to implement an occupational choice" (p. 563). Thus, an understanding of the complex process by which individuals choose vocations can be useful in making inferences about the types of people who are likely to enter and remain in an organization.

Many vocational choice theories share the assumption that life history variables influence vocational choice. For example, Neiner and Owens (1985) assert that a common theme implicit in most vocational choice theories is that life experiences have a direct or indirect effect on the decision to pursue a certain vocation. They argue that life experiences are determinants of vocational personality, orientation, values, and interests, which, in turn, result in vocational choice. Lipset, Bendix, and Malm (1962) concluded that "family background, education, and other background variables may be discerned in a person's first job" (cited in Neiner & Owens, 1985, p. 127).

Holland's (1966, 1985) theory of vocational choice is the most popular and most heavily researched theory of its kind (see Spokane, 1985, for a review). The theory is based on the assumption that striving for person–situation congruence drives a person's vocational choice. Individuals seek a vocational environment that corresponds to their strongest personality orientation. Holland (1985) explicitly argues that the development of personality is highly influenced by life history experiences (e.g., home, school, friends)—"Members of a vocation have similar personalities and similar histories of personal development" (p. 10)—and that "people's vocational interests flow from their life history and personality" (p. 7). Thus, Holland's theory acknowledges the role of life history experiences as determinants of vocational choice.

Holland's theory provides a vocational classification system that categorizes vocational environments into six types: realistic, investigative, artistic, social, enterprising, and conventional. Each environment is conceptualized as placing different demands on, and providing different opportunities to, individuals. For example, a social vocational environment is characterized by demands for and opportunities to inform, train, develop, cure, or enlighten others. Some examples of occupations included in the social category are sociologist, psychologist, high school teacher, and school principal. Each vocational environment is hypothesized to be sought by persons who will fit it. Thus, Holland proposes that people can also be categorized into six personality types, which correspond to the six vocational environment types discussed previously. For example, social types prefer activities such as training, developing, curing, and enlightening others (i.e., prefer social environments). Thus, social personality types are predicted to seek and fit into social vocational environments. Holland (1985) argues that "if a person enters a given vocation because of a particular personality and history, it follows that each vocation attracts and retains people with similar personalities" (p. 10).

The theory asserts that each personality type is the product of a series of life history events. Examples of life history influences cited by Holland are family, high school, religious institutions, college, and one's first job. Life history experiences are said to influence the opportunities available to individuals, which, in turn, result in the development of preferences for certain activities, interests, competencies, and values (Holland, 1985). Life history events, then, influence vocational choice through their influence on an individual's personality development.

Because of the prominent position that life history experiences occupy in Holland's and others' theories of vocational choice, many researchers have assessed the value of biodata in predicting vocational choice (Neiner & Owens, 1985). For example, Smart (1989) argued that "vocational type development is a function of a long series of life history experiences that extend from individuals' family background through their experiences at different kinds of colleges and universities" (p. 83).

Biodata are useful for classifying people into types based on similar patterns of life experiences (Owens, 1968, 1971). Owens (1971, 1976) has argued that grouping individuals on the basis of similarities in their patterns of life experience (i.e., through the use of biodata) is useful for predicting and interpreting human behavior. It follows that biodata should be useful for assessing the types of people likely to enter one vocation rather than another.

Holland's vocational classification scheme has been the leading typology for testing the biodata–vocational choice relationship. Studies of this type typically correlate individual responses to a biodata questionnaire with information about their vocational choice. A wide variety of life history variables has been assessed in studies investigating the biodata–vocational choice relationship. Information about vocational choice in these studies has been obtained in two different ways: by assessing vocational preference and by assessing actual vocational choice.

BIODATA AND VOCATIONAL PREFERENCE

In studies that investigate the biodata–vocational preference relationship, respondents are asked to describe various life history experiences and indicate the types of occupations they prefer. Participants complete both the biodata and vocational preference questionnaires concurrently.

The relationship between vocational preference and biodata does not provide direct information about the types of people who *actually enter* one vocation rather than another (Eberhardt & Muchinsky, 1982, 1984). Other factors, such as opportunities, skills, or abilities, may be involved in one's decision to pursue a vocation. Consequently, studies using vocational preference as a criterion are not as strong a test of the biodata–vocational choice relationship as are studies using actual vocational choice as a criterion (Eberhardt & Muchinsky, 1982). Nonetheless, vocational preference studies are still useful for enhancing an understanding of the types of people who are characteristic of one vocation rather than another.

In general, research has demonstrated a relationship between biodata and vocational preference (Eberhardt & Muchinsky, 1982, 1984; Mumford & Owens, 1982; Owens & Schoenfeldt, 1979). For example, Eberhardt and Muchinsky (1982) examined the relationship of vocational subgroup membership to life history experiences. This study is a good example of the career approach to biodata research. College students completed Owens' *Biographical Questionnaire* (BQ; Owens & Schoenfeldt, 1979; it covers such areas as family life, academic achievement, school-related activities, interests and attitudes derived from life experiences, sports participation, religious activities) and indicated the types of occupations they liked and disliked on Holland's *Vocational Preference Inventory* (Holland, 1975). Responses on the inventory were used to form vocational subgroups.

Muchinsky and Eberhardt found that up to 35 percent of the variance in people's vocational preferences could be explained by their life history experiences. More importantly, they also concluded that life history measures have the potential for predicting vocational preference to a greater degree than other measures, such as personality inventories.

Mumford and Owens (1982) also provided support for the relationship between biodata and vocational preferences. They argued that biodata may be useful for enhancing an understanding of the antecedents of vocational interests. Undergraduates were administered Owens' *Biographical Questionnaire* and also completed an interest blank requiring them to indicate their preference for various activities and occupations (e.g., business management, science, adventure). Mumford and Owens found that life history experiences were related to these vocational interests. For example, individuals who expressed an interest in business management were characterized by such life history experiences as enjoyment and interest in business courses, leadership activities, popularity/sociability, part-time employment, well-educated parents, and high socioeconomic status.

BIODATA AND VOCATIONAL CHOICE

Some studies have examined the relationship between biodata and actual vocational choice. For the most part, these studies have been of the concurrent validity type, in that they assess individuals on various life history experiences as well as the types of vocations/occupations in which they already are members. Studies vary in the level of analysis used in classifying vocations. For example, some studies broadly categorized jobs according to Holland's six vocational environments. Other studies classified jobs into occupations or job families. Some studies were even more specific, investigating the life history experience differences between people in closely related jobs and even positions within jobs. Regardless of the level of specificity with which vocations are classified, research strongly supports the conclusion that different vocations are characterized by individuals with different types of life history experiences (Albright & Glennon, 1961; Baehr & Williams, 1967; Brush & Owens, 1979; Neiner & Owens, 1985; Smart, 1989).

Albright and Glennon's (1961) study of supervisory and research-oriented scientists is an example of the position-within-job approach. Employees completed a personal history questionnaire, along with a questionnaire assessing their desire to advance in research or supervisory functions. Albright and Glennon found that 43 personal history items differentiated the research group from the supervisory group. More impressively, these same items were also found to discriminate between actual job incumbents in research and supervisory positions.

With regard to the ability of biodata to make vocational choice distinctions, Brush and Owens (1979) used a sample of more than 2,000 employees occupying 19 job groups (verified through job analysis) in a large oil company. Participants completed an inventory of life history experiences, as well as interest and personality variables, and they were subgrouped according to similarity in life history. Brush and Owens found a significant relationship between subgroup membership (each subgroup was characterized by individuals with similar patterns of life experiences, personality, and interests) and job family membership. This is a good example of the cluster approach to biodata research.

Baehr and Williams (1967) examined personal history items and their ability to discriminate between widely different occupational groups. Participants consisted of employees in 10 occupations (e.g., chemists, middle and upper management, salespersons, line managers, and school administrators) who completed a biographical questionnaire. Responses to the questionnaire were factor-analyzed, resulting in 15 biographical factors (e.g., high school achievement, higher educational achievement, leadership, early family responsibility). Baehr and Williams found that virtually all biographical factors discriminated between the occupational groups.

Some studies on the biodata–vocational choice relationship have been predictive in nature. For example, Neiner and Owens (1985) examined the validity of biodata in predicting vocational choice among a sample of college undergraduates. Participants completed Owens' *Biographical Questionnaire* in their first year of college; four years later, following graduation, participants' actual jobs were categorized under Holland's six vocational types. Neiner and Owens found that biographical information was significantly related to vocational choice, accounting for 22 and 24 percent of the variance in vocational group membership for females and males, respectively.

Smart (1989) conducted an extensive longitudinal study to determine the influence of life history variables on vocational choice. He had first-year college students complete an extensive biodata survey, and participants continued to provide information for nine years regarding their college and job experiences (e.g., educational and occupational achievements, quality of undergraduate institution, distribution of majors at the college). In Smart's study, as in that of Neiner and Owens (1985), vocational choice was obtained by classifying people's current jobs into one of Holland's six vocational environments.

Smart found that life history variables had a significant influence on vocational choice. For example, people who were working in enterprising vocations were characterized by the following life history profile: parents employed in nonenterprising occupations, parents of high socioeconomic status, attendance at high-quality colleges with a large proportion of business majors, an undergraduate major incongruent with an enterprising vocation, and an enterprising orientation. More impressively, life history variables predicted vocational choice up to nine years after the surveys were administered.

Summary

Research suggests that biodata have considerable concurrent and predictive validity in predicting the types of individuals likely to enter various vocations. Along with influencing vocational choice, life history variables also seem to be strongly and consistently related to the types of occupations, jobs, and positions people prefer and actually choose.

BIODATA AND VOCATIONAL STABILITY

Holland's (1985) theory not only makes predictions regarding the types of people likely to enter vocations; it also specifies the types of people likely either to leave or remain in vocations. Thus, Holland's (1985) theory includes the concept of vocational stability.

Holland (1973) argues that people tend to remain in vocations compatible with their personality structure. Thus, he proposes that people with personality types that are incongruent with their vocational environment will eventually leave their job in search of a more congruent one (i.e., they will not only change jobs but also vocations). On the other hand, people with personality types that are congruent with their vocational environment remain in the same job or move between jobs that belong to the same vocational category. Through this process of people seeking personality–environment congruence, different vocations tend to retain different types of people.

Some evidence suggests that personality–vocational environment congruence is related to vocational stability (Rose & Elton, 1982; Villwock, Schnitzen, & Carbonari, 1976; Weiner & Vaitenas, 1977). For example, Rose and Elton (1982) examined the vocational stability of a sample of college students over a four-year period. First-year students completed a vocational interest inventory (to assess their personality) and provided information about their intended college major (to be used as evidence for their vocational choice). Intended majors were classified into one of Holland's six vocational environments. They found that students whose vocational interests were congruent with their expressed college major tended to remain in that major four years later, whereas students whose vocational interests were incongruent with their expressed college major tended to switch majors by the end of four years. Thus, congruence between one's personality and one's vocational environment was predictive of vocational stability (i.e., whether they remained in the same major).

Weiner and Vaitenas (1977) provided even more convincing evidence for the proposition that people who remain in a particular vocation share similar characteristics. They used a sample of workers in enterprising occupations (e.g., sales and management jobs) and found that people who expressed intent to remain in enterprising occupations could be distinguished from people who expressed intent to leave enterprising occupations by some of the following personality characteristics: dominance, endurance, order, responsibility, ascendancy, and sociability.

Some vocational choice studies discussed earlier may provide evidence that life history experiences can predict the types of people who remain in and leave certain vocations. For example, some vocational choice studies identified the life history experiences of people who may have been in a particular occupation for some time (e.g., Albright & Glennon, 1961; Baehr & Williams, 1967; Brush & Owens, 1979) versus people who have recently entered an occupation (e.g., Neiner & Owens, 1985; Smart, 1989). These studies may capture the life history experiences of people attracted to particular occupations/jobs initially *and* who have decided to remain in these occupations/jobs. In Holland's terms, those with personal characteristics congruent with their occupational environment might stay, whereas those with personal characteristics incongruent with their occupational environment might leave. Obviously, this process would yield a homogeneous group of people in a particular occupation.

The vocational stability literature provides another useful piece of support for our thesis that certain types of people are characteristic of certain types of organizations for two reasons. First, the idea that people who do not fit in a particular vocation are likely to leave that vocation can be applied to the organizational level of analysis as well. That is, people who do not fit in an organization are likely to leave that organization (Chatman, 1989). Second, not only does evidence suggest that biodata can predict the types of people who enter a vocation, but indirect evidence also suggests that biodata may help predict the types of people who remain in a vocation.

IMPLICATIONS OF A BIODATA–VOCATIONAL
CHOICE RELATIONSHIP

The biodata–vocational choice literature suggests that people's life history experiences strongly influence their vocational preference and subsequent choice of a vocation. Thus, vocations are composed of similar types of people. The fact that individuals with similar patterns of life history experiences are likely to be characteristic of certain vocations may be the result of two processes: (a) People's life history experiences are likely to determine which type of vocation they are attracted to initially; and (b) the fit between individual and vocational characteristics is likely to determine whether individuals remain in a vocation.

In this chapter we take the finding that vocations are characterized by individuals with similar patterns of life history experiences one step further—to the organizational level. We propose that biodata may be useful in assessing the types of people who are likely to be attracted to and remain in a particular organization. This is based on the following two propositions: (a) The same type of "fit" process characteristic of Holland's vocational theory and related research is likely to operate at the organizational level; and (b) the vocational choice process can enhance an understanding of the organizational choice process, particularly in vocation-specific organizations.

To better understand how biodata may be useful for predicting the types of people characteristic of an organization, we shall turn our attention now to the biodata–turnover literature.

THE BIODATA–TURNOVER RELATIONSHIP

The biodata–turnover literature may be particularly useful for enhancing our understanding of the types of people characteristic of a particular organization. As with the vocational choice process discussed previously, we assume that the fit between individuals and their organizational environment influences the organization turnover/retention process.

Many models of turnover acknowledge that the interaction between individual and job/organizational characteristics influence the turnover process (Mobley, 1982; Sheridan, 1992). Just as individuals who do not fit certain vocations are likely to leave that vocation, individuals who do not fit certain organizations are likely to leave that organization. As discussed earlier, biodata are one technique for capturing the types of personal characteristics that may predict whether individuals fit in certain vocations, jobs, and organizations.

In general, research has consistently demonstrated a relationship between biodata and turnover (Brown, 1978; Cascio, 1976; Muchinsky & Tuttle, 1979; Owens & Schoenfeldt, 1979; Reilly & Chao, 1982). For example, Reilly and Chao (1982) used meta-analytic techniques to investigate the validity of biodata for predicting various outcomes, such as tenure. They concluded that the average validity of biodata for predicting tenure was .30 for military personnel, .52 for clerical personnel, and .50 for scientific and engineering personnel. Results from the biodata literature provide evidence that certain types of people are more likely than others to leave or remain in organizations.

Unfortunately, it is not clear from this literature whether biodata identify the types of people likely to leave one organization and/or job rather than another, or whether biodata predict turnover across organizations and/or jobs (i.e., whether biodata identify the types of people likely to leave *any* organization). In addition, it is not clear from the literature if the criterion being predicted is *job* turnover or *organizational* turnover. That is, studies typically fail to indicate whether the criterion is leaving a job but staying in the organization or leaving both the job *and* the organization.

Two characteristics of biodata–turnover research contribute to the lack of clarity regarding the type of turnover that is associated with biodata. First, many studies use demographic variables (e.g., age, marital status, tenure, educational level, number of children) to predict turnover (Cascio, 1976; Federico, Federico, & Lundquist, 1976; Jackson, Brett, Sessa, Cooper, Julin, & Peyronnin, 1991; Minor, 1958; Muchinsky & Tuttle, 1979; Parasuraman & Futrell, 1983). Many demographic variables found on a typical application blank may predict the types of individuals likely to leave *any* organization or job. In fact, Schuh (1967) concluded that some items in an applicant's personal history can relate to tenure in most jobs. Because these types of life history items are not useful for identifying the types of people likely to fit or not fit in *particular organizations,* they are not of interest to us.

Second, our focus is of necessity on issues related to turnover from the organization, not just the job. This created problems, however, because turnover studies are typically done *within* an organization. But whenever the variance studied is obtained from within one organization, data on variables that might distinguish turnover *between* organizations (i.e., which people might leave one organization but stay in another organization) are unavailable.

In what follows, we shall focus on studies that include the types of life history variables that we believe have the potential for predicting employee turnover from a specific organization. We shall review available studies that use biodata measures that assess a wide range of prior behaviors and experiences. We do this under the logic that organizations are characterized, for example, by different job demands and requirements, practices, and policies and procedures that may determine the types of individuals who are likely to fit in a particular organization and, subsequently, remain in or leave that organization (Chatman, 1989). Where they exist, we shall also describe single-organization studies.

RESEARCH ON BIODATA AND TURNOVER

The most extensive research on biodata and turnover has been conducted by the Life Insurance Marketing and Research Association (LIMRA). LIMRA developed a life history measure called the *Aptitude Index* using a large sample of life insurance agents hired in the 1930s. Initial research on the validity of the *Aptitude Index* indicated that a weighted combination of 10 life history items yielded the best prediction of life insurance agents remaining in a company. Some examples of predictive items were membership in and offices held in organizations, minimum current living expenses, and amount of life insurance owned (cf. Brown, 1978). This research exemplifies the individual approach to biodata research.

Since the early 1930s, the *Aptitude Index* has undergone numerous revisions (it is now called the *Aptitude Index Battery*) and has generated much research. For example, Brown (1978) investigated the long-term validity of the instrument. He found that the same biodata key that predicted life insurance agents remaining in a company in 1933 also predicted the same characteristic for agents hired up to 38 years later. Although organization-specific research on the validity of the *Aptitude Index Battery* was not conducted by Brown (1978) or earlier researchers, *Aptitude Index Battery* research was conducted on one job (life insurance agent) in one industry. Thus, this research should be applicable for predicting turnover/retention in vocation-specific organizations, such as life insurance companies.

The biodata–turnover relationship has also been investigated using biographical information blanks. For example, Brush and Owens (1979) used a large sample of employees in a wide variety of jobs within an oil company to investigate the biodata–turnover relationship. Based on participants' responses to such biographical information blank items as educational and work experiences, leadership activities, interests, perceived self-confidence, and introversion, 18 biodata subgroups were formed. They found that cluster membership significantly predicted turnover from the oil company. Different life history clusters also predicted turnover in different job categories. Because a large oil company is likely to be characterized by diverse jobs, results of this study are consistent with using biodata to predict turnover in vocation-specific organizations, such as law firms.

Biodata have also been used to predict military attrition (Laurence & Means, 1985). Because the military can be conceptualized as one type of organization, findings in this research support the idea that biodata and turnover from a specific organization may be related. Laurence and Means (1985) reviewed the validity of various biodata instruments and life history items for predicting attrition of diverse military samples. They concluded that the following types of life history variables predicted military attrition: school behaviors/attitudes, family experiences, self-reports of personal characteristics (e.g., self-concept, ability to get along with others, athletic ability), and educational achievement.

Drakeley, Herriot, and Jones (1988) conducted a study to determine whether biodata could predict voluntary turnover from a naval training program. They found that the following life history variables predicted retention in the training program: participation in uniformed youth activities, stability of home background, and orientation toward science rather than the arts.

Some research on the weighted application blank also has provided evidence for the relationship between nondemographic-type life history variables and turnover. For example, Buel (1964) studied a sample of clerical workers in a large petroleum company and found that a weighted application blank predicted voluntary turnover. Some examples of predictive life history variables were schooling, participation in class organizations, participation in school-sponsored sports, participation in other school-related activities, and the way summer vacations were spent. Mosel and Wade (1951) also investigated the validity of a weighted application blank and found that principal selling experience and years of previous selling experience predicted the tenure of sales clerks in a large department store.

Biodata and Job Satisfaction

Research demonstrating that biodata predicts job satisfaction provides indirect support for a biodata–turnover relationship because the literature consistently demonstrates a negative relationship between job satisfaction and turnover (Locke, 1975; Mobley, Griffeth, Hand, & Meglino, 1979; Porter & Steers, 1973; Vroom, 1964). Mobley et al.'s (1979) model of turnover also proposes that job attitudes influence an individual's decision to leave an organization.

Sides, Feild, Giles, Holley, and Armenakis (1984), for example, conducted a study examining the relationship between biodata and job satisfaction. Supervisors at a large textile company completed a biodata instrument that assessed some of the following life history variables: perceived ability to communicate with others, athletic interests and abilities, school activities, and mechanical interests and abilities. Sides et al. found that the biodata key significantly predicted job satisfaction.

Mumford and Owens (1984) conducted a longitudinal study to determine whether biodata subgroup membership predicted various postcollege behaviors, including job satisfaction. First-year college students completed Owens' *Biographical Questionnaire* and the *College Experience Inventory*. The *College Experience Inventory* measures behaviors and experiences from the college years, such as reading habits, academic experiences, academic achievement, and religious involvement. Mumford and Owens found that biodata cluster membership predicted job satisfaction six to eight years after college graduation, regardless of the kind of job or organization the sample entered.

Childs and Klimoski (1986) conducted a study to determine whether biodata predicted career/occupational success. One component of career/occupational success studied was job satisfaction. Undergraduates completed a biodata instrument, and career/occupational success was assessed two years later. They found that life history variables significantly predicted job satisfaction. The most predictive variables were academic achievement, perceived self-confidence, and self-reported sociability. This study, like Mumford and Owens' (1984), predicted the job satisfaction of individuals in diverse organizations and jobs.

Although current research on the biodata–job satisfaction relationship provides some support for the hypothesis that specific organizations are likely to be characterized by individuals with similar patterns of life history experiences, stronger evidence may be provided by studies that examine the influence of biodata on *organizational satisfaction* versus job satisfaction. A person's decision to leave an organization may be determined not only by his or her satisfaction with the job itself, pay, or supervision (i.e., some commonly studied facets of satisfaction) but also by his or her satisfaction with specific aspects of the organization (e.g., the climate of the organization).

Studies that investigate the biodata–job satisfaction relationship within one organization (Sides et al., 1984) provide more support for our thesis than those using large samples of employees in different jobs and organizations (Childs & Klimoski, 1986; Mumford & Owens, 1984). No studies to date, however, have made organizational-level comparisons regarding the types of life history experiences that are associated with the job satisfaction of employees in different organizations. This would provide more powerful evidence that different organizations are likely to retain or lose different types of people.

IMPLICATIONS OF A BIODATA–TURNOVER RELATIONSHIP

The biodata–turnover and biodata–job satisfaction literatures provide a basis for conceptualizing turnover at the organizational level of analysis—

that is, we can better understand the types of people likely to leave and, thus, the types of people likely to remain within a particular organization. As will be discussed shortly, future research is necessary to reach this goal.

Turnover research has focused on the individual level of analysis and thus on making predictions regarding the types of employees that are likely to leave an organization. Researchers seek to determine whether such variables as age, education level, and job attitudes are related to whether or not an individual leaves an organization. Many recent reviews of the turnover literature, however, have argued for extending turnover research to the organizational level of analysis (e.g., understanding organizational-level turnover rates). For example, Teborg and Lee (1984) argued that if age is negatively related to individual turnover, then turnover rates should be negatively correlated with the average age of the organization's work force. Taken one step further, if life history experiences—such as educational experiences, academic achievements, sports participation, and leadership activities—predict individual turnover within an organization, then it can logically be argued that these variables would predict the types of people who remain within that organization.

Studies investigating the relationship between biodata and turnover/job satisfaction would benefit from sampling more than one organization to determine whether different types of people are satisfied with and leave different types of organizations. Although some biodata studies do sample many organizations, biodata are typically used to predict turnover across organizations rather than to make turnover comparisons between organizations. Thus, researchers fail to address whether different biodata items predict job satisfaction and retention in different organizations. Future research could be conducted to determine whether different patterns of life history experiences predict job satisfaction and turnover in different organizations. This would require using an organizational level of analysis (i.e., comparing biodata predictors of turnover between various organizations) rather than an individual level of analysis. Studies of this type would provide further evidence to support the hypothesis of this chapter: An organization is characterized by similar types of people, who in turn influence the climate and culture of that organization, and these people differ from people in other organizations.

Stronger support for the usefulness of biodata in predicting the types of people who will remain within and subsequently shape an organization would be provided by conducting more turnover research using nondemographic-type biodata items to identify who is likely to fit and remain in a particular organization (see Jackson et al., 1991). Differences may be captured by conducting more biodata–turnover studies using the diverse life history variables employed in the biodata–vocational choice literature (e.g., academic achievement, school-related activities, religious experiences, and interest in various academic disciplines).

SUMMARY AND CONCLUSION

The literature we have summarized on biodata correlates of vocational choice and organizational turnover seems to warrant support for our contention that organizations, particularly vocation-specific organizations, are likely to contain people with common life history experiences. Thus, the numerous studies that have been conducted on vocational choice lend support to the idea that, whether accomplished from an individual, cluster, or career methodology, life history predicts both vocational preference and actual vocational choice. In addition, the comparatively small literature on the biodata–turnover relationship was equally encouraging; biodata predict who will remain in and who will leave an organization.

It is not much of an inferential leap to conclude that vocation-specific organizations are likely to attract, select, and retain persons with similar life history experiences. One may legitimately question the implications of this conclusion. For instance, does life history similarity have implications for our understanding of leadership, groups, motivation, and so forth? Or does life history similarity tell us something new about communication in work organizations or the cohesion and morale that can be expected in a setting?

These are difficult questions to confront. Our present position is that, because of the relationships existing among life history experiences, careers, turnover, and job satisfaction, we are far more likely to find consistent patterns of life history in relation to more affective outcomes at work. By this, we mean that, *at the organizational level of analysis,* predictions based on life history variables will more likely be reflected in affect and withdrawal issues rather than in productivity issues. This prediction follows from Schneider's (1983b) caution that a tendency toward homogeneity is dangerous for an organization because it can yield an inability to respond to a changing environment. Such an inability will be reflected in poorer rather than enhanced organizational productivity. Simultaneously, however, any *individuals* joining such an organization who do not fit it can still be predicted to have lower job satisfaction and to withdraw (Chatman, 1989). Thus, the fit process itself should influence the withdrawal and affective responses of organizational members. The homogeneity of life history experiences resulting from this fit process may negatively affect the productivity of the organization as a whole.

With regard to the internal processes existing in organizations, a life history homogeneity perspective like the one presented here implies that organizations will differ in the way they lead, motivate, and reward people. But this prediction is not different from one that suggests that organizations differ in the personality of their members and, as such, that one can expect to find different patterns of internal organizational processes (Schneider, 1983a).

What is different about the life history perspective presented here is that we may be able to specify the kinds of experiences people *should* have in order to be effective in particular kinds of organizations. Such specification would permit the introduction of practices into organizations, or in society at large, that would enable people to have relevant experiences. In this way, a focus on life history experiences provides a more tangible avenue for making change than that provided by studies of "personality" or "values." Thus, to this point in the chapter, our focus has been explicitly on the predictive power of life history experiences, not their etiology. Obviously, life history experiences emerge as the natural process of development occurs (e.g., Roe, 1957; Roe & Baruch, 1967). Not included in our presentation has been the use of these data for intervening in the life history experiences of persons.

An analogy to the kinds of experiences managers have as they grow and develop may be helpful. McCall, Lombardo, and Morrison (1988) have documented the kinds of experiences managers have in their managerial careers and some consequences—positive and negative—of those experiences. Under the hypothesis that interventions to provide experiences can serve as substitutes for naturally occurring experiences, they encourage organizations to take advantage of these findings by designing positive experiences for managers that may yield the kinds of outcomes that will promote high performance. McCall et al., then, are arguing for interventions in managers' lives that will promote effectiveness and success for managers.

In like manner, as we build a data base of the kinds of life history experiences that yield persons and organizations that are effective, we can begin to suggest models and designs for creating these types of experiences for people. This type of intervention may, we hypothesize, facilitate the attainment of positive outcomes for people and their future organizations.

We could, of course, be accused of social programming for making such a suggestion. Our preference, however, is to view it as a natural outcome of the collection of a sufficiently large data base suggesting the kinds of life history experiences likely to yield effectiveness at work. Leaders in particular kinds of organizations will probably require certain life history experiences, and reward systems from organization to organization will need to be targeted on enhancing the probability that people will seek particular kinds of activities and/or training. The McCall et al. book (1988), then, introduces the idea that organizations may be able to formalize the previously ad hoc by capitalizing on the idea that data on life history experiences lend themselves to change more readily than more abstract labels like the "personality" or "values" labels noted earlier.

CAUTIONS

There are a number of cautions that accompany the main thesis of this chapter regarding life history similarity in vocation-specific organizations. First, although the evidence summarized here leads to the conclusion that people in different professional firms might differ in their life history experiences, what is not clear is how different firms *within* a profession might be from each other. That is, suppose we were able to demonstrate that law firms contain people who differ in their life history experiences from people in accounting firms. Is it reasonable to also expect that people in law firm A will differ in life history experiences from people in law firm B? We suspect, based on the literature reviewed here, that the latter prediction would be more difficult to make than the former but that there would be within-vocation, between-organizational differences in life history experiences, too.

And what of the different jobs people occupy in law firms or medical practices? That is, not only lawyers work in law firms—there are clerical people, accountants, and so forth. Do they also share life history experiences with the lawyers? Again, we call on Holland (1985) for a potential explanation. He proposes that persons in what he calls career environments share that environment as a function of their primary, secondary, and/or tertiary vocational codes. Thus, he would argue that clerical people who work in law firms differ from those who work in medical practices because their secondary and/or tertiary vocational interests indicate law or medicine, respectively. We also would accept this kind of logic here. That is, we hypothesize that clerical people in different vocation-specific organizations would share some attributes with other clerical people and share some attributes with the vocation-specific organization in which they choose to work.

One consequence of focusing on life history experiences rather than the six interests in Holland's typology, then, may be the much greater variety of issues on which people can be similar or different. Life history experiences can vary on so many dimensions that it would seem possible to show how persons in a law firm are *both* similar and different as a function of the kind of job they occupy there.

As we noted in the conclusion to the biodata–turnover relationship section, the kind of research necessary to substantiate our hypotheses has yet to be accomplished. What we have not yet noted are some of the practical implications of our conceptualization and inferences. First, life history variables are powerful for making valid inferences about people. This characteristic makes it possible to simultaneously counsel people into particular kinds of organizations in which they are most likely to fit, make accurate predictions about who should not join particular organizations, and create opportunities for people to have the kinds of experiences that might suit them for particular organizational environments.

At present, we know relatively little about making these kinds of predictions and changes, and, while we can make gross predictions about the vocations in which people may be satisfied, the range of potential environments in which they can implement their vocational interests is very broad indeed. Biodata provide a potentially useful strategy for making these more fine-grained distinctions for people (as in counseling them) and about people (as in making valid organizationally relevant predictions).

Second, Schneider (1987) has hypothesized that the kinds of people in an organization determine its climate or culture. Such a proposition makes sense on the surface, but it is a hypothesis that has yet to receive empirical verification. If it turns out to be true, then it should be possible to change an organization's climate or culture by selecting people with different patterns of life history experiences. Thus, if we were able to demonstrate that different kinds of organizational climates are associated with identifiable patterns of life history experiences of the people in the organizations, we would have a basis for designing organizational climate or culture through the selection of the kind of mix we need in order to have the climate or culture desired.

It probably is true that much of this kind of fitting or matching already naturally occurs in organizations. However, it is one thing for it to naturally occur and another to *make* it occur. There is one very strong reason for making it occur. Schneider (1987) has argued that organizations that become overly homogeneous may be unable to respond appropriately to changing environments. If the kind of data we are proposing to be collected were available, it would be possible to continually fine-tune the qualities of newly hired persons to keep homogeneity from reaching such stultifying levels.

Finally, life history experiences are themselves interesting in that they constitute the nature of people's developmental history. To psychologists, there is little that is more interesting than such history. Our hope is that we have presented a new vantage point from which to view life history variables—from the organization.

REFERENCES

Albright, L. E., & Glennon, J. R. (1961). Personal history correlates of physical scientists' career aspirations. *Journal of Applied Psychology, 45*(5), 281–284.

Baehr, M. E., & Williams, G. B. (1967). Underlying dimensions of personal background data and their relationship to occupational classification. *Journal of Applied Psychology, 51*(6), 481–490.

Bem, D. J., & Allen, A. (1974). On predicting some of the people some of the time: The search for cross-situation consistencies in behavior. *Psychological Review, 81,* 506–520.

Bowers, K. S. (1973). Situationism in psychology: An analysis and critique. *Psychological Review, 80,* 307–336.

Bretz, R. D., Jr., Ash, R. A., & Dreher, G. F. (1989). Do people make the place? An examination of the attraction-selection-attrition hypothesis. *Personnel Psychology, 42,* 561–581.

Brown, S. H. (1978). Long-term validity of a personal history item scoring procedure. *Journal of Applied Psychology, 63*(6), 673–676.

Brush, D. H., & Owens, W. A. (1979). Implementation and evaluation of an assessment classification model for manpower utilization. *Personnel Psychology, 32,* 369–383.

Buel, W. D. (1964). Voluntary female clerical turnover: The concurrent and predictive validity of a weighted application blank. *Journal of Applied Psychology, 48,* 180–182.

Byrne, D. (1971). *The attraction paradigm.* New York: Academic Press.

Cascio, W. F. (1976). Turnover, biographical data, and fair employment practices. *Journal of Applied Psychology, 61,* 576–580.

Chatman, J. A. (1989). Improving interactional research: A model of person–environment fit. *Academy of Management Review, 14*(3), 333–349.

Childs, A., & Klimoski, R. J. (1986). Successfully predicting career success: An application of the biographical inventory. *Journal of Applied Psychology, 71*(1), 3–8.

Drakeley, R. J., Herriot, P., & Jones, A. (1988). Biographical data, training success and turnover. *Journal of Occupational Psychology, 61*(2), 145–152.

Eberhardt, B. J., & Muchinsky, P. M. (1982). Biodata determinants of vocational typology: An integration of two paradigms. *Journal of Applied Psychology, 67*(6), 714–727.

Eberhardt, B. J., & Muchinsky, P. M. (1984). Structural validation of Holland's hexagonal model: Vocational classification through the use of biodata. *Journal of Applied Psychology, 69*(1), 174–181.

Endler, N. S., & Magnusson, D. (Eds.). (1976a). *Interactional psychology and personality.* Washington, DC: Hemisphere.

Endler, N. S., & Magnusson, D. (1976b). Personality and person by situation interactions. In N. S. Endler & D. Magnusson (Eds.), *Interactional psychology and personality.* New York: Hemisphere.

Epstein, S. (1980). The stability of behavior: II. Implications for psychological research. *American Psychologist, 35,* 790–806.

Epstein, S., & O'Brien, E. J. (1985). The person–situation debate in historical and current perspective. *Psychological Bulletin, 98,* 513–537.

Federico, J. M., Federico, P., & Lundquist, G. W. (1976). Predicting women's turnover as a function of extent of met salary expectations and biodemographic data. *Personnel Psychology, 29,* 559–566.

George, J. M. (1989). Mood and absence. *Journal of Applied Psychology, 74,* 317–324.

Holland, J. L. (1966). *The psychology of vocational choice.* Waltham, MA: Blaisdell.

Holland, J. L. (1973). *Making vocational choices: A theory of careers.* Englewood Cliffs, NJ: Prentice-Hall.

Holland, J. L. (1975). *Manual for the Vocational Preference Inventory.* Palo Alto, CA: Consulting Psychologists Press.

Holland, J. L. (1985). *Making vocational choices: A theory of vocational personalities and work environments.* Englewood Cliffs, NJ: Prentice-Hall.

Hunter, J. E., & Hunter, R. F. (1984). Validity and utility of alternative predictors of job performance. *Psychological Bulletin, 96*(1), 72–98.

Jackson, S. E., Brett, J. F., Sessa, V. I., Cooper, D. M., Julin, J. A., & Peyronnin, K. (1991). Some differences make a difference: Individual dissimilarity and group heterogeneity as correlates of recruitment, promotions and turnover. *Journal of Applied Psychology, 76,* 675–689.

Journal of Vocational Behavior (1987). Vol. 31, Whole No. 4

Keon, T. L., Latack, J. C., & Wanous, J. P. (1982). Image congruence and the treatment of difference scores in organizational choice research. *Human Relations, 35,* 155–166.

Kohn, M. L., & Schooler, C. (Eds.). (1983). *Work and personality.* Horwood, NJ: Ablex.

Kuder, G. F. (1946). *Revised manual for the Kuder Preference Record.* Chicago: Science Research Associates.

Laurence, J. H., & Means, B. (1985). *A description and comparison of biographical inventories for military selection.* Alexandria, VA: Human Resources Research Organization.

Laurent, H. (1970). Cross-cultural cross-validation of empirically validated keys. *Journal of Applied Psychology, 54,* 417–423.

Lewin, K. (1935). *Dynamic theory of personality.* New York: McGraw-Hill.

Lipset, S. M., Bendix, R., & Malm, F. T. (1962). Job plans and entry into the labor market. In S. Nosow & W. H. Form (Eds.), *Man, work, and society.* New York: Basic Books.

Locke, E. A. (1975). Personnel attitudes and motivation. *Annual Review of Psychology, 25,* 457–480.

Magnusson, D., & Endler, N. S. (1977). Interactional psychology: Present status and future projects. In D. Magnusson & N. S. Endler (Eds.), *Personality at the crossroads: Current issues in interactional psychology.* Hillsdale, NJ: Erlbaum.

McCall, M. W., Jr., Lombardo, M. M., & Morrison, A. M. (1988). *The lessons of experience: How successful executives develop on the job.* Lexington, MA: Lexington Books.

Minor, F. J. (1958). The prediction of turnover of clerical employees. *Personnel Psychology, 11,* 393–402.

Mobley, W. H. (1982). *Employee turnover: Causes, consequences, and control.* Reading, MA: Addison-Wesley.

Mobley, W. H., Griffeth, R. W., Hand, H. H, & Meglino, B. M. (1979). Review and conceptual analysis of the employee turnover process. *Psychological Bulletin, 86,* 493–522.

Mosel, J. N., & Wade, R. R. (1951). A weighted application blank for reduction of turnover in department stores sales clerks. *Personnel Psychology, 4,* 177–184.

Muchinsky, P. M., & Tuttle, M. L. (1979). Employee turnover: An empirical and methodological assessment. *Journal of Vocational Behavior, 14,* 43–77.

Mumford, M. D., & Owens, W. A. (1982). Life history and vocational interests. *Journal of Vocational Behavior, 21,* 330–348.

Mumford, M. D., & Owens, W. A. (1984). Individuality in a developmental context: Some empirical and theoretical considerations. *Human Relations, 27,* 84–108.

Mumford, M. D., & Owens, W. A. (1987). Methodology review: Principles, procedures, and findings in the application of background data measures. *Applied Psychological Measurement, 11*(1), 1–31.

Neiner, A. G., & Owens, W. A. (1985). Using biodata to predict job choice among college graduates. *Journal of Applied Psychology, 70,* 127–136.

Owens, W. A. (1968). Toward one discipline of scientific psychology. *American Psychologist, 23,* 782–785.

Owens, W. A. (1971). A quasi-actuarial basis for individual assessment. *American Psychologist, 26,* 992–999.

Owens, W. A. (1976). Background data. In M. D. Dunnette (Ed.), *Handbook of industrial and organizational psychology.* Chicago: Rand McNally.

Owens, W. A., & Schoenfeldt, L. F. (1979). Toward a classification of persons. *Journal of Applied Psychology Monograph, 65,* 569–607.

Parasuraman, A., & Futrell, C. M. (1983). Demographics, job satisfaction, and propensity to leave of industrial salesmen. *Journal of Business Research, 11,* 33–48.

Porter, L. W., & Steers, R. M. (1973). Organizational, work, and personal factors in employee turnover and absenteeism. *Psychological Bulletin, 80,* 151–176.

Reilly, R. R., & Chao, G. T. (1982). Validity and fairness of some alternative employee selection procedures. *Personnel Psychology, 35*(1), 1–62.

Roe, A. (1957). Early determinants of vocational choice. *Journal of Counseling Psychology, 4,* 212–217.

Roe, A., & Baruch, R. (1967). Occupational changes in adult years. *Personnel Administration, 30,* 26–32.

Rose, H. A., & Elton, C. G. (1982). The relation of congruence, differentiation, and consistency to interest and aptitude scores in women with stable and unstable vocational choices. *Journal of Vocational Psychology, 20,* 162–174.

Schneider, B. (1983a). Interactional psychology and organizational behavior. In L. L. Cummings & B. M. Staw (Eds.), *Research in organizational behavior* (Vol. 5). Greenwich, CT: JAI Press.

Schneider, B. (1983b). Organizational effectiveness: An interactionist perspective. In D. Hetten & K. S. Cameron (Eds.), *Multiple models of organizational effectiveness.* New York: Academic Press.

Schneider, B. (1987). The people make the place. *Personnel Psychology, 40*(3), 437–453.

Schuh, A. J. (1967). The predictability of employee tenure: A review of the literature. *Personnel Psychology,* 133–151.

Sheridan, J. E. (1992). Organizational culture and employee retention. *Academy of Management Journal, 35,* 1036–1056.

Sides, E. H., Feild, H. S., Giles, W. F., Holley, W. H., & Armenakis, A. A. (1984). *Human Resource Planning, 7,* 151–156.

Smart, J. C. (1989). Life history influences on Holland vocational type development. *Journal of Vocational Behavior, 34,* 69–87.

Spokane, A. R. (1985). A review of research on person–environment congruence in Holland's theory of careers. *Journal of Vocational Behavior, 26,* 306–343.

Spokane, A. E. (1987). Research on person–environment fit. *Journal of Vocational Behavior, 31(6).*

Strong, E. K., Jr. (1943). *Vocational interests of men and women.* Stanford, CA: Stanford University Press.

Teborg, J. R., & Lee, T. W. (1984). A predictive study of organizational turnover rates. *Academy of Management Journal, 27,* 793–810.

Villwock, J. D., Schnitzen, J. P., & Carbonari, J. P. (1976). Holland's personality constructs as predictors of stability of choice. *Journal of Vocational Behavior, 9,* 77–85.

Vroom, V. H. (1964). *Work and motivation.* New York: Wiley.

Vroom, V. H. (1966). Organizational choice: A study of pre- and post-decision processes. *Organizational Behavior and Human Performance, 1,* 212–226.

Wanous, J. P. (1980). *Organizational entry.* Reading, MA: Addison-Wesley.

Weick, K. E. (1979). *The social psychology of organizing* (2d ed., pp. 147–169). Reading, MA: Addison-Wesley.

Weiner, Y., & Vaitenas, R. (1977). Personality correlates of voluntary midcareer change in enterprising occupations. *Journal of Applied Psychology, 62(6),* 706–712.

Biodata Applications in Career Development Research and Practice

Robert F. Morrison

Navy Personnel Research and Development Center[*]

INTRODUCTION

Until the 1970s, the field of developmental psychology applied very limited resources to adult developmental processes and concentrated on childhood with brief side trips into the geriatric period of life. This emphasis on early development made it appear that children grew physically, psychologically, socially, and mentally until early adulthood when they made their life decisions. Using these decisions as bases, adults stagnated for the next 40 years—until adjustment to the aging process began to dominate their lives. This philosophy has changed markedly with the discovery that adults change, leading to a mushrooming interest in the field of adult career development.

CAREER DEVELOPMENT

Evolution through usage has taken the term *career* from its French origin, *carriere,* meaning "a road or race course," to its current interpretation as

---

[*]The opinions expressed in this chapter are those of the author, are not official, and do not necessarily reflect the views of the Navy Department.

"one's progress in a particular vocation" (Dalton, 1989, p. 89). Such progress can be represented by a work history so that "all people who work acquire work histories, and thus have careers" (Adams, 1991, p. 1). In this vein, a career can be described by a sequence of work roles that are related to each other in such a way that some of the knowledge, skills, abilities, personal characteristics, or experiences acquired in one role are perceived as relevant to the next.

The developmental process associated with the career is a personal change that occurs as a result of "the individual's experiences, roles, and relationships in work-related organizations—and other situations—as developing, or having the possibility of developing along some course" (Dalton, 1989, p. 89). In more specific terms, career development can be considered "a system of change in behavior and personal characteristics related to learning at work or in work-related contexts. The focus is on intraindividual change as a learning process and on the type of interindividual differences in learning histories that produce different developmental outcomes" (Morrison & Hoch, 1986, p. 238). The interaction between the individual and the work environment makes each career unique. The individual aspect of career development is represented by the internal self-image—or felt identity. The environmental aspect concerns official position, jural relations, and style of life, which are part of a publicly accessible institutional complex (Dalton, 1989).

BIOGRAPHICAL DATA (BIODATA)

A purist may emphasize that biodata should consist only of objective, verifiable information about an individual's past. Examples of this position are present in scored application blanks that request information about level of education, academic major, amount of life insurance owned, grade-point average, memberships, and so on. In this chapter, individuals' interpretations and self-reports of personal life histories and the related environments will be considered relevant along with objective life histories (see Owens, 1976). This combination of objective and subjective life history information will be included as *biographical data,* although, in fact, much will be autobiographical.

The importance of adding subjective interpretation of personal life events and situations to objective data sets was strongly evidenced by recent research on the factors that enhance or inhibit experienced naval officers in learning to perform a specific set of new jobs (Morrison & Brantner, 1992). Starting with the premise that fidelity between the content of past experiences and the present job would directly enhance the process of learning the new job (Baird, 1982), independent judges were asked to rate the similarity of the task content between officers' distal subordinate past positions and their present positions. When directly comparable previous experiences (same jobs, different ships) immediately preceded the new jobs, learning was enhanced. When other work-oriented experiences (e.g., training, education, or trouble-shooting assignments) of more than five months duration were inserted between prior experiences and the new jobs, the only significant direct relationship between the fidelity of distal prior work experiences and the facility with which learning the new jobs took place was a small negative one. This indicated that such experience had inhibited, not enhanced, learning. In the latter case, the officers' perceptions of the suitability of their experiences and performance in past jobs to the new jobs, a measure of *self-efficacy* (Wood & Bandura, 1989), were inserted as moderators between their objective work histories and their positions on the learning curves for their new positions. This relationship was positive and significant. Those officers who perceived more relevance between their high-fidelity distal prior experiences and their new jobs learned their new jobs significantly faster than those officers who perceived less relevance. Only when very high fidelity experiences immediately preceded reporting to the new jobs was learning markedly enhanced. These results are consistent with Wood and Bandura's (1989) position that past performance is the best predictor of initial managerial performance but falls into second place behind self-efficacy for experienced managers.

Continuing this line of reasoning, it is possible for two individuals to interpret similar work histories as different careers and two other individuals to interpret different work histories as similar careers. Thus, if biodata are interpreted as only the objective reporting of prior life events, those events probably will not demonstrate the anticipated high relationship with present or future behavior. Such data need to be mediated via the individual's personal career schema (Ilgen & Klein, 1989; Mumford & Owens, 1987). Such personal interpretations would mean that biodata may be able to capture "trade-offs" in the career and noncareer life paths that provided experiential learning alternatives in preparation for future career roles. The perception that one has successfully practiced some elements, decisions, and so forth, of a future role in a prior experience may form a *likelihood* hierarchy of learning (Morrison & Hoch, 1986) in the eyes of the beholder. Perceiving this prior success in similar situations as relevant to the new one may increase self-efficacy, developing the confidence that the future role can be performed successfully.

"Experience at work or in a work-related environment is *the* primary source of career learning for each individual" (Morrison & Hoch, 1986, p. 237). As past experiences are perceived as contributing to learning and successfully performing new experiences, such experiences contribute to the achievement of psychological success (Hall, 1976) and enhance personal self-esteem. In this way, biodata based on the perceptions of past experiences capture a key personality characteristic, self-esteem, that has demonstrated relationships with different career events across time and different populations (e.g., Morrison, Owens, Glennon, & Albright, 1962; Morrison & Sebald, 1974).

BIODATA AND CAREER DEVELOPMENT

To link biodata and career development, the term *career* needs to be placed in perspective.

MUDDLING THROUGH THE CAREER

Careers do not evolve in the orderly manner that appears to be assumed by most career theorists and researchers (e.g., Levinson, Darrow, Klein, Levinson, & McKee, 1978; Super, 1990). Individual careers are not planned over long periods of time. They evolve step-by-step as situations and opportunities arise in the environment. This process is akin to managers "muddling through" the sequence of decisions that establishes the strategic path of their organizations (Lindblom, 1959). Most adults react to such experiences and opportunities because they are short-term, intuitive decision makers rather than long-term, planful ones. Since each person has uniquely different situations to which she or he reacts, a cohort of individuals who demonstrate relative homogeneity in their major attributes (e.g., knowledge, skills, abilities, interests, values, attitudes, personalities, gender, and socioeconomic status) in early adulthood diverge significantly in their careers and life experiences as the cohort matures. While such divergence creates differences in knowledge, skills, and socioeconomic status, leading one to assume that the cohort's members also have become differentiated in their abilities and other characteristics (AOs), this may not be true. As individuals transition from one experience, one position, and one organization or occupational site to others, new and more complex levels of knowledge and skill develop. Because the persona provides a stable framework for the decision process, whether it is planful, intuitive, or other, the individuals' AOs may mature but not necessarily change during the sequential transitions (Morrison & Hoch, 1986). This combination of maturation and individual development would appear to be linear, varying from individual to individual primarily in the speed with which it occurs and only diluting the impact of age (Mumford & Owens, 1987). However, such a linear effect is overridden by situational effects that create marked differences in the cohort's opportunities for career transitions (Austin & Hanisch, 1990; Hall & Richter, 1990; Scarr & McCartney, 1983). For example, a cohort of new college graduates may choose organizations that require very similar personalities for successful membership. However, the organization's initial placements may represent the first steps in different organizational or occupational career paths. Such paths could diverge to an increasing extent over an entire career and become quite disparate in the task knowledge and skills content of the positions but be very similar in the AOs required for the positions. Furthermore, an observer may detect very little apparent similarity in the terminal positions occupied by two individuals who have been in the different career paths for 30 years. While the prior statements hold true for planful and intuitive career decision makers, they would not be true for dependent career decision makers, that is, those who depend on others to make their decisions for them. Adults who respond to the environment in a dependent way may take career paths that are inconsistent with their persona. Such careers may be maladaptive since the individuals respond to the desires of others rather than their own. Dependent decision makers who are in career paths that are inconsistent with their persona would introduce error into any data base used to investigate careers via biographical data.

While maturation and individual differences in AOs combine to produce variation in career experiences, the variety of career opportunities due to situational effects creates even greater deviations among the career experiences that could be captured with biodata. When career development research goes beyond following a single cohort and starts contrasting several cohorts, generational differences (Howard & Bray, 1988) in opportunities add even more variation to the career experiences expressed via biodata.

The impact of generational factors on organizational programs that use life history information to predict future career behaviors was demonstrated by biodata research used in a large corporation (Morrison, Ginsburg, & Trammell, 1968). Different sets of items from a scored application blank were used to predict whether the firm's consumer sales personnel would remain in the organization and/or whether they would be promoted during their first five years after employment. While the cross-validated correlations for the initial two-year applicant cohort were in the mid .60s and .50s, respectively, validity coefficients for each of the next five annual cohorts of new applicants decreased linearly to the mid .30s for both and became of little practical use.* As a consequence of the generational effect, greater fidelity between recent (proximal) past experiences and present/future experiences than between distal past experiences and present/future ones should be expected (Owens, 1976).

PROXIMAL VERSUS DISTAL EXPERIENCES

The results of the research presented above suggest that the best technique to use in predicting an individual's career progression may be the *moving average* approach of the economist. This procedure would take advantage of the more proximal biodata and put only indirect weight on the more distal biodata. Typically, more rapid transitions on the diverging career paths occur in the first half of the career. As a result, the period used for the moving average procedure might be shorter (e.g., 5 years) early in one's career but longer (e.g., 10 years) in the latter portion of one's career. Thus, while past behavior and experience remains the best predictor of future behavior (Goodenough, 1949; Owens, 1968), this axiom could be adapted as follows: *The more proximal the past experience of adults is to the behavior that we desire to predict, the more we enhance our ability to predict future behavior.*

There are, however, times when the most proximal experience is not the best predictor of future behavior. One exception is when a proximal experience is consistent with the organizational culture and decision processes but includes few behaviors that are relevant to some future performance. For example, a technical degree is not considered relevant when a newly commissioned naval officer is assigned to a *primary* warfare specialty position in aviation or surface warfare. At this career step, manpower management decisions consider only the primary specialty (warfare), even though performing in some warfare positions earns the officers qualifications in *secondary* technical specialties (e.g., oceanography or electronic warfare) that may become important later in their careers. If an assignment decision was partially driven by the presence of a technical background, development might be enhanced because of the appropriate academic preparation. However, the Navy's strong cultural value system in these two warfare communities emphasizes general leadership skills and a primary warfare skill (e.g., flying) without reference to other potentially

---

*One explanation for this change may have been the impact of the 1960s ethos and Vietnam War problems on the societal factors that affected the newer cohorts of college graduates applying for the positions.

relevant ones. The culture of the Navy's submarine community is very different; it emphasizes a technical degree in preparation for becoming nuclear-power qualified. As a result, newly commissioned submariners' most proximal experience (academic major) is an excellent predictor of future behaviors, whereas academic major would not be a good predictor for newly commissioned aviation and surface warfare officers. This situation highlights the fact that organizational or situational concerns may be moderators of the relationship between biodata and a dependent variable. Therefore, the axiom noted in the previous paragraph should be adapted even further: *The more proximal and relevant the past experience of adults is to the behavior that we desire to predict, the more we enhance our ability to predict future behavior.*

As biographical data are used to track the development of individuals throughout their career lives, the content of the data must change. Different behaviors are salient at different periods in career development, depending upon the occupational and organizational requirements and the maturation and development of individuals. Some individuals plateau relatively early in their careers and do not transition into new career roles or develop significant new skills. In some occupations (e.g., medicine or dentistry) and organizations, early plateauing may be acceptable and seen as a mark of a successful career as assessed by society. The majority of the people plateau at midcareer, but some plateau later or not at all. In each instance, the behaviors and experiences that underlie biographical data change markedly as career transitions take place (Dalton & Thompson, 1986; Morrison & Hoch, 1986). Thus, the constructs underlying the biographical data used to map careers need to be assessed using different content as the career evolves.

How can measures of psychological constructs be developed using biographical data that change in concert with the many transitions that individuals go through during a career? The traditional approaches are to relate responses or clusters of responses to career issues such as turnover, promotability, performance, occupational group, or groups with homogeneous response sets on a biodata form (e.g., see Albright & Glennon, 1961; Morrison, 1977a; Morrison et al., 1962; Morrison et al., 1968; Owens & Schoenfeldt, 1979; Schoenfeldt, 1974).

Using the empirical approach pioneered by Schoenfeldt (1974) and Owens and Schoenfeldt (1979), it is possible to develop insights into how "nonintellective" characteristics either adapt across a career to life/work experiences or are reflected in various behaviors that are internally consistent in their representation of "nonintellective" characteristics. However, such an approach is not parsimonious. It requires long time periods to follow individuals throughout their careers; huge samples to represent special groups covering gender, race, socioeconomic status, and so forth; and an extremely large number of variables to cover all possible predictors. Considerable theory covering early career decisions (e.g., Holland, 1985; Mitchell & Krumboltz, 1990), career transitions (Latack, 1984; Nicholson & West, 1989) such as socialization processes (Berlew & Hall, 1966; Feldman, 1989; Louis, 1980) and voluntary withdrawal (e.g., Mobley, 1982; Mowday, Porter, & Steers, 1982), career adjustment and personality development (Dawis & Lofquist, 1984; Hall, 1986), and life span career development processes (Dalton & Thompson, 1986; Levinson et al., 1978; Super, 1990) has been formulated. These theories are sufficiently advanced to allow research on career issues to incorporate biodata measures of psychological constructs that can contribute to the refinement/revision of these embryonic theories and to problem identification and solving. Biographical data have been used very successfully to test and support Holland's (1985) theory of career decision making (Eberhardt & Muchinsky, 1982b, 1984; Smart, 1989). Such data have contributed to tests of the generalizability of turnover theory (Murphy & Morrison, 1991) and to its application. Using a specific career transition element, that is, turnover theory, research incorporating biographical data has demonstrated that such theory is generalizable across time and occupational groups (Burch, Sheposh, & Morrison, 1991; Murphy & Morrison, 1991) and can aid in problem solving (Breaugh & Dossett, 1989; Murphy & Morrison, 1991).

BIODATA'S RELEVANCE TO A
CAREER DEVELOPMENT SYSTEM

In order to make the discussion of biodata more relevant to career development, in this section the organizational/occupational context of a career development system (Schein, 1978) will be discussed. Whether it is part of an organization or an occupation, a career development system (Figure 1) needs to be examined from two perspectives—organizational/occupational and individual—and from three stages—input, process, and outcome. Both individual and organizational sets of inputs are dynamic in an open system such as the one shown in Figure 1. Inputs change as a result of career development processes, and such change results in outcomes that contribute to new/altered inputs. In addition, the outside world (e.g., the family for the individual and competition for the organization) and changes in the individual and organization (e.g., growth and new products) also contribute to new/modified inputs, increasing the system's dynamic nature.

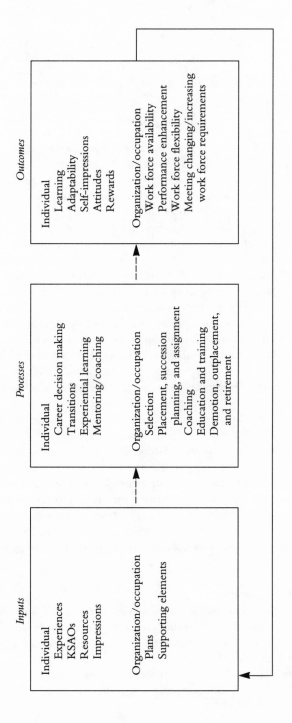

FIGURE 1   A Career Development System

CAREER DEVELOPMENT SYSTEM INPUTS

There are two primary classes of imputs to a career development system. One is individual, and the other is a combination of organizational and occupational.

Individual

The individual's inputs to the career development processes include prior experiences, knowledge, skills, abilities, and other characteristics (KSAOs), resources, and personal impressions of these inputs and the context surrounding them. Prior experiences include not only work experiences but also all of the experiences of life, education, childhood, and so forth that occurred before individuals entered the career development system. A detailed description of how the relevance of those experiences are established was provided in the previous section. The knowledge, skills, and abilities that individuals contribute to the career development system have been systematically analyzed and assessed by psychometricians and educators for many years. However, much less effort has been made to identify, measure, and introduce the other characteristics of the individual to the career development system. Interests have received considerable consideration via the introduction of Holland's (1985) theory of careers. But personality, values, attitudes, and motives have not been as carefully investigated. Personal resources (e.g., time, effort, and money) are significant individual contributions to the career development system. Such resources are dependent on two factors: their availability to the individual and, when available, the individual's motivation to contribute them to the career development system. Personal impressions of their potential contributions and the context surrounding them also become individual inputs to the career development system. For example, if the individual perceives that the opportunities for career growth are limited, then resources will be withheld from the system; if past experiences are perceived as irrelevant, their contribution to the career development system will be greatly constrained. Such inputs are the foundation of biodata.

Organization / Occupation

The organization/occupation's inputs to the system can be summarized in two classes—plans and supporting elements. There are three types of organizational plans. The first plan projects how the organization will be structured at a future date and the steps that will be made to achieve the new structure. The plan for the new organization can be translated into many career development system requirements, such as career paths, new KSAO requirements, and mobility/transition needs. Biodata could be used to represent career paths formed from subgroups (Mumford & Owens, 1984), KSAO requirements (Mumford & Owens, 1987), and adaptable personnel (Morrison, 1977b).

The second plan is a human resource plan that should include a forecast of the organization's future needs for numbers of personnel within each hierarchical level and skill type and a series of steps that lays out how the organization expects to fulfill its future needs. If the human resource plan is complete, it will contain an inventory of current human resources with the status of the inventory projected for each planning period (e.g., two and five years into the future). While manpower models using historical data (Jackson & Schuler, 1990) are typically used in such forecasts, biodata could enhance the accuracy of such models by helping predict the mobility of classes of work force members both within the organization and to the outside. Biodata collected on the present work force could be used to see if upward mobility (Howard & Bray, 1988; Laurent, 1968), allocation among work groups (Morrison & Arnold, 1974; Morrison & Vosburgh, 1987), turnover (Bruce & Burch, 1989; Morrison et al., 1968), and early retirements would follow historical trends.

The third is a succession plan (Jackson & Schuler, 1990) that identifies high potential employees, delineates generic competencies, and prescribes learning experiences to develop those competencies. Generic competencies such as adaptability (Morrison, 1977b) can be described, and high-potential employees (Howard & Bray, 1988; Laurent, 1968; Morrison & Sebald, 1974) can be predicted by biodata. It appears that biodata in conjunction with other techniques (McCall, Lombardo, & Morrison, 1988) can help identify learning experiences relevant in the development process.

Plans cannot be made or translated into action without supporting elements such as policies and programs, resources, and leadership. Policies and programs will not support the career development system unless the components are developmentally and future-oriented. Developmental processes take concentrated effort and time, producing no impact in a year and little in two years. Resources consisting of time, money, facilities, and information are required to implement the plans. Research about the optimum application of historical inputs is a key information resource. A final supporting element consists of the organizational/occupational leadership, who should have been trained in managing and participating in the career development system processes.

CAREER DEVELOPMENT SYSTEM PROCESSES

The individual's basic inputs to career development processes are present regardless of what the organization does. The organization's inputs provide the technology and context used to interpret and modify individual inputs during the implementation of the organizational/occupational career development processes.

Individual

CAREER DECISION MAKING AND PLANNING PROCESSES: Proactive individuals can have major influences on their careers, especially if they seek opportunities that are compatible with their KSAOs. The self-assessment process is a key initial step in career decision making and planning. In one individual differences (IDs) model (Bell & Staw, 1989), individuals who exert proactive personal control over their career outcomes accrue strong feelings of self-efficacy and career satisfaction plus significant organizational rewards. More dependent, reactive individuals progress toward withdrawal from their careers and organizations and learned helplessness. Six of the model's seven IDs—that is, self-monitoring, risk-seeking, dominance (need for power), work as a central life interest, career anchor, and history of control—can be captured via biodata. Such a model can help individuals look at themselves and determine why their careers are in limbo and why they do not make career decisions—the first step in taking control of their careers. Self-efficacy in the learned helplessness state may be so low that individuals will not be able to move out of it without intervention from their work or nonwork environment.

Most career counseling processes assume that there is only one correct way, the rational, systematic one, to make career decisions. Super (1990), Harren (cited in Phillips, Pazienza, & Ferrin, 1984), and Driver (1991) not only propose a rational or hierarchic style but also introduce intuitive (decisive), integrative, flexible, impulsive, and conforming (dependent) styles. All but the latter two are considered effective techniques, indicating that career counseling processes need to be made more adaptable to the style of the decision maker. Biodata could be used to discover decision makers' decision styles and guide them to the use of more compatible counseling procedures. This approach would be especially useful as the first step in a computer-aided counseling system. Then, an intuitive (decisive) or flexible decision maker could take a shorter, less complete path than the rational (hierarchic) one would. Both groups might find the approach acceptable and tend to use it more often than a system built only upon a rational hierarchical/integrative model.

The importance of effective career decision making to the individual is brought out in several theories that emphasize career choice (Brown, 1990;

Ginzberg, 1990; Hotchkiss & Borow, 1990; Miller-Tiedeman & Tiedeman, 1990; Mitchell & Krumboltz, 1990; Roe & Lunneborg, 1990; Super, 1990; Weinrach & Srebalus, 1990). As the match between personal characteristics and job requirements becomes closer, the likelihood of success increases (Brown, 1990). An increase in success increases self-efficacy (Bandura, 1989; Wood & Bandura, 1989) and self-esteem (Coopersmith, 1981; Mumford, Snell, & Reiter-Palmon, 1990) and aids in career subidentity development (Hall, 1971). All of these can or have been assessed using biodata (Mumford & Owens, 1987).

Measures of interests have been used for many years to aid individuals, primarily students, in their career choices. Over the last three decades, considerable research on vocational interests has been conducted using Holland's theory of career choice (Weinrach & Srebalus, 1990). The applicability of biodata to vocational classification has been demonstrated using Holland's (1985) theory in concert with Owens' developmental theory (Betz, Fitzgerald, & Hill, 1989; Eberhardt & Muchinsky, 1982b, 1984). Biodata should receive even more attention in the career decision-making process since they capture a much wider array of personal characteristics than interest measures alone. Values, attitudes, and personality characteristics that are assessed in biodata measures differentiate among occupations (Morrison, 1977a; Morrison & Arnold, 1974; Schein, 1985) in addition to interests and abilities (Holland, 1985; Schneider & Schmitt, 1986; Smart, 1989; Super, 1953). Betz and Fitzgerald (1987) introduce a wide range of factors influencing the career choices of women that have been or could be captured by biodata. Along with the ability to adapt to new requirements (Morrison & Brantner, 1992; Morrison & Hoch, 1986), knowledge and skills of adults can be assessed by biodata because there is sufficient life history. Biodata have been used successfully to identify creativity in scientists and engineers (Barron & Harrington, 1981), and the results have been adapted for use in the personal career decision making process in either a paper-and-pencil (Morrison & Vosburgh, 1987) or a computer-based (Edwards, 1991) mode.

Biodata can serve as a key source of information for career development planning (Avolio & Gibbons, 1988). If biodata are available from individuals who have been successful in a chosen career, the information can be used to plan sequences of actions that can be taken to follow such role models (Bandura, 1977). Since successful individuals will have taken a variety of career paths, activities can be selected that are feasible and consistent with the planner's self-concept (Dawis & Lofquist, 1984).

A basic premise underlying this discussion of individual career decision making and planning is that individuals must have the opportunity to be involved in the career decisions affecting them (Super, 1953). Many individuals do not have accurate information about career opportunities or are not allowed to participate in decisions about their career. In these instances, neither biodata nor other measures will show coherent relationships between apparently relevant antecedents and career choices (Morrison & Wilcove, 1991). Thus, the associated motivational component represented in biodata may disappear.

Just as in career decision making, most, but not all, career transtions are volitional, and the proportion of acceptable career transitions may be dependent on the proactive nature of the individuals involved.

CAREER TRANSITION PROCESSES: Working adults are faced constantly with transitions during their careers by events such as entry into a school, career, or organization; transferring jobs, occupations, or locations; reorganization; promotion or demotion; significant special assignments; interruptions and reentry due to child rearing, poor health, or other circumstances; plateauing; job loss; and retirement. Each transition includes adjustment and development that theorists (Thomae, 1979) postulate can modify some personality characteristics over the life span. For example, gains and losses in social competence are posited as the result of changing roles and physical conditions. Such changes are expected to be orderly and necessary, or adjustment to changing career situations is inhibited. While individuals vary greatly, there is an orderly sequence of change in most adult career and life histories (Thomae, 1979) that can be assessed using biodata measures.

In their theory of work adjustment, Dawis and Lofquist (1984) propose that adjustment is a process of achieving and maintaining correspondence between individual and environmental requirements as assessed by both parties' level of satisfaction. They postulate that individuals' work personalities develop from their experiences in responding in certain ways and under different conditions of reinforcement in social, educational, and work settings. Biodata are used to capture different adjustment styles and individuals' needs and values (Dawis & Lofquist, 1984). Bruce (1991) has used biodata effectively to evaluate the process of adjusting to transitions that place stress on individuals.

In a similar vein, biodata can be used to capture the "rites of passage" (Trice & Morand, 1989) that are often part of the initial entry into an occupation, organization, or elite group. Each candidate who enters the new organization, moves from specialist to manager, changes from bench scientist to one with national or world recognition, moves from middle management to the executive suite, and so forth, must survive a "testing" process to become an accepted member of the new group. Biodata can represent both the literal process elements and the individuals' interpretations of them—a key to successful transition.

If the term *work histories* denotes sequences of job experience and *careers* denotes how people interpret the meaning of their work histories (Nicholson & West, 1989), *biodata* represent a combination of the two. Biodata can measure an individual's perceptions of transitions in their work histories by covering issues such as the following:

- *Discretion*: How much control did the individual have over the transition process?
- *Speed*: How rapid was the transition?
- *Amplitude*: Was the transition major or minor?
- *Propulsion*: Did the individual or external forces initiate the transition? That is, was it done willingly? Was it planned? Did it make sense?
- *Significance:* How personally or organizationally important were the outcomes of the transition?

EXPERIENTIAL LEARNING: The adaptation and learning process occurs throughout the time at work, not just during transitions. The majority of adult career development occurs at work, not in the training or education situation (Morrison & Hoch, 1986). The mastery motivation that is important to human learning (Dweck, 1986) can be identified using biodata (M. D. Mumford, personal communication, October 7, 1991). An adaptive, mastery-oriented learning pattern is characterized by challenge-seeking, effective persistence in the face of obstacles, and enjoyment in working at task mastery. For example, the simple accumulation of a training program history in biodata would not aid in the identification of adaptive, master-oriented learners. The purpose behind the training would need to be identified because such adults would participate in training only when they perceived a need (London & Bassman, 1989) to acquire new knowledge and skill for an upcoming transition or resolve a problem in their present work.

A single event cannot identify developmental progress. Progress can be charted by biographical evidence because coherence and continuity within a temporal framework are demonstrated (Howe, 1982). Even information about leisure pursuits needs to be acquired since they may be the source of development supporting a move from one occupation to another (Super, 1986).

People develop in their careers not only through direct experience and reinforced repetition but also by the use of cognitive aids such as vicarious experiences and symbolic processes (Bandura, 1977; Wood & Bandura,

1989). They learn via reading, observing others' behavior, and modeling others' actions. These experiences are processed and preserved in representational forms, using verbal and imagined symbols to serve as guides for future behavior. Thus, to provide an adequate description of the individual's developmental life history, biodata must provide the opportunity to record vicarious experiences of the individual and his or her interpretations of these experiences as well as the individual's direct experiences and interpretations. Since the developmental process continues throughout the adult's career, the historical record of career development must be constantly updated and revised.

MENTORING AND COACHING: In order to develop a new skill, an individual must not only notice a new behavior, remember it, and interpret it but he or she must also *try out* the new behavior. A training program may impart knowledge and even initiate the first faltering steps in developing some skill, but a mentor (Kram, 1985) or coach can provide guidance while attempts are made to try out and gain new skills (Wood & Bandura, 1989). The mentoring process has received little comprehensive research (Kram, 1986), and its constructs are poorly defined and measured. Biodata can be used to include descriptions of the developmental history of voluntary mentoring relationships so that distinctions between effective and ineffective relationships can be determined. Such data can help establish whether naturally evolving mentoring relationships and/or assigned ones (i.e., coaching [Noe, 1988]) are effective contributors to the career development process (Dreher & Ash, 1990; Whitely, Dougherty, & Dreher, 1988).

Organizational/Occupational

SELECTION: Biodata have been used effectively in the selection of applicants for a wide variety of jobs (see chapters by Pannone and Stokes & Cooper in this volume). This application is sufficiently mature to have demonstrated validity generalization (Rothstein, Schmidt, Erwin, Owens, & Sparks, 1990). In traditional selection procedures, applicants provide information to the organization that makes the decision for them. Biodata provide information on conative aspects of the applicants that complement traditional measures of knowledge, skills, and abilities (KSAs) since the overlap between the biodata and KSA measures is minor (Barge & Hough, 1987). Entering the organization or occupation is a key career decision and transition, especially in organizations and occupations that try to minimize losses across a full career, such as military, government, police, medicine, and crafts. Such organizations use success in entry-level training and turnover as criteria for selection program validation. Biodata typically do very well in these instances (Laurence & Means, 1985; Malouff & Schutte, 1985; Roomsburg, 1988; Sager & Johnston, 1989; Trent, Quenette, & Pass, 1989) but not always (Parker, Wiskoff, McDaniel, Zimmerman, & Sherman, 1989).

Although seldom interpreted in such a way, biodata from experienced, midcareer personnel describe past behaviors in a context that reflects the value system and culture of their organization or occupation as perceived by its members (Bowen, Ledford, & Nathan, 1991). If they desire to stay therein, the members will have accepted the values of the culture, contributing to clear differentiation among organizations and occupations (Morrison, 1977a; Morrison & Arnold, 1974; Schein, 1975). Thus, in the selection of new employees, an organization can use biodata to create a work group with personalities that are consistent with the organizational culture (Schneider, 1987). Such homogeneity aids in the development of cohesion and cooperative behavior by enhancing organizational and occupational commitment, leading to work-group stability (minimal turnover; Murphy & Morrison, 1991). Depending on the work, the potential for enhanced performance also exists in such a situation.

While there have been concerns that systematic, validated selection decision aids will produce an organizational or occupational membership that is homogeneous and inflexible, this does not appear to be the case (Bowen et al., 1991). For example, membership in three disparate biodata subsets has produced effective performance in a single corporate occupational group—sales (Taylor, 1968).

PLACEMENT, SUCCESSION PLANNING, AND ASSIGNMENT: The technology is available to use biodata in the selection and assignment of personnel in a wide variety of organizational career paths (Schoenfeldt, 1974) from blue collar (Morrison, 1977a) to professional, technical, and managerial (Laurent, 1968) employees. Avolio and Gibbons (1988) have described the antecedent events and conditions to the development of transformational leadership. Such information could be used to construct a biodata instrument that would help identify individuals who could be placed on a transformational leadership career path and have increased opportunities for career success on such a path. Succession plans could be developed by using biodata and other measures to predict successful placement and promotion of candidates.

A personal history record and biodata for individuals (Avolio & Gibbons, 1988) could aid considerably in reassignment decisions. If sets of alternative developmental patterns of successful personnel for a career path were identified rigorously, individuals could be assigned to those positions providing similar developmental opportunities. To date, this technique has been applied subjectively in most organizations, although it might be applied objectively using alternative career paths or assignments produced via pattern analysis or policy capturing.

Not every effective application of biodata for succession planning continues to be successful. In one instance (R. S. Wonder, personal communication, September 6, 1984), a battery that included biodata and had effectively predicted executive success for many years was dropped from use for several reasons:

- There was differential prediction among special groups.
- Executives wanted complete control over rewards such as promotion without the "interference" of a battery of tests.
- No feedback was available for participants.
- The firm had not developed an aura of sophisticated technology so that the external environment provided positive feedback about the "state-of-the-art" status of the program.

COACHING: If members of the organization are going to aid individuals in their career development, they need to have information about both the organization's career opportunities and the individual's background and KSAOs. Biodata provide basic inputs to such a career coaching process. The organizational representative's prime contribution to the process is to aid in interpreting how the organization and individual inputs can be meshed to provide an optimum combination of the two. At the same time, a coach can aid in identifying career gaps in the individual's background, suggesting approaches that are available to help fill such gaps, and finding programs in the organization that might help in the process.

EDUCATION AND TRAINING: The application of biodata in the educational process has focused on the initial choice of a college major as described earlier in the section on individual career decision making and planning processes. Although this would be applicable when an organization selects personnel for the educational programs it sponsors, such use does not appear to be made. Both corporations and government expend large amounts of money in long-term residential or release educational programs without using biodata or other sophisticated technologies to determine whether most applicants to such programs should be sponsored.

Personal characteristics have a strong impact on performance in training (Fleishman & Mumford, 1989). While most research in this area looks at success in initial training in the military (e. g., Fleishman & Mumford, 1989; Roomsburg, 1988), biodata could be used to predict success in training for mid- to late-career adults as well. In addition, biodata could be used to spot previous training or experience that would provide adequate substitutes for new training, thereby reducing training costs. In other instances, biodata could be used to identify where training was needed by contrasting an individual's pattern of career events with a pattern typical of successful organizational or occupational participants.

DEMOTION, OUTPLACEMENT, AND RETIREMENT: Although not presently used by organizations in a systematic way, biodata could be very helpful in the career change process. Skills, interests, adaptability, values, and so forth, could be brought out in a way that would aid individuals to accept career changes in the organization as well as outside. Reassignment or demotion could be used to initiate progress on a new career path that may be more compatible with the individual's attributes. In outplacement, as well as in those instances of retirement in which there is a desire to continue a career, the organization can use biodata input to help the individual decide on a new organization, self-employment, or even a new occupation since the opportunity for such a transition has arisen. It is possible that a major change may help individuals improve their career outcomes.

CAREER DEVELOPMENT SYSTEM OUTCOMES

The outcomes of the career development system cover a wide array and can vary in emphasis depending upon the level of effort expended on different input and process elements. Some outcomes are valued primarily by the individual or by the organization or occupation, while many are valued by both.

Both parties should find learning, the central ingredient of the system, a valued outcome. For the individual, learning can be associated with enhanced feelings of personal and career success (Childs & Klimoski, 1986)—for example, career identity, self-efficacy, and achievement. These can translate into good attitudes toward the organization or occupation and the job as represented in career and job satisfaction, organizational or occupational commitment, and enjoyment in retirement (Feldman, 1988). In such instances, learning may result not only in new or improved job performance KSAs but also in successful adjustment to work requirements (Barge & Hough, 1987), the social system (Bloom, 1964; Nelson, 1975), and even job loss (Feldman, 1988). In many instances, the system leads to organizational rewards such as pay increases and promotion (Childs & Klimoski, 1986; Dreher & Ash, 1990).

For the organization, the outcomes (Feldman, 1988) are reflected in two ways—in the continuous presence of the work force via reduced turnover (Daniel, 1980; Murphy & Morrison, 1991) and absenteeism and in a higher performing and more promotable, creative, and flexible work force that is up to date in its KSAs and willing to move (Feldman, 1988). Both help the organization to meet its immediate and long-term staffing requirements. Most historical, empirical biodata-based research has been focused on solving organizational problems such as plateauing (Brantner, 1989; Feldman & Weitz, 1988), obsolescence of KSAs among technical, scientific, and professional personnel (Kaufman, 1974), inability to adapt to a major organizational change (Morrison, 1977b), turnover (Feldman, 1988; Morrison et al., 1968), insufficient promotable personnel (Laurent, 1968), and inhibitors, as well as enhancers, of the experiential learning process (Morrison & Brantner, 1992).

Biodata have been useful predictors of all of these outcomes as described throughout the previous pages. More references to the research using such criteria are scattered throughout this chapter and the rest of the book. Additional emphasis here would be redundant; however, it should be noted that most historical research has been short-term and atheoretical, aimed at solving an immediate problem. Career development, by its nature, is long term and heavily emphasizes positive outcomes associated with the adult developmental process. Future efforts should emphasize the positive side of career development and longitudinal research, focusing on developmental processes (Mumford & Owens, 1987; Owens, 1968; Owens & Schoenfeldt, 1979) supported by theory building (Mumford & Owens, 1984; Mumford, Reiter-Palmon, & Snell, 1990; Mumford, Snell, & Reiter-Palmon, 1990) and empirically constructed biodata measures (Eberhardt & Muchinsky, 1982a; Morrison et al., 1962; Neiner & Owens, 1982; Owens & Schoenfeldt, 1979).

SPECIAL GROUPS AND THE CAREER DEVELOPMENT SYSTEM

The three major career theories that provide insight into the adult career development process (Holland, 1985; Levinson et al., 1978; Super, 1990) have been criticized (Brown, 1990; Greenhaus & Parasuraman, 1986) because of their lack of attention to gender, race, ethnic background, religion, low socioeconomic status, and physical or mental handicaps as factors in career development. Of the three theories, Holland's (1985) is the only one to specifically include gender and the socioeconomic status of the family background. His theory minimizes the impact of age by concentrating on a limited cross section of life, youth, and early adulthood.

More specifically, it emphasizes the career decision processes of high school and college populations.

Although there is dissent by those who feel that discrimination is the only factor that makes women's careers different from men's (Lemkau, 1984; Powell, 1990), gender must be considered a significant factor in career development (Brooks, 1990; Jordaan, 1967; Mumford & Owens, 1987; Rounds, Dawis, & Lofquist, 1977). The use of biographical data in longitudinal research (Austin & Hanisch, 1990; Barge & Hough, 1987; Davis, 1984; Dawis & Lofquist, 1984; Eberhardt & Muchinsky, 1984; Neiner & Owens, 1985; Smart, 1989) demonstrates significant differences between the sexes in the occupational choice and behavior of different college populations while in college and during the first years after graduation. Research must be extended so that more is learned about any career differences that men and women face throughout their adult lives. If dual-career and family linkages cause asynchronous career development patterns between husband and wife (Sekaran & Hall, 1989), biographical data can help capture those differences. Gender differences in self-concept have been identified (Brooks, 1990; Metcalfe, 1987). If career growth and identity are based on autonomy (detachment) and task achievement or mastery for men and on interdependence and relationships (linkages) for women (Gallos, 1989; Sekaran & Hall, 1989), these differences can be identified using biographical data. Additional issues, such as career preparation and societal opportunities (Gallos, 1989), should also be investigated using biographical data.

Biographical data can aid in the investigation of differences not only in the career development of men and women but also within gender. For example, the proportion of adult women working outside the home has increased dramatically over the last 20 years. Although the child-rearing role has been shared increasingly with the fathers and childcare facilities, it becomes very difficult for upwardly mobile women to be as wholly dedicated to their careers as organizations have demanded of their executives throughout history (Metcalfe, 1987). Biographical data can capture the differences within a gender (Morrison & Sebald, 1974) as both women and men struggle with the revolutionary changes occurring in traditional career and life roles (Brett & Yogev, 1988; Yogev & Brett, 1985).

The progress achieved in research on gender differences in career development has not occurred for other special groups. Little is known about career development in different racial, ethnic, religious, physically and mentally handicapped, low income (Greenhaus & Parasuraman, 1986), and age groups. In a few instances, biographical data have been used to identify differences in developmental patterns between groups that are college educated and those that are not (Howard & Bray, 1988; Morrison

& Arnold, 1974), but much more needs to be discovered about the magnitude of the influence that education level has on differential career development. Race is a major facet of the social context that affects the individual's career success in American and similar cultures and thereby influences the individual's identity (Thomas & Alderfer, 1989). Biographical data can aid in capturing information about the impact of race on the career development process. For example, in America, race and gender may interact to produce different career development effects for Caucasian versus African-American women (Thomas & Alderfer, 1989) or men. Although the career theories based on age-defined stages (Levinson et al., 1978) are on the wane, the affect of age in limiting the time of entry into various occupations is a neglected area of research. Biographical data can be used to establish the career paths of effective occupational members, the time taken to achieve their status, and the age they left their fields. By determining how long members must practice their occupations to prepare for retirement and repay society's investment in them, the oldest age at which individuals can enter those fields and have successful careers can be calculated.

The problem becomes even more complex when cultures (organizational, ethnic, etc.) are added to the developmental progress equation (Schein, 1986). In some instances the culture of a multinational corporation can interact with the culture of the host country to make the development of its expatriate managers and their families complex (Zeira & Banai, 1985). While ethnic group differences have not been obtained in many studies (Barge & Hough, 1987; Mumford & Owens, 1987), organizational (Laurent, 1970), occupational, or national cultures represented in selection systems or socialization processes may be so dominant that ethnic group differences are masked when a study is conducted within a single corporation, occupation, or country. The key career issue underlying human resource management concerns may be the career adaptability of individuals and their families to changes not only within the organization's culture (Morrison, 1977b) but also outside the organization, while conducting business or relocating. Biodata can capture aspects of career adaptability (Morrison, 1977b), but items such as childhood and preadult experiences may represent specialized adaptability in a culture like Canada's and may need to be revised or omitted when used to study cross-cultural developmental patterns (Laurent, 1970).

In summary, we should keep in mind that society's discriminatory and socialization practices create different levels of career development opportunity based on membership in one or more special groups (Brooks, 1990). However, the culture may also create differences in needs, values, and so forth, that cause members of special groups to gravitate toward unique occupations and to be absorbed into informal networks more readily. Such competing factors need to be identified if they are present.

SUGGESTIONS FOR THE FUTURE

With such an extensive list of requirements, where should future efforts be replaced? If we can assume that theory and practice are symbiotic (Murphy & Morrison, 1991) in nature, we will need to emphasize both research and application.

RESEARCH

The most glaring problem present in tying biodata and career development together is the omission of biodata measures from most research on theories of adult career development. Consistent with the requirements of career theory, background data can be used to assess (a) the individual, (b) his or her career environment, and (c) the outcomes of this interaction. Biodata should be considered explicitly in the development of career theory as Levinson and his colleagues (Bujold, 1990; Levinson, 1986) could have done using material from their autobiographical narratives. Other theories to which biodata could be introduced to a greater extent are those of Dalton and Thompson (1986) and Super (1990). Biodata's promise should be extended into broader theoretical frameworks than initial occupational choice (Eberhardt & Muchinsky, 1984; Holland, 1985).

A possible constraint on the ability of theorists to include biodata within their formulations is the lack of information available about the underlying meaning of biodata (Barge & Hough, 1987). More theoretically based research (Mumford, Snell, & Reiter-Palmon, 1990) needs to go into the construction of biodata measures. For example, better insight is required into the underlying classes of constructs (e.g, motivation and values) represented by biodata as initiated by Mumford and Owens (1987). Simultaneously, parsimony in the number of constructs assessed needs to be introduced so that biodata measures are not too long to be included in research with a broader perspective (Morrison & Brantner, 1992).

To aid in the process, biodata items should be designed to be developmental in content. Such items should focus on discrete elements of prior behaviors and experiences and the individual's personal interpretations of those events (Mumford & Owens, 1987) that have been hypothesized to represent developmental antecedents of later career decisions, personal states, or behaviors. The prediction of the latter outcomes is based on a developmental strategy (Mumford & Owens, 1987), a central ingredient of career development theory, research, and application. An approach that would be helpful in this arena is the use of intensive studies of individual careers over the life span (Levinson, 1986). These in-depth studies should introduce continuous socialization and macroenvironmental issues with their situational and cohort effects into the design of biodata. Maturation is not the only cause of individual development. People develop and function in dynamic and reciprocal interactions with their environments (Bandura, 1982; Magnusson & Bergman, 1989; Mumford, Snell, & Reiter-Palmon, 1990) as well as at different rates (Mumford, Wesley, & Shaffer, 1987). Because of the wide variety of life experiences required to capture the developmental process, an interdisciplinary approach including developmental psychologists, sociologists, organization behaviorists, and human resource specialists along with industrial and organizational psychologists may provide optimum results (Herr, 1990).

More longitudinal research (e.g., Block,1971; Neiner & Owens, 1982) is required, especially in middle and late careers. In today's dynamic environment, career adaptability might be the appropriate central theme of such future research (Morrison, 1977b; Mumford, Reiter-Palmon, & Snell, 1990). A possible approach would be to identify major transition points (e.g., entry, change to management, plateauing, and outplacement or retirement) for divergent occupations (e.g., carpentry, engineering, and medicine), and organization types (e.g., military, large corporation, and self-employment). Cohorts would be assessed before the transition and after the event to capture the process, its impact, and how different subsets (based on homogeneous patterns of behaviors and experiences; see Mumford & Owens, 1984) develop and progress in their careers. A major challenge will be identifying different sets of experiences and their interpretations (biodata) that are relevant antecedents of the career period under study since the content of the sets changes with maturation and experience (Davis, 1984; Mumford & Owens, 1987; Neiner & Owens, 1982; Russell, 1991). To compress the time required to obtain results, it may be necessary to use specialized research designs with multiple cohorts and a few repeated measures (Horn & McArdle, 1980).

Future research should include more noncollege occupation and career groups. Data collection, including much more biodata, should start in high school rather than college, as was done in Super's (1953) and Block's (1971) research and Project Talent (Flanagan et al., 1962).

APPLICATIONS

For many years, biodata have been successfully applied in the selection of new employees for jobs and job clusters and in identifying potential candidates for management positions. Where do we go from here? With biodata's already significant contribution, emphasis on selection of applications should continue. However, adaptations of the measures should be made to cope with the unique career issues of special groups. For example, some previous career experiences (developmental antecedents) represented in biodata may not be available to women who have been caring for young children or to handicapped persons. Surrogate experiences that are valid indicators of the desired career outcome and are available to special groups should be included in alternate forms.

Continuing in the selection mode, the organization could emphasize developmental outcomes in selection decisions—something that has received little previous attention. If biodata measures, validated for classes of positions or levels in the hierarchy, were scored for significant omissions, high potential employees lacking that experience could be given assignments that would complete the biodata experience portion of their background. Then, further assignments, promotions, or moves would be based on biodata covering a complete combination of the objective experience and its personal interpretation related to the new position's requirements.

The previous proposal is based on the premise that biodata measures could be designed as compliments to or substitutes for assessment centers that identify developmental needs (Drakeley, Herriot, & Jones, 1988). Using biodata, the subgroup membership of individuals could be identified (Owens, 1971). Then, as in the assessment center process, biodata results could be fed back to the participant for personal use in career decision making and planning (Morrison & Vosburgh, 1987).

If the labor supply, especially the skilled portion, dwindles as forecasted, selection ratios and the effectiveness of selection techniques will decrease. The need to optimize placements for new and experienced employees should increase. The technology to use biodata in such decisions has been developed (Schoenfeldt, 1974) and shown to be practical (Brush & Owens, 1979; Morrison, 1977a). While the decision may include assignment to a specific job, it may involve placement in an organization, function, or occupation with unique personnel attributes (Edwards, 1991; Schneider, 1987). However, it is also possible to identify individuals with specialized attributes and plan an environment that develops and nurtures those characteristics (Michael & Colson, 1979).

Biodata describe past behavior in the context of an occupational or organizational value system and culture as perceived by the typical occupational or organizational member who has accepted those values and committed to the group. Thus, biodata can aid in the following:

- Placing unskilled personnel within a context of common interests, values, personality, and abilities that enhances their development of new skills and knowledge (Morrison, 1977a); such placement should produce cooperative behavior and provide an opportunity to learn in a lower risk environment (Morrison & Brantner, 1992)
- Building a context (Schneider, 1987) that develops satisfaction with work and the employment situation by responding to the members' desires for developmental opportunities, rewards, and human resource development policies and practices

Using the ideas of Owens (1976) for guidance, it is possible to form biodata subsets, identify the subsets that individuals are in, and choose one or more alternate subsets that individuals may want to be in. Individuals could then plan experiences that are representative of the other subsets to try out and assess whether they want to change and/or develop in a direction similar to the members of an alternate subset. It would seem that the process would be most effective if the individuals' distal past experiences were similar to those of the new subset, and deviations had occurred only in proximal past experiences.

CONCLUSION

Both theory and research support the adage that our past history influences us at the present time and will continue to do so in the future. However, we are not controlled by our past to such an extent that we cannot and do not develop and change. Much of this developmental progress in our adult life is not clearly delineated, but biographical data have the ability to aid in the clarification of unique developmental patterns and the factors that influence them. This chapter has taken a systems and interaction approach to linking career development with biographical data as it is known today and as it might be spelled out in the future.

REFERENCES

Adams, J. (1991). Issues in the management of careers. In R. F. Morrison & J. Adams (Eds.), *Contemporary career development issues*. Hillsdale, NJ: Erlbaum.

Albright, L. E., & Glennon, J. R. (1961). Personal history correlates of physical scientists' career aspirations. *Journal of Applied Psychology, 45,* 281–284.

Austin, J. T., & Hanisch, K. A. (1990). Occupational attainment as a function of abilities and interests: A longitudinal analysis using Project Talent data. *Journal of Applied Psychology, 75,* 77–86.

Avolio, B. J., & Gibbons, T. C. (1988). Developing transformational leaders: A life span approach. In J. A. Conger, R. N. Kanungo, and Associates (Eds.), *Charismatic leadership* (pp. 276–308). San Francisco: Jossey-Bass.

Baird, L. L. (1982). *The role of academic ability in high-level accomplishment and general success* (CB-R-82-6/ETS-RR-82-43). New York: College Board Publications.

Bandura, A. (1977). *Social learning theory.* Englewood Cliffs, NJ: Prentice-Hall.

Bandura, A. (1982). The psychology of chance encounters and life paths. *American Psychologist, 37,* 747–755.

Bandura, A. (1989). Human agency in social cognitive theory. *American Psychologist, 44,* 1175–1184.

Barge, B. N., & Hough, L. M. (1987). Utility of biographical data for predicting job performance. In L. M. Hough (Ed.), *Literature review: Utility of temperament, biodata, and interest assessment for predicting job performance* (ARI Research Note). Alexandria, VA: U.S. Army Research Institute for the Behavioral Sciences.

Barron, F., & Harrington, D. M. (1981). Creativity, intelligence, and personality. *Annual Review of Psychology, 32,* 439–476.

Bell, N. E., & Staw, B. M. (1989). People as sculptors versus sculpture: The roles of personality and personal control in organizations. In M. B. Arthur, D. T. Hall, & B. S. Lawrence (Eds.), *Handbook of career theory* (pp. 232–251). Cambridge: Cambridge University Press.

Berlew, D. E., & Hall, D. T. (1966). The socialization of managers: Effects of expectations on experience. *Administrative Science Quarterly, 11,* 207–223.

Betz, N. E., & Fitzgerald, L. F. (1987). *The career psychology of women.* New York: Academic Press.

Betz, N. E., Fitzgerald, L. F., & Hill, R. E. (1989). Trait-factor theories: Traditional cornerstone of career theory. In M. B. Arthur, D. T. Hall, & B. S. Lawrence (Eds.), *Handbook of career theory* (pp. 26–40). Cambridge: Cambridge University Press.

Block, J. (1971). *Lives through time.* Berkeley, CA: Bancroft.

Bloom, B. S. (1964). *Stability and change in human behavior.* New York: Wiley.

Bowen, D. E., Ledford, G. E., Jr., & Nathan, G. R. (1991). Hiring for the organization, not the job. *The Executive, 5*(4), 35–51.

Brantner, T. M. (1989). *Differences between plateaued and nonplateaued Navy officers in career attitudes and career related issues.* Unpublished master's thesis. San Diego State University, San Diego, CA.

Breaugh, J. A., & Dossett, D. L. (1989). Rethinking the use of personal history information: The value of theory-based biodata for predicting turnover. *Journal of Business and Psychology, 3,* 371–385.

Brett, J. M., & Yogev, S. (1988). Restructuring work for family: How dual-earner couples with children manage. *Journal of Social Behavior and Personality, 3,* 159–174.

Brooks, L. (1990). Recent developments in theory building. In D. Brown, L. Brooks, and Associates (Eds.), *Career choice and development* (2d ed., pp. 364–394). San Francisco: Jossey-Bass.

Brown, D. (1990). Trait and factor theory. In D. Brown, L. Brooks, and Associates (Eds.), *Career choice and development* (2d ed., pp. 13–36). San Francisco: Jossey-Bass.

Bruce, R. A. (1991). *The career transition cycle: Antecedents and consequences of career events* (NPRDC TR-91-8). San Diego, CA: Navy Personnel Research and Development Center.

Bruce, R. A., & Burch, R. L. (1989). *Officer career development: Modeling married aviator retention* (NPRDC-TR-91-8). San Diego, CA: Navy Personnel Research and Development Center.

Brush, D. H., & Owens, W. A. (1979). Implementation and evaluation of an assessment classification model for manpower utilization. *Personnel Psychology, 32,* 369–383.

Bujold, C. (1990). Biographical-hermeneutical approaches to the study of career development. In R. A. Young & W. A. Borgen (Eds.), *Methodological approaches to the study of career* (pp. 57–69). New York: Praeger.

Burch, R. L., Sheposh, J. P., & Morrison, R. F. (1991). *Officer career development: Surface warfare officer retention* (NPRDC-TR-91-5). San Diego, CA: Navy Personnel Research and Development Center.

Childs, A., & Klimoski, R. J. (1986). Successfully predicting career success: An application of the biographical inventory. *Journal of Applied Psychology, 71,* 3–8.

Coopersmith, S. (1981). *The antecedents of self-esteem.* Palo Alto, CA: Consulting Psychologists Press.

Dalton, G. W. (1989). Developmental views of career in organizations. In M. B. Arthur, D. T. Hall, & B. S. Lawrence (Eds.), *Handbook of career theory* (pp. 89–109). Cambridge: Cambridge University Press.

Dalton, G. W., & Thompson, P. H. (1986). *Novations: Strategies for career development.* Glenview, IL: Scott Foresman.

Daniel, J. (1980). *Life path as a predictor of performance in the Navy.* Kensington, MD: Richard A. Gibbony Associates.

Davis, K. R., Jr. (1984). A longitudinal analysis of biographical subgroups using Owens' developmental-integrative model. *Personnel Psychology, 37,* 1–14.

Dawis, R. V., & Lofquist, L. H. (1984). *A psychological theory of work adjustment.* Minneapolis: University of Minnesota Press.

Drakeley, R. J., Herriot, P., & Jones, A. (1988). Biographical data, training success and turnover. *Journal of Occupational Psychology, 61,* 145–152.

Dreher, G. F., & Ash, R. A. (1990). A comparative study of mentoring among men and women in managerial, professional, and technical positions. *Journal of Applied Psychology, 75,* 539–546.

Driver, M. J. (1991, October 17). *Decision styles.* Presentation to the staff of the Navy Personnel Research and Development Center, San Diego, CA.

Dweck, C. S. (1986). Motivational processes affecting learning. *American Psychologist, 41,* 1040–1048.

Eberhardt, B. J., & Muchinsky, P. M. (1982a). An empirical investigation of the factor stability of Owens' Biographical Questionnaire. *Journal of Applied Psychology, 67,* 138–145.

Eberhardt, B. J., & Muchinsky, P. M. (1982b). Biodata determinants of vocational typology. *Journal of Applied Psychology, 67,* 714–727.

Eberhardt, B. J., & Muchinsky, P. M. (1984). Structural validation of Holland's hexagonal model: Vocational classification through the use of biodata. *Journal of Applied Psychology, 69,* 174–181.

Edwards, J. E. (1991). Classification in a changing organization: Initial career concerns. In R. F. Morrison (Chair), *Shifting placement decisions from the organization to the individual.* Symposium conducted at the annual conference of the Society for Industrial and Organizational Psychology, St. Louis, MO.

Feldman, D. C. (1988). *Managing careers in organizations.* Glenview, IL: Scott, Foresman.

Feldman, D. C. (1989). Socialization, resocialization, and training: Reframing the research agenda. In I. L. Goldstein (Ed.), *Training and development in organizations* (pp. 376–416). San Francisco: Jossey-Bass.

Feldman, D. C., & Weitz, B. A. (1988). Career plateaus reconsidered. *Journal of Management, 14,* 69–80.

Fleishman, E. A., & Mumford, M. D. (1989). Individual attributes and training performance. In I. L. Goldstein (Ed.), *Training and development in organizations* (pp. 183–255). San Francisco: Jossey-Bass.

Flanagan, J. C., Dailey, J. T., Shaycoft, M. F., Gorham, W. A., Orr, D. B., & Goldberg, I. (1962). *The talents of American youth: Vol. 1. Design for a study of American youth.* Boston: Houghton Mifflin.

Gallos, J. V. (1989). Exploring women's development: Implications for career theory, practice, and research. In M. B. Arthur, D. T. Hall, & B. S. Lawrence (Eds.), *Handbook of career theory* (pp. 110–132). Cambridge: Cambridge University Press.

Ginzberg, E. (1990). Career development. In D. Brown, L. Brooks, & Associates (Eds.), *Career choice and development* (pp. 169–191). San Francisco: Jossey-Bass.

Goodenough, F. (1949). *Mental testing: Its history, principles, and applications.* New York: Holt, Rinehart, and Winston.

Greenhaus, J. H., & Parasuraman, S. (1986). Vocational and organizational behavior, 1985: A review. *Journal of Vocational Behavior, 29,* 115–176.

Hall, D. T. (1971). A theoretical model of career subidentity development in organizational settings. *Organizational Behavior and Human Performance, 6,* 50–76.

Hall, D. T. (1976). *Careers in organizations.* Glenview, IL: Scott, Foresman.

Hall, D. T. (1986). Breaking career routines: Midcareer choice and identity development. In D. T. Hall & Associates (Eds.), *Career development in organizations* (pp. 120–159). San Francisco: Jossey-Bass.

Hall, D. T., & Richter, J. (1990). Career gridlock: Baby boomers hit the wall. *Academy of Management Executive, 4*(3), 7–22.

Herr, E. L. (1990). Issues in career research. In R. A. Young & W. A. Borgen (Eds.), *Methodological approaches to the study of careers* (pp. 3–21). New York: Praeger.

Holland, J. L. (1985). *Making vocational choices* (2d ed.). Englewood Cliffs, NJ: Prentice-Hall.

Horn, J. L., & McArdle, J. J. (1980). Perspectives on mathematics/statistical model building (MASMOB) in research on aging. In L. F. Poon (Ed.), *Aging in the 1980s: Selected contemporary issues in the psychology of aging* (pp. 503–541). Washington, DC: American Psychological Association.

Hotchkiss, L., & Borow, H. (1990). Sociological perspectives on work and career development. In D. Brown, L. Brooks, & Associates (Eds.), *Career choice and development* (2d ed., pp. 262–307). San Francisco: Jossey Bass.

Howard, A., & Bray, D. W. (1988). *Managerial lives in transition.* New York: Guilford Press.

Howe, M. J. A. (1982). Biographical evidence and the development of outstanding individuals. *American Psychologist, 37,* 1071–1081.

Ilgen, D. R., & Klein, H. J. (1989). Organizational behavior. *Annual Review of Psychology, 40,* 327–351.

Jackson, S. E., & Schuler, R. S. (1990). Human resource planning: Challenges for industrial/organizational psychologists. *American Psychologist, 45,* 223–239.

Jordaan, J. P. (1967). Career development theory. *International Review of Applied Psychology, 26*(2), 107–114.

Kaufman, H. G. (1974). *Obsolescence and professional career development.* New York: AMACOM.

Kram, K. E. (1985). *Mentoring at work: Developmental relationships in organizational life.* Glenview, IL: Scott, Foresman.

Kram, K. E. (1986). Mentoring in the workplace. In D. T. Hall & Associates (Eds.), *Career development in organizations* (pp. 160–201). San Francisco: Jossey-Bass.

Latack, J. (1984). Career transitions within organizations: An exploratory study of work, nonwork, and coping strategies. *Organizational Behavior and Human Performance, 34,* 296–322.

Laurence, J. H., & Means, B. (1985). *A aescription and comparison of biographical inventories for military selection* (TR-FR-PRD-85-5). Alexandria, VA: Human Resources Research Organization.

Laurent, H. (1968). Research on the identification of management potential. In J. A. Myers, Jr. (Ed.), *Predicting managerial success* (pp. 1–34). Ann Arbor, MI: Foundation for Research on Human Behavior.

Laurent, H. (1970). Cross-cultural cross-validation of empirically validated tests. *Journal of Applied Psychology, 54,* 417–423.

Lemkau, J. P. (1984). Men in female-dominated professions: Distinguishing personality and background features. *Journal of Vocational Behavior, 24,* 110–122.

Levinson, D. J. (1986). A conception of adult development. *American Psychologist, 41,* 3–13.

Levinson, D. J., Darrow, C. N., Klein, E. B., Levinson, M. H., & McKee, B. (1978). *The seasons of a man's life.* New York: Knopf.

Lindblom, C. E. (1959). The science of "muddling through." *Public Administration Review, 19*(2), 79–88.

London, M., & Bassman, E. (1989). Retraining midcareer workers for the future workplace. In I. L. Goldstein (Ed.), *Training and development in organizations* (pp. 333–375). San Francisco: Jossey-Bass.

Louis, M. R. (1980). Surprise and sense making: What newcomers experience in entering unfamiliar organizational settings. *Administrative Science Quarterly, 25,* 226–251.

Magnusson, D., & Bergman, L. R. (1989). Longitudinal studies: Individual and variable based approaches to research on early risk factors. In M. Rutter (Ed.), *Studies of psycho-social risk.* New York: Cambridge University Press.

Malouff, J. M., & Schutte, N. S., (1985). *A review of validation research on psychological variables used in hiring police officers.* Paper presented at the annual convention of the Rocky Mountain Psychological Association, Phoenix, AZ.

McCall, M. W., Jr., Lombardo, M. M., & Morrison, A. M. (1988). *The lessons of experience.* Lexington, MA: Lexington Books.

Metcalfe, B. A. (1987). Male and female managers: An analysis of biographical and self-concept data. *Work and Stress, 1*(3), 207–219.

Michael, W. B., & Colson, K. R. (1979). The development and validation of a life experience inventory for the identification of creative electrical engineers. *Educational and Psychological Measurement, 39,* 463–470.

Miller-Tiedeman, A., & Tiedeman, D. V. (1990). Career decision making: An individualistic perspective. In D. Brown, L. Brooks, & Associates (Eds.), *Career choice and development* (2d ed., pp. 308–337). San Francisco: Jossey-Bass.

Mitchell, L. K., & Krumboltz, J. D. (1990). Social learning approach to career decision making: Krumboltz's theory. In D. Brown, L. Brooks, & Associates (Eds.), *Career choice and development* (2d ed., pp. 145–196). San Francisco: Jossey-Bass.

Mobley, W. H. (1982). *Employee turnover: Causes, consequences, and control.* Reading, MA: Addison-Wesley.

Morrison, R. F. (1977a). A multivariate model for the occupational placement decision. *Journal of Applied Psychology, 62,* 271–277.

Morrison, R. F. (1977b). Career adaptivity: The effective adaptation of managers to changing roles. *Journal of Applied Psychology, 62,* 549–558.

Morrison, R. F., & Arnold, S. J. (1974). A suggested revision in the classification of nonprofessional occupations in Holland's theory. *Journal of Counseling Psychology, 21,* 485–488.

Morrison, R. F., & Brantner, T. M. (1992). What enhances or inhibits learning a new job? A basic career issue. *Journal of Applied Psychology, 77,* 926–940.

Morrison, R. F., Ginsburg, L. R., & Trammell, G. B. (1968). *Selection of nontechnical salesmen.* Unpublished manuscript.

Morrison, R. F., & Hoch, R. R. (1986). Career building: Learning from cumulative work experience. In D. T. Hall & Associates (Eds.), *Career development in organizations* (pp. 236–273). San Francisco: Jossey-Bass.

Morrison, R. F., Owens, W. A., Glennon, J. R., & Albright, L. E. (1962). Factored life history antecedents of industrial research performance. *Journal of Applied Psychology, 46,* 281–284.

Morrison, R. F., & Sebald, M. L. (1974). Personal characteristics differentiating female executive from female nonexecutive personnel. *Journal of Applied Psychology, 59,* 656–659.

Morrison, R. F., & Vosburgh, R. M. (1987). *Career development for engineers and scientists.* New York: Van Nostrand Reinhold.

Morrison, R. F., & Wilcove, G. L. (1991). Roadblocks to warrior subspecialty development. *Military Psychology, 3,* 41–59.

Mowday, R. T., Porter, L. W., & Steers, R. M. (1982). *Employee organization linkages: The psychology of commitment, absenteeism, and turnover.* New York: Academic Press.

Mumford, M. D., & Owens, W. A. (1982). Life history and vocational interests. *Journal of Vocational Behavior, 21,* 330–348.

Mumford, M. D., & Owens, W. A. (1984). Individuality in a developmental context: Some empirical and theoretical considerations. *Human Development, 27,* 84–108.

Mumford, M. D., & Owens, W. A. (1987). Methodology review: Principles, procedures, and findings in the application of background data measures. *Applied Psychological Measurement, 11,* 1–31.

Mumford, M. D., Reiter-Palmon, R., & Snell, A. F. (1990). *Background data and development: Structural issues in the application of life history measures.* Unpublished manuscript, George Mason University, Fairfax, VA.

Mumford, M. D., Snell, A. F., & Reiter-Palmon, R. (1990). *Personality and background data: Life history and self concepts in an ecological system.* Unpublished manuscript, George Mason University, Fairfax, VA.

Mumford, M. D., Wesley, S. S., & Shaffer, G. S. (1987). Individuality in a developmental context. II. The crystallization of developmental trajectories. *Human Development, 30,* 291–321.

Murphy, K., & Morrison, R. F. (1991). *The competing requirements of theory and application: Modeling naval warfare officer turnover.* Manuscript submitted for publication.

Neiner, A. G., & Owens, W. A. (1982). Relationships between two sets of biodata with 7 years separation. *Journal of Applied Psychology, 67,* 146–150.

Neiner, A. G., & Owens, W. A. (1985). Using biodata to predict job choice among college graduates. *Journal of Applied Psychology, 70,* 127–136.

Nelson, P. D. (1975). *Biographical constructs as predictors of adjustment to organizational environments.* Paper presented at the Research Seminar on Social Psychology of Military Service, Chicago.

Nicholson, N., & West, M. (1989). Transitions, work histories, and careers. In M. B. Arthur, D. T. Hall, & B. S. Lawrence (Eds.), *Handbook of career theory* (pp. 181–201). Cambridge: Cambridge University Press.

Noe, R. A. (1988). An investigation of the determinants of successful assigned mentoring relationships. *Personnel Psychology, 41,* 457–479.

Owens, W. A. (1968). Toward one discipline of scientific psychology. *American Psychologist, 23,* 782–785.

Owens, W. A. (1971). A quasi-actuarial basis for individual assessment. *American Psychologist, 26,* 992–999.

Owens, W. A. (1976). Background data. In M. D. Dunnette (Ed.), *Handbook of industrial and organizational psychology* (pp. 609–644). New York: Wiley.

Owens, W. A., & Schoenfeldt, L. F. (1979). Toward a classification of persons. *Journal of Applied Psychology, 64,* 569–607.

Parker, J. P., Wiskoff, M. F., McDaniel, M. A., Zimmerman, R. A., & Sherman, F. (1989). *Development of the Marine security guard life experiences questionnaire* (PERS-SR-89-008). Monterey, CA: Defense Personnel Security Research and Education Center.

Phillips, S. D., Pazienza, N. J., & Ferrin, H. H. (1984). Decision-making styles and problem-solving appraisal. *Journal of Counseling Psychology, 31,* 497–502.

Powell, G. N. (1990). One more time: Do female and male managers differ? *Academy of Management Executive, 4*(3), 68–75.

Roe, A., & Lunneborg, P. W. (1990). Personality development and career choice. In D. Brown, L. Brooks, & Associates (Eds.), *Career choice and development* (2d ed., pp. 68–101). San Francisco: Jossey-Bass.

Roomsburg, J. D. (1988). *Biographical data as predictors of success in military aviation training* (AFIT/CI/CIA-88-220). Wright-Patterson AFB, OH: AFIT/CIA.

Rothstein, H. R., Schmidt, F. L., Erwin, F. W., Owens, W. A., & Sparks, C. P. (1990). Biographical data in employment selection: Can validities be made generalizable? *Journal of Applied Psychology, 75,* 175–184.

Rounds, J. B., Jr., Dawis, R. V., & Lofquist, L. H. (1977). *Biographical factors related to vocational needs: Sex differences.* Paper presented at the annual meeting of the American Psychological Association, San Francisco.

Russell, C. J. (1991). On prescriptions derived from oversimplifications. *The Industrial-Organizational Psychologist, 29*(2), 55–56.

Sager, J. K., & Johnston, M. W. (1989). Antecedents and outcomes of organizational commitment: A study of salespeople. *Journal of Personal Selling and Sales Management, 9*(1), 30–41.

Scarr, S., & McCartney, K. (1983). How people make their own environments: A theory of genotype —> environment effects. *Child Development, 54,* 424–435.

Schein, E. H. (1978). *Career dynamics.* Reading, MA: Addison-Wesley.

Schein, E. H. (1985). *Career anchors: Discovering your real values.* San Diego, CA: University Associates.

Schein, E. H. (1986). A critical look at career development theory. In D. T. Hall & Associates (Eds.), *Career development in organizations* (pp. 310–331). San Francisco: Jossey-Bass.

Schneider, B. (1987). The people make the place. *Personnel Psychology, 40,* 437–453.

Schneider, B., & Schmitt, N. (1986). *Staffing organizations* (2d ed.). Glenview, IL: Scott, Foresman.

Schoenfeldt, L. F. (1974). Utilization of manpower: Development and evaluation of an assessment-classification model for matching individuals with jobs. *Journal of Applied Psychology, 59,* 583–595.

Sekaran U., & Hall, D. T. (1989). Asynchronism in dual-career and family linkages. In M. B. Arthur, D. T. Hall, & B. S. Lawrence (Eds.), *Handbook of career theory* (pp. 159–180). Cambridge: Cambridge University Press.

Smart J. C. (1989). Life history influences on Holland vocational type development. *Journal of Vocational Behavior, 34,* 69–87.

Super, D. E. (1953). A theory of vocational development. *American Psychologist, 8,* 185–190.

Super, D. E. (1986). Life career roles: Self-realization in work and leisure. In D. T. Hall & Associates (Eds.), *Career development in organizations* (pp. 95–119). San Francisco: Jossey-Bass.

Super, D. E. (1990). A life-span, life-space approach to career development. In D. Brown, L. Brooks, & Associates (Eds.), *Career choice and development* (2d ed., pp. 197–261). San Francisco: Jossey-Bass.

Taylor, L. R. (1968). *A quasi-actuarial approach to assessment.* Unpublished doctoral dissertation, Purdue University, West Lafayette, IN.

Thomae, H. (1979). The concept of development and life-span psychology. In P. B. Baltes & O. G. Brim (Eds.), *Life-span development and behavior* (Vol. 2, pp. 281–312). New York: Academic Press.

Thomas, D. A., & Alderfer, C. P. (1989). The influence of race on career dynamics: Theory and research on minority career experiences. In M. B. Arthur, D. T. Hall, & B. S. Lawrence (Eds.), *Handbook of career theory* (pp. 133–158). Cambridge: Cambridge University Press.

Trent, T., Quenette, M. A., & Pass, J. J. (1989). *An old-fashioned biographical inventory.* Paper presented at the annual meeting of the American Psychology Association, New Orleans.

Trice, H. M., & Morand, D. A. (1989). Rites of passage in work careers. In M. B. Arthur, D. T. Hall, & B. S. Lawrence (Eds.), *Handbook of career theory* (pp. 397–416). Cambridge: Cambridge University Press.

Weinrach, S. G., & Srebalus, D. J. (1990). Holland's theory of careers. In D. Brown, L. Brooks, & Associates (Eds.), *Career choice and development* (2d ed., pp. 37–93). San Francisco: Jossey-Bass.

Whitely, W., Dougherty T. W., & Dreher, G. F. (1988). The relationship of mentoring and socioeconomic origin to managers' and professionals' early career progress. In F. Hoy (Ed.), *Academy of Management best paper proceedings* (pp. 58–62). Athens, GA: Academy of Management.

Wood, R., & Bandura, A. (1989). Social cognitive theory of organizational management. *Academy of Management Review, 14,* 361–384.

Yogev, S., & Brett, J. (1985). Patterns of work and family involvement among single- and dual-earner couples. *Journal of Applied Psychology, 70,* 754–768.

Zeira, Y., & Banai, M. (1985). Selection of expatriate managers in MNCs: The host-environment point of view. *International Studies of Management and Organization, 15*(1), 33–51.

The Utility of Biodata

Terry W. Mitchell

MPORT Management Solutions

OVERVIEW

Although the effectiveness of biodata in predicting a diverse array of criteria has been demonstrated by over a century of research, biodata may currently be the least understood and most underutilized of the available alternatives for fair, cost-effective, and valid selection of personnel.

After briefly reviewing the history of biodata in this chapter, I will attempt to describe the many potential advantages of using biodata as an alternative for personnel programs. I will then discuss the meaning of utility and present rules of thumb for estimating the utility of biodata across a broad range of situations. Finally, I will discuss several threats to the future use and utility of biodata.

The oldest and most effective selection procedures include what we now call *biodata*. Actuarial techniques for weighting and combining application blank data were used in the insurance industry as early as the mid-1890s (Mumford & Owens, 1987). By the 1920s, weighted application data were routinely used to screen for insurance sales jobs (Kenagy & Yoakum, 1925), and impressive results of increasing sales productivity and decreasing turnover were commonly reported (Goldsmith, 1922; Manson, 1925). In 1971, England reviewed 200 studies validating the use of weighted application blanks for personnel selection against an extensive range of criteria across a variety of jobs and industries. More recently, Barge and Hough (1988) concluded that evidence from over 100 rigorous studies strongly supports the validity of biodata to predict important job criteria, including job performance, trainability, job involvement, and adjustment to work.

Indeed, biodata have been used to predict an extremely broad range of criteria. A partial list of criteria that have been predicted with biodata was presented by van Rijn (1992). That list includes job performance, employee turnover, managerial effectiveness, creativity, vocational interest, student achievement, credit risk, honesty, training success, and career success. Moreover, reviews of the personnel selection literature have consistently shown biodata to be among the most effective predictors for *any given criterion* (Ghiselli, 1966; Hunter & Hunter, 1984; Reilly & Chao, 1982; Schmitt, Gooding, Noe, & Kirsch, 1984).

Ironically, the use of biodata would be new to most public and private sector organizations outside of the insurance industry. A 1988 survey of 718 personnel directors estimated that less than 15 percent had ever used biodata (Hammer & Kleiman, 1988), and biodata may be used even less at this time in the public sector (van Rijn, 1992). A more recent survey may show somewhat greater use of biodata in larger private-sector companies (depending on what sorts of data are considered to be biodata); nonetheless, even the most liberal estimates of the use of any sort of biodata for any type of job would be well under 30 percent (HRStrategies, 1991).

Biodata may be new in another sense as well: The development of methodologies for understanding and measuring biodata constructs may still be in its infancy. In the past, theory-oriented approaches to biodata have been dominated by *rational-empirical* methods, where responses to biodata items are subjected to various types of internal variance analysis, generally based on the components model of factor analysis (Mitchell & Klimoski, 1982). In this approach, researchers attempt to impose post hoc interpretations on empirically derived dimensions of internal variance. In truth, however, this approach may be more akin to rationalization than to rationality. Moreover, internal variance analyses of biodata items keyed against a criterion would undoubtedly yield different underlying structures than analyses of rationally keyed items (van Rijn, 1992). Only recently have researchers attempted to develop and validate a priori biodata scales to predict specific criterion dimensions, such as teamwork, learning rate, and retention (Mitchell, 1992).

POTENTIAL ADVANTAGES OF BIODATA

From a utility viewpoint, biodata has the potential of offering many advantages. These include improving the validity and fairness of personnel selection programs, while at the same time decreasing the adverse impact of those programs. Biodata may offer these potential gains at a time when literacy and other basic skills of the work force may be declining, making the current reliance on tests of basic skills and general mental ability less defensible.

PREDICTOR-CRITERION FIDELITY

Unlike most selection procedures, such as tests, simulation exercises, or interviews, biodata may be used to measure not only what a person *can* do under maximum performance demands but also what a person *will* do under typical circumstances. For this reason, biodata measure typical behavior as opposed to maximum performance (Cronbach, 1960). Thus, in contrast to tests of mental ability, skill, or proficiency, biodata capture typical rather than maximal performance. Therefore, one psychometric basis for the observed predictive validity of biodata might be called *predictor-criterion fidelity:* Biodata uses a person's typical behavior in past situations to predict that person's typical behavior in future situations.

CAPTURING CURVILINEAR RELATIONSHIPS

There is a second important psychometric basis for the validity of biodata in predicting a broad range of criteria: Biodata keying methods capture *curvilinear* as well as linear relationships between biodata predictor items and criterion measures (Weiss, 1976). As we will see, this may be a major foundation for both the predictive validity and utility of biodata, as well as a major advantage for biodata compared to traditional skill and ability tests.

Scoring tests usually involves simply adding together the number of items answered correctly to compute a total score. This type of scoring is based on an underlying assumption of *linearity*. In psychometric terms, we refer to this type of test score as a *linear composite* of item scores. The underlying assumption is that the test score will be linear with respect to the level of the knowledge, skill, ability, or other trait the test measures. In other words, as the test score increases, the level of the characteristic measured by the test is also assumed to increase. Thus, the test score is assumed to vary as a linear function of the underlying characteristic that the test was developed to measure. For properly developed tests, this assumption may be true.

However, even when this assumption is true, it is not always true that the test score will, in turn, have a linear relationship with the criterion. Many criteria, such as personnel turnover, quantity or quality of work, and creativity, *may not have linear relationships with traditional skill or ability test scores*. For example, maximum performance tests, such as intelligence or general mental ability, tend to correlate poorly with personnel turnover (Guion, 1965; Schmitt et al., 1984). This may be because mental or cognitive abilities are often important in learning how to do a job and, thus, may be predictive of criteria such as trainability, rates of learning, advancement, or proficiency. However, mental abilities are likely to have a curvilinear relationship with turnover for several reasons (Guion, 1965). For one, individuals at higher levels of mental ability may become bored, dissatisfied, or lose interest in a job once it is learned, especially when the cognitive demands of the job are below the individual's cognitive capabilities. Also, individuals who have relatively high levels of mental ability are often presented with many opportunities for advancement and upward mobility, either within or outside the employing organization, making turnover a greater possibility for those individuals (Gerhart, 1990).

On the other hand, biodata have often been used to predict turnover and have been validated against turnover criteria for many different jobs (Schuh, 1967). In addition to turnover, biodata have been used across a wide variety of occupations to predict a diverse range of job-relevant criteria. To a large extent, biodata prediction of these criteria may rely on the use of curvilinear as well as linear relationships between predictor items and criterion variables.

Empirical keying methods that are most commonly used to develop biodata scoring algorithms, such as the vertical percent method (England, 1971), scale each option of each biodata item in direct proportion to its criterion-related validity. With England's method, the magnitude of the score assigned to each option is based on the linear relationship between the item and the criterion. As a result, this empirical scaling imposes linear relationships between item scores and the criterion, even for items that have underlying curvilinear relationships with that criterion. Therefore, biodata scores based on linear composites of empirically keyed biodata items will always have a linear relationship with the criterion that they were derived to predict, as a direct product of the empirical keying method.

An Example of Empirical Keying

An example of empirical keying for one biodata item may be helpful to illustrate how the keying process results in linear scaling. Table 1 shows the results of empirical keying methods when applied to a commonly used biodata item. This item is a variation of one published in *A Catalog of Life History Items* (Glennon, Albright, & Owens, 1966). It asks: "During your youth, when teams were chosen for games, were you usually (a) the one doing the choosing, (b) chosen near the first, (c) chosen near the middle,

TABLE 1   An Example of Empirical Keying With One Item

Item Stem: During your youth, when teams were chosen for games, were you usually…

Options	Cases	Percentage	Percentage High	Percentage Low	Percentage Hztl	OIW	HPM	VPM	OCC	MSC
a. The one doing the choosing	373	37	36	39	48	1	5	−1	−0.04	−0.05
b. Near the first chosen	345	34	36	33	53	2	5	1	0.08	0.11
c. Chosen near the middle	208	21	21	21	50	3	5	0	−0.02	−0.05
d. Chosen near the end	55	6	5	6	47	4	5	0	−0.04	−0.18
e. Not involved in games	19	2	2	2	53	5	5	0	0.00	−0.01
Total	1,000	100	100	100						
Mean					50	2.0	5.0	0.03	0.01	0.00
r						−.01		.06	.08	.08
F						.12	N/A	4.08	6.06	6.92
Significance F						.72	N/A	.04	.01	.01
Percentage linear component						1.45	N/A	68.33	98.36	100.00

Note: Percentage High = Vertical percentage above criterion median
Percentage Low = Vertical percentage below criterion median
Percentage Hztl = Horizontal percentage above criterion median
OIW = Ordinal integer weighting

HPM = Horizontal percentage method
VPM = Vertical percentage method
OCC = Option criterion correlation
MSC = Mean standardized criterion score

(d) chosen near the end, or (e) not involved in games?" The alternatives are mutually exclusive, and the item requires a choice of a single option. Thus, the options for this type of item are not independent variables. Rather, they are statistically dependent because the item has but a single degree of freedom.

For this illustration, the item is keyed against a criterion of *teamwork effectiveness,* based on supervisory ratings of 1,000 employees. The validity of this item is not especially strong. However, if properly keyed, it is strong enough to be of some practical value when used in combination with other valid items. Furthermore, the item has several properties that are useful for the purposes of this example.

Table 1 shows results for four empirical keying methods, as well as for an "intuitive" scale. The intuitive scale is created by first judgmentally ordering the options as they might relate to some underlying predictor construct, then assigning sequential integer weights to each option based ordinal position (Mitchell & Klimoski, 1986). For the example shown in Table 1, the intuitive construct underlying the ordering of the options might be something like *social influence,* such that attaining a position to do the choosing requires most influence, being chosen first requires the next most, and so forth. Accordingly, the options may be assigned integer values based on ordinal position. The result is similar to a Likert-type of scale, and this type of scaling is often used for *criterion-free* factor analysis of biodata items. In Table 1, options a through e are scaled 1 through 5, respectively, under the heading OIW (ordinal integer weighting).

The first two empirical keying methods represent the most commonly used approaches—the horizontal percentage method (HPM) and the vertical percentage method (VPM). The first method, HPM, keys items in reference to the probability of success indicated for each option of the item. Conversely, VPM weights each option based on its discrimination between high versus low groups (see Guion, 1965, for a more detailed discussion). However, in spite of whatever conceptual differences there may be between the HPM and VPM approaches, from a practical viewpoint there tends to be very little difference. Keys developed using the two approaches for the same predictor items against the same criterion and on the same sample are often correlated in the high .90s.

Both HPM and VPM approaches require a dichotomous criterion. For this example, a median split was used to create high versus low criterion groups. With HPM, the horizontal percentage (i.e., the percentage of those in the high criterion group who endorse each option labeled "Percentage HZTL" in Table 1) is simply rounded to the nearest whole integer to calculate the scale weight for that option. For VPM, the vertical percentage for the low criterion group (labeled "Percentage Low") is subtracted from the vertical percentage for the high criterion group (labeled "Percentage High"). Strong's tables (see Guion, 1965, p. 388, or England, 1971, p. 27) are then used to convert the obtained difference, in high versus low vertical percentages, to a signed numerical "unit" weight. Thus, both of these approaches scale the options of an item in relation to the validity of each option in predicting the dichotomous criterion.

Two additional empirical keying approaches are shown in Table 1. Both of these have the advantage of use for continuous criteria, enabling the key to capture variance across the full range of the criterion. The first is computed by correlating each option of the item (coded as a dichotomous variable where 1 = endorsement and 0 = nonendorsement) with the continuous criterion. This correlation (labeled OCC in Table 1 for *option criterion correlation*) may be equivalent to a *point biserial* correlation for instances where the option is a true dichotomy and the criterion is a true continuum. For each option, the empirical scale weight simply becomes the signed correlation of the option with the criterion. The OCC approach is conceptually similar to the VPM approach, in that each option is weighted with a signed value corresponding to its relation to high or low criterion status. The last method is merely the mean standardized criterion (MSC) score for each option. The MSC approach is conceptually similar to HPM, in that each option is weighted in direct reference to the level of criterion success with which it is associated.

As shown in Table 1, the initial *intuitive* weights (OIW) are improperly ordered with respect to the criterion ($r = -0.01$), and the five-point OIW scale captures a mere 1.45 percent of the linear trend in criterion means (i.e., using ANOVA for linear trend). The HPM scale is also disappointing because the method is too crude to capture the low level of validity for this item. As a result, all of the options have the same weight, and the resulting HPM scale has but a single value. As such, this constant can have no validity against the criterion. On the other hand, the VPM scale does show significant validity against the continuous criterion ($r = .06$, $F = 4.08$, $p < .05$). Furthermore, 68.33 percent of the trend in criterion means is linear with respect to the resulting three-point VPM scale ($-1, 0, 1$). In turn, the resulting four-point OCC scale ($-0.04, -0.02, 0.00,$ and 0.08) also shows significant validity against the criterion ($r = .08$, $F = 6.06$, $p < .01$), and 98.36 percent of the trend in criterion means is linear with this scale. Finally, the five-point MSC scale has similar validity against the criterion ($r = .08$, $F = 6.92$, $p < .01$), and, of course, 100 percent of the trend in criterion means is linear with respect to this scale.

Furthermore, the empirical scales presented in this example are highly intercorrelated. Although correlations for the HPM scale could not be computed, the OCC scale was highly correlated with both the VPM

($r = .93$, $p < .001$) and the MSC scales ($r = .94$, $p < .001$), and the VPM and MSC scales were also substantially correlated ($r = .78$, $p < .001$).

Thus, all of the empirical keying methods impose linear relationships between item scores and the criterion. The magnitude and order of the resulting *validity weights* are based on the sensitivity of each of the various methods in estimating the validity of each option. However crudely, depending on the method used, the empirically keyed item scale will be linearly related to the criterion. This will be true even for items that have underlying curvilinear relationships with the criterion, such as the item shown in this example. Therefore, as a direct result of the empirical keying process, biodata scores based on linear composites of empirically keyed biodata items, each of which is linearly related to the criterion, will necessarily have a linear relationship to the criterion that they were derived to predict.

PERSONNEL SELECTION

Predictive Validity for a Broad Range of Criteria

Another advantage of biodata relates to what has been called the *principle of equipollence* (Mitchell, 1990). This simply means that opposite personalities may be equally successful. An example of this principle is often seen among sales personnel, where two very different styles may be equally successful. Although they are often viewed as opposite extremes, the aggressive, hard-sell style versus the low pressure, soft-sell style may be equally effective in producing sales. This phenomenon is difficult for trait-oriented approaches to accommodate because high levels of certain traits are considered necessary for certain types of success to occur. However, this phenomenon is readily handled by biodata because past success predicts future success, irrespective of the way in which the success was achieved.

Test-Retest Reliability

Because biodata are often factual, objective, and verifiable, they tend to have excellent test–retest reliabilities. Test–retest reliability coefficients ranging from .85 to .91 have often been reported (Chaney & Owens, 1964; Erwin & Herring, 1977). Moreover, biodata may show high test-retest reliabilities over a period of many years (Shaffer, Saunders, & Owens, 1986). Indeed, we should expect high test-retest reliability for facts from a person's life history. For example, once established, one's GPA at the point of graduation from high school never changes. With this sort of factual item, the predictor *construct* has near perfect reliability and stability.

However, the heterogeneous content of biodata items makes internal consistency estimation of reliability generally inappropriate for biodata.

This may make it difficult to estimate reliability for biodata in many situations where test-retest designs are not feasible. Under such circumstances, internal consistency estimates will produce downwardly biased estimates of biodata reliability. Nonetheless, internal consistency (e.g., KR-20) might be used to establish lower-bound estimates for the reliability of factorially derived biodata scales (Baehr & Williams, 1967).

Fairness, Avoidance of Adverse Impact, and Legal Defensibility

Personnel specialists may be surprised to learn that biodata is among the most favorable of assessment techniques for women, minorities, and older applicants. On average, these groups tend to score about as well on biodata as the highest-scoring groups (Reilly & Warech, 1989). Most studies have found no significant differences in average scores for different demographic groups. When average biodata predictor scores do differ across demographic groups, those differences appear merely to reflect true differences between groups on the criterion. Actually, biodata generally show less than half as much difference across demographic groups as do tests of general mental ability such as the *General Aptitude Test Battery* (GATB). This becomes an important advantage for biodata as a selection technique, compared to tests of general mental ability, which tend to show extensive adverse impact, especially on blacks, Hispanics, and persons over age 40, and compared to special ability tests, such as mechanical reasoning and spatial ability, that tend to show severe adverse impact on women. At a time when the available applicant pool is increasingly composed of women and minority groups, biodata offers an alternative to ability testing that can be both fair and valid.

Also, because biodata result in little or no adverse impact on protected groups, biodata can be very advantageous from the viewpoint of legal defensibility. Plainly, if there is no evidence of adverse impact, there is no prima facie case for discrimination (Bureau of National Affairs, 1978). Consequently, there is no basis for a discrimination complaint. Furthermore, with the passage of the Civil Rights Act of 1991, it is no longer legal to use within-group normative adjustments to decrease the adverse impact of general mental ability tests such as the GATB. Thus, avoiding adverse impact becomes a particular advantage for biodata.

Incremental Validities When Added to Existing Programs

Biodata also combine very well with other assessment techniques. This is partly because biodata tend to show low correlations with traditional tests of ability or skill. Indeed, unless biodata are intentionally developed to predict specific ability or personality constructs, biodata predictors of job success tend to show very low correlations with selection tools that are based on measures of these constructs (Merenda & Clarke, 1959; Rush,

1953; Sparks, 1971). This means that the validity of biodata will most often combine directly with the validities of these other selection devices, resulting in *incremental validity*. For this reason, a biodata form will generally add to the validity of any existing selection process, and it will be likely to decrease the adverse impact of that process as well.

In fact, the addition of biodata can double the validity of existing selection programs. For example, Booth, McNally, and Berry (1978) found that the addition of three biodata items to the navy's cognitive aptitude test increased the multiple correlation with training performance from .35 to .48, increasing R^2 from .12 to .23. Similar findings have often been reported in the military and private sector (Barge & Hough, 1988).

Cost Effectiveness

Compared to other assessment techniques, biodata may be highly cost-effective. The developmental costs of biodata may be modest compared with assessment centers, work samples, and proficiency tests (Hunter & Hunter, 1984). However, even the most miserly approaches to biodata may result in predictive validity equal to the most costly assessment programs (Hinrichs, 1978). Furthermore, biodata may be inexpensively administered, either to large groups or to individuals as needed.

Generalizability Across Time and Organizations

Usually, biodata have been developed to predict specific criteria within a limited set of circumstances. However, the validity of biodata has been shown to endure across the changes that occur over time (Brown, 1978). Furthermore, biodata may be made generalizable across organizations, if generalizability is a primary objective of the development process (Rothstein, Schmidt, Erwin, Owens, & Sparks, 1990).

Resistance to Faking

Personnel administrators may be surprised to learn that biodata can be highly resistant to exaggeration or faking by applicants. This resistance to faking may be partly due to the nonintuitive scoring for empirically keyed biodata. In fact, item scores based on empirical keying are often counter-intuitive, making it nearly impossible for an applicant to give the "right" answer to a biodata item (Trent, 1987). In contrast to tests, biodata questions do not have right or wrong answers. Instead, scoring keys for biodata are most often developed using criterion-based techniques to weight each possible answer to each question in direct reference to a job-relevant criterion such as job performance or turnover.

Responses to biodata items may resist falsification for another reason as well. Because many biodata items appear to be verifiable, they may create an inherent demand for accurate and careful responses. Applicants are much less likely to exaggerate potentially verifiable and factual data (Cascio, 1975).

THE MEANING OF UTILITY

A Problem of Definition

With the many advantages of biodata, the prospects for its future use would seem to be very good. Unfortunately, biodata is in danger of becoming a victim of its own success. Interest in using biodata as an alternative to ability testing is increasing, yet there seems to be little regard for the expertise needed for the development and validation of biodata (van Rijn, 1992).

Over the years, biodata has suffered from a critical lack of consensus in both conceptual and operational definitions. The definition of biodata was controversial 20 years ago (Asher, 1972). Now, more than ever, a heterogeneous mix of qualitatively diverse data are collected through a variety of methods and from a variety of sources, subjected to a variety of analytic techniques, and interpreted in a variety of ways (Mael, 1991). Today, the lack of clear conceptual and operational definitions for biodata may be a major threat to its future utility.

However, before we turn to definitional problems of biodata and the resulting threats to its future utility, we must first face the issue of defining utility. Like biodata, our concept of utility has evolved through a long and rich history. The term may now imply numerous parameters and complex formulations bearing little resemblance to its original intent.

Utility Analysis: An Overview

The need to demonstrate the value of personnel programs probably began with the development of the very first program. Clearly, any program that consumes the resources of an organization must justify its worth. To this end, the original objective for what we now call *utility analysis* was to assess and communicate the value of our programs to personnel managers and other decision makers.

By now, an extensive literature exists on the topic of utility theory and analysis, and several comprehensive reviews are available (Boudreau, 1991; Cascio, 1987; Hunter & Schmidt, 1982). Some of the following discussion in this section draws from Zeidner and Johnson's (1989) review of the utility literature.

This discussion does not apply exclusively to estimating the utility of biodata. However, as it has evolved, utility analysis is especially applicable to biodata, due to the criterion-oriented designs that are used most often for developing and validating biodata.

The earliest efforts to assess utility were founded on understanding a very basic principle: Utility increases as a direct function of validity. The first statistical indexes were based on the square of the validity coefficient (r^2) as a measure of predictable criterion variance. These include a statistic that Kelley (1923) called the *coefficient of alienation* (cited in Zeidner & Johnson, 1989):

$$\sqrt{1 - r^2_{xy}}$$

and Hull's *index of forecasting efficiency* (1928):

$$E = 1 - \sqrt{1 - r^2_{xy}}$$

More simply, the single term r^2_{xy} was popularly known as the *coefficient of determination* and was often used during the 1930s as the basic index for utility. Likewise, the coefficient of alienation was simplified in later years to become merely $1 - r^2_{xy}$ (Guion, 1965). An advantage of using r^2_{xy} based statistics as indexes is that r^2_{xy} increases directly with increases in predictable criterion variance. However, it also has several disadvantages.

Because r^2_{xy} is the basic measure of the accuracy for predicting an individual's criterion score used in these statistics, it imposes an extremely stringent standard for utility. For example, Kelley's coefficient of alienation computes an index based on decreasing the standard error of estimate as a function of increasing the coefficient of determination. With this index, incredibly high levels of validity are needed to show gains in utility. For example, a validity of $r = .86$ is needed to reduce the standard error by just 50 percent. Likewise, using Hull's index of forecasting efficiency, a validity of $r = .50$ is only 13 percent better than chance!

The r^2_{xy} approach has other disadvantages. For one, it is a crude measure that does not consider the external context or the relative costs of different kinds of decision error. What's more, decision makers may have difficulty understanding the meaning and practical implications of r^2_{xy}. More to the point, this index certainly does not provide for very compelling demonstrations of the value of personnel programs.

The Taylor and Russell (1939) decision-theoretic model provides two important advances. First, it reformulates utility from measuring the accuracy of individual predictions to measuring the proportion of successful outcomes as a consequence of an organizational decision. This reformulation changes the basic issue from one of the accuracy of individual prediction to a question of the consequences of an organization's choice between two alternatives. Second, in addition to validity, the model incorporates the importance of two additional parameters: (a) base rate and (b) selection ratio. As such, this model recognizes that under some circumstances, even very low validities can be very useful to organizations. As the selection ratio improves (i.e., as the number of applicants for a job increases), and as the base rate approaches .50 (i.e., as we approach the point where no more and no fewer than half the applicants chosen at random would succeed on the job), utility increases substantially, even for low levels of validity.

Today, the Taylor and Russell tables remain useful aids in assessing and communicating the basic concepts of utility to decision makers. However, there are some basic limitations of the Taylor-Russell model. The foremost limitation may be the need to use a dichotomous criterion, which ignores differences that occur along continuous criterion dimensions, such as performance, because all employees within a group must be assigned an equal level of success. Furthermore, the decision as to where to draw the line between successful and unsuccessful employees may be arbitrary. Nonetheless, these concerns do not limit the Taylor-Russell approach when it is applied to naturally occurring dichotomous criteria such as pass/fail training outcomes or employee turnover.

In response to the limitations of the Taylor-Russell approach, Brogden (1946, 1949) greatly advanced the theory and practice of utility analysis. His formulations eliminate the problem of forcing a two-point distribution for job performance criteria or other continuous criteria. Rather, this index uses the full range of variations along the criterion distribution. Brogden's index of utility is simply the increase in a continuous criterion score. Brogden showed that, based on the general equation for linear prediction, the best predictor of the average criterion score is expressed as:

$$\bar{Z}_y = (r_{xy})(\bar{Z}_x)$$

where:

r_{xy} = the validity coefficient

$\bar{Z}_x$ = the mean predictor standard score for those selected

$\bar{Z}_y$ = the mean criterion standard score for those selected

Brogden's index for the increase in mean criterion performance is a practical index for utility that may be more generally relevant than the Taylor-Russell approach. Because the increase is expressed in standard score units, meaningful comparisons across studies using different criteria can be made. This formulation led, in turn, to the development of the basic formula for calculating the mean gain in utility per selectee:

$$\Delta U_{per\ selectee} = r_{xy}SD_y\bar{Z}_x$$

where:

SD_y = the criterion standard deviation among randomly selected employees

One feature of this index is generally considered a limitation. Because it is being expressed in standard score units rather than in terms of dollars, decision makers may find that the index does not provide the direct comparability that they would find using a dollar metric for weighing various alternatives. Thus, Brogden (1949) later expanded the components of the equation to include payoff in dollar terms, as well as other parameters of the situational context, such as the costs of testing. As such, the following equation forms the basis for most utility analyses conducted today.

$$\Delta U = N_sSD_yr_{xy}\frac{\lambda}{\phi} - N_{app}\ C$$

where:

$$\frac{\lambda}{\phi} = \bar{Z}_x$$

λ = the ordinate for the normal distribution at the predictor cutoff score
ϕ = the selection ratio
N_s = the number of employees selected
N_{app} = the number of applicants
C = the cost of administering the predictor per applicant

The implication of subtracting dollar costs in this equation is that SD_y must now be measured as the standard deviation of the criterion in a dollar metric. In Brogden's equation, utility improves with increases in (a) the validity coefficient, (b) the standard deviation of dollar-valued performance, and (c) the mean predictor score for those selected. Selection costs, however, increase with decreases in selection ratios and are subtracted to estimate total net economic benefit. Conceptually, economic benefit is thus defined as the difference between the mean criterion score for the selected group versus the mean for the applicant population. Amazingly, Brogden's landmark equation requires only the assumption of linearity between the predictor and the criterion (Zeidner & Johnson, 1989).

Cronbach and Gleser (1965) expanded Brogden's formulations by adding many new utility concepts. However, their formulas for traditional selection utility, with single-stage fixed job selection decisions, are identical to those developed by Brogden (1946, 1949). Actually, Cronbach and Gleser's equations are derived in terms of mean gain per applicant, whereas Brogden's equations are derived in terms of mean gain in utility per selectee. However, Cronbach and Gleser's equations are equivalent to Brogden's for total utility. Thus, collectively, these equations are often referred to as the *Brogden-Cronbach-Gleser* (or BCG) *utility model*.

In addition to the fundamental assumption of linearity between the predictor and the criterion, the BCG model also assumes that utility can be measured in a dollar metric. This assumption has been the focus of great effort and concern over the past three decades. In addition to the original cost-accounting approach (Brogden & Taylor, 1950), Cascio (1987) describes other major approaches to estimating the standard deviation of the dollar-valued criterion (SD_y). These include the 40 percent rule (Hunter & Schmidt, 1982), global estimation (Schmidt, Hunter, McKenzie, & Muldrow, 1979), CREPID (Cascio & Ramos, 1986), and superior equivalent techniques (Eaton, Wing, & Mitchell, 1986). A major issue for the BCG utility formulation is that differing interpretations result from different approaches to measuring SD_y because each approach yields somewhat different values. Also, it may be argued that none of the estimates provides truly adequate accuracy and that unrealistic assumptions have led to incredible estimates of utility (Vance & Colella, 1990). Moreover, these methods involve complicated procedures that may be difficult to explain to decision makers.

Indeed, the history of utility analysis is one of ever increasing complexity. Starting with the development of the first decision theoretic models, a new language began to emerge. Unfortunately, that language and the concepts to which it refers may be foreign and difficult to understand for decision makers in most organizations. Ironically, experts have resorted to this language and its complex concepts in an effort to communicate the practical value of the programs we offer to organizations. Yet the very complexity of utility analysis is often contrary to its most basic objectives: to assess and communicate the value of personnel programs.

Moreover, this trend toward increasing complexity of models for utility analysis is continuing. Indeed, Cronbach and Gleser (1965) greatly contributed to this trend. Their formulations actually went well beyond Brogden by advancing a more complex decision-theoretic framework for estimating utility. Their comprehensive model includes new utility concepts for situations where placement and selection procedures involve sequential decisions and multivariate data. However, to solve the resulting complex formulations, it often becomes necessary to introduce strong assumptions. Generally, as the complexity of the utility formulation increases, the stringency of the necessary assumptions also increases (Zeidner & Johnson, 1989).

Increasing complexity of the utility model has had many contributors. Schmidt et al. (1979) added a parameter for the longevity of utility gains by including the average tenure of employees. Boudreau (1983) expanded the utility model by assessing total marginal utility for the entire duration of the personnel program. Boudreau and Berger (1985) further expanded the model to include the effects of downsizing. Murphy (1986) adjusted the utility model by estimating the likelihood of job offer rejections. Cronshaw and Alexander (1985) have modified the model to include capital budgeting variables such as discounting for the time value of money and estimating return on investment. More recently, Bobko, Colella, and Russell (1990) formulated a hybrid model for utility, encompassing multiple predictors and multiple criteria from different points in time.

However, relying on inaccurate estimates for basic parameters such as SD_y within the context of these highly complex mathematical models may have become a classic example of the *error of misplaced precision*. More basically, as complex as these expansions of the utility model have become, they may nonetheless fail to include some of the more significant, albeit less measurable, parameters.

These missing parameters could include very real costs to organizations, such as legal fees for defending a personnel program, damage to the corporate image, alienation of customers or future recruits, or losses due to imposing procedures that lack acceptance by recruiters, employees, and applicants. In the absence of these parameters, the current complex utility formulations may reduce to the estimation of a single parameter, SD_y, in comparing the relative utility of alternatives selection procedures. For example, using the kind of utility analysis that is typically conducted in our profession as a means to compare the relative utilities for integrity testing versus ability testing, Sackett (1992) concluded that the question reduces to a very simple comparison. Because most of the other parameters in the utility equation tend to cancel each other out, the question reduces to a comparison of the relative magnitudes of (a) the standard deviation of the *performance* criterion most often predicted by ability tests versus (b) the standard deviation of the *counter-productivity* criterion that is most often predicted by integrity tests. However, this comparison ignores issues of invasiveness, user resistance, legal defensibility, corporate image, employee morale, and other issues of very real concern to organizations.

Our use of utility analysis must not lose sight of its original objectives. We must assess and communicate the value of our personnel programs, and we must be prepared to do it in language that organizations understand and in the context of issues that are of most importance to those organizations.

Indeed, at times we may find it advantageous to trade off whatever precision may result from expanding complexity, in favor of simplicity and relevance.

RULES OF THUMB FOR ESTIMATING UTILITY

The following rules of thumb for estimating utility are based on two basic observations. The first observation is that the BCG utility model, and each of its subsequent expansions, reduces to a simple conceptual formula (Bobko et al., 1990):

$$\text{Utility} = \text{gains} - \text{costs}$$

Thus, estimating utility is most fundamentally based on subtracting the total estimated costs and losses resulting from a personnel program from the total estimated gains resulting from that program. Conceptually, then, this suggests a simple cost accounting process that is intuitively appealing and understandable for decision makers (Cascio, 1987).

The second observation is one first made by Brogden (1946) that went largely unappreciated for over 20 years (Curtis & Alf, 1969). Although it is now well regarded among academics (e.g., Landy, Farr, & Jacobs, 1982), its importance has still not received the attention it deserves among practitioners. Brogden's basic formula shows (a) the validity coefficient is a direct index of the proportional improvement (over chance) that is possible for a given selection ratio, and (b) r_{xy} is a linear function of the difference between the criterion means for the selected group versus the population of applicants (Zeidner & Johnson, 1989). For example, when a predictor and a criterion (a) are continuous, (b) are linearly related, and (c) have identical distributions, a validity of .40 for a constant selection ratio would produce 40 percent of the gain that would result from a selection device that is perfectly correlated with the criterion.

Curtis and Alf (1969) compared the validity coefficient, r_{xy}, with the actual increase in the criterion mean and the subsequent proportion of successful employees. They found r_{xy} to be a linear function of the increased criterion mean, and they found r_{xy} highly related to other measures of practical significance. Likewise, Schmidt and Hoffman (1973) employed cost accounting procedures to compare actual savings resulting from the use of a selection device to those predicted by Brogden's interpretation of the validity coefficient. They found Brogden's simple formulation was accurate in estimating actual savings, even when statistical assumptions were violated.

These two simple but powerful observations may be combined to create elementary yet compelling estimates for utility across a broad range of situations. In fact, these rules of thumb may be readily applied in any situation where the relationship between the predictor and the criterion can be estimated by a validity coefficient (r_{xy}) and where the relationship between the predictor and the criterion is linear. Thus, the use of these rules of thumb is particularly suited to empirically keyed biodata, where the keying process guarantees predictor-criterion linearity, and where the predictor-criterion relationship is expressed in the form of a criterion-related validity coefficient.

In this simple approach, we first use Brogden's interpretation of the validity coefficient to estimate the gain in criterion units resulting from the personnel program. This criterion may be expressed in dollars, or it may be initially expressed in other criterion-relevant units (e.g., increasing productivity, savings in training time, decreasing downtime, reducing accidents, etc.) that may have particular importance to the decision maker. Very simply, the validity coefficient represents the improvement resulting from the use of a predictor, as a percentage of the total gain that is possible on the criterion.

For example, if eliminating the bottom third of current employees would improve productivity by 50 percent, we would estimate utility for the use of a cutoff score set at that level. For a predictor that has a .40 validity, this cutoff score will improve the productivity of new employees by 20 percent (i.e., .4 x .5 = .2). Thus, in this example, a 20 percent gain becomes our approximate estimate for the improvement that we expect to occur on this productivity criterion as a result of using the predictor. Furthermore, assuming that gains on this and other criteria could be converted to a common metric (e.g., dollars), gains on several criteria that result from using the same predictor may be similarly estimated and then combined to compute a rough estimate for the total gain in dollars resulting from use of that predictor. Likewise, in situations where incremental utility is the primary focus, this may also be roughly estimated by calculating gains as the percentage improvement resulting from incremental validity.

Next, we list and estimate all of the various costs and losses resulting from the use of a predictor. Here, it is generally more important to list all of the relevant costs and losses than it is to achieve highly precise estimates for each. In other words, all relevant costs and losses should be represented on the list for the benefit of the decision maker, even if only best guess estimates can be made. As suggested previously, costs might include program development and administration, ongoing maintenance, consumption of program materials, consulting fees, legal fees, or any other relevant costs. Costs may also include anticipated losses due to factors such as increased recruiting requirements, alienation of customers, litigation, or loss of good will.

As suggested by the conceptual formula, the next step is to subtract the costs from the gains to compute an estimate for utility. If all of the component gains and costs can be converted to a common metric such as dollars, it will be possible to show utility as a single bottom-line value and to express it in terms of this common metric. If so, this has the advantage of allowing for direct comparisons among alternative programs or among competing strategies. However, in some instances, this single value cannot be computed, either because some gains could not be converted to a dollar metric or because some losses could not be estimated beyond probabilistic terms. In those instances, the information provided by this process will nevertheless be of value to decision makers, who may have surprisingly little difficulty weighing the gains and costs subjectively, even when they cannot be combined mathematically.

However, if a single bottom-line value can be computed, this has another advantage. If desired, the total estimated utility can be averaged for the number of employees selected to compute an average utility per selectee. Or, alternatively, this value may be averaged by the number of applicants to compute an average utility per administration.

A second quick and ready approach to estimating utility involves the old but reliable use of the Taylor and Russell tables (1939). This approach is somewhat less generally applicable because the tables are based on assumptions of bivariate normality, linearity, and homoscedasticity between the predictor and criterion, and because they require dichotomization of the criterion to form a success ratio. However, if the validity, selection ratio, and base rate are known, the tables can provide convenient and practical estimates for utility. For example, if the base rate is 50 percent and the selection ratio is .20, a predictor with a validity of $r = .45$ will increase the percentage of successful new hires from 50 percent to 75 percent, for a gain of 25 additional successful employees per hundred selected. Furthermore, if the differential value of hiring successful versus unsuccessful employees can be estimated, this gain can be evaluated against the corresponding costs.

For some naturally occurring dichotomous criteria such as turnover, this approach to estimating utility may be very straightforward. Assuming the same validity, selection ratio, and base rates as in the above example, the organization would experience one more success (i.e., survivor) for every four employees it hires than it would have had without the use of the predictor. For purposes of illustration, let's assume the total investment made by the organization in each new employee is valued at an average of $20,000 (including recruitment, personnel and administrative costs, moving expenses, orientation, training and development, etc.) and, thus, this represents the dollar value of the gain (i.e., savings) per each added survivor. However, the average gain per new hire is $5,000 (i.e., 20,000 ÷ 4), and the average gain per applicant is $1,000 (selection ratio = 1/5; $5,000 ÷ 5 = $1,000). If the average cost for developing and administering the predictor is $100 per applicant, then the average utility per applicant is $900. In other words, in this example, the organization saves $900 *for every time the predictor is administered to an applicant*. If the organization tests 1,000 applicants in hiring 200 new employees, it saves $900,000 in reduced turnover costs. Clearly, this provides a simple but compelling demonstration of the utility for this kind of personnel program.

Furthermore, validities of the magnitude given in the preceding example are certainly attainable for empirically keyed biodata. For instance, Mitchell and Klimoski (1982) obtained a cross-validity of $r = .46$ using biodata to predict a dichotomous criterion of early career survival in real estate sales. In that study, all 88 biodata items were keyed using a textbook application of the vertical percent method (England, 1971), and naturally occurring, sequential samples were used for derivation and cross-validation in a longitudinal design. The survival criterion was also naturally occurring and had a near optimal .44 base rate for early career survival. In the sequential design, the total sample size of $N = 644$ was adequate, both for calculating stable scoring weights and for estimating the predictive validity of the scoring algorithm. Altogether, the major features of this study were very favorable to the development and validation of biodata. Unfortunately, biodata are often used under much less favorable circumstances.

THREATS TO THE FUTURE UTILITY OF BIODATA

Today there are several threats to the future utility of biodata. These threats include inadequate validation designs, misguided methodologies, misdirected legal developments, and demands within the professional community for inappropriate psychometric properties. This section briefly discusses some of the major challenges to the future utility of biodata.

The greatest threat to the future utility of biodata, and perhaps the root of all other threats, stems from confusion regarding the conceptual and operational definitions of biodata. At this time, a growing army of researchers is studying qualitatively different types of data, using a chaotic variety of methods and imposing an ever widening assortment of sociopsychological conceptions, all in the name of biodata (Mael, 1991). The resulting diversity of conceptualizations and incongruence of methods may make it impossible to formulate meaningful generalizations in the future.

For example, take the issue of reliability. Are biodata reliable? Yes, of course, and, in fact, this is one of the major potential advantages of biodata.

However, not all of the qualitatively different types of items currently being called biodata are necessarily reliable. Indeed, some suffer from very poor reliability. Increasingly, soft items measuring self-perceptions and self-evaluations of personal attributes are being construed by many as a type of biodata. In the past, these types of items were more often used as an approach to measuring personality, but we find these items increasingly included in biodata forms. Indeed, Ashworth (1989) and Hough (1989) have argued that current biodata items are essentially equivalent to those traditionally used for personality measurement. However, the poor reliability of these types of items is notorious in the testing literature (Kaplan & Saccuzzo, 1989). Thus, in stark contrast to the exceptional item reliabilities of biodata, which are founded on factual content, objectivity, and verifiability, these soft, self-perceptual items are more likely to measure mood states (versus traits) based on self-impressions at a moment in time, providing a very poor basis for reliability.

This issue is very much related to other important concerns about biodata, such as face validity and faking (Crosby & Mitchell, 1988). Do biodata resist faking and dissimulation? Yes, and, again, this is one of the major potential advantages of biodata. As opposed to tests that have right and wrong answers to items (making them vulnerable to compromise and manipulation over time), the nonintuitive nature of biodata scoring keys makes them highly resistant to faking and manipulation, assuming the keys are kept secure (Brown, 1978). However, self-perception and self-evaluation items are essentially transparent to the respondent, making them susceptible to exaggeration, faking, and manipulation.

As discussed by Crosby and Mitchell (1988) and Kaplan and Saccuzzo (1989), this problem was well known in the evolution of personality testing. In practical applications of biodata to personnel selection, counterintuitive biodata item keys (of the sort that typically result from empirical keying) are resistant to falsification by both applicants and recruiters in field settings (Pannone, 1987). This field research finding corroborates research using experimental manipulations (Klein & Owens, 1965; Lautenschlager, 1985; Trent, 1987). Conversely, transparent items (for which the "good" answer is logical and obvious to the respondent) are highly vulnerable to loss of validity due to faking. For example, a study of a forced-choice adjective checklist done 30 years ago found that loss of validity due to faking was greatest for face-valid items, which were most obviously related to the job (Dunnette, McCartney, Carlson, & Kirchner, 1962).

This problem was well known in an even earlier era, in the context of logical-content approaches to structured personality testing. In such an approach, the item content was logically and obviously related to the construct that it was intended to measure. If one wanted to know whether a subject was outgoing, one would simply ask the subject. When the subject responded "true" to the item "I am outgoing," it was assumed to be true. Kaplan and Saccuzzo (1989, p. 370) summarize:

> Indeed, structured personality tests based on the logic of face validity were so sharply criticized (Landis, 1936; Landis, Zubin, & Katz, 1935; McNemar & Landis, 1935) that the entire structured approach to personality was all but discarded until it was finally rescued by the introduction of a new conceptualization in personality testing, the empirical criterion group strategy (Dahlstrom, 1969).

Cronbach (1970) discusses the problem as a distinction between sign versus sample interpretations of self-reports. The actuarial interpretation of responses as signs is in contrast to the assumption of honest self-reports, which is necessary to the sampling or logical-content approach. Cronbach (1970) writes:

> These two approaches have been characterized as the "sample" and "sign" approaches. If self-reports are seen as frank reports of an observer, we present transparent items sampling various content areas and pay primary attention to the content of the responses. We are at the mercy of the subject who wants to mislead us. But if responses are signs, we can use items the surface content of which is irrelevant to our concern. Even distorted responses may have significance. (pp. 506–507)

A similar vulnerability to response distortion may underlie loss in validity for self-perceptual items when validities based on data collected for research purposes are later examined under real-life selection situations (Bass, 1957; Heron, 1956), or under differing conditions of accountability (Doll, 1971). Clearly, applicants may be motivated to present a different, perhaps maximally desirable, picture of themselves since a job often hangs in the balance.

Thus, nonintuitive biodata scoring keys are highly resistant to faking, dissimulation, manipulation, and other forms of compromise over time. However, logical content items that are obvious and transparent to applicants are likely to be highly vulnerable to all of the various forms of falsification. Generally, in practical situations, there is likely to be an inverse relationship between the face validity versus the predictive validity of biodata (Crosby & Mitchell, 1988).

In view of this relationship, current methods involving the use of panels of applicants, employees, or supervisors to prescreen biodata items could easily become misdirected. Such a method for prescreening biodata items has been generally recommended (Mumford & Owens, 1987). This method relies on panels to assess the logical content of biodata, screening out any that may appear objectionably non–job relevant (Mumford, Cooper, & Schemmer, 1983). Others have followed Mumford and Owens (1987), advocating the use of content review panels to prescreen biodata items (Reilly & Warech, 1989). Following these recommendations, an extensive set of rules, including a requirement for face-valid job relevance, was used to prescreen items as an initial step in the development of the *Individual Achievement Record* (IAR), a biodata instrument developed by the U.S. Office of Personnel Management (Gandy, Outerbridge, Sharf, & Dye, 1989).

However, due to the nonintuitive nature of biodata, this kind of prescreening methodology could easily run the proverbial risk of throwing out the baby with the bath water. Data presented by Crosby and Mitchell (1988) suggest that unaided employees and supervisors may have difficulty understanding relationships between biodata items and subsequent success on the criterion. Their studies conducted in two separate industries showed that the job experts' estimations of the validity of biodata items were negatively correlated with the empirical validities for those items ($r = -0.38$ in the real estate industry, and $r = -0.30$ in the insurance industry). Thus, if job experts are allowed to "object" to particular biodata items solely due to the poor face validity of those items, this may unwittingly eliminate many valid biodata items from the pool. These eliminated items are likely to have been among the most robust and durable over time because these are the very items that would have been most resistant to faking. To this point, although Gandy et al. (1989) were able to attain a modest but practically useful validity for the IAR in spite of the use of this prescreening strategy ($r = .32$), it will be interesting to see how this validity may hold up over time.

In addition to prescreening methods, there seems to be a more general and growing demand for face validity of biodata within our profession. This may stem, in part, from a widespread misconception concerning the job relevance of biodata. Pace and Schoenfeldt (1977) are popularly cited as being the first to distinguish between criterion-related validity versus the job relevance of biodata. However, although these concepts can be conceptually distinguished, they are also logically interdependent. Assuming the criterion is job relevant, either because it is obviously related to the job (e.g., sales productivity is clearly a proficiency criterion for sales jobs), or because job relevance of the criterion is demonstrated through job analysis, *the job relevance of the predictor score is technically and legally demonstrated through an appropriate validation design.* In other words, if a biodata item effectively predicts a job-relevant criterion measure, then that item must also be job relevant. This is the fundamental logic of criterion-related validation, which, in turn, is the basis for all of the various forms of utility estimation.

The federal interpretation of Title VII of the 1964 Civil Rights Act was still evolving when the Pace and Schoenfeldt article was published in 1977. A year later, the central question of that article was clarified with the publication of the 1978 Uniform Guidelines. With that publication came a clear provision for criterion-related validation as a principle means for establishing the job relevance of a selection procedure. That provision has now held for 14 years.

Unfortunately, however, the confusion between criterion-related validity and job relevance has persisted. For example, it was revisited in the *Amicus Curiae* Brief (1988) filed by the American Psychological Association in *Watson v. Fort Worth Bank and Trust*. Citing Pace and Schoenfeldt (1977), that brief implies a conceptual distinction between logical and empirical justifications for using biodata and suggests that both are necessary.

Other major threats to the future utility of biodata stem from the often misguided efforts of legislators and regulators, particularly at the state government level (Ash, 1988; Mitchell, 1989). Interpretations of state civil rights laws, such as the various preemployment inquiry guidelines issued by most states, often disallow asking questions that have been extensively validated by biodata researchers (Mitchell, 1989). This matter is thoroughly discussed in another chapter in this handbook (see Sharf's chapter on legal and EEO issues) and, thus, will not be covered in detail here. However, an example may be helpful.

One example of an extensively validated biodata item that has been disallowed by many state guidelines is the number of dependents who rely on an individual for primary financial support. This item has been validated as predictor for either performance or retention in at least 14 published studies, yet it has been disapproved in guidelines issued by at least 10 states (Mitchell, 1989). This item may be interpreted as an objective indicator of the individual's motivation to secure a sufficient and stable source of income. Empirical keying for this item typically gives higher scores for more dependents and lower scores for no dependents. Furthermore, empirical keys for this item are essentially the same for women (England, 1971) and men (Goldsmith, 1922) and for minority groups (Thayer, 1977). As such, use of this item actually favors minority groups, such as blacks and Hispanics, who may tend to have greater numbers of dependents. Ironically, however, state guidelines disallow this inquiry on the mistaken assumption that it would be used to discriminate against minorities and women who have children. Clearly, these kinds of misguided attempts will not help disadvantaged groups, but they will threaten the future use and utility of biodata.

A number of additional threats to the future utility of biodata might be listed under a broad category relating to inappropriate validation designs and procedures. These include improper job analyses, inadequate validation designs, inappropriate use of formula estimation of cross-validity, the haphazard use of concurrent validation designs, and the inappropriate use of statistical corrections used to compare the validities of alternative selection procedures.

Job analysis is generally the first step in developing a personnel program of any kind, and so it usually is with biodata. Unfortunately, conventional task- or worker-oriented job analyses do not directly provide the data needed to logically link biodata items to job criteria (Mitchell, 1986). Often, subjective and tenuous inferences provide the only logical foundation available for the development of biodata items. Although some recent effort has been made (see Hough and Paulin, and Russell in this volume), this continues to be a major weakness in the typical biodata development process. As it now stands, the use of inappropriate job analyses represent a significant threat to the future utility of biodata.

The use of improper or inadequate validation designs is another major threat to the utility of biodata. The empirical development of biodata demands large samples (*minimum* $N = 300$ to 400) to allow scoring keys to be properly derived and cross-validated. Furthermore, the use of formula estimates for cross-validity are generally inappropriate as substitutes for the empirical cross-validation of empirically keyed biodata (Mitchell & Klimoski, 1986). Like formula estimation of cross-validity, concurrent validation designs are commonly used shortcuts that may be problematic for empirically keyed biodata.

In validating some types of tests, such as cognitive and general mental ability tests, concurrent designs may be perfectly appropriate (Barrett, Phillips, & Alexander, 1981). However, in developing biodata, these designs must be used with great care. In concurrent development and validation designs, procedures intended for eventual use in selecting applicants are initially developed and validated on current employees. Concurrent designs are often used by practitioners because they can be much more quickly and economically conducted compared to predictive validation designs. However, concurrent designs may cause serious problems for the unwary biodata developer.

One such problem is a kind of predictive tautology that is difficult to avoid when using concurrent designs for developing biodata. This occurs when the same underlying variable is inadvertently used as both a biodata predictor and as a criterion within the concurrent sample. For example, a person's income for the previous year is often found to be a fairly good predictor of that person's first year sales commissions, even though the person has changed jobs or even careers between the two years. However, in the context of a concurrent validation design, the predictor (last year's income) and the criterion (last year's sales commissions) may often be the same or overlapping operational measures of the same underlying variable. As a result, this item will be improperly weighted in the resulting scoring key, and the validity of this item will be grossly inflated. Given this phenomenon, it is not surprising that concurrent designs have consistently estimated higher criterion-related validities for biodata compared to predictive validation designs (Barge & Hough, 1988). It should be clear, however, that inaccurately estimated validities, whether too high or too low, will inevitably serve to undermine the future utility of biodata.

Another inappropriate methodology may underestimate the validity and utility of biodata. This involves the use of statistical corrections for validity estimates, which, in turn, are used to compare validities for alternative selection procedures. For example, Hunter and Hunter (1984) used corrections for restriction of range when the necessary data were available to compare average validities for general mental ability tests versus biodata. Comparing average corrected validity estimates against job performance ratings as the criterion, Hunter and Hunter (1984) concluded that "the average validity of biodata measures is .37 in comparison with .53 for ability measures" (p. 87). On the other hand, Schmitt et al. (1984) compared average *uncorrected* validities against the same criterion, finding an average validity of .32 for biodata versus an average validity of .22 for general mental ability tests. How can this be?

It seems the statistical corrections used by Hunter and Hunter (1984) favored general mental ability tests. Why? One major reason is the "availability" of the necessary data. Estimates of unrestricted predictor variance are widely available for general mental ability measures. However, because biodata are most often specially devised against specific criteria within single organizations, estimates of unrestricted predictor variance tend not to be available for biodata. Consequently, statistical corrections for restriction of range can be readily applied to general ability measures but cannot be readily applied to biodata. Therefore, using validities corrected for range restriction to compare the utility of biodata versus general mental ability places biodata at a severe disadvantage. Interestingly, this point was not considered by Hunter and Hunter (1984). Unfortunately, due to inappropriate methods used to compare the validities of alternative selection procedures, many in our profession have accepted the dubious conclusion that biodata have generally lower utility compared to general mental ability tests.

In summary, there are many threats to the potential utility of biodata. How psychology, as a profession, responds to these many critical challenges will determine how *and even if* we will continue to use and reap the utility of this powerfully predictive technology.

CONCLUSION

Biodata may offer a cost-effective means to help accomplish the two most important goals we face at this point in the evolution of human resources management. First, biodata may add to the validity and accuracy of our programs for selecting and placing personnel. Biodata may contribute by capturing and predicting unique criterion variance and, thus, may directly increase the overall accuracy of our programs when combined with existing procedures. Increasing the predictive accuracy of these programs benefits everyone because hiring personnel who will become productive and satisfied in their jobs benefits everyone. It benefits both the employer, who gains a more effective worker, and the employee, who experiences a successful and fulfilling work life. Furthermore, today's employers are driven by international competition. They have compelling business interests for hiring effective workers and avoiding the many costs of poor performance, including inefficiency, waste, defects, downtime, and accidents. Biodata may have greater potential for affecting this broad range of critical criteria than any other currently available technology.

Biodata also offer a cost-effective means to promote a second but equally important goal for the continuing evolution of our society, as we move forward from this point in history. The biodata technology offers a fair and valid mechanism for decreasing the adverse impact of our selection programs and for increasing employment opportunities for members of traditionally disadvantaged groups. Biodata may be used to substantially lower the adverse impact of our personnel programs while at the same time maintaining or even improving the validity of those programs. From the perspective of our society, the simultaneous accomplishment of these two goals may be the ultimate utility.

REFERENCES

Amicus Curiae Brief for the American Psychological Association. (1988). In the Supreme Court of the United States: Clara Watson v. Fort Worth Bank & Trust. *American Psychologist, 43,* 1019–1028.

Ash, P. (1988). *The legality of pre-employment inquiries: A guide to state and other jurisdictional rules and regulations.* Park Ridge, IL: London House.

Asher, J. J. (1972). The biographical item: Can it be improved? *Personnel Psychology, 25,* 251–269.

Ashworth, S. D. (1989). Distinctions…between biodata and personality measurement are no longer meaningful. In T. W. Mitchell (Chair), *Biodata vs. personality: The same or different classes of individual differences?* Symposium conducted at the annual meeting of the Society for Industrial and Organizational Psychology, Boston.

Baehr, M., & Williams, G. B. (1967). Underlying dimensions of personal background data and their relationship to occupational classification. *Journal of Applied Psychology, 51,* 481–490.

Barge, B. N., & Hough, L. M. (1988). Utility of biographical data for the prediction of job performance. In L. M. Hough (Ed.), *Literature review: Utility of temperament, biodata, and interest assessment for predicting job performance* (ARI Research Note 88–020). Alexandria, VA: U.S. Army Research Institute.

Barrett, G. V., Phillips, J. S., & Alexander, R. A. (1981). Concurrent and predictive validity designs: A critical reanalysis. *Journal of Applied Psychology, 66,* 1–6.

Bass, B. M. (1957). Faking by sales applicants on a forced-choice personality inventory. *Journal of Applied Psychology, 41,* 403–404.

Bobko, P., Colella, A., & Russell, C. J. (1990). *Estimation of selection utility with multiple predictors in the presence of multiple performance criteria, differential validity through time, and strategic goals* (Contract No. DAAL03–86–D–0001, DO 1717). San Diego: Navy Personnel Research and Development Center.

Booth, R. E., McNally, M. S., & Berry, N. H. (1978). Predicting performance effectiveness in paramedical occupations. *Personnel Psychology, 31,* 581–593.

Boudreau, J. W. (1983). Economic considerations in estimating the utility of human resource productivity improvement programs. *Personnel Psychology, 36,* 551–576.

Boudreau, J. W. (1991). Utility analysis for decisions in human resource management. In M. D. Dunnette & L. M. Hough (Eds.), *Handbook of Industrial and Organizational Psychology* (2d ed., vol. 2., pp. 621–745). Palo Alto, CA: Consulting Psychologists Press.

Boudreau, J. W., & Berger, C. J. (1985). Decision-theoretic utility analysis applied to external employee movement [Monograph]. *Journal of Applied Psychology, 70,* 581–612.

Brogden, H. E. (1946). On the interpretation of the correlation coefficient as a measure of predictive efficiency. *Journal of Educational Psychology, 37,* 65–76.

Brogden, H. E. (1949). When testing pays off. *Personnel Psychology, 2,* 171–183.

Brogden, H. E., & Taylor, E. K. (1950). The dollar criterion: Applying the cost accounting concept to criterion construction. *Personnel Psychology, 3,* 133–154.

Brown, S. H. (1978). Long-term validity of a personal history item scoring procedure. *Journal of Applied Psychology, 63,* 673–676.

Bureau of National Affairs. (1978). *Uniform guidelines on employee selection procedures adopted by the EEOC, Civil Service Commission, Departments of Labor and Justice* (43 FR 38290). Washington, DC: Author.

Cascio, W. F. (1975). Accuracy of verifiable biographical information blank responses. *Journal of Applied Psychology, 60,* 767–769.

Cascio, W. F. (1987). *Costing human resources: The financial impact of behavior in organizations* (2d ed.). Boston: Kent.

Cascio, W. F., & Ramos, R. (1986). Development and application of a new method for assessing job performance in behavioral/economic terms. *Journal of Applied Psychology, 71,* 20–28.

Chaney, F. B., & Owens, W. A. (1964). Life history antecedents of sales, research, and general engineering interest. *Journal of Applied Psychology, 48,* 101–105.

Cronbach, L. J. (1960). *Essentials of psychological testing* (2d ed.). New York: Harper & Row.

Cronbach, L. J. (1970). *Essentials of psychological testing* (3d ed.). New York: Harper & Row.

Cronbach, L. J., & Gleser, G. C. (1965). *Psychological tests and personnel decisions* (2d ed.). Urbana: University of Illinois Press.

Cronshaw, S. F., & Alexander, R. A. (1985). One answer to the demand for accountability: Selection utility as an investment decision. *Organizational Behavior and Human Decision Processes, 35,* 102–118.

Crosby, M. M., & Mitchell, T. W. (1988, April). The obscurity of biodata predictor-criterion relationships: A blessing in disguise? In T. W. Mitchell (Chair), *Advancing the theory and method of biodata.* Symposium conducted at the annual meeting of the Society for Industrial and Organizational Psychology, Dallas.

Curtis, E. W., & Alf, E. F. (1969). Validity, predictive efficiency, and practical significance of selection tests. *Journal of Applied Psychology, 53,* 327–337.

Dahlstrom, W. G. (1969). Invasion of privacy: How legitimate is the current concern over this issue? In J. N. Butcher (Ed.), *MMPI: Research developments and clinical applications.* New York: McGraw-Hill.

Doll, R. E. (1971). Item susceptibility to attempted faking as related to item characteristics and adopted fake set. *Journal of Applied Psychology, 77,* 9–16.

Dunnette, M. D., McCartney, J., Carlson, H. C., & Kirchner, W. K. (1962). A study of faking behavior on a forced-choice self-description checklist. *Personnel Psychology, 15,* 13–24.

Eaton, N. K., Wing, H., & Mitchell, K. J. (1985). Alternate methods of estimating the dollar value of performance. *Personnel Psychology, 38,* 27–40.

England, G. W. (1971). *Development and use of weighted application blanks* (Rev. ed.). Minneapolis: University of Minnesota.

Erwin, F. W., & Herring, J. W. (1977). *The feasibility of the use of autobiographical information as a predictor of early army attrition* (TR–77–A67). Alexandria, VA: U.S. Army Research Institute.

Gandy, J. A., Outerbridge, A. N., Sharf, J. C., & Dye, D. A. (1989). *Development and initial validation of the Individual Achievement Record (IAR).* Washington, DC: U.S. Office of Personnel Management.

Gerhart, B. (1990). Voluntary turnover and alternative job opportunities. *Journal of Applied Psychology, 75,* 467–476.

Ghiselli, E. E. (1966). *The validity of occupational aptitude tests.* New York: Wiley.

Glennon, J. R., Albright, L. E., & Owens, W. A. (1966). *A catalog of life history items.* Greensboro, NC: Richardson Foundation.

Goldsmith, D. B. (1922). The use of personal history blanks as a salesmanship test. *Journal of Applied Psychology, 6,* 149–155.

Guion, R. M. (1965). *Personnel testing.* New York: McGraw-Hill.

Hammer, E. G., & Kleiman, L. S. (1988). Getting to know you. *Personnel Administrator,* *33(5),* 86–92.

Heron, A. (1956). The effects of real-life motivation on questionnaire response. *Journal of Applied Psychology, 40,* 65–68.

Hinrichs, J. R. (1978). An eight-year follow-up of a management assessment center. *Journal of Applied Psychology, 63,* 596–601.

Hough, L. (1989). Biodata and the measurement of individual differences. In T. W. Mitchell (Chair), *Biodata vs. personality: The same or different classes of individual differences?* Symposium conducted at the annual meeting of the Society for Industrial and Organizational Psychology, Boston.

HRStrategies. (1991). *Survey of human resource trends.* Grosse Pointe, MI: Author.

Hull, C. L. (1928). *Aptitude testing.* Yonkers, NY: World.

Hunter, J. E., & Hunter, R. F. (1984). Validity and utility of alternative predictors of job performance. *Psychological Bulletin, 96,* 72–98.

Hunter, J. E., & Schmidt, F. L. (1982). Fitting people to jobs: The impact of personnel selection on national productivity. In E. A. Fleishman & M. D. Dunnette (Eds.), *Human performance and productivity: Vol. 1: Human capability assessment.* Hillsdale, NJ: Erlbaum.

Kaplan, R. M., & Saccuzzo, D. P. (1989). *Psychological testing: Principles, applications, and issues.* Monterey, CA: Brooks/Cole.

Kelley, T. L. (1923). *Statistical methods.* New York: Macmillian.

Kenagy, H. G., & Yoakum, C. E. (1925). *The selection and training of salesmen.* New York: McGraw-Hill.

Klein, S. P., & Owens, W. A. (1965). Faking of a scored life history blank as a function of criterion objectivity. *Journal of Applied Psychology, 49,* 451–454.

Landis, C. (1936). Questionnaires and the study of personality. *Journal of Nervous and Mental Disease, 83,* 125–134.

Landis, C., Zubin, J., & Katz, S. E. (1935). Empirical evaluation of three personality adjustment inventories. *Journal of Educational Psychology, 26,* 321–330.

Landy, F. J., Farr, J. L., & Jacobs, R. R. (1982). Utility concepts in performance measurement. *Organizational Behavior and Human Performance, 30,* 15–40.

Lautenschlager, G. (1985). Within subject measures for the assessment of individual differences in faking. *Educational and Psychological Measurement, 46,* 309–316.

Mael, F. A. (1991). A conceptual rationale for the domain and attributes of biodata items. *Personnel Psychology, 44,* 763–792.

Manson, G. E. (1925). What can the application blank tell? Evaluation of items in personal history records of four thousand life insurance salesmen. *Journal of Personnel Research, 4,* 73–99.

McNemar, O. W., & Landis, C. (1935). Childhood disease and emotional maturity in the psychopathic woman. *Journal of Abnormal and Social Psychology, 30,* 314–319.

Merenda, P. F., & Clarke, W. V. (1959). The predictive efficiency of temperament characteristics and personal history variables in determining success in life insurance agents. *Journal of Applied Psychology, 43,* 360–366.

Mitchell, T. W. (1986, April). Specialized job analysis for developing rationally oriented biodata prediction systems. In S. Gael (Chair), *Advances in tailoring job analysis methods for specific applications.* Symposium conducted at the annual meeting of the Society for Industrial and Organizational Psychology, Chicago.

Mitchell, T. W. (1987). Electronic mechanisms for controlling false biodata in computerized selection testing. In L. J. Stricker (Chair), *Problems of distortion in personnel selection systems.* Symposium conducted at the annual meeting of the American Psychological Association, New York.

Mitchell, T. W. (1989). Are weighted application blanks valid and legal? *Proceedings of the 1989 National Assessment Conference.* Minneapolis: Personnel Decisions, Inc.

Mitchell, T. W. (1990). Can biodata predict personality? *Proceedings of the 14th Annual Conference of the International Personnel Management Assessment Council (IPMAAC),* San Diego.

Mitchell, T. W. (1992, May). *A priori biodata to predict teamwork, learning rate, and retention.* Paper presented at the annual meeting of the Society for Industrial and Organizational Psychology, Montreal.

Mitchell, T. W., & Klimoski, R. J. (1982). Is it rational to be empirical? A test of methods for scoring biographical data. *Journal of Applied Psychology, 71,* 411–418.

Mitchell, T. W., & Klimoski, R. J. (1986). Estimating the validity of cross-validity estimation. *Journal of Applied Psychology, 71,* 311–317.

Mumford, M. D., Cooper, M., & Schemmer, F. M. (1983). *Development of a content valid set of background data measures.* Bethesda, MD: Advanced Research Resources Organization.

Mumford, M. D., & Owens, W. A. (1987). Methodology review: Principles, procedures, and findings in the application of background data measures. *Applied Psychological Measurement, 11,* 1–31.

Murphy, K. R. (1986). When your top choice turns you down: Effects of rejected offers on the utility of selection tests. *Psychological Bulletin, 99,* 133–138.

Pace, L. A., & Schoenfeldt, L. F. (1977). Legal concerns in the use of weighted applications. *Personnel Psychology, 30,* 159–166.

Pannone, R. D. (1987, August). Effects of faking on biodata validity coefficients. In L. J. Stricker (Chair), *Problems of biodata distortion in personnel selection systems.* Symposium conducted at the annual meeting of the American Psychological Association, New York.

Reilly, R. R., & Chao, G. T. (1982). Validity and fairness of some alternative employee selection procedures. *Personnel Psychology, 35,* 1–62.

Reilly, R. R., & Warech, M. A. (1989). *The validity and fairness of alternative predictors of occupational performance.* Paper invited by the National Commission on Testing and Public Policy, Washington, DC.

Rothstein, H. R., Schmidt, F. L., Erwin, F. W., Owens, W. A., & Sparks, C. P. (1990). Biographical data in employment selection: Can validities be made generalizable? *Journal of Applied Psychology, 75,* 175–184.

Rush, C. H. (1953). A factorial study of sales criteria. *Personnel Psychology, 6,* 9–24.

Sackett, P. R. (1992, May). Utility issues in integrity testing. In D. L. Stone (Chair), *Honesty testing in organizations: Utility, construct validity and privacy issues.* Symposium conducted at the annual meeting of the Society for Industrial and Organizational Psychology, Montreal.

Schmidt, F. L., & Hoffman, B. (1975). Empirical comparison of three methods of assessing utility of a selection device. *Journal of Industrial and Organizational Psychology, 1*, 13–22.

Schmidt, F. L., Hunter, J. E., McKenzie, R. C., & Muldrow, T. W. (1979). The impact of valid selection procedures on workforce productivity. *Journal of Applied Psychology, 64*, 609–626.

Schmitt, N., Gooding, R. Z., Noe, R. A., & Kirsch, M. (1984). Meta-analyses of validity studies published between 1964 and 1982 and the investigation of study characteristics. *Personnel Psychology, 37*, 407–422.

Schuh, A.J. (1967). The predictability of employee tenure: A review of the literature. *Personnel Psychology, 20*, 133–152.

Shaffer, G. S., Saunders, V., & Owens, W. A. (1986). Additional evidence for the accuracy of biographical data: Long-term retest and observer ratings. *Personnel Psychology, 39*, 791–809.

Sparks, C. P. (1971). Using life history items to predict cognitive test scores. *Experimental Publication System, American Psychological Association, 12* (477–2), 1–7.

Taylor, H. C., & Russell, J. T. (1939). The relationship of validity coefficients to the practical effectiveness of tests in selection: Discussion and tables. *Journal of Applied Psychology, 23*, 565–578.

Thayer, P. W. (1977). Somethings old, somethings new. *Personnel Psychology, 30*, 513–524.

Trent, T. (1987, August). Armed forces adaptability screening: The problem of item response distortion. In L. J. Stricker (Chair), *Problems of biodata distortion in personnel selection systems.* Symposium conducted at the 95th Annual Convention of the American Psychological Association, New York.

Vance, R. J., & Colella, A. (1990). The utility of utility analysis. *Human Performance, 3*, 123–139.

van Rijn, P. (1992). Biodata: Potentials and challenges in public sector employee selection. *Personnel Assessment Monograph, 2*(4). Alexandria, VA: International Personnel Management Association Assessment Council (IPMAAC).

Weiss, D. J. (1976). Multivariate procedures. In M. D. Dunnette (Ed.), *Handbook of industrial and organizational psychology.* Chicago: Rand McNally.

Zeidner, J., & Johnson, C. D. (1989). *The utility of selection for military and civilian jobs.* (IDA Paper P-2239). Alexandria, VA: Institute for Defense Analysis.

SECTION

V

THEORETICAL ISSUES

The four chapters in this section on theoretical issues are diverse, but their common theme involves the integration of biodata theory and practice to enhance our understanding of biodata and its meaning. Moreover, each demonstrates the contribution of biodata to enhancing our understanding of individual differences. The chapter authors each do so in different substantive areas. Tenopyr's chapter begins this section, and she reviews new concepts in measurement that we may use to enhance our understanding of the meaning of biodata dimensions and their construct validity. She incorporates work in the area of personality on the Big Five personality dimensions into her discussion, where it becomes evident that personality research can both provide a general framework for biodata research *and* contribute to our understanding of personality development. The need for a taxonomic system is substantial, and Tenoypr uses the Big Five as an example for developing a taxonomic system. At the same time there is recognition of our need for process models. She discusses the use of structural models and latent factor models and their usefulness, noting that "the road from theory to practice is often rocky and ill charted."

Muchinsky discusses the large amount of research in the area of life history and vocational interests and job choices. He systematically reviews the studies using life history for predicting both interests and choices. His focus on substantive and methodological issues is particularly interesting and suggestive of avenues for future research. Work in this area can provide substantial background for the development of biodata forms for selection purposes as well as for career development and personnel classification.

The final chapters, written by Mumford and his colleagues Snell and Reiter-Palmon, focus on two areas: developmental psychology and personality. In both chapters the theories in each area are used to provide recommendations for item development, scaling, and validation of biodata inventories. The first of two by Mumford, Reiter-Palmon, and Snell focus on the rich source of information for biodata form development available in developmental psychology. The authors review models of development, including issues of environmental influences and continuity and change. They then examine the applications of developmental theories to biodata form item development and scaling, noting that developmental psychology provides not only guidance regarding the kinds of constructs that may be useful for measurement, but their implications for important item characteristics as well.

The second chapter, by Mumford, Snell, and Reiter-Palmon, examines the relationship between background data and personality constructs. They discuss the distinction between biodata inventories and personality inventories, and they argue that background data items are not the exclusive property of any construct domain. Still, the authors recognize that there is a meaningful relationship between biodata and personality constructs. Mumford et al. propose a theoretical model, called the *ecology model,* for how personality becomes manifest in life history responses. The practical applications of the model are outlined, including the use of biodata items to assess key personality constructs and methods for developing such biodata items. The implications of the ecology model for differential classification, team performance, and prescribing organizational change are discussed.

Big Five, Structural Modeling, and Item Response Theory

Mary L. Tenopyr
AT&T

There are several new developments in measurement that have impact on research and development in the life history area. First, there is convergence of the results of factor analytic research in the area of personality theory. There is increasing acceptance of essentially the same limited set of personality constructs. This event leads to confirmation of some of the major findings of life history research by industrial psychologists and points the way toward even more understanding of the role of background in affecting employee behavior. Until such construct understanding of major techniques such as life history data is reached, our efforts at applying advanced measurement techniques may not yield optimal results.

The second development is the continuing work on enhancing structural modeling. This work clearly facilitates determination of the construct validity of biodata and allows the opportunity for developing more sophisticated models. Related to this work are new perspectives on determining cross-validities. A final set of developments, which has yet to receive much attention in background data research, includes item response theory and its applications. These, it is proposed, will become increasingly meaningful as the construct validity of background data measures takes form and more homogeneous scales are developed.

CONSTRUCT VALIDITY

FIVE-FACTOR THEORY

As investigations of personality structure have continued over the past decade, the progress toward convergence of theories, particularly those based on factor analysis, has progressed to the point at which it appears that human personality may be described parsimoniously in terms of five major factors, often referred to as the "Big Five" (Digman, 1990). The interesting fact is that the dominant personality researchers in this area have all but ignored the research work on background data.

The stream of research leading to convergence appears to have started with the work of Fiske (1949), who reanalyzed Cattell's data and found only five factors, not the complex personality system Cattell (1947) had postulated. A separate development was the work of Tupes and Christal (1961), who supported Fiske's findings. Other investigators soon corroborated the findings of the seminal works (e.g., Borgatta, 1964; Norman, 1963; Smith, 1967).

The five factors have been named differently by different investigators, but all labels convey similar, if not identical, meanings. For example, Tupes and Christal called the factors *surgency, agreeableness, dependability, emotional stability,* and *culture.* Digman (1990) referred to the factors as *extroversion/intraversion, friendliness/hostility, conscientiousness, neuroticism/emotional stability,* and *intellect.*

Also, it is apparent from accumulated research that these five factors prevail under a wide range of measurement methods (Digman 1990). They are apparent when teachers rate children, when either officer candidates or college students rate one another, and when persons respond to inventories. It is also clear that the five-factor model of personality is gaining so much acceptance that soon personality researchers may have to defend results that do not conform to this model. However, Norman (1963) expressed a caution that bears reiteration today: There is more to theory development and refinement than the construction of a taxonomic observation language.

ECOLOGY MODEL

Mumford, Stokes, and Owens (1990), as a result of their research on biographical data, caution against attempting to describe and predict individual human behavior solely in terms of traits. They believe that individuality can only be described as it emerges over time, and it is subject to a host of complex moderating effects and can only be assessed by describing the situational context in which it emerges. They support their contentions with an extensive series of integrated research efforts carried out by Owens and associates.

The Mumford, Stokes, and Owens (1990) model has been designated an *ecology model*, which assumes that people select situatins and potential activities in these situations based on their associated affordances, which are in turn described as those aspects of the situation presenting good or evil for the individual. As a person engages in specific activities, he or she will begin to develop those attributes or resources required for affordance maintenance (Mumford & Nickels, 1990). Some patterns of situation selection will emerge more frequently than others for a given individual. The patterns of a given person's situation selection should, to some extent, be maintained over time.

Consequently, future behavior relative to the selection of situations can be predicted from data on past selection. As pointed out by Stokes, Mumford, and Owens (1989), the tenets of the model are consistent with those of researchers in the area of developmental psychology.

Thus, one is presented with divergent views relative to the theoretical aspects of human personality. One view suggests that human behavior can be explained in terms of five broad constructs. An opposing view is that a developmental approach, taking into consideration the context in which individual characteristics emerge, is more appropriate for explaining behavior. The former approach strives for parsimony in the most rigorous scientific tradition. The parsimony is most welcome in view of the confusion that has surrounded the research on human traits. On the other hand, the search for parsimony, as is argued by proponents of a developmental approach, can eliminate almost all mining of the rich data pertaining to individuality.

RECONCILING MODEL

Is it possible to reconcile the two views? One possible general model under which both views could be incorporated suggests that these are different levels of generality in the description of behavior. Guilford (1959) has suggested a hierarchical model of personality with specific behaviors at the lowest level and above them progressively more general levels, such as habits, until a level of general personality traits is reached. According to Guilford, it is probable that many investigators have reached such markedly different conclusions from the results of factor analytic studies because they have worked simultaneously with items at all of the levels in the hierarchy.

One can envision future investigations involving biographical data incorporating a hierarchical model that acknowledges the Big Five as the

TABLE 1   Hypothesized Congruence of Big Five Factors and Biodata Factors

Big Five Factor[*]	Factor Number in Schoenfeldt (1974)	Biodata Factors
Surgency	3.	Social introversion[+]
	6.	Aggressiveness/independence[+]
	5.	Social extroversion and popularity[t]
	11.	Independence/dominance[t]
Agreeableness (9)[t]	9.	Social desirability[+]
	1.	Warmth of parental relationship[+]
	7.	Negative social adjustment[t]
Dependability (3)[t]	2.	Academic achievement[+] (2)[t]
	5.	Intellectualism[+]
	10.	Extracurricular activity[t]
	8.	Parental control versus freedom[+]
Emotional stability		
Culture	10.	Scientific interest[+] (8)[t]
	11.	Positive academic attitude[+]
	3.	Academic interest[t]

Note: Number in parentheses represents factor number used by authors.
[*]Adapted from Tupes and Christal (1961)
[+]Adapted from Schoenfeldt (1974)
[t]Adapted from Eberhardt and Muchinsky (1982)

highest level of generality. Since biodata usually are at a lower level of generality and emphasize life history material at the behavioral and habit level, the next logical step, as far as construct validity is concerned, could be definition of a set of narrower constructs that fall beneath the Big Five in the generality hierarchy. Although it is possible that biodata may extend beyond this parsimonious system and include other concepts such as practical intelligence, this approach could be extended to find even more rules that account for the development of the Big Five. Perhaps it will be found that development even in childhood can be conceptualized in a hierarchical model based on the Big Five.

The possibility of a model of this sort is not that remote. It appears that there is considerable superficial congruence between the factors found by Owens, his associates, and other biodata researchers and the Big Five. Owens and Schoenfeldt (1979) and Schoenfeldt (1974) identified 13 factors in biodata for males. Eberhardt and Muchinsky (1982) found highly congruent factors in a separate sample, as did Lautenschlager and Shaffer (1987). A hypothesized model involving these factors and the Big Five is reported in Table 1.

The comparisons of the biodata factors with the Big Five, although hypothetical, do point to a great degree of order. The fact that in many biodata studies there has not been an apparent counterpart for Tupes and Christal's emotional stability factor probably just reflects the fact that the biodata researchers have used few items having content that would reflect such a dimension in a factor analysis. An exception might be the findings of an adjustment factor for females by Owens and associates (Owens & Schoenfeldt, 1979).

However, as far as the other four dimensions are concerned, it appears that there is at least superficial congruence and that the constructs derived from biodata are comparable to those derived from personality inventories and ratings. There is also some evidence to suggest that the biodata factors represent a lower order of factor than the Big Five.

Certainly the question of documenting congruence of Big Five factors and biodata factors is a matter for research, which can be expedited by the recent development of inventories to measure the Big Five (e.g., Costa & McCrae, 1985).

A total theory of personality and its associated measurement methods would probably include both the trait approach and the ecology approach advocated by Mumford, Stokes, and Owens (1990). The possibilities for merging these two approaches seem strong. A total theory of personality must not only describe an end result, as in trait theory, but also incorporate developmental aspects. To that end, Mumford and Nickels (1990) have developed a triadic conceptualization relative to the construct validity of biodata. A set of constructs would indicate the resources possessed by the individual. These are selectively developed and applied. Here a key to relationships with the Big Fve might be found. The predictive power of background data is affected by two other categories of variable that condition the way these resources are applied. These latter categories were designated as (a) *choice processes*, which reflect preferences in seeking certain affordances, and (b) *filter processes*, which influence perceptions of affordances or their attainability. Mumford and Nickels (1990) and Nickels (1990) have developed data supporting this conceptualization, which is also presented as a "transactional resource allocation model." This promising model deserves further exploration.

Relative to preferences and biodata, there appears to be another avenue that might be investigated further with a view toward incorporating it in the model presented by Mumford, Stokes, and Owens (1990) or in a modification of that model. Holland's (1973) hexagonal model of vocational type has become so well accepted that any model of individual development or personality probably must take the model into account. Eberhardt and Muchinsky (1984) have related biodata to vocational type in an attempt to assess the structural validity of the Holland model, but further work remains to be done relating biodata to preferences in a broad context. This suggestion is not meant to imply that there is a "Big Eleven" that should be related to life history data, but rather that it appears appropriate as models are refined to make more effort to account for preferences, both vocational ones and more general ones.

Other recent empirical work relative to the construct validity of biographical information includes that of Russell and Domm (1990), who evaluated a theory-based method of item generation.

One necessary but not sufficient condition for construct validity is generalizability of validity for the instruments across relevant situations. Prediction specific to a situation would suggest the lack of measurement of any broad constructs. Rothstein, Schmidt, Erwin, Owens, and Sparks (1990) showed that for one well-developed biodata blank, validities do generalize across organizational situations and settings. However, the authors caution that the results should be interpreted to indicate that the validities of biodata can generalize, not that they invariably do. One would like to see further relevant work along these lines to determine what constructs account for the generalizability.

In another recent study relative to construct validity and generalizability, Crosby, Dalessio, and McManus (1990) used confirmatory factor analysis to determine whether the factor structure of the career profile used in the life insurance industry in the United States was replicated with a sample from the United Kingdom. Results indicated that a seven-factor structure based on a U. S. sample was essentially confirmed in the U.K. sample.

SUMMARY

In summary, much progress has been made in the definition of constructs associated with life history data, particularly in the last two decades. However, as factor analytic work in the area of personality and preference measurement has progressed, there appear to be opportunities for refinement of the primary theory (Mumford, Stokes, & Owens, 1990), affording more construct-based meaning to biographical information. Parsimony, in the form of the Big Five personality characteristics, has been achieved in the field of personality measurement. Holland's hexagonal theory of vocational preference types appears to have endorsement in psychology. It is not suggested that the richness of human development can be encapsulated in a simple descriptive taxonomy, yet it appears that the research in personality has much to offer in terms of modifying and amplifying existing life history models.

STRUCTURAL MODELING

Structural modeling, as well as one of its predecessors, factor analysis, has become widely used in psychology. Both, however, present some problems, more in application than in theory.

As a theory-building tool, factor analysis has a long history. Its early development was hindered largely by the extensive computations involved and the lack of modern data processing equipment. Starting in the 1960s when programs for extracting factors and rotating them became accessible, factor analysis became a standard tool in psychology. Then, as now, there was much misuse of the technique, and, consequently, theoretical research in all areas of psychology, including those involving life history, suffered. For example, often factor analyses have been done on experimentally dependent data or with samples too small to ensure replicable results.

Several common inappropriate actions on the part of researchers have led to confusion about constructs, particularly in the area of biodata. One sees results of factor analyses where the item scoring has involved multiple responses for each individual. Often the responses within items represent ipsative measures, whereas those between items represent normative data. Consequently, some factor analyses are based on a combination of ipsative and normative measurement, with unknown degrees of experimental dependence in parts of the data set.

A second problem, not limited to applications with life history data, is the use of principal components analysis instead of principal factors analysis. In the former procedure, when 1.00 is placed in the principal diagonal, specific and error variance, as well as common factor variance, are analyzed. Therefore, results can be misleading and unstable. Snook and Gorsuch (1989) have reported a Monte Carlo study that indicated the superiority of common factor analysis. Despite the problems of making communality estimates, it is recommended that these be used.

A third problem that appears to manifest itself particularly with biodata applications is the frequent lack of hypotheses to inform the analyses. Unless there are hypotheses, and marker items are constructed to conform to these hypotheses, it makes little sense to use factor analyses for theory building. Often when life history items are subjected to factor analysis, only those items predictive of a criterion of unknown factorial composition are used. It is little wonder that results of factor analyses of these selected items yield little in the way of theoretical information.

Furthermore, the possibility of differences in factor structure emerging from concurrent and predictive validation in operational settings has not been considered adequately. Also, the question of possible different factor structures for males and females and for other groups needs to be taken into account. Perhaps this is best done, however, in the context of causal modeling. The difficulties of obtaining sufficiently large samples so that replicated differences between predictive and concurrent applications can be compared has hindered this effort. Possibly the problem could be better conceptualized as one involving differences between research data for which an effort has been made to minimize response style and data from actual applications in which response styles (e.g., responding in a socially desirable direction) are operating to an unknown degree. Thus, we have another problem attributable to trying to make the same data set serve two purposes. It would seem advisable, until sufficient research has been done so that theoretical findings converge, that validation efforts and theory-building efforts be separated. This is not to say that existing theory should not inform validation efforts, but it does suggest that researchers should be clear in what their main goals are and not attempt to have the same data serve too many purposes.

A final problem associated with factor analysis is the perennial problem of the nature of rotation to be done. Probably oblique rotation is used more than it should be, and results in more confusion than necessary in determining the construct validity of biodata. Certainly advocates of oblique rotation can offer cogent arguments as to why factors should be correlated; however, in an area in which meaning is as obscure as it has been with life history data, orthogonal rotation results should be reported along with those of oblique rotation, so that there is a more reasonable basis for making comparisons among studies.

Confirmatory factor analysis based on analysis of covariance structures (Jöreskog, 1970) is a powerful tool in theory building and can form the basis for theory-based generalization of findings. Over the last two decades, the early theory has evolved, its uses have been extended, and its computational options have become extraordinarily elaborate (Jöreskog & Sörbom, 1986). The analysis of covariance structures has become a widely used method for research on structural modeling involving a variety of models and types of data. For tutorial technical discussions, the reader is referred to James, Mulaik, and Brett (1982), Hayduk (1987), Loehlin (1987), or Long (1983).

The relatively simple application of the causal modeling techniques to confirmatory factor analysis, despite its theoretical and computational sophistication, is complicated by many of the issues that plague exploratory common factor analysis. For example, construct interpretations are often attempted without viable hypotheses and sufficient marker variables to provide information about the plausibility of such hypotheses. The difficulties have many parallels with the failure to use appropriate controls in experimental studies. Another problem is the use of samples and items that were collected in an operational predictive setting or for a validation study in confirmatory factor analysis. For example, in an employee selection study, item responses may be affected by response bias. Other problems, such as interdependence of item responses, also present difficulties.

However, one of the most serious problems one finds in the use of confirmatory factor analysis is the apparently widespread practice of using confirmatory factor analysis as if it were exploratory factor analysis. Some investigators go through several iterations, letting the fit of each attempted model inform successive models investigated. Thus, the whole intent of using confirmatory factor analysis is perverted. One wonders how many journal articles have been based on unreported iteration involving multiple models. Specifically, Breckler (1990) strongly criticizes those who develop their model and confirm it on the same set of data. The cross-validation strategy of theory building is paramount. Different sets of data should be used in the exploratory and confirmatory stages of the analysis. Breckler (1990) also mentions several other problems with the use of covariance structure modeling. These include (a) potential violations of distributional assumptions, (b) failure to recognize the existence of equivalent models, and (c) poorly justified causal inferences.

Cudeck (1989) has cautioned against the assumption that covariance structure models can arbitrarily in all cases be applied to sample correlation matrices, as they are to sample covariance matrices. He has developed examples of the various problems that can arise.

A major technical problem with covariance structure models has been evaluating the goodness of fit in the confirmatory analysis portion of the research. Various investigators have developed goodness-of-fit indices. None of these appears to be completely satisfactory in all cases, and often different indices yield contradictory results. Among the indices developed are those of Bentler and Bonett (1980), Hoetler (1983), Jöreskog and Sörbom (1986), and Mulaik et al. (1989). The latter authors criticize all previous goodness-of-fit indices, but their recent contribution has yet to be thoroughly evaluated in the literature. Marsh, Balla, and Roderick (1988) have pointed out that most existing goodness-of-fit indices are affected by sample size. Bentler and Mooijaart (1989) suggest parsimony as a major consideration when choosing between two competing models when the sample size is large.

Satorra (1989) has proposed a unified approach to addressing the validity of the restrictions that a model specification imposes on a more general (less restricted) model.

In general, covariance structure analysis holds great promise for facilitating much of the theory building so necessary relative to life history data. Not only is the method an asset in determining construct implications of the data, but the procedures also provide the means for testing the applicability of more complicated models beyond simple categorical descriptions. Covariance structure analysis is not without its problems. Many of these are associated with improper research procedures, but the technical problem of assessing goodness of fit remains a vexing one. In many ways, there is still much art that needs to be applied in confirmatory factor analysis and the other applications of covariance structure analysis.

CROSS-VALIDATION

Cross-validation, which is a standard procedure in the development of life history inventories, has a number of limitations. By dividing the sample into two parts, then developing the key on one part and applying the key to the other part, one encounters a significant loss of information. When the sample size is large (e.g., several thousand people), this loss is likely to be minor. However, for moderate-sized data sets, which typify the usual research applications with biodata, splitting the data can yield seriously unstable estimates of validity. In another context, this has been shown by Picard and Cook (1984).

Over the years, numerous investigators have developed formulas to assess cross-validity. Kennedy (1988) has provided the most recent simulation study involving a number of formulas commonly used for estimating the squared cross-validity coefficient of a sample regression equation in the context of best subset regression. He found that a formula by Stein (1960) would be expected to yield estimates as good as or better than cross-validation or several more recently developed formula estimators for the populations he considered.

The most recent formulation of a single sample cross-validity coefficient is that of Cudeck and Browne (1983). More recently these authors (Browne & Cudeck, 1989) have shown that their formula produces a result that is a simple linear function of the Akaike Information Criterion (Akaike, 1983).

LATENT VARIABLE MODELS

No discussion of measurement relative to life history information would be complete without discussion of item response theory (IRT). Certainly, for the last twenty years, manuscripts on IRT have occupied much of the space in the psychometrically oriented journals. There are two main points that need to be made about IRT. First, with some exceptions (Henley, Klebe, McBride, & Cudeck, 1989), one sees few applications of IRT other than in ability testing, where the theory is most appropriate. Costs and logistical and hardware considerations appear to be dominant factors preventing widespread practical application, despite the fact that the mathematical procedures and appropriate associated software for such application have long been available.

The second problem in applying IRT to life history data is the one to which much of this chapter has been devoted—the need to determine the constructs underlying life history information. IRT cannot be applied to biodata unless latent variables that can be measured by homogeneous sets of items are obtained. Even with a set of constructs, it will be necessary to reformulate some of the measurement bases for IRT before applying the theory to life history information. Also, there needs to be further research on the circumstances under which the model does not apply. In the future, we will probably see latent variable models studied in the context of prediction situations to which much research involving biodata has been devoted. An example may be found in the work of Rosenbaum (1989).

PREDICTIVE BIAS

The question of predictive bias in the use of selection procedures has been a topic of considerable interest for nearly three decades. It is apparent that practical selection researchers, dealing with large item pools, can select items in such a way as to minimize group differences and provide similar validities for different groups (Richardson, Bellows, Henry, & Co., 1981). Whether such selection of items alters the construct-based meaning of the total set of items is a subject for further research. Again, there are problems in using biographical questionnaires developed for a purpose other than the one for which they were intended.

Despite the fact that life history data appear to present fewer equal employment opportunity problems than other data, such as results of ability tests, there are new issues emerging concerning civil rights. One issue I have personal experience with is the request by government agencies for validity data for every item on every test. Requiring item-by-item justification causes major problems for all types of measurement, but life history items are particularly vulnerable. It would be a rare biographical questionnaire in which every item was valid to a significant and useful degree. Otherwise, researchers could use one or two items and not have the large number of scored items usually needed.

Also, government agencies have been known to demand the examination of alternative selection procedures with equal construct validity, even when a study clearly follows a criterion-related model and results in significant criterion-related validity for an instrument. This again poses special problems for life history data, especially when items are selected mainly on the basis of predictive validity.

DEVELOPING LIFE HISTORY QUESTIONNAIRES

Obviously, there have been many new developments concerning constructs in relation to life history data. In the theoretical sense, models to use as a basis for item development are converging; in the mathematical area, new methods for studying life history data relative to constructs are reaching new levels of sophistication.

In the practical sense, life history data have been shown to be useful for predicting many practical criteria and to be amenable to reducing adverse consequences for various groups.

However, several times in this chapter the role of purpose in the development of biographical questionnaires has been mentioned. It is clear that an instrument developed for one purpose is not necessarily useful for other purposes. Also, different research designs and sampling schemata may lead to different results.

The question then becomes how to develop biographical questions within a given context. As in all measurement, a strategy that is all empiricism or one that is all theory is probably not optimal. My preference is to have at least some theoretical underpinning, even when the purpose is purely practical, such as in selecting life history items to predict production output. In practice, however, there are many factors other than theory that must be taken into account. These include results of studies of job requirements, knowledge of characteristics of the applicant pool, past predictive performance of the items in other settings, and various contextual variables, such as whether the organization is unionized or not.

The road from theory to practice is often rocky and ill-charted. Despite the gains in research in the area of life history measurement, the translation of theory into practice remains something of a multifaceted art.

SUMMARY

Life history information is a rich source not only for predicting future behavior but also for building theories so that developmental processes can be better understood and perhaps modified. To develop and test the needed theories, we should understand better and thoroughly study the constructs or latent variables underlying life history data. We should work toward not only taxonomic systems, such as the Big Five personality traits, but also toward refinement of process models, such as the ecology model.

There is still much to be achieved in translating theory into practice, and new developments in the equal employment opportunity field need to be considered, but with the new developments in both construct definitions and mathematics relative to theory building, life history data appear to have a promising and long future.

Life history data have an important role in all psychology, and researchers in the area of biodata should continue coordinating their work with that of researchers in other areas of psychology. Only when life history research is integrated into the mainstream of psychology can the current research base in life history yield its full contribution to psychological theory.

REFERENCES

Akaike, H. (1983). Information measures and model selection. *Bulletin of the International Statistical Institute: Proceedings of the 44th Session, 1,* 277–290.

Bentler, P. M., & Bonett, D. G. (1980). Significance tests and goodness-of-fit in the analysis of covariance structures. *Psychological Bulletin, 88,* 588–606.

Bentler, P. M., & Mooijaart, A. B. (1989). Choice of structural model via parsimony: A rationale based on precision. *Psychological Bulletin, 106,* 315–317.

Borgatta, E. F. (1964). The structure of personality characteristics. *Behavioral Science, 12,* 8–17.

Breckler, S. J. (1990). Applications of covariance structure modeling in psychology: Cause for concern? *Psychological Bulletin, 107,* 260–273.

Browne, M. W., & Cudeck, R. (1989). Single sample cross-validation indices for covariance structures. *Multivariate Behavioral Research, 24,* 445–455.

Cattell, R. B. (1947). Confirmation and clarification of primary personality factors. *Psychometrika, 12,* 197–220.

Costa, P. T., Jr., & McCrae, R. R. (1985). *The NEO personality inventory.* Odessa, FL: Psychological Assessment Resources.

Crosby, M. M., Dalessio, A. T., & McManus, M. A. (1990). *Stability of biodata dimensions across English-speaking cultures: A confirmatory investigation.* Paper presented at the annual meeting of the American Psychological Association, Boston.

Cudeck, R. (1989). Analysis of correlation matrices using covariance structure models. *Psychological Bulletin, 105,* 317–327.

Cudeck, R., & Browne, M. W. (1983). Cross-validation of covariance structures. *Multivariate Behavioral Research, 18,* 147–167.

Digman, J. M. (1990). Personality structure: Emergence of the five-factor model. *Annual Review of Psychology, 41,* 417–440.

Eberhardt, B. J., & Muchinsky, P. M. (1982). An empirical investigation of the factor stability of Owens' Biographical Questionnaire. *Journal of Applied Psychology, 67,* 138–145.

Eberhardt, B. J., & Muchinsky, P. M. (1984). Structural validation of Holland's hexagonal model: Vocational classification through the use of biodata. *Journal of Applied Psychology, 69,* 174–181.

Fiske, D. W. (1949). Consistency of the factorial structures of personality ratings from different sources. *Journal of Abnormal and Social Psychology, 44,* 329–344.

Guilford, J. P. (1959). *Personality.* New York: McGraw-Hill.

Hayduk, L. A. (1987). *Structural equation modeling with LISREL.* Baltimore, MD: John Hopkins University Press.

Henley, S. J., Klebe, K. J., McBride, J. R., & Cudeck, R. (1990). Adoptive and conventional versions of the DAT: The first complete test battery comparison. *Applied Psychological Measurement, 13,* 363–371.

Hoetler, J. V. (1983). The analysis of covariance structures: Goodness-of-fit indices. *Sociological Methods and Research, 11,* 325–344.

Holland, J. L. (1973). *Making vocational choices: A theory of careers.* Englewood Cliffs, NJ: Prentice-Hall.

James, L. R., Mulaik, S. A., & Brett, J. M. (1982). *Causal analysis, assumptions, models and data.* Beverly Hills, CA: Sage.

Jöreskog, K. G. (1970). A general method for the analysis of covariance structures. *Biometrika, 57,* 239–251.

Jöreskog, K. G., & Sörbom, D. (1986). *LISREL VI* (4th ed.). Mooresville, IN: Scientific Software.

Kennedy, E. (1988). Estimation of the squared cross-validity coefficient in the context of best subset regression. *Applied Psychological Measurement, 12,* 231–237.

Lautenschlager, G. J., & Shaffer, G. S. (1987). A reexamination of the component stability of Owens's Biographical Questionnaire. *Journal of Applied Psychology, 72,* 149–152.

Loehlin, J. C. (1987). *Latent variable models: An introduction to factor, path, and structural analysis.* Hillsdale, NJ: Erlbaum.

Long, J. S. (1983). *Covariance structure models: An introduction to LISREL.* Beverly Hills, CA: Sage.

Marsh, H. W., Balla, J. R., & Roderick, P. M. (1988). Goodness-of-fit indices in confirmatory factor analysis: The effect of sample size. *Psychological Bulletin, 105,* 391–410.

Mulaik, S.A., James, L.R., Van Alstine J., Bennett, N., Lind, S., & Stilwell, C. D. (1989). Evaluation of goodness-of-fit indices for structural equation models. *Psychological Bulletin, 105,* 430–445.

Mumford, M. D., & Nickels, B. J. (1990). *Applying principles of content and construct validity to background data.* Paper presented at the annual conference of the Society for Industrial and Organizational Psychology.

Mumford, M. D., Stokes, G. S., & Owens, W. A. (1990). *Patterns of life history: The ecology of human individuality.* Hillsdale, NJ: Erlbaum.

Nickels, B. J. (1990). *The construction of background data measures: Developing procedures which optimize construct, content. and criterion-related validities.* Unpublished doctoral dissertation, Georgia Institute of Technology, Atlanta.

Norman, W. T. (1963). Toward an adequate taxonomy of personality attributes: Replicated factor structure in peer nomination personality ratings. *Journal of Abnormal and Social Psychology, 66,* 574–583.

Owens, W. A., & Schoenfeldt, L. F. (1979). Toward a classification of persons [Monograph]. *Journal of Applied Psychology, 64,* 569–607.

Picard, R. R., & Cook, R. D. (1984). Cross-validation of regression models. *Journal of the American Statistical Association, 79,* 575–583.

Richardson, Bellows, Henry, & Co., Inc. (1981). *Supervisory profile record: Technical reports 1, 2, and 3.* Washington, DC: Author.

Rosenbaum, P. R. (1989). Criterion-related construct validity. *Psychometrika, 54,* 625–633.

Rothstein, H. R., Schmidt, F. L., Erwin, F. W., Owens, W. A., & Sparks, C. P. (1990). Biographical data in employment selections: Can validities be made generalizable? *Journal of Applied Psychology, 75,* 175–184.

Russell, C. J., & Domm, D. R. (1990). *On the construct validity of biographical information: Evaluation of the theory-based method of item generation.* Paper presented at the annual meeting of the Society for Industrial and Organizational Psychology, Boston.

Satorra, A. (1989). Alternate test criteria in covariance structure analysis: A unified approach. *Psychometrika, 54,* 131–151.

Schoenfeldt, L. F. (1974). Utilization of manpower: Development and evaluation of an assessment classification model for matching individuals with jobs. *Journal of Applied Psychology, 59,* 583–595.

Smith, G. M. (1967). Usefulness of peer ratings of personality in educational research. *Educational and Psychological Measurement, 27,* 967–984.

Snook, S. C., & Gorsuch, R. L. (1989). Component analysis versus common factor analysis: A Monte Carlo study. *Psychological Bulletin, 106,* 148–154.

Stein, C. (1960). Multiple regression. In I. Olkin, H. Hotelling, S. S. Gupta, M. Sobel, & M. E. Terry (Eds.), *Contributions to probability and statistics.* Stanford, CA: Stanford University Press.

Stokes, G. S., Mumford, M. D., & Owens, W. A. (1989). Life history prototypes in the study of individuality. *Journal of Personality, 57,* 509–545.

Tupes, E. C., & Christal, R. E. (1961). *Recurrent personality factors based on trait ratios* (USAF ASD Tech. Rep. No. 61–97). Lackland Air Force Base, TX: Personnel Laboratory, Aeronautical Systems Division.

The Influence
of Life History Experiences
on Vocational Interests
and Choices

Paul M. Muchinsky
University of North Carolina at Greensboro

INTRODUCTION

Since the inception of research on vocational behavior, scholars have documented the relationship between our early life experiences and our subsequent vocational interests and choices as adults. In a classic article written almost fifty years ago, Berdie (1944) discussed how vocational interests were influenced by school and work experiences and family activities. Theorists such as Roe (1956), Super (1957), Osipow (1973), and Holland (1985) have acknowledged life history experiences as one of the origins of our vocational interests, although the nature of their influence is often unspecified. The purpose of this chapter is to review the published literature on life history experiences and vocational behavior and to discuss several substantive and methodological issues associated with this area of research.

While most studies of vocational behavior are directed toward interests or preferences, some are not. I have identified two types of criteria used in vocational behavior research. The first is *interest* and refers to the study of the vocations individuals prefer to enter. Subjects in these studies are typically students in college or high school. This is the most common type

535

of study. The second is *choice* and refers to the study of the actual vocations that individuals have entered. Subjects in these studies are vocational incumbents and typically are under 40 years of age.

The research on life history experiences is divided in terms of the extensiveness with which life experiences are measured. Some studies utilize a comprehensive assessment of life history experiences, as reflected by Owens' *Biographical Questionnaire* (BQ). Other studies assess only one or two life history factors (e.g., parental support). The former studies tend to be more exploratory in nature, while the latter often involve the testing of specific hypotheses.

There are approximately 30 studies that comprise the literature base of life history experiences and vocational behavior. These studies can be classified in a variety of ways. The classification I have used is to group studies that are primarily concerned with gender-related issues in vocational interest development from those where gender is not the primary issue in the research. Following a review of the empirical studies that comprise the literature, I will discuss major substantive and methodological issues that pervade this body of research.

GENDER-RELATED STUDIES

The most pervasive theme to this body of research is the study of the factors that lead females to express interest in or choose vocations traditionally populated by males. A few studies examined both males and females, and two studied the backgrounds of males who entered traditionally female-dominated vocations.

Green and Parker (1965) examined whether the parent-child relationship influenced the child's preference for an occupation in a sample of seventh grade boys and girls. Boys were more likely to enter "person-oriented" occupations when their relationship with either parent was positive. Girls were more likely to enter "non–person-oriented" occupations when their relationship with either parent was negative.

Standley and Soule (1974) examined the backgrounds of women who had entered one of four traditionally male-dominated professions: architecture, law, medicine, and psychology. The women reported they were raised by their parents as "special" children. In general, their parents were well educated, were in high-status occupations, and earned above average incomes. The women reported they engaged in more "boyish" acts and independent activities than affiliative or nurturant activities.

Burlin (1976) asked a sample of adolescent females their preference for entering vocations that varied as a function of the percentage of women in the vocation. Burlin classified the vocations as *innovative* (less than 30 percent female), *moderate* (30 to 50 percent female), and *traditional* (over 50 percent female). The vocational aspirations of the subjects were positively related to the father's education and the mother's occupational status. Most fathers with daughters pursuing traditional vocational goals had high school or less education. Most fathers with daughters pursing innovative vocational goals held graduate or professional degrees.

Peng and Jaffe (1979) examined data from the National Longitudinal Study of High School Classes. The authors studied women who had graduated in 1972. They reported that women in male-dominated fields of higher education had higher academic ability, more coursework in science and math in high school, and were more work-oriented than women in traditional fields of employment. Family influence was not found to be related to women's entry into male-dominated fields.

Greenfeld, Greiner, and Wood (1980) reported that women in male-dominated jobs were more likely to be older, be better educated, have fathers with more education, and be childless, as compared to women in female-dominated jobs. The best predictors of whether women would hold a male-dominated job were college attainment, age, feelings about achieving a very high salary, importance of work, and being regarded as an authority on the job.

Zuckerman (1980) studied a sample of females in a private, elite college. She found the women to have nontraditional educational and career goals, but the sample was traditional with regard to marriage and motherhood goals. Their vocational preferences were related to religious upbringing and mother's educational attainment, but not to father's educational attainment, parent's occupation, or their own self-esteem.

In a review article, Auster and Auster (1981) identified six factors that were associated with women's entry into nontraditional occupations: (a) mother works in a high-level, nontraditional occupation; (b) father is an achievement role model; (c) parents are supportive of daughter's career orientation; (d) family is of high socioeconomic status; (e) child placed early in birth order; and (f) peer-group influence is supportive.

Zuckerman (1981) studied a sample of 308 male and 455 female college students. She found the traditional/nontraditional career plans of men were not influenced by the educational requirements of the careers. In contrast, however, women who planned nontraditional careers were more likely to aspire to careers that require more education. Zuckerman reported that the level of parents' educational attainment, mother's career, and religious upbringing most strongly predicted the gender-typed occupational goals of women. She suggested that in the 1980s, nontraditional goals for women were becoming more popular and acceptable, which suggested different predictors of women's vocational aspirations in the 1980s compared to the 1960s and 1970s.

Houser and Garvey (1983) classified women in a vocational training program into those with nontraditional versus traditional occupational interests. Those women with nontraditional interests consistently received more support and encouragement than the women with traditional interests. The traditional women said they expected to receive more discouragement than the nontraditional women indicated they actually received.

Lemkau (1984) conducted a study of the background characteristics of men in female-dominated professions. Such men were found to have had employed mothers and distant relationships with their fathers and were positively influenced in their career choices by women. Compared to a sample of men working in traditional male professions, men in female-dominated professions more frequently experienced the death of a par -ent or sibling or parental divorce or separation, and they frequently mentioned such stresses as sensitizing them to their nuturant and emotional capabilities.

In the second research study of this type, Hayes (1989) obtained data from the 1981 National Longitudinal Surveys of Work Experience (Young Male Cohort). Men who worked in female-concentrated jobs ($n = 171$) were compared to men who worked in male-concentrated jobs ($n = 181$). The results indicated that men in female-concentrated occupations were not more likely to have experienced the loss of a parent due to death, nor to have experienced father absence. However, Hayes suggested the *timing* of father absence and parental death, particularly in childhood, might be related to subsequent vocational choice.

Jagacinski (1987) examined data from a national survey of professional engineers. The sample consisted of 840 women and 1,167 men, categorized into four cohorts—those who had graduated from college (a) 5 years previously or less, (b) 6 to 10 years previously, (c) 11 to 15 years previously, and (d) 16 to 20 years previously. She reported that the parents of female engineers were more likely to have college degrees and be employed in professional positions than were the parents of male engineers. It was also found that more recent women graduates were more likely to have considered engineering as a career possibility while still in high school than were the older graduates. This cohort effect was not found for men.

In a study of 12th-grade boys and girls, Hannah and Kahn (1989) reported that boys uniformly expressed interest in male-dominated occupations. However, girls from high socioeconomic families were more likely than girls from low socioeconomic families to be interested in male-dominated occupations.

Fitzpatrick and Silverman (1989) compared background and motivational factors of 113 high-achieving college women in engineering, science, and humanities and social sciences in factors affecting career choice. Areas of investigation included family composition and parental characteristics, childhood socialization, sources of support for career choice, and work characteristics. Engineering majors perceived stronger support for career choice from both parents than did women in other majors. The authors concluded that when samples of women in traditional versus nontraditional careers are comparable in terms of achievement orientation and ability, differences in family background and childhood socialization diminish. Also, women choosing traditional and nontraditional careers do not differ as much in research in the 1980s as they did in research in the 1970s.

In a review article that was published prior to most of the studies just cited, Lemkau (1979) examined background characteristics of women in male-dominated occupations. She reported that the vocational choices of women were related to their sibling status, parental education and employment, and parental values and identification. The more recently published research also underscores the importance of these characteristics, along with females' involvement with science courses and activities and the extent of their social popularity.

OVERVIEW

It is somewhat difficult to draw comparisons across studies because of differences in life history factors examined and samples used. Nevertheless, certain life history factors repeatedly emerge as being influential in affecting vocational criteria.

Perhaps the life history factor having the most consistent effect on vocational behavior is relationship with one's parents. The magnitude of relationship appears particularly strong for females involving the relationship they have with their mothers. Most studies of females entering male-dominated occupations point to the importance of parental influence. The nature of the influence may be in the form of the psychosocial relationship between the child and parents or may be related to the status/income of the parents. It is somewhat less clear whether parents serve as role models who themselves crossed gender-linked occupational lines, or whether the parents provide encouragement to the child to do so. Furthermore, not all of the parental influence appears deliberate or positive, as some individuals express interests (and/or make choices) seemingly in contrast to the treatment afforded them by their parents.

It is also clear that early academic experiences influence vocational preferences and choices. Exposure to certain types of coursework (e.g., the physical sciences) in high school was cited as one of the reasons behind the selection of a particular vocation. Also, the level of performance in high school was related to the selection of certain vocations. It appears the development of vocational preferences and choices begins in the home and is nurtured by activities and interests experienced in high school.

Socioeconomic status has consistently emerged as an influential factor in the vocational interests of women. Women from families of low socioeconomic status tend to pursue more traditional occupations (e.g., teaching, clerical work, and selected blue collar jobs), while women from families of high socioeconomic status seemingly have more latitude in selecting vocations, with a relatively high proportion of women selecting nontraditional vocations. A few studies suggest that first or early-born children are more likely to enter nontraditional occupations than children born late in the birth order. Research from developmental psychology (Forer, 1969) indicates that first-born children often exhibit the highest level of intelligence of all their siblings, and nontraditional occupations for women (e.g., engineering, science) often require high levels of intellectual ability.

While the studies reviewed in this section have gender-related issues as the focal point of the research, the same pattern of results can be observed for other studies investigating the influence of life history factors on vocational behavior.

NON–GENDER-RELATED STUDIES

The studies comprising the body of literature span a 30-year period. While the researchers may have studied both men and women, gender-related issues (per se) were not of singular interest to the investigation. The studies previously reviewed that addressed gender-related issues tended to assess a few selected life history factors through a variety of nonstandardized surveys. The studies in this section are divided between studies predictive of specific occupations versus general predictive studies.

SPECIFIC PREDICTION STUDIES

Kulberg and Owens (1960) assessed a sample of 111 freshmen engineering majors with a 100-item BQ and the *Strong Vocational Interest Blanks*® (SVIB®). Subjects with a marked interest in engineering had a history of academic superiority and more satisfactory experiences with things and ideas than with people and social situations. This finding was more pronounced for subjects with interests in research engineering and less so for subjects with interests in sales engineering.

Nachmann (1960) studied male students in professional schools of law, dentistry, and social work. Nachmann found differential responses to BQ items by academic major. Lawyers and dentists reported stronger father figures, while social workers identified more with their mothers. Also, dentists were found to be more formally religious than either lawyers or social workers.

Albright and Glennon (1961) surveyed a sample of petroleum research scientists with a 484-item life history survey. The items were cross-validated against the criteria of rated job performance, creativity, and number of patents earned over a five-year period. The authors found 43 items that differentiated research scientists who desired administrative positions from those who aspired to remain as active scientists. Scientists with administrative aspirations had significantly higher overall performance ratings and creativity ratings, while scientists who wished to remain in research had a significantly greater number of patent disclosures. The pattern of predictive life history variables indicated research scientists were somewhat more introverted and work-oriented, while administrative aspirants were more outgoing and status seeking.

Chaney and Owens (1964) assessed 900 freshman engineering majors with interests in either sales, research, or general engineering, as measured by the Engineer scale of the SVIB, along with a 170-item life history questionnaire. Sales engineering interest was predicted by a liking for school in general, and was negatively related to enjoyment of natural and biological sciences. Individuals with high research interests enjoyed math and physical science courses and reported that their parents allowed them to participate in very limited social activities.

Werts (1968) studied the vocational interests of 76,000 male college freshmen as assessed through applications to the National Merit Scholarship Program. He wanted to determine what types of occupations get passed from father to son as determined by SVIB scores. Werts discovered that sons are most likely to pursue the occupation of their father in the physical sciences, social sciences, and the medical occupations within the biological sciences. However, the findings were limited by the relatively high percentage of students who had undecided vocational interests.

Klimoski (1973) administered Owens' BQ to 920 engineers employed in either R & D, management, or nonengineering positions. Ten life history factors were found to differentiate the three groups. Among the major findings were that R & D engineers scored the highest on having an impoverished childhood environment, professional orientation, and research interest orientation, while those individuals in nonengineering positions scored the lowest on these factors. Engineering managers scored the highest in favorable self-impression, while R & D engineers scored the lowest. Finally, individuals in nonengineering positions scored highest on athletic/physical activities, while R & D engineers scored the lowest.

Schoenfeldt (1974) was able to differentiate a sample of 1,934 college students majoring in either the arts or sciences (e.g., fine arts, social sciences) versus applied studies (e.g., agriculture, business). Subgroups formed on the basis of BQ responses in the freshman year differed with respect to membership and academic performance measurements taken four years later. The results were differentiated by gender. Males interested in arts or sciences scored high in intellectualism, academic achievement, and introversion, while males interested in applied studies scored high in control and adjustment and low on warmth, introversion, and radicalism. Females interested in arts or sciences scored high on academic achievement and maladjustment and low on popularity and social leadership. Females interested in applied studies scored high on warmth, simplicity, and social leadership and low on achievement, reading, and academic attitude.

GENERAL PREDICTION STUDIES

Eberhardt and Muchinsky (1982) assessed 437 female and 379 male college students with Owens' BQ and Holland's *Vocational Preference Inventory* (VPI). The subjects were classified into one of Holland's RIASEC types according to their vocational interests. The authors discovered that significantly different life history experiences differentiated the lives of the six vocational types. Up to 35 percent of the variance in the subjects' vocational interests could be explained by their life history experiences. For males, three discriminant functions differentiated Holland vocational types. Investigative males scored significantly higher in scientific interest and lower in social introversion and popularity than Social or Enterprising types. Artistic males scored significantly higher on independence/dominance than other vocational types. Social types scored significantly higher than Investigative and Conventional types on warmth of parental relations and significantly lower on negative social adjustment and religious activity. For females, two discriminant functions differentiated Holland vocational types. Investigative females scored the highest on scientific interest, academic achievement, positive academic attitudes, and socioeconomic status. Artistic females scored high in school and cultural activities and low in warmth of maternal and paternal relations and freedom from parental control. Effect sizes (ω^2) ranged from .02 to .16 for males and .02 to .19 for females for the differentiation of group membership on the basis of the life history factors.

Mumford and Owens (1982) correlated 389 BQ items with 22 basic interest scales of the SVIB on a sample of 847 males and 847 females. Results were reported for three scales. The authors found significant clusters of BQ items that differentiated scores on the business management, science, and adventure interest scales. Students interested in business management scored very high in sociability, leadership, acceptance of parental and social ideals, and material concerns. Students with science interests participated frequently in science courses and activities, had high academic achievement, and disliked verbal activities. Females expressing an interest in science rejected the social pressures of adolescence and exhibited a more mature and slightly more masculine pattern of behavior than females with low scientific interest. Students scoring high in adventure avoided conventional activities, exhibited a preference for nonroutine interests, and scored high in athletics and object manipulation.

Eberhardt and Muchinsky (1984) assessed the structural validity of Holland's hexagonal model of vocational interests via Owens' BQ. Factored life history items were used to predict RIASEC group membership for a sample of over 800 males and females. Hit rates (based on congruence between actual and predicted group membership) of 40.4 percent for males and 51.8 percent for females were found. Both hit rates far exceeded chance expectation. However, the results differed markedly by vocational type. For males, the hit rate was 59 percent for the Investigative and Enterprising types, but only 6 percent for the Conventional type. For females, the hit rate was 86 percent for the Social type, but 0 percent for the Enterprising and Conventional types. Errors of classification were *not* evenly distributed across the hexagonal model, with adjacent-type errors being more common than errors two steps or three steps removed in the model.

Neiner and Owens (1985) assessed the vocational choices of 531 females and 464 males three to four years after college. Owens' BQ factor scores were able to explain 24 percent of the variance in vocational choices for males and 20 percent for females, as indexed by ω^2. Neiner and Owens identified two discriminant functions that differentiated the vocational choices of females and males. For females, the first function reflected having a warm relationship with one's mother, having strong interest in both scientific and artistic subjects, and being less active than others in heterosexual social activities. The second function involved the expression of negative emotions, infrequent participation in physical activities and sports, and frequent participation in heterosexual social activities. For males, the first function reflected being noncompetitive and relatively less successful in academic endeavors. These men displayed little or no interest in science-oriented subject matter but were socially active and had many friends. The second function reflected poor academic achievers who had an attraction for physical activities and athletic events, with little or no interest in intellectual challenges. The authors noted research that reports that only 33 percent of males and 55 percent of females are engaged in the same vocation five years after college. As such, predicting the vocational choices of recent college graduates is like "trying to hit a moving target." The authors speculated that predictions of job choice may be more successful with older and more mature populations.

Mumford (1985) analyzed the relationship between life history information and SVIB scores for a sample of 847 male and 847 females, data originally collected as part of a study by Owens and Schoenfeldt (1979). The responses to a 389-item BQ were clustered on the basis of similarity of content and then correlated with the SVIB scale scores. Three vocational interest scales were of interest to Mumford (business management, sales, and office practices), reflecting a unified set of interests in the applied field. Interest in business management was correlated ($\bar{r} \cong .20$) with sociability, leadership, acceptance of parental and social ideals, and material concerns, and correlated ($\bar{r} \cong .10$) with parental sociability, parental socioeconomic status, and parental emphasis on achievement. Interest in sales was not as predictable as business management, but modest positive relationships were evidenced for material concerns, extroversion, and social conformity, and moderate negative relationships occurred for science courses and activities and general academic achievement. Interest in office practices was as predictable as interest in sales. Positive relationships were evidenced for social desirability and preference for structure, and negative relationships were found for independence and intellectual pursuits. Mumford hypothesized that success in clerical work is likely to require a willingness to follow standard operating procedures and carry out tasks defined by others. He believes the life history predictors of vocational interest illustrate the relationship between the characteristics of individuals and the demands occupations make and the rewards they offer.

Graef, Wells, Hyland, and Muchinsky (1985) conducted a study that examined a criterion other than vocational interest or choice, that of vocational uncertainty. Vocational uncertainty was indexed by three constructs: decidedness, identity, and maturity. The sample consisted of 97 female and 103 male undergraduate students. Owens' BQ factor scores produced R^2 values for decidedness, identity, and maturity of .33, .36, and .34 for females and .14, .16, and .31 for males, as measured by *My Vocational Situation,* the *Careeer Decision Scale,* and the *Career Development Inventory,* respectively. The vocationally uncertain male was found to have a high grade point average, be socially introverted and not well adjusted, and have little scientific interest. The vocationally uncertain female was found to have a low grade point average, a poor academic attitude, poor relationships with siblings, and a cold paternal relationship, and to participate in few high school or cultural activities.

Smart (1989) analyzed life history and vocational interest data from respondents to the 1971 and 1980 Cooperative Institutional Research Program surveys. Information was available on three Holland types: Investigative (490 individuals), Social (1,421), and Enterprising (707), including both males and females in the sample. Smart used causal modeling techniques to assess the effects of life history experiences on vocational interests. Vocational type development was found to be a function of a complex series of events resulting from family backgrounds and initial personal orientation. The relative importance of life history experiences varied among Investigative, Social, and Enterprising types. Family background was most influential in the development of Social types, while initial personal orientation, career aspirations, and educational preparation were most influential in the development of Investigative types. While Social types tend to be predominantly women from less affluent backgrounds and whose parents tend to be employed in social occupations, Investigative and Enterprising types tend to be men from more affluent backgrounds whose parents are not as likely to be employed in these occupational groups.

Reichel (1990) assessed the effect of life history experiences, sex-role orientation, and self-esteem on the vocational interests of 296 undergraduate female college students. Life history experiences were assessed via Owens' BQ, and vocational interests were assessed via the *Strong Interest Inventory*. Life history experiences were found to have a greater effect on vocational interests than either sex-role orientation or self-esteem. Investigative females exhibited much greater scientific interest and participated less in athletics, exhibited less social leadership and popularity, and were less feminine than Social females. Artistic and Enterprising women were most differentiated from the Investigative type. Artistic and Enterprising females exhibited much less scientific interest and academic achievement, had more younger siblings close to their age, and had lower socioeconomic status than Investigative females.

OVERVIEW

Research addressing life history antecedents of vocational interests and choices has produced consistent results. Life history experiences are associated with vocational interests not only across different types of vocations (e.g., artists vs. engineers) but also across different types of jobs within the same vocation (e.g., research vs. sales engineering).

Although researchers have used a wide variety of instruments to assess life history experiences, Owens' BQ provides a convenient framework for identifying those life history factors found most influential in the formation of vocational interests. Certain life history factors emerge that are common to both genders in affecting vocational behavior; some factors appear unique to each gender; and other life history factors do not appear to exert consistent or heavy influence on vocational behavior.

For both genders, academic achievement, academic interest, socioeconomic status, and parental control versus freedom appear to be the dominant life history factors affecting vocational interests. The literature shows that individuals who performed well in school, had parents who pushed for academic excellence, liked academic activities, and came from families with high parental educational levels were most influenced by these factors in the development of their own vocational interests. Such individuals tended to be interested in higher prestige, higher income, and more autonomous vocations than the population at large.

For males, athletic involvement, negative social adjustment, scientific interest, and warmth of parental relationship were found to exhibit significant effects on vocational interests. Males who expressed high negative social adjustment, had cool and aloof relationships with their parents, and had strong scientific interests tended to pursue vocations having greater involvement with things than with people. Conversely, males who participated in athletics, were well adjusted, exhibited little scientific interest, and were close to their parents tended to be attracted to vocations having more involvement with people than with things. The factors of sibling friction, extracurricular activities, religious activities, and social extroversion and popularity appear to be less influential, although some studies report the latter two factors did exert some mild influence on vocational interests.

For females, the factors of position in family, academic achievement, warmth of maternal relationships, religious activity, and social leadership and popularity appear to be most critical. Females who were first-born, were good students in high school, didn't get along with their mother, were not religiously active, and were not social leaders tended to pursue vocations that are nontraditional for women. Although measured in a variety of ways across the studies, the relationship females have with their mothers consistently emerges as being influential in their lives. The factors of warmth of paternal relationship, athletic participation, and school and cultural activities seem to exert less influence on vocational interests in general but are predictive of interest in artistic areas.

A broad perspective of this body of literature seems to suggest two general patterns of relationship between life history experiences and vocational behavior. The first and foremost pattern relates to the degree to which academic interests and pursuits played a major role in the life of the individual as a child. Individuals who as children performed well in school, liked school, and received parental support for their academic experiences tend to be interested in vocations that are characterized by higher degrees of status, prestige, and income than the population of vocations in general. This effect holds for both males and females.

The second pattern is gender specific. For males, interests tend to be directed either toward vocations that require greater involvement with people and social situations or toward vocations directed more toward involvement with things and ideas. Males who as children were close to their parents, well adjusted, and socially popular are inclined to be more interested in vocations requiring close interaction with people. Males who as children were distant from their parents, not well adjusted, and socially unpopular are more inclined to be interested in vocations requiring less interactions with people.

For females, the pattern is different than for males, and somewhat more complex. Females appear to have their vocational interests shaped more by their relationships with other people than do males. Compared to males, females are more influenced by the relationships they had with their siblings, mothers, and peers. Women are more likely to pursue nontraditional vocations (e.g., Investigative and Enterprising) if they experienced less positive social relationships in adolescence, while more positive social relationships are associated with interest in vocations traditional for women (e.g., Social and Conventional). It might be argued that the patterns of vocational interest development for males and females are equivalent but in opposite directions. That is, females are traditionally socialized to be interested in nurturing, people-oriented vocations, while males are not. However, I feel this conclusion would misrepresent the development of vocational interests. Vocations such as sales, for example, are just as traditional for males as would be engineering. However, for females, the degree of latitude in what is "traditional" is not so broad. Within the bounds of traditional interests, males seem to express interests along a continuum of vocations associated with different degrees of people involvement. For females, the boundaries of traditional vocations are more narrow, with the boundaries not being determined by just people-involvement parameters. Furthermore, the evolutionary process by which the vocational interests of men and women occurs seems to differ by gender. The vocational interests of women (particularly interests in the nontraditional vocations) appear to be strongly influenced by their relationships with other people, while the vocational interests of men do not appear influenced in this manner to such a comparable degree.

SUBSTANTIVE AND METHODOLOGICAL ISSUES

In this final section, I would like to address a number of substantive and methodological issues associated with biodata research on vocational behavior. In my opinion, these issues are critical to our understanding the constructs and processes we investigate.

Expanding the criteria. By far the most common criterion in this area of research is vocational interests, as typically measured by a standardized interest inventory such as the SVIB, VPI, or SII. Studies of vocational choice are relatively rare, with Neiner and Owens (1985) being a notable exception. Since the actual vocation individuals enter is a function of abilities and employment opportunities as well as interests, vocational choices are less predictable than vocational interests. Nevertheless, it appears advisable to expand our criteria beyond interests and choices. To date there has been but one study of vocational uncertainty (which did yield promising results). We should also study occupational satisfaction (apart from job satisfaction), as well as intra- and intervocational mobility. For example, Albright and Glennon (1961) successfully differentiated scientists who wanted to remain as active scientists versus those who aspired to administrative positions. Smart (1989) reported that Investigative types of people were more likely to aspire to Investigative occupations, while Enterprising types of people were more likely to aspire to careers in other types of occupations. In addition, we could more intensely study performance within an occupation, particularly the life history antecedents of outstanding performers or exemplars within an occupation. While the research published to date on vocational interests has provided us with a valuable body of literature, there are other constructs worth investigating that transcend interests.

Effect size. I feel the issue of effect size is particularly intriguing. I am of the opinion that the effect sizes for biodata predictors of vocational interests are large, and, in fact, may be larger than any other type of predictor. For example, Eberhardt and Muchinsky (1982) were able to account for 35 percent of the variance in the vocational interests of Investigative females on the basis of life history information. Reichel (1990) also found life history information to be more predictive of vocational interests than personality variables. Furthermore, the effect sizes appear to vary as a function of vocational type. Smart (1989) reported larger effect sizes for family background factors for Social types, while educational preparation had the largest effect on the development of Investigative types. Both the magnitude of the effect size and the particular patterning of the life history factors help to map the origins of vocational interest development across the various types.

Reliability and validity. The issues of reliability and validity are critical to all fields of psychological measurement, but seem particularly salient to predicting vocational interests from biodata. Vocational interest measurement can consist of indicating preference for a job title (e.g., chemist), or a description of the behaviors performed in that job (e.g., mixing chemicals in a laboratory). Let us assume an individual expresses interest in the field of chemistry. One item on Owens' BQ is, "In high school how much did you enjoy courses in each of the following areas?" One of the areas is science. In the classic criterion–related validity paradigm, scores on the predictor measure (i.e., the biodata item) are correlated with scores on the criterion measure (e.g., the question about chemistry). Evidence of the validity of the biodata item for predicting the response to the vocational interest question is shown by the size of the correlation between the two. Fiske (1978) has stated that reliability and validity are not distinct concepts, but reflect different points on a continuum. In the foregoing example, it could be argued that the correlation between the two items is a measure of the consistency (i.e., reliability) of the subject's response, since both deal with the individual's affective judgment of a single class of activity.

It is not my point to assert that biodata items lack validity. It is my point to assert that when both the predictor and criterion variable assess preference, and the objects in question are highly similar, we should be temperate in concluding that life history information is predictive of vocational interests, since in this example the two constructs are virtually identical in composition.

Analytic procedures. Most studies assessing the relationship between life history experiences and vocational interests have utilized correlational and multiple regression statistical analyses. One study (Smart, 1989) used causal modeling techniques and was able to partition the results into direct and indirect effects. For example, Smart found that 40 percent of the variance in socioeconomic status was exerted in an indirect manner. It appears that efforts to trace the process by which vocational interests develop are aided by the use of sophisticated analytic procedures, and that simpler analytic strategies run the risk of mischaracterizing this developmental process.

Assessing the role of the mentor. The typical life history questionnaire usually devotes several questions to the influence of parents in one's life. The vocational behavior literature has identified a critical life history experience (for some people) that serves to shape vocational interests, but is not typically included in life history questionnaires. That experience is the influence of a role model, mentor, or significant referent in a person's life, apart from parents, who was instrumental in affecting vocational interests. Given the frequency with which individuals cite others as influencing their choice of a vocation, it is somewhat surprising that such an omission in item specification has occurred. It is possible that the timing of this experience occurs *after* adolescence for some individuals, which is why it is not included in a survey of adolescent experiences. That is, some people adopt role models or mentors in college, shortly thereafter, or perhaps early in their first job. Nevertheless, many individuals have cited family members (uncles, aunts, siblings), neighbors, friends, teachers, and people reported in the media as inspiring them to select a particular vocation. I feel it could be potentially of great value to include such items in a biographical questionnaire. I believe they would have predictive value, and I also believe they would exhibit differential influences across vocational types.

Impact of negative life events. Many studies report findings that individuals were drawn to or *pulled toward* a particular vocation because of a parent they wished to emulate, positive experiences in childhood, and the like. However, a few studies have indicated that some individuals select vocations as a *push from* negative experiences in childhood, such as Lemkau (1984), who found males who entered traditionally female vocations as reporting a distant relationship with their father as a reason for their choice. Tyler (1965) noted the impact of negative life events on vocational interests, but to date this topic has not attracted a great deal of research. What little evidence we have on this topic suggests this phenomenon is most often found in Social type vocations. While we need more research on this topic in general, we have virtually no data at all on the satisfaction and vocational stability of these people.

Effect of value judgment and economic factors on nontraditional occupational preference. The labeling of occupations as *traditional* or *nontraditional* is in part a value judgment based on what one considers to be traditional (Hayes, 1986). Zuckerman (1981) and Fitzpatrick and Silverman (1989) noted that the so-called nontraditional occupational preferences of females in the 1970s weren't so nontraditional in the 1980s. If that trend continues, such preferences will be even less nontraditional in the 1990s. While we do not have equivalence of vocational preferences between males and females, societal changes in the past 30 years have greatly altered the social acceptability of crossing traditional gender lines in pursuing vocations. The effect of these social changes may serve to weaken the predictive relationships evidenced in the previous literature between differential life history experiences for men and women and their vocational preferences.

I also believe that economic as well as social factors may alter the pattern of predictability between life history experiences and vocational choice. Harmon (1989) suggested one reason more women are preparing for nontraditional jobs is that such jobs are associated with higher pay and better potential for advancement than the jobs traditionally held by women. Also, current economic conditions are such that two-income families are becoming increasingly more common, and problems of professional obsolescence are grossly skewed across the various occupations. Individuals enter and exit occupations for economic reasons in different patterns compared to the past. Changing national demographics have shifted to produce more single heads of households, individuals marrying later in life, and women bearing children later in life, compared to past cohorts. In short, the classic criterion variables of vocational preference and choice are undergoing considerable changes in this country. It should not be surprising to us to witness new predictive relationships between life history experiences and vocational criteria as broad-based societal changes filter down to the individual level of analysis.

Effects of "opportunity to engage." Mumford (1985) has proposed a cognitive social reinforcement conception as the theoretical basis for explaining how life history antecedents influence vocational interests. The theory proposes that vocational interests emerge as a result of an individual's engagement in occupationally relevant activities. "Subsequent positive or negative social reinforcement following engagement in these activities will facilitate or inhibit the individual's future engagement in these activities and his or her interests" (p. 30). Mumford interpreted his findings as suggesting a close relationship between inventoried interests in an occupational field and past behavior or experiences to the extent these are relevant to engagement and success in vocationally related endeavors. While I do not argue with this conclusion or interpretation, I believe we have underestimated the power of the "opportunity to engage" in the activities and experiences that influence vocational interests. Throughout my research in life history experiences I have been struck by the fact that biodata information measures more of *what one did* than *what one could have done*, that is, the concept of opportunity to engage. For example, adolescents in southern geographic areas have the opportunity to engage in outdoor activities year round because of the warm weather conditions, while adolescents in the more northern areas do not. Boys have more opportunity to participate in team sports than girls simply because there are more sporting events for boys than girls. Children raised in rural areas may develop a greater sense of independence than children raised in urban areas because there are fewer social and recreational activities for rural children. Warmth of paternal (or maternal) relations will be a meaningless life history factor for a child raised solely by the other parent. In short, I believe the cognitive social reinforcement perspective is correct—given the engagement in certain activities—but the initial opportunity to engage in certain activities greatly limits one's choices. As in personnel selection, one can only select from those applicants who have applied for a job. In vocational interest development, one can only nurture those activities and interests to which one is exposed. If my perspective is valid, we need to consider the range of opportunities afforded to individuals in tracing antecedents of vocational interest as well as how we grow from the activities we experienced.

Sample representativeness—educational. The issue of sample representativeness is a long-held concern in biodata research. Its effects are particularly acute in the area of vocational interests and choices. Because of the availability of advantageous samples, most biodata studies have examined college students. While we have amassed a large data base on college-educated people, we have scant information on people who terminate their education at high school or before. People who are factory workers, waitresses, secretaries, carpenters, plumbers, and so forth (i.e., the constellation of jobs that college graduates don't typically assume) are grossly underrepresented in biodata research. Not only is this a major shortcoming of biodata research in general, it also masks intergenerational vocational choices that we know exist from other bodies of research. For example, it is not uncommon for the coal mining industry to attract family members across many generations. There are complex sociologies of vocational choices among blue collar workers that biodata studies dwelling on college students have ignored. As a discipline we may have underestimated the magnitude and consistency of intergenerational vocational choices by excluding from our research those types of people for whom it is most prevalent.

Sample representativeness—cultural. Finally, the published research on biodata is derived almost exclusively from U.S. samples. We do not have much data on the lives of people from cultures other than our own. We do not know if the factorial structure of BQ items would generalize, if the same types or clusters of people (e.g., Schoenfeldt, 1974) would materialize, or if the associations between life history experiences and vocational behavior found for individuals from this country would hold elsewhere. As world events have painfully taught us, other cultures and nationalities of people don't necessarily think, behave, and hold the same values as Americans. We may discover there is a far stronger association between life history experiences and vocational behavior than we have come to believe if we could expand the arena in which we study both.

REFERENCES

Albright, L. E., & Glennon, J. R. (1961). Personal history correlates of physical scientists' career aspirations. *Journal of Applied Psychology, 45,* 281–284.

Auster, C. J., & Auster, D. (1981). Factors influencing women's choice of nontraditional careers: The role of family, peers, and counselors. *Vocational Guidance Quarterly, 29,* 253–263.

Berdie, R. F. (1944). Factors related to vocational interests. *Psychological Bulletin, 41,* 137–155.

Burlin, F. D. (1976). The relationship of parental education and maternal work and occupational aspiration in adolescent females. *Journal of Vocational Behavior, 9,* 99–104.

Chaney, F. B., & Owens, W. A. (1964). Life history antecedents of sales, research, and general engineering interest. *Journal of Applied Psychology, 48,* 101–105.

Eberhardt, B. J., & Muchinsky, P. M. (1982). Biodata determinants of vocational typology: An integration of two paradigms. *Journal of Applied Psychology, 67,* 714–727.

Eberhardt, B. J., & Muchinsky, P. M. (1984). Structural validation of Holland's hexagonal model: Vocational classification through the use of biodata. *Journal of Applied Psychology, 69,* 174–181.

Fiske, D. W. (1978). *Strategies for personality research.* San Francisco: Jossey-Bass.

Fitzpatrick, J. L., & Silverman, T. (1989). Women's selection of careers in engineering: Do traditional-nontraditional differences still exist? *Journal of Vocational Behavior, 34,* 266–278.

Forer, L. K. (1969). *Birth order and life roles.* Springfield, IL: Charles C. Thomas.

Graef, M. I., Wells, D. L., Hyland, A. M., & Muchinsky, P. M. (1985). Life history antecedents of vocational indecision. *Journal of Vocational Behavior, 27,* 276–297.

Green, L. B., & Parker, H. J. (1965). Parental influence upon adolescents' occupational choice: A test of Roe's theory. *Journal of Counseling Psychology, 12,* 379–383.

Greenfeld, S., Greiner, L., & Wood, M. M. (1980). The "feminine mystique" in male-dominated jobs: A comparison of attitudes and background factors of women in male-dominated versus female-dominated jobs. *Journal of Vocational Behavior, 17,* 291–309.

Hannah, J. A. S., & Kahn, S. E. (1989). The relationship of socioeconomic status and gender to the occupational choices of grade 12 students. *Journal of Vocational Behavior, 34,* 161–178.

Harmon, L. W. (1989). Longitudinal changes in women's career aspirations: Developmental or historical? *Journal of Vocational Behavior, 35,* 46–63.

Hayes, R. (1986). Gender nontraditional or sex atypical or gender dominant or...research: Are we measuring the same thing? *Journal of Vocational Behavior, 29,* 79–88.

Hayes, R. (1989). Men in female-concentrated occupations. *Journal of Organizational Behavior, 10,* 201–212

Holland, J. L. (1985). *Making vocational choices* (2d ed.). Englewood Cliffs, NJ: Prentice-Hall.

Houser, B. B., & Garvey, C. (1983). The impact of family, peers, and educational personnel upon career decision making. *Journal of Vocational Behavior, 23,* 35–44.

Jagacinski, C. M. (1987). Engineering careers: Women in a male-dominated field. *Psychology of Women Quarterly, 11*, 97–110.

Klimoski, R. J. (1973). A biographical data analysis of career patterns in engineering. *Journal of Vocational Behavior, 3*, 103–113.

Kulberg, G. E., & Owens, W. A. (1960). Some life history antecedents of engineering interests. *Journal of Educational Psychology, 51*, 26–31.

Lemkau, J. P. (1979). Personality and background characteristics of women in male-dominated occupations. A review. *Psychology of Women Quarterly, 4*, 221–240.

Lemkau, J. P. (1984). Men in female-dominated professions: Distinguishing personality and background characteristics. *Journal of Vocational Behavior, 24*, 110–122.

Mumford, M. D. (1985). The development of vocational interests: Life history antecedents of interest in three business careers. *International Journal of Management, 2*, 16–33.

Mumford, M. D., & Owens, W. A. (1982). Life history and vocational interests. *Journal of Vocational Behavior, 21*, 330–348.

Nachmann, B. (1960). Childhood experience and vocational choice in law, dentistry, and social work. *Journal of Counseling Psychology, 7*, 245–250.

Neiner, A. G., & Owens, W. A. (1985). Using biodata to predict job choice among college graduates. *Journal of Applied Psychology, 70*, 127–136.

Osipow, S. H. (1973). *Theories of career development* (3d ed.). Englewood Cliffs, NJ: Prentice-Hall.

Owens, W. A., & Schoenfeldt, L. F. (1979). Toward a classification of persons. *Journal of Applied Psychology, 64*, 569–607.

Peng, S. S., & Jaffe, J. (1979). Women who enter male-dominated fields of study in higher education. *American Educational Research Journal, 6*, 285–293.

Reichel, L. S. (1990). *Life history and developmental correlates of female vocational preferences: A multivariate study.* Unpublished doctoral dissertation, Iowa State University, Ames.

Roe, A. (1956). *The psychology of occupations.* New York: Wiley.

Schoenfeldt, L. F. (1974). Utilization of manpower: Development and evaluation of an assessment-classification model for matching individuals with jobs. *Journal of Applied Psychology, 59*, 583–595.

Smart, J. C. (1989). Life history influences on Holland's vocational type development. *Journal of Vocational Behavior, 34*, 69–87.

Standley, K., & Soule, B. (1974). Women in male-dominated professions: Contrasts in their personal and vocational histories. *Journal of Vocational Behavior, 4*, 245–258.

Super, D. E. (1957). *The psychology of careers.* New York: Harper & Row.

Tyler, L. E. (1965). *The psychology of human difference.* Englewood Cliffs, NJ: Prentice-Hall.

Werts, C. E. (1968). Paternal influences on career choices. *Journal of Counseling Psychology 15*, 48–52.

Zuckerman, D. M. (1980). Self-esteem, personal traits, and college women's life goals. *Journal of Vocational Behavior, 17*, 310–319.

Zuckerman, D. M. (1981). Family background, sex-role attitudes, and life goals of technical college and university students. *Sex Roles, 7*, 1109–1126.

Background Data and Development

Structural Issues in the Application of Life History Measures

Michael D. Mumford
George Mason University

Roni Reiter-Palmon
George Mason University

Andrea F. Snell
University of Georgia

Theories of human behavior differ in countless ways. Nevertheless, most theoretical efforts start with the proposition that behavior is a joint function of the individual and the situation (Schneider, 1987). One must recognize, however, that the individual attributes conditioning behavior do not arise in a vacuum. Rather, the historical accretions of past experiences and heredity leave individuals with a set of behavior predispositions conditioning the manner in which they perceive, select, act on, and react to their environmental surroundings (Buss, 1989; Kendrick & Funder, 1988; Magnusson, 1988). Fiske (1979) and Sontag (1971) note that unraveling the manner in which these historic accretions condition later behavior and experiences represents one of the more crucial tasks confronting developmental psychologists.

Due to their focus on current job performance, industrial psychologists have not, on the whole, been overly concerned with individual life history and its impact on differential development. An important exception to this rule may be found in the background data literature (Mumford & Owens, 1982; Mumford & Stokes, 1992). Background data items present people with a common set of questions concerning their behavior and experiences in certain kinds of situations likely to have occurred earlier in their lives (Mumford & Owens, 1987). In responding to these questions, people are asked to recall their typical behavior in, or reactions to, the referent situation and then select from the available response options the one that best describes the overall pattern of their prior behavior and experiences. This historic information concerning pertinent prior behavior and experiences is used to define a developmental pattern in which items or item response options are weighted on the basis of their ability to discriminate good and poor performances on the criteria of interest (Mumford & Owens, 1987). Subsequently, the individuals' fit to this quantitatively defined developmental pattern is used to make predictive statements about later job performance (Mumford & Owens, 1987; Schoenfeldt, 1974).

It is not at all surprising that industrial psychologists continue to employ this expressly developmental assessment technique. Prior reviews of the literature by Asher (1972), Ghiselli (1973), Mumford and Owens (1987), Owens (1976), and Reilly and Chao (1982) indicate that these quantitative patterns of developmental events represent highly effective predictors of differential job performance yielding cross-validities in the .30 to .40 range against criteria ranging from leadership performance to employee theft. Although few would dispute the predictive significance of the developmental information captured by background data items, rote application of this technique has been criticized (Mumford & Owens, 1987; O'Leary, 1973; Pace & Schoenfeldt, 1977; Schwab & Oliver, 1974; Wernimont, 1962).

An important source of many of these criticisms is the limited understanding of exactly why certain kinds of prior behavior and experiences enter into the definition of a meaningful developmental pattern. Without some kind of overarching substantive framework, it is difficult to specify the kind of developmental events likely to contribute to later performance or formulate procedures for effective measurement of these events. By virtue of its focus on developmental information as a potential source of predictive information, one might wonder, of course, whether our general understanding of differential development could be used to formulate principles pertinent to the construction and application of background data measures. Thus, the ensuing discussion will consider certain select issues in the developmental literature bearing on the application of background data.

DEVELOPMENTAL THEORY

MODELS OF DEVELOPMENT

Perhaps the most appropriate starting point for this discussion is to consider the general paradigmatic models commonly employed in attempts to understand the life course. Reese and Overton (1970) and Overton and Reese (1973) draw a distinction between two general kinds of models. *Organismic* models stress holistic movement toward a final end state in which hereditary and motivational factors lead to a series of progressive, stagelike transformations in behavior. Within organismic theories, environmental influences are viewed as moderators acting only to govern and channel this predetermined pattern of growth and change. The theories of Freud (1940), Erikson (1959), Kohlberg (1968), and Piaget (1950) all represent variations on this basic approach. In direct contrast, *elementalist* models typically do not assume a fixed pattern of movement to some idealized endstate. Instead, development is thought to proceed as a result of a combination of environmental events that, through mechanisms such as learning and skill acquisition, induce changes in people's behavior. Illustrations of this approach may be found in Skinner's (1957) work on language acquisition or Pines' (1987) discussion of the development of self-concepts. Although each theoretical model seems better suited for explaining some forms of behavior than others, strict organismic models have not proven widely applicable in the postadolescent years, when strong biomaturational influences diminish in importance and learning becomes progressively more important to individual development.

This statement should not be taken to imply, however, that current theories of adult development espouse a strict elementalist viewpoint. The contextual, dynamic, or strong interactional models of development stress the point that both biological and historic properties of the organism interact with environmental conditions in determining behavior and behavioral change. These dynamic interchanges lead to a sequence of progressive changes in the individual, just as the individual's perceptions of, selections of, reactions to, and actions on the environment lead to progressive changes in the environment confronting the individual (Lerner, 1978; Lerner & Tubman, 1989; Riegel, 1975; Tobach, 1981). Support for the tenets of the interactional models have been obtained in longitudinal studies by Block (1971), Caspi (1987), Elder and Clipp (1989), Magnusson

(1988), Thomas and Chess (1981), and Vaillant and McArthur (1972). In addition to this empirical support, recent theoretical work by Buss (1989), Bandura (1986, 1989) and Kendrick and Funder (1988), which emphasizes the individual's active construction of environments, the systematic action on situational features, and overt selection of alternative situations, further supports the applicability of the interactional theory to understanding differential development in adulthood. Given these varied sources of support, as well as the models' emphasis on the individual's construction of a life through active, purposeful, and meaningful situational interchanges, interactional models provide an especially appropriate heuristic for understanding life history in the context of background data measures.

ENVIRONMENTAL INFLUENCES

Strong interactional models invariably emphasize the importance of the environment in shaping people's lives. These models do not view the environment as a simple matter of randomized situational exposures. Rather, the environment is thought to represent an organized coherent whole. Thus, exposure to, potential entry into, and effective exploitation of certain kinds of situations occurs in a selective and integrated fashion, leading to ongoing and progressive change in both the individual and the character of his or her environment. This dynamic organization of the individual's environmental surround has a number of important implications for differential development.

To begin, Havighurst (1953) and Neugarten (1979) note that society imposes normative, age-related expectations concerning the kinds of situations to which people are exposed and their expected behavior in these situations. There are, for instance, strong normative expectations pertaining to schooling and requisite behaviors in the classroom environment. Similar normative expectations are also associated with more nebulous events such as marriage and child rearing. As a result, not all situations are open to people of all ages, and developmental importance of their behavior in these situations may vary with age and the developmental tasks imposed by society. This age grading of developmental tasks, when coupled with the progressive nature of individual development and the organized nature of the environmental surroundings, may result not only in some systematic discontinuities but also in the kind of phase- or stagelike transformations remarked upon by Levinson (1978). More centrally, however, Levinson's (1978, 1986) and Vaillant and McArthur's (1972) findings indicate that the individual's relative success in coping with these socially imposed developments may have a marked impact on later development (Brim & Ryff, 1980).

The age grading of behavior and experiences represents one way society imposes some organization on individual development and situational exposure while providing an important mechanism forwarding development and preparing individuals for later tasks. Another mechanism society employs in structuring situational exposures may be found in certain central life roles, such as sex, occupation, social class, and ethnic background. These roles are of substantial import as stable social stimuli, which vis-à-vis others' reactions and intrinsic role demands tend to channel situational exposures while interacting with normative expectations (Buhler, 1968; Tyler, 1978).

A third mechanism serving to structure situational exposures may be found in socially induced interdependency in situational exposures. That is, an individual cannot adopt the role of a lawyer unless he or she has graduated from high school and college and, following competition for access to this socially valued role, has been admitted to law school. After applying Project Talent data in a study of educational and occupational choices, Abeles, Steel, and Wise (1980) found that choices made relatively early in the course of people's lives tended to exert a marked impact on later development by prohibiting later role access. Similarly, in the case of vocational interest development, the work of Tyler (1965) has served to underscore the impact of activity rejection in channeling individual development away from certain kinds of situational exposures, especially those explicitly or implicitly linked to the rejected activity.

CONTINUITY AND CHANGE

Even granting that powerful environmental structuring mechanisms do exist, the strong interactionist position nevertheless suggests that the individual exists in a constant state of change, albeit coherent change. As Lerner and Tubman (1989) note, however, change in the individual does not necessarily imply a lack of coherence in differential behavior and experiences, nor does it imply a lack of differential stability in at least some attributes. As Schaie and Geiwitz (1982) point out, individuals tend to enter situations and select behaviors in these situations so as to maximize fit or congruence with extant characteristics. This not only minimizes demands for qualitative change but may also, over time and repeated selection of congruent situations, lead to developmental change which reinforces the individual's extant characteristics.

Some support for these notions may be found in Pulkkinen's (1982) study of a group of Finnish youth at ages 8, 14, and 20. Initially, 8-year-olds were assessed with respect to two variables: excitation and response control. Later assessments indicated that, despite shifts in environmental opportunities brought about by age grading, individuals commonly drifted into activities consistent with their patterning of excitation and control scores at age 8. In adolescence, excitable, uncontrolled individuals, for instance, tended to do poorly in school, use drugs and alcohol, and have many friends of the opposite sex. In another set of investigations, Gustafson (1987), Holland (1973), Neiner and Owens (1985), and Wesley (1989) have provided evidence indicating that individuals possessing certain personality characteristics selectively enter certain kinds of occupations and tend to display higher levels of performance and satisfaction when entering congruent, as opposed to incongruent, occupations. Similarly, Thomas and Chess (1981), in a study of temperament development, found that temperament was associated with maladjustment only when there was a poor fit between children's temperamental characteristics and environmental demands.

Additional support for these propositions may be found in a series of studies by Costa and McCrae (1976, 1977, 1980). Here, measures of neuroticism, openness, extroversion, agreeableness, and conscientiousness were administered to adults between ages 25 and 80 as part of the Baltimore Longitudinal Study. Ten-year retest reliabilities in the .50 to .80 range were obtained, indicating substantially more stability in adult personality than one might expect based on Mischel's (1968, 1973) observations. Similar results have been obtained by Mumford, Snell, and Hein (1993) in a longitudinal study of continuity and change in religious involvement. In this study, a series of structural equation models yielded stability coefficients in the .70 to .90 range, with moderators exerting progressively less impact on religious involvement as individuals aged.

Mumford, Wesley, and Shaffer (1987) have provided a potential explanation for this stability in adults' differential characteristics. They argue that, following a period of adolescent exploration, individuals will find a set of roles that are congruent with their characteristics and capable of facilitating personal adaptation. Subsequent repetitive entry into role-relevant activities will tend to develop those characteristics contributing to initial choice and adaptation, thereby inducing stability through a self-propagating pattern of environmental transactions. Furthermore, Abeles, Steel, and Wise (1980) note that situational exposure and initial adaptive efforts will contribute to emergence of the knowledge, skills, abilities, and personality characteristics, or human capital, required to perform well in certain classes of situations. The implied exploitation advantage here would tend to facilitate movement into other capital-relevant situations, while opportunity costs would drive individuals away from situations associated with or requiring capital demands different from those they possess. Finally, Caspi, Bem, and Elder (1989) have argued that others' expectations for role-appropriate and self-consistent behavior, as well as the individual's tendency to seek out, elicit, and attend to information congruent with one's self-concept, will tend to induce further stability in people's patterns of situational exposure and their behavior in these situations. In fact, Caspi (1987) and Caspi, Bem, and Elder (1989) have examined the impact of shyness and ill-temperedness on situational interchange and obtained some support for these interactional postulates using data gathered as part of the Berkeley Longitudinal Study.

Given the potential operation of all these mechanisms, there would seem to be substantial reason to expect stability in adult behavior, due to the self-limiting and self-propagating character of situational choice and activity preferences in a structured environment. The ability of developmental change to bring about differential stability has five other implications worthy of mention. First, certain attributes, such as intelligence (Terman & Oden, 1959), self-esteem (Bandura, 1989), attractiveness (Livson & Peskin, 1972), shyness (Caspi, Bem, & Elder, 1989), and personal control (Brandtstadter, 1989), may have a marked impact on both the attractiveness of and potential adaptation to the demands made by many situations that are themselves interdependent. Thus, measures of these kinds of attributes or events contributing to their development (McCrae & Costa, 1988) may prove to have some broad predictive power. Second, despite stable expression of these characteristics, situational changes and the age grading of behavior may lead to changes in the specific behavioral outcomes associated with these characteristics. This point has been illustrated in Brooks-Gunn, Rock, and Warren's (1989) and Costa and McCrae's (1977) studies of stability and change, as well as Hein and Mumford's (1988) finding that, although the outcomes of religious involvement varied with age, a relatively stable set of behaviors could be used to provide direct measures of religious involvement. Third, prediction and stability will depend on overall fit, along with the meaning individuals ascribe to situational exposure and behavior in a situation. These characteristics of the choice process may, in turn, result in the inclusion of extraneous, nonfunctional elements in an interactional pattern, while giving rise to maladaptive patterns of behavior resulting from misguided attributions concerning the self and significant situational features (Caspi, Bem, & Elder, 1989). Fourth, because individuals will differ in developmental history, available resources, and desired outcomes, different people will not necessarily ascribe the same meaning to a common situation, choosing to enter this situation for very different reasons, thereby producing distinct developmental patterns (Mumford, Snell, & Hein, 1993; Rauste-VonWright, 1986). Fifth, and finally, some characteristics, such as openness and self-monitoring, may increase the individual's likelihood of exposure to new situations or predispose the individual to seek new, hopefully more adaptive behavior patterns (Zuckerman, Bernieri, Koestner, & Rosenthal, 1989). Differences of this sort should, in turn, lead some individuals to be more volatile or malleable than others.

SITUATIONAL CHANGES

To this point, our discussion of development has emphasized the structured, predictable nature of situational exposures and the coherence arising from the individual's attempts to cope with these situational opportunities through a systematic and self-propagating pattern of choice behavior. This line of argument, however, ignores a particularly salient feature of life. The nature of the situations to which individuals are exposed may shift as a result of unanticipated events arising from past situational interchanges or socially induced discontinuities brought about by normal movement through the life course.

In a recent analysis of autobiographical data, Handel (1987) has marshaled a variety of biographical evidence indicating that chance exposure to unanticipated, new situations not only plays an important role in shaping differential development, but also tends to stand out in people's minds. Howe (1982) reached similar conclusions in an analysis of how unanticipated life events, such as illness, act to shape the careers of highly creative individuals. The developmental import and apparent diagnosticity of these unanticipated or chance events are, in some senses, not especially surprising, since they may encourage entry into new kinds of situations and lead to the development of new capacities. Furthermore, the structured nature of situations and situational dependencies may result in chance events having substantially more far-reaching consequences than one might otherwise anticipate. This point has been illustrated in a recent study by Elder and Clipp (1989), in which it was found that exposure to intense combat led not only to initial emotional and behavioral problems in the immediate postwar years but also to greater long-term resilience and coping skills as initial stress effects faded away. It should, however, be recognized that the effects induced by these chance events will, to some extent, also depend on the meaning imported to them, and, thus, while they may induce change, this change will not be completely independent of prior character (Bandura, 1982).

Chance encounters or unanticipated life events in this sense represent a potential source of growth and change. These events, however, also induce strong coping demands and carry some threat connotations by virtue of their novelty. Thus, unanticipated life events, especially those associated with strong adaptive demands, will induce some stress (Headley & Wearing, 1989) as well as growth. Prior research by Headley and Wearing (1989), Hotard, McFatter, McWhirter, and Steggall (1989), and Kahn and Antonucci (1980), however, suggests that the degree of debilitation observed will depend on the meaning ascribed to the event, its controllability, and personality attributes that would provide individuals with stabilizing buffers and strong competency beliefs.

These growth effects are not, however, solely a property of growth in response to discrete life events. As Erikson (1959) notes, society induces discontinuities in life, such as entry into the occupational world. Discontinuities may also arise when previous patterns of environmental transaction become maladaptive or outlive their usefulness (Levinson, 1986; Stokes, Mumford, & Owens, 1989). Under these conditions, individuals are likely to undergo substantial stress and display some growth as they seek new patterns of interchange capable of facilitating individual adaptation. Consequently, strong predictive statements may prove difficult to formulate. Some prediction, however, will be provided by buffering attributes—core characteristics, such as intelligence and self-esteem—that condition effective interaction in a variety of situations. Finally, the individual's prior pattern of environmental transactions, as it relates to demands in this new environment, might also prove of some general predictive value, since it can be anticipated that individuals will generally seek situations and activities in this new environment providing the best available fit with prior transactional patterns.

Not only do situations change due to chance events or developmental discontinuities, but historical forces also lead to changes in the nature and structure of situational opportunities. Traditionally, developmental psychologists have discussed these historic influences on situational exposures under the general rubic of *cohort effects*. Cohort effects represent an amalgam of many potential kinds of changes in situational exposure. For instance, cohort effects brought about by historic changes in situational exposure might arise from (a) changes in the frequency with which individuals are exposed to certain situations, (b) the emergence of new qualitatively different situations, (c) changes in the interdependencies among situations, (d) changes in the requirements for effective adaptation to situations, and (e) shifts in the rewards and punishments associated with various situations, roles, or behavioral acts.

Numerous prior studies (Elder, 1974; Schaie, 1984; Owens, 1953) have demonstrated the aggregate impact of these cohort effects on various forms of differential characteristics. These historic changes in situational opportunities can also have marked impact on the nature and structure of the life course, as illustrated by the effects of historic changes in women's roles. These observations, in turn, imply that there is not and cannot be a single, absolute mapping of people's lives. Rather, attempts to understand differential development in adulthood must take a relativistic, nonabsolute approach, recognizing the possibility of progressive coherence embedded in a system subject to ongoing change.

BACKGROUND DATA AND DEVELOPMENT

STABILITY

Because background data items focus on the recall of certain behavioral and experiential events, one might expect that our foregoing discussion of differential development would have some important implications for the construction and application of background data measures. In fact, the existence of cohort effects has some important implications for the stability concerns brought to the fore in prior reviews of the background data literature (Mumford & Stokes, 1992). Although few would dispute the predictive power of background data scales, the stability of prediction has been cause for concern. In a series of studies, Dunnette, Kirchner, Erickson, and Banas (1960), Roach (1971), and Wernimont (1962) reexamined the predictive power of items included in background data keys initially formulated by Kirchner and Dunnette (1957) and Minor (1958). It was found that items yielding significant prediction in initial keying efforts were not likely to maintain their predictive power when administered to new cohorts in later years.

Of course, many factors contribute to the stability of background data measures, including scaling procedures (Schoenfeldt, 1989), sample size (Schmidt, personal communication, 1988), capitalization on chance (Schwab & Oliver, 1974), and test security (Hughes, Dunn, & Baxter, 1956). Even granting adequate control for these influences, however, the existence of cohort effects indicates that there will be some intrinsic instability in any background data scale, due to changes in the nature and structure of situations contributing to differential development. Thus, there is a need to monitor changes in item predictive power and periodically revise scales to control for potential cohort effects. As a rule of thumb, it would seem prudent to reestablish item predictive power every five to ten years, shortening this interval whenever there have been changes in the applicant pool or when changes in the job environment have led to shifts in position requirements or potential rewards.

Cohort effects might arise from many sources, ranging from the addition of new developmental events (e.g., television) to changes in the rewards and punishments associated with actions taken in certain situations (e.g., marijuana use in 1970 and 1990). Although research pertinent to this point is not available, one might expect items to differ in their sensitivity to cohort effects, whereas various kinds of cohort effects might differ in terms of their impact on predictive stability. For instance, items focusing on simple situational exposure or fixed situational outcomes may display greater instability than items focusing on the behaviors, reactions, and motivations associated with situational entry. Similarly, given the evidence compiled by Hall and Jones (1950) and Deeg and Paterson (1947) concerning the historic stability of occupational demands and reinforcers, it seems likely that items targeted on enduring situations that call for the application of job-relevant capacities would display greater stability than items focusing on social attributes and demographic characteristics.

Some support for this notion may be found in Brown (1978). Using background data items constructed in 1933 to predict sales performance, he reassessed the predictive power of these items using individuals hired in 1968 and 1971. Stable prediction was produced by items examining life events such as organizational membership, offices held in organizations, amount of life insurance owned, and number of dependents. Because these items reflect factors such as extroversion, sociability, dominance, and financial need, which are likely to be central to sales performance, these findings are not at all surprising. They do suggest that predictive stability might be improved by targeting items on historically stable life situations (e.g., organizational membership) calling for or contributing to the development of occupationally relevant skills and motivational characteristics.

PREDICTIVE CONSTRUCTS

Our comments with regard to predictive stability lead to a second question of some practical significance. More specifically, one might ask what the nature of differential development tells us about the kind of constructs that might prove useful to measure through background data items. Given Abeles, Steel, and Wise's (1980) observations concerning the importance of human capital or personal resources in guiding movement into various situations, it would seem useful to focus background data items on prior behavior and experiences expressing or contributing to the development of job-relevant knowledge, skills, abilities, and personality constructs required for or contributing to the effective performance of core occupational tasks, as opposed to specific features of the job situation. While we would not dispute this conclusion, it should be recognized that occupations and job situations differ in the rewards they provide and the values they encourage. Mumford and Stokes (1992) have underscored the significance of these motivational influences in performance prediction, and so it would seem desirable to formulate items reflecting an attraction to and liking for prior life situations involving the expression of these values, goals, or reward preferences.

This extended human capital approach is, of course, likely to prove useful in many situations. One should recognize, however, that new jobs often involve a major life transition for individuals in which they are confronted with multiple new situations, and resources for coping with these new situational demands must be developed. Under these conditions, new kinds of predictive dimensions concerned with attributes capable of facilitating developmental growth are likely to come into play. Here, dimensions such as self-esteem (Bandura, 1989), practical intelligence (Sternberg & Wagner, 1986), conscientiousness (Costa & McCrae, 1980), ego control (Block, 1971), resistance to stress (Pulkkinen, 1982), openness to new experiences (McCrae & Costa, 1987), and certain social skills (Snyder, 1974) may play an important role in conditioning a favorable developmental trajectory. In fact, some support for this notion may be found in Bray, Campbell, and Grant's (1974) study of managerial lives. Here, it was found that *enlargers,* who engage new situations, displayed better adaptation to managerial jobs than *enfolders,* who withdraw from new situations, despite comparability in initial assessments of managerial potential. Similar findings have been reported by Russell and Domm (1990) and by Russell, Mattson, Devlin, and Atwater (1988).

A third kind of predictive construct suggested by the developmental literature pertains to assessment of the self-system or self-concepts by which individuals import meaning to events occurring in their lives. Kuhnert and Russell (1990) have made a similar point, using a stage theory of development in which individuals progress to broader, less personal subject–object relations. Although we question the value of stage theories, the issue at hand is an important one, and, given the personal fit model implied by the strong interactionist approach, overlap of self-concepts with job demands may provide a useful source of predictive information. Although techniques for defining *core meaning* constructs are in their infancy (Krietler & Krietler, 1987; Little, 1987), one approach might involve assessing affective, evaluative reactions to prior situations and behavior in these situations that are analogous to crucial aspects of the job. Alternatively, one might contrast the life experiences of motivated, satisfied individuals with the less satisfied or motivated and use the resulting differences to define core meaning dimensions.

Prior to concluding this section, two other kinds of predictive constructs suggested by the developmental literature need to be considered. First, as noted earlier, situational choices exist in an integrated network. Thus, developmental constructs, which have the ability to markedly shape initial environmental transactions by providing individuals with crucial values or capacities, may have substantial predictive value. This point has been illustrated in a recent study by McCrae and Costa (1988), who found that broad personality dimensions such as neuroticism, extroversion, openness, agreeableness, and conscientiousness were strongly related to dimensions of parental warmth, parental control, and parental attention. Interestingly, these same three dimensions have emerged in multiple factor analyses of background data items, and so there is reason to suspect that they reflect crucial aspects of parental behavior. It should, however, be recognized that other aspects of family life (e.g., sibling relations), early socialization (childhood peers), and initial schooling (teachers' attitudes) may also be of some import in this regard. Finally, because the developmental literature emphasizes the importance of choice, especially the channeling effects brought about by rejections of certain situational or behavioral alternatives, it might prove useful to seek dimensions and items indicating a dislike for or unwillingness to undertake the kind of activities called for on a job (Reiter-Palmon, DeFilippo, & Mumford, 1990; Tyler, 1965).

ITEM CHARACTERISTICS

Not only does the developmental literature provide guidance concerning the kinds of constructs that might be profitably assessed using background data items, it also has some important implications with respect to item characteristics. Perhaps the most important of these pertains to the contextualistic nature of background data items. Because individual development proceeds as a result of situational interaction, background data items should focus on people's behavior and experiences in a situational context. This observation, in turn, suggests that in defining situations in which construct-relevant behavior and experiences will be assessed, an attempt should be made to identify situations in which expression of construct-relevant behavior and experiences are crucial to situational entry and/or behavior in these situations. It should be recognized that many constructs are likely to condition behavior and experiences in any situation, and these same behaviors and experiences might contribute to the development of multiple constructs. Thus, to ensure accurate assessment of the construct at hand, an attempt should be made to identify multiple eliciting situations (Epstein & O'Brien, 1985). Typically, adequate measurement will require an assessment of behavior and experiences in 10 to 15 situations (Mumford & Owens, 1987).

The situational bounding of background data items constitutes an advantageous characteristic with regard to both realism and recall. This situational bounding, however, may constitute something of a problem when differential statements require comparability and when individuals have not been exposed to comparable environments. For instance, the age grading of developmental tasks and behavioral expectations implies that people of different ages may not have been exposed to similar situational opportunities, nor will their behavior in these situations necessarily have identical implications. Ferguson (1967) has provided a classic illustration of this principle by noting that owning $10,000 of insurance does not have the same meaning at 25 and 55. Thus, in generating item specifications, attention must be given to the age range of the target population and their common experiences during the course of development.

This point also pertains to other kinds of social stereotyping, such as race and sex, that might influence situational exposure or behavior in these situations. Under these conditions, an attempt might be made to generate items equally applicable to the members of all groups or, alternatively, one might develop group-specific measures. Based on the comments of Reilly and Chao (1982) and Hunter and Hunter (1984), it appears that the former strategy is effective in controlling race differences due to obvious marked commonalities in the course of differential development. For males and females, however, this strategy may prove more problematic, especially when the construct at hand is heavily sex-typed, resulting in difficulties in identifying common items. Under these conditions, within-group scaling may be necessary.

In specifying situations eliciting pertinent behaviors and experiences, four other points should be kept in mind. First, our intent in constructing background data measures is to describe differential development. Thus, one should avoid extremely powerful, low locus of control situations in which the individual has little discretion in potential behavior and experiences, since here behavior and experiences are a property of the situation, not the individual's interchange with this situation. Second, situations should be sought where there is relatively little ambiguity about exactly what is of concern. Third, because other people constitute a key aspect of many interpersonal situations, one might wish to target some questions on other peoples' relations to the individual's behavior. Fourth, given the fact that prediction diminishes over time in accordance with a simplex structure (Fleishman & Mumford, 1989; Owens, 1978), it may prove desirable to focus items on proximate situations.

When generating items intended to assess one or more performance-relevant constructs, investigators might employ either a direct or an indirect approach. In the direct approach, items are formulated to capture prior behavior and experiences that would reflect direct outcomes of the constructs in the situations at hand. The indirect approach, on the other hand, attempts to identify behavior and experiences in situations that would contribute to development of the construct. Although both these item development strategies have been profitably employed in prior research (Mumford & Stokes, 1992) and need not be treated as mutually exclusive approaches, recent research by Redmond and Nickels (1989) has shown that these two kinds of items display different characteristics. In an empirical keying study examining criteria, such as academic achievement and social adjustment, they found that both approaches yielded effective prediction. However, a larger number of items was required when the indirect approach was in use, due to the many factors contributing to development of these complex criterion constructs. These indirect items, however, were found to be less transparent and therefore potentially robust with respect to faking (Lautenschlager, 1985).

Our foregoing observations point to an important application of developmental theory in background data research. Traditionally, discussions of item characteristics have focused on manifest content issues, such as objectionability, verifiability, and response option characteristics (Asher, 1972; Barge, 1988; Owens, Glennon, & Albright, 1962). We do not wish to debate the value of this research with regard to item construction. We do, however, wish to point out that it might prove useful to approach item construction issues from a developmental perspective, as illustrated in the Redmond and Nickels (1989) study.

One particularly promising avenue applying this developmental process approach would be a search for key events. More specifically, given the embedded contingencies implied by some situational exposures, it seems likely that items that assess multiple exposures will prove to be useful predictors. Similarly, the importance of situational choice within this developmental framework suggests that it might be useful to appraise dislike for others engaging in certain behaviors. Alternatively, one might examine the predictive power of items reflecting willingness to enter or liking for situations comparable to those found on the job.

In addition to these relatively straightforward process implications, this developmental framework suggests a number of other kinds of item characteristics that might be profitably examined. One might, for instance, contrast the predictive power of human capital and motivational items in predicting different kinds of criteria. In a related vien, one might contrast affective, reactive items to performance capacity items. On a somewhat more subtle level, where there is a concern with predicting growth, the utility of items formulated to appraise perceptions of and reactions to novel situations occurring earlier in people's lives or items that draw out the specific resources used to adapt to these situations might be assessed.

Although other examples of this sort might be described, one particularly significant issue bears on the importance of unusual, rare, or chance events in conditioning the life course. It was noted earlier that events of this sort appear to play a crucial role in shaping people's lives. Unfortunately, due in part to the pattern dependence of these effects and in part to the use of parametric procedures, the utility of background data items intended to capture these non-normal developmental influences has received little attention in the literature. Thus, techniques are required for specifying when items of this sort will be pertinent to performance prediction and how one should go about applying this descriptive information.

ITEM GENERATION AND APPLICATION

Although the principles of human development discussed above have some important implications for the characteristics of background data items, they also suggest some alternative techniques that might be used in generating items intended to measure certain kinds of performance-relevant constructs. Mumford and Owens (1987) note that three basic techniques might be used in generating background data items: (a) the known predictive characteristics and factor loadings of these items, (b) developmental or general psychological theory, and (c) information gathered from incumbents through interviews or other life-record techniques. Given the availability of relatively powerful developmental theories intended to describe the ontogeny of certain characteristics such as authoritarianism and self-esteem, it would seem appropriate to apply this literature in formulating both direct and indirect item specifications.

Although theory and prior research findings may provide a useful basis for many item generations, in many applied situations the nature of the constructs at hand may prohibit efficient application of this approach. Under these conditions, Russell and Domm (1990) and Russell, Mattson, Devlin, and Atwater (1988) note that retrospective life history essays might provide a cost-efficient and apparently effective method for generating background data items. Typically, this approach begins by presenting people with definitions of each dimension, and subsequently they are asked to write essays about their behavior in prior situations in which this attribute had an impact on performance.

Because current theory in differential development indicates that individuals have adequate recall of prior life events relevant to self-concepts and performance, this approach seems well justified. The theoretical issues sketched out earlier, however, suggest certain extensions of this technique that might prove useful. First, prior research, while supporting the accuracy of autobiographical descriptions (Bronson, Katten, & Livson, 1959; Costa & McCrae, 1988; Shaffer, Saunders, & Owens, 1986), nonetheless indicates that certain types of information tend to be recalled. More specifically, people seem better able to recall prior life events of some import with regard to their self-concept, but they have difficulty in specifying the exact timing of events and subtle emotional reactions (Freeman, Csikszentmihalyi, & Larson, 1986; Handel, 1987). Furthermore, information recalled appears to be organized around existing self-concepts, not the self-concept operating at the time of the event (Handel, 1987). Although this does not necessarily indicate a problem with retrospective essay techniques, at least when applied in samples whose self-concepts have stabilized and are reinforced by self-propagating patterns of environmental transactions, this—with the foregoing observations—does suggest a need for research delineating the kinds of information captured by essay techniques vis-à-vis that which might be obtained from other sources.

Not only does the theory sketched out here indicate the need for some research specifying the kind of information captured by different item generation techniques, it suggests some promising new techniques for item generation. One potentially useful approach would be to identify the key roles more or less successful employees filled at different points in their lives, and the roles or role-relevant activities differentiating more and less successful individuals might then be used to provide guidelines for item generation. Another potentially promising approach would be to specify items based on their ability to condition exposure to multiple situations contributing to development of a given construct. In cases in which the primary concern at hand was adaptation to a new environment, prior life transitions might be identified, and items intended to measure the effective expression of relevant constructs might then be formulated by asking about pertinent behaviors and experiences in these transitory periods. Finally, individuals might be presented with construct definitions and asked to generate critical incidents describing situations and behaviors in which application of this construct proved crucial to personal adaptation or well-being.

It should be recognized that current research in differential development has some important implications for the application of these item generation techniques and, more broadly, background data items. Research by Chandler, Boyes, Ball, and Hala (1987) using story problems indicates that young children do not organize self-relevant information in a narrative biographical form. Rather, this capacity emerges only as individuals reach the later stages of concrete operations or the early stages of formal operations. Thus, there seems to be little point in seeking biographical information from children much below the age of 9 or 10. On the other hand, the exploratory nature of adolescent behavior and experiences and the relatively slow emergence of self-propagating patterns of environmental transactions suggests that background data items should not be used to make strong predictors until individuals have reached late adolescence.

The need for coherent, self-propagating patterns of environmental transactions also points to the other issues in the generation and application of background data measures. First, when there is substantial variability in the situations posed by a job such that adaptive demands are changing rapidly over time, it may prove difficult to apply background data measures in performance prediction, except under conditions where item content focuses on constructs facilitating adaptation to new situations. Second, the utility of background data items will decline whenever broader environmental changes have led to marked disruptions in the individual's prior pattern of environmental transactions. Third, in generating and applying items, item content focusing on adaptation to these social situations should be applied to enhance the stability of prediction.

With regard to the general application of background data items, one further implication of developmental theory merits some consideration. In essence, when background data items predict, our foregoing observation· indicate that they capture elements of a general pattern of differenti: development, which somehow contributes to differential performance ·· the predictive situation. This rather straightforward observation has tw important implications. First, in item generation and application, attempt should be made to obtain an accurate assessment of people's li history as they perceive it and act on the basis of these perceptions. Thu although endemic distortion may not be a salient problem, every attemp. should be made to minimize intentional faking through the use of techniques such as stereotype masking, control keys, and the inclusion of verifiable items. Further, when items are developed in a concurrent setting, it would seem desirable to reestablish their validity in a predictive setting in which there are substantial incentives for faking. Second, it should be recognized that not all forms of performance differences are attributable to differential developmental influences. For instance, high turnover might be attributed to poor pay or a highly aversive climate rather than to the attributes of a person and his or her developmental history. Under these conditions, there is obviously little point to applying background data items in performance prediction.

SCALING

Perhaps the most clear-cut implication that can be drawn from the developmental literature as it pertains to item scaling concerns the notion of fit. As Lerner and Lerner (1983) point out, a strong interactional model implies that the outcomes of situational entry depend on the fit of people's developed characteristics to the adaptive demands made by the situation. Because virtually all techniques for scaling background data items seek weights for multiple items or item dimensions reflecting relationships with criterion performance, and the individual's fit to this idealized score pattern provides a basis for selection, it appears that most current scaling procedures are in line with developmental theory.

Beyond this general conclusion, however, the developmental literature has a few additional implications for application of our more common scaling procedures. With regard to empirical keying, two points come to the fore. First, patterns should be defined with respect to the criterion construct, not a single operationalized criterion measure that is subject to some degree of deficiency, contamination, and bias. Thus, to ensure effective and stable prediction, substantial effort should be devoted to criterion measurement and careful assignment of individuals to the high and/or low performers categories. Second, percentage weighting keying strategies should be preferred to pattern weighting whenever it is anticipated that relatively rare events will have a significant impact on the development of differential performance capacities. However, when these conditions do not apply, the bulk of the psychometric literature argues for the application of pattern weighting techniques (Mumford & Owens, 1987).

In recent years, rational scales have emerged as a viable alternative to the more traditional empirical keying procedure (Schoenfeldt, 1989; Schrader, 1975; Uhlman, Reiter-Palmon, & Connelly, 1990). Perhaps the most salient implication of developmental theory in this regard concerns the generation of alternate strategies for formulating rational scales. The procedures typically employed in rational scaling group items into clusters based on manifest similarity in item content or underlying theoretical considerations. Our foregoing observations, however, suggest that from time to time it may prove profitable to consider alternative strategies for grouping items, such as similarity in the outcomes of situational entry and crucial demands for adapting to new situations. Beyond expanding the construct frameworks underlying rational scaling, we believe that our preceding observations might explain a puzzling finding. Recently, Schoenfeldt (1989) contrasted strict rational scales with post hoc rational scales constructed using procedures piloted by Mumford and Owens (1982) involving the assessment of intraitem and item–criterion relationships. He found that the post hoc rational scales performed somewhat better than rational scales. This finding might be explained by the many complex factors capable of influencing differential development and the need for some sensitivity to local situational influences in formulating content scales.

With regard to factorial scaling and subgrouping, one relatively straightforward point comes to the fore. More specifically, as illustrated in our discussion of adaptation to new situations, careful application of developmental principles may do much to spur the application of confirmatory factor analytic and causal modeling procedures in the construction of background data measures. Some caution must be exercised in efforts along these lines, however, because developmental theory, the formulation of coherent patterns of interchange, and the notion of fit to the environment provide a compelling argument for the extended application of subgrouping procedures. If these subgroups display different causal structures, as illustrated in a recent study by Mumford, Snell, and Hein (1993), then aggregate average-person structures may be somewhat distorted. More centrally, these observations suggest that Schoenfeldt's (1974) and Owens and Schoenfeldt's (1979) assessment classification, looking at prediction through subgroup–environment fit, deserves substantially more attention than it has received to date.

CONCLUSION

Our observations should not be taken as an absolute definitive statement on the potential applications of developmental theory to background data. Rather, our intent was to delineate the existence of a strong, substantive relationship between the principles of differential development and the characteristics of background data measures. Not only does it appear that a strong relationship exists that has some heuristic value in attaining an understanding of background data measures, it also appears that developmental theory has some promise as a vehicle for extending current theory and methods.

Taken by themselves, these observations should be sufficient to convince both researchers and practitioners that truly effective application of background data measures demands some attention to the principles of differential development. To some, this may represent a troublesome reorientation. It should, however, be recognized that application of this approach may serve to provide a much-needed, substantive foundation to our measurement efforts. In addition, the comments of Costa and McCrae (1988), Fiske (1979), and Mumford and Owens (1982) point to an important, albeit often overlooked advantage of substantively oriented background data measures. More specifically, by using well-constructed item pools intended to capture the developmental antecedents of performance, we shall acquire a new information base likely to prove crucial in enhancing our understanding of the nature and ontogeny of human performance.

We would like to thank Bill Owens, Bernie Nickels, Tim Clifton, Shane Connelly, and Ed Fleishman for their comments concerning earlier drafts of this manuscript.

REFERENCES

Abeles, R. P., Steel, L., & Wise, L. L. (1982). Patterns and implications of life-course organization: Studies from Project Talent. In P. B. Baltes & O. G. Brim, Jr. (Eds.), *Life span development and behavior.* New York: Academic Press.

Asher, E. J. (1972). The biographical item: Can it be improved? *Personnel Psychology, 25,* 251–269.

Bandura, A. (1982). The psychology of change encounters and life paths. *American Psychologist, 37,* 747–755.

Bandura, A. (1986). *The social foundations of thought and action.* Englewood Cliffs, NJ: Prentice-Hall.

Bandura, A. (1989). Human agency in social cognitive theory. *American Psychologist, 44,* 1175–1184.

Barge, B. N. (1988). *Characteristics of biodata items and their relationship to validity.* Unpublished doctoral dissertation, University of Minnesota, Minneapolis.

Block, J. (1971). *Lives through time.* Berkeley, CA: Bancroft.

Brandstadter, J. (1989). Personal self-regulation of development: Cross-sequential analyses of development-related control beliefs and emotions. *Developmental Psychology, 25,* 96–108.

Bray, D. W., Campbell, R. J., & Grant, D. L. (1974). *Formative years in business.* New York: Wiley.

Brim, O. G., Jr., & Ryff, C. D. (1980). On the properties of life events. In P. B. Baltes & O. G. Brim, Jr. (Eds.), *Life span development and behavior* (Vol. 3). New York: Academic Press.

Bronson, W. C., Katten, E. S., & Livson, N. (1959). Patterns of authority and affection in two generations. *Journal of Abnormal and Social Psychology, 58,* 143–152.

Brooks-Gunn, J., Rock, D., & Warren, M. P. (1989). Comparability of constructs across the adolescent years. *Developmental Psychology, 25,* 51–60.

Brown, S. H. (1978). Long-term validity of a personal history item scoring procedure. *Journal of Applied Psychology, 63,* 673–676.

Buhler, C. (1968). The course of human life as a psychological problem. *Human Development, 11,* 1–15.

Buss, A. H. (1989). Personality as traits. *American Psychologist, 44,* 1378–1388.

Caspi, A. (1987). Personality in the life course. *Journal of Personality and Social Psychology, 53,* 1203–1213.

Caspi, A., Bem, D. J., & Elder, G. H. (1989). Continuities and consequences of interactional styles across the life course. *Journal of Personality, 57,* 375–406.

Chandler, M., Boyes, M., Ball, L., & Hala, S. (1987). The conservation of selfhood: A developmental analysis of children's changing conceptions of self-continuity. In T. Honess & K. Yardley (Eds.), *Self and identity: Perspectives across the life span.* New York: Rutledge & Kegan Paul.

Costa, P. T., & McCrae, R. R. (1976). Age differences in personality structure: A cluster analytic approach. *Journal of Gerontology, 31,* 564–570.

Costa, P. T., & McCrae, R. R. (1977). Age differences in personality structure revisited: Studies in validity, stability, and change. *International Journal of Aging and Human Development, 8,* 261–275.

Costa, P. T., & McCrae, R. R. (1980). Still stable after all these years: Personality as a key to some issues in adulthood and old age. In P. B. Baltes & O. G. Brim, Jr. (Eds.), *Life span development and behavior.* New York: Academic Press.

Costa, P. T., & McCrae, R. R. (1988). Personality in adulthood: A six-year longitudinal study of self-reports and sparse ratings on the NEO Personality Inventory. *Journal of Personality and Social Psychology, 54,* 853–863.

Deeg, M. E., & Paterson, D. G. (1947). Changes in the social status of occupations. *Occupations, 25,* 205–208.

Dunnette, M. D., Kirchner, W. K., Erickson, J., & Banas, P. (1960). Predicting turnover among female office workers. *Personnel Administration, 23,* 45–50.

Elder, G. H. (1974). *Children of the Great Depression.* Chicago: University of Chicago Press.

Elder, G. H., & Clipp, E. C. (1989). Combat experience and emotional health: Impairment and resilience in later life. *Journal of Personality, 57,* 311–342.

Epstein, S., & O'Brien, E. J. (1985). The person–situation debate in historical and current perspective. *Psychological Bulletin, 98,* 513–537.

Erikson, E. H. (1959). Identity and the life cycle. *Psychological Issues, 1,* 18–164.

Ferguson, L. W. (1967). Economic maturity. *Personnel Journal, 46,* 22–26.

Fiske, D. W. (1979). Two worlds of psychological phenomena. *American Psychologist, 34,* 733–739.

Fleishman, E. A., & Mumford, M. D. (1989). Individual attributes and training performance. In I. L. Goldstein & Associates (Eds.), *Training and development in organizations.* San Francisco: Jossey-Bass.

Freeman, M., Csikszentmihalyi, M., & Larson, R. (1986). Adolescence and its recollection: Toward an interpretive model of development. *Merrill-Palmer Quarterly, 32,* 167–185.

Freud, S. (1940). *Outline of psychoanalysis.* New York: Norton.

Ghiselli, E. E. (1973). The validity of aptitude tests in personnel selection. *Personnel Psychology, 26,* 461–477.

Gustafson, S. B. (1987). *Person and situation subgroup membership as predictors of job performance and job perceptions.* Unpublished doctoral dissertation, Georgia Institute of Technology, Atlanta.

Hall, J., & Jones, D. C. (1950). Social grading of occupations. *British Journal of Sociology, 1,* 31–55.

Handel, A. (1987). Personal theories about the life span development of one's self in autobiographical self-presentations of adults. *Human Development, 30,* 83–98.

Havighurst, R. (1953). *Human development and education.* New York: Longman.

Headley, E. Y., & Wearing, A. (1989). Personality, life events, and subjective well-being: Toward a dynamic equilibrium model. *Journal of Personality and Social Psychology, 57,* 731–739.

Hein, M. B., & Mumford, M. D. (1988). *Continuity and change in religious involvement.* Paper presented at the annual meeting of the American Psychological Association, Atlanta.

Holland, J. L. (1973). *Making vocational choices: A theory of careers.* Englewood Cliffs, NJ: Prentice-Hall.

Hotard, S. R., McFatter, R. M., McWhirter, R. M., & Stegall, M. E. (1989). Interactive effects of extravention, neuroticism, and social relationships on subjective well-being. *Journal of Personality and Social Psychology, 57,* 321–331.

Howe, M. J. (1982). Biographical evidence and the development of outstanding individuals. *American Psychologist, 37,* 1071–1081.

Hughes, J. F., Dunn, J. F., & Baxter, B. (1956). The validity of selection instruments under operating conditions. *Personnel Psychology, 9,* 321–324.

Hunter, J. E., & Hunter, R. F. (1984). Validity and utility of alternative predictors of job performance. *Psychological Bulletin, 96,* 72–98.

Kahn, R. C., & Antonucci, T. C. (1980). Convoys over the life course: Attachment, roles, and social support. In P. B. Baltes & O. G. Brim, Jr. (Eds.), *Life span development and behavior.* New York: Academic Press.

Kendrick, D. T., & Funder, D. C. (1988). Profiting from controversy: Lessons from the person–situation debate. *American Psychologist, 43,* 23–34.

Kirchner, W. K., & Dunnette, M. D. (1957). Applying the weighted application blank technique to a variety of office jobs. *Journal of Applied Psychology, 41,* 206–208.

Kohlberg, L. (1968). Early education: A cognitive developmental view. *Child Development, 34,* 1013–1062.

Kreitler, S., & Kreitler, H. (1987). The psychosemantic aspects of the self. In T. Honess & K. Yardley (Eds.), *Self and identity: Perspectives across the life span.* New York: Rutledge & Kegan Paul.

Kuhnert, K. W., & Russell, C. J. (1990). Using constructive developmental theory and biodata to bridge the gap between personnel selection and leadership. *Journal of Management, 16,* 1–13.

Lautenschlager, G. J. (1985). Within subject measures for the assessment of individual differences in faking. *Educational and Psychological Measurement, 46*, 309–316.

Lerner, J. U., & Lerner, R. M. (1983). Temperament and adaptation across life: Theoretical and empirical issues. In P. B. Baltes & O. G. Brim, Jr. (Eds.), *Life span development and behavior* (Vol. 5). New York: Academic Press.

Lerner, R. M. (1978). Nature, nurture, and dynamic interactionism. *Human Development, 21*, 1–20.

Lerner, R. M., & Tubman, J. G. (1989). Conceptual issues in studying continuity and discontinuity in personality development across life. *Journal of Personality, 57*, 343–373.

Levinson, D. J. (1978). *Seasons of a man's life.* New York: Knopf.

Levinson, D. J. (1986). A conception of adult development. *American Psychologist, 41*, 3–13.

Little, B. R. (1987). Personal projects and fuzzy selves: Aspects of self identity in adolescence. In T. Honess & K. Yardley (Eds.), *Self and identity: Perspectives across the life span.* New York: Rutledge & Kegan Paul.

Livson, N., & Peskin, H. (1972). The prediction of adult psychological health in a longitudinal study. *Journal of Abnormal Psychology, 72*, 509–518.

Magnusson, D. (1988). Individual development from an interactional perspective. In D. Magnusson (Ed.), *Paths through life (1–18).* Hillsdale, NJ: Erlbaum.

McCrae, R. R., & Costa, P. T. (1987). Validation of the five-factor model across instruments and observers. *Journal of Personality and Social Psychology, 52*, 81–90.

McCrae, R. R., & Costa, P. T. (1988). Recalled parent–child relations and adult personality. *Journal of Personality, 56*, 417–433.

Minor, F. T. (1958). Prediction of turnover of clerical employees. *Personnel Psychology, 11*, 393–402.

Mischel, W. (1968). *Personality and assessment.* New York: Wiley.

Mischel, W. (1973). Toward a cognitive social learning reconceptualization of personality. *Psychological Review, 80*, 252–283.

Mumford, M. D., & Owens, W. A. (1982). Life history and vocational interests. *Journal of Vocational Behavior, 21*, 330–348.

Mumford, M. D., & Owens, W. A. (1987). Methodology review: Principles, procedures, and findings in the application of background data measures. *Applied Psychological Measurement, 11*, 1–31.

Mumford, M. D., Snell, A. F., & Hein, M. B. (1993). Varieties of religious experience: Continuity and change in religious involvement. *Journal of Personality, 61*, 69–88.

Mumford, M. D., & Stokes, G. S. (1992). Developmental determinants of individual action: Theory and practice in the application of background measures. In M. D. Dunnette & L. M. Hough (Eds.), *Handbook of industrial and organizational psychology* (2d ed., vol. 3, pp. 61–138). Palo Alto, CA: Consulting Psychologists Press.

Mumford, M. D., Wesley, S. S., & Shaffer, G. S. (1987). Individuality in a development context II: The crystallization of developmental trajectories. *Human Development, 30*, 291–321.

Neiner, A. G., & Owens, W. A. (1985). Using biodata to predict job choice among college graduates. *Journal of Applied Psychology, 70*, 129–136.

Neugarten, B. L. (1979). Time, age, and the life cycle. *American Journal of Psychiatry, 136,* 887–894.

O'Leary, L. R. (1973). Fair employment, sound psychometric practice, and reality. *American Psychologist, 23,* 782–785.

Overton, W. F., & Reese, H. W. (1973). Models of development: Methodological implications. In J. R. Nesselroade & H. W. Reese (Eds.), *Life span developmental psychology: Methodological issues.* New York: Academic Press.

Owens, W. A. (1953). Age and mental abilities: A longitudinal study. *Genetic Psychological Monographs, 48,* 3–54.

Owens, W. A. (1976). Background data. In M. D. Dunnette (Ed.), *Handbook of industrial and organizational psychology.* Chicago: Rand McNally.

Owens, W. A. (1978). Moderators and subgroups. *Personnel Psychology 31,* 243–247.

Owens, W. A., Glennon, J. R., & Albright, L. E. (1962). Retest consistency and the writing of life history items. *Journal of Applied Psychology, 46,* 329–332.

Owens, W. A., & Schoenfeldt, L. F. (1979). Toward a classification of persons. *Journal of Applied Psychology, 64,* 569–607.

Pace, L. A., & Schoenfeldt, L. F. (1977). Legal concerns in the use of weighted application blanks. *Personnel Psychology, 30,* 159–166.

Piaget, J. (1950). *The psychology of intelligence.* New York: Harcourt Brace.

Pines, G. M. (1987). Mirroring and child development: Psychodynamic and psychological interpretations. In T. Honess & K. Yardley (Eds.), *Self and identity: Perspectives across the life span.* New York: Rutledge & Kegan Paul.

Pulkkinen, C. (1982). Self control and continuity from childhood to adolescence. In P. B. Baltes & O. G. Brim, Jr. (Eds.), *Life span development and behavior* (Vol. 4). New York: Academic Press.

Rauste-VonWright, M. (1986). On personality and educational psychology. *Human Development, 29,* 328–340.

Redmond, M. R., & Nickels, B. J. (1989). *Assessing the utility of empirical keys constructed using direct and indirect background data items.* Paper presented at the annual meeting of the Southeastern Psychological Association, Washington, DC.

Reese, H. W., & Overton, W. F. (1970). Models of development and theories of development. In L. R. Goulet & P. B. Baltes (Eds.), *Life span developmental psychology: Research and theory.* New York: Academic Press.

Reilly, R. N., & Chao, G. T. (1982). Validity and fairness of some alternative employee selection procedures. *Personnel Psychology, 35,* 1–62.

Reiter-Palmon, R., DeFilippo, B., & Mumford, M. D. (1990). *Differential predictive validity of positive and negative response options to biodata items.* Paper presented at the annual meeting of the Southeastern Psychological Association, Atlanta.

Riegel, K. F. (1975). Toward a dialectical theory of development. *Human Development, 18,* 50–64.

Roach, P. E. (1971). Double cross-validation of a weighted application blank over time. *Journal of Applied Psychology, 55,* 157–166.

Russell, C. J., & Domm, D. R. (1990). *On the construct validity of biographical information: Evaluation of a theory-based method for item generation.* Unpublished manuscript.

Russell, C. J., Mattson, J., Devlin, S. E., & Atwater, D. (1988). *Predictive validity of biodata items generated from retrospective life experience essays.* Paper presented at the annual meeting of the Society of Industrial and Organizational Psychology, Dallas.

Schaie, K. W. (1984). Historical time and cohort effects. In K. A. McClusky & H. W. Reese (Eds.), *Life span developmental psychology: Historical age generational effects*. New York: Academic Press.

Schaie, K. W., & Geiwitz, J. (1982). *Adult development and aging*. Boston: Little, Brown.

Schneider, B. (1987). The people make the place. *Personnel Psychology, 40,* 437–454.

Schoenfeldt, L. F. (1974). Utilization of manpower: Development and evaluation of an assessment-classification model for matching individuals with jobs. *Journal of Applied Psychology, 59,* 583–595.

Schoenfeldt, L. F. (1989). *Biographical data as the new frontier in employee selection research*. Paper presented at the annual meeting of the American Psychological Association, New Orleans.

Schrader, A. D. (1975). *A comparison of the utility of several rational and empirical strategies for forming biodata dimensions*. Unpublished doctoral dissertation, University of Houston, Houston, TX.

Schwab, D. P., & Oliver, R. L. (1974). Predicting tenure with biographical information: Exhuming buried evidence. *Personnel Psychology, 27,* 125–128.

Shaffer, G. S., Saunders, V., & Owens, W. A. (1986). Additional evidence for the accuracy of biographical information. *Personnel Psychology, 39,* 791–809.

Skinner, B. F. (1957). *Verbal behavior*. New York: Appleton-Century-Crofts.

Snyder, M. (1974). The self monitoring of expressive behavior. *Journal of Personality and Social Psychology, 30,* 526–537.

Sontag, L. W. (1971). The history of longitudinal research: Implications for the future. *Child Development, 42,* 987–1002.

Sternberg, R. J., & Wagner, R. K. (1986). *Practical intelligence: Nature and origins of competence in the everyday world*. New York: Cambridge University Press.

Stokes, G. S., Mumford, M. D., & Owens, W. A. (1989). Life history prototypes and the study of human individuality. *Journal of Personality, 57,* 509–545.

Terman, L. M., & Oden, N. C. (1959). *The gifted group at mid-life*. Stanford, CA: Stanford University Press.

Thomas, A., & Chess, S. (1981). The role of temperament in contributions of individuals to their development. In R. M. Lerner & N. A. Busch-Rossnagel (Eds.), *Individuals as producers of their own development: A life span perspective*. New York: Academic Press.

Tobach, E. (1981). Evolutionary aspects of the activity of the organism and its environment. In R. M. Lerner & N. A. Busch-Rossnagel (Eds.), *Individuals as producers of their own development: A life span perspective*. New York: Academic Press.

Tyler, L. E. (1965). *The psychology of human differences*. New York: Appleton-Century-Crofts.

Tyler, L. E. (1978). *Individuality*. San Francisco: Jossey-Bass.

Uhlman, C. E., Reiter-Palmon, R., & Connelly, M. S. (1990). *A comparison and integration of empirical keying and rational scaling of biographical data items*. Paper presented at the annual meeting of the Southeastern Psychological Association, Atlanta.

Vaillant, L. L., & McArthur, C. C. (1972). Natural history and male psychological health in the adult life cycle. *Seminars in Psychiatry, 4,* 415–427.

Wernimont, P. F. (1962). Reevaluation of a weighted application blank for office personnel. *Journal of Applied Psychology, 46,* 417–419.

Wesley, S. S. (1989). *Background data subgroups and career outcomes: Some developmental influences on person–job matching.* Unpublished doctoral dissertation, Georgia Institute of Technology, Atlanta.

Zuckerman, M., Bernieri, F., Koestner, R., & Rosenthal, R. (1989). To predict some of the people some of the time: In search of moderators. *Journal of Personality and Social Psychology, 57,* 279–293.

Personality and Background Data
Life History and Self-concepts in an Ecological System

Michael D. Mumford
George Mason University

Andrea F. Snell
University of Georgia

Roni Reiter-Palmon
George Mason University

Any piece of psychological research is predicated on a straightforward assumption. More specifically, our research paradigms assume that people's prior behavior and experiences condition their future behavior and experiences (Owens, 1968, 1971). Cognizance of this fact has led to an abiding, albeit haphazard, interest in the potential applications of life history information (Allport, 1937, 1942; Galton, 1902; Howe, 1982).

Although background data items can be scaled in a number of ways (Mumford & Owens, 1987; Schoenfeldt, 1989), the vagaries of history have led to a reliance on an empirical keying strategy. Few would dispute the predictive efficiency of empirically keyed background data scales (Asher, 1974; Ghiselli, 1973; Owens, 1976; Reilly & Chao, 1982). By virtue of its focus on prediction to the exclusion of explanation, however, this technique has led to some trenchant criticisms of background data measures (Korman, 1968; O'Leary, 1973; Pace & Schoenfeldt, 1977; Schwab & Oliver, 1974; Thayer, 1977; Wernimont, 1962).

Although differing in specifics, these criticisms seem bound together by a common thread. The comments of these investigators imply that simple predictive efficiency is not a fully adequate basis for appraising meaningfulness. Rather, their observations indicate that background data measures should be embedded in a broader, nomothetic net permitting inferences of content and construct validity (Mumford & Nickels, 1990; Nickels, 1990). With the recent resurgence of interest in background data (Fleishman, 1988), a number of investigators have responded to this challenge. Schoenfeldt (1989) and Hough (1984), for instance, have provided evidence arguing for the utility of alternative, theoretically driven scaling procedures taking into account constructs of substantive import. Work by Quaintance (1981), Redmond and Nickels (1989), Russell, Mattson, Devlin, and Atwater (1988), and Stricker (1989) has served to indicate that better prediction and stronger inferences of meaningfulness are provided by background data items explicitly formulated to capture developmental antecedents of performance-relevant constructs.

Of course, to apply these new techniques for item development and scaling, one must have some understanding of the kind of constructs that can be captured by background data items. In this search for an appropriate nomothetic net, attempts have been made to relate background data to measures of other kinds of psychological constructs, such as vocational interests (Eberhardt & Muchinsky, 1984; Klimoski, 1973; Neiner & Owens, 1985) and creativity (Buel, Albright, & Glennon, 1966; Ellison & Taylor, 1962). In recent years, the relationship between background data measures and personality constructs has been of particular concern.

The intent of this chapter is to examine the relationship between background data and personality constructs. We will begin this effort by first considering the nature of background data measures in the context of personality assessment. Our attention will subsequently turn to delineating the general nature of background data measures and specifying how personality constructs condition the predictive efficiency of these measures. In the final section of this chapter, we will consider some of the practical implications of these observations with respect to the development and application of background data scales.

BACKGROUND DATA AND PERSONALITY

MEASUREMENT CONSIDERATIONS

Perhaps the most straightforward answer to the question we have posed concerning the relationship between background data and personality is to argue that background data represent little more than an alternative format for personality assessment. At a macro-theoretical level, there is certainly some support for this proposition. Allport (1937, 1942), for instance, has defined personality as the sum total of a person's behavior and experiences. Other theorists, such as Adler (1927), have also emphasized the crucial role of life history in conditioning the nature of personality. Because background data are used to generate a life history description based on recall of past events, these comments might easily lead one to conclude that background data measures are synonymous with personality.

When one looks at background data measures from a broader content perspective, however, this conclusion becomes suspect. Personality measures typically ask individuals to describe generalized behavioral tendencies pertinent to some specified construct or stimulus set (Fiske, 1973). Thus, an authoritarianism item might ask, "Do you believe in astrology?" Background data items, on the other hand, require individuals to recall and report prior behavior and experiences in developmentally significant situations. Thus, items might ask, "How often did you go out on dates in high school?" or "How often were you picked first for sports teams?" or "Have you ever fixed a piece of electronic equipment?"

These items illustrate three important points concerning the relationship between personality and background data measures. First, background data items do not ask for global evaluations of projected behavioral tendencies, but instead focus on behavior and experiences. By focusing on what was done or what has happened, it seems likely that background data items capture somewhat different information than personality items. Second, unlike personality items, background data items capture a significant element of situational choice (Mumford & Owens, 1982). Third, as illustrated in the athletics and electronics items, responses to background data items may be influenced by a variety of constructs, such as physical and mechanical abilities, not traditionally subsumed under the rubric of personality. In fact, background data items are often used to assess job-relevant knowledge and skills (Hough, 1984; Levine & Zachert, 1951; Pannone, 1984). Mumford and Stokes (1992) have also argued that these items represent a particularly attractive vehicle for capturing certain cognitive attributes, such as planning skills and practical intelligence.

We emphasize this last point because, as a developmental assessment technique, background data items are not the exclusive property of any construct domain. Rather, they are likely to prove adequate markers of any differential characteristic that develops as a result of prior behavior and experiences or is manifest in people's earlier behavior and experiences. Thus, background data encompass a larger domain than personality. To compound matters, McCrae and Costa (1988) note that the relationship between developmental events, such as child-rearing practices and personality traits, is sufficiently complex that it is difficult to make unambiguous statements about developmental markers. Furthermore, the work of Epstein and O'Brien (1985), Mischel (1968), Snyder (1974), and Zuckerman, Bernieri, Koestner, and Rosenthal (1989) indicates that the expression of personality attributes in prior behavior and experiences may itself be moderated by a variety of intrinsic and extrinsic factors. Given these observations, it seems unwise to equate background data and personality measures in an absolute, operational sense.

SUBSTANTIVE CONSIDERATIONS

Although our foregoing observations argue against arbitrarily equating background data and personality measures, these comments should not be taken to imply that there is no substantively meaningful relationship between background data and personality constructs. Although evidence is available indicating that certain personality traits such as inhibition and extraversion may have been influenced by biological or genetic factors, the amount of variance accounted for is not great (Buss & Plomin, 1975; Eysenck & Eysenck, 1985; Kagan, 1989; Loehlin, Willerman, & Horn, 1985; Price, Vandenberg, Iyer, & Williams, 1982). Thus, it seems likely that the development of these attributes will be influenced, or at least shaped, by certain life history events. In fact, research by Atkinson (1979), Block (1971), Strickland (1989), and Witkin and Berry (1975), among others, indicates that early life events condition the later expression of personality attributes, such as achievement motivation, ego resiliency, locus of control, and field independence.

A recent study by McCrae and Costa (1988) examined how parental behaviors influenced the ontogeny of personality characteristics, such as extraversion, neuroticism, and openness. Their findings indicated that parental warmth was positively related to extraversion and openness, but negatively related to neuroticism. Parental casualness or leniency was, however, negatively related to extraversion, but positively related to openness. Although other evidence of this sort might be cited, it appears that certain patterns of developmental events condition later expression of a given personality characteristic. Thus, one might expect some relationship between background data items measuring relevant developmental influences and scores on pertinent trait indices. In fact, the existence of these relationships suggests that background data items capable of capturing relevant developmental influences might be used to measure certain personality characteristics (Redmond & Nickels, 1989).

The relationship between developmental events and the later expression of personality characteristics is not the only potential linkage between background data and personality constructs. Once developed, these personality characteristics might also condition people's later behavior and experiences. Hence, background data items might also capture the prior operation of these constructs in determining the individual's life course. With regard to this point, the literature is somewhat more ambivalent. After reviewing the consistency of trait measures and their ability to predict "real-world" behaviors, Mischel (1968) concluded that personality traits are not systematically related to later behavior and experiences, thereby bringing to question the import of dispositional variables, as opposed to situational factors, in shaping the course of human life.

Mischel's (1968) observations triggered an ongoing debate concerning the relative influence of personality traits and situational variables in determining people's later behavior and experiences. An important outcome of this debate is that it has served to clarify a number of issues bearing on how people's dispositions influence their lives. Magnusson and Endler (1977) and Magnusson (1988) have pointed out that behavior in any situation is likely to arise from a dynamic interaction of multiple attributes of the person and the situation. As might be expected under these conditions, trait influences can be most readily identified when behavioral indices are aggregated over multiple situations, thereby taking into account the limited reliability of behavioral markers obtained in a single situation (Epstein, 1979; Epstein & O'Brien, 1985). Powerful situational constraints permitting little choice among alternative courses of action or situations are, however, likely to mask dispositional effects (Buss, 1989; Kenrick & Funder, 1988). Furthermore, certain attributes of the individual or situation may condition people's sensitivity to certain kinds of situational influences and thereby moderate the impact of personality characteristics on behavior (Bem & Allen, 1974; Mischel & Peake, 1982; Snyder, 1974; Zuckerman, Koestner, DeBoy, Garcia, Maresca, & Sartoris, 1988). It also appears that broad, second-order personality characteristics, such as extraversion, neuroticism, openness, agreeableness, and conscientiousness, display greater stability and have a stronger impact on people's later behavior and experiences than more narrow dimensions (Jackson & Paunonen, 1985; McCrae & Costa, 1987; Zuckerman, Kuhlman, & Camac, 1988). Finally, as so eloquently pointed out by Cheek and Buss (1981), no single personality characteristic is likely to fully condition behavior in any situation; rather, a multivariate combination of trait variables is likely to condition perception, entry, and behavior in a given situation.

When one examines longitudinal studies in which many of the conditions required for effective dispositional expression are met, evidence of the stability of personality characteristics and their impact on later behavior and experiences is more impressive than one typically finds in laboratory studies. For instance, Olweus (1979) examined a number of longitudinal studies concerned with aggressive behavior. Although the magnitude of stability coefficients diminished over time, in accordance with a simplex structure, the degree of stability observed, near .80, was impressive. Costa and McCrae (1980), in longitudinal study of adults, have compiled evidence indicative of the stability of broad personality characteristics such as extraversion and neuroticism. Similar findings have also been reported by Bronson (1966) and Block (1971). Not only have these longitudinal studies provided evidence for stability, they also indicate that these attributes can have a marked impact on later behavior and experiences. For instance, Pulkkinen (1982), in a longitudinal study of 135 Finnish youths, found substantial stability in measures of self-control and reactivity between the ages of 8 and 20. More centrally, these indices were found to influence life events such as dating, smoking, and school achievement. In a related study, employing the Berkeley Longitudinal Sample, Caspi (1987) found that early explosiveness was related to later occupational difficulties. Given these observations, it seems reasonable to conclude that personality constructs can affect life events and therefore can influence responses to, and be measured by, background data items.

EMPIRICAL CONSIDERATIONS

When one examines the results obtained using background data measures, some support exists for a strong, substantive relationship between background data measures of life history and personality constructs. One line of evidence derives from studies examining the relationship between background data items and scores on personality inventories. In an initial investigation along these lines, Rawls and Rawls (1968) showed that empirically keyed background data scales predicted scores on standard personality inventories. A study by Mikesell and Tesser (1971) demonstrated that not only were background data items effective predictors ($r = .50$) of scores on the California F Scale, but the content of the items yielding significant correlations with this measure of authoritarianism, such as parental harshness and socioeconomic status, were also consistent with the known developmental antecedents of authoritarianism.

A later study by Mumford and Stokes (1982) took this logic one step further. Initially, the responses of 1,037 men and 890 women to 389 background data items were correlated with scores on measures of positive and negative emotionality. These items were then grouped into content clusters by the first investigator (Mumford) using the procedures suggested by Mumford and Owens (1982) to form post-hoc rational scales. The average item correlation within each scale was then determined. Prior to seeing these results, the second investigator (Stokes) reviewed the developmental literature on positive and negative emotionality to identify (a)characteristic expressions of these traits in life history and (b)significant developmental influences. When these results were compared, it was found that 80 percent of the relationships identified in the personality literature were confirmed by the item clusters. Not only does this study underscore the existence of strong, interpretable relationships between background data and personality measures, it provides some support for Baltes and Goulet's (1971) and Costa and McCrae's (1988) contention that retrospective self-reports garnered from background data might be used to obtain crucial information bearing on the ontogeny of personality characteristics, especially given the available evidence on the accuracy of recall data when there is no motive for faking (Block, 1971; Bronson, Katten, & Livson, 1959; Shaffer, Saunders, & Owens, 1986).

A more comprehensive assessment of the relationship between background data measures and personality measures has been provided by Owens (1976). In this study, 1,037 men and 890 women completed a 389-item background data form. Men's and women's item responses were then subjected to a principal components analysis to derive a set of factorial scales. These scales were correlated with some 30 personality measures examining constructs such as extraversion, neuroticism, tough-mindedness, authoritarianism, and values. The background data scales were found to yield an interpretable, substantively meaningful pattern of relationships with the personality scales. For example, a cultural/literary interest background data factor was positively related to cognitive values ($r = .32$) and integrative complexity ($r = .29$), but negatively related to indices of authoritarianism ($r = .15$) and economic values ($r = .19$). More centrally, when the personality scales were regressed on the background data scales, multiple R's on the order of .50 to .60 were obtained, indicating a substantial degree of overlap attributable to either the expression of these attributes in life events or their impact on the development of personality characteristics.

Not only is there evidence of a relationship between background data and personality in correlational data; there is also some support for this relationship in the structural characteristics of background data and personality measures. Although many considerations influence the nature of the dimensions identified in factor analytic investigations, it appears that five factors consistently emerge in studies of personality measures: (a) neuroticism, (b) extraversion, (c) openness or cultural interests,

TABLE 1   Number of Factor Analytic Studies (N = 21)
Identifying Generic Dimensions

Dimension	Number
1. Introversion vs. Extroversion	13
2. Social Leadership	12
3. Independence	8
4. Self-esteem	7
5. Achievement Motivation	7
6. Social Conformity	8
7. Personal Conservatism	6
8. Maturity	11
9. Adjustment	18
10. Academic Achievement	16
11. Parental Warmth	7
12. Parental Control	6
13. Parental SES	8
14. Sibling Relationships	3
15. Religious Involvement	9
16. Family Commitment	4
17. Urban/Rural Background	1
18. Health	3
19. Athletic Pursuits	8
20. Scientific/Engineering Pursuits	7
21. Intellectual Cultural Pursuits	13
22. Work Values	4
23. Organizational Commitment	6
24. Professional Skills	7
25. Trade Skills	5
26. Career Development	10

From "Methodology Review: Background Data Measures" by M. D. Mumford and W. A. Owens, 1987, *Applied Psychological Measurement, 11,* 20. Copyright 1987 by *Applied Psychological Measurement.* Reprinted by permission.

(d) agreeableness, and (e) conscientiousness (Buss, 1989; Eysenck & Eysenck, 1985; McCrae & Costa, 1987; Norman, 1963; Zuckerman, Kuhlman, & Camac, 1988). In a recent review of the factors commonly identified in the background data literature, Mumford and Owens (1987) found that factors such as adjustment, extraversion, cultural interests, social leadership, and social maturity were commonly identified. These factors are listed in Table 1 along with the frequency with which they were identified in 21 factor analyses. Despite some differences in terminology, these factors share much in common with those identified in the personality literature. This congruence in structure has been remarked upon by other investigators as well. It should be noted, however, that background data measures often reveal other kinds of factors, such as academic achievement and athletic pursuits, in accordance with our earlier observation that background data reflect a somewhat broader domain of differential characteristics.

Studies in which an attempt was explicitly made to measure personality constructs through background data items provide another line of evidence indicating a strong, substantive relationship between these two domains. In an initial investigation along these lines, Torrance and Ziller (1957) formulated a rational background data scale composed of items expressly intended to capture prior life events, such as playing poker, which would reflect risk taking. In a subsequent validation effort, Himelstein and Blaskovics (1960) found that scores on this scale would predict performance in combat leadership positions. Schoenfeldt (1989) employed a similar approach in generating background data items to measure sociability, responsibility, calmness, resistance to stress, concentration, and work ethic. When these scales were administered to a sample of 699 customer service workers, they were found to yield cross-validated multiple R's on the order of .30 for predicting performance and withdrawal criteria. Russell and Domm (1990) employed a somewhat different strategy in item generation in which retrospective essays were used to generate items for background data scales intended to measure personality attributes such as energy, social sensitivity, forcefulness, judgment, and leadership. In a sample of 140 store manager positions, these scales were found to predict both assessment center and performance ratings at the .30 level, while showing substantial convergent and discriminant validities with respect to the substantive implications of scale content.

Taken as a whole, these attempts to measure personality characteristics using background data items appear to have met with a surprising degree of success. Not only did these scales yield sizable predictive validity coefficients, the magnitude of these validities was far larger than that commonly obtained from standard personality inventories and ability measures in comparable job families (Ghiselli, 1973; Schoenfeldt, 1989). These findings, of course, underscore the utility of background data in personality assessment, as well as the existence of strong, substantive relationships between these two domains. It seems to us, however, that they also pose a somewhat more intriguing question. Apparently, personality constructs measured through background data items yield better prediction than measures of these same constructs generated through the personality items tapping beliefs about future behavior. This trend might be attributable to the advantageous psychometric characteristics evidenced by background data items such as freedom from response biases (Ames, 1983; French, Lewis, & Long, 1976; Shaffer, Saunders, & Owens, 1986), high reliability (Cascio, 1975; Keating, Paterson, & Stone, 1950; Mosel & Cozan, 1952; Shaffer, Saunders, & Owens, 1986), the nontransparent nature of item content (Klein & Owens, 1965; Lautenschlager, 1985), and relative item independence (Owens, 1976). It is also possible, however, that by assessing trait expression in earlier life events, a more realistic assessment of operational trait influences and their salience to the individual is obtained, thereby leading to more meaningful measurement and better prediction in operational settings.

Our final line of evidence indicating an important substantive relationship between personality and life history pertains to a specific construct that has received some attention in both background data and personality research. Recent work by Bandura (1986, 1989) has emphasized the importance of self-esteem in determining people's behavior in and reactions to various situations by relating this construct to the motivation to perform challenging or frustrating tasks, affective responses, and situational selection. This self-esteem construct has also been identified in a number of factorings of background data items. These background data measures of self-esteem appear, furthermore, to be effective predictors of real-world performance criteria. Morrison, Owens, Glennon, and Albright (1962), for instance, found that scores on a background data self-esteem factor were effective predictors of scientific productivity in a sample of petroleum scientists. In another study, Dye (personal communication, 1989) found that a background data self-esteem factor accounted for a sizable proportion of the variance in responses to a set of background data items used in selecting entry-level managers while proving to be a highly effective predictor of job performance.

The apparent import of the self-system as manifest in efficacy beliefs has been confirmed in a recent study by Nickels (1990). In this investigation, a sample of undergraduates was asked to rate the extent to which 389 background data items reflected constructs such as verbal ability, agreeableness, morality, persistence, and self esteem, among some 40 other variables. The ability of items receiving high ratings on each dimension to discriminate the general life history patterns identified by Owens and Schoenfeldt (1979) was then assessed in a series of policy-capturing analyses. It was found that self-esteem was the single best predictor of the background data item's ability to discriminate general patterns of differential development. Items yielding high scores on this construct were also found to be effective predictors of such diverse criteria as academic achievement, adjustment, and job satisfaction. Although the reasons for the apparent power of self-esteem may not be immediately apparent, these observations suggest that the self-system may be just as important a determinant of life history as the more discrete behavioral dispositions discussed earlier.

A THEORETICAL MODEL

CONCEPTUAL BACKGROUND

Our preceding observations indicate that personality is closely related to, if not completely synonymous with, life history as measured by background data items. Unfortunately, the available evidence provides little information indicating exactly when, where, how, and why personality comes to manifest itself in people's life history and, therefore, their responses to background data items. Without at least a preliminary answer to this question, it is difficult to draw any clear-cut conclusions concerning the application of personality constructs in developing background data measures. Of course, one potential solution to this problem would be to delineate the general nature of background data measures and then proceed to elaborate on the implications of personality constructs within this general framework.

Based on its status as a life history measure, Owens (1976) concluded that whenever a background data item predicts performance, it must also represent a developmental antecedent, or a "sign," for later performance. This observation led Mumford and Owens (1987) to conclude that the predictive power of any background data scale is contingent on the quantitative definition of a pattern of developmental events. Cognizance of this fact suggested to Owens (1968, 1971, 1976, 1978) that a general understanding of background data measures might be obtained through the identification and analysis of modal patterns of differential development without defining these patterns in terms of a particular criterion performance, as is commonly the case (Mumford & Owens, 1987).

To implement this approach, Owens and Schoenfeldt (1979) administered 389 background data items to 1,037 men and 890 women entering the University of Georgia. These items primarily measured childhood and adolescence experiences. After men's and women's item responses had been factored and used to form a profile of scores, a Ward and Hook (1963) clustering procedure was used to group together more or less similar individuals. These analyses yielded 23 male and 15 female subgroups intended to reflect modal patterns of differential development.

Subsequent examination of the characteristics of these subgroups indicated that most individuals (75%) could be adequately described by virtue of assignment to a single subgroup (Schoenfeldt, 1974). This subgroup structure proved, moreover, to be a stable one, such that it could be applied in new samples with no more than a 10 percent loss in the number of individuals assigned to a single subgroup. With regard to the topic at hand, however, Owens and Schoenfeldt's (1979) finding that members of each subgroup displayed an interpretable, substantively mean-ingful pattern of differential characteristics on a set of academic achieve-ment, interest, and personality reference measures is of somewhat greater import. These data are illustrated in Table 2. As may be seen, the Analytical Independents, characterized by low parental control and scientific interests on the background data items, evidenced high emotional exposure, cognitive complexity, and long-term goals on the reference measures. Not only are these results in line with Costa and McCrae's (1988) observations, they indicate that the developmental pattern reflected a coherent organi-zation of personality attributes.

To determine whether these developmental patterns actually provided the general description of differential development that was sought, their ability to account for a variety of criterion performances was assessed. In the 50 feedback studies conducted using these criteria, select subgroups were identified and hypotheses were formulated about how subgroup members should perform. In accordance with this generality hypothesis, subgroup status was found to predict a remarkably wide range of criterion perfor-mances, including academic over and underachievement (H. A. Klein, 1972), Rorschach responses (Frazier, 1971), vocational interests (Jones, 1970; L. L. Thomas, 1982), and drug use (Strimbu & Schoenfeldt, 1973). Overall, it was found that subgroup status was an effective predictor of performance in roughly 90 percent of these studies and was especially likely to capture differences on motivationally and dispositionally loaded criteria.

Subsequent research has sought to elucidate the characteristics of these subgroups. In one set of investigations, Feild and Schoenfeldt (1975) and Davis (1984) administered background data inventories intended to capture significant behavior and experiences occurring in college and the immediate postcollege years to members of the initial Owens and Schoenfeldt (1979) sample. The results obtained in these investigations indicated that (a) meaningful subgroups could be formulated using other background data questionnaires, (b) subgroups could be established in later develop-mental periods, and (c) the background data information obtained in earlier developmental periods predicted later subgroup membership, although the power of these predictive relationships diminished over time. In an extension of these initial efforts, Jackson (1982), Snell and Stokes (1990), and Stokes, Mumford, and Owens (1989) examined patterns of movement across the subgroups identified in different developmental periods. Their results indicated that members in an initial adolescent subgroup tended to enter only two or three of some ten college subgroups, while members of a given collegiate subgroup entered two or three of the

TABLE 2   Description of Male Biographical Subgroups in Terms of
Distinctive Stands on Selected Biographical Factors, References,
Measures, and Feedback Data Identifying Generic Dimensions

Group	Subgroup	Description
Indifferent, low-achieving artists	Biodata	(H) SES; (L) pseudointellectualism, scientific and athletic interest
	Reference	(H) music teacher (strong); (L) long-term goals, cognitive values
	Feedback	(H) music majors, drug users; college GPA = 2.73
Traditional, science-oriented leaders	Biodata	(H) academic achievement; (L) social achieving introversion
	Reference	(H) social-religious conformity, high school grade point, Reverse F; (L) inhibition
	Feedback	(H) biological science, physical science majors, campus leaders; college GPA = 3.08
Cognitively simple, non-achieving business majors	Biodata	(H) pseudointellectualism; (L) aggressiveness-independence
	Reference	(H) negative emotionality, conceptual simplicity; (L) SAT
	Feedback	(H) business, law, health, and physical education majors, careless in completion of BQ; college GPA = 2.55
Unconventional, overachieving, self-directed leaders	Biodata	(H) academic achievement; (L) religious activity
	References	(H) radicalism, advertising man, psychiatrist, librarian (strong); (L) tender-minded, F scale, external-ization, social-religious conformity, negative emotionality, conceptual simplicity, neuroticism
	Feedback	(H) law majors, campus leaders, drug users, overachievers, homosexuals, college GPA = 3.07
Analytical independents	Biodata	(H) scientific interest; (L) parental control
	Reference	(H) emotional exposure, cognitive complexity, long-term goals
	Feedback	(H) speech pathology and education, biological science majors, probation, drug users; college GPA = 2.81

TABLE 2   Description of Male Biographical Subgroups in Terms of Distinctive
Stands on Selected Biographical Factors, References, Measures, and
Feedback Data Identifying Generic Dimensions (continued)

Group	Subgroup	Description
Cognitively complex religious converters	Biodata	(H) aggressiveness–independence, academic attitude, religious activity; (L) social introversion, scientific interest
	Reference	(H) F scale, social–religious conformity, long-term goals, emotional exposure, cognitive complexity, extroversion, neuroticism, occupational level (strong); (L) computer programmer and osteopath (strong)
	Feedback	(H) music, speech, and journalism, social science majors, careful in completing BQ; college GPA = 3.04
"Egghead" leaders	Biodata	(H) social introversion, positive adjustment response bias; (L) parental control, athletic interest
	Reference	(H) high school grade point, SAT, printer (strong); (L) physical goals, positive emotionality, and emotional exposure, extraversion, life
	Feedback	(H) language, physical science, agriculture, dramatic arts, pharmacy majors, leaders; college GPA = 3.16
Business-oriented "Fraternity Joe"	Biodata	(H) academic attitude, SES
	Reference	(H) economic values, physical goals, extraversion; community recreation director, Chamber of Commerce executive; credit manager (strong); (L) physicist, dentist, artist (strong)
	Feedback	(H) business, humanities majors; college GPA = 2.79

Note: Only a limited number of the male subgroups are presented here for the purpose of illustration. More detailed information may be obtained by consulting Owens and Schoenfeldt (1979). (H) = scores above mean; (L) = scores below mean.

From "Toward a Classification of Person" by W. A. Owens and L. F. Schoenfeldt, 1979, *Journal of Applied Psychology, 64*, 569–607. Copyright 1979 by *Journal of Applied Psychology*. Reprinted by permission.

nine postcollege subgroups. Not only did these studies indicate that prior life history channeled later life history, but the results obtained in these investigations also indicated that departures from a trajectory were to some extent conditioned by maladjustment, as well as the strength of a person's prior expression of the developmental pattern.

The existence of these systematic relationships suggested to Mumford and Owens (1984) and Mumford, Stokes, and Owens (1990) that it might be possible to formulate subgroups extending across these three developmental periods. Correspondingly, background data responses from 417 men and 358 women who completed all three questionnaires were used to construct a set of subgroups. It was found that 84 percent of the men and 87 percent of the women could be fitted to one of the 15 male and 17 female subgroups. Examination of subgroup members' differential characteristics on the background data items and reference measures indicated that (a) these subgroups captured meaningful patterns of differential development yielding a complex, albeit an integrated and interpretable, set of differential characteristics; (b) across periods, there were some changes in characteristic behavior and experience; but (c) these changes tended to be consistent with their earlier pattern of behavior and experiences.

ECOLOGY MODEL

The question flowing from these findings was how individuals would go about constructing a coherent pattern of behavior and experiences that maintained itself over time despite marked changes in developmental tasks, situational demands, and potential opportunities. To address this issue, Mumford and Owens (1984) and Mumford, Stokes, and Owens (1990) proposed a theoretical framework they have referred to as the *ecology model*. This model takes its point of departure from the proposition that the individual is an active, purposive entity who, through learning, cognition, and action, seeks to maximize personal adaptation under conditions of shifting environmental demands (Bandura, 1986; Bergman & Magnusson, 1987; Caspi, 1987; Endler, 1982; R. M. Lerner, 1978; Magnusson, 1988; Mischel, 1973; Riegel, 1975; Tobach, 1981). Although the channeled nature of early development will constrict life history differences, heredity, early experiences, and the cognitive structures one uses to construe the world will give rise to an initial differential structure (Adler, 1927; Thomas & Chess, 1981). As children mature, adolescence will then bring to the fore a problem endemic to human life (Buhler, 1968; Erickson, 1963). That is, the broader environment will present a variety of situations and potential activities that might satisfy a person's needs and values. Because individuals have only limited time and energy available, however, they must choose among these alternatives in such a way as to maximize long-term adaptation. These choices are assumed to be guided by affordances, or perceived goals (Baron & Boudreau, 1987; Gibson, 1979).

In entering a situation and initiating actions intended to bring about certain affordances, however, a person will begin to develop those resources required for goal attainment while becoming more knowledgable about and sensitive to the affordance-laden implications of the associated class of situations. The individual should tend to seek out situations and activity sequences that have in the past been linked to the attainment of goals, just as he or she will avoid situations and activities leading to negative outcomes. Over time, this process of choice, development, and choice should lead to the emergence of a highly refined set of characteristics contributing to exploitation of certain types of situations contributing to goal attainment.

Of course, no one class of situations is likely to provide the outcomes required to satisfy all of a person's operative needs and values. Thus, people must seek out multiple situations having different affordance-laden implications. The individual's resources, beliefs, knowledge, and perceptual sensitivities will be developing in all these situations. Situational exposure and potential affordance-seeking actions in these situations exist in a network of structural interdependencies induced by broader socioenvironmental conditions and the common adaptive demands confronting human beings. Under these conditions, overall long-term adaptation can be maximized only to the extent that the situations sought and the affordance-seeking actions taken in these situations are complementary and compensatory, rather than competing. Individuals will select a coherent set of situations, initiating in them a coherent set of affordance seeking actions. This chain of behaviors results in the creation of a coherent niche of available adaptive situations in the environmental surround, along with an integrated set of personal resources, or an adaptive style, facilitating exploitation of this niche. Through situation perception, affordance seeking, environmental structuring, and the development of capital resources from past environmental transactions, this niche and style will condition entry into and success in exploiting new situations. This process thereby gives rise to the formation of coherent patterns of differential development and, due to the structured nature of human differences and the broader social environment, the kind of modal patterns of differential development identified by Block (1971), Magnusson (1988), Mumford and Owens (1984), Owens and Schoenfeldt (1979), and Wesley (1989).

NEEDS, VALUES, AND AFFORDANCES

Not only does this model explain the emergence of the coherent patterns of differential development underlying the application of life history measures, it also accounts for another common observation concerning background data measures. More specifically, its emphasis on choice and affordances is consistent with the tendency of background data measures to capture motivationally loaded criteria (Mumford & Stokes, 1992; Owens & Schoenfeldt, 1979). Given its import to life history measures, and the ecology model generally, it would seem desirable to elaborate this point.

Broadly speaking, human motivation is held to emerge from basic needs. Although it is possible to postulate many potential need states (Murray, 1938), we believe that based on the work of Maslow (1970) and studies of primate behavior, three basic kinds of needs are likely to condition human behavior: (a) physiological maintenance needs, (b) social or esteem needs, and (c) mastery needs. Although these first two categories are unlikely to stir up much debate, to allay any skepticism we have added this third category in recognition of the importance of play, exploration, and environmental control to primates (Kawai, 1965) and in response to Dweck's (1986) findings concerning the importance of mastery motivation to human learning.

Except under conditions of extreme deprivation, it seems unlikely to us that needs are directly manifested in behavior and experiences. Rather, as a child develops his or her early socialization, experiences will lead to need satisfaction for some kinds of actions and a withdrawal of need satisfaction for other kinds of actions. These early experiences should, in turn, lead to the emergence of prescriptive cognitive structures or schema reflecting beliefs about the value of certain activities (instrumental values) and beliefs about the desirability of certain situations (terminal values; Braithwite & Law, 1985; Rokeach, 1973). Coupled with this prescriptive structure will be a proscriptive structure composed of beliefs about situations and activities leading to the withdrawal of need satisfaction. This proscriptive structure may represent an important screen for operation of the prescriptive values (Dunkleberger & Tyler, 1961). The value and belief schema may be modified by the accommodation of later experiences due to the self-propagating nature of choice behavior, early environmental regularities, and a preference for assimilation. However, these values are likely to prove quite stable following their initial formation (Kelly, 1955; Rokeach, 1973).

Because individuals will differ in the strength of operative needs and other differential characteristics such as intelligence and temperament (Lerner & Lerner, 1983; Thomas & Chess, 1981), children will develop different, highly complex value schema, which differ from child to child. These differential value schema are of great import with regard to affordances. More specifically, real-life situations offer multiple potential outcomes, and in recognizing and reacting to these outcomes to specify self-set goals, individuals will apply their unique value schema. Thus, the differential value-laden implications of projected situational outcomes or affordances will drive situational selection, and value schema will mediate the impact of needs on situational choice and action selection. Furthermore, given the implications of the ecology model, these choices will contribute to differential resource development, knowledge, and situational sensitivities causing value schema to have a broad, diffuse impact on the character of the individual's life history.

This point has been underscored in a recent study by James and James (1989) concerning the relationship between climate perceptions and job satisfaction. Here, support was obtained for the notion that the value-laden meaning ascribed to situational events conditioned climate perceptions and job satisfaction and thus, presumably, the tendency of individuals to stay in or leave this situation. Similarly, these postulates would lead one to expect that different patterns of causal variables would operate for individuals reacting to different kinds of affordances. To investigate this possibility, Mumford, Snell, and Hein (1993) obtained a set of background data subgroups. For each subgroup of similar individuals, the personality variables related to high and low levels of religious involvement, as measured by background data items, were established in a series of two-way chi-square tests. After phi coefficients had been signed for directionality without respect to level, they were used to form a meaning profile for each subgroup, and a Ward and Hook (1963) procedure was used to cluster together subgroups for whom involvement in religious institutions had similar meaning, as indexed by its correlates. This analysis yielded two clusters of subgroups, one labeled *expressives,* who apparently accepted or rejected religion based on its value as a vehicle for evaluative emotional expression, and one labeled *instrumentals,* who apparently accepted or rejected religion based on its ability to provide personal services.

Not only did this study provide support for the notion that qualitatively different affordances could operate to condition situational entry across individuals, it also indicated that the nature of the affordances influenced the ontogeny of religious involvement. When moderated simplex models were constructed to describe continuity and change in religious involvement within each cluster, it was found that very different models were required to describe the ontogeny of this behavior. These models are presented in Figure 1. As may be seen, variables such as collegiate bohemianism ($p = -.12$) and literary pursuits ($p = -.21$) contributed to the rejection of religious involvement only in the expressive cluster, while variables such as adolescent social skills ($p = .20$) and family demands in young adulthood ($p = .17$) contributed to religious involvement in the instrumental cluster.

Given our foregoing observations concerning needs, values, affordances, and goals, five additional points seem worthy of consideration. First, because any situation provides only certain potential outcomes and the affordance-laden implications of these outcomes differ for individuals, different individuals will be attracted to different situations (Gustafson, 1987; Schneider, 1987). Second, the affordances reacted to by the individual and the requirements for affordance attainment condition differential development, not the situation per se, as an absolute entity. Third, because situational outcomes are reacted to based on their affordance-laden implications, the goals set and the actions taken in a situation will be strongly influenced by past life history, the individual's idiosyncratic value pattern, and the values ascribed to recognized outcomes. Fourth, value cannot be ascribed to a situational outcome or a potential course of action in a situation if the individual is not aware that the outcome exists or does not understand the action contingencies required to attain this outcome. Thus, information about the environment and self, especially expertise and perceived personal resources, are likely to have a marked impact on situational selection, action in this situation, the affordances pursued, and continued development (Ekehammer, 1974). Fifth, and finally, it should be pointed out that many information processing and judgment biases may operate to distort these appraisals from time to time, including factors such as the use of spurious, self-perpetuating diagnostics for encoding information (Hill, Lewicki, Czyzewski, & Boss, 1989), the overestimation of rare events (Einhorn & Hogarth, 1981; Hogarth, 1980), and localized excitation factors (Kosson & Newman, 1989). Although environmental feedback may limit the impact of some of these biases, people's choices will not always adequately reflect their values or serve their needs, especially under conditions of low expertise. Thus, as suggested by Sears' (1977) data, the good life may require some intelligence and experience.

SELF-CONCEPTS

Our foregoing observations concerning the impact of motivational and life history factors on choice and development pose a significant problem. More specifically, each day individuals are confronted with hundreds, if not thousands, of choices with regard to situational entry and potential actions in these situations. It seems to us unlikely that individuals consciously appraise each of these alternatives by carefully analyzing each outcome and its affordance-laden implications. It appears, therefore, that some kind of

Total Group

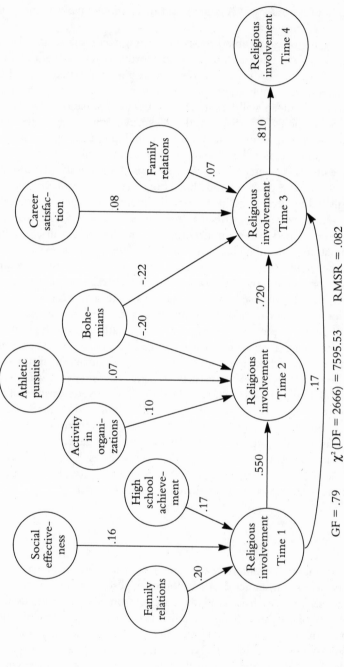

FIGURE 1   Continuity and Change in Religious Involvement

GF = .79 χ^2 (DF = 2666) = 7595.53   RMSR = .082

Instrumentals

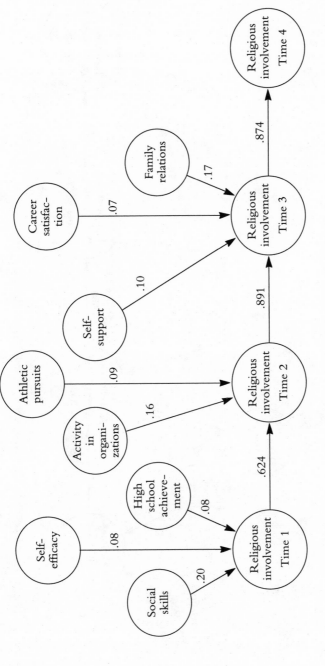

GF = .782 χ^2 (DF = 1859) = 3932.04   RMSR = .089

FIGURE 1   Continuity and Change in Religious Involvement (continued)

Expressives

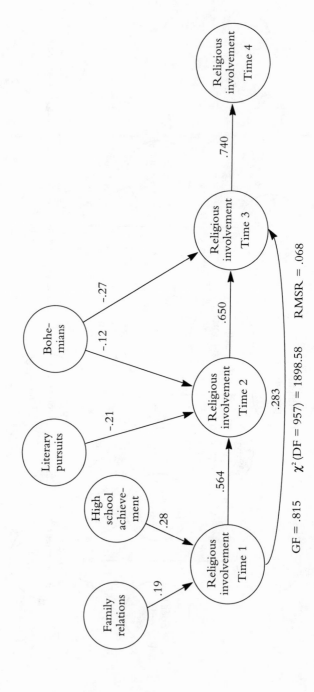

FIGURE 1   Continuity and Change in Religious Involvement (continued)

GF = .815 χ^2(DF = 957) = 1898.58   RMSR = .068

structure is required that permits people to process choice-relevant information in an automatic or unconscious fashion.

Not only does the demand for automatic processing constitute a problem within this model, three other issues in situational selection point to a need to extend this model. First, although not inherently reactive, it does not seem to us that the model captures the substantial proactive component evident in individual development. To wit, many of us went to graduate school, where we suffered long hours of work at low wages coupled with substantial negative feedback in the hope of some greater gain in the future. Second, because the situations confronting individuals change over time as a function of developmental tasks and changes in the broader cultural environment, it seems that people must engage in some form of opportunistic planning in order to choose among multiple situations and prepare for the future (Hayes-Roth & Hayes-Roth, 1979; Nutt, 1984). Therefore, some form of cognitive template is required to project and adjust action choices. Finally, some mechanism is required that will integrate these choices into a coherent adaptive whole.

This general template guiding situational selection appears to be tied up in the individual's self-concept. Broadly speaking, the self-concept may be viewed as the individual's understanding of him or herself as a unique and continuous being (Honess & Yardley, 1987). In its initial, most primitive form, the self-concept is seen as unfolding from the child's early social interactions involving the mirroring of others and the manipulation of significant environmental stimuli, particularly those related to initial need satisfaction (Harwood, 1987; Kohut, 1977; Wannicott, 1960). Formation of the self-concept is apparently a slow process influenced not only by interactional outcomes, but also by those dispositional and temperament factors conditioning the nature of these outcomes (Thomas & Chess, 1981; Wylie, 1987) and those cognitive capacities that make possible judgments of constancy (Aboud & Ruble, 1987; Chandler, Boyes, Ball, & Hala, 1987).

Recently, Hart and Damon (1985) have presented a systematic description of development of the self-system linked to Piaget's (1967) views on cognitive development. In the first stage of this process, the self is defined in terms of a set of unrelated surface features, overt actions, and current thoughts. The second stage involves comparisons of the self with others, especially in terms of abilities and requisite social roles, and therefore plays a key role in self-definition. In the third stage, near adolescence, this template image is tested and elaborated in direct social contact, while in the fourth and final stage it is integrated into broader personal systems conditioning people's view of life. Not only does this sequence seem consistent with Aboud and Ruble's (1987) comments concerning the import of concrete and formal operations in the development of self-concepts, Hart, Maloney, and Damon (1987) have provided some evidence indicating the validity of this model through the content of 6- to 15-year-olds' spontaneous self-descriptions. In a similar study, Peevers (1987) asked children and adolescents to describe themselves, and their subsequent responses were coded in terms of temporal orientation, distinctiveness, agency, and self-reflection. Temporal orientation comments, especially those concerned with future roles, predominated the comments of 9-year-olds, but sharply decreased as individuals moved into adolescence, when self-reflection increased.

These observations concerning the ontogeny of the self-system point to an important conclusion with regard to the ecology model. Specifically, the values and capacities developing in early childhood appear to be used in later childhood to construct an idealized template vis-à-vis specification of a set of future social role preferences. This generalized role preference reflects an integration of the individual's values and capacities into a template guiding situational selection and action preferences through specification of the affordances to be sought in the future. This initial template will, of course, be a rather crude and poorly articulated image of the good life and will obviously be substantially influenced by both prior life history and the social and historic conditions operating at the time of its formation. Thus, it is not surprising that an exploratory period follows initial formation of this template, during which it is tested, refined, and elaborated in direct social interaction, resulting in increasing differentiation and substantial self-monitoring of the affordances flowing from template application (Krietler & Krietler, 1987a, 1987b). Further, it cannot be expected that this future-oriented self-template will be fully effective until the individual has identified a set of roles that promise to provide affordances consistent with this refined template (Krietler & Krietler, 1987b).

In recent years, a series of longitudinal and retrospective life history studies have provided some support for this notion. For instance, after a series of interviews with middle-aged adults, Levenson (1978) concluded that an individual's choices of life events were often influenced by what he or she refers to as a dream state or an idealized image of life roles. More recently, Ochberg (1988), in an analysis of career histories, found that individual's choices were guided by scripts, stories, or plots created by people in later childhood as a function of their values and life situation. Thomkins (1987) and Carlson (1988) have described and provided some biographical evidence for a similar construct referred to as commitment scripts in which initial cognitions concerning actions and values are organized into an integrated set of role preferences conditioning later situational selection and life history. In a longitudinal study of gifted children, Albert (personal communication, 1990) found that individuals who changed career orientation in college, despite substantial resources, typically moved into career fields consistent with their self-image in childhood.

There does seem to be reason to suspect that the creation of a goal-oriented, socially defined self-concept integrating values and perceived abilities constitutes an important force shaping human life. These templates, however, may be better articulated for some individuals than others (Markus, 1977). Practical application of this template structure will allow automatic processing of the affordance-laden implications of situations while integrating choices into a coherent whole, permitting opportunistic exploitation of new situational opportunities. More centrally, however, this concept suggests that life events are both pushed by prior history and pulled by an image of one's future self. Not only does this dualism permit coherent preparatory activities, it integrates past, present, and future into a continuously unfolding whole. Because operative rewards and goals are template-driven vis-à-vis affordances, any event—even a large, objective reward—that induces a discrepancy in template congruence or a conflict between being and becoming is likely to be demotivating. This will lead individuals to enter situations congruent with their template (Gustafson, 1987; Holland, 1973; Schneider, 1987) that reflect a patterning of values as operationalized by the individual in their life context. It can also be expected that when one's life situation or career is thought to block movement toward or expression of this template, maladjustment, stress, and coping will occur. However, due to inclusion of extraneous or unrealistic elements in one's template and less than perfect environmental contingencies, these reactions need not always be consistently correct or rational.

Affect and Judgment

Given the complex and diffuse nature of this template construct, at first it may be difficult to see how individuals monitor its routine application. It seems likely, however, that much of this guidance is provided by affective responses. Based on Heider's (1958) discrepancy theory, Higgins (1987) has provided a model for relating self-concepts to affective reactions, arguing that this cognitive self-image will include an ideal or positive state (related to prescriptive values) and an ought state (related to proscriptive values). Within this framework, individuals are assumed to evaluate the discrepancy between their own behavior as construed through self-observation and to contrast this to these central template elements.

Not only are discrepancies between one's actual self and template ideal assumed to induce discomfort and therefore be motivating, specific affective states are assumed to arise contingent on the perceived nature of the discrepancy. For instance, a discrepancy between actual and prescriptive elements is assumed to result in dejection-related emotions such as disappointment and dissatisfaction, while discrepancies between proscriptive elements is thought to engender agitation-related emotions such as fear or threat. Finally, it is thought that the nature of the discrepancies identified will depend on activation of these cognitive structures as determined by their relevance to the situation and the recency and frequency of their prior activation.

Although one might debate the specifics of this theory, it seems to capture a grain of truth. For instance, Strauman and Higgins (1987) presented subjects with an adjective-priming manipulation in which adjectives were either (a) irrelevant to self-values or (b) mismatched with positive or negative values such that they activated discrepancy evaluation. Affect measures taken four weeks later indicated that mismatched priming induced emotional reactions, with dejection emotions being associated with positive value discrepancies and agitation emotions being associated with negative value discrepancies. Other support for this model has been obtained by Strauman (1989) and Hildebrand-Saints and Weary (1989), indicating that dejection and depression may be related to evaluative activation tendencies.

With regard to the issues at hand, however, these findings seem to have two central implications. First, it appears that rapid, unconscious cueing of discrepancy evaluations can occur and that these evaluations induce emotional reactions. Second, it seems likely that these affective emotional reactions will provide important guidelines for situational entry and action selection.

EXPLORATION, STABILITY, AND CHANGE

Although situational choice may be guided by unconscious processes and their affective outcomes, this need not always be the case. Rosenberg (1987) points out that when unexpected events occur leading to outcomes that cannot be readily incorporated in the existing self-structure, individuals experience depersonalization. This depersonalization, or loss of a sense of continuity, implies controlled processing or an attempt to understand and incorporate the meaning of events into one's self-concept.

Because new environments present multiple, novel situations and often require new kinds of actions in these situations, this controlled processing is likely to be called forth, and a period of exploration will ensue (Ackerman, 1986; Fleishman & Mumford, 1989). During exploration, individuals will seek to attain an understanding of the available situations, their action requirements, and the affordance-laden implications of situational outcomes. Initially, this exploration is likely to be predominantly vicarious in nature, using observational strategies (e.g., reading and watching others) to elaborate the nature of the situation in terms of its affordance implications and action requirements. The success of such endeavors is likely to be strongly influenced by the individual's general cognitive capacities. Provided that some congruence with the individual's template is reached, this process is likely to move into a new stage of direct situational exploration.

As individuals enter these situations, both vicariously and in actuality, they will begin to develop those resources required for affordance attainment. This exploratory process should, furthermore, be coupled with strong, active self-monitoring tendencies, in which the individuals carefully appraise actions and affordance attainment with regard to their cognitive template. This intense, active monitoring has a number of important consequences. One is that this intensive monitoring characteristic of exploration will provide a basis for change and reorganization of the self-concept. Another is that during this exploratory period, individuals may be especially sensitive to negative feedback due to limited task-specific self-esteem (Kernis, Brockner, & Frankel, 1989). In fact, research by Tyler (1965) indicates that interest development may be strongly channeled by the rejection of activities leading to negative outcomes.

These observations also point to the reasons why self-esteem has a strong impact in guiding life history. Self-esteem, or a generalized belief in one's ability to cope with the environment, develops along with the self-concept as a function of past environmental transactions. As Bandura (1986, 1989) points out, individuals with a strong sense of self-esteem are more likely to choose to enter new situations, set higher goals in these situations, perform effectively, and continue performance under frustrating conditions. Thus, it can be expected that self-esteem would lead to more thorough exploration of environmental alternatives while simultaneously encouraging development of those resources required for affordance attainment. Under these conditions, it is hardly surprising that background data items reflecting self-esteem have been found to have a broad, diffuse impact on differential development patterns, or that they would predict performance as individuals move into new occupational settings.

Self-esteem has been consistently held to be an important determinant of adolescent behavior (Simmons, 1987). Given the fact that adolescence represents an exploratory period during which an initial, rather crude template is elaborated and refined in an interpersonal context and an attempt is made to identify roles actually congruent with this template, effects of this sort might be anticipated. As this exploration proceeds, however, individuals are likely to monitor situations, self, and outcomes intensely and thereby induce some degree of affect through discrepancy awareness. This process will produce some changes in their behavior as this template is adjusted to fit social reality. Due to the predispositions developed earlier in life and the self-propagating nature of situational selections, this change will not always be radical, and some prediction should be possible. However, as exploration proceeds and individuals form a clear idea of available affordances and develop the resources required to attain these affordances, stability should increase over time, barring unexpected events causing a previous interactional pattern to become maladaptive.

As exploration proceeds, individuals should at some point come to identify a set of stable, interrelated social roles that permit adequate expression of and movement toward this refined self-template. This merger of the individual's self-concept into stable social roles permitting adequate personal expression has been remarked upon by other authors (Krietler & Krietler, 1987b) and has been referred to as a process of crystallization (Mumford, Wesley, & Shaffer, 1987). In an initial investigation into this phenomenon using life history data, Mumford, Wesley, and Shaffer (1987) defined crystallized individuals as people who had a high probability of following a developmental pattern derived from adolescent, collegiate, and postcollege background data items. When scores on background data factors derived in these three periods were used as predictors of subgroup membership, it was found that an individual's probability of subgroup membership tended to increase markedly in the period immediately following crystallization, indicating a tendency of individuals to become more like themselves with repeated situational exposures. More centrally, in a comparison of early and late crystallizers, it was found that individuals tended to crystallize in an environment that provided roles permitting expression of their unique needs and values such that traditional, socially oriented women crystallized in adolescence while more independent, intellectually oriented women crystallized during the college years.

In an extension of this initial study, Wesley (1989) hypothesized that members of a background data subgroup would typically move into job environments congruent with their prior life history. It was argued, however, that the effects of occupational congruence would be moderated by crystallization. After forming a set of subgroups using background data items targeted on adolescent and collegiate behavior and experiences, Wesley (1989) found that subgroup members tended to move into occupational environments congruent with their prior life history. The effects of this congruence, however, were moderated by crystallization such that crystallized individuals moving into incongruent environments were less successful and less satisfied than uncrystallized individuals moving into incongruent environments. In a related set of investigations, Snell (1990) found that variables such as family relations and social effectiveness influenced continuity in religious involvement in the developmental periods preceding crystallization. Thus, these variables had the greatest impact before a self-propagating pattern of environmental transactions had developed. Clifton and Mumford (1990) found that individuals crystallizing in a bad family environment tended to maintain a pattern of maladaptive behavior in later years, apparently as a result of their tendency to choose situations, initiate behavior, and interpret outcomes based on a distorted template constructed and finalized under adverse and unrealistic conditions.

PRACTICAL APPLICATIONS

Our foregoing observations concerning continuity and change point to an important characteristic of the ecology model. More specifically, it appears that this model can account for a number of findings in the background data literature, such as the emergence of coherent self-propagating developmental patterns (Mumford & Owens, 1984), the developmental significance of items loading on self-esteem (Nickels, 1990), and the tendency of background data subgroups to capture motivationally and dispositionally loaded criteria (Owens & Schoenfeldt, 1979). Of course, the model's ability to account for these diverse findings represents one characteristic of a good theory. Cook and Campbell (1979) and Fleishman and Quaintance (1984) note, however, that an adequate theory should also have significant practical implications. Thus, in the ensuing discussion, an attempt will be made to sketch out some of the model's practical implications.

PERSONALITY ASSESSMENT

As noted earlier, traditional personality inventories have not proven to be highly effective predictors of job performance criteria. Thus, one of the more salient practical implications of this model is that background data items might be used to measure key personality constructs. To accomplish this, one must begin by specifying the outcomes or reinforcers available in the job environment, as well as those attributes that would contribute to the individual's attainment of positive outcomes and/or avoidance of negative outcomes. This may, of course, be accomplished using standard job analysis techniques, such as Fleishman's (1975) ability requirements approach or Borgen's (1988) occupational reinforcers analysis.

Having specified a set of available outcomes, as well as dispositional variables conditioning the likely attainment of these outcomes, the next obvious step is to generate a set of background data items capable of capturing either the prior expression of these constructs or the variables influencing their development. In the case of outcome variables, it is unlikely that investigators will focus on developmental influences due to their early distal nature. Instead, items are likely to be generated reflecting the affordance-laden implications of these outcomes, either positive or negative, as they have occurred in people's past lives. Thus, for each potential outcome, multiple prior life situations having similar effects might be specified. Items might then be formulated asking individuals about (a) their willingness to enter these situations, (b) their reactions to each situation, or (c) their desire to strive for the pertinent rewards afforded by the situation. In formulating these value-laden motivational items, however, two additional points should be borne in mind. First, given the importance rejection plays in situational choice, it might be useful to formulate items indicating a dislike or rejection of relevant outcome classes. Second, although objective, verifiable items offer certain advantages in terms of reliability (Asher, 1974), it may prove useful, given the importance of affective reactions to situational choice, to ask for evaluations of, or emotional reactions to, situational outcomes, as well as the requisite behaviors for outcome attainment.

In the case of dispositional variables, a somewhat wider range of techniques is available for assessment. Essentially, one should attempt to identify multiple situations in which these variables might act to condition the attainment of certain outcomes. Items might then be formulated asking (a) How often was the outcome attained? (b) To what extent did you enter situations calling for this behavior? (c) How likely were you to enjoy or dislike situations calling for this behavior? (d) Were you confident in your ability to handle this situation? and (e) To what extent have you been exposed to situations influencing the development of this behavior? Again, it seems likely, given the model sketched out above, that items focusing on evaluation, rejection, and failure may prove useful.

While the ecology model provides some valuable recommendations about the general item formats that might be used in assessing the values and dispositional constructs reflected in people's developmental patterns, it is true that research is still required assessing the relative merits of these item formats in construct measurement. Furthermore, it should be clear that these general structures must be fleshed out with respect to particular dimensions such that pertinent situations, behaviors, and outcomes are clearly specified. Mumford and Owens (1987) have suggested a number of sources of information that might be used in generating item content specifications, including available theory and developmental findings, the known predictive characteristics and factor loadings of background data items, and retrospective data gathered from incumbents. Research by Russell and Domm (1990) and Russell et al. (1988) has indicated the value of retrospective life histories in generating items, particularly critical incident essays oriented around motivational and dispositional dimensions. Given the content of the ecology model, there is much to recommend this technique, since it integrates item content with experienced and successful incumbents' self-concepts. This observation, moreover, suggests that other retrospective procedures, such as Little's (1987) personal projects technique for eliciting dimensions of environmental attributes relevant to self-concepts, might also prove useful, as well as Krietler and Krietler's (1987a) techniques for defining core meaning constructs for interpreting life events.

SCALING

Obviously, background data items intended to tap personality constructs may be scaled in a number of ways. For instance, Himelstein and Blaskovics (1960) employed a rational scaling technique in their measure of risk taking. Other work by Schoenfeldt (1989) argues for the utility of factorial or post-hoc rational scales. Mumford and Stokes (1992) have pointed out that all of these techniques have certain strengths and weaknesses, so the choice of a particular technique is somewhat contingent on the practical concerns at hand. Nonetheless, we believe that the nature of the ecology model, as it applies to the manifestation of personality in behavior, points to an important, albeit often overlooked, issue in scaling.

Within the ecology model, individuals are held to operate as wholistic, adaptive entities. An individual's behavior flows from the template being applied when selecting situations and actions in an integrated fashion with respect to current environmental opportunities. This suggests that the essential issue at hand in scaling background data measures is to make predictive statements about the fit of the individual's life history template to the situations at hand. The notion of fit is implicit in Schoenfeldt's (1974) assessment classification model, in which prior subgroup performance is used as an index of the likelihood of an individual who displays a similar life history to other subgroup members entering and performing well in certain situations. Similarly, it can be argued that regression weighting of rational scales or empirical keying also attempt to define an optimal life history pattern with respect to some criterion and thus reflect more limited patterns of fit to a single criterion.

These more limited dimensionally oriented procedures work well within certain limits. More specifically, these approaches will work when core motivational and dispositional elements required of all individuals are assessed, most individuals possess these attributes to some extent, the operation of these attributes is not markedly moderated by broader template characteristics, and individuals are not permitted much discretion in situational exposure or potential actions. These conditions obviously apply in many selection situations, so simple dimensional fit procedures should prove effective. As time, discretion, criteria, and the breadth of adaptive demands increases, however, one would expect that general assessments of fit will yield better prediction than more narrow dimensional assessments. Recent work by Wesley (1989) and MacLane (1990) using subgrouping techniques tend to support this hypothesis.

The question arising at this junction, however, is whether there are other techniques that might be used in fit assessment. One potential approach here would be to use multidimensional scaling techniques to reveal the organization of life events characterizing successful, as opposed to unsuccessful, incumbents drawn from different subgroups and/or different situations. Another approach might involve definition of outcomes and action demands characterizing alternate situations and then assessing individuals in terms of their expression of pertinent affordances or dispositional characteristics in relation to those outcomes. A third approach, based on the perceptual developmental aspect of the ecology model, might entail having individuals project the outcomes and necessary action sequences in which more or less effective adaptation could be specified a priori. A fourth approach might involve contrasting the templates employed by applicants with those characterizing successful incumbents or, perhaps more appropriately, less successful incumbents. Given Lerner and Lerner's (1983) comments concerning our limited understanding of environmental fit and the need for more appropriate environmental measures and fit assessment techniques, these recommendations must be approached cautiously. Nonetheless, as is characteristic of any good theory, these observations suggest a compelling need for some novel and innovative approaches to the assessment of environmental fit vis-à-vis background data measures.

EXTENDED APPLICATIONS

The notion of fit assessment points to an important implication of background data measures suggested by the ecology model. To the extent that background data measures reflect situational preferences and preferred actions, one might expect that these measures would provide a heuristically appropriate vehicle for the differential classification of individuals into occupations. In fact, research by Lunneborg (1968) and Schoenfeldt (1974) suggests that, when general ability is not a factor due to common requirements or prior selection, background data measures provide a particularly attractive vehicle for differential classification. The ecology model, furthermore, suggests two ways in which the efficiency of background data measures in differential classification might be improved. First, an attempt might be made to specify discriminating situational outcomes and requisite actions, and then background data items might be formulated to tap the prior expression of pertinent affordances and dispositional characteristics. Second, the structure of life history, current history, or the template characterizing individuals who are uniquely successful or unsuccessful and who particularly like or dislike one field as opposed to others might be used in item specification. The hypotheses flowing from these analyses of environmental demands and the characteristics of good and poor fits might then be used to generate an item pool capable of maximizing differential prediction.

Another potential application of background data measures suggested by the ecology model pertains to the enhancement of team performance through the assessment of individual fit to the group. However, due to the complex manner in which an individual's characteristics are expressed in interactional settings, it has proven difficult to find viable mechanisms for measuring these characteristics and relating them to team performance. Yet, because the ecology model suggests that individuals generate a general template guiding a variety of situational and action selections, it seems possible that background data subgroups might be used to obtain an index of this template. Subsequent studies examining the task and outcome conditions in which members of different subgroups work well together might then be used to generate a model indicating what types of people should be assigned to the various roles in different group settings.

In a related view, Schneider (1987) has argued that organizational culture is to some extent a function of the personality of the organization's founder and its members. Further, he notes that the rigidities induced by the attraction of similar types of people to the affordances offered in this interpersonal environment may contribute to organizational decline. Of course, one source of evidence for this hypothesis might be provided by background data studies showing that individuals having similar templates systematically enter and remain in certain organizational environments. More centrally, however, it might also be possible, vis-à-vis organizational change goals and their implications, for this analysis of situational outcomes to help specify when and where new types of individuals should be added to an organizational environment to offset this rigidity and to stimulate adaptive change. Thus, this theory and the ability of background data to capture core elements of personality might allow such measures to be used as a tool for organizational development efforts.

CONCLUSIONS

Of course, many of the applications sketched out in this chapter represent more a promise for the future than current reality. Nonetheless, it does appear that the ecology model and its implications for the assessment of personality through background data has some far-reaching implications. Not only will this technique permit us to address the pressing problem of developing valid personality measures for use in industrial settings, it also appears that the use of background data measures in personality assessment will allow us to address some perennial problems in the assessment-classification area while indicating some necessary extensions to our current methodology. When situational affordances are considered in light of both the many things background data measures have told us and the many things they will eventually reveal about the nature of human personality, we believe it is reasonable to conclude that the application of background data in personality assessment represents an area of great potential to both applied psychologists and the discipline of psychology as a whole.

We would like to thank Ralph Barocas, John Riskind, Tim Clifton, Bernie Nickels, Bill Owens, and Jack Feldman for various comments that helped clarify our thoughts on this issue.

REFERENCES

Aboud, F. E., & Ruble, D. N. (1987). Identity constancy in children: Developmental processes and implications. In T. Honess & K. Yardley (Eds.), *Self and identity: Perspectives across the life span*. New York: Rutledge & Kegan Paul.

Ackerman, P. O. (1986). Individual differences in information processing: An investigation of intellectual abilities and task performance during practice. *Intelligence, 10*, 101–139.

Adler, A. (1927). *The practice and theory of individual psychology*. New York: Harcourt, Brace.

Allport, G. W. (1937). *Personality: A psychological interpretation*. New York: Holt, Rinehart & Winston.

Allport, G. W. (1942). The use of personal documents in psychological science. *Social Science Research Council Bulletin, 49*.

Ames, S. D. (1983). *Prediction of research vs. applied interests in veterinarians*. Unpublished master's thesis, University of Georgia, Athens.

Asher, E. J. (1974). The biographical item: Can it be improved? *Personnel Psychology, 25*, 251–269.

Atkinson, J. (1979). Achievement strivings. In H. Lowdow & D. Ender (Eds.), *Dimensions of personality*. New York: Wiley.

Baltes, P. B., & Goulet, L. R. (1971). Exploration of developmental variables by manipulation and simulation of age differences in behavior. *Human Development, 14*, 149–170.

Bandura, A. (1986). *Social foundations of thought and action: A social cognitive theory*. Englewood Cliffs, NJ: Prentice-Hall.

Bandura, A. (1989). Human agency in social cognitive theory. *American Psychologist, 44*, 1175–1184.

Baron, R. M., & Boudreau, L. A. (1987). An ecological perspective on integrating perso-ality and social psychology. *Journal of Personality and Social Psychology, 53*, 1222–1228.

Bem, D. J., & Allen, A. (1974). On predicting some of the people some of the time: The search for cross-situational consistencies. *Psychological Review, 81*, 506–520.

Bergman, L. R., & Magnusson, D. (1987). A person approach to the study of the development of adjustment problems: An empirical example of some research strategy considerations. In D. Magnusson & Ohman (Eds.), *Psychopathology: An interactional perspective*. New York: Academic Press.

Block, J. (1971). *Lives through time*. Berkeley, CA: Bancroft.

Borgen, F. H. (1988). Occupational reinforcer patterns. In S. Gael (Ed.), *The job analysis handbook for business, government, and industry*. New York: Wiley.

Braithwaite, V. A., & Law, H. G. (1985). Structure of human values: Testing the adequacy of the Rokeach Value Survey. *Journal of Personality and Social Psychology, 49*, 250–263.

Bronson, W. C. (1966). Central orientation: A study of behavior organization from childhood to adolescence. *Child Development, 37*, 125–155.

Bronson, W. C., Katten, E. S., & Livson, N. (1959). Patterns of authority and affection in two generations. *Journal of Abnormal and Social Psychology, 58*, 143–152.

Buel, W. D., Albright, L. E., & Glennon, J. R. (1966). A note on the generality and cross-validity of personal history for identifying creative research scientists. *Journal of Applied Psychology, 50,* 217–219.

Buhler, C. (1968). The course of human life as a psychological problem. *Human Development, 11,* 1–16.

Buss, A. H. (1989). Personality as traits. *American Psychologist, 44,* 1378–1388.

Buss, A. H., & Plomin, R. (1975). *A temperament theory of personality development.* New York: Wiley.

Carlson, R. (1988). Exemplary lives: The uses of psychobiography for theory development. *Journal of Personality, 56,* 105–138.

Cascio, W. F. (1975). Accuracy of verifiable biographical information blank responses. *Journal of Applied Psychology, 60,* 767–769.

Caspi, A. (1987). Personality in the life course. *Journal of Personality and Social Psychology, 53,* 1203–1213.

Chandler, M., Boyles, M., Ball, L., & Hala, S. (1987). The conservation of self-hood: A developmental analysis of children's changing conceptions of self-continuity. In T. Honess & K. Yardley (Eds.), *Self and identity: Perspectives across the life span.* New York: Rutledge & Kegan Paul.

Cheek, J. M., & Buss, A. H. (1981). Shyness and sociability. *Journal of Personality and Social Psychology, 41,* 330–339.

Clifton, T., & Mumford, M. D. (1990). *Family history as an influence on adjustment.* Paper presented at the annual meeting of the Southeastern Psychological Association, Atlanta.

Cook, D. T., & Campbell, D. J. (1979). *Quasi-experimentation: The design and analysis of experiments in field settings.* Chicago: Rand McNally.

Costa, P. T., & McCrae, R. R. (1980). Still stable after all these years: Personality as a key to some issues in adulthood and old age. In P. B. Baltes & O. G. Brim, Jr. (Eds.), *Life span development and behavior.* New York: Academic Press.

Costa, P. T., & McCrae, R. R. (1988). Personality in adulthood: A six-year longitudinal study of self-reports and sparse ratings on the NEO Personality Inventory. *Journal of Personality and Social Psychology, 54,* 853–863.

Davis, K. R. (1984). A longitudinal analysis of biographical subgroups using Owens' developmental integrative model. *Personnel Psychology, 37,* 1–14.

Dunkleberger, C. J., & Tyler, L. E. (1961). Interest stability and personality traits. *Journal of Counseling Psychology, 8,* 70–74.

Dweck, C. S. (1986). Motivational processes affecting learning. *American Psychologist, 41,* 1040–1048.

Eberhardt, B. J., & Muchinsky, P. M. (1984). Structural validation of Holland's Hexagonal Model: Vocational classification through the use of background data. *Journal of Applied Psychology, 69,* 174–181.

Einhorn, H. J., & Hogarth, R. M. (1981). Behavioral decision theory. In M. R. Rosenzweig & L. W. Porter (Eds.), *Annual Review of Psychology.* Palo Alto, CA: Annual Reviews.

Ekehammer, B. (1974). Psychological cost benefit as an intervening construct in career choice models. *Journal of Vocational Behavior, 12,* 279–284.

Ellison, R. L., & Taylor, C. W. (1962). The development and cross-validation of a biographical inventory for predicting success in science. *American Psychologist, 17,* 391–392.

Endler, N. S. (1982). Interactionism: A personality model, but not yet a theory. *Nebraska Symposium on Motivation, 30,* 155–200.

Epstein, S. (1979). The stability of behavior: I. On predicting most of the people most of the time. *Journal of Personality and Social Psychology, 37,* 1097–1126.

Epstein, S., & O'Brien, E. J. (1985). The person-situation debate in historical and current perspective. *Psychological Bulletin, 98,* 513–537.

Erikson, E. H. (1963). *Childhood and society.* New York: Wiley.

Eysenck, H. J., & Eysenck, M. W. (1985). *Personality and individual differences.* New York: Plenum.

Feild, H. S., & Schoenfeldt, L. F. (1975). Development and application of a measure of students' college experiences. *Journal of Applied Psychology, 60,* 491–497.

Fiske, D. W. (1973). *Personality assessment.* Chicago: Aldine.

Fleishman, E. A. (1975). Toward a taxonomy of human performance. *American Psychologist, 30,* 1127–1149.

Fleishman, E. A. (1988). Some new frontiers in personnel selection research. *Personnel Psychology, 41,* 679–701.

Fleishman, E. A., & Mumford, M. D. (1989). Abilities as causes of individual differences in skill acquisition. *Human Performance, 2,* 201–222.

Fleishman, E. A., & Quaintance, M. K. (1984). *Taxonomies of human performance: The description of human tasks.* Orlando, FL: Academic Press.

Frazier, R. W. (1971). *Differential perception of individuals subgrouped on the basis of biodata responses.* Unpublished doctoral dissertation, University of Georgia, Athens.

French, N. R., Lewis, M. A., & Long, R. E. (1976). *Social desirability responding in a multiple-choice background data questionnaire.* Paper presented at the meetings of the Southeastern Psychological Association, New Orleans.

Galton, R. (1902). *Life history album* (2d ed.). New York: Macmillan.

Ghiselli, E. E. (1973). The validity of aptitude tests in personnel selection. *Personnel Psychology, 26,* 461–477.

Gibson, J. J. (1979). *An ecological approach to visual perception.* Boston: Houghton-Mifflin.

Gustafson, S. B. (1987). *Individual and situational determinants of job outcomes: A typological approach.* Unpublished doctoral dissertation, Georgia Institue of Technology, Atlanta.

Hart, D., & Damon, W. (1985). Contrasts between understanding self and others. In R. Leahy (Ed.), *The development of the self.* New York: Academic Press.

Hart, D., Maloney, J., & Damon, W. (1987). The meaning and development of identity. In T. Honess & K. Yardley (Eds.), *Self and identity: Perspectives across the life span.* New York: Rutledge & Kegan Paul.

Harwood, I. H. (1987). The evolution of the self: An integration of Wannicott's and Kohut's concepts. In T. Honess & K. Yardley (Eds.), *Self and identity: Perspectives across the life span.* New York: Rutledge & Kegan Paul.

Hayes-Roth, B., & Hayes-Roth, F. (1979). A cognitive model of planning. *Cognitive Science, 3,* 275–310.

Heider, F. (1958). *The psychology of interpersonal relations*. New York: Wiley.

Higgins, T. E. (1987). Self-discrepancy: A theory relating self and affect. *Psychological Review, 94,* 319–340.

Hildebrand-Saints, L., & Weary, G. (1989). Depression and social information gathering. *Personality and Social Psychology Bulletin, 15,* 150–160.

Hill, T., Lewicki, P., Czyzewski, M., & Boss, A. (1989). Self-perpetuating development of encloding biases in person perception. *Journal of Personality and Social Psychology, 57,* 373–387.

Himmelstein, D., & Blaskovicks, T. L. (1960). Prediction of an intermediate criterion of combat effectiveness with a biographical inventory. *Journal of Applied Psychology, 44,* 166–168.

Hogarth, R. M. (1980). *Judgment and choice*. New York: Wiley.

Holland, S. L. (1973). *Making vocational choices: A theory of careers*. Englewood Cliffs, NJ: Prentice-Hall.

Honess, T., & Yardley, K. (1987). Perspectives across the life span. In T. Honess & K. Yardley (Eds.). *Self and identity: Perspectives across the life span*. New York: Rutledge & Kegan Paul.

Hough, L. M. (1984). Development and evaluation of the accomplishment record method of selecting and promoting professionals. *Journal of Applied Psychology, 69,* 135–146.

Howe, M. J. (1982). Biographical evidence and the development of outstanding individuals. *American Psychologist, 37,* 1071–1081.

Jackson, D. N., & Paunonen, S. U. (1985). Construct validity and the predictability of behavior. *American Psychologist, 43,* 23–34.

Jackson, K. E. (1982). *A further look at life history defined subgroup homogeneity across time.* Unpublished doctoral dissertation, University of Georgia, Athens.

James, L. A., & James, L. R. (1989). Integrating work environment perceptions: Explorations into the measurement of meaning. *Journal of Applied Psychology, 74,* 739–757.

Jones, E. L. (1970). *The affinity of biodata subgroups for vocational interests*. Paper presented at the annual meeting of the Georgia Psychological Association, Atlanta.

Kagan, J. (1989). Temperamental contributions to social behavior. *American Psychologist, 44,* 668–674.

Kawai, M. (1965). Newly acquired pre-cultural behavior of the natural troop of Japanese monkeys on Koshima Islet. *Primates, 6,* 1–30.

Keating, E., Paterson, D. G., & Stone, C. H. (1950). Validity of work histories obtained by interview. *Journal of Applied Psychology, 66,* 233–241.

Kelly, G. A. (1955). *The psychology of personal constructs*. New York: Norton.

Kenrick, D. T., & Funder, D. C. (1988). Profiting from controversy: Lessons from the person situation debate. *American Psychologist, 43,* 23–34.

Kernis, M. H., Brockner, J., & Frankel, B. S. (1989). Self-esteem and reactions to failure: The mediating role of overgeneralization. *Journal of Personality and Social Psychology, 57,* 707–714.

Klein, H. A. (1972). *Personality characteristics of discrepant academic achievers*. Unpublished doctoral dissertation, University of Georgia, Athens.

Klein, S. P., & Owens, W. A. (1965). Faking of a second life history blank as a function of criterion objectivity. *Journal of Applied Psychology, 49,* 452–454.

Klimoski, R. J. (1973). A biographical data analysis of career patterns in engineering. *Journal of Vocational Behavior, 3,* 103–113.

Kohut, H. (1977). *The restoration of the self.* New York: International Universities Press.

Korman, A. K. (1968). The prediction of managerial performance: A review. *Personnel Psychology, 21,* 295–322.

Kosson, D. S., & Newman, J. P. (1989). Socialization and attentional deficits under focusing and divided attention conditions. *Journal of Personality and Social Psychology, 57,* 87–99.

Krietler, S., & Krietler, H. (1987a). Plans and planning: Their motivational and cognitive antecedents. In S. L. Friedman, E. K. Scholnick, & R. R. Cockling (Eds.), *Blueprints for thinking: The role of planning in cognitive development.* New York: Cambridge University Press.

Krietler, S., & Krietler, H. (1987b). The psychosemantic aspects of the self. In T. Honess & K. Yardley (Eds.), *Self and identity: Perspectives across the life span.* New York: Rutledge & Kegan Paul.

Lautenschlager, G. J. (1985). Within subject measures for the assessment of individual differences in faking. *Educational and Psychological Measurement, 46,* 309–316.

Lerner, J. V., & Lerner, R. M. (1983). Temperament and adaptation across life: Theoretical and empirical issues. In P. B. Baltes & O. G. Brim, Jr. (Eds.), *Life span development and behavior.* New York: Academic Press.

Lerner, R. M. (1978). Dialectics and development. *Human Development, 21,* 1–20.

Levenson, D. (1978). *Seasons of a man's life.* New York: McGraw-Hill.

Levine, A. S., & Zachert, V. (1952). Use of a biographical inventory in the air force classification program. *Journal of Applied Psychology, 35,* 241–244.

Little, B. R. (1987). Personal projects and fuzzy selves: Aspects of self identity in adolescence. In T. Honess & K. Yardley (Eds.), *Self and identity: Perspectives across the life span.* New York: Rutledge & Kegan Paul.

Loehlin, J. C., Willerman, L., & Horn, J. M. (1985). Personality resemblances in adoptive families when children are late adolescent or adult. *Journal of Personality and Social Psychology, 48,* 376–392.

Lunneborg, C. E. (1968). Biographic variables in differential versus absolute perediction. *Proceedings of the 76th Annual Convention of the American Psychological Association, 3,* 233–234.

MacLane, C. N. (1990). *Configural scoring: Enhancing the validity of biodata through a developmental approach.* Washington, DC: Office of Personnel Management.

Magnusson, D. (1988). *Individual development from an interactional perspective: A longitudinal study.* Hillsdale, NJ: Erlbaum.

Magnusson, D., & Endler, N. S. (1977). Interactional psychology: Present status and future prospects. In D. Magnusson & N. S. Endler (Eds.), *Personality at the cross roads: Current issues in interactional psychology.* Hillsdale, NJ: Erlbaum.

Markus, H. (1977). Self-schemata and processing information about the self. *Journal of Personality and Social Psychology, 35,* 63–78.

Maslow, A. H. (1970). *Motivation and personality.* New York: Harper & Row.

McCrae, R. R., & Costa, P. T. (1987). Validation of the five factor model across instrumens and observers. *Journal of Personality and Social Psychology, 52,* 81–90.

McCrae, R. R., & Costa, P. T. (1988). Recalled parent-child relations and adult personality. *Journal of Personality, 56,* 417–433.

Mikesell, R. H., & Tesser, A. (1971). Life history antecedents of authoritarianism: A quasi-longitudinal approach. *Proceedings of the 74th Convention of the American Psychological Association, 6,* 136–137.

Mischel, W. (1968). *Personality and assessment.* New York: Wiley.

Mischel, W. (1973). Toward a cognitive social learning reconceptualization of personality. *Psychological Review, 80,* 252–283.

Mischel, W., & Peake, P. K. (1982). Beyond déjà vu in the search for cross-situational consistency. *Psychological Review, 89,* 730–755.

Morrison, R. F., Owens, W. A., Glennon, J. R., & Albright, L. E. (1962). Factored life history antecedents of industrial research performance. *Journal of Applied Psychology, 46,* 281–284.

Mosel, J. L., & Cozan, L. W. (1952). The accuracy of application blank work histories. *Journal of Applied Psychology, 46,* 281–284.

Mumford, M. D., & Nickels, B. J. (1990). Making sense of people's lives: Applying principles of content and construct validity to background data. *Forensic Reports, 3,* 143–167.

Mumford, M. D., & Owens, W. A. (1982). Life history and vocational interests. *Journal of Vocational Behavior, 21,* 330–348.

Mumford, M. D., & Owens, W. A. (1984). Individuality in a developmental content: Some empirical and theoretical considerations. *Human Development, 27,* 84–108.

Mumford, M. D., & Owens, W. A. (1987). Methodology review: Principles, procedures, and findings in the application of background data measures. *Applied Psychological Measurement, 11,* 1–31.

Mumford, M. D., Snell, A. F., & Hein, M. B. (1992). Varieties of religious experience: Person influences on continuity and change in religious involvement. *Journal of Personality, 61,* 69–88.

Mumford, M. D., & Stokes, G. S. (1982). *Life history correlates of positive and negative emotionality.* Paper presented at the annual meeting of the Southeastern Psychological Association, Atlanta.

Mumford, M. D., & Stokes, G. S. (1992). Developmental determinants of individual action: Theory and practice in the application of background data measures. In M. D. Dunnette (Ed.), *Handbook of industrial and organizational psychology* (2d ed., vol. 3, pp. 61–138). Palo Alto, CA: Consulting Psychologists Press.

Mumford, M. D., Stokes, G. S., & Owens, W. A. (1990). *Patterns of life history: The ecology of human individuality.* Hillsdale, NJ: Erlbaum.

Mumford, M. D., Wesley, S. S., & Shaffer, G. S. (1987). The origins of developmental trajectories: An empirical examination of the crystallization phenomenon. *Human Development, 30,* 291–321.

Murray, H. A. (1938). *Explorations of personality.* New York: Oxford University Press.

Neiner, A. G., & Owens, W. A. (1985). Using biodata to predict job choice among college graduates. *Journal of Applied Psychology, 70,* 127–136.

Nickels, B. J. (1990). *The construction of background data measures: Development procedures which optimize construct, content, and criterion related validities.* Unpublished doctoral dissertation, Georgia Institute of Technology, Atlanta.

Normal, W. T. (1963). Toward an adequate taxonomy of personality attributes: Replicated factor structure in peer nominations of personality ratings. *Journal of Abnormal and Social Psychology, 66*, 574–583.

Nutt, P. C. (1984). Planning process archetypes and their effectiveness. *Decision Sciences, 15*, 221–247.

Ochberg, R. L. (1988). Life stories and psychosocial construction of careers. *Journal of Personality, 56*, 173–204.

O'Leary, L. R. (1973). Fair employment, sound psychometric practice, and reality. *American Psychologist, 28*, 147–150.

Olweus, D. (1979). Stability of aggressive reaction patterns in males. *Psychological Bulletin, 86*, 852–875.

Owens, W. A. (1968). Toward one dicipline of scientific psychology. *American Psychologist, 23*, 782–785.

Owens, W. A. (1971). A quasi-actuarial basis for individual assessment. *American Psychologist, 26*, 992–999.

Owens, W. A. (1976). Background data. In M. D. Dunnette (Ed.), *Handbook of industrial and organizational psychology* (1st ed.). Chicago: Rand McNally.

Owens, W. A. (1978). Moderators and subgroups. *Personnel Psychology, 32*, 243–247.

Owens, W. A., & Schoenfeldt, L. F. (1979). Toward a classification of persons. *Journal of Applied Psychology, 64*, 569–607.

Pace, L. A., & Schoenfeldt, L. F. (1977). Legal concerns in the use of weighted application blanks. *Personnel Psychology, 30*, 159–166.

Pannone, R. D. (1984). Predicting test performance: A content valid approach to screening applicants. *Personnel Psychology, 37*, 507–519.

Peevers, B. H. (1987). The self as observer of the self: A developmental analysis of the subjective self. In T. Honess & K. Yardley (Eds.), *Self and identity: Perspectives across the life span*. New York: Rutledge & Kegan Paul.

Piaget, J. (1967). *The psychology of intelligence*. London: Routledge & Paul.

Price, R. A., Vandenberg, S. G., Iyer, H., & Williams, J. S. (1982). Components of variation in normal personality. *Journal of Personality and Social Psychology, 43*, 328–340.

Pulkkinen, L. (1982). Self-control and continuity from childhood to late adolescence. In P. B. Baltes & O. G. Brim, Jr. (Eds.), *Life span development and behavior*. New York: Academic Press.

Quaintance, M. K. (1981). *Development of a weighted application blank to predict managerial assessment center performance*. Unpublished doctoral dissertation, George Washington University, Washington, DC.

Rawls, D., & Rawls, J. R. (1968). Personality characteristics and personal history data of successful and less-successful executives. *Psychological Reports, 23*, 1032–1034.

Redmond, M. R., & Nichels, B. J. (1989). *Comparison of the validity of direct and indirect background data items*. Paper presented at the annual meeting of the Southeastern Psychological Association, Washington, DC.

Reilly, R. R., & Chao, G. T. (1982). Validity and fairness of some alternative employee selection procedures. *Personnel Psychology, 35*, 1–62.

Riegel, K. F. (1975). Toward a dialectical theory of development. *Human Development, 18*, 50–64.

Rokeach, M. (1973). *The nature of human values.* New York: Free Press.

Rosenberg, M. (1987). Depersonalization: The loss of personal identity. In T. Honess & K. Yardley (Eds.), *Self and identity: Perspectives across the life span.* New York: Rutledge & Kegan Paul.

Russell, C. J., & Domm, D. R. (1990). *On the construct validity of biographical information: Evaluation of a theory-based method for item generation.* Unpublished manuscript.

Russell, C. J., Mattson, J., Devlin, S. E., & Atwater, D. (1988). *Predictive validity of biodata items generated from retrospective life experience essays.* Paper presented at the annual meeting of the Society for Industrial and Organizational Psychology, Dallas.

Schneider, B. (1987). The people make the place. *Personnel Psychology, 40*, 437–452.

Schoenfeldt, L. F. (1974). Utilization of manpower: Development and evaluation of an assessment classification model for matching individuals with jobs. *Journal of Applied Psychology, 59*, 583–595.

Schoenfeldt, L. F. (1989). *Biographical data as the new frontier in employee selection research.* Paper presented at the annual meeting of the American Psychological Association, New Orleans.

Schwab, D. P., & Oliver, R. L. (1974). Predicting tenure with biographical data: Examining buried evidence. *Personnel Psychology, 27*, 125–128.

Sears, R. R. (1977). Sources of life satisfaction of the Terman gifted men. *American Psychologist, 32*, 119–128.

Shaffer, G. S., Saunders, V., & Owens, W. A. (1986). Additional evidence for the accuracy of biographical data: Long-term retest reliability and observer ratings. *Personnel Psychology, 39*, 791–809.

Simmons, R. G. (1987). Self-esteem in adolescence. In T. Honess & K. Yardley (Eds.), *Self and identity: Perspectives across the life span.* New York: Rutledge & Kegan Paul.

Snell, A. F. (1990). *Crystallization as a moderator of continuity and change in religious involvement.* Unpublished master's thesis, Georgia Institute of Technology, Atlanta.

Snell, A. F., & Stokes, G. S. (1990). *Crystallization as a moderator of patterns of subgroup movement.* Paper presented at the annual meeting of the Southeastern Psychological Association, Atlanta.

Snyder, M. (1974). The self-monitoring of expressive behavior. *Journal of Personality and Social Psychology, 30*, 526–537.

Stokes, G. S., Mumford, M. D., & Owens, W. A. (1989). Life history prototypes in the study of human individuality. *Journal of Personality, 49*, 341–386.

Strauman, T. J. (1989). Self-discrepancies in clinical depression and social phobias: Cognitive structures that underlie emotional disorders. *Journal of Abnormal Psychology, 98*, 14–22.

Strauman, T. J., & Higgins, E. T. (1987). Automatic activation of distinct self-discrepancies and emotional syndromes. *Journal of Personality and Social Psychology, 53*, 1004–1014.

Stricker, L. J. (1989). *Assessing leadership potential at the Naval Academy with a biographical measure* (Tech. Rep. No. RR-89-14). Princeton, NJ: Educational Testing Service.

Strickland, B. R. (1989). Internal-external control expectancies: From contingency to creativity. *American Psychologist, 44,* 1–12.

Strimbu, J. L., & Schoenfeldt, L. F. (1973). Life history subgroups in the prediction of drug usage patterns and attitudes. *JSAS Catalog of Selected Documents in Psychology, 3,* 83.

Thayer, P. W. (1977). Something's old, something's new. *Personnel Psychology, 30,* 513–524.

Thomas, A., & Chess, S. (1981). The role of temperament in the contributions of individuals to their development. In R. M. Lener & N. A. Busch-Rossnagel (Eds.), *Individuals as producers of their own development: A life span perspective.* New York: Academic Press.

Thomas, L. L. (1982). *Biographical antecedents of vocational choice.* Unpublished doctoral dissertation, University of Georgia, Athens.

Thomkins, S. S. (1987). Script theory. In J. Aronoff, A. I. Rabin, & R. A. Zuker (Eds.), *The emergence of personality.* New York: Springer.

Tobach, E. (1981). Evolutionary aspects of the activity of the organism and its environment. In R. M. Lerner & N. A. Busch-Rossnagel (Eds.), *Individuals as producers of their own development: A life span perspective.* New York: Academic Press.

Torrance, J. P., & Ziller, R. C. (1957). *Risk and life experience: Developing a scale for measuring risk taking tendencies.* Lackland AFB, TX: U.S. Air Force Personnel Training Research Center.

Tyler, L. E. (1965). *The psychology of human differences.* Englewood Cliffs, NJ: Prentice-Hall.

Wannicott, D. W. (1960). The theory of parent infant relationships. In D. W. Wannicott (Ed.), *The maturational processes and the facilitating environment.* New York: International Universities Press.

Ward, J. J., & Hook, M. E. (1963). Application of an hierarchical grouping procedure to the problem of grouping profiles. *Educational and Psychological Measurement, 23,* 69–81.

Wernimont, P. F. (1962). Re-evaluation of a weighted application blank for office personnel. *Journal of Applied Psychology, 46,* 417–419.

Wesley, S. S. (1989). *Background data subgroups and career outcomes: Some developmental influences on person-job matching.* Unpublished doctoral dissertation, Georgia Institute of Technology, Atlanta.

Witkin, H. A., & Berry, J. W. (1975). Psychological differentiation in cross-cultural perspective. *Journal of Cross-Cultural Psychology, 6,* 4–87.

Wylie, R. C. (1987). Mother's attribution to young children. In T. Honess & K. Yardley (Eds.), *Self and identity: Perspectives across the life span.* New York: Rutledge & Kegan Paul.

Zuckerman, M., Bernieri, F., Koestner, R., & Rosenthal, R. (1989). To predict some of the people some of the time: In search of moderators. *Journal of Personality and Social Psychology, 57,* 279–293.

Zuckerman, M., Koestner, R., DeBoy, T., Garcia, T., Marecsa, B. C., & Sartoris, J. M. (1988). To predict some of the people some of the time: A re-examination of the moderator variable approach in personality theory. *Journal of Personality and Social Psychology, 54,* 1006–1019.

Zuckerman, M., Kuhlman, D. M., & Camac, C. (1988). What lies beyond E and N? Factor analyses of scales believed to measure basic dimensions of personality. *Journal of Personality and Social Psychology, 54,* 96–107.

Credits

Acknowledgment is made to the following authors and publishers for their kind permission to reprint material from the copyrighted sources as follows:

Chapter 3 Fine and Cronshaw

Pages 47 and 48 From *Principles for the Validation and Use of Personnel Selection Procedures* (3d ed., pp. 24 and 22) by the Society for Industrial and Organizational Psychology, 1987, College Park, MD: Author. Copyright 1987 by the Society for Industrial and Organizational Psychology. Reprinted by permission. **50–51** From "Functional Job Analysis" by S.A. Fine in *The Job Analysis Handbook for Business, Industry and Government* (p. 1024), S. Gael, Ed. (1988), New York: Wiley. Copyright 1988 by Wiley. Reprinted by permission. **53–54** G. S. Stokes, M. D. Mumford, and W. A. Owens, "Life History Prototypes." *Journal of Personality*, Vol. 57, No. 3, p.542. Copyright Duke University Press, 1989. Reprinted with permission of the publisher.

Chapter 13 Sharf

Page 352 From *Patterns of Life History: The Ecology of Human Individuality* by M. D. Mumford, G. S. Stokes, and W. A. Owens, 1990, Hillsdale, NJ: Erlbaum. Copyright 1990 by Erlbaum. Reprinted by permission. **355, 359, and 369** From "The Validity and Fairness of Alternatives to Cognitive Tests" by R. Reilly and M. Warech in *Employment Testing and Public Policy*, L. Wing, Ed. (in press), Berkeley, CA: Kluwer Press. Reprinted by permission. **363** Reprinted with permission from *Employee Relations Law Journal*, V15N3, Winter 1989/90. Copyright 1990 by Executive Enterprises, Inc., 22 West 21st Street, New York, NY 10010-6990. 212-645-7880. All rights reserved. **383** From *Standards for Educational and Psychological Testing* (p. 78) by AERA, APA, and NCME, 1985, Washington, DC: American Psychological Association. Copyright 1985 by the American Psychological Association. Reprinted by permission.

Chapter 17 Mitchell

Page 506 From *Essentials of Psychological Testing* (pp. 506-507) by L. Cronbach, 1970, New York: Harper and Row. Copyright 1970 by Harper and Row. Reprinted by permission.

Index

627